Malaysia, Singapore & Brunei
a travel survival kit

Geoff Crowther
Tony Wheeler

Malaysia, Singapore & Brunei - a travel survival kit
3rd edition

Published by
Lonely Planet Publications
Head Office: PO Box 88, South Yarra, Victoria 3141, Australia
US Office: PO Box 2001A, Berkeley, CA 94702, USA

Printed by
Singapore National Printers Ltd, Singapore

Photographs by
Vicki Beale (VB), Michael Clark (MC), Joe Cummings (JC), Brendon Hyde (BH), Colleen Kennedy (CK),
Mark Lightbody (ML), Richard Nebeski (RN), Alan Samagalski (AS), Sue Tan (ST), Tony Wheeler (TW)
Front cover: Market, Kuala Trengganu (TW)
Back cover: Omar Ali Saifuddin Mosque, Brunei (BH)

First published
May 1982

This edition
May 1988

National Library of Australia Cataloguing in Publication Data

Crowther, Geoff, 1944- Malaysia, Singapore & Brunei, a travel survival kit.

3rd ed.
Includes index.
ISBN 0 86442 022 6.

1. Malaysia – Description and travel –
Guide-books. 2. Singapore – Description and travel – Guide-books. 3. Brunei – Description and travel – Guidebooks. I. Wheeler, Tony, II. Title

915.95

© Copyright Geoff Crowther, Tony Wheeler, 1982, 1985, 1988

Geoff Crowther

Geoff was born in Yorkshire, England and started his travelling days as a teenage hitch-hiker. Later, after many short trips around Europe, two years in Asia and Africa, Geoff got involved with the London underground information centre BIT. He helped put together their first, tatty, duplicated overland guides and was with them from their late '60s heyday right through to the end. Since his first LP guide, to Africa, Geoff has written or collaborated on many others in the series. Geoff now lives with Hyung Pun, whom he met in Korea, in the rainforests of northern New South Wales.

Tony Wheeler

Tony Wheeler was born in England, but spent most of his youth overseas in places like Pakistan, the West Indies and all of his high school years in the US due to his father's occupation with British Airways. He returned to England to do a university degree in engineering, worked for a short time as an automotive design engineer, returned to university and did an MBA then dropped out on the Asian overland trail with his wife Maureen. They've been travelling, writing and publishing guidebooks ever since having set up Lonely Planet Publications in the mid-70s. Travel for the Wheelers is now considerably enlivened by their children Tashi and Kieran.

Joe Cummings

Joe Cummings has been involved in South-East Asian studies for many years and was a Peace Corps volunteer in Thailand during the '70s. Since then he has been a translator/interpreter of Thai in San Francisco, a graduate student in Thai language and Asian art history (MA 1981) at the University of California (Berkeley), an East-West Center Scholar in Hawaii, a university lecturer in Malaysia and most recently a bilingual consultant for public schools in Oakland, California.

For this new edition, Joe visited Singapore and the west coast of Peninsular Malaysia. Joe is also the author of Lonely Planet's *Thailand – a travel survival kit* and *Thai phrasebook* as well as having worked on the *Burma – tsk* update.

Sue Tan

Sue Tan, *Update* editor at Lonely Planet, went to the jungles of Brunei and East Malaysia, and to the beaches of the east coast of the Malaysian Peninsula to work on this latest edition. Sue has visited Malaysia a number of times.

Sue was born in Melbourne and after completing study in psychology at Monash University, travelled through Europe and Asia for 2½ years. Whilst living in London, Sue worked in the travel 'bucket' shops. On returning to Australia, Sue worked for Student Travel before joining LP where she has been reading travellers' letters for the past 2½ years.

Lonely Planet Credits

Editor	Susan Mitra
Maps & cover design	Vicki Beale
Design	Valerie Tellini
Illustrations	Joanne Ryan
Typesetting	Ann Jeffree
	Debbie Lustig

Thanks also to: Lindy Cameron for the final preparation of the disks; to Joanne Ryan who started off the paste up and to Adrienne Ralph for proof reading and corrections.

Acknowledgements

Joe Cummings would like to thank Michael and Janet Clarke of Casa Elephant, Nassar Rasool, Victor Chin, Julie Corty, Doug Glenn, Michael Harvey, the Petersons, Alang and Sim for their assistance.

Sue Tan would like to thank Tan Kim Hock & Siew Ying, Kang Sam Chuan, Choy Wong, Johnny Tan Bon Bok, Rose Tan, Bob Tungku Ibrahim, Naraja Dorsamy and Shuco Sumatras all from Malaysia, as well as Ingrid Bremer from West Germany, Tony Yates from the UK, Roxy Timm from USA and Roy Wiedemeyer from Australia.

Producing this Book

Researching this guide was originally a two part operation. While Geoff Crowther covered Sarawak, Sabah and Brunei in north Borneo, Tony and Maureen Wheeler roamed around Singapore and up and down the Malay peninsula.

Researching the second edition was handled by Mark Lightbody, author of Lonely Planet's *Canada – a travel survival kit* and updater of several LP guidebooks. This third edition was again a joint effort. Sue Tan tackled the east coast of the peninsular along with Sabah, Sarawak and Brunei. Meanwhile Joe Cummings worked his way along the west

coast and covered Singapore. Finally Tony Wheeler made a last minute visit to Penang, Kuala Lumpur and Singapore, to try out the recently opened subway and tick off how many old buildings had fallen to the wreckers. His photograph shows him checking out a bathtub in the E&O Hotel, Penang!

Thanks must also go to Tony Jenkins, whose delightful cartoons and sketches you can also see in *India – a travel survival kit*. To Murray D Bruce and Constance S Leap Bruce who wrote the section on national parks.

Last, but not least, a special thanks to 'our travellers' who took the time and energy to write to us from places large and small from all over the region. These people's names are at the back of the book.

A Warning & a Request

Things change – prices go up, schedules change, good places go bad and bad places go bankrupt – nothing stays the same. So if you find things better or worse, recently opened or long since closed, please write and tell us and help make the next edition better! All information is greatly appreciated and the best letters will receive a free copy of the next edition, or any other Lonely Planet book of your choice.

Extracts from the best letters are also included in the *Lonely Planet Update*. The *Update* helps us make useful information available to you as soon as possible – it's like reading an up-to-date noticeboard or postcards from a friend. Each edition contains hundreds of useful tips, and advice from the best possible source of information – other travellers. The *Lonely Planet Update* is published quarterly in paperback and is available from bookshops and by subscription. Turn to the back pages of this book for more details.

Contents

Introduction

Malaysia, Singapore and Brunei are three independent South-East Asian nations offering the visitor a taste of Asia at its most accessible. In all of Asia only Japan has a higher per capita income than these countries so, as you might expect, they are relatively prosperous and forward looking. Transport facilities are good, accommodation standards are high, the food excellent (often amazingly good in fact) and for the visitor there are very few problems to be faced.

Yet despite these high standards these are not expensive countries – Singapore may be able to offer all the air-conditioned comforts your credit cards can handle and East Malaysia may at times be a little pricey due to its jungle-frontier situation, but in Peninsular Malaysia the costs can be absurdly cheap if you want them to be.

More important than simple ease of travel this region offers amazing variety both geographically and culturally. If you want beaches and tropical islands it's hard to beat the east coast of the peninsula. If you want mountains, parks and wildlife then you can climb Mt Kinabalu, explore the rivers of Sarawak or watch for wildlife in the huge Taman Negara (national park) on Peninsular Malaysia.

If you want city life then you can try the historic old port of Melaka, the easy going back streets of Georgetown in Penang or the modern-as-tomorrow city of Singapore. When it comes to people you've got Malays, Chinese, Indians and a whole host of indigenous tribes in Sabah and Sarawak. Last, but far from least, you have got a wonderful selection of food to choose from which alone brings people back to the region over and over again. There is no question in many people's minds that Singapore is deservedly the food capital of Asia.

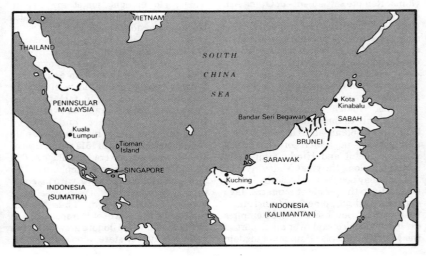

Facts about the Region

HISTORY

It is only since WW II that Malaysia, Singapore and Brunei have emerged as three separate independent countries. Prior to that they were all loosely amalgamated as a British colony, Sarawak excepted, and earlier still they might have been independent Malay kingdoms, or part of the greater Majapahit or Srivijaya empires of what is now Indonesia. In the dim mists of time it's possible that Malaysia was actually the home for the earliest homo sapiens in Asia. Discoveries have been made in the gigantic Niah Caves of Sarawak which indicate that stone age man was present there, and in other caves of north Borneo and the Malay peninsula, as long as 40,000 years ago.

Early Trade & Empires

Little is known about these stone age Malaysians, but around 10,000 years ago the aboriginal Malays – the Orang Asli – began to move down the peninsula from a probable starting point in south-west China. Remote settlements of Orang Asli can still be found in parts of Malaysia, but 4000 years ago they were already being supplanted by the Proto-Malays, ancestors of today's Malays, who at first settled the coastal regions, then moved inland. In the early centuries of the Christian era Malaya was known as far away as Europe. Ptolemy showed it on his early map with the label 'Golden Chersonese'. It spelt gold not only to the Romans for it wasn't long before Indian and Chinese traders also arrived in search of that most valuable metal and Hindu mini-states sprung up along the great Malay rivers.

The Malay people were basically similar ethnically to the people of Sumatra, Java and even the Philippines and from time to time various South-East Asian empires extended their control over all or part of the Malay peninsula. Funan, a kingdom based in modern day Kampuchea, at one time controlled the northern part of the peninsula. From the 7th century the great Sumatran based Srivijaya empire, with its capital in Palembang, held the whole area and even extended its rule into Thailand.

In turn the Srivijayans fell to the Java based Majapahit empire, then in 1403 Paramesvara, a Sumatran prince, established himself at Melaka which soon became the most powerful city state in the region. At this time the spice trade from the Moluccas was beginning to develop and Melaka, with its strategic position on the straits which separate Sumatra from the Malay peninsula, was a familiar port for ships from the east and west.

In 1405 the Chinese admiral Cheng Ho arrived in Melaka with greetings from the 'Son of Heaven' and, more important, the promise of protection from the encroaching Siamese to the north. With this support from China the power of Melaka extended to include most of the Malay peninsula. Cheng Ho brought something else to Melaka – the Islamic religion which also began to spread through Malaya.

The Portuguese Period

For the next century Melaka's power and wealth expanded to such an extent that the city became one of the wealthiest in the east. So wealthy in fact that the Portuguese began to take an over-active interest in the place and after a preliminary skirmish in 1509 Alfonse de Albuquerque arrived in 1511 with a fleet of 18 ships and overpowered Melaka's 20,000 defenders and their war elephants. The Sultan of Melaka fled south with his court to Johore where the Portuguese were unable to dislodge him. Thus Melaka came to be the centre of European power in the region while Johore grew to be the main Malay city state, along with other

Malay centres at Brunei in north Borneo and Acheh in the north of Sumatra.

The Portuguese were to hold Melaka for over 100 years although they were never able to capitalise on the city's fabulous wealth and superb position. Portuguese trading power and strength was never great enough to take full advantage of the volume of trade that used to flow through Melaka but, more important, the Portuguese did not develop the complex pattern of influence and patronage upon which Melaka had based its power and control. Worse, the Portuguese reputation for narrow-mindedness and cruelty had preceded them and they gained few converts to Christianity and little support for their rule.

Thus the other Malay states were able to grow into the vacuum created by the Portuguese takeover of Melaka and while they squabbled and fought between themselves they also had the strength to make attacks on Melaka. Gradually Portuguese power declined and after long skirmishes with the Dutch, who supported the rulers of Johore, Melaka eventually fell, after a long and bitter siege, in 1641.

The Dutch Period

Like the Portuguese the Dutch were to rule Melaka for over a century but, also like the Portuguese, the Dutch failed to recognise that Melaka's greatest importance was as a centre for entrepôt trade. To an even greater extent than their predecessors the Dutch tried to keep Melaka's trade totally to themselves and as a result Melaka continued to decline. Also the greatest Dutch interest was reserved for Batavia, modern day Jakarta, so Melaka was always the poor sister to the more important Javan port.

The British Arrive

Meanwhile the British were casting eyes at Malaya again. They had shown an interest in the area then decided to concentrate on their Indian possessions,

but in 1786 Captain Francis Light arrived at Penang and this time British intentions were firm ones. Light followed a free trade policy at Penang, a clear contrast to the monopolistic intentions of the Portuguese and then the Dutch in Melaka. As a result Penang soon became a thriving port and by 1800 the population of the island, virtually uninhabited when Light took over, had reached 10,000.

While Penang was a success story locally it did not meet the high expectations of the British East India Company and in 1795 the company also found itself controlling Melaka due to events in Europe. When Napoleon overran the Netherlands the British temporarily took control of Melaka and later on the other Dutch possessions in the region. In 1814, with Napoleon defeated, an agreement was reached on the return of these possessions and by 1818 Melaka and Java had been returned to Dutch control.

During the years of British rule, however, there had been a number of advocates for greater British power in the region – one of the most outspoken being Thomas Stamford Raffles. He had decided that Britain, not the Dutch, should be the major power in the region, but was unable to convince his superiors in London that this was a wise plan. In 1818, however, the re-establishment of Dutch power had caused sufficient worry to the company officials in Calcutta that Raffles was told to go ahead and establish a second British base further south than Penang. In early 1819 Raffles arrived in Singapore and decided this should be the place.

Raffles' Singapore

More than 1000 years earlier Singapore, then known as Temasek or 'Sea Town', had been a small outpost of the Srivijaya empire. Around 1100 AD the place had been renamed Singapura or 'Lion City' by a visiting Sumatran prince who fancied he had seen a lion there. Later other Malay kings ruled the swampy island, but with the defeat of Singapura's last Sumatran prince, Iskandar Shah in the mid-1300s, Singapore sank into backwater oblivion.

Thus when Raffles arrived the population of the island consisted of little more than a few sea gypsies and some Chinese farmers. Raffles' first problem was to find somebody to buy the island from since his instructions were not to provoke any dispute with the Dutch and if anyone could lay claim to Singapore it would probably be a sultan who owed allegiance to the Dutch. Raffles turned up an uncommitted local ruler, announced that he was the ruling sultan and then contracted to pay him a yearly stipend for ownership of the island. Thus Singapore became the second British settlement in Malaya and the Dutch became highly annoyed.

Fortunately for Raffles communications were slow and by the time a few letters had crawled their way back and forth between Singapore, Calcutta, London and Amsterdam a new agreement had been hammered out between the British and Dutch. Bengkulu in Sumatra was transferred to the Dutch in exchange for Melaka. In 1826 Singapore, which by this time had a population already approaching 100,000, became part of the British Straits Settlement, governed from Bengal in India along with Melaka and Penang. The agreement with the Dutch had a further effect on the region – the Malay peninsula and Sumatra, which had so long been connected by a common culture, religion and language and often politically connected as well, were now divided. Sumatra was clearly under Dutch control and Malaya was equally clearly destined to be ruled by the British.

The British Period

Despite British rule the straits continued to be a fairly frontier-like area. Piracy, long a popular activity, still thrived although the British eventually got around to cracking down on it. Curiously piracy has had a revival in the 1980s and a number of ships have been boarded and the ship's safes ransacked or the crew robbed as they approached the Indonesian islands around Singapore!

In Singapore and Malaysia the developments through the balance of the 19th century were chiefly economic ones, but in their wake they brought enormous changes to the racial make up of the region. There had been Chinese settlers in Malaya from the time of Cheng Ho's visit to Melaka in the early 1400s, but in the 1800s they began to flood in much greater numbers. The main attraction was tin and at mining towns around Kuala Lumpur and Perak fortunes were quickly won and lost. In 1877 rubber plantations began to spring up all over the peninsula. Since the indigenous supply of labour was not sufficient, labourers were imported from the British plantations in India. Thus by the turn of the century Malaya had a burgeoning economy, but also a vastly different racial mix than a century before. Whereas Malaya had been predominantly populated by Malays now it also had large groups of Indians and Chinese. Furthermore with the arrival of women settlers the labourers who had come there only to work now began to think of settling down and staying on.

As in India the British managed to bring more and more of the country under their control without having to fight for it or even totally govern it. Internal government was left up to the local sultans while the British provided 'advisers' and managed external affairs. In 1867 the Straits Settlements became a crown colony and was no longer governed from India. In 1895 Perak, Selangor, Negri Sembilan and Pahang became the Federated Malay States. Johore refused to join the federation while Kelantan, Trengganu, Perlis and Kedah were still controlled by the Thais until 1909.

Meanwhile in Borneo

Across in north Borneo events sometimes read more like Victorian melodrama than hard fact. In 1838 James Brooke, a British adventurer, arrived in Borneo with his armed sloop to find the Brunei aristocracy facing rebellion from the dissatisfied inland tribes. He quelled the rebellion and in gratitude was given power over part of what is today Sarawak. Appointing himself 'Rajah Brooke' he successfully cooled down the fractious tribes, suppressed head-hunting, eliminated the dreaded Borneo pirates and founded a personal dynasty that was to last for over 100 years. The Brooke family of 'White Rajahs' gradually brought more and more of Borneo under their power until the Japanese arrived during WW II.

The development of British power in Sabah was much more prosaic. Once part of the great Brunei empire, Sabah came under the influence of the British North Borneo Company after centuries of being avoided due to its unpleasant pirates. At one time Kota Kinabalu was known as Api Api, 'Fire, Fire', from the pirates' tiresome habit of repeatedly burning it down. Eventually in 1888 the whole north Borneo coast was brought under British protection although Mat Salleh, a Sabah rebel, held out against British power until his death in 1900.

World War II

From the turn of the century until WW II Malaya became steadily more prosperous although the peninsula continued to forge ahead of the north Borneo states. The various peninsula states came more under British influence, whilst more and more Chinese and Indian immigrants flooded into the country eventually outnumbering the indigenous Malays. By the time WW II broke out in Europe Malaya supplied nearly 40% of the world's rubber and 60% of its tin.

When the war arrived in Malaya its impact was sudden and devastating. A few hours before the first Japanese aircraft was sighted over Pearl Harbor the Japanese landed at Kota Bahru in the north of Malaya and started their lightning dash down the peninsula. British confidence that they were more than a match for the Japanese soon proved to be sadly misplaced and it took the Japanese little over a month to take Kuala Lumpur and a month after that they were at the doors of Singapore. On 15 February 1942 Singapore fell and the remaining British inhabitants who had not managed to escape were to spend the rest of the war in prison camps. North Borneo had fallen to the Japanese with even greater speed.

The Japanese were unable to form a cohesive policy in Malaya since there was not a well organised Malay independence movement which they could harness to their goals. Furthermore many Chinese were bitterly opposed to the Japanese who had invaded China in the 1930s. Remnants of the British forces continued a guerrilla struggle against the Japanese throughout the war and the predominantly Chinese Communist Malayan People's Anti-Japanese Army also continued the struggle against the Japanese.

Post War & the Emergency

Following the sudden end of WW II Britain was faced with reorganising its position in Malaya. There had not been the same concerted push towards independence which India had been through in the inter-war years so while independence and the end of colonial rule was clearly a long term programme, in the short term British rule was likely to continue.

At first the plan was to take over the rule of Sabah, Sarawak and Brunei, to form the Malay states into a Malay Union and to rule Singapore as a crown colony. This plan faced one major obstacle – all prior British plans for Malaya had been based on the premise that the country was Malayan despite the increased population of people from either Chinese or Indian descent. With their increase this premise became less and less realistic. Through WW II the population of Indians and Chinese had become much more settled than before and now there was even less likelihood of them returning to their 'homelands'. British acceptance of this fact of life naturally provoked strong Malay opposition.

Faced with these difficulties the British soon had an even greater problem to grapple with – the Emergency. In 1948 the Malayan Communist Party, which had fought against the Japanese throughout the war, decided the time had come to end British colonial rule and launched a guerrilla struggle which was to continue for 12 years. Although there are still sporadic outbreaks of Communist violence the threat was eventually declared over in 1960. In part this was because the Communists were never able to gain a broad spectrum of support. They were always predominantly a Chinese grouping and while the Malays might have wanted independence from Britain they certainly did not want rule by the Chinese. Nor were all Chinese in favour of the party, it was mainly an uprising of the peasantry and lower classes.

Independence

In 1955 Britain agreed that Malaya would become fully independent within two years, but in the same year Singapore was torn by strikes, riots and demonstrations over low wages, terrible housing conditions, unemployment and education. Nevertheless in 1956 Britain also agreed that Singapore should have internal self government by 1959. Malaya duly achieved independence (merdeka) in 1957 despite unsuccessful meetings with Chin Peng, leader of the Communist forces, in an attempt to end the now merely smouldering Emergency. Tunku Abdul Rahman was the leader of the new nation which came into existence with remarkably few problems.

In Singapore things went nowhere near as smoothly and politics became increasingly more radical. The election in 1959 swept Lee Kuan Yew's People's Action Party (PAP) into power, but they faced a whole series of major problems. When the Federation of Malaya was formed in 1948 the Malay leaders were strongly opposed to including Singapore because this would have tipped the racial balance from a Malay majority to a Chinese one. Furthermore while politics in Malaya were orderly, upper class and gentlemanly, in Singapore they were anything but.

Nevertheless to Singapore merger with Malaya seemed to be the only answer to high unemployment, a soaring birthrate and the loss of its traditional trading role with the growth of independent South-East Asian nations. Malaya was none too keen to inherit this little parcel of problems, but when it seemed possible that the moderate PAP party might be toppled by its own left wing the thought of a moderate Singapore within Malaysia became less off-putting than the thought of a communist Singapore outside it. Accordingly in 1961 Tunku Abdul Rahman agreed to work towards the creation of Malaysia which would include Singapore. To balance the addition of Singapore, discussion also commenced on adding Sarawak, Sabah and Brunei to the union. This proposal was welcomed by Britain who had been facing the problem of exactly what to do with their north Borneo possessions.

Confrontation

Accordingly in 1963 Malaysia came into existence although at the last moment Brunei, afraid of losing its oil wealth, refused to join. No sooner had Malaysia been created than problems arose. First of all the Philippines laid claim to Sabah, which had been known as North Borneo prior to the union. More seriously Indonesia laid claim to the whole place and Sukarno, now in the final phase of his megalomania, commenced his ill-starred 'Confrontation'. Indonesian guerrilla forces crossed the borders from Kalimantan (Indonesian south Borneo) into Sabah and Sarawak and landings were made in Peninsular Malaysia and even in Singapore.

British troops, having finally quelled the Emergency only four years earlier, now found themselves back in the jungle once again.

Singapore Departs

At the same time relations between Malaya and Singapore soured almost as soon as Malaysia was formed. The ogre of Chinese domination reared its ugly head, and Singapore refused to extend the privileged position held by Malays in Malaya to Malays in Singapore. In August 1965, exactly two years after Malaysia was created, Singapore was kicked out.

Fortunately for Singapore the breathing space had been a valuable one. Lee Kuan Yew had tamed the PAP's left wing and Singapore radicals who spoke out against his policies soon found themselves off the streets indefinitely. The economy had started to grow and with Sukarno's dramatic fall from power and the end of Confrontation Singapore was soon able to plot a path towards prosperity.

Lee Kuan Yew went all out on his campaign to turn Singapore into a tough, resilient country where enterprise and hard work would win the day. It worked – by the late '70s Singapore, a country devoid of natural resources and with massive problems of unemployment and squalid living conditions, had become the second most prosperous country in Asia with negative unemployment and a much praised government housing plan. Nor was Malaysia doing so badly – abundant natural resources, self-sufficiency in oil and a reasonable population level all helped to give Malaysia economic prospects not far behind Singapore.

Problems in Malaysia

By 1968 the PAP in Singapore had changed their precarious electoral position at the beginning of the decade so dramatically that they now held every single seat in the Singapore parliament! When a solitary opposition representative was elected in 1981 it made headlines. Despite its economic stability, things were not so smooth politically in Malaysia. One of the cornerstones of the government's policy had been to right the imbalance between the various elements of Malaysia's population.

In 1969 only 1.5% of company assets in Malaysia were owned by Malays and per capita income amongst Malays was less than 50% of that of non-Malays. Attempts to unify Malaysia by making Bahasa Malay the one national language also created resentment amongst the non-Malays as did the privileges Malays had in land ownership, business licences, educational opportunities and government positions. In 1969 violent intercommunal riots broke out, particularly in Kuala Lumpur. Hundreds of people were killed.

Following these riots the government moved to improve the position of Malays in Malaysia with much greater speed. The title *bumiputra* or 'sons of the soil' was created to define the indigenous Malay people; this meant not only Malays, but also the aboriginal inhabitants and the indigenous peoples of Sarawak and Sabah. New guidelines were instituted stipulating how much of a company's shares must be held by *bumiputras* and in other ways enforcing a Malay share in the nation's wealth.

Although many Chinese realised that Malaysia could never attain real stability without an equitable distribution of the country's wealth there was also much resentment and many talented people either left the country or simply withdrew their abilities and capital. Fortunately Malaysia's natural wealth has enabled it to absorb these inefficiencies, but the problems of bringing the Malays to an equal position in the nation, economically as well as politically, remains a thorny one. Travellers in Malaysia will have ample opportunity to discuss the problem – either with expats or with Malaysians, when they know there is no possibility of them being overheard.

Malay, Malays & Malaysia

Malays are the indigenous people of Malaysia although they are not the original inhabitants. Malaya is the old name for the country which, prior to 1963, consisted only of peninsular Malaya. With the amalgamation of Malaya, Sarawak and Sabah the title Malaysia was coined for the new nation and the peninsula is now referred to as Peninsular Malaysia while Sarawak and Sabah are referred to as East Malaysia.

GEOGRAPHY

Malaysia, Singapore and Brunei consist of two distinct parts. Peninsular Malaysia is the long finger of land extending down from Asia as if pointing towards Indonesia and Australia. Singapore is the island at the very tip of this peninsula. Much of the peninsula is covered by dense jungle, particularly in its northern half where there are also high mountains, and the central area is very lightly populated. While on the western side of the peninsula there is a long fertile plain running down to the sea, the mountains descend more steeply on the eastern side where there are also many more beaches.

The other part of the region, making up more than 50% by area, is East Malaysia – the northern part of the island of Borneo. The larger, southern part is the Indonesian state of Kalimantan. East Malaysia is divided between Sarawak and Sabah with Brunei a small enclave between them. Both parts are covered by dense jungle with many large river systems, particularly in Sarawak. Mt Kinabalu in Sabah is the highest mountain in South-East Asia; indeed it is the highest mountain from Papua New Guinea to the Himalaya.

CLIMATE

Malaysia and Singapore have a typically tropical climate – it's hot and humid year round. Once you've got used to the tropics it never strikes you as too uncomfortable though, it's simply almost always warm and sunny. The temperature rarely drops below 20°C even at night and usually climbs to 30°C or more during the day.

Rain, when it comes, tends to be short and sharp and is soon replaced by more of that ever present sunshine. At certain times of the year it may rain every day but it's rare that it rains all day. Although the region is monsoonal it's only on the east coast of Malaysia that you have a real rainy season – elsewhere it's just a time of year when the average rainfall is heavier than at other times of the year.

Singapore is at its wettest from November through January, west coast Malaysia gets heavier rainfall from September through December. On the east coast, and also in Sarawak and Sabah, October through February is the wet season. Throughout the region the humidity tends to hover around the 90% mark, but on the peninsula you can always escape from heat and humidity by retreating to the delightfully cool hill stations.

NATIONAL PARKS

Malaysia, Singapore and Brunei are part of the region possessing the most ancient rainforests in the world, having remained virtually unchanged for many millions of years. Particularly in Malaysia we can see the entire spectrum – from the extensive, lowland rainforest tracts, to the summits of several mountainous areas (Mt Kinabalu in Sabah is the highest mountain between the Himalaya and New Guinea at 4101 metres). West Malaysia sits at the centre of what has evolved into the most complex, diverse animal and plant communities ever known. Situated along the north of the great island of Borneo, East Malaysia and Brunei are more on the periphery of this tropical lushness, but have not missed much of this diversity.

It is the remarkable climatic stability of this region which has made its forests such a major focal point of scientific interest for many years. Within these vast jungles nature has run rampant for so long that just about every type of bizarre animal or plant known today has survived somewhere there. In fact, scientists are still far from knowing even a significant percentage of the mysteries concealed in these forests. Regrettably, the focal point has shifted to one of concern to understand this living laboratory before it is irretrievably consumed by uncontrolled development and inadequate conservation measures.

In Peninsular Malaysia alone there are over 8000 species of flowering plants, including 2000 trees, 800 orchids and 200 palms. Here is found the world's tallest tropical tree species, the Tualang, reaching to a height of 80 metres, with a base diameter of over three metres. The *Rafflesia* is the world's largest flower measuring up to one-metre across and weighing up to nine kg.

There are over 200 species of mammals, 450 of birds, 250 of reptiles (including 100 snakes, 14 tortoises and turtles and three crocodiles), 90 frogs, and 150,000 insects (including the giant birdwing butterflies and the Atlas moth). There are snakes, lizards and frogs which can 'fly', spiders that eat birds, giant (as well as flying) squirrels, and many smaller creatures which have 'giant' versions. Even the leeches can seem huge after a day on some of the jungle trails!

Mammals include elephants, rhinos (very rare now), tapirs, tigers, leopards, honey bears, several kinds of deer, seladang (forest cattle), various gibbons and monkeys (including in Borneo the orang-utan and the bizarre proboscis monkey in which the male has a huge, pendulous nose), scaly anteaters (pangolins) and porcupines, to name a few.

The bird life features spectacular pheasants, hornbills (including the rare helmeted hornbill, prized for its 'ivory' – actually the base of its 'horn' or casque), and many groups of colourful birds, such as kingfishers, sunbirds, pittas, woodpeckers, trogons and barbets. Snakes include cobras, notably the spitting cobra, which shoots venom into the eyes of its prey, vipers (the kind seen in snake temples), pythons (including the reticulated python, the world's longest snake, with some

growing over 10 metres), and colourful tree snakes (most are harmless to man).

The Orang Asli (original people) still living in the forests survive in scattered groups. They are allowed to hunt in protected areas, such as parts of Taman Negara, as long as they only practise traditional hunting methods, such as the blowgun, with darts poisoned by the sap of the ipoh tree, a relative of the South American curare.

The British had established the first national park, in Malaysia, in 1938, which is now included in Taman Negara, Malaysia's major (and Peninsular Malaysia's only) national park. Its future is still not secured as sections are threatened by various development plans. East Malaysia has several national parks, forming a valuable, but still inadequate network. Singapore contains several nature reserves, particularly for the protection of water catchment areas, while Brunei is in the stage of developing a protected areas system.

The greatest concern today is to see more areas protected in Peninsular Malaysia, because the diversity of the flora and fauna is the richest, containing much that does not extend to Borneo. Many areas have been proposed for protection, with the most important area being the lowland forests of Endau-Rompin (perhaps the last refuge for the Sumatran rhinoceros, photographed in the wild only in December 1983), straddling the borders of Pahang and Johore. Today we can see an increase in public awareness of these and other environmental problems. In the 1970s the region of Gunung Mulu, in east Sarawak, was the centre of what became the most intensively studied tropical forest area in the world, leading to the establishment of a national park there. Visitor facilities, however, are still underdeveloped.

For those who wish to experience the primeval world of the ancient rainforests, Taman Negara offers a spectacular introduction, but there are other places which can be visited in Peninsular Malaysia, and a visit to East Malaysia is recommended, if only to see (and perhaps climb) Mt Kinabalu. Details are provided here for the main national parks and several other places.

Accommodation is not a problem when visiting most national parks, and various categories, from hostel to chalet, are available. In Peninsular Malaysia, contact River Park Sdn Bhd (tel 03-2915299), 260-H 2nd Mile, Jalan Ipoh, Kuala Lumpur, to arrange your dates, transport, accommodation and pay a deposit. Best times: June through September (east coast, including Taman Negara); October through March (west coast).

In Sabah contact the Sabah Parks Office (tel 211585), Box 10626, Kota Kinabalu. It's in Block L of Sinsuran Kompleks, opposite the waterfront. In Sarawak, contact the National Parks & Wildlife Office (tel 2466477), opposite the Sikh temple on Jalan Mosque, Kuching. It is always advisable to settle all arrangements and fees in advance. Best time is April through October. Basic and other information is available in all areas, and may be found in tourist offices also.

Taman Negara

A scenic region of forested plateau, hills and mountains covering 4343 square km, the national park ranges from 120 to 2150 metres (the summit of Gunung Tahan, the highest mountain in Peninsular Malaysia). It is traversed by several rivers, and of these, the Tembeling provides access to the park headquarters. From Kuala Lumpur take a bus or taxi to Kuala Tembeling via Jerantut. Here you meet the park boat for the 60-km trip into the park, taking three to four hours. Around the headquarters are several trails, and a number of observation hides can be visited. For the adventurous, it's a nine-day return trip to Gunung Tahan; otherwise there is much to do walking the trails, watching at the hides, or arranging a river trip.

Templar Park

This park of 12 square km was originally established as a botanical reserve in 1955, but is now a fully protected area, about 30 minutes from Kuala Lumpur. Signs of former tin-mining operations can be seen but today it is a popular place for a day trip. The dominant feature of the area is the 305-metre limestone hill Bukit Takun. The main trail to the summit is the centre of activity for many visitors and offers good views. There are many caves there, too, with little known about them. A good place to go if you're contemplating Kinabalu. It is reached on the Rawang road, turning off at the 13th milestone. The road forks ahead, with a right turn indicating the main Templar Park area, while Bukit Takun is straight ahead. Also near there are the Kancing Falls and Serendah Forest Reserve.

Bukit Lagong Forest Reserve

This 607-hectare reserve, close to Kuala Lumpur, includes a Forest Research Institute. There are several attractions for visitors, including a picnic area near a waterfall, a small museum and an arboretum. The 300-metre peak of Bukit Lagong can be climbed on a good trail through undisturbed forest (about two hours up). A visit may be arranged by contacting the Director, Forest Research Institute, Kepong, Selangor. A guide is needed for Bukit Lagong.

Bukit Timah Nature Reserve

A piece of primary forest measuring 75 hectares, the nature reserve is located at the south-west fringe of the catchment area in Singapore. In land-short Singapore this and other small reserves are being increasingly used for public recreation. Facilities are much improved and access is easy to organise through the island's efficient bus services.

Gunung Mulu National Park

This is Sarawak's largest national park, covering an area of 544 square km. The park contains Sarawak's second highest peak, Gunung Mulu, 2376 metres of sandstone and Gunung Api, 1750 metres of limestone. The surrounding vegetation varies from peat swamp to limestone and forest terrain.

This national park contains about 1500 species of flowering plants, including 10 species of the famous pitcher plant. The pitcher plants attract many scientists and students of botany to Gunung Mulu. Removing these plants from the national park, or from the country, is strictly prohibited – there is a smuggling network.

Another feature of Gunung Mulu National Park is the underground cave system, apparently, the most extensive cave network in the world. At present, you can only visit the Deer Cave and part of the Clearwater Cave. The Deer Cave runs through an entire mountain and is the largest cave passage known to man. Clearwater Cave, the longest cave in South-East Asia, has a length of 51½ km. There are many other caves in the park but, authorities are still in the process of 'preparing' them for the public.

Gunung Mulu is becoming one of the most popular destinations in Sarawak, though it is an expensive place to visit. To get there, take a bus to Kuala Baram, then an express boat from Kuala Baram to Marudi. From Marudi, charter a longboat to Kuala Apoh and from there, take another to park headquarters. Package tours can also be arranged in Miri.

Bako National Park

A small park of 26 square km in west Sarawak, the Bako National Park is on the peninsula at the mouth of the Bako River. It features sandstone cliffs and sandy bays, with a range of forest types, including mangroves. Access is only by boat, about 30 minutes from Kuching to Kampung Bako, from where you take another boat into the park. The park has beach areas and a network of paths. Camping gear can be hired, but all food must be brought with you. A pleasant way to spend a few days.

Niah National Park

This 31 square km park has only recently been established to protect the valuable Niah caves, made famous by the discoveries of traces of early man dating back 35,000 years. The caves are also remarkable for the millions of bats and swiftlets which roost there. The swiftlets are famous, as their nests made of saliva are collected for bird's nest soup. The mass movements of these bats and swiftlets through the mouth of the Great Cave are a spectacular sight at dawn and dusk. Other examples of cave life can be seen, and if you are lucky you may see the black-and-white bat hawk at the entrance waiting to pounce on a bat or swiftlet.

The park, in east Sarawak, can be reached from Bintulu or Miri via nearby Batu Niah. Hostel space and boat access can be arranged in advance, or just stay at Batu Niah and walk in. The walk includes the famous plank trail, which can take 45 minutes to one hour, if not too slippery. (If you're not sure about your shoes you can walk the planks barefoot.) There are other trails in the park and a longhouse nearby. It's a good detour if you're travelling overland to Brunei and Sabah.

Tunku Abdul Rahman National Park

This park covers five islands off Kota Kinabalu, Sabah, and has an area of about 49 square km. The main features are coral reefs and beaches that can only be visited by making arrangements with private boat operators, which is good if you can organise a small group. Park headquarters are on Pulau Gaya, the largest island. There are also forest trails, and camping can be arranged, but all food must be brought in. Facilities for day visitors are available and plans to increase tourism, such as a rest house on Pulau Mamutik, are well underway.

This park partly developed from the notion that protecting offshore islands also protected the flora and fauna of Sabah until it was demonstrated that most of it is not found off the mainland. Fortunately, it led to the establishment of the first valuable marine park, with the hope that Malaysia will protect more of its marine resources.

Kinabalu National Park

This magnificent park of about 770 square km was established in 1964 to protect the massif of Mt Kinabalu and its environs. The region has been a focal point of exploration and scientific investigation in Borneo for over 100 years. Today the focus has shifted more towards tourism as the climb to the summit offers such an exciting enticement to the visitor.

The park headquarters (1560 metres) is about 50 km from Kota Kinabalu at Simpangan. Getting there takes about two hours, it's close to the road. Buses stop there on the way to Ranau or Sandakan, but there are also minibuses and Land Rovers available. It is advisable to book ahead for accommodation at the headquarters in case large groups of summit seekers may be arriving. Also, the army uses the mountain for hiking exercises and can quickly fill up the available space. While it is not so essential to book ahead for the high-altitude huts, it is worth checking at headquarters about groups which may have gone up just before you arrived.

There is plenty of information available at park headquarters for planning your ascent, including a recently published book by the Sabah Society. Plan to spend at least two or more nights on the mountain in case fickle weather conditions force you to wait for a clear morning to reach the top. The best time to be there is at or near sunrise. On a clear morning the vista is incredible and exhilarating and is definitely worth all the time spent getting there.

The trail, starting on a road, is well marked all the way up, with steeper sections graded and other aids provided nearer the top. The Panar Laban huts and those just below it (around 3340 metres) are the main stop for climbers and a good base for exploring the upper terrain, but Sayat Sayat hut (3800 metres), although smaller, can give you more time to reach the summit and await the sunrise. All food and cooking fuel must be carried up, so it is always better to allow provisions for at least one day more than you intend to stay. Also be sure to have enough warm clothing and sleeping gear. Guides are recommended for all visitors, although it is possible to join up with others once you are at the upper huts.

At least a week is needed at the park. Around the headquarters are several shorter trails, and a day or overnight trip can be made to the Poring Hot Springs, about 20 km by road on the other side of Ranau. Kinabalu offers one of the best opportunities to see the changes in the forests, which become very stunted near the top. The famous pitcher plants can be seen along the trail, with the largest ones capable of holding two litres of water. There are many fascinating animals found in the upper levels of Kinabalu, with the most obvious being squirrels and birds, notably the mountain blackbird and the Kinabalu friendly warbler. A native rat species has found the huts to be a good food source and some have learned to lift the lid on rice pots and steal leftovers.

Sepilok Reserve & Orang-Utan Rehabilitation Centre

If you go to Sandakan, it is worth visiting this centre. Take a No 14 Batu bus. This centre was originally designed for looking after orang-utans before releasing them back into the wild, but it has become a little touristy and the animals are the main attraction. Some other animals are also kept there, and there is a very good visitor centre. Through the compound there are some forest trails which offer good walking in lowland forest. The forest on the seaward side of the reserve contains proboscis monkeys and it is possible to organise a boat to try and see them. Check with the centre or at the National Parks office in Sandakan.

In 1983, a devastating fire burned for six months in east Borneo, including parts of east Sabah.

- Murray D Bruce
- Constance S Leap Bruce

PEOPLE

The ethnic groups that comprise the people of Singapore and Malaysia are essentially the same – Malays, Chinese, Indian, indigenous Orang Asli and the various tribes of Sarawak and Sabah. The Malays are the majority indigenous people of the region although they were preceded by aboriginal people, small pockets of whom still survive. The Malays are Muslim and despite major changes in the last decades are still to some extent 'country' rather than 'city' people.

The Chinese are later arrivals. Although some have been there since the time of Admiral Cheng Ho's visit to Melaka in 1403, the vast majority of the region's Chinese settlers have arrived since the beginning of the 19th century. The biggest group of Chinese are Hokkiens who comprise 40% of the population of Singapore. Another 20% are Teochews and slightly less than that percentage, Cantonese. The remainders are Hakkas, Hainanese and other groups. Although all Chinese use a similar script the dialects can be quite different and a Hokkien and a Hakka speaker may well have to resort to English to communicate!

The region's Indian population arrived later still and in a more organised fashion. Whereas the Chinese flooded in of their own volition the Indians were mainly brought in to provide plantation labour for the British colonists. In Singapore approximately 60% of the Indian population are Tamils and a further 20% are Malayalis from the other southern state of

Kerala. The remainder include Kashmiris, Sikhs, Punjabis and Bengalis.

There are still small scattered groups of Orang Asli, 'original people', in Peninsular Malaysia. The indigenous people of Sarawak and Sabah are much greater in number, approaching one million in total. They include Ibans and Land Dyaks in Sarawak and the Muruts of Sabah – all of whom are noted for the longhouses they live in. In this form of communal living a whole village effectively shares one 'long house' with individual houses opening out onto the shared verandah. The Kadazan of Sabah and the Punan of Sarawak are other groups. Of course there are also other minority groups including expatriate westerners, Japanese, Sri Lankans, Filipinos and Indonesians (many of the Filipino and Indonesian people are illegal immigrants or refugees).

RELIGIONS

The variety of religions found in Malaysia and Singapore is a direct reflection of the diversity of races living there. Although Islam is the state religion of Malaysia, freedom of religion is guaranteed. The Malays are almost all Muslims and there are also some Indian Muslims. The Chinese are predominantly Buddhists, though some are Christians. The majority of the region's Indian population come from south India and are Hindu. Although Christianity has made no great inroads into Peninsular Malaysia it has had a much greater impact upon Sarawak and Sabah where many of the indigenous people have converted to Christianity.

FESTIVALS & HOLIDAYS

With so many cultures and religions there is a quite amazing number of occasions to celebrate in Malaysia and Singapore. Although some of them have a fixed date each year, the Hindus, Muslims and Chinese all follow a lunar calendar which results in the dates for many events varying each year. In particular Muslim festivals can change enormously over a period of years. Each year, the TDC puts out a *Calendar of Events* booklet with specific dates and venues of various festivals and parades.

The major Muslim events each year are connected with Ramadan the 30 days during which Muslims cannot eat or drink from sunrise to sunset.

Fifteen days before the commencement of Ramadan the souls of the dead are supposed to visit their homes on Nisfu Night. During Ramadan Lailatul Qadar, the 'Night of Grandeur', celebrates the arrival of the Koran on earth from heaven before its revelation by Mohammed. A Koran reading competition is held in Kuala Lumpur (and extensively televised) during Ramadan.

Hari Raya Puasa marks the end of the month-long fast with three days of joyful celebration. This is the major holiday of the Muslim calendar and it can be difficult to find accommodation in Malaysia, particularly on the east coast. Hari Raya Puasa commences 10 days earlier each year (in 1988, this festival begins in mid-May and in 1989, early May).

14 January
Thai Pongal A Hindu harvest festival marking the beginning of the Hindu month of Thai, considered the luckiest month of the year.

January-February
Chinese New Year Dragon dances and pedestrian parades mark the start of the new year. Families hold open house, unmarried relatives (especially children) receive *ang pows* (money in red packets), businesses traditionally clear their debts and everybody wishes you a Kong Hee Fatt Choy (a happy & prosperous new year).
Birthday of Chor Soo Kong Six days after the new year the number of snakes at Penang's snake temple, dedicated to Chor Soo Kong, is supposed to be the greatest.

Birthday of the Jade Emperor Nine days after the new year a Chinese festival honours Yu Huang, the Supreme Ruler of Heaven, with offerings at temples.
Ban Hood Huat Hoay A 12-day celebration for the Day of Ten Thousand Buddhas is held at the Kek Lok Si Temple in Penang.
Chap Goh Meh On the 15th day after Chinese New Year the celebrations officially end.
Chingay In Singapore and Johore Bahru processions of Chinese flag bearers, balancing bamboo flag poles six to 12-metres long, can be seen on the 22nd day after the new year.
Thaipusam One of the most dramatic Hindu festivals in which devotees honour Lord Subramaniam with acts of amazing masochism. In Singapore they march in a procession to the Chettiar Temple carrying *kavadis*, heavy metal frames decorated with peacock feathers, fruit and flowers. The kavadis are hung from their bodies with metal hooks and spikes driven into the flesh. Other devotees pierce their cheeks and tongues with metal skewers or walk on sandals of nails. Along the procession route the kavadi carriers dance to the drum beat while spectators urge them on with shouts of 'Vel, Vel'. In the evening the procession continues with an image of Subramaniam in a temple car.

In Penang, Thaipusam is celebrated at the Waterfall Temple and in KL at the Batu Caves. This festival is now officially banned in India.

Late February
Kwong Teck Sun Ong's Birthday Celebration of the birthday of a child deity at the Chinese temple in Kuching.

March-April
Tua Peck Kong Paper money and paper models of useful things to have with you in the after life are burnt at the Sia Sen Temple in Kuching.
Easter On Palm Sunday a candlelight

procession is held at St Peter's in Melaka. Good Friday and Easter Monday also witness colourful celebrations at St Peter's and other Melaka churches and in the Church of St Joseph in Singapore.

Panguni Uttiram On the full moon day of the Tamil month of Panguni, the marriage of Shiva to Shakti and of Lord Subramaniam to Theivani is celebrated.

Birthday of the Goddess of Mercy Offerings are made to the very popular Kuan Yin at her temples in Penang, Kuala Lumpur and Singapore.

Cheng Beng On All Soul's Day Chinese traditionally visit the tombs of their ancestors to clean and repair them and make offerings.

Sri Rama Navami A nine-day festival held by the Brahman caste to honour the Hindu hero of the Ramayana, Sri Rama.

Birthday of the Monkey God The birthday of T'se Tien Tai Seng Yeh is celebrated twice a year. In Singapore mediums pierce their cheeks and tongues with skewers and go into a trance during which they write special charms in blood.

Birthday of the Saint of the Poor Kong Teck Choon Ong is honoured with a procession from the White Cloud Temple on Ganges Avenue in Singapore.

April-May

Songkran Festival A traditional Thai Buddhist New Year in which buddha images are bathed.

Chithirai Vishu Start of the Hindu New Year.

Puja Pantai A large three-day beach festival held five km south of Kuala Trengganu.

Birthday of the Queen of Heaven Ma Cho Po, the Queen of Heaven and Goddess of the Sea, is honoured at her temples.

Vesak Day Buddha's birth, enlightenment and death are celebrated by various events including the release of caged birds to symbolise the setting free of captive souls.

Early May

Sipitang Tamu Besar Annual market celebration at Sipitang near Beaufort in Sabah. Blowpipe competitions feature among the events.

May

Start of the turtle season; from then, through to September giant turtles come ashore along the beach at Rantau Abang on the east coast of the peninsula each night to lay their eggs.

10 to 11 May

Kadazan Harvest Festival A thanksgiving harvest festival by the Kadazan farmers of Sabah, marked by the sumazau Kadazan dance.

30 to 31 May

Kota Belud Tamu Besar Bajau horsemen feature in this annual market festival at Kota Belud, near Kota Kinabalu in Sabah.

May-June

Birthday of the Third Prince The child-god is honoured with a procession from the Taoist temple dedicated to him in Singapore – it's near the junction of Clarke St and North Boat Quay.

1 to 2 June

Gawai Dayak Annual Sarawak festival of the Dayaks to mark the end of the rice season. War dances, cockfights and blowpipe events all take place.

4 June

Birthday of the Yang di Pertuang Agong Celebration of the official birthday of Malaysia's Supreme Head of State.

29 June

Festa de San Pedro Christian celebration in honour of the patron saint of fishermen, particularly celebrated by the Eurasian-Portuguese community of Melaka.

June
Birthday of the God of War Kuan Ti, who has the ability to avert war and protect people during a war, is honoured on his birthday.

June-August
Dragon Boat Festival Commemorating the death of a Chinese saint who drowned, this festival is celebrated with boat races in Singapore.

June-September
Isra Dan Mi'Raj A Muslim holiday in mosques and homes to celebrate the prophet's ascension.

1 July
Keningau Tamu Besar Market festival at Keningau in Sabah with buffalo races, blowpipe competitions and other events.

29 July
Tuaran Tamu Besar Tuaran, only 35 km from Kota Kinabalu, celebrates its annual market festival with boat races as well as Bajau horsemen and other events.

Late July
Lumut Sea Carnival At Lumut, the port for Pangkor Island, boat races, swimming races and many other events are held.

July
Birthday of Kuan Yin The Goddess of Mercy has another birthday!

July-August
Sri Krishna Jayanti A 10-day Hindu festival celebrating popular events in Krishna's life is highlighted on day eight by celebrations of his birthday. The Laxmi Narayan Temple in Kuala Lumpur is a particular focus.

July-September
Market Festival Month-long festival in the markets of Singapore with wayangs (street operas).

9 August
Singapore National Day A series of military and civilian processions and an evening firework display celebrate Singapore's independence in 1965.

31 August
National Day Hari Kebangsaan Malaysia celebrates Malaysia's independence with events all over the country, but particularly in Kuala Lumpur where there are parades and a variety of performances in the Lake Gardens.

31 August
Beaufort Tamu Besar Another annual market festival in Sabah.

August
Festival of the Seven Sisters Chinese girls pray to the Weaving Maid for good husbands.
Festival of the Hungry Ghosts The souls of the dead are released for one day of feasting and entertainment on earth. Chinese operas and other events are laid on for them and food is put out, which the ghosts eat the spirit of but thoughtfully leave the substance for mortal celebrants.

August-September
Vinayagar Chathuri During the Tamil month of Avani prayers are offered to Vinayagar, another name for the extremely popular elephant-headed god Ganesh.

1 to 22 September
Feast of Santa Cruz A month-long pilgrimage season at the Church of Santa Cruz at Malim, Melaka.

15 to 20 September
Papar Tamu Besar Annual market festival in an area of Sabah renowned for its beautiful Kadazan girls.

September
Moon Cake Festival The overthrow of the Mongol warlords in ancient China is celebrated by eating moon cakes and

lighting colourful paper lanterns. Moon cakes are made with bean paste, lotus seeds and sometimes a duck egg.

September-October
Thimithi – Fire Walking Ceremony Hindu devotees prove their belief by walking across glowing coals at the Gajah Berang Temple in Melaka or the Sri Mariamman Temple in Singapore.

Navarathri In the Tamil month of Purattasi the Hindu festival of 'Nine Nights' is dedicated to the wives of Shiva, Vishnu and Brahma. Young girls are dressed as the goddess Kali. The Chettiar Temple in Singapore is a centre of activities.

Festival of the Nine Emperor Gods Nine days of Chinese operas, processions and other events honour the nine emperor gods. At the Kau Ong Yah Temple in Kuala Lumpur a fire walking ceremony takes place on the evening of the ninth day.

September-November
Pilgrimage to Kusu Island Tua Pek Kong, the God of Prosperity, is honoured by Taoists in Singapore by making a pilgrimage to the shrine on Kusu Island.

1 to 31 October
Puja Ketek Offerings are brought to Buddhist shrines or keteks in the state of Kelantan. Traditional dances are often performed.

Menggatal Tamu Besar Another Sabah market festival.

7 October
Universal Children's Day A rally for children in Kuala Lumpur.

Mid-October
Kudat Tamu Besar Another Sabah market festival.

October-November
Kantha Shashithi Subramaniam, a great

fighter against the forces of evil, is honoured during the Hindu month of Aipasi.

Deepavali Later in the same month Rama's victory over the demon King Ravana is celebrated with the 'Festival of Lights' where tiny oil lamps are lit outside Hindu homes.

Birthday of Kuan Yin The birthday of the popular Goddess of Mercy is celebrated yet again.

Kartikai Deepam Huge bonfires are lit to commemorate Shiva's appearance as a pillar of fire following an argument with Vishnu and Brahma. The Thandayuthapani Temple in Muar is a major site for this festival.

22 November

Guru Nanak's Birthday The birthday of Guru Nanak, founder of the Sikh religion, is celebrated on this day.

December

Pesta Pulau Penang Month-long carnival on Penang Island featuring many water events including dragon boat races towards the end of the festival.

Winter Solstice Festival Chinese festival to offer thanks for a good harvest.

25 December

Christmas Day

LANGUAGE

You can get along quite happily with English throughout Malaysia and Singapore. Although it is not the official language in either country it is still the linking language between the various ethnic groups. When a Tamil wants to speak to a Chinese or a Chinese to a Malay it's likely they'll speak in English. Officially Bahasa Malay or 'bahasa' is the language in both countries. In Malaysia the government is trying to make that edict a reality, but in Singapore only lip service is paid to it. There the everyday languages are either English or one of the Chinese dialects like Hakka or Hokkien. The government is,

however, waging a campaign to persuade people to speak Mandarin, the main non-dialectal Chinese language. The majority of the region's Indians speak Tamil although there are also groups who speak Malayalam, Hindi or another Indian language.

Bahasa is, as near as it makes no difference, the same as Indonesian. So if you are also visiting Indonesia you'll find a little knowledge worthwhile since English is not so widely spoken. Picking up enough Bahasa to get by on is remarkably easy and also good fun. Bahasa is, at least in its most basic form, very simple. There are no tense changes for example; you indicate the tense by using words such as yesterday or tomorrow or you just add *suda* (already) to make anything past tense. Many nouns are pluralised simply by saying them twice – thus *buku* is 'book', *buku buku* is 'books'. Or *anak* is 'child', *anak anak* is 'children'. They are often written *buku 2* or *anak 2*.

The everyday street language is often referred to as *pasar* or market language. Other language simplifications include the omission of the articles 'the', 'a' or 'an'. Thus you just say *buku baik* rather than 'a good book' or 'the good book'. The verb 'to be' is also omitted so again it would be *buku baik* rather than 'the book is good'. Bahasa is also a very musical and evocative language – 'the sun', for example, is *mata hari* or 'the eye of the day'!

Just as many Hindi words have found their way into Indian-English so many Malay terms are used in everyday English in Malaysia. You'll often read in the papers or see ads with the word *bumiputra*, which literally means 'sons of the soil' but is used to specify that the job or whatever is open only to Malay-Malays not Indian-Malays or Chinese-Malays. Papers occasionally complain about *jaga keretas* – they are people who operate car parking rackets – pay them to 'protect' your car while it is parked or you'll wish you had. Or you may hear of a couple being accused of *khalwat* – literally 'close proximity' and something unmarried Muslims should not be suspect of!

One thing to note about pronunciation is that in Bahasa Malay 'c' is pronounced as 'ch' in the English word 'church'.

Lonely Planet also publishes the pocket-size *Indonesian Phrasebook*. It is a handy introduction to Bahasa Indonesian or Malay.

Civilities

thank you (very much)
terima kasih (banyak)
please
silakan
good morning
selamat pagi
good day
selamat siang
goodbye (to person staying)
selamat tinggal
goodbye (to person going)
selamat jalan
good afternoon/evening
selamat sore
good night
selamat malam
sorry
ma'af
excuse me
permisi

Questions

How are you?
apa khabar?
What is this?
apa ini?
What is your name?
siapa nama saudara?
My name is . . . .
nama saya . . . .
How many km?
berapa kilometre?
where is/which way?
dimana ada/kemana?
How much (money)?
berapa (harga)?

Getting Around

ticket	*tikit*
ticket window	*tempat tikit*
bus	*bus*
train	*kereta-api*
ship	*kapal*
town	*bandar*
small town	*pekan*
city	*negri*

Numbers

1	*satu*
2	*dua*
3	*tiga*
4	*empat*
5	*lima*
6	*enam*
7	*tujuh*
8	*delapan*
9	*sembilan*
10	*sepuluh*
11	*sebelas*
12	*duablas*
20	*duapuluh*
21	*duapuluh satu*
30	*tigapuluh*
53	*limapuluh tiga*
100	*seratus*
1000	*seribu*
½	*setengah* (say *stinger*)

Time

when?	*kapan?*
tomorrow	*besok*
yesterday	*kelmarin*
hour	*jam*
week	*minggu*
year	*tahun*
what time?	*jam berapa?*
how long?	*berapa pukul?*
7 o'clock	*jam tujuh*

Days of the Week

Monday	*hari senen*
Tuesday	*hari selasa*
Wednesday	*hari rabu*
Thursday	*hari kamis*
Friday	*hari jum'at*
Saturday	*hari sabtu*
Sunday	*hari minggu*

Some Useful Phrases

I want to go to . . . . *saya mau ke . . . .*

bank	*bank*
street	*jalan*
post office	*pejabat pos*
immigration	*immigresen*

How much for . . .? *berapa harga . . .?*

one night	*satu malam*
one person	*satu orang*

I don't understand.
   saya tidak mengerti

Some Useful Words

sleep	*tidur*
bed	*tempat tidur*
room	*bilik*
bathroom	*bilik mandi*
toilet	*tandas*
soap	*sabun*
shop	*toko, kedai*
this/that	*ini/itu*
big/small	*besar/kecil*
here	*disini*
stop	*berhenti*
another	*satu lagi*
no, not, negative	*tidak*
open/closed	*buka/tutup*
see	*lihat*
good, very nice	*bagus*
no good	*tidak baik*
alright, good, fine	*baik*
finished	*habis*
dirty	*kotor*
expensive	*mahal*

Food – *makan*

fried rice	*nasi goreng*
boiled rice	*nasi putih*
rice with odds & ends	*nasi campur*
fried noodles	*mee goreng*
noodle soup	*mee kuah*
soup	*sup*

fried vegetables with crispy noodles	*cap cai tami*
sweet & sour omelette	*fu yung hai*
fish	*ikan*
chicken	*ayam*
egg	*telur*
pork	*babi*
frog	*kodok*
crab	*kepiting*
beef	*daging lembu*
prawns	*udang*
potatoes	*kentang*
vegetables	*sayur*

Drink – *minum*

drinking water	*air minum*
orange juice	*air jeruk*
coffee	*kopi*
sweet tea	*teh manis*
plain tea	*teh-o*
milk	*susu*
cordial	*stroop*

Extras

butter	*mentega*
sugar	*gula*
salt	*garam*
ice	*air batu*
hot peppers	*sambel*

Description

sweet	*manis*
no sugar	*pahat*
hot hot	*panas*
hot spicy	*pedas*
cold	*sejoh*
delicious	*enak*
special, usually means an egg on top	*istemiwa*

Finally for vegetarians *tidak mahu ikan, ayam, daging* means 'I do not want fish, chicken or meat'.

Facts for the Visitor

VISAS & IMMIGRATION – SINGAPORE

Commonwealth citizens, western Europeans and Americans do not require a visa to visit Singapore. In general you will be given a 14-day stay permit on arrival and this can be extended at the Immigration Department (tel 324031) at Empress Place. The Singapore government has decided that 14 days is enough for anybody to get their duty-free shopping done and unless you can provide a guarantee from a Singapore sponsor you'd better plan on being on your way by day 14.

Singapore used to be famed for its 'anti long hair and hippy' attitudes but these have somewhat relaxed of late. You're unlikely to be given a free haircut on arrival unless you look really outrageous. Nor, despite the signs in post offices and the like announcing that 'long-haired males will be served last', are you likely to find yourself perpetually at the end of the queue if your hair reaches your collar. Nevertheless it's wise not to look too scruffy on arrival in Singapore – but that's simple good manners in any Asian country.

Some Singaporean consulates and embassies overseas include:

Australia
    81 Mugga Way, Red Hill, Canberra ACT 2603
Germany
    Ubierstrasse 45, 5300 Bonn-Bad, Godesberg
Hong Kong
    19th floor, Wang Kee Building, 36 Connaught Rd, Central
India
    48 Golf Links, New Delhi 110003
Indonesia
    23 Jalan Proklamasi, Jakarta
    3 Jalan Suryo, Medan
Japan
    12-2 Roppongi, 5 Chome, Minato-ku, Tokyo

Malaysia
    5th floor, Straits Trading Building, Leboh Pasar Besar, Kuala Lumpur
New Zealand
    17 Kabul St, Khandallah, Wellington
Philippines
    6th floor, ODC International Plaza, 217-219 Salcedo St, Legaspi Village, Makati, Rizal
Sweden
    Banergathan 10, 5 Tr S-11522 Stockholm
Thailand
    129 Sathorn Tai Rd, Bangkok
UK
    2 Wilton Crescent, London SW1
USA
    1824 R St NW, Washington DC 20009

VISAS & IMMIGRATION – MALAYSIA

Commonwealth citizens, citizens of the Republic of Ireland, Switzerland, the Netherlands and Liechtenstein do not require a visa to visit Malaysia. Citizens of the United States, West Germany, France, Italy, Norway, Sweden, Denmark, Belgium, Finland, Luxembourg and Iceland do not require a visa for a visit not exceeding three months. Seven-day visas are granted to citizens of Czechoslovakia, Hungary, Poland, Russian, Yugoslavia, Rumania and Bulgaria.

Recently the immigration regulations for visitors have been eased and now you normally get a 30-day stay permit on arrival. Previously you only got 14 days and if you wanted to stay longer had to hunt out an immigration office, fill in a form, hand in your passport and hang around for half an hour to have your length of stay extended. The extension was quite straightforward, just time consuming.

Note that Sabah and Sarawak are treated in some ways like separate countries. Your passport will be checked again on arrival in each state and a new stay permit issued. Travelling directly from either Sabah or Sarawak back to Peninsular Malaysia, however, there are no formalities and you do not start a new entry period.

Malaysia is very unhappy about 'hippy' visitors. The regulations state that:

Malaysia welcomes bona fide tourists but not hippies. If you are found dressed in shabby, dirty or indecent clothes, or living in temporary or makeshift shelters you will be deemed a hippy, your visit pass will be cancelled and you will be ordered to leave Malaysia within 24 hours, failing which you will be prosecuted under the immigration laws, furthermore you will not be permitted to enter Malaysia again.

In the mid-70s this ruling was used on a number of occasions as a pretext to round up westerners staying with villagers at the kampung at Batu Ferringhi in Penang since they were in 'makeshift' shelters. Similar events have occurred at Telok Bahang in Penang and at the Tanjung Kling beach centre near Melaka. Fortunately this attitude seems to have improved, however, Malaysia is a predominantly Muslim country with conservative attitudes towards dress and behaviour. Backpackers should follow the policy of dressing sensibly and behave in a manner that fits in with local attitudes.

Some Malaysian consulates and embassies overseas include:

Australia
    7 Perth Avenue, Yarralumla, Canberra ACT 2600
Canada
    60 Boteler St, Ottawa, Ontario K1N 8Y7
Germany
    Rheinallee 23, 5300 Bonn 2
Hong Kong
    24th floor, Lap Heng House 47-5, Gloucester Rd, Wanchai
India
    50M Satya Marg, Chanakyapuri, New Delhi 110021
    23 Khader Nawaz Khan Rd, Madras
Indonesia
    17 Jalan Imam Bonjol, Jakarta
    11 Jalan Diponegoro, Medan

Japan
    20/16 Nempedai Machi, Shibuya-ku, Tokyo
Netherlands
    Adries Bickerweg 5, The Hague
New Zealand
    Chase-NBA House, 163 The Terrace, Wellington
Philippines
    2nd & 3rd floor, Republic Glass Building, Tordesillas & Galardo Sts, Salcedo Village, Makati
Singapore
    301 Jervois Rd, Singapore 1024
Thailand
    35 South Sathorn Rd, Bangkok
    4 Sukum Rd, Songkhla
UK
    45 Belgrave Square, London SW1
USA
    2401 Massachusetts Avenue NW, Washington DC 20008

VISAS & IMMIGRATION - BRUNEI

For visits of up to 14 days, visas are not necessary for citizens of France, Switzerland, Canada, Japan, Thailand, Philippines, Indonesia and the Republic of Korea. British citizens do not require a visa for visits of 30 days or less. All other nationalities, including British overseas citizens and British dependent territories citizens must have visas to visit Brunei. Citizens of Malaysian and Singapore do not require a visa to enter Brunei.

If entering from Sarawak or Sabah there's no fuss on arrival - no money showing, no requirement for an onward ticket and it's unlikely your bags will even be looked at - and a one-week stay permit is more or less automatic. If you ask you can usually get two weeks; it might be useful, you never know. At the Brunei/Sarawak border there are some yellowing-with-age and quite hilarious sketches of 'acceptable' and 'unacceptable' hair styles, but no-one cares.

MONEY

A$1	= S$1.42	M$1.82
US$1	= S$2.02	M$2.58
UK£1	= S$3.55	M$4.55

DM1	= S$1.18	M$1.51
NZ$1	= S$1.33	M$1.71
HK$1	= S$0.26	M$0.33

The Brunei dollar is on par with the Singapore dollar. Coins in use in Malaysia, Singapore and Brunei are 1c, 5c, 10c, 20c and 50c while notes are $1, $5, $10, $50, $100, $1000 and Singapore also has a S$10,000 note – not that you'll see too many. All major credit cards are widely accepted in Singapore and Malaysia although you're not going to make yourself too popular after a hard bargaining session for a new camera if you then try to pay for it with your Amex card.

Originally the Singapore, Malay and Brunei currencies were all directly interchangeable but nowadays a fixed exchange rate is no longer maintained. The Singapore and Brunei currencies are fairly comparable in value while Singapore dollars are now worth much more than Malaysian dollars. There is no chance that anybody would accept Malay dollars in Singapore, and on the other hand, it would be very extravagant to use Singapore dollars in Malaysia.

Until recently, Malaysian and Singapore coins were identical in size and shape so it didn't matter which currency you used in a pay phone, etc. Now that Singapore has completely changed their coins it is a different story.

The banks are efficient and there are also plenty of money changers, but see the special notes in the Singapore section about service charges on travellers' cheques and varying exchange rates.

For cash you will generally get a better rate at a money changer than in a bank. A money changer will probably be much quicker also. Singapore is also an excellent place to buy other foreign currencies, should you want to arrive (illegally) in India with a pocketful of rupees.

Normal banking hours in Singapore are 10 am to 3 pm from Monday to Friday and 9.30 to 11.30 am on Saturdays. The Development Bank of Singapore branches stay open until 4.30 pm on Saturdays. There is 24 hour banking at Changi Airport. There used to be a bank at the Tourist Promotions Board office but it has closed down.

In Malaysia banking hours are the same except that Sabah banks open 30 minutes earlier on weekdays and they also close 30 minutes earlier. Money changers are open much longer hours and generally offer equally good or better rates for cash than banks, but will not (usually) change travellers' cheques. Note that the exchange rate for cash in banks is usually considerably inferior to that offered for travellers' cheques. Major hotels and some major shops will also change cash and travellers' cheques, but usually at a very poor rate.

COSTS

Singapore and Malaysia can pretty much cost you what you want. If you're travelling on a shoestring budget then Malaysia has lots of hotels where a couple can get a quite decent room for around US$6 (more like US$10 in Singapore). On the other hand, if you want to spend US$100 a night on accommodation alone that is no problem either, especially in Singapore.

Food is a delight, and an economical delight at that, in Singapore and Malaysia. There's an incredible variety of restaurants, particularly in Singapore, offering excellent food at amazingly cheap prices. You'll wonder if anyone ever eats at home when you can get an excellent meal in a small restaurant for not much over US$1 – in Singapore chicken rice with soup, a soft drink, a cup of coffee and a couple of varieties of tropical fruit to finish up with will set you back less than US$3 in any food centre. Meanwhile at the other end of the scale the fancy hotels and restaurants offer French cuisine at Parisian prices.

It's the same story when it comes to getting around. If you want to travel by chauffeur-driven air-conditioned car you can, but there are lots of cheaper and quite comfortable means of getting around. In Malaysia and Singapore there are plenty of reasonably priced and reasonably honest taxis for local travel – there's no need to get into the frantic bargaining sessions or fear the subsequent arguments that taxi travel in some Asian countries entails. Longer distance, Malaysia has excellent buses, trains and surprisingly economical long-distance taxis, all at very reasonable prices.

On top of these travel essentials – accommodation, food and transport – you will also find nonessentials and luxuries are moderately priced, even downright cheap. After all, shopping is what a lot of people come to Singapore for.

TIPPING

Tipping is not normally done in Singapore or Malaysia. More expensive hotels and restaurants have a 10% service charge. In that case in Singapore tipping is actually prohibited, as it is at Singapore airport. You do not tip taxi drivers.

TOURIST INFORMATION

Both Singapore and Malaysia have efficient tourist offices with a wide range of literature and brochures available and offices around the world. In Malaysia there are also a number of local tourist promotion organisations, such as the Penang Tourist Association, who back up the national Tourist Development Corporation's activities. Some offices of the Singapore Tourist Promotion Board and the Malaysian Tourist Development Corporation include:

Singapore Tourist Promotion Board

Australia
18th floor, Goldfields House, 1 Alfred St, Circular Quay, Sydney 2000 (tel 02 241-3771)
2nd floor, Grainpool Building, 172 St George's Terrace, Perth 6000 (tel 06 322-6996)

Germany
Poststrasse 2-4, D-6000 Frankfurt/Main (tel 0611 231456)

Hong Kong   2598 9290
19th floor, Wang Kee Building, 36 Connaught Rd Central, Hong Kong (tel 5-268538)

New Zealand
c/o Rodney Walsh Ltd, 2nd floor, Dingwall Building, 87 Queen St, Auckland 1 (tel 9 793 708)

Singapore
36-04 Raffles City Tower, 250 North Bridge Rd (tel 3396622)

UK
33 Heddon St, off Regent St, London W1R 7LB (tel 01 437 0033)

USA
Suite 1008, 10th floor, 342 Madison Ave, New York, NY 10017 (tel 212 687-0385)
251 Post St, San Francisco, CA 94108 (tel 415 391-8476)

Malaysian Tourist Development Corporation

Australia
12th floor, R&W House, 92 Pitt St, Sydney 2000 (tel 02 232-3751)

Germany
Rossmarkt 17, Am Salzhaus 6, 6000 Frankfurt/Main (tel 0611 283782)

Hong Kong
Ground Floor, Shop 1, Malaysia Building, 47-50 Gloucester Rd (tel 5 285810)

Singapore
G3 Ocean Building, Collyer Quay, Singapore 0104 (tel 02 96351)

Thailand
285/9 Silom Rd, Bangkok 10500 (tel 2349808)

UK
17 Curzon St, London W1 (tel 01 499-7388)

USA
c/o MAS, Suite 2148, 420 Lexington Ave, New York, NY 10017 (tel 212 697-8994)
36th floor, Transamerica Pyramid Building, 600 Montgomery St, San Francisco, CA 94111 (tel 415 788-3344)
c/o MAS, Suite 417, 510 West Sixth St, Los Angeles, CA 90014 (tel 213 627-1301)

Brunei Darussalam Brunei does not have a tourist promotion organisation. Try writing to the Information Department, Ministry of Culture, Youth & Sport, Box 2318, Bandar Seri Begawan, Brunei. They may not reply.

GENERAL INFORMATION
Post

Singapore and Malaysia have efficient postal systems with good poste restantes at the major post offices. In Singapore the GPO is open 8 am to 6 pm Monday to Friday, 9 am to 1 pm on Saturday. The Killiney Rd post office is open 8 am to 9 pm daily. In Malaysia post offices are open 8 am to 6 pm from Monday to Friday and 8 am to 12 noon on Saturdays. Costs for aerogrammes and postcards are as follows, light air letters cost the same as aerogrammes from Singapore:

	Singapore	Malaysia
aerogramme	35c	40c
postcard to Australasia	25c	25c
Americas	55c	55c
Europe	40c	40c

Telephone

There are good telephone communications throughout Singapore and Malaysia. You can direct dial long distance calls between all major towns in Malaysia. Local calls cost 10c for three minutes in Singapore, and in Malaysia unlimited time from phone boxes, but in Singapore local calls are free from private phones. A trunk call to Singapore from KL costs M$5 before 6 pm, M$2.50 after 6 pm.

Overseas calls can be direct dialled from Singapore or Kuala Lumpur. In Singapore there are a number of telecom offices from where you can make international calls and pay by time rather than in three minute blocks. Dialling codes in Malaysia include Singapore 02, Kuala Lumpur 03, Penang 04, Ipoh 05, Melaka 06, Kuantan 095, Kuala Trengganu 096, Kota Bahru 097, Sarawak 082, Sabah 088.

In Sabah and Sarawak, you can not use public pay phones to make international calls (including collect calls).

Electricity

Electricity supplies are dependable throughout Singapore and Malaysia. Supply is 220-240 volts, 50 cycles.

Time

Singapore and Malaysia are on the same time, two hours behind Australian eastern standard time (Sydney and Melbourne), eight hours ahead of GMT (London), 13 hours ahead of American eastern standard time (New York) and 16 hours ahead of American western standard time (San Francisco and Los Angeles). Thus 12 noon in Singapore is 2 pm in Sydney, 4 am in London, 11 pm in New York and 8 pm the previous day in Los Angeles.

Business Hours

In Singapore government offices are usually open Monday to Friday and Saturday mornings. Hours vary, starting around 7.30 to 9.30 am and closing between 4 and 6 pm. On Saturdays closing time is 11.30 am to 1 pm. Hours are similar in Malaysia. Shop hours are also somewhat variable although Monday to Saturday from 9 am to 6 pm is a good rule of thumb. In Singapore major department stores, Chinese emporiums and some stores catering particularly to tourists are open until 9 pm seven days a week. The story is similar in Malaysia.

MEDIA
Newspapers & Magazines

There are Chinese, Tamil, Malay, Malayalam and even English-language papers in Singapore and Malaysia.

The *Nanyang Siang Pau*, a Singapore Chinese-language daily, is the most widely read but for visitors the *Straits Times* (Singapore) and the *New Straits Times* (Malaysia) are the two main dailies. Although they look remarkably alike they're actually quite separate and, believe it or not, the customs officials at the causeway will confiscate copies of the Singapore *Straits Times* as you cross into Malaysia.

There are other English-language papers including the popular afternoon *New Nation* in Singapore.

Asian and western magazines are readily available throughout the region.

Radio & Television

Radio and television are equally cosmopolitan in their languages and programming. Singapore and Malaysia each have two TV channels and in Singapore you can generally receive all four. Programmes

Top: Temple art (ST)
Left: Thian Hock Keng Temple door, Singapore (TW)
Right: Chinese temple, BSB, Brunei (ST)

Top: Chinese temple, Melaka (ML)
Bottom: Ice cream vendor, Tanjung Kling (JC)

range from local productions in the various languages to imports from the US and UK. Hardly surprisingly *Dallas* is very popular in Singapore!

HEALTH

Singapore and Malaysia both enjoy good standards of health and cleanliness. In Singapore you can safely eat in virtually any street food stall and you can drink water directly from the tap. In the major towns and cities of Malaysia you can drink tap water but it is still wise to ensure that water has been boiled in kampungs or off the beaten track.

Vaccinations against cholera or yellow fever are only required if you've recently come from an infected area – there are no other health requirements on arrival. Although Singapore and Peninsular Malaysia are not malarial you should take precautions if you're visiting Sarawak or Sabah, particularly if you will be travelling up-river. Your doctor will prescribe a daily or weekly anti-malarial drug. Keeping mosquitoes away also helps – insect repellents, mosquito coils and mosquito nets are all extra protection.

The usual rules for healthy living in a tropical environment apply. Ensure that you do not become dehydrated, particularly before you have acquired some acclimatisation, by keeping your liquid intake up. Wear cool, lightweight clothes and avoid prolonged exposure to the sun. Treat cuts and scratches with care since they can easily become infected.

Dr Ann Faraday and Professor John Wren-Lewis recommend that:

If you are in need of medical services in any of the smaller towns, we strongly recommend the government hospitals, which are either completely free or make a nominal M$1 charge and go out of their way to be helpful to travellers. Medical staff and most of the senior nursing staff speak good English and there is rarely any need to wait for long. We especially commend the staff at the General Hospitals in Tapah, Tanah Rata (Cameron Highlands) and Kuala Lipis.

In major cities the queue situation is likely to be a very different story, though staff are in our experience no less helpful and may help a helpless-looking foreigner to jump the huge lines. However, it may be simpler (especially in Kuala Lumpur) to resort to a private clinic, in which case the minimum charge for a visit is about M$20. If you are contemplating visits to jungle areas you should certainly go to a hospital for anti-malarials.

There are many efficient dentists in Singapore and Kuala Lumpur. One dentist recommended as being cheap as well as competent, is Dr Chua (tel 3361463), Rochore Community Centre, Prinsep St, Singapore.

DRUGS

In both Singapore and Malaysia the answer is simple – don't. Drug trafficking can result in the death penalty in either country.

Under Malaysian law all drug offenders are considered equal and being a foreigner will not save you from the gallows, as the 1987 execution of two Australians found guilty of charges relating to heroin possession proved.

The penalties are severe and the authorities seem to catch a steady stream of unsuccessful peddlers, smugglers and users. Mere possession can bring down a lengthy jail sentence and a beating with the rotan.

There was a period in the '70s when Malaysia was a major staging post for heroin coming down from Thailand and continuing on to the west and also had manufacturing laboratories in its own right. There still seems to be plenty of it around, especially in Penang where numerous trishaw riders offer to pedal far more than their bicycles.

Recently, due to bumper opium crops, local use has also become a problem. The odd old opium den still continues a precarious existence too. Due to these factors baggage of travellers coming from South-East Asia has become particularly suspect to customs inspectors.

CONDUCT & CUSTOMS

Like many Muslim countries Malaysia has been going through a period of increasing concentration on religion and religious activity in the past 10 years or so. It's wise to be appropriately discreet in dress and behaviour, particularly on the Muslim east coast of the peninsula. Unfortunately some people also seem to be taking a staunchly Muslim view of women and a number of women travellers have written to complain of hotel peeping toms and other forms of harassment.

FILM & PHOTOGRAPHY

Singapore and Malaysia are, of course, delightful areas to photograph. There's a lot of natural colour and activity and the people have no antipathy to being photographed. It is, of course, polite to ask permission before photographing people or taking pictures in mosques or temples. There is usually no objection to taking photographs in places of worship, in Chinese temples virtually anything goes.

The usual rules for tropical photography apply: try to take photographs early in the morning or late in the afternoon. By 10 am the sun will already be high in the sky and colours are easily washed out. Try to keep your camera and film in a happy environment – don't leave it out in direct sunlight, try to keep film as cool as possible and have it developed as soon as possible after use. Colour film can be developed quickly, cheaply and competently, but Kodachrome colour slides are usually sent to Australia for developing. Ektachrome, however, can be developed in Singapore.

Film is readily available in both Singapore and Malaysia, but there is a considerable price difference. Even 'duty-free' a Kodachrome 64 36-exposure slide film costs 50% more in Malaysia than in Singapore. If you buy a reasonable number of films at a time the price in Singapore will probably beat anything you could do in the west – as low as S$15 for Kodachrome 64 36-exposure including

developing. Singapore is, of course, an excellent place for camera equipment and there are competent camera shops in both countries.

ACCOMMODATION

Malaysia and Singapore have a very wide range of accommodation possibilities – you can still find many places to stay for less than US$5 per person per night while at the other end of the scale some of Singapore's more luxurious 'international standard' hotels are well over US$100 a night for a room. Student Travel have special discount rates negotiated at a number of hotels in Malaysia and Singapore. These hotels tend to be rather more expensive than most real students could afford since they are predominantly upper bracket places. Check with Student Travel in KL or Singapore. Accommodation possibilities include:

International Hotels

There are modern, multi-storey, air-con, swimming pool, all mod-cons hotels of the major international chains (Hyatts, Holiday Inns, Hiltons) and of many local chains (the Singapore Goodwood group, the Merlin Hotels found all over Malaysia). In these hotels nightly costs are generally from S$100 and up for a double in Singapore with standard doubles in the upper notch establishments running to well over S$200. Although you can approach these levels in Kuala Lumpur or Penang you'll generally find Malaysia hotel prices somewhat lower. In most places it's possible to get an air-con, fully equipped room in a modern hotel for as low as M$50 and rarely do prices go over M$100.

Traditional Chinese Hotels

At the other end of the price scale are the traditional Chinese hotels found in great numbers all over Malaysia and Singapore. They're the mainstay of the budget travellers and backpackers and in Malaysia you can generally find a good room for

M$10 to M$16, in some places even less than M$10. In Singapore they will start somewhat more expensive, there's not much available for less than S$20 these days.

Chinese hotels are generally fairly spartan – bare floors, just a bed, a couple of chairs and a table, a wardrobe and a sink. The showers and toilets (which will almost inevitably be Asian squat style) will generally be down the corridor. A couple of catches and points to watch for: couples can generally economise by asking for a single since in Chinese hotel language single means one double bed, double means two beds. Don't think this is being tight, in Chinese hotels you can pack as many into one room as you wish.

The main catch with these hotels is that they can sometimes be terribly noisy. They're often on main streets and the bottom rung of the Chinese hotel ladder has a serious design problem – the walls rarely reach the ceiling. The top is simply meshed or barred in. This is great for ventilation but terrible for acoustics. Every noise carries throughout the hotel and Chinese hotels all awake to a terrible dawn chorus of hawking, coughing and spitting like only the Chinese know how.

That apart these hotels are delightfully traditional in style (all swishing ceiling fans and old furniture), are almost always spotlessly clean (there are exceptions) and they're great fun to stay in. They're very often built on top of coffee bars or restaurants so food is never more than a few steps away. And they're cheap.

There are also many older-style Chinese places a notch up from the most basic places, where M$10 to M$20 will get you a fan-cooled room with common facilities. For M$20 to M$30 you can often find air-conditioned rooms with attached bathroom – but still basically Chinese in their spartan style.

Other Possibilities – Singapore
In Singapore there are a number of YMCAs and YWCAs, but for the budget traveller the crash pads are the important accommodation story. In part these are a result of the frantic pace of Singapore's modernisation. As more and more of the traditional old parts of Singapore disappear the traditional old hotels disappear with it. There are certainly no plans in Singapore to build new hotels not equipped with swimming pools, air-con and wall-to-wall carpet – which leaves budget travellers out in the cold.

Naturally some bright young entrepreneurs have jumped into this yawning gap in the accommodation market. Their answer is to get a large flat or apartment and divide the rooms up into smaller rooms and dormitories into which they pack lots of backpackers at rock bottom prices. Of course this is probably mildly illegal but in free enterprise Singapore who cares? Some people enjoy the atmosphere, informality and useful exchange of information these handy meeting places provide but other travellers still prefer the less crowded atmosphere of the old hotels.

Other Possibilities – Malaysia
There are also a number of alternatives to the cheap hotels in Malaysia. For a start some of the old British-developed rest houses are still in operation. During the colonial era these were set up to provide accommodation for travelling officials and later provided excellent shelter for all types of tourists and travellers. Now the remaining rest houses are all privately operated although still government owned. Many have now closed down but there are still a number of rest houses offering excellent accommodation standards in traditional style and often at pleasantly low prices.

There are a number of YMCAs and YWCAs around Malaysia and at one time there were also a string of youth hostels. Unfortunately some of them were inconveniently situated and almost all of them suffered from extremely indifferent operators. Combined with the competition from cheap hotels most of the hostels have now closed; a shame since some of them were very pleasant.

Finally Malaysia has a number of cheap local accommodation possibilities, usually at beach centres. Unfortunately some of this village level accommodation has suffered from official harassment. Immigration regulations describe in detail how unpopular 'hippies' are in Malaysia and how you can be unceremoniously hustled out of the country if they should decide you are a 'hippie'. One definition of this unwanted creature is 'a person who stays in temporary or makeshift shelter'. Since many of these village level places are not government registered, local officials could, if the mood was upon them, accuse people staying there of being in a 'temporary or makeshift shelter'.

In the mid-70s a series of highly publicised raids were made on the Penang village of Batu Ferringhi and many travellers were given orders to depart Malaysia immediately. Fortunately these policies have been curbed today but it's worth bearing in mind. Places with village level accommodation include Batu Ferringhi and Telok Bahang on Penang Island, Tanjung Kling near Melaka, Cherating village on the east coast and Tioman Island off the east coast.

Taxes & Service Charges In Singapore the more expensive hotels are all subject to a government 3% tax. In Malaysia there's a 5% tax which applies to all hotels. In Singapore there's a 10% service charge and in Malaysia a 5% service charge for the more expensive places. You are not expected to tip in addition. More expensive places always quote prices exclusive of service charge and tax so you can add 13% in Singapore, 10% in Malaysia.

Cheap Malaysian hotels, however, generally quote a price inclusive of the 5% government tax – hence prices like M$7.35 or M$16.80. Most hotel prices quoted in this guide have been rounded off to the nearest dollar. This 5% plus 5% business also applies to food and drink in the more expensive places – a cup of tea or coffee in an expensive place might cost you M$1.80 plus 9 sen plus 9 sen whereas in a cheap hotel coffee bar it would be 30 sen or 40 sen with no taxes.

FOOD
While travelling around some parts of Asia is as good as a session with weight watchers Singapore and Malaysia are quite the opposite. The food is simply terrific, the variety unbeatable and the costs pleasantly low. Whether you're looking for Chinese food, Malay food, Indian food, Indonesian food or even a Big Mac (巨無霸) you'll find happiness!

Chinese Food
You'll find the full range of Chinese cuisines in Singapore and Malaysia although if you're kicking round the backwoods of Sabah or Sarawak Chinese food is likely to consist of little more than noodles and vegetables. In Singapore you'll find variety to send any epicure into raptures.

Cantonese When people in the west speak of Chinese food they probably mean Cantonese food. It's the best known and most popular variety of Chinese cooking even in Singapore where the majority of Chinese are not Cantonese, as they are in Hong Kong. Cantonese food is noted for the variety and freshness of its ingredients. The food is usually stir-fried with just a touch of oil to ensure that the result is crisp and fresh. All those best known 'western Chinese' dishes fit into this category – sweet & sour dishes, won ton soup, chow mein, spring rolls.

With Cantonese food the more people you can muster for the meal the better because dishes are traditionally shared so that everyone manages to sample the greatest variety. A corollary of this is that Cantonese food should be balanced –

traditionally all foods are said to be ying – 'cooling' – like vegetables, most fruits, and clear soups or yang – 'heaty' – starchy foods and meat. A cooling dish should be balanced by a heaty dish, too much of one or the other is not good for you.

Another Cantonese speciality is dim sum or 'little heart'. Dim sum is usually eaten at lunchtime or as a Sunday brunch. Dim sum restaurants are usually large, noisy affairs and the dim sum, little snacks, fried, steamed, dumplings, buns, small bowls or whatever, are whisked around the tables on individual trolleys or carts. As they come by you simply ask for a plate of this or a bowl of that. At the end of the meal your bill is toted up from the number of empty containers on your table.

Cantonese cuisine can also offer real extremes – shark's fin soup or bird's nest soup are expensive delicacies from one end of the scale; mee (noodles) or congee (rice porridge) are cheap basics from the other end.

North & West China Far less familiar than the dishes of Canton are the cuisines from the north and west of China – Sichuan, Shanghai and Beijing. Sichuan food is the fiery food of China, the food where the peppers really get into the act. Whereas the tastes of Cantonese food are delicate and understated, in Sichuan food the flavours are strong and dramatic – garlic and chillies play their part in dishes like diced chicken or sour & hot soup.

Beijing food is, of course, best known for the famous Peking duck where the specially fattened ducks are basted in syrup and roasted on a revolving spit. The duck skin is served as a separate first course. Like the other northern cuisines Beijing food is less subtle, more direct than Cantonese food. Although Beijing food is usually eaten with noodles or steamed buns in China, because rice does not grow in the cold northern Beijing region, in Singapore it's equally likely to come with rice.

Food from Shanghai is to some extent a cross between northern and Cantonese cuisines – combining the strong flavours of the north with the ingredients of Canton. It is not easy to find, however, in Singapore.

South China Cantonese is, of course, the best known southern Chinese cuisine but it is quite easy to find a number of other regional styles in Singapore – particularly since so many of the region's Chinese are Hokkiens or Hakkas. One of the best known of these southern dishes comes from the island of Hainan. Throughout Singapore and Malaysia one of the most widespread and also most economical meals you can find is Hainanese chicken rice. It's one of those dishes whose very simplicity ensures its quality. Chicken rice is simply steamed chicken, rice boiled or steamed in the chicken stock, a clear soup and slices of cucumber. Flavour this delicate dish with soy or chilli sauce and you've got a delicious meal for Singapore or Malaysian $2.50 to $3.50. The Hainanese also produce steamboat, a sort of oriental variation on a Swiss fondue where you have a boiling stockpot in the middle of the table into which you dip pieces of meat, seafood or vegetables.

The Hokkiens come from Fukien province and make up the largest dialect group in Singapore. Although Hokkien food is rated way down the Chinese gastronomic scale they have provided the unofficial national dish of Singapore – Hokkien fried mee. It's made of thick egg noodles cooked with pork, seafood and vegetables and a rich sauce. Hokkien popiah spring rolls are also delicious.

Teochew food, from the area around Swatow, is another style noted for its delicacy and natural flavour. Teochew food is also famous for seafood and a popular food-centre dish is char kway teow – broad noodles, clams and eggs fried in chilli and black bean sauce. Hakka food is noted for its simple ingredients and the best known Hakka dish, again easily found in food-centres, is yong tau foo – bean curd stuffed with minced meat.

Taiwanese food includes rice porridge, a healthy and economical meal, often with small side dishes of oysters, mussels or pork stewed in a rich sauce.

Indian Food

Indian food is one of the region's greatest delights, indeed it's easier to find really good Indian food in Singapore or Malaysia than in India! Very approximately you can divide Indian food into southern and northern – food from the south tends to be hotter with the emphasis more on vegetarian food while from the north the food tends to be more subtle in its spicing, more Muslim in its influences and uses more meat. Common to all Indian food are the spices or masala, the lentil soup known as dahl, the yoghurt and water drink known as lassi and the sauces or condiments known as chutneys.

The typical south Indian dish is a rice plate. If you ask for one in a vegetarian restaurant you won't get a plate at all, instead a large banana leaf is placed in front of you and on this a large mound of rice is placed then scoops of a variety of vegetable curries are added around the rice and a couple of papadums tossed in for good measure. With your right hand, for south Indian vegetarian food is never eaten with utensils, you then knead the curries into the rice and eat away. When your banana leaf starts to get emptier you'll suddenly find it refilled – for rice plate is always an 'as much as you can eat' meal. When you've finished fold the banana leaf in two, with the fold towards you, to indicate that you've had enough.

Other vegetarian dishes include the popular masala dosa. A dosa is a thin pancake which, when rolled around the masala (spiced vegetables) with some rasam on the side, provides about the cheapest light meal you could ask for. An equivalent snack meal in the north would be a murtabak, made from a paratha

(paper thin dough) which is then folded around egg and minced mutton and lightly grilled with oil. Or a roti chanai – simply a chopped up paratha which you dip into a bowl of dahl. This is a very popular and filling breakfast throughout the region. Or perhaps a samosa – roughly an Indian equivalent of a Chinese spring roll.

A favourite north Indian dish, and one which is easy to find at low cost and of excellent standard, is biriyani. Served with a chicken or mutton curry the dish takes its name from the saffron coloured rice it is served with. Another particular favourite in the north is tandoori food which takes its name from the clay tandoor oven in which meat is cooked after an over-night marinade in a complex yoghurt and spice mixture. Tandoori chicken is the best known tandoori dish. Although rice is also eaten in the north it is not so much the ever present staple it is in the south. North Indian food makes wide use of the delicious Indian breads like chappatis, parathas or rotis.

Indonesian, Malay & Nonya Food

Surprisingly Malay food is not all that easily found in Malaysia or Singapore although many Malay dishes, like satay, are essentially the same as Indonesian. Some Malay dishes you may have a chance to try include tahu goreng – fried soy bean curd and bean curd sprouts in a peanut sauce; ikan bilis – tiny fish fried whole; ikan assam – fried fish in a sour tamarind curry; sambal udang – fiery curry prawns.

Indonesian, or rather Javanese, food includes dishes like nasi goreng – nasi is rice and goreng is fried and nasi goreng is a close cousin to Chinese fried rice. Gado gado is an Indonesian salad dressed with a peanut sauce. Peanut sauce again finds its way on to satay – tiny kebabs of chicken, mutton or beef. Ayam goreng is fried chicken, soto ayam is a thin chicken soup, rendang is a sort of spiced curried beef. In Sumatra the Indonesian food bends much more towards curries and chillies. The popular Sumatran dish is nasi padang – rice from the town of Padang. In a nasi padang restaurant all the different dishes are on display in the window and you select as many as you want to share amongst your group. The Dutch developed a variation on nasi padang called rijstaffel or 'rice table'. You can find rijstaffel at many major hotels.

Nonya cooking is a local variation on Chinese and Malay food – it uses Chinese ingredients, but with local spices like chillies and coconut cream. Nonya cooking is essentially a home skill, rather than a restaurant one – there are few places where you can find nonya food.

Other Cuisine

Western fast food addicts will find Ronald McDonald, the Colonel from Kentucky and A&W have all made inroads into the regional eating scene. At big hotels you can find all the usual western dishes. In Singapore you will also find Japanese, Korean and other regional restaurants. Both countries have modern air-con supermarkets where you can find anything from yoghurt to packaged muesli.

Tropical Fruit

Once you've tried rambutans, mangosteens, jackfruit and durians how can you ever go back to boring old apples and oranges? If you're already addicted to tropical fruit, Singapore and Malaysia are great places to indulge the passion. If you've not yet been initiated then there could hardly be a better place in the world to develop a taste for exotic flavours. In Singapore in particular the places to head for an easy introduction are the fruit stalls which you'll find in food centres or even just on the streets. Slices of a whole variety of fruits (including those dull old apples and oranges) are laid out on ice in a colourful and mouth-watering display which you can make a selection from for just 30c and up. You can also have a fruit salad made up on the spot from as many fruits as you

care to choose. Some tastes to sample include:

Rambutan The Malay name means 'spiny' and that's just what they are. Rambutans are the size of a large walnut or small tangerine and they're covered in soft red spines. You peel the skin away to reveal a very close cousin to the lychee with cool and mouth watering flesh around a central stone.

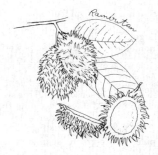

Pineapple Probably the most popular tropical fruit, a slice of pineapple is always a delicious thirst quencher. You've not really tasted pineapple until you're handed a whole one, skin sliced away and with the central stem to hold it by while the juice runs down your arm!

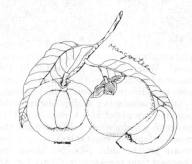

Mangosteen One of the finest tropical fruits, the mangosteen is about the size of a small orange or apple. The dark purple outer skin breaks open to reveal pure white segments shaped like orange segments – but with a sweet-sour flavour which has been compared to a combination of strawberries and grapes. Queen Victoria, so the story goes, offered a considerable prize to anybody able to bring a mangosteen back intact from the east for her to try.

Durian The region's most infamous fruit, the durian is a large oval fruit about 20 to 25 cm long although it may often grow much larger. The durian is renowned for its phenomenal smell, a stink so powerful that first timers are often forced to hold their noses while they taste. In fact durians emanate a stench so redolent of open sewers that in season you'll see signs in hotels all over Malaysia warning that durians are expressly forbidden entry.

When the hardy, spiny shell is cracked open pale white-green segments are revealed with a taste as distinctive as their smell. Durians are so highly esteemed that great care is taken over their selection and you'll see gourmets feeling them carefully, sniffing them reverently and finally demanding a preliminary taste before purchasing. Durians are also expensive and unlike other fruits which are generally ying (or cooling) durians are yang (or heaty). So much so that the durian is said to be a powerful aphrodisiac. It's no wonder that durians are reputed to be the only fruit which a tiger craves!

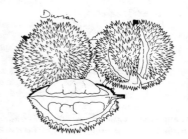

Jackfruit or Nangka This enormous watermelon-size fruit hangs from trees and when opened breaks up into a large number of bright orange-yellow segments with a slightly rubbery texture. Externally the nangka is covered by a green pimply skin, but it's too big and too messy to clean to make buying a whole one worthwhile. From street fruit stalls you can often buy several nangka segments skewered on a stick.

Papaya The papaya or paw paw originated in Central America but is now quite common throughout South-East Asia and is very popular at breakfast time when, served with a dash of lemon juice, a slice of papaya is the perfect way to start the day. The papaya is about 30 cm or so in length and the bright orange flesh is somewhat similar in texture and appearance to pumpkin but related in taste to a melon. The numerous black seeds in the centre of a papaya are said to have a contraceptive effect if eaten by women.

Starfruit Known in Indonesia as blimbing, the starfruit takes its name from the fruit's cross-sectional star shape. A translucent green-yellow in colour, starfruit has a crisp, cool, watery taste.

Custard Apple or Zirzat Sometimes known as soursop or white mango the custard apple has a warty green outer covering and is ripe and ready to eat when it begins to look slightly off – the fresh green skin begins to look blackish and the feel becomes slightly squishy. Inside the creamy white flesh has a deliciously thirst quenching flavour with a hint of lemon in it. This is another fruit you can often find at fruit stalls.

Other Fruit Then there are coconuts, mangoes, lychees, bananas, jambu, buah duku, chiku, jeruks, even strawberries up in the Cameron Highlands. Plus all the temperate climate fruits which are imported from Australia, New Zealand and further afield.

Desserts

Although desserts are not a really big deal in the region you can find some interesting after dinner snacks like *pisang goreng* (banana fritters) or even *bo-bo cha-cha*, which is similar to ais kacang and chendol (refer to the section on drinks). Ice cream addicts will be relieved to hear they can find excellent ice cream all over the region. You can choose from the soft-serve, multi-flavour gelati-style, or packaged ice cream on a stick.

DRINKS

Life can be thirsty in Singapore and Malaysia so you'll be relieved to hear that drinks are excellent, economical and readily available. For a start water can be drunk straight from the taps in Singapore and in most larger Malaysian cities (which is a far cry from many Asian countries where drinking water without elaborate sterilising preparations is foolhardy).

Secondly, there is a wide assortment of soft drinks available. There is everything from Coca-Cola, Pepsi, 7-Up and Fanta to a variety of F&N flavours including sarsaparilla (for root beer fans). Soft drinks generally cost around $1.

You can also find those fruit juice-in-a-box drinks all over the region with both normal fruit flavours and also oddities like chrysanthemum tea.

Beer drinkers will probably find Anchor Beer or Tiger Beer to their taste although the minimum price for a bottle of beer is now nearly M$2.50. Travelling Irishmen may be surprised to find that Guinness has a considerable following – in part because the Chinese believe it has a strong medicinal value. ABC Stout is a cheaper priced local equivalent of the dark black brew.

Sipping a coffee or tea in a Chinese cafe is a time honoured pursuit at any time of day or night. If you want your tea, which the Chinese and Malays make very well, without the added thickening of condensed milk, then ask for *teh-o*. Shout it – as it's another of those words which cannot be said quietly. If you don't want sugar either you have to ask for *teh-o kosong*, but you're unlikely to get it, they simply cannot believe anyone would drink tea that way!

Fruit juices are very popular and very good, particularly in Singapore where, with the aid of a blender and crushed ice, delicious concoctions like watermelon juice can be whipped up in seconds. Old fashioned sugar cane crushers, which look like grandma's old washing mangle, can still be seen in operation.

Halfway between a drink and a dessert are chendol and ais kacang. An ais (ice) kacang is rather like an old fashioned sno-cone but the shaved ice is topped with syrups and condensed milk, and it's all piled on top of a foundation of beans and jellies! It tastes terrific! Chendol is somewhat similar.

Other oddities? Well, the milky white drink in clear plastic bins at street drink sellers is soybean milk which is also available in soft drink bottles. Medicinal teas are a big deal with the health-minded Chinese.

BOOKS & BOOKSHOPS

There are a wide variety of books available on the region and a number of good bookshops in which to find them.

Singapore's main bookshop chain is MPH and their shop at 71-77 Stamford Rd is probably the best general bookshop in the region. They have others on Robinson Rd, at Changi Airport, in the basement level at Plaza Singapura on Orchard Rd and other places around the city. Select Books, 215 Tanglin Shopping Centre (near the Tourist Office) has an excellent collection specialising in South-East Asia.

Other good bookshops include Times Bookshops at Lucky Plaza on Orchard Rd, in Robinson's department store in the Specialists' Centre also on Orchard Rd and at other locations. Marican have branches at DBS Building on Shenton Way and Supreme House on Penang Rd. In Plaza Singapura, Shizuoka Yajimaya is another excellent bookshop. There are also book and magazine stalls in many of the larger hotels.

Along Bras Basah Rd there are a number of small bookshops several of which specialise in secondhand books. Two good bookshops in this street are Jimmy Ho's Bookshop at No 40, and the Oriental Bookstore next door.

In KL, the best bookshops are on Jalan Bukit Bintang, in the Sungei Wang Plaza where MPH and Berita can be found. There are other bookshops on Bukit Bintang. The Central Market and Daya Bumi Complex also have Berita bookshops.

In Penang there are several good bookshops along Beach Rd (Pantai St) and the E&O Hotel also has a good bookshop. Major hotels also often have book stalls, but on the east coast the selection of bookshops is not as good as elsewhere.

People & Society

Kampong Boy, and the more recently published *Town Boy*, by Lat (Straits Times Publishing) provide a delightful introduction to Malay life. They're a humorous autobiographical cartoon series on growing up in a village (kampung) and then moving to the town of Ipoh.

Tales of Chinatown, Sit Yin Fong (Heineman Asia, 1983) is a readable and informative piece on Chinese life. Fong was a newspaper man in Singapore for many years and writes anecdotal short stories about Chinese customs and beliefs.

Culture Shock, JoAnn Craig (Times Books International, 1979) is an attempt to explain the customs, cultures and lifestyles of Singapore's polyglot population to expatriates working there.

Living in Singapore (American Association of Singapore, 1979), handy for westerners planning to set up house in Singapore, this is a useful introduction to life in the tropical city-state.

History

There are a great number of books on the history of Singapore and Malaysia.

A Short History of Malaysia, Singapore & Brunei, C Mary Turnbull (Cassell Australia, 1980), may fit the bill if you simply want a straightforward and not over-long history from early civilisation to modern politics.

A History of Malaya by R Winstedt (Porcupine Press, 1979) is another standard history.

Raffles, Maurice Collins (Day, 1968) is the story of the man who founded Singapore.

Recently there has been a great deal of interest in the fall of Malaysia and Singapore and the subsequent Japanese occupation and the internal and external struggles of the '50s and '60s. These include:

Sinister Twilight - The Fall of Singapore, Noel Barber (originally published 1968; now available in a Fontana paperback). It recounts the bunglings, underestimations and final heroics that culminated in the rapid collapse of Singapore.

The Jungle is Neutral, F Spencer Chapman (originally published 1949; now available in a Mayflower paperback), recounts the hardships and adventures of a British guerrilla force that fought on in the jungles of Malaya for the rest of the war.

Out in the Midday Sun, Kate Caffrey (Andre Deutsch, 1973), tells of the hardships of those who were captured and spent the rest of the war years in prison camps like the notorious Changi camp.

The War of the Running Dogs – Malaya 1948-1960, Noel Barber (first published 1971; now a Fontana paperback) recounts the events of the long running Communist insurrection.

The Undeclared War – The Story of the Indonesian Confrontation, Harold James and Denis Sheil-Small (originally published 1971; now a paperback from the University of Malaya Co-Operative Bookshop). No sooner had the Communist struggle ended than the confrontation with Indonesia commenced. This book tells the story of that strange and disorganised argument.

Lee Kuan Yew – The Struggle for Singapore, Alex Josey (first published 1968; updated and republished a number of times). It covers all the twists and turns of Lee Kuan Yew's rise to power and the successful path which his People's Action Party has piloted Singapore along.

The Malay Dilemma, written in 1970 by Mahathir bin Mohamed who became Prime Minister in 1981. It is interesting both for its not altogether optimistic analysis of the problems facing Malaysia and the fact that it was banned for a

number of years. It has now been republished in a Federal Publications paperback.

Fiction

Singapore and Malaysia have always provided a fertile setting for novelists and Joseph Conrad's *The Shadow Line* and *Lord Jim* both use the region as a setting. Somerset Maugham also set many of his classic short stories in Malaya – look for the *Borneo Stories*.

The Malayan Trilogy, Anthony Burgess (Penguin paperback) is a classic series of long stories of life in Malaya during the declining years of Britain's colonial management.

The Consul's File, by Paul Theroux, is a very readable collection of short stories set in, of all places, Ayer Hitam near KL. Theroux's *Saint Jack* is set in Singapore.

The Singapore Grip, J G Farrell (Fontana paperback, 1979) was a local bestseller and provides an almost surreal view of life in Singapore as the Japanese stormed down the peninsula in WW II. A certain amount of 'fiddling while Rome burnt' appeared to be going on.

Turtle Beach, Blanche d'Alpuget (Penguin, 1981), is an Australian award winning novel which gives an insight into the Vietnamese boat people, the impact of their arrival in Malaysia and the racial tension those events engendered – with flashbacks to the horrors of 1969.

North Borneo

Nineteenth Century Borneo – A Study in Diplomatic Rivalry, Graham Irwin (Donald Moore Books, Singapore), is the best book on the fascinating history of Sarawak, Sabah and Brunei.

Rajah Charles Brooke – Monarch of all he Surveyed, Colin N Criswell (Oxford University Press, 1978), tells you more about the white rajahs.

Vanishing World, the Ibans of Borneo, Leigh Wright (Weatherhill, 1972), has some beautiful colour photographs.

A Stroll Through Borneo, James Barclay (Hodder & Stoughton, 1980), is a delightful tale of a long walk and river trip through Sarawak, Sabah and Indonesian Kalimantan. The contrasts between Malaysian bureaucracy and the Indonesian variety are enlightening, with the Malaysians coming off distinctly second best.

Into the Heart of Borneo, Redmond O'Hanlon (Random House, New York 1984), is the story of five travellers as they journey by foot and boat into Borneo.

Travel Guide

Insight Singapore and *Insight Malaysia*, part of the Apa guide series, features their usual collection of text and photographs.

Jalan Jalan, (also from the Singapore-based Apa company) is a coffee-table book on Malaysia. It's as much a photographic book as a travel book since it covers Malaysia with a series of photographs taken with a 8 x 10 large format studio camera. The description of how the photographs were taken and the travels around Malaysia (by motorcycle) to take them is as interesting as the pictures themselves.

South-East Asia on a Shoestring, (Lonely Planet) is our overall guidebook to the region. If you're travelling further afield there are other LP guides to most South-East and North-East Asian countries.

Time Travel in the Malay Crescent by Wayne Stier is an unusual guidebook, written in the second person, present tense. There are some maps and travel information at the back of the book, but most of the text consists of tales gathered and events which occurred while the author was in Malaysia. Some of the stories about the more remote areas of Sarawak and Sabah are very interesting.

MAPS

It's not possible to get the detailed maps of Malaysia which were available during the colonial period because of fears that they will fall into communist hands. You can, however, get good road maps from petrol stations. Probably the best is the Shell one which is larger scale since it is two-sided. On the other hand the Mobil map also shows relief.

An excellent map for Malaysia is the *Malaysia* map produced by Nelles Verlag for APA Maps. The scale is 1:1.5 million and it details the Peninsula and East Malaysia together with a number of city maps. It is widely available in Malaysia.

A very good map, particularly for roads, is the *Asian Highway Route Map – Singapore, Malaysia, Thailand, Laos* which is published by the United Nations, Escap, Transport & Communications Division. It's available from the Singapore Automobile Association headquarters for just S$1.

Two maps recommended for travellers in Singapore, are the *Clyde Leisure Map for the Tourist* which shows hotels, shopping areas, embassies, places of interest, banks and important buildings, and *The Secret Map of Singapore* which points out the more unusual places to visit on the island.

The TDC publish an excellent map to Kuala Lumpur called *Lani's KL Discovery Map*. It costs M$3.30 and is sold in most bookshops.

WHAT TO BRING

There's really very little you need to worry about forgetting when you come to Malaysia or Singapore. There are none of those problems of finding your favourite brand of toothpaste or even common medicines. If you want a film for your camera it will be cheaper in Singapore than at home.

Clothes are readily available and very reasonably priced. Some people reckon that Singapore is better for off-the-shelf clothing than Hong Kong, as there's more variety and lower costs.

The best advice is to bring as little with you as possible; travelling light is the only way to travel. In any case you don't need too much to start with as the weather is perpetually of the short sleeve variety.

Although if you're planning to head up to the hill stations you may appreciate a sweater or light jacket in the evenings.

Dress is casual throughout the region – budget travellers may find a set of 'dress up' gear sensible for dealing with officialdom but you're highly unlikely to need a coat and tie or equivalent too often.

Sensible accessories include sunglasses, a hat, a water bottle/canteen, pocket knife, a day pack, a basic first aid kit and a money belt or pouch.

TAKE THE CHILDREN

Researching the first edition of this book was familiar in one respect and totally unfamiliar in another. It was familiar in that we'd pretty well covered Malaysia in the past. We'd made one trip all over the country on a motorcycle and in subsequent years had returned to Malaysia on a number of occasions, travelling by air, train, bus, long-distance taxi and even by thumb. So we felt pretty well at home in Malaysia and knew our way round fairly well. The trip was totally unfamiliar in that it was the first time out with our daughter, who was seven months old when we arrived in Singapore at the start of our travels.

The end verdict? Harder work than we might have expected but quite possible and in many ways great fun. For starters Malaysia is a very civilised country for travelling with kids. It's clean and hygienic by Asian standards and travel is relatively easy. Equally important the people of Singapore and Malaysia love kids, especially blonde blue-eyed ones, so Tashi was thoroughly spoilt. The pleasant surprises were how well equipped many places were to deal with children. Even the tiniest little coffee-shop restaurants seemed to have a high chair ready to be whisked out when we appeared. And, of course, Chinese food is designed to be messed with – you're bound to end up with prawn shells and fish bones littered all around you, so any additional mess a baby can make hardly seems to matter.

As far as the western necessities of dealing with babies went everything was pretty simple. Milk is, of course, hard to obtain, as in most of Asia, but we did find plenty of fruit juice, soy milk drinks and often did find milk too. Our initial intention to wash nappies (diapers) as we went along soon went out the window.

Perhaps if you're travelling slowly you could manage that, but when you're covering a lot of ground (as you have to when researching a guidebook) it simply wasn't possible to get them dried in time to move on. But finding disposable nappies was no trouble in the big cities (Singapore, KL, Penang, etc) and prices were not much more than in the west. They were usually American (higher stick failure) or Japanese (pretty, but not always effective).

As for Tashi, she had a great time, loved Chinese food (especially baby sweet corn), delighted in the water (beach or pool) and generally enjoyed herself. The biggest problem, and this would have been a problem anywhere, not just in Asia, was that she was too big to take along after she'd reached her bedtime but too small to keep up late. At times we had to miss meals or rush out for take-aways because she was asleep and could not be stirred. Plus the constant moving, every second night a new hotel room, did unsettle her a bit and we had rather too many middle-of-the-night wake-ups for comfort. But then Tashi has never been a great sleeper. We've subsequently made several more trips in Asia with Tashi and, when he came along, her younger brother Kieran. For more information on taking the kids see Maureen's book *Travel with Children*.

– **Tony Wheeler**

Getting There

AIRLINE TICKETS – A WARNING

Singapore and Malaysia both have a reputation as good centres for buying discounted airline tickets. As in many other places in the world ticket discounting can be a slightly shady activity – it may be under the counter, quietly tolerated or even openly tolerated but it's never totally free and open. Additionally the official attitudes towards it can blow hot and cold – one year it's OK (happy days, the prices drop); the next year it's a no no (disaster, the prices soar). It can also go in and out of official favour depending on where you want to fly to – one year tickets to Europe may be a bargain, tickets around Asia very expensive. The next year the opposite may apply.

So don't expect anything when it comes to cheap tickets – what applies this week certainly may not apply next. Nevertheless Singapore, Kuala Lumpur and Penang are certainly three of the best places around to find bargains on airline tickets. Beware, however, of unscrupulous people in this field. There are many fly by night operators and the agent everybody speaks highly of one year can all too easily do a midnight flit the next. As did one ticket agent that we recommended in the first edition of this book. Many travellers have written to us recommending particular agents and where appropriate we have mentioned agents who have been highly and frequently recommended. Curiously enough, however, some agents, in Penang in particular, seem to simultaneously get 'great guy, very reliable' recommendations and 'danger, avoid at all costs' warnings!

The only suggestion we can make from direct experience is that over the years we have bought a number of tickets for Lonely Planet researchers from Airmaster Travel in Singapore. From time to time we've had letters from people saying that other Singapore agents are cheaper, but we have never received a letter from any traveller saying that they had any trouble with tickets purchased from Airmaster Travel.

FROM/TO EUROPE

Tickets are available from travel agents in London to Kuala Lumpur or Singapore from around UK£200 to UK£250 or return from around UK£400 to UK£450. It's possible to get flights from London to Australia with stop-overs in Singapore or KL from around UK£400. To Auckland with a Singapore stop-over costs around UK£425. For more information check the travel ad pages in *Time Out* or the *Australasian Express*. Two good agents for cheap airline tickets are Trailfinders at 46 Earls Court Rd or STA at 74 Old Brompton Rd.

FROM/TO AUSTRALIA

Air Advance purchase one-way fares from the Australian east coast to Singapore vary from A$559 off-peak to A$675 in the peak season. To Kuala Lumpur the variation is A$619 to A$747. There are also advance purchase round-trip fares varying from A$826 to A$998 to Singapore; A$897 to A$1083 to Kuala Lumpur. The regular one-way economy fare to Singapore is A$1096 and to Kuala Lumpur A$1147.

Shopping around travel agents you can probably find one-way tickets to Singapore at around A$380 (A$780 return) or to KL for about A$400 (A$800 return).

Boat There are no longer any regular shipping services between South-East Asia and Australia, even the Singapore-Fremantle service no longer operates. Mansfield Travel (tel 737 9688), G8 Ocean Building Shopping Centre, Collyer Quay, Singapore is the most likely agent to know if there is any change in the situation.

FROM/TO NEW ZEALAND

Air New Zealand and Singapore Airlines fly from Auckland to Singapore. If you shop around, you can get fares from Auckland to Singapore for around NZ$550 one-way and NZ$1000 return. Some fares will allow you to stop-over in Australia on the way.

FROM/TO THE USA

There is now a lot of ticket discounting with Asian airlines from the US west coast to Asia. Whereas this used to be basically a closed shop operation for Asians only it's now fairly wide open. It's possible to find fares from the US west coast to Singapore for around US$550 one-way or US$900 return. Scan the Sunday travel section of west coast newspapers like the *LA Times* or the *San Francisco Chronicle-Examiner* for agents handling discounted tickets. Some cheap fares include a stop-over in Hong Kong. There are also budget and super Apex fares available out of the west coast. Similar deals from the east coast can be found in the Sunday papers there.

FROM/TO THAILAND

There are a number of ways of getting from Singapore or Malaysia into Thailand. You can fly from Singapore, Kuala Lumpur or Penang. You can cross the border by land at Padang Besar (rail or road), Changlun-Sadao (road) or Keroh-Betong (road) in the west or at Rantau Panjang-Sungai Golok in the east. There's also a rather unusual route by sea from Kuala Perlis on the west coast.

Air You can fly from Singapore to Bangkok for about S$220. You can fly from Penang to Hat Yai for M$80 or from Penang to Phuket for slightly more. Add on a Phuket to Bangkok flight and it works out no more expensive than flying to Bangkok directly. Flying from Penang to Hat Yai or Phuket can save a lot of time wasted in crossing the border by land.

Train The rail route into Thailand is on the Butterworth-Alor Setar-Hat Yai route which crosses into Thailand at Padang Besar. You can take the International Express from Butterworth all the way to

		Singapore	*Kuala Lumpur*	*Butterworth*
Hat Yai	1st class	M$116.50	M$ 69.10	M$ 24.20
	2nd class	M$ 52.80	M$ 31.50	M$ 11.20
Bangkok	1st class	M$175.60	M$128.20	M$ 83.30
	2nd class	M$ 80.30	M$ 59.00	M$ 38.70

1		*2*
13.35	Butterworth	12.10
14.53	Alor Star	10.51
16.40	Hat Yai	07.05
08.35	Bangkok	15.15

1 International Express from Butterworth runs daily
2 International Express from Bangkok runs daily

In addition there is a small express surcharge on the International Express.
Additional cost for berths range from around M$6 to M$25 depending on whether you want a 2nd class upper, 2nd class lower, 1st class ordinary or 1st class air-con.

Bangkok with connections from Singapore and KL. On Sunday nights there is a special 1st class coach attached to the night express from KL which is then attached to the Monday International Express from Butterworth. Once in Hat Yai there are frequent train and bus connections to other parts of Thailand.

Road - West Coast Although there are border points at Padang Besar and Keroh the majority of travellers cross by road between Changlun and Sadao for Hat Yai. There's a long stretch of no-man's land between these two points so although you can easily get a bus or taxi up to Changlun on the Malay side and on from Sadao to Hat Yai on the Thai side, crossing the actual border is difficult. There are two easy alternatives – one is a Thai taxi from Georgetown (see Penang) for around M$25 to Hat Yai. The other is to cross at Padang Besar, where the railway also crosses and where the border is an easy walk across. Note that the Sadao-Changlun border is only open to 6 pm. From Hat Yai there are plenty of buses and trains to Phuket, Bangkok or other places.

Road - East Coast From Kota Bahru you can take a No 29 bus to Rantau Panjang – the 45-km trip takes 1½ hours and costs about M$2. Once there you've got a half-km walk to the Thai train station at Sungai Golok. An express train departs Sungai Golok for Bangkok everyday at 10.55 am and arrives in Bangkok at 7.05 am the next day. There is a 'rapid' train every-day at 10.05 am which arrives at 6.35 am the next day. These trains pass through Hat Yai.

A number of travellers have pointed out in the past that the Malay immigration post at Rantau Panjang is very slack and it's quite easy to miss them, but it seems to be more efficient now. Local buses would zip straight by, since locals did not need special clearance to go to Sungai Golok. It's your responsibility to make sure your passport is stamped on entry. Failure to do so can mean a stiff fine for 'illegal entry'.

Boat - West Cost You can often get yachts between Penang and Phuket in Thailand. Look for advertisements in the cheap hotels and restaurants in Georgetown. Encounter Overland used to run a regular yacht trip costing around UK£200 for a 10-day voyage between Penang and Phuket. Although it appears that operation has stopped now there are other yachts still sailing.

Cheaper and more frequent are the small boats that skip across the border from Kuala Perlis in the north-west corner of Malaysia to Setul in Thailand. There are customs and immigration posts there so you can cross quite legally although it's an unusual and rarely used entry/exit point. The boats will be those open long boats, unique to Thailand, with a car engine mounted on gimbels on the back and a long, solid shaft from the end of the engine driving the prop. The whole engine is swivelled to steer the boat. Fare for the short trip is around M$3 and from Setul you can bus to Hat Yai. Make sure you get your passport stamped on entry.

Thai Visas

You can get Thai visas from the embassies in Singapore or Kuala Lumpur or the consulates in Penang or Kota Bahru. The consulates are quick and convenient. We've had reports of shabbily-dressed travellers being refused Thai visas at the consulate in Kota Bahru. Apparently, the staff are very strict as far as dress code goes; one traveller said she was refused a visa because of her passport photo, in which she wore a sleeveless summer dress! There are three types of Thai visa: If you have an onward air ticket and will not be staying in Thailand for more than 14 days then you do not need to prearrange a visa and can get a free entry permit on arrival by air or land. For M$15 you can get a one month transit visa or for M$30 a two month tourist visa. Three photos are required.

FROM/TO INDONESIA

Air There are several interesting variations from Indonesia to Singapore or Malaysia. Simplest is to fly from Jakarta to Singapore with tickets available from around US$110 to US$150 depending on the the airline. Medan, in Sumatra, to Penang will cost around US$50. These are the two standard flight possibilities but others also exist – such as Pekanbaru, Medan or Padang to Singapore.

There is also a weekly flight between Kuching in Sarawak and Pontianak in Kalimantan, which is the Indonesian, southern half of the island of Borneo. Similarly at the eastern end of Borneo there is a rather more irregular flight between Tawau in Sabah and Tarakan in Kalimantan. The latter route tends to open and close depending on the attitude of the moment.

Boat – Singapore-Indonesia Curiously there is no direct shipping service between the main ports in Indonesia and near neighbour Singapore but it is possible to travel between the two nations via the islands of the Riau Archipelago.

The Riau Archipelago is the cluster of Indonesian islands immediately south of Singapore. Once you get to these islands

there is a variety of ways of continuing to other parts of the country. Starting from Singapore there are two ways of taking the first step. The longer route is to take a regular ferry service to Sekumpang on Batam Island where you go through Indonesian immigration. The fare is S$20 (16,000 rp from Sekumpang). From there you take a bus for 500 rp to Nagoya and a taxi for 2000 rp to Kabil. From Kabil a ferry crosses to Tanjunguban on Bintan Island for 1700 rp. A bus runs from there to Tanjung Pinang, the major town of the whole archipelago, for 1750 rp. Total cost of this expedition is about 22,000 rp and it takes quite a time.

The faster alternative is to take a direct ferry from Singapore to Tanjung Pinang. The cost is S$60 or S$65 and there are departures at 9 and 10.30 am and at around 2 or 3 pm daily. The trip takes about 2½ hours via Batam, where you clear immigration. Departures are from Finger Pier on Prince Edward Rd in Singapore, phone 336 0528 for details.

From Tanjung Pinang there used to be a regular weekly Pelni service to Jakarta which in its heyday was something of a legend amongst Asian travellers. It no longer operates but there are a variety of ways of continuing your travels from the Riau islands. Easiest is to fly with Garuda as they have a variety of regular flights to and from Batu Besar on Batam including

two daily flights to Jakarta and a daily flight to Pekanbaru, continuing to Medan. The Jakarta-Batam fare is about 50,000 rp which makes it a very economical way to travel to or from Singapore.

Merpati also have flights between Tanjung Pinang and Jakarta, Pekanbaru or Surabaya or from Batam to a variety of cities in Sumatra or Java. A more time-consuming route is to take a boat between Tanjung Pinang and Pekanbaru, a 40 hour trip costing 17,500 rp. There are other possibilities if you're willing to wait including irregular ships to ports in Java or Sumatra.

Boat - Malaysia-Indonesia There are now two regular services between Malaysia and Indonesia - Penang-Medan and Melaka-Dumai. After years out of operation the Penang-Medang ferry once again crosses to Sumatra twice a week in about 15 hours at a fare of M$45. Sanren Delta Marine is the Penang agents for the service on the ferry *Gadis Langkasuka*. The other alternative is the Melaka-Dumai service, also twice a week which costs about M$70.

Land There is currently no easily accessible land border between Malaysia and Indonesia but in early 1988 it was announced that a new road would be built between Kuching in Sarawak and Pontianak in Kalimantan.

Indonesian Visas
For most western nationalities no visa is required on arrival in Indonesia, as long as you have a ticket out (not always rigidly enforced) and do not intend to stay for more than two months. The only catch is that the 'no visa' entry only applies if you both enter and leave Indonesia through certain recognised gateways. These entry and exit points include all the usual airports and seaports, but there are some places, like Jayapura in Irian Jaya, not on the list. If you intend to arrive or leave

Indonesia through one of the oddball places then you have to get a visa in advance.

When the new regulations were first introduced some travellers discovered to their expense that Indonesian diplomatic offices did not know the full story on the new plan and happily told them that entering without a visa at Jakarta was fine, failing to add if you then tried to leave from Jayapura you would be told no. These days the regulations are well understood.

FROM/TO INDIA & OTHER PLACES IN ASIA
Air Although Indonesia and Thailand are the two 'normal' places to travel to or from there are plenty of other possibilities including India, Sri Lanka, Burma, Hong Kong and the Philippines. For details on cheap air fares check the relevant sections in Singapore and Penang - these are the two airline ticket centres.

Boat The *MV Chidambaram* used to travel from Penang to Madras every alternate week until it was destroyed by fire in 1985. The service is to be resumed by the Greek-built *MV Vigneswara* which is operated by the Singapore-based Greenseas Shipping Company. The *MV Vigneswara* will make two voyages per month between Madras, Singapore and Penang. The ship has all the necessary amenities such as a casino, swimming pool, bar, TV lounge and duty-free shop. Return tickets from Madras cost Rs 8100 in deluxe cabins, Rs 6300 in 1st class and Rs 3350 in economy.

AIRPORT TAXES
Both Singapore and Malaysia levy airport taxes on all their flights. From Singapore the tax is S$5 on flights to Malaysia, S$12 on longer international flights. From Malaysia it's M$3 on domestic flights, M$5 to Singapore or Brunei and M$15 on other international flights. There is no airport tax out of Brunei.

Getting Around

AIR

Three airlines operate regional routes in this area – Singapore International Airlines, Malaysian Airlines System and Royal Brunei Airlines. Since every Royal Brunei or Singapore Airlines flight is an international flight it's Malaysian Airlines who have the major regional network. The chart details some of the main regional routes and their fares in M$. MAS have many other regional routes in Sarawak and Sabah. They operate Airbuses, Boeing 737s and Fokker F27 Friendships on their domestic routes plus Britten Norman Islanders on some of their remote Sarawak and Sabah routes. On some sectors the economy F27 fare is somewhat cheaper than the 737 fare.

You can also save quite a few dollars if flying to Sarawak or Sabah by flying from Johore Bahru rather than Singapore. To Kuching the regular economy fare is M$147 from JB against M$170 from Singapore. To KK the respective fares are M$301

against M$346. To persuade travellers to take advantage of these lower fares MAS offer a bus service directly from their Singapore downtown office to the JB airport.

MAS also have a number of special night flights and advance purchase fares. The 14-day advance purchase tickets are available for one-way/return flights from Johore Bahru to Kuching – M$125/250; JB to Kota Kinabalu – M$256/512; Kuala Lumpur to Kuching – M$197/394; and Kuala Lumpur to Kota Kinabalu – M$323/646. There are also economy night flights between Kuala Lumpur and Kota Kinabalu M$266/532, Kuching M$162/324 and Penang M$61/112.

If you are travelling with two other people, you can save 50% on regular MAS economy airfares between West and East Malaysia by booking and paying as a group (group must comprise three people) at least seven days in advance. For flights within West Malaysia or within East Malaysia

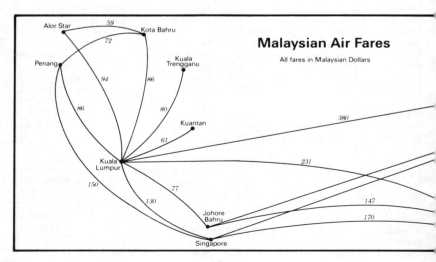

Malaysian Air Fares

All fares in Malaysian Dollars

(but not between the two), groups of three people can travel for 75% of the regular economy fare if they book and pay together, at least seven days in advance.

In north Borneo, where air transport is much more important than on the peninsula, there are many local flights which are often cancelled on short notice. Don't count too heavily on flight schedules here. Don't believe too implicitly that flights are fully booked either. In Sarawak and Sabah you can often go out to the airport and find seats readily available on a supposedly full flight.

Warning

Fares on flights between Singapore and Malaysia cost the same dollar figure whether bought in Malaysia or Singapore. Thus a Penang-Singapore or Singapore-Penang ticket costs M$150 in Malaysia, S$150 in Singapore. Since the Singapore dollar is worth 20% more than the Malaysian dollar you can save a lot of money by buying tickets in Malaysia.

RAIL

Malaysia has a modern, comfortable and economical rail service although there are basically only two rail lines. One runs from Singapore to Kuala Lumpur, Butterworth and on into Thailand. The other branches off from this line at Gemas and runs through Kuala Lipis up to the north-east corner of the country near Kota Bahru. A road is now being pushed through paralleling this second 'jungle' line and it's probable that eventually it will be closed down. Other lines are just minor branches off these two routes and are not much used. The line to Port Dickson from Kuala Lumpur is only used for weekend excursions, for example.

Malaysia's first railway line was a 13-km route from Taiping to Port Weld which was laid in 1884, but is no longer in use. By 1903 you could travel all the way from Johore Bahru to near Butterworth and the extension of the line to the Thai border in 1918 and across the causeway to Singapore in 1923 meant you could travel by train from Singapore right into Thailand. In 1931 the east coast line was completed, effectively bringing the rail system to its present state.

The KTM, Keretapi Tanah Melayu,

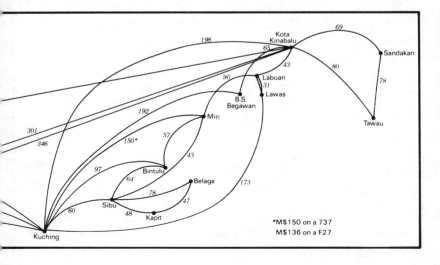

offers a number of concessions to rail travellers including a Railpass entitling the holder to unlimited travel for 30 days for M$175 or 10 days for M$85. The pass entitles you to travel on any class of train, but does not include sleeping berth

Fares From Butterworth

	1st	2nd	3rd	ER/ES AC	non-AC
Padang Besar	20.70	9.30	5.80		
Alor Star			3.50		
Butterworth					
Taiping	11.70	5.30	3.30		
Ipoh	22.50	10.20	6.30	17.00	10.00
Kuala Lumpur	47.40	21.40	13.20	28.00	17.00
Gemas	69.20	31.20	19.20		
Johore Bahru	92.30	41.60	25.60	48.00	29.00
Singapore	96.00	43.30	26.60	50.00	30.00
Kuala Lipis	96.00	43.30	26.60		
Tumpat	132.40	59.70	36.70		

Fares From Kuala Lumour

	1st	2nd	3rd	ER/ES AC	non-AC
Padang Besar	65.60	29.60	18.20		
Alor Star	57.10	25.80	15.80		
Butterworth	47.40	21.40	13.20	28.00	17.00
Ipoh	25.50	11.50	7.10	18.00	11.00
Kuala Lumpur					
Gemas	21.90	9.90	6.10		
Johore Bahru	45.00	20.30	12.50	27.00	16.00
Singapore	48.60	21.90	13.50	28.00	17.00
Kuala Lipis	49.80	22.50	13.80		
Tumpat	86.20	38.90	23.90		

Fares From Singapore

	1st	2nd	3rd	ER/ES AC	non-AC
Padang Besar	113.00	50.90	31.30		
Alor Star	105.70	47.60	29.30		
Butterworth	96.00	43.30	26.60	50.00	30.00
Ipoh	74.10	33.40	20.50	40.00	24.00
Kuala Lumpur	48.60	21.90	13.50	28.00	17.00
Gemas	28.00	12.60	7.80		
Johore Bahru	3.40	1.50	1.00	8.00	4.00
Singapore					
Kuala Lipis	54.70	24.70	15.20		
Tumpat	91.10	41.10	25.20		

ER/ES – Ekspres Rakyat/Ekspres Sinaran
AC – air-conditioned
non-AC – non-air-conditioned

Supplementary berth charges are M$20 for 1st class with air-conditioning, M$10 1st class ordinary, M$8 for 2nd class lower berth, M$6 for 2nd class upper berth.

charges. Railpasses are only available to foreign tourists and can be purchased at a number of main railway stations.

Malaysia has two types of rail services. There are the conventional 1st, 2nd and 3rd class trains with both express and slower ordinary services. On these trains you can reserve seats on 1st and 2nd class up to 90 days in advance and there are day and overnight trains. On the overnight trains sleeping berths are available in 1st and 2nd class. The other trains are known as the Ekspres Rakyat (People's Express) and the Ekspres Sinaran. These trains only have air-con or non air-con carriages, and only stop at main stations. Consequently they are faster than the regular express trains. In fact in most respects these

---

Timetables for the main express train services are as follows. There are also a number of ordinary train services.

	ER	ES	ES	ORD
Butterworth	07.14	07.45	14.15	20.15
Ipoh	09.53	10.36	17.14	00.30
Kuala Lumpur	13.10	13.45	20.15	05.30

	ER	ES	ES	ORD
Kuala Lumpur	07.30	13.50	14.45	20.30
Ipoh	10.29	16.53	17.44	00.55
Butterworth	13.30	20.00	20.50	05.30

	ES	ER	ES	ORD
Kuala Lumpur	07.30	13.30	14.50	20.20
Gemas		16.20		00.15
Johore Bahru	13.23	19.32	20.40	04.57
Singapore	14.10	20.20	21.40	06.15

	ES	ER	ES	ORD
Singapore	07.00	07.45	15.00	20.30
Johore Bahru	07.28	08.13	15.28	21.58
Gemas	10.39			01.51
Kuala Lumpur	13.30	14.25	21.45	06.15

	ORD	ORD
Tumpat	10.30	
Wakaf Bahru	10.58	
Kuala Lipis	18.33	06.36
Jerantut	20.10	08.30
Gemas	23.40	

	ORD	ORD
Gemas	02.30	
Jerantut		
Kuala Lipis	07.00	08.30
Wakaf Bahru	14.57	17.40
Tumpat	15.35	18.15

ER – Ekspres Rakyat, ES – Ekspres Sinaran, ORD – Ordinary

services are definitely the ones to take. Fares on the Ekspres Rakyat and Ekspres Sinaran are very reasonable, not much more than 3rd class for the non air-con carriages, and not much more than 2nd for air-con. Ekspres Rakyat and Ekspres Sinaran services only operated between Singapore and KL or KL and Butterworth.

There are a number of other ordinary (biasa) train services, particularly on the central route to the east coast where there are numerous local trains. For details on the fares and schedules to Hat Yai and Bangkok in Thailand see the From/To Thailand section in Getting There.

LONG-DISTANCE TAXIS

Malaysia's real travel bargain is the long-distance taxis. They make Malaysian travel, already easy and convenient even by the best Asian standards, a real breeze. A long-distance taxi is usually a diesel Mercedes, Peugeot or, more recently, Japanese car. In almost every town there will be a 'teksi' stand where the cars are lined up and ready to go to their various destinations. As soon as a full complement of four passengers turns up off you go. Between major towns the wait will rarely be long.

You can often get the taxis to pick you up or drop you off at your hotel or for four times the single fare you can 'charter' the whole taxi. You can also take a taxi to other destinations at charter rates. Taxi fares generally work out at about twice the comparable bus fares. Thus from KL to Butterworth it's M$30, KL to Melaka is M$12. Of course there has to be a drawback to all this and that is the frightening driving which the taxi pilots often indulge in. They don't have as many head-on collisions as you might expect, but closing your eyes at times of high stress certainly helps.

BUSES

Malaysia has an excellent bus system. There are public buses on local runs and a variety of privately operated buses on the longer trips as well as the big fleet of MARA express buses. In larger towns there may be a number of bus stops – a main station or two plus some of the private companies may operate directly from their own offices.

Buses are fast, economical, reasonably comfortable and seats can be reserved. On many routes there are also air-conditioned buses which usually cost just a few dollars more than the regular buses. They make mid-day travel a sweat-free activity, but beware – as one traveller put it, 'Malaysian air-conditioned buses are really meat lockers on wheels with just two settings: cold and suspended animation'.

CAR RENTAL & DRIVING

Rent-a-car operations in Malaysia and Singapore are still in their infancy, but they're bound to grow. In many Asian countries driving is either a fraught experience (ever seen the rush hour in Bangkok or Jakarta?), full of local dangers (I'd hate to think what would happen if you collided with a cow in India), or the roads are terrible, cars unavailable or for some other reason

driving yourself is not really possible. None of these drawbacks apply in Malaysia and Singapore. The roads are generally of a high standard, there are plenty of new cars available and driving standards are not too hair raising.

Basically driving in Singapore and Malaysia follows much the same rules as in England or Australia – cars are right-hand drive, you drive on the left side of the road. The only additional precaution one needs to take is to remain constantly aware of the possible additional road hazards of stray animals, the large number of cyclists and the occasional suicidal motorcyclist.

Although most drivers in Malaysia are relatively sane, safe and slow there are also a fair few who specialise in overtaking on blind corners and otherwise trusting in divine intervention. Long-distance taxi drivers are particular specialists in these activities. Malaysian drivers also operate a curious signalling system where a left flashing indicator means 'you are safe to overtake' . . . or 'I'm about to turn off' . . . or 'I've forgotten to turn my indicator off' . . . or something.

Petrol is more expensive than in the US, more comparable with the price in Australia, and a bit cheaper than in Europe at around M$4.60 an imperial gallon. Remember that wearing safety belts *is* compulsory in both countries. Parking regulations are a little curious in both Singapore and Malaysia. Singapore has its coupon parking system and central business district entry regulations. In Malaysia they have a strange human parking meter system where your car collects a stack of little tickets under its wiper and you then have to find somebody to pay for them at so many cents per ticket.

Major rental operators in Singapore and Malaysia include Sintat, Avis, Hertz and Mayflower Acme although there are numerous others including many local operators only found in one city. Singapore in particular has a simply phenomenal number of local operators. Rates are quoted both for unlimited distance and with an additional mileage charge, cheaper rates are available by the week. Unlimited distance rates with Sintat vary from around M$120 a day for a Toyota Corolla to M$330 for a Mercedes.

The Automobile Association of Malaysia (tel 417137) is at Lot 20/24 Hotel Equatorial, Jalan Sultan Ismail, Kuala Lumpur. They will let you join their organisation if you have a letter of introduction from your own automobile association.

HITCHING

Malaysia has long had a reputation for being an excellent place for hitch-hiking and it's generally still true. You'll get picked up both by expats and by Malaysians and Singaporeans, but it's strictly an activity for foreigners – a hitch-hiking Malaysian would probably just get left by the roadside! So the first rule of thumb in Malaysia is to look foreign. Look neat and tidy too, a world-wide rule for successful hitching, but make sure your backpack is in view and you look like someone on their way around the country.

Apart from the basic point of hitching, getting from A to B cheaply, hitching in Malaysia has the additional benefit that it's a fine way to meet the local people. Foreign hitch-hikers are also looked upon as a neutral ear – you're likely to find out much more about the *bumiputra* situation from disgruntled Chinese when you're in their car. Or hear much more about the Chinese from disgruntled Malays!

Don't try hitching in Singapore, it's too small, too built up and the government probably doesn't approve of it. On the west coast of Malaysia, particularly on the busy Johore Bahru-Kuala Lumpur-Butterworth route, hitching is generally quite easy. Much of the traffic is businessmen, the sort of people interested in conversation and likely to pick up hitch-hikers. On the east coast traffic can often be quite light and there may be long waits between rides. Hitching in north Borneo also depends on the traffic although it's quite possible. Hitching into Bandar Seri Begawan from the Sarawak-Brunei border is very easy.

BOAT

Feri Malaysia commutes between the peninsula and East Malaysia twice weekly. From Kuching, you can take the ferry to Singapore for M$200 (standard cabin), M$235 (deluxe cabin) or M$355 (suite). Return fares are double these one-way fares. Alternatively, you can go from Kuching to Kota Kinabalu for M$140 (standard cabin), M$195 (deluxe cabin) or M$300 (suite). For reservations or more information, contact Malaysia Shipping Agencies (tel 429480) Block E, Lot 33 Taman Sri Sarawak Mail, Jalan Tuanku Abdul Rahman.

LOCAL TRANSPORT

Local transport varies widely from place to place. Almost everywhere there will be taxis and in most cases these will be metered. In major cities there will be buses – in Singapore they are all government operated, in Kuala Lumpur the government buses are backed up by private operators. In many towns there are also bicycle-rickshaws – while they are dying out in KL and have become principally a tourist gimmick in most of Singapore they are still a viable form of transport in many Malaysian cities. Indeed in places like Georgetown, with its convoluted and narrow streets, a bicycle-rickshaw is probably the best way of getting around. See the relevant city sections for more details on local transport.

SINGAPORE

SINGAPORE

Singapore is an island at the tip of the Malay peninsula. It was once just a small fishing kampung on a rather swampy island. It took its improbable name, 'Lion City', from a Sumatran prince who thought he saw a lion – even though there have probably never been lions there. Singapore would have drifted quietly on if Sir Stamford Raffles had not decided, in 1819, that it was just the port he needed to ensure Britain's pre-eminent position in the east.

His choice proved to be a sound one because today Singapore not only thrives on trade but has become a jet age travel crossroads with one of the busiest airports in Asia. Under its efficient and forward looking government, Singapore has become the most affluent country in Asia after Japan and a model for developing nations. Singapore celebrated 20 years of independence in 1985. For the visitor it's promoted as 'instant Asia'. An island/city which offers enormous variety in terms of people, food and religions as well as being colourful, exciting and atmospheric – all in a small, handy package.

Population

Singapore's polyglot population numbers 2.5 million. It's made up of 76% Chinese, 15% Malay, 7% Indian and Pakistani and the remaining 2% a variety of races. Singapore's population density is high but the government has waged a particularly successful birth control campaign. Great emphasis is placed on the two child family being the ideal (two girls or not) and there are a number of financial disincentives to larger families. In fact the birth control campaign has been so successful with certain groups that the government has done a complete reversal and is now actively encouraging women with university degrees to have children!

Geography

Singapore is a low-lying island of 616 square km, not much over 100 km from the equator. Apart from the main island there are also about 50 smaller islands. Singapore is connected with Peninsular Malaysia by a km-long causeway. Bukit Timah (Hill of Tin) is the highest point on the island at an altitude of 166 metres,

Economy

Singapore's economy is based on trade, shipping, banking and tourism with a growing programme of light industrialisation. Singapore has a major oil refining business producing much of the petroleum for the South-East Asian region. Other important industries include ship building and maintenance and electronics. Singapore's port is the third busiest in the world.

There are few social programmes in Singapore although medical care is heavily subsidised. As part of the government's 'rugged society' programme there are no unemployment payments or programmes – but unemployment is negligible and the government insists that anyone who wants to work can find work. In fact Singapore actually has negative unemployment and has to import workers from neighbouring countries, particularly to do the hard, dirty work which Singaporeans no longer want any part of.

Strikes are virtually unknown in Singapore but the government has a policy to actually push wages up in order to drive the inefficient labour intensive industries out and force more capital intensive industries to the fore. At a time when some western countries are trying to protect their inefficient 'twilight' industries it's quite a different policy! All Singaporeans have to save money with the Central Provident Fund, a form of superannuation that is returned to them on retirement. They can, however, invest their CPF savings in the purchase of government housing.

Immigration & Health

If you plan to stay in Singapore for longer than your initial two-week entry permit the immigration office is on Empress Place, just across the river from the GPO. For cheap immunisations go to the vaccination centre at 5th floor, 1226 Outram Rd. Phone 222 7711 for information or get there on a No 123 bus from Orchard Rd.

Orientation

It is relatively easy to find your way around Singapore Island. At the top it is joined to Malaysia by the causeway which carries both road and rail traffic. At the bottom centre of the island is Singapore city. Changi Airport is at the extreme eastern tip of the island while the major industrial centre, Jurong, is towards the western tip. If you thought of the island as having a north, south, east and west corner, which in essence it does, those four places (causeway, city, airport and Jurong) would define it.

In the city itself Orchard Rd and Bras Basah Rd make a very useful dividing line. Orchard Rd continues more or less directly on to Bras Basah Rd and they run more or less perpendicularly towards the waterfront. Both are one way so a parallel road carries traffic in the opposite direction away from the waterfront.

Bras Basah Rd is the watershed for cheap hotels – backpackers almost always stay in the modern crashpads or the older hotels to the east of Bras Basah Rd. This area is not only less expensive it also holds more of historical interest.

On the other hand Orchard Rd is the address of a large percentage of Singapore's multi-storey international hotels and interspersed with them are a number of Singapore's major shopping centres. From Bras Basah Rd to the Singapore River there are a number of parks and greens and some of Singapore's major colonial buildings.

The modern office centre of Singapore is to the south-west of the river where you'll also find the GPO and most of the banks. North-east of this modern centre is Chinatown, the oldest part of Singapore city, while north-east again are many new housing blocks and shopping centres.

Information

There are two tourist information centres in town. One is on the ground floor of the new Raffles City Tower, it's beside the Singapore Airlines office on the North Bridge Rd side of the block. The second office is at the ~~Singapore Handicraft~~ Centre on the corner of Tanglin Rd and Grange Rd. The office is open from 8.30 am to 5 pm Monday to Friday, 8.30 am to 1 pm on Saturday. They can provide a variety of useful leaflets and information including the *Singapore Official Guide* which provides a useful and colourful run down on the entire island.

There is a hotel booking desk at the airport but the cheapest they go is about S\$30 to S\$40 so it does not cover any of the bottom end bracket. Student Travel have an office in the Ming Court Hotel on the mezzanine level. They can provide advice on student cards, cheap airline tickets and also offer discounts on a number of middle and upper range hotels.

The famous anti-long-hair campaign is pretty much a thing of the past. You're unlikely to be turned away on arrival or given short back and sides on the spot unless you look really outrageous.

Singapore remains heavy on a number of other issues, however. The successful anti-littering campaign continues – up to S\$500 fine for dropping even a cigarette butt on the street. Actually nobody does get fined that amount but the idea is effective – Singapore is amazingly clean.

You can also get hit for a S\$500 fine for smoking in a public place – buses, lifts, cinemas and even government offices. Jaywalking is the latest activity to get the Singapore treatment – walk across the road within 50 metres of a designated crossing and it could cost you S\$50.

Maps The American Express/STPB *Map of Singapore* is an excellent free map, available at the airport on arrival, at most middle and top-end hotels and at some shopping centres. The *Map of Singapore,* another giveaway map, is also good.

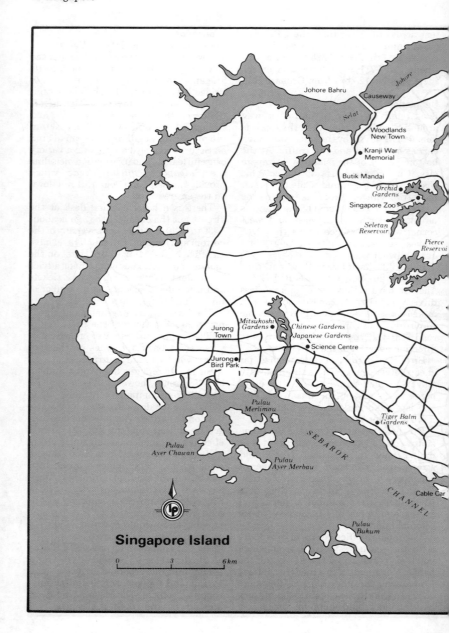

Singapore Island

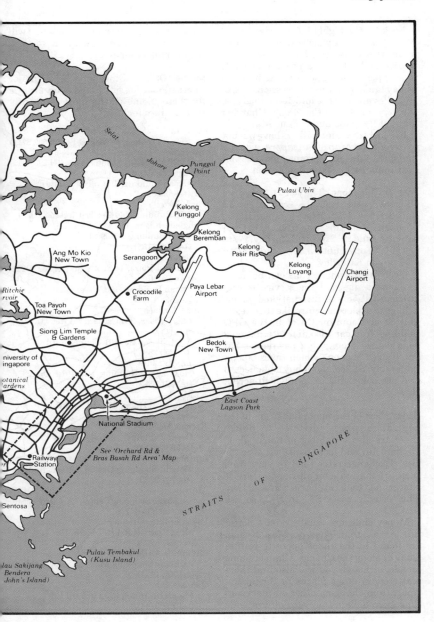

Look for the highly informative *Secret Map of Singapore* which can be purchased in most bookstores which cater to the tourist trade. This is especially valuable to shoppers seeking such exotic items as Malay bridal costumes, professional mahjong tiles and clothes for Mecca pilgrims. It's very similar to the Nancy Chandler maps of Bangkok and Chiang Mai.

Recently the same authors have put out a *Secret Food Map of Singapore*, which is indispensable for people looking for maximum eating experimentation.

Post & Telephone The GPO, with its efficient poste restante service, is on Raffles Quay close to the Singapore River. It's open for stamps from 8.30 am to 6 pm weekdays and till 2 pm on Saturday. Poste restante is open until 5.30 weekdays and 1.30 pm on Saturday.

Overseas telephone calls can be made 24 hours a day and the service is very efficient. To make international phone calls go to a telecom centre like the ones on Hill St or Robinson Rd or in the GPO building. You can also dial international calls yourself from public pay phones but you'll need a phone which takes 50c or, preferably, S$1 coins. Or buy a phonecard and use one of the phones which accept these cards.

Banks Most of the major banks are in the central business district although there are also a number of banks along Orchard Rd and local banks all over the city. Exchange rates tend to vary from bank to bank and some also make a service charge on each exchange transaction. This usually costs S$2 to S$3, so ask first.

Money changers usually offer a better rate for cash than banks do. Most of them are found in the shops opposite Raffles Quay or along the Change Alley shopping arcade, although you will also find them scattered in other places in Singapore. Apart from changing other currencies to Singapore dollars they also offer a wide variety of other currencies for sale and will do amazing multiple currency transactions in the blink of an eye.

Airline Offices Singapore is a major international crossroads and many airlines fly there. Some of the most frequently used airlines include:

Aeroflot
   Sinsov Building, 55 Market St (tel 532 6711)
Air India
   UIC Building, 5 Shenton Way (tel 225 9411)
Air New Zealand
   Ocean Building, 10 Collyer Quay
   (tel 535 8266)
Air Lanka
   PIL Building, 140 Cecil St (tel 223 6026)
Bangladesh Biman
   Fidvi Building, 97-99 Market St
   (tel 535 2155)
British Airways
   Far East Plaza, 14 Scotts Rd (tel 253 5922)
Cathay Pacific
   Ocean Building, 10 Collyer Quay
   (tel 533 1333)
China Airlines
   Lucky Plaza, 304 Orchard Rd (tel 737 2211)
Garuda
   Goldhill Square, 101 Thomson Rd
   (tel 250 2888)
Japan Air Lines
   Hong Leong Building, 16 Raffles Quay
   (tel 221 0522)
KLM
   Mandarin Hotel, 333 Orchard Rd
   (tel 737 7622)
Korean Air Lines
   Ocean Building, 10 Collyer Quay
   (tel 534 2111)
Lufthansa
   Tanglin Shopping Centre, 19 Tanglin Rd
   (tel 737 9222)
MAS
   Singapore Shopping Centre, 190 Clemenceau
   Ave (tel 336 6777)
Pakistan International
   Ming Court Hotel, 1 Tanglin Rd
   (tel 737 3233)
Philippine Airlines
   Parklane Shopping Mall, 35 Selegie Rd
   (tel 336 1611)
Qantas
   Mandarin Hotel, 333 Orchard Rd
   (tel 737 3744)

Top: Restored house, Singapore (JC)
Left: Sultan Mosque, Singapore (TW)
Right: Modern government apartments, Singapore (TW)

Top: Goodwood Park Hotel, Singapore (AS)
Left: Singapore River & the central business district (TW)
Right: Coffee shop, Singapore (JC)

Royal Brunei Airlines
   Orchard Towers, 400 Orchard Rd
   (tel 235 4672)
Royal Nepal Airlines
   SIA Building, 77 Robinson Rd (tel 225 7575)
Scandinavian Airlines System
   Finlayson House, 4 Raffles Quay
   (tel 225 1333)
Singapore Airlines
   77 Robinson Rd (tel 223 8888)
   Mandarin Hotel, Orchard Rd (tel 229 7291)
   Raffles City, North Bridge Rd (tel 229 7128)
Thai International
   Keck Seng Towers, 133 Cecil St
   (tel 224 9977)
United Airlines
   Hong Leong Buiding, 16 Raffles Quay
   (tel 220 0711)
UTA
   Orchard Towers, 400 Orchard Rd
   (tel 737 6355)

Consulates & Embassies The addresses of some embassies in Singapore include:

Australia
   25 Napier Rd (tel 737 9311)
Bangladesh
   Goldhill Square, 101 Thomson Rd
   (tel 250 6323)
Brunei
   7A Tanglin Hill (tel 474 3393)
Burma
   15 St Martin's Drive (tel 235 8704)
Canada
   Faber House, 230 Orchard Rd (tel 737 1322)
Denmark
   Goldhill Square, 101 Thomson Rd
   (tel 250 3383)
West Germany
   Far East Shopping Centre, 545 Orchard Rd
   (tel 737 1355)
India
   31 Grange Rd (tel 737 6809)
Indonesia
   7 Chatsworth Rd (tel 737 7422)
Japan
   16 Nassim Rd (tel 235 8855)
Republic of Korea
   Goldhill Square, 101 Thomson Rd
   (tel 256 1188)
Malaysia
   301 Jervois Rd (tel 235 0111)
Netherlands
   Liat Towers, 541 Orchard Rd (tel 737 1155)

New Zealand
   13 Nassim Rd (tel 235 9966)
Pakistan
   20A Nassim Rd (tel 235 9966)
Philippines
   20B Nassim Rd (tel 737 3977)
Sri Lanka
   Goldhill Plaza, 51 Newton Rd (tel 254 4595)
Sweden
   PUB Building, 111 Somerset Rd
   (tel 734 2771)
Thailand
   370 Orchard Rd (tel 737 2644)
UK
   Tanglin Rd (tel 473 9333)
USA
   30 Hill St (tel 338 0251)
USSR
   51 Nassim Rd (tel 235 1834)

Laundries There aren't many of them yet but self-service laundries do seem to be more easily found these days. Close to the cheap hotel and crashpad enclave, Systematic is on the 5th floor of Plaza Singapura in Orchard Rd, hidden away behind Yaohan's near the car park entrance. There are only two machines and it's open 10 am to 8 pm. They have a drop off wash, dry and fold service for S$8 a load. Up the other end of Orchard Rd is Washy Washy in the basement of Forum Galleria by the Ming Court Hotel. It costs S$3 per load to wash and another S$3 to dry.

AROUND THE CITY
Singapore's greatest attraction is probably the sheer variety it offers – you can walk in minutes from the modern business centre with its towering air-conditioned office blocks into the narrow streets of Chinatown where the bicycle rickshaw is still the best way to get around. Meanwhile across the river there are areas known as little India (Serangoon Rd) and the Muslim centre of Arab St while further out are the new housing complexes and industrial centres.

City, River & Harbour

Singapore's city centre straddles the Singapore River and runs parallel to the waterfront along Raffles Quay, Shenton Way, Robinson Rd and Cecil St. The Singapore River was once one of the most picturesque areas of Singapore with old shops and houses along the river and soaring office buildings right behind them.

Sadly, it doesn't look like the old places will be around much longer. All the bustling activity along this stretch of river – the loading and unloading of sampans and bumboats – has ceased. The cranes are gone and the yelling, sweating labourers, too. All boats have been kicked out of the area and relocated to the Pasir Panjang wharves away from the city centre. You can still sit in the hawkers centres by the river, but rather than watch all the activity you can bet on which building will be next under the wrecking ball.

On the Empress Place side of the river a statue of Sir Stamford Raffles stands imperiously by the water. It's in the approximate place where he first set foot on Singapore island. There is a second statue of Raffles in front of the clock tower by Empress Place. Nearby is the Supreme Court and City Hall, across from which is the open green of the Padang, site for cricket, hockey, football and rugby matches. There are also memorials to civilians who died as a result of the Japanese occupation and to Lim Bo Seng, a resistance leader killed by the Japanese.

If you continue up Coleman St from the Padang you pass the Armenian Church and come to Fort Canning Hill, a good viewpoint over Singapore. Once known as 'Forbidden Hill', the hill is now topped by the old Christian cemetery which has many gravestones with their poignant tales of hopeful settlers who died young. There too is the tomb of Sultan Iskander Shah, the last ruler of the ancient kingdom of Singapura. At the mouth of the river, or at least what used to be the mouth before the most recent bout of land reclamation, stands Singapore's symbol, the Merlion.

Change Alley, Singapore's most famous place for bargains has survived or rather adapted to modernisation. It still cuts through from Collyer Quay to Raffles Place, but has become a pedestrian bridge and is known as 'Aerial Change Alley'. It's still lined with shops and money changers although now it's air-conditioned! The older alley runs below.

Further along the waterfront you'll find large office blocks, airline offices and more shops. Here too is the popular Telok Ayer Transit Food Centre by the waterfront. Singapore's disappearing Chinatown is inland from this modern city centre.

You can hire a boat to go out onto the harbour from Clifford Pier or you can take a tour boat. Singapore's harbour is the third busiest in the world and there are always many boats anchored offshore, with at least one arriving or leaving every 15 minutes.

Chinatown

One of the most fascinating areas of Singapore is also, unfortunately, one of the most rapidly disappearing. Any time you can spare an hour or two it's worth devoting it to wandering the tightly packed streets of Chinatown because in a few years it's quite probable there will be very little left to explore.

Meanwhile any time of day is a good time, but you'll probably find the early morning hours not only the most interesting but also the coolest. Chinatown is roughly bounded by the Singapore River to the east, New Bridge Rd to the north, Maxwell Rd and Kreta Ayer Rd to the west and Cecil Rd to the south. Roughly, because already urban renewal and new office blocks are nibbling at the edges of Chinatown and wider roads are being ploughed right through the middle of it.

You could start a Chinatown walking tour from Boon Tat St beside the Telok Ayer food centre. This is still a narrow street lined with typical Chinese shopfronts and at the junction with Telok Ayer St you'll find the

Nagore Durgha Shrine (1), an old mosque built by Muslims from south India during 1829 and 1930. It's not that interesting, but just a little down the street is the Chinese Thian Hock Keng or Temple of Heavenly Happiness (2) – one of the most interesting in Singapore. See Temples, Mosques & Churches for more details.

Continue walking along Telok Ayer St and you'll soon come to the Al-Abrar Mosque (3) which was originally built in 1827 and rebuilt in its present form from 1850 to 1855. A right turn and another right turn will bring you into Amoy St where once again there are rows of typical Chinese shop fronts with their convoluted 'five-foot ways'.

Walking on these covered walkways is always a continuous obstacle course. It's amazing how, on many of these old Chinese houses, bushes and even large trees seem to sprout straight out of the walls – an indication of the amazing fertility which Singapore's steamy climate seems to engender.

Continue over Cross St, a wide new road which has been ruthlessly pushed right through the middle of Chinatown, and then turn up Pekin St to China St. This whole street is a fascinating conglomeration of shops and shopfront activity. Old men ride by on bicycle rickshaws, shops sell provisions and Chinese groceries, you can peer into a darkened Chinese wine shop where old men cluster around equally old marble-topped tables. Further along there are shops making and selling temple equipment and the paraphernalia you burn for good luck. Another shop deals in eggs – brown eggs, white eggs, chicken eggs, duck eggs and even 100-year-old eggs.

If you cross back over Cross St the name changes to Club St, a curious street because it seems to go steeply uphill when you would think this part of Singapore was all pancake flat. On the corner with

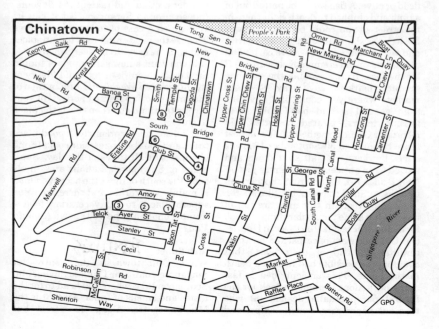

Mohamed Ali Lane a tiny hole-in-the-wall shop (4) makes 'popiah' skins – the outer covering for Chinese spring rolls. Across the road are a couple of places where Chinese religious figures and temple furniture are carved and painted (5).

At the top of Club St you meet Ann Siang Hill and on the corner there you'll find a place making paper transport for the after life – anything from a bicycle rickshaw to a car (6).

Continue up to South Bridge Rd and you enter the real heart of Chinatown although there too urban renewal is cutting its swath. Many of the most interesting sights in this area could only be seen very early in the morning, when the food and produce markets were operating, or in the evening when the night markets would swing into action.

Along Trengannu, Smith and Banda Sts you could see fish stalls selling fish, turtles, snails, frogs and even snakes – dead or alive. A fish would be netted out of a tank and clubbed to death right there in the street so you could be certain it was fresh. Vegetable stalls sold glistening fruit and vegetables. Chickens were carried off in baskets or unceremoniously carted off by the legs. In the evening the daytime produce markets gave way to night markets where you could find anything from general second hand rubbish to fortune tellers, pirated cassettes, old records or Chinese medicines. It's all past tense because on 30 September 1983 the street hawkers were all shut down and moved to an antiseptic new centre just off New Bridge Rd, hammering another nail into the coffin of colourful old Singapore.

All the streets in this area are full of interest but some particular things to look for include the last few old 'Death Houses' (7). Old folk were once packed off there towards the end of their lives, thus avoiding the possible bad luck of a death in the home. This ancient idea is fast dying out! Along Temple St look for the funeral paraphernalia dealers (8) who turn out paper cars, houses, ships, and other equipment just in case you can take it with you. Also in this area is the Sri Mariamman Temple (9) which is described later on.

Other things you may see in the bustling streets of Chinatown include calligraphers who will quickly pen a message in Chinese script for you. Chinese delicacies like shark's fins, abalone, sea slugs or deer horns can be seen in some shops. Across the New Bridge Rd is the huge People's Park Complex – a modern shopping centre, but with much more local appeal than the general run of Orchard Rd centres.

Serangoon Rd INDIAN FOOD + CLOTHING

Although Singapore is a predominantly Chinese city it does have its minority groups and the Indians are probably the most visible – particularly in the colourful streets of 'little India'. This is another area, like Chinatown, where you simply wander around and take in the flavours. Indeed around Serangoon Rd it can be very much a case of following your nose because the heady aromas of Indian spices and cooking seem to be everywhere.

If you want a new sari, a pair of Indian sandals, a recent issue of *India Today* or the *Illustrated Weekly of India*, a tape of Indian music or a framed portrait of your favourite Hindu god then this is the place to go.

It's also, not surprisingly, a good place to eat and you'll see streetside cooks frying chappatis at all times of the day. Since many of Singapore's Indians are Tamils from the south of India the accent on food is mainly vegetarian and there are some superb places to eat vegetarian food – number one being the well known *Komala Vilas*.

Arab Street TEXTILES

While Chinatown is the centre for Singapore's old-time Chinese flavour and Serangoon Rd is where you head to for the tastes and smells of India, Arab St is the Muslim centre. Along this street but especially along North Bridge Rd and adjoining side streets with Malay names like Pahang Rd, Aliwal St, Jalan Pisang, and Jalan Sultan, you'll find batiks from Indonesia and sarongs, hookahs, rosaries, flower essences, Haj caps, songkok hats, basketware and rattan goods.

The Sultan Mosque, focus for Singapore's Muslim community, is at the junction of Arab St and North Bridge Rd. You'll also find good north Indian food at restaurants along North Bridge Rd.

Other Areas

Singapore's international tourists and its wealthy residents also have whole areas of Singapore to themselves. Orchard Rd is where the high-class hotels predominate and beyond it you enter the area of the Singapore elite. Prior to independence the mansions of the colonial rulers were built there and today Singapore's wealthy elite, as well as many expatriate personnel, live in those fine old houses.

Still another side of Singapore is found in the modern HDB (Housing & Development Board) satellite cities like Toa Payoh. A high percentage of Singaporeans already live in these government housing blocks and it is intended to raise the figure to 80% by the end of the decade. Once again it is a programme that Singapore manages to make work. While high-rise flats have become a dirty word in many countries, in Singapore they are almost universally popular. In many cases the occupants actually own their own flats and, Singapore being Singapore once again, with prices escalating it's often possible to sell your flat at a profit before you even move in.

Jurong Town, to the west of the island, is more than just a new housing area. There, a huge industrial complex has been built from the ground up on land that was still a swamp at the end of WW II. Today it's the power house of Singapore's economic success story.

Temples, Mosques & Churches

Singapore's polyglot population has resulted in an equally varied collection of places of worship. There are mosques, churches and Chinese, Hindu and Buddhist temples. The churches chiefly date from the English colonial period, though Singapore's oldest church is Armenian, as Armenian traders were visiting Singapore at about the same time as Raffles. The Hindu temples are basically of the south Indian Dravidian style since many of Singapore's Indian settlers are Tamils from that region.

Thian Hock Keng

The temple of Heavenly Happiness on Telok Ayer St in Chinatown is the oldest and also one of the most colourful temples in Singapore – in part due to a restoration in 1979. The temple was originally built in 1840 and dedicated to Ma-Cho-Po, the Queen of Heaven and protector of sailors.

At that time it was on the waterfront and since many Chinese settlers were arriving in Singapore by sea it was inevitable that a joss house be built where they could offer thanks for a safe voyage. As you wander the courtyards of the temple look for the rooftop dragons, the intricately decorated beams, the burning joss sticks, the gold leafed panels and, best of all, the beautifully painted doors. It's open from 5.30 am to 9 pm.

Sri Mariamman Temple

On South Bridge Rd, right in the heart of Chinatown, the Sri Mariamman Temple is the oldest Hindu temple in Singapore. It was originally built in 1827, but its present form dates from 1862 when the original wooden temple was rebuilt. With its colourful gopuram, or tower, over the entrance gate this is clearly a temple in the south Indian Dravidian style. A superb collection of colourfully painted Hindu figures gaze out from the gopuram.

In October of each year the temple is the scene for the Thimithi festival during which devotees walk barefoot over burning

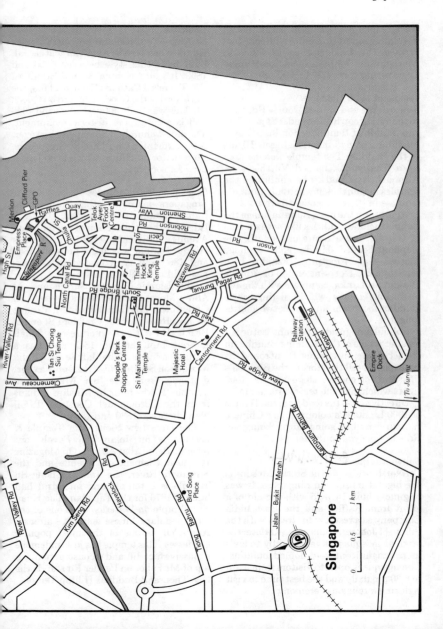

Singapore

Merlion
Clifford Pier
GPO
Raffles Quay
Empress Place
Singapore R
High St
Telok Ayer Food Centre
Shenton Way
Robinson Rd
Cecil St
Chulia
St
North Canal Rd
South Bridge Rd
Thian Hock King Temple
Maxwell Rd
Anson Rd
Tanjung Pagar Rd
Neil Rd
Tan Si Chong Siu Temple
River Valley Rd
Clemenceau Ave
People's Park Shopping Centre
Sri Mariamman Temple
Majestic Hotel
Cantonment Rd
New Bridge Rd
Railway Station
Keppel Rd
Empire Dock
To Jurong
River Valley Rd
Kim Seng Rd
Havelock Rd
Tiong Bahru Rd
Bird Song Place
Jalan Bukit Merah
Kampong Bahru Rd

0   0.5   1 km

coals – supposedly feeling no pain although spectators report that quite a few hot-foot it over the final few steps! The Sri Mariamman Temple is open from 6 am to 12 noon and from 4.30 to 8.30 pm.

Temple of 1000 Lights

Towards the end of Race Course Rd, close to the Serangoon Rd/Lavender St junction, this Buddhist temple is dominated by a brightly painted 15-metre-high seated figure of the Buddha. The temple was inspired by a Thai monk named Vutthisasara. Although it is said to be similar to the temples in Bangkok it's actually far more Chinese in its technicolour flavour.

Apart from the huge Buddha image the temple includes oddities like a wax model of Gandhi and a figure of Ganesh, the elephant-headed Hindu god. A huge mother-of-pearl footprint is said to be a replica of the footprint on top of Adam's Peak in Sri Lanka, complete with the 108 auspicious marks which distinguish a Buddha foot from any other two-metre-long foot.

Behind, and inside, the giant statue is a smaller image of the reclining Buddha, in the act of entering nirvana. Right round the base models tell the story of the Buddha's life, and, of course, there are the 1000 lights which give the temple its name.

Directly across the road from the Temple of 1000 Lights is a colourful new Chinese temple. Any bus going down Serangoon Rd will take you to the temple.

Sultan Mosque BEAUTIFUL

On North Bridge Rd the Sultan Mosque is the biggest mosque in Singapore. It was originally built in 1825 with the aid of a grant from Raffles and the East India Company as a result of his treaty with the Sultan of Johore. A hundred years later the original mosque was replaced by today's more magnificent gold-domed building. The mosque is open to visitors from 5 am to 8.30 pm daily and the best time to visit is during a religious ceremony.

Churches

St Andrew's Cathedral on North Bridge Rd is Singapore's Anglican cathedral, built in Gothic style between 1856 and 1863. It's on Coleman St and Stamford Rd. There's a Catholic Cathedral too, the Cathedral of the Good Shepherd on Queen St. This was built between 1843 and 1846 and is a Singapore historic monument. The oldest church in Singapore, however, is the Armenian Church of St Gregory the Illuminator on Hill St which is no longer used for services.

Other Temples & Mosques

Singapore has many other Chinese and Indian temples and mosques. On Tank Rd, near the intersection of Clemenceau Avenue and River Valley Rd, the Chettiar Hindu Temple was built between 1855 and 1860 and is dedicated to the six-headed Lord Subramaniam.

The Islamic Durgha Shrine and Al Abrar Mosque are on Telok Ayer St in Chinatown. The Hajjah Fatimah Mosque on Java Rd is near the Crawford St end of Beach Rd. It's a picturesque small mosque built around 1845 and has a leaning minaret. The Jamae or Chulia Mosque on South Bridge Rd is only a short distance from the Sri Mariamman Temple. It was built by Muslim Indians from the Coromandel Coast of Tamil Nadu between 1830 and 1855.

The large new Siong Lim Temple & Garden is on Jalan Toa Payoh, out towards Paya Lebar Airport. On Magazine Rd, near Clemenceau Avenue and the Singapore River, the Tan Si Chong Su Temple is a temple and ancestral hall built in 1876 for the Tan clan. The Kuan Yin Temple on Waterloo St is one of the most popular Chinese temples – after all Kuan Yin is one of the most popular goddesses. This temple has just undergone a massive face-lift and reconstruction. On top of Mt Faber on Pender Rd stands the One Thousand Buddhas Hilltop Temple.

Places to Go & Things to Do

Apart from the parks, islands, gardens temples and colourful city areas Singapore also has a whole list of conventional attractions from museums and galleries to an aquarium, the Instant Asia show, and the famous Raffles Hotel.

Instant Asia & Other Shows

For jet set tourists who want to see it all in one fast, painless performance the Instant Asia show is just the ticket. In 45 action packed minutes you'll see everything from lion dances to Indian snake charmers and Chinese opera. Some of the costumes and dances you are unlikely to see elsewhere. It's very popular with photographers. The show is presented at 11.45 am daily at the Raffles Hotel and admission is S$5 (children S$2).

Other shows include ASEAN Night at the Mandarin Hotel, Malam Singapura at the Hyatt Regency, the nightly Cultural Show at the Raffles and the Chinese operas or wayangs which you might stumble across anywhere but which also take place on Saturdays and Sundays from 7.30 to 9.30 pm at the Singapore Handicraft Centre on Tanglin Rd.

National Museum & Art Gallery

The National Museum, on Stamford Rd, traces its ancestry back to Mr Raffles himself who first brought up the idea of a museum for Singapore in 1823. The original museum was finally opened in 1849 then moved to another location in 1862 before being rehoused in the present building in 1887.

Exhibits include archaeological artefacts from the Asia region, articles relating to Chinese trade and settlement in the region, Malaysian and Indonesian arts and crafts and a wide collection of items relating to Raffles. These include his manuscripts plus maps and paintings of old Singapore.

The art gallery includes contemporary paintings from both Singaporean and other South-East Asian artists. A recent addition to the museum is the superb jade collection from Haw Par House which has now been closed. The Aw brothers, of Tiger Balm fame, amassed not only this priceless collection of jade pieces but also a variety of other valuable pieces of art. The museum is open from 9 am to 4.30 pm daily and admission is S$1.

Van Kleef Aquarium

On River Valley Rd in Central Park the Van Kleef Aquarium has 71 tanks displaying nearly 5000 fish and other creatures including crocodiles and turtles. The aquarium is open from 9.30 am to 9 pm daily and admission is 60c.

Singapore Science Centre

On Science Centre Rd, off Jurong Town Hall Rd, the Science Centre is great fun. It attempts to make science come alive by providing countless opportunities to try things out yourself. There are handles to crank, buttons to push, levers to pull, microscopes to look through, and films to watch. The centre is open from 10 am to 6 pm from Tuesday to Sunday and admission is S$2 (children 50c). You can get there on a No 143 or 158 bus.

Raffles Hotel   EVENING JAZZ

The Raffles Hotel is far more than just an expensive place to stay or even just the best known hotel in Singapore. It's a Singapore institution, an architectural landmark which has been classified by the government as a part of Singapore's 'cultural heritage' and a place that virtually oozes the old fashioned atmosphere of the east as Somerset Maugham would have known it.

Originally the Raffles started as a tiffin house run by a Captain Dare. Later he expanded it into a hotel which in 1886 was taken over by the Sarkies brothers, three Armenians who built a string of hotels which were to become famous throughout the east. They include the Strand in Rangoon and the E&O in Penang as well as the Raffles.

The Raffles soon became a byword for oriental luxury and was featured in novels by Joseph Conrad and Somerset Maugham. It was also recommended by Rudyard Kipling as the place to 'feed at' when in Singapore (but stay elsewhere he added!) and in its Long Bar one Ngiam Tong Boon created the Singapore Sling in 1915. You can still front the bar and order a Singapore Sling today.

More recently the Raffles was threatened by redevelopment, it had lost its waterfront location to land reclamation and more modern hotels could offer better facilities and far lower running costs. Fortunately there are enough discerning visitors to keep the Raffles balance sheet in the black and future developments will be in the form of extensions, not replacement of the existing building.

Meanwhile a visit to the Raffles is well worthwhile even if you're not staying there. You can sip a drink in the bar or order tea on the immaculate lawn – and turn the clock back a century.

Sunday Morning Bird Singing
One of the nicest things to do on a Sunday morning in Singapore is to go and hear the birds sing. The Chinese love caged birds as their beautifully ornate bird cages indicate. The birds – thrushes, merboks, sharmas, and mata putehs – are treasured for their singing ability. To ensure the quality of their song the doting owner will feed his bird a carefully prepared diet and once a week crowds of bird fanciers get together for a bird song session.

The bird cages are hung up on wires strung between trees or under verandahs. They're not mixed indiscriminately – sharmas sing with sharmas, merboks with merboks – and each type of bird has its own design of cage. Tall pointy ones for tall pointy birds, short and squat ones for short squat birds. Having assembled the birds the proud owners then congregate around tables, sip coffee and listen to their birds go through their paces. It's a delightful scene both musically and visually.

You'll find bird concerts on Sunday mornings from around 8 to 11 am at the junction of Tiong Bahru and Seng Poh Rds and at Sturdee Lane by Petain Rd, just off Jalan Besar near the Lavender St intersection.

Other Attractions
The Thong Chai Medical Institution building on Wayang St was built in 1892 and now houses, among other things, a display of Chinese medicines. On Clemenceau Avenue the House of Tan Yeok Nee is now the headquarters of the Salvation Army, but in 1885 it was built as the townhouse of a prosperous merchant in a style then common in the south of China.

Near the Malaysia Causeway off Woodlands Rd the Kranji War Memorial includes the graves of thousands of Allied servicemen who died in the region during WW II.

There are a number of art galleries and displays apart from the major National Museum Art Gallery. On Clemenceau Avenue the National Theatre also has a gallery with paintings and ceramics. The Alpha Gallery at 7 Alexandra Avenue displays work by local and Balinese artists. Sculptures and batik paintings can be seen in the Seah Gallery in the Shangri-La Hotel. The three Centre of Fine Arts displays (see Things to Buy) also have a wide variety of artwork.

Peranakan Place is a complex of old Nonya-Baba shop-houses at Orchard Rd and Emerald Hill Rd. Peranakan culture is that of the Straits-born Chinese who spoke a Malay dialect and developed their own customs which were sort of a hybrid of Chinese and Malay. 'Nonya' is the word for an adult Peranakan woman, 'Baba' her male counterpart. There is a restaurant, a small museum, and a coffee shop which exhibit Peranakan culture. Due to its location on Orchard Rd, it tends to be a bit touristy, but if traditional Straits Chinese culture interests you, it shouldn't be missed.

Parks & Gardens

Singapore has been dubbed the Garden City and with good reason – it's green and lush with parks and gardens scattered everywhere. In part this fertility is a factor of the climate – you only have to stick a twig in the ground for it to become a tree in weeks! The government has backed up this natural advantage with a concentrated programme that has even turned the dividing strip on highways into flourishing gardens – you notice it even as you drive into Singapore from the Malaysia causeway.

Botanic Gardens

Singapore's 127-year-old Botanic Gardens are on Cluny and Holland Rds, not far from Tanglin Rd and the tourist office. They're a popular peaceful retreat for Singaporeans.

The Botanic Gardens also house the herbarium where much .work has been done on breeding orchids for which Singapore is famous. The orchid enclosure contains over 2500 examples of orchids representing 250 species and hybrids in

all. In an earlier era the gardens pioneered the development of Brazilian rubber plants that were to spread all over South-East Asia.

The 47-hectare gardens are open from 5 am to 11 pm on weekdays, to midnight on weekends, and admission is free. Early in the morning you'll see hundreds of Singaporeans jogging there.

Tiger Balm Gardens

About 10 km out from the city centre on Pasir Panjang Rd the Tiger Balm Gardens are a magnificent tribute to bad taste. An exotic collection of concrete and plaster figures cover six hillside hectares. It's a delight to children of all ages, a gaudy grotesquerie of statues illustrating the pleasures and punishments of this life and the next, scenes from Chinese legends and a whole series of 'international displays' such as a group of kangaroos to represent Australia.

Favourite displays include, inevitably, the 'torture chamber', where sinners get their gory come-uppance in the after life,

or the 'moral lessons' aisle, where sloth, indulgence, gambling and even wine, women & song lead to their inevitable unhappy endings. More curious groups even include collections of giant lobsters and frogs tumbling over one another.

The gardens are financed by the fortune the Aw brothers made from their miracle cure-all Tiger Balm and the odd bottle of amazing Tiger Oil duly makes its appearance in some displays.

The gardens are open from 8 am to 6 pm daily and admission is free. To get there take either bus Nos 10, 30, 143, 145, 146 or 192.

Chinese & Japanese Gardens

Off Yuan Ching Rd at Jurong Park the adjoining Chinese and Japanese gardens each cover 13.5 hectares. The Japanese gardens, known as Seiwaen, are calm and reflective while the Chinese gardens (Yu Hwa Yuan), which occupy an island by the Jurong Lake, are exuberant and colourful with attractions like the 'Cloud-Piercing Pagoda' or the 'White Rainbow Bridge'.

The gardens are open from 9.30 am to 6 pm Monday through to Saturday but they are open an hour earlier Sundays and holidays. Admission to the Chinese gardens is S$2 adults, $1 children; to the Japanese gardens, S$1 adults, 50c for children. A combined ticket is S$2.50 adults, S$1.20 children. There is a 50c charge for cameras.

To get there take a bus to Jurong Interchange then bus No 242 to Yuan Ching Rd. On Sundays and public holidays bus No 406 will take you there directly.

Jurong Bird Park   INTERESTING

The bird park is on Jalan Ahmad Ibrahim. The 20-hectare park has over 7000 birds and includes a two-hectare walk-in aviary with an artificial waterfall at one end. This aviary, which has over 3000 birds including 100-plus peacocks, is the largest in the world. Exhibits include everything from cassowaries, birds of paradise and macaws to penguins in air-conditioned comfort.

You can walk around the park or take the tram service that shuttles around the park dropping people off and picking them up. The park is open from 9 am to 6 pm. It's suggested that you visit the park early in the morning or late in the afternoon since the birds tend to be less active during the heat of the day. Admission to the park is S$5 for adults, S$2.50 for children, and the tram service costs an additional S$1. A camera permit is 50c.

You can get there by taxi or by any of the many buses that run to Jurong Interchange from where bus No 250 will take you to the bird park. You can climb up Jurong Hill, beside the park, from where there is a good view over Jurong.

There is also a special bus shuttle service twice a day to the Bird Park from the following hotels: Boulevard Hotel, Glass Hotel, King's Hotel, Mandarin Hotel, Orchard Hotel, River View Hotel, Royal Holiday and the Inn Hotel. Return fares are S$10 per adult, S$6 per child. Bookings and departure times can be obtained by calling Journey Express (tel 339 7738).

Zoological Gardens

Located at 80 Mandai Lake Rd in the north of the island, Singapore's zoo has over 1600 animals on display in conditions as natural as possible – wherever possible moats replace bars. Exhibits of particular interest include the orang-utan colony (the largest zoo colony in the world) and the tiny mousedeer, the smallest hoofed animals in the world. They now have a breakfast programme where you get a feeding and are joined by one of the orang-utans! There is also a children's zoo and an elephant work performance.

The zoo is open from 8.30 am to 6.30 pm daily and admission is S$4 adults, S$1.50 kids, plus 50c for still cameras and S$2 for movie/video cameras. To get there you can take any bus going to Bukit Timah Rd then a bus No 171 to the zoo, or any bus to Toa Payoh and then bus No 137 to the zoo. Several major hotels also have Zoo

Express shuttle buses which go to the zoo daily – call 235 3111 for information.

CN West Leisure Park

Formerly known as the Mitsukoshi Garden, the CN West Leisure Park at 9 Japanese Garden Rd, Jurong has a restaurant, pool, water slide and so on. Hours are 10 am to 6 pm on weekdays, 9 am to 8 pm on weekends. Weekday admission is S$3 (children S$1) and at weekends it is S$4 (children S$2).

To get there take a bus to Jurong Interchange then a bus No 242 from there to Yuan Ching Rd. On Sundays and public holidays bus No 406 runs directly there.

Other Parks

Despite Singapore's dense population there are many small parks and gardens and, of course, every traffic island or highway divide is turned into a green plantation. Central Park off Clemenceau Avenue provides 40 hectares of green right in the city – the National Theatre and the Van Kleef Aquarium are here. At 790 Upper Serangoon Rd, there's a crocodile farm.

Off Kampung Bahru Rd the 116-metre-high Mount Faber provides fine views over the harbour and the city. To get there just take the cable car up from the World Trade Centre, it's conveniently visited in conjunction with Sentosa Island. Singapore has a major business in cultivating orchids and the Orchid Gardens, beside the zoo on Mandai Lake Rd, is the best place to see them – four hectares of solid orchids! The gardens are open from 9 am to 6 pm daily and admission is S$1.

Bukit Timah Nature Reserve on the Upper Bukit Timah Rd boasts the highest point in Singapore, 177-metre Bukit Timah. MacRitchie Reservoir provides good walking tracks around the reservoir and is popular with joggers. Close to the centre there's Elizabeth Walk, across from the Padang, and the small Merlion Park at the mouth of Singapore River. There the merlion, symbol of Singapore, spouts a fountain of water out into the river.

The East Coast Park, out of town toward the airport, is built on reclaimed land and has swimming, windsurfing with rentals, bike hire, a food centre and the Singapore Crocodilarium with 1000 of the friendlies.

After Dark

Singapore has plenty of night time activity although it is certainly not of the Bangkok or Manila sex and sin variety. Even Bugis St, Singapore's raucous transvestite parade ground, was first cleaned up and has now totally disappeared in the construction of the new MRT subway system. It was never, officially, more than simply another food stall centre but, in practice, at the witching hour certain young men turned into something much more exotic than pumpkins. There's talk of making a new (no doubt highly sanitised) Bugis St when the MRT is complete.

Still, if you're worried that Singapore is simply too squeaky clean for belief, you may be relieved to hear that there's a real locals-only low-class red light district stretching along a narrow alley from Jalan Besar to Serangoon Rd. It's an interesting area to browse around in the evening. Chinese men hawk powerful medicines and smash bricks with their bare hands to show what they will do for your sexual potency. Astrologers and fortune tellers set up their cards, gamblers run shell games that appear so easy to win it's a joke and various novelties are displayed.

The transvestite scene is now in the vicinity of Orchard Mall between Orchard Towers and the parking lot of the infamous Rasa Sayang, a bar in the Tropicana nightclub complex on Scotts Rd which is known for its Thai hookers.

Many of the Chinese supper clubs such as the Neptune Theatre near Clifford Pier and the Oasis Theatre in Kallang feature singers from Taiwan who are in the high end of the flesh business. And the predominantly Malay district of Geylang is full of houses and apartments operated by organised Chinese gangs who employ women of all nationalities including Indonesians, Indians, and the occasional Caucasian. So it's really a matter of visibility these days.

There are many more mundane ways you can spend the night in Singapore. There are plenty of cinemas although Singaporean taste in western films runs very much to the action-packed spectaculars, despairing Singaporean movie fans occasionally pen letters to the *Straits Times* asking why one acclaimed film or another has never (and may never) be shown in Singapore. Or you can kung fu it in Chinese films or see an all-singing all-dancing Indian movie.

The big hotels have cocktail lounges, cabarets, discos and theatre restaurants. At the Mandarin there is an ASEAN night four times a week. It features activities from all over the region – rather like the Instant Asia show. The Raffles Hotel also puts on a nightly cultural show which you can combine with dinner.

Trishaw tours, lasting 1½ to three hours, start at the Raffles Hotel each evening and include a visit to Chinatown before depositing patrons on Orchard Rd.

There are also night-time harbour cruises lasting two to three hours including a cheap S$2 cruise from the World Trade Centre ferry terminal.

The impecunious can find free entertainment by simply wandering the streets. In Chinatown or in the older streets around Serangoon Rd and Jalan Besar you may well chance upon a wayang – the brilliantly costumed Chinese street operas. In these noisy and colourful extravaganzas overacting is very important; there's nothing subtle about it at all.

At the many food centres eating can be combined with entertainment – the food preparation is all out front and it goes on fairly late in many centres.

Islands, Beaches & Water Sports

Singapore is, of course, an island, but there are a number of other islands around Singapore. The best known is Sentosa, 'tranquillity' in Malay, which has been developed into a locally popular resort. Other islands include Kusu and St John's, the Sisters' Islands and islands such as Pulau Bukom, which are used as refineries and for other commercial purposes. South of Singapore's southern islands are many more islands – the scattered Indonesian islands of the Riau Archipelago.

There are other islands to the north and east, between Singapore and Malaysia. There you will also find the *kelongs*, long arrow shaped fences erected to trap fish. The fish swim down the 'shaft' of the arrow into the 'arrowhead' then cannot find their way out. You can clearly see a number of these kelongs if your flight into Singapore approaches Changi Airport from the north. They're another disappearing sight since the Singapore government doesn't want any of these untidy things in the water. Permits for kelongs are not renewed once they expire.

You don't have to cross the sea to find beaches and water sport activities. Although the construction of Changi Airport destroyed one of Singapore's favourite stretches of beach there is still the huge East Coast Lagoon on the East Coast Parkway, not to mention the CN West Leisure Park at Jurong. Skin diving enthusiasts will find coral reefs at Sisters' Islands and Pulau Semakan, while if you want to water ski head to Ponggol Point on the north coast.

Sentosa Island

Sentosa Island has been through a major development programme to turn it into a tourist attraction but the idea has only been half successful. Sentosa attracts few overseas tourists (who can find the real thing in the tropical island line when they get to Malaysia), but has proved a big hit with Singaporeans, particularly on weekends when it can get very crowded.

Once used as a military base, the gun emplacements and underground tunnels of Sentosa's Fort Siloso, which date from the late 19th century, can be explored. The guns were all pointing in the wrong direction when the Japanese invaded in WW II and the island was then used by the victorious Japanese as a prisoner of war camp.

Other Sentosa attractions include the Surrender Chamber with 27 wax-work figures recreating the formal surrender by the Japanese forces in 1945. The Maritime Museum has exhibits recording the history of Singapore as a port while the Sentosa Arts Centre displays local art works. In the Coralarium there is, not surprisingly, a display of live corals. These attractions are all open from 10 am to 6 pm, Mondays to Saturdays and from 9 am to 6 pm on Sundays and public holidays.

There are a wide variety of sporting facilities on Sentosa including an 18-hole golf course, a swimming lagoon, a canoeing centre and a roller-skating centre. Major improvements are taking shape with plans for a family entertainment park by the middle of 1985. Also work is being done on upgrading the swimming lagoon and wax museum. An oceanarium is being planned.

You can get around Sentosa by bicycle – hire a bike for S$3 per day (9 am to 4.30 pm) from the hire kiosk by the ferry terminal. Or you can take the free bus service which runs around the island roads with departures every 10 minutes. Or you can take the five-stop monorail loop service which costs S$3.

To get to Sentosa take a bus or taxi to the World Trade Centre from where ferries operate and where the Jardine Steps Cable Car terminal is also located. There are three types of admission tickets. Ticket 1 is S$7 (S$3.50 child) and covers return ferry trip, monorail and all attractions including the Surrender Chambers and Pioneers of Singapore. Ticket 2 is S$3.50 (S$2 child) and covers return ferry trip and all attractions except the Surrender Chambers/Pioneers of Singapore. Ticket 3 includes the same as ticket 2 but is only valid from 5 pm to closing.

Ferries leave the World Trade Centre every 15 minutes starting at 7.30 am. The last ferry back from Sentosa is at 6.45 pm except on weekends and holidays when this is extended to 11.15 pm.

By cable car you can also go to Mt Faber and then make the longer return trip via Jardine Steps to Sentosa Island. There is a complete four-sector round trip, a two-sector trip (Mt Faber, Jardine Steps, Sentosa or Jardine Steps, Sentosa, Jardine Steps) or a one-sector trip (Jardine Steps, Sentosa or Mt Faber). The cost varies from S$2.50 to S$5 and they run from 10 am to 7 pm Mondays to Saturdays and 9 am to 7 pm Sundays and holidays.

The cable car ride, with its spectacular views, is the best part of a visit to Sentosa so take it at least one-way. In 1983 a ship managed to run into the cable car line but additional precautions have been taken to ensure such a disaster could not occur again.

Accommodation is available on Sentosa either at the *Apollo Sentosa Hotel* or at the camping site.

St John's & Kusu Islands

Although Sentosa is Singapore's most well known island there are two others which are also locally popular as city escapes. On weekends they can become rather crowded, but during the week you'll find St John's and Kusu fairly quiet and good places for a peaceful swim. Both islands have cafeterias, changing rooms, toilet facilities, grassy picnic areas and swimming areas.

St John's is much bigger than Kusu which you can walk around in 10 minutes. Kusu has a Chinese temple and a Malay shrine.

To get there take a ferry from the World Trade Centre. It costs S$5 for the round trip and takes 45 minutes to reach Kusu and one hour to St John's. On weekdays a visit to both islands is an all day trip since there are only three services. If you left at 9 am you wouldn't be able to continue on to St John's until 3 pm, unless you continued straight through. There are far more departures on weekends:

Mondays to Saturdays		
WTC	Kusu	St John's
10.00 am	10.45 am	11.15 am
1.30 pm	2.15 pm	2.45 pm

Sundays & Public Holidays		
WTC	Kusu	St John's
9.00 am	10.00 am	10.20 am
10.00 am	11.00 am	11.20 am
11.20 am	12.20 pm	12.40 pm
12.20 pm	1.20 pm	1.40 pm
1.40 pm	2.40 pm	3.00 pm
2.40 pm	3.40 pm	4.00 pm
4.00 pm	5.00 pm	5.20 pm
5.00 pm	6.00 pm	6.20 pm
7.20 pm	8.00 pm	8.20 pm

Other Islands

There are other islands both to the north and to the south of Singapore. To get to the northern islands like Pulau Seletar go to Ponggol Boatel at Ponggol Point or to Sembawang. A five-passenger speedboat will cost about S$25. Kusu and St John's are both part of the southern islands group. These also include Sisters' Islands, Pulau Hantu, Lazarus Island, Buran Darat, Terumbu Retan Laut and Pulau Renggit.

By special arrangement (tel 271 2211) you can hire a ferry to Pulau Seking, Pulau Hantu or Sisters' Islands for S$5 return. Otherwise you can charter a motorised 'bumboat' (sampan) from Jardine Steps or Clifford Pier for about S$60 per day. These boats are big enough for six to 12 people, but finding one is simply a matter of going down to the waterfront and asking.

Weekend boat trips around the southern islands on the 43-foot cruiser, *Farah*, can be arranged by phoning 41 8082. One day is S$48 with lunch. Swimming and snorkelling are featured.

Off the eastern end of Singapore Island, Pulau Tekong is Singapore's largest island, but tends to be forgotten because it is often cut off the edge of Singapore maps (including the one in this book). To get there, take a ferry from Changi Point to the delightfully old-fashioned village of Kampung Salabin. There's great seafood at a dilapidated waterfront restaurant on stilts, close to the dock. The best way to get around the island is on a bicycle brought with you. There are no private cars here, just a few ancient and run down unofficial taxis.

From the east end of the island you can also take the 1½-hour trip to Pengerang in Malaysia where you have to go through customs and immigration. I don't know where you'd go to from there though!

Riau Archipelago

South of the southern islands are the Indonesian islands of the Riau Archipelago. The largest of these islands, which stretch across to Sumatra, is Pulau Bintang and it covers three times the area of Singapore. The entire island group is lightly populated, many of the islands having no permanent population at all, and there are fine opportunities for scuba diving or simply exploring. The simple, quiet and poor way of life on the islands is a dramatic contrast to the bustle of downtown Singapore.

Tanjung Pinang is the main town in the Riau Archipelago and is also the port for the weekly shipping service to Indonesia. You can visit Tanjung Pinang either by chartering a bumboat, by taking the regular ferry boats from Singapore or by going on a tour. The ferry boats are inexpensive. German Asian Travels (tel 915116) at room 1303/4, Straits Trading Building, 9 Battery Rd, operate round trip tours which cost about S$150 per person including overnight accommodation and tours from Tanjung Pinang.

There are a number of small hotels at Tanjung Pinang, which also has an interesting market, a Chinese temple and a mosque. Nearby you can see the ruins of ancient Sea Dayak capitals or you can take excursions to other islands like Pulau Mapor or Pulau Terkulai. If you're energetic you can even climb Gunung Bintang Besar, the highest hill on Pulau Bintang. The ferry trip to Tanjung Pinang takes about two hours and you have to obtain an Indonesian visa in order to visit the Riau Archipelago. November to March is the best time to visit as the water is clearest.

Places to Stay

Singapore has a wide variety of accommodation in all price categories – you can get a dorm bed in a 'crash pad' for S$5, a reasonable room in a cheap Chinese hotel for around S$20 or pay over S$200 for a room in an 'international standard' hotel, even over S$1000 for some super deluxe suites.

Over the last couple of years Singapore's accommodation squeeze has changed into an accommodation surplus and as a result prices have been fairly static. At the top end it's a result of a great number of new hotels recently built or under construction. At the bottom end, where the cheap Chinese hotels were disappearing to redevelopments, the proliferation of crash pads has taken the strain of the old hotels and provided lots of new accommodation possibilities. There still may be times when accommodation is a little tight. Chinese New Year is a bad time of year as everything tends to be full and the cheaper hotels may push their prices up.

In the major hotels there will be a 3% government tax and a 10% service charge added to your bill. The hotels stipulate that you should not tip. The 3% government tax also applies to the cheaper hotels with a minimum of S$1 but this is usually added straight into the original quoted price.

Hotels have been approximately categorised into three groups. 'Top end' hotels are roughly from S$120 for a double and up. The main centre for these large hotels is along Orchard Rd. At the other extreme most 'bottom end' hotels cost under S$40, often under S$20. They can chiefly be found to the east of Bras Basah Rd; particularly along Beach Rd, Middle Rd, Bencoolen St and Jalan Besar. 'Middle' range hotels cover the middle ground – some of them are bigger and better

cheaper Chinese hotels, some of them are smaller air-con hotels. They tend to be scattered widely over Singapore. For reservations you can call an agency at 542 6955 which coordinates bookings for 62 different middle and upper-class hotels.

Places to Stay – bottom end

Singapore's rapid modernisation is even hitting the cheap places to stay. Many of these small, family-run hotels are in areas destined for eventual redevelopment and already some popular cheapies have gone – to be replaced by ever more air-conditioned shopping centres. You can be certain that there are no new hotels planned without air-con, bars and restaurants, high speed lifts, swimming pools and all the other necessities of modern tourism.

Meanwhile, the Singapore answer for backpackers seems to be crash pads which have sprung up like wildfire. Bencoolen St is the main crash pad centre and it is also the main centre for cheap hotels.

Singapore's cheap accommodation is mainly concentrated in the streets that run off Bras Basah Rd to the north-east. Amongst the buses that run out that way from the city centre are Nos 101, 131 and 146 down Serangoon Rd; Nos 94, 100 and 120 along Victoria St; Nos 125, 161, 172 and 175 start off down Victoria St but then split across Middle Rd while Nos 130 and 141 continue further down before turning off across Jalan Besar. Jalan Besar, which becomes Bencoolen St at Rochor Rd, runs one way – the wrong way if you're coming from the city centre, the docks or the railway station.

Coming in from the airport public bus No 390 will drop you right on Bencoolen St, conveniently close to most of the Bencoolen St and Beach Rd hotels.

Crash Pads Singapore's crash pads are all mildly illegal since they're just residential flats which have been broken up into dormitories and cubicle-like rooms. But then this is Singapore and free enterprise

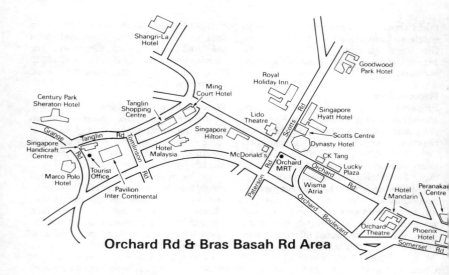

Orchard Rd & Bras Basah Rd Area

is what counts! The trouble with them is that the jam-packed crowds tend to overstretch the limited facilities and the rooms really are small. Plus everybody else there will be another traveller, just like yourself. On the other hand they're good information sources and good places to meet people – since so many other travellers stay there – and you won't find any cheaper accommodation in Singapore.

Almost down at the Bras Basah end of Bencoolen St you'll find the *Peony Mansions* crash pad, longest running of these places. It's at 46-52 Bencoolen St, on top of a furniture store. There's no sign at all, go around the back and take the lift to the 6th floor and knock on the door at 50E. Like all the crash pads it's rather anonymous. Inside you can stay for as little as S$5 a night; simple dormitory-style accommodation that has seen better days. As in nearly all the crash pads some private rooms are also available, costing S$15 to S$18. There are other flats in the block, like *Latin House* (tel 339 6308) at 46 on the 3rd floor.

On the other side of Bencoolen between the Strand and Bencoolen hotels is *Bencoolen House* (tel 338 1206) at number 27. The reception area is on the 7th floor. Dorm beds cost S$5, single rooms are available for S$10, and doubles are S$20, or S$28 with air-con. Accommodation is clean and fairly quiet. Hot showers are available. They have laundry facilities and do air tickets.

Across the road and up a bit at 173/175 is another centre for crash pads in the newish Hong Guan Building. There are no outside signs there either, again go around the back and up the elevator by the parking lot.

The first place you'll come to, on the 2nd floor, is the *Hawaii Guest House*. Dorm accommodation is S$5; share rooms with four beds are S$8 per person and six-bed rooms are S$6. The staff seems friendly and there are free lockers, laundry service (S$5 a load), storage services, a notice board and a travel service. The Hawaii has rooms on the 2nd, 3rd, 5th, and 7th floors.

Goh's Homestay has a reception desk on the 6th floor, but also has rooms on the

1	Sweet Home Cafeteria	9	Tai Loke Hotel
2	Tiong Hoa & Rendezvous Restaurant	10	Fortune Centre
3	Strand Hotel	11	South-East Asia Hotel
4	Bencoolen Hotel	12	Hong Guan Building
5	Airmaster Travel	13	Swee Kee Restaurant
6	Kian Hua Hotel	14	Shang Onn
7	San Wah Hotel	15	Soon Seng Long
8	Peony Mansions	16	Hai Hin Hotel

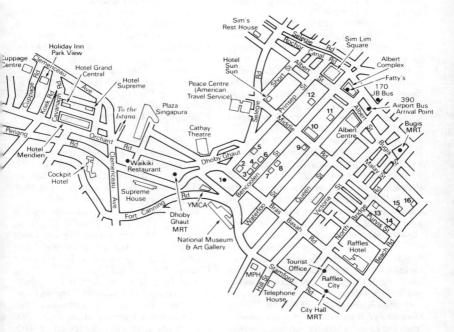

5th. In their dorm you get a bed and a locker for S\$5 to S\$8, depending on how many beds are in a room. Private rooms go for S\$23 to S\$26. They've got a good notice board with bus guides.

On the 3rd floor is *Philip Choo's*. Dorm rates are the same as at Goh's; rooms go for S\$20 to S\$22. Again the dorm has lockers and there's a notice board, but the general conditions are not quite as good as Hawaii or Goh's.

Nearby, another of these central crash pads is *Airmaster Travel Centre* (tel 338 3942) at 36B Prinsep St, a block over from Bencoolen and down towards Bras Basah Rd. Dorm beds are S\$5 and a washing machine and TV is available for your use. Travellers report that this is a friendly, convenient place with an excellent notice board. Airmaster Travel is a popular travel agent for cheap tickets and you enter through their office.

Not too far away is *Sim's Rest House* (tel 336 4957, 336 0176) at 114A Mackenzie Rd. Mackenzie Rd becomes Albert St across Serangoon. It's a bit of a walk from Serangoon along the sort of industrial/factory-lined Mackenzie Rd but the location is good since that end of MacKenzie is quiet. The owner is a friendly guy and if you phone him from the bus terminus he'll pick you up. Dorm beds cost S$4 to S$5 (lockers available) and real rooms for S$20.

The *Friendly Rest House* (tel 294 0847) is at 357A Serangoon Rd, just past Kitchener Rd, but the door is actually around the corner from Serangoon on Perumal Rd. Look for Fong Tat Auto – it's below the guest house which is on the 1st floor. Rooms with attached bathroom are S$23 but this place isn't so popular with travellers. Bus No 390 from the airport takes you in the general area, then bus No 131 or 140 will take you down Serangoon Rd. Bus No 146 from the railway station will take you practically to the door.

Sandy's Place (tel 252 6711) at 355 Balestier Rd, on the 4th floor of the Goodwill Mansion has mattresses for S$6 on the floor and beds for S$8. Rooms are available for S$12 to S$20. It's clean and the management are friendly.

The *Das Travellers Inn* (tel 338 7460) at room 5-2, 67 Beach Rd has been recommended by travellers although they really pack them in here. You can easily reach there on bus No 390 from the airport (get off at Rochore Rd), or bus No 20 from the railway station, or if you are coming from the Melaka bus station you can take either bus No 82 or 120; if you ring them they will pick you up. Facilities include free coffee and tea, TV, laundry services and help in purchasing cheap plane tickets. Dorm accommodation ranges from S$5 to S$7 and doubles from S$16 to S$20.

Other crash pad possibilities include *Traveller's Lodge* at 16 Penhaus St off Lavender St at the far end of Jalan Besar. This is a slightly run-down industrial area. Rooms with fan cost S$14 to S$17.

Sunseeker's Rest House is next to the Neptune Building on the 2nd floor of 20 South Quay.

Chinese Hotels – Bras Basah Rd to Rochor Canal Rd Many travellers would prefer to spend a few dollars more for the cheap Chinese hotels. Your money will get you a fairly spartan room with a bare floor, a few pieces of furniture, a sink and a fan. Toilets are usually shared, but you might even get hot water in the showers. Couples should always ask for a single room – a single usually means just one double bed, whereas a double would have two. As for the crash pads Bencoolen St is a good place to start looking.

Towards Bras Basah Rd at 81 Bencoolen is the *Kian Hua* (tel 338 3492) with single rooms for S$21 and doubles from S$27 to S$30. It's a fairly typical old Chinese hotel.

Other places around Bencoolen St include the slightly more expensive *San Wah* (tel 336 2428) at 36 Bencoolen St with singles at S$25 and doubles at S$28, or S$32 with air-con. It's a little up market from the cheapest Chinese hotels.

Round on Prinsep St (next one over) is the *Tiong Hoa* (tel 338 4522) at No 4. Rooms in this very pleasantly run hotel are S$22 with fan or S$30 with air-conditioning – good value for a classic Chinese hotel.

The Park Hotel is around the corner from Bencoolen St at 239B Victoria St at the corner where Albert becomes Bugis St. It's the freshly-painted white place with blue shutters. Inside it's very clean with lots of tilework but also likely to be noisy since this is one of the old places with meshed top to the walls. Singles are S$20, doubles cost from S$22.

The *South-East Asia Hotel* (tel 338 2394) at 190 Waterloo St, parallel to Bencoolen, is a bit more costly, but if you really need a rest it has air-con and is quiet and rather newer with singles/doubles at S$34/41.

Beach Rd, a few blocks over towards the

(ever-receding) waterfront, is another centre for cheap hotels although some of them have already fallen prey to redevelopment. If you aspire to the Raffles but can't afford to stay there, at least you can stay nearby at these places! Somehow the several blocks along Beach Rd from the Raffles have managed to stay a little enclave, uneffected by all the demolition around them.

The *Shang Onn* (tel 338 4153) at 37 Beach Rd, on the corner of Purvis St, has singles at S$24, doubles at S$26 and is clean and friendly. The good looking *Hai Hin* (tel 336 3739) with its balconies is at 97 Beach Rd on the corner of Liang Seah St. Rates are the same as the Shang Onn.

If you follow Middle Rd from Beach Rd back towards Bencoolen St, you'd find a few more cheapies like the rather inconspicuous *Soon Seng Long* (tel 337 6318) at 26 Middle Rd where rooms are also around S$20. Big rooms, if you can wake the proprietor up from his slumbers, or pry him away from that mahjong table.

Others on Middle Rd include the *Lido* (tel 337 1872) at 54 with singles/doubles at S$24/28. Nearly back at Bencoolen is the *Tai Loke* (tel 337 6209), at 151. There are big, airy rooms with fine old furniture for S$22 to S$26. By that time you're almost back at Bencoolen St.

Continuing up Middle Rd near the corner of Selegie at Nos 260 and 262 is the clean and very nice *Sun Sun Hotel* (tel 338 4911). It's reasonable with singles/doubles at S$25/30 and there's a bar and restaurant downstairs.

Rochor Rd also runs from Beach Rd to Bencoolen St, parallel to Middle Rd. At 228/229 the *New 7th Storey Hotel* (tel 337 0251/4) is an up market cheapie with singles/doubles at S$45/59 or with bath S$55/69.

Chinese Hotels - Rochor Canal Rd to Lavender St Another batch of cheap hotels is across Rochor Rd down to Lavender St on and around Jalan Besar.

Only a few steps from Rochor Canal Rd and Sungei Rd, on the corner of Mayo St and Jalan Besar is *Sim Lim Lodging House*, a typically clean and painted Chinese hotel with rooms for S$25. Across the street on Mayo St is *South Seas Hotel*, same rates and conditions as Sim Lim.

Continuing up Jalan Besar there's the *International* (tel 258 3347) at 290 Jalan Besar, on the corner with Allenby Rd. It costs S$22 single, S$25 double or S$30 for a double with bath. Right across the street at 10 Allenby Rd is the *Central Hotel*.

Further down Jalan Besar at 383 is the *Kam Leng* (tel 258 2289). It's upstairs and has good, clean rooms at S$22 single or double and also has an excellent restaurant with an English menu and fish tanks where you select your fish while it's still swimming.

Right down at the end of the street near Lavender at 407A-B Jalan Besar is the spotlessly clean *Palace Hotel* (tel 258 3108) with singles/doubles at S$14/16, probably the cheapest in town. The front rooms can be very noisy due to the round-the-clock traffic along Jalan Besar. Traffic noise is quite a problem in most of these central hotels.

There are quite a few other places in this area; many about halfway down Jalan Besar around Kitchener Rd. The *Siong Cheong* (tel 294 7147) is at 18 Verdun, near the big President Merlin Hotel. Verdun runs parallel to Serangoon Rd and Jalan Besar, midway between them. It's a quiet street and pleasant rooms cost S$20 single or double, S$28 with air-con. The *Tai Hoe Hotel*, close by on the corner of Verdun and Kitchener Rd, has air-con and looks pleasant.

Chinese Hotels - Other Places Oddly, there are few hotels to speak of in Chinatown, nearly all are in the areas already mentioned east of Bras Basah Rd. An exception of note is the *Majestic Hotel* (tel 222 3377) at 31 Bukit Pasoh Rd near Chinatown. Bukit Pasoh runs between New Bridge Rd and Neil Rd. It's a quiet street lined with traditional houses and buildings, but all are well maintained, in good condition and brightly painted. There's a pleasant park nearby and in the morning and evening people do tai chi and tai kuan do exercises there. The hotel is immaculate and rooms are pleasant, some with a balcony. Singles/doubles are S$29/37 without bath, S$39/54 with bath.

The *New Asia* is on Maxwell Rd at Peck Seah, a couple of blocks up from Robinson. Rooms here are S$25/32 or with air-con and bath they're S$28/36. A couple of doors down at 10 Peck Seah St there's the *Air View Hotel* (tel 225 7788) with rooms at S$35/45.

Remember that at Chinese New Year it can be very difficult to find a room in Singapore and some places are prone to sudden price increases. Student Travel, in the Ming Court Hotel, offer substantial discounts at some of Singapore's 'International Standard' hotels – which means they will still cost something like S$70 for a single and up.

The Ys Singapore has a number of YMCAs and YWCAs, although the cheap old YMCA Katong has now been redeveloped. All of the YMCAs in Singapore take men, women and couples.

The *YMCA International House* (tel 337 3444) is at 1 Orchard Rd and has rooms for S$45 single, S$55 double, and S$70 triple, plus 10% service charge. All rooms have air-con, TV and telephone. The facilities at this YMCA are exceptionally good with a fitness centre, swimming pool (on the roof), squash and badminton courts, and a billiards room. There's also a restaurant which offers a daily set meal at S$5.50 and there's a *McDonald's* actually in the YMCA building which offers room service!

The *Metropolitan YMCA* (tel 737 7755) at 60 Stevens Rd is less conveniently located and lacks the facilities of the Orchard Rd YMCA. They have singles/doubles with attached bathroom, TV and air-con for S$37/44.

Finally there's the *Metropolitan YMCA International Centre* (tel 222 4666), also called the Chinese YMCA, at 70 Palmer Rd. If you want to be near Chinatown or the waterfront this is your place. They have singles with air-con but common shower at S$22. Singles/doubles with air-con and shower are S$31/37.

The *YWCA Hostel* (tel 336 1212) at 6-8 Fort Canning is behind Supreme House, quite close to the Orchard Rd YMCA. It costs S$24/30 for rooms with common bathroom. Air-con rooms are S$28/35. Nice dorm rooms are available, for women at S$13. They take women or couples only. This place has been recommended by solo women travellers as a safe and secure place.

Camping There's no sign of an official YHA hostel in Singapore as yet. You can, however, camp out at Sentosa Island where there are pre-erected tents available from S$6 per night.

There's also the good *East Coast Campsite* on East Coast Parkway, at the five km marker. Unfortunately there are no buses stopping on this expressway so you have to get off at the bus stop in Upper East Coast Rd and then walk 15 minutes; from the end of Bedok Rd a walking track leads under the expressway right to the camp. The site has a clean, well-lit reading and TV room and there are a few shops and a hawkers' centre nearby. The site is deserted during the week but very busy on weekends and school holidays. A four-person tent costs S$5 per night Monday to Friday, S$6 on weekends and holidays.

Places to Stay – middle
Middle range places include higher-class Chinese cheapies, a few colonial-era hangovers and some smaller or second string modern hotels. The boom in new hotel construction, combined with the slow down in tourist arrivals, has combined to depress hotel prices. There are often special deals available and these days you can even find modern hotel

rooms with air-conditioning and even a swimming pool for S$40 to S$70. It's worth enquiring at the hotel counter at Singapore airport on arrival if there are any special deals on offer. Or ask at the reception desk if there's any special discount on offer, competition is fierce! The Student Travel office in the Ming Court Hotel also often has special discounts available at certain middle range hotels.

Some of the bottom-end hotels listed like the excellent Orchard Rd YMCA are really good quality middle-range hotels. Others like the Majestic in Chinatown or the South-East Asia have had their prices pushed down by the plethora of modern new hotels.

The *Station Hotel* has seen better days and is a little inconveniently located for most things in modern Singapore. If, however, you've just arrived after a long train trip and can't face heading straight into the city it might be ideal.

Most of the older Chinese-style hotels are down in the bottom end category, in price at least. Smaller modern hotels include the *Bencoolen Hotel* on Bencoolen St, situated amongst the rock-bottom Chinese hotels, but it's nothing special. Better is the rather new *Strand Hotel* (tel 338 1866) at 25 Bencoolen, practically next door to the Hotel Bencoolen, where all rooms are S$59 and have air-con, hot water, TV, telephone and a free safety deposit box. The *Broadway* is on Serangoon Rd, where you will also find the *New Serangoon Hotel*. 734 3344

~~The *Morningside*~~ (tel ~~7373344~~), 322 River Valley Rd near the Killeney Rd intersection, is in a class by itself. Very large rooms in an old 16-room mansion start at S$35 and include private bath, air-con, TV, telephone, and fridge. There is a terrace in front with tables and chairs and the location is quiet. For some reason the area around the building has been cemented over – some nice landscaping would make it even more idyllic.

The *Premier Hotel*, on Nassim Hill not far from the handicraft centre tourist office, is a small hotel also used as a training centre for hotel and catering staff – the standards of service are therefore usually better than the small size might indicate.

The *RELC International Centre* (RELC stands for Regional Language Centre) has a hotel in its complex next to the Shangri-La on Orange Grove Rd. There is no service charge or government tax at this hotel.

All the hotels that follow have air-con and add a 10% service charge and 3% government tax to the rates given here.

Hotel Asia (tel 737 8388), 37 Scotts Rd, 146 rooms, singles S$60, doubles S$70
Hotel Bencoolen (tel 336 0822), 47 Bencoolen St, 69 rooms, singles S$44, doubles S$54
Broadway Hotel (tel 292 4661), 195 Serangoon Rd, 63 rooms, singles S$45 to S$55, doubles S$50 to S$60
Duke Hotel (tel 345 3311), 42/46 Meyer Rd, 170 rooms, singles S$55 to S$65, doubles S$65 to S$85
Great Eastern Hotel (tel 284 8244), 401 MacPherson Rd, 151 rooms, singles S$50 to S$55, doubles S$55 to S$60
Lion City Hotel (tel 345 8111), 15 Tanjong Katong Rd, 168 rooms, S$48 to S$55
Lloyd House Hotel (tel 737 7011), 2 Lloyd Rd, 19 rooms, singles S$30, doubles S$35
Metropole Hotel (tel 336 3611), 41 Seah St, 54 rooms, singles S$45 to S$50, doubles S$55 to S$60
Mitre Hotel (tel 737 3811), 145 Killiney Rd, 19 rooms, singles S$29, doubles S$32
~~*Morningside Hotel* (tel 737 3344), 322~~ River Valley Rd, 16 rooms, S$40 to S$50
Hotel Negara (tel 737 0811), 15 Claymore Drive, 104 rooms, swimming pool, S$70 to S$85
Queen's Hotel International (tel 737 6088), 24 Mount Elizabeth Rd, 61 rooms, swimming pool, singles S$45, doubles S$50
RELC International House (tel 737 9044), 30 Orange Grove Rd, 128 rooms, S$49
Sloane Court Hotel (tel 235 3311), 17 Balmoral Rd, 37 rooms, singles S$40, doubles S$50
Station Hotel (tel 222 1551), Railway Station, Keppel Rd, 34 rooms, singles S$35, doubles S$40
Strand Hotel (tel 338 1866), 25 Bencoolen St, singles/doubles S$55

Hotel Supreme (tel 737 8333), 15 Kramat Rd, 86 rooms, S$55

Tanglin Court Hotel (tel 737 3581), 2/4 Kim Yam Rd, 28 rooms, S$40

Hotel VIP (tel 235 4277), 5 Balmoral Crescent, 41 rooms, S$45

Places to Stay - top end

Singapore has a huge number of 'international standard' hotels, many of them built in the mid-80s, just when Singapore's explosive growth in number of visitors had topped out! As a result there can be some real bargains in this price category. Many of these hotels are intended for expense account travellers and are luxurious and expensive.

The project which garnered the most attention was the US$475 million *Raffles City* – a complex of offices, a convention centre and two luxury class hotels. One of them at 73 stories is the world's tallest hotel. Together they've added about 2000 rooms to the local hotel scene.

Due to the many new hotels opening the severe price escalation of the late '70s and early '80s has slowed down dramatically. Occupancy rates have been dropping from the 90% range of the late '70s and with all the new hotels it's expected to continue sliding to as low as 50%. Some investors may take a bath, but for visitors the increased competition means lower prices, added incentives and of course less difficulty in finding a room. In fact, in researching the last two editions of this book we've had to lower just about all of the hotel rates in all categories!

When Price Waterhouse did a comparison study of hotel rates in 11 international cities recently Singapore was next to the lowest (Kuala Lumpur held the bottom position).

If you're arriving independently at a hotel in the top end category (ie you're not on a tour, pre-paid voucher or something similar) then it's always worth asking if there is any sort of discount available. The 'rack rates' listed here will often drop if you ask.

These hotels have a number of characteristics in common. For a start a great many of them are strung along Singapore's 'hotel alley', known as Orchard Rd. This is very much the tourist centre of Singapore with hotels, airline offices and shopping centres in profusion. Quite a few more hotels are in roads off Orchard Rd – like Scotts Rd, Tanglin Rd, Somerset Rd or Orange Grove Rd.

As a rough demarcation line 'top end' refers to hotels where a double is something over S$80 to S$100 a night. Singapore's best hotels will generally cost over S$200 a night for a double! Naturally all these hotels will be air-conditioned, all rooms will have attached bathrooms and in almost all cases there will be a swimming pool. These places are further subdivided into 'super-luxury', 'other big hotels' and 'old fashioned'.

Super-Luxury Singapore has a number of hotels that in price and standards esteem themselves a cut above the mere international-standard hotels. They include the twin-towered *Mandarin Hotel* on Orchard Rd – with 1200 rooms it is also (currently) the biggest hotel in Singapore and is topped by a revolving restaurant. The *Shangri-La* is set in five hectares of garden on Orange Grove Rd, just a few minutes walk from Orchard Rd. The rooms in the Garden Wing each have their own balcony overflowing with plants.

The *Marco Polo* is at the Grange Rd-Orchard Rd intersection just a short distance from the tourist office. The smaller *Singapore Hilton* on Orchard Rd is also edging towards the upper-notch bracket. The new *Dynasty Hotel* on Orchard Rd by the junction with Scotts Rd is a strange skyscraper-topped-by-a-pagoda building. Just off Tanglin Rd the equally new *Pavilion Inter-Continental* also fits in this category.

Other Big Hotels The hotels of the international chains are all in this category, which includes places like the

Hyatt Regency and the *Royal Holiday Inn* which face each other across Scotts Rd, just off Orchard Rd. The *Century Park Sheraton* is a relatively new hotel on Grange Rd, just off Tanglin Rd. The *Oberoi Imperial* on Jalan Rumbia enjoys a hilltop location near River Valley Rd.

At the intersection of Tanglin Rd, Orange Grove and Orchard Rd the *Ming Court* is one of Singapore's better-known hotels, in part because of their superb doormen. Many Singapore hotels vie with one another to have the most exotic doormen, but the Ming Court's take the blue ribbon. Where else can you be ushered into a taxi by a towering, bearded Sikh dressed as a Ming warrior?

Sandwiched between the Ming Court and the Hilton on Orchard Rd the *Singapura Forum* was one of the first international chain hotels in Singapore, but is now a relatively small hotel compared to the huge new hotels of the '80s. The *York Hotel* on Mount Elizabeth, behind Scotts Rd, is one of a Singapore chain which includes the old-world Goodwood Park and the Boulevard Hotel Singapore.

Further down Orchard Rd the *Phoenix Hotel* sits on top of the Specialist's Shopping Centre. On Somerset Rd, parallel to Orchard Rd, the *Cockpit Hotel* was much used by airline crew at one time – hence the name. Then there's the tallest hotel in the world, the 73-storey *Westin Stamford*, with 17 restaurants and lounges and two rooftop swimming pools.

On Coleman St, over towards the business centre of Singapore, is the *Peninsula Hotel* while the *Tai Pan Hotel Ramada*, which bridges the middle to top gap, is on Victoria St off Bras Basah Rd. The *President Merlin Hotel* has an unusual but interesting location on Kitchener St, across from the New World Amusement Park.

Other hotels include the *Apollo Singapore* at the Havelock-Outram Rds intersection; the *Cairnhill*; the *Equatorial*, further out from Orchard Rd; the circular *King's Hotel* on Havelock Rd; the *Boulevard Hotel Singapore* on Orchard Boulevard; the *Miramar*, once again on Havelock Rd; the *Royal* on Newton Rd; the *Novotel Orchid Inn*; the smaller *Garden Hotel* and the *Orchard Hotel*.

The *Ladyhill Hotel* has a particularly pleasant garden setting. Out on Sentosa Island there is also the *Apollo Sentosa*, for those who really want to get away from it all.

Old Fashioned Singapore also has a couple of hotels with definite old eastern flavour and style. Close to the waterfront at the junction of Bras Basah Rd and Beach Rd the venerable *Raffles* is as much a superb tourist attraction as it is a fine old hotel. The bars and restaurants conjure up all the mysteries of the orient and what other hotel can claim that a tiger was once shot in the billiards room? The Raffles is built around a beautiful central courtyard complete with fan-shaped travellers' palms – the only two-dimensional tree.

On Scotts Rd is the larger, but nearly as old, *Goodwood Park*. If anything, its architecture is even more delightful than the Raffles.

Amara Hotel Singapore (tel 733 2666), 352 rooms, S$70 to S$170
Apollo Sentosa (tel 63 3377), Sentosa Island, 161 rooms & chalets, singles S$60, doubles S$70
Apollo Singapore (tel 733 2081), Havelock & Outram Rds, 332 rooms, singles S$60, doubles S$70
Boulevard Hotel Singapore (tel 737 2911), Cuscaden Rd, 528 rooms, singles S$75 to S$125, doubles S$100 to S$145
Cairnhill Hotel (tel 734 6622), 19 Cairnhill Circle, 220 rooms, S$75 to S$85
Century Park Sheraton (tel 737 9677), Nassim Hill, 461 rooms, S$160 to S$220
Cockpit Hotel (tel 737 9111), 6/7 Oxley Rise & Penang Rd, 182 rooms, singles S$50, doubles S$60
Crown Prince Hotel (tel 732 1111) 270 Orchard Rd, 303 rooms, S$110
Dynasty Hotel (tel 734 9900), 320 Orchard Rd, 400 rooms, S$150 to S$180

Hotel Equatorial (tel 732 0431), 429 Bukit Timah Rd, 224 rooms, singles S$80 to S$105, doubles S$90 to S$125

Excelsior (tel 338 9644), Coleman St, 300 rooms, singles S$78, doubles S$88

Furama Singapore (tel 533 2177), Eu Tong Sen St, 354 rooms, singles S$75, doubles S$85

Garden Hotel (tel 235 3344), 14 Balmoral Rd, 216 rooms, singles from S$70 to S$80, doubles S$80 to S$90

Glass Hotel (tel 733 0188), 317 Outram Rd, 509 rooms, singles S$80, doubles S$88

Goodwood Park Hotel (tel 737 7411), 22 Scotts Rd, 300 rooms, singles S$190 to S$220

Hotel Grand Central (tel 737 9944), 22 Orchard Rd & Cavanagh Rd, 365 rooms, singles S$65 to S$75, doubles S$75 to S$88

Hilton International Singapore (tel 737 2233), 581 Orchard Rd, 463 rooms, singles S$140 to S$180, doubles S$160 to S$200

Hyatt Regency Singapore (tel 733 1188), 10-12 Scotts Rd, 824 rooms, S$110 to S$170

King's Hotel (tel 733 0011), Havelock Rd, 319 rooms, singles S$80, doubles S$100

Ladyhill Hotel (tel 737 2111), Ladyhill Rd, 175 rooms, S$65

The Mandarin Singapore (tel 737 4411), 333 Orchard Rd, 1200 rooms, S$135 to S$155

The Marco Polo (tel 474 7141), Tanglin Rd, 603 rooms, singles S$140, doubles S$160

Hotel Meridien Singapore (tel 733 8855), 100 Orchard Rd, 419 rooms, singles S$120, doubles S$140

Hotel Meridien Changi-Singapore (tel 734 3863), 2 Netheravon Rd, 280 rooms, singles S$95, doubles S$105

Ming Court Hotel (tel 737 1133), Tanglin Rd, 300 rooms, S$120 to S$160

Hotel Miramar (tel 733 0222), 401 Havelock Rd, 214 rooms, singles S$65, doubles S$85

Hotel New Otani Singapore (tel 339 2941), 177A River Valley Rd, 408 rooms, singles S$100, doubles S$120

Novotel Orchid Inn (tel 250 3322), 214 Dunearn Rd, 321 rooms, singles S$85, doubles S$95

Hotel Oberoi Imperial (tel 737 1666), Jalan Rumbia, 600 rooms, S$80 to S$120

Orchard Hotel (tel 734 7766), 442 Orchard Rd, 350 rooms, S$80 to S$85

Paramount Hotel (tel 344 5577), 25 Marine Parade Rd, 250 rooms, singles S$68, doubles S$78

Pavilion Inter-Continental Singapore (tel 733 8888), 1 Cuscaden Rd, 450 rooms, S$155

Peninsula Hotel (tel 337 8091), Coleman St, 315 rooms, singles S$68, doubles S$78

Hotel Phoenix Singapore (tel 737 8666), Orchard & Somerset Rds, 300 rooms, singles S$79, doubles S$92

Plaza Hotel (tel 298 0011), Beach Rd, 355 rooms, singles S$90 to S$150, doubles S$110 to S$170

President Merlin Hotel (tel 295 0122), 181 Kitchener Rd, 525 rooms, singles S$65, doubles S$75

Raffles Hotel (tel 337 8041), 1-3 Beach Rd, 127 rooms, singles S$100 to S$140, doubles S$110 to S$150

Royal Holiday Inn (tel 737 7966), 25 Scotts Rd, 543 rooms, S$85

Hotel Royal (tel 253 4411), Newton Rd, 331 rooms, singles S$79, doubles S$92

Sea View Hotel (tel 345 2222), Amber Close, 460 rooms, singles S$48 to S$96, doubles S$60 to S$96

Shangri-La Hotel (tel 737 3644), 22 Orange Grove Rd, 700 rooms, singles S$140 to S$265, doubles S$165 to S$295

Hotel Tai-Pan Ramada (tel 336 2526), 101

Victoria St, 269 rooms, singles S$87 to S$126, doubles S$98 to S$136

Westin Plaza (tel 338 8585), 2 Stamford Rd, singles S$160 to S$230, doubles S$190 to S$260

Westin Stamford (tel 338 8585), 2 Stamford Rd, 1253 rooms, singles S$140 to S$200, doubles S$170 to S$230

The York Hotel (tel 737 0511), 21 Mount Elizabeth, 400 rooms, S$80 to S$95

Places to Eat

Singapore is far and away the food capital of Asia. When it comes to superb Chinese food, Hong Kong may actually be a step ahead but it's Singapore's sheer variety and low prices which make it so good. Equally important, Singapore's food is so accessible – you haven't got to search out obscure places, you don't face communication problems, and you don't need a big bankroll.

On the other hand, if you want to make gastronomic discoveries there are lots of out-of-the-way little places where you'll find marvellous food that nobody else knows about. The Singaporeans' enthusiasm for food (and economical food at that) is amply illustrated by the competitions newspapers run every so often to find the best hawker's stall in the city. To get to grips with food in Singapore, you first have to know what types of food are available in Singapore, then where to find them.

There are plenty of guides to finding the best eating places. *The Secret Food Map of Singapore* is an excellent reference for finding countless interesting possibilities. Pick up a copy of the free *Singapore 101 Meals* booklet which lists 101 interesting dining out possibilities, subdivided into breakfast, lunch, tea, dinner and supper categories. The recommendations are excellent and range all the way from hawkers' centres to flashy international hotel restaurants. It's available at the airport on arrival or from the tourist offices. The *Singapore Official Guide*, another free booklet, also has an excellent food section.

Hawker's Food Hawkers are the mobile food stalls, pushcarts which set their tables and stools up around them and sell their food right on the streets. This is the base line for Singapore food, the place where it all starts, where the prices are lowest and the eating quite possibly the most interesting.

Real, mobile, on-the-street hawkers are a disappearing species, but they've been replaced by hawkers' centres where a large number of non-mobile hawkers can all be found under the one roof. Scattered amongst them are tables and stools and you can sit and eat at any one you choose – none of them belong to a specific stall. Indeed a group of you can sit at one table and all eat from different stalls and at the same time have drinks from another.

It's one of the wonders of food centre eating how the various operators keep track of their plates and utensils – and manage to chase you up with the bill. The real joy of food centres is the sheer variety; while you're having Chinese food your companion can be eating a biriyani and across the table somebody else can be trying the satay. As a rough guide most one-dish meals cost from S$1.20 to S$3. Higher for more elaborate dishes.

There are hawkers' centres all over Singapore and more are being built as areas are redeveloped and the hawkers moved off the streets. In the business centre one of the best is the waterfront *Telok Ayer Transit Food Centre*, built in an old Victorian market building between Robinson Rd and Shenton Way. Other business centre places are *Empress Place* beside the Singapore River and *Boat Quay* directly across from it on the other bank. Telok Ayer and others in the business district are very busy at lunch, but tend to be quiet or closed in the evenings, apart from the ones by the river.

The *Satay Club* area by the waterfront at the foot of Stamford Rd has gone through a rejuvenation now the frantic construction all around it has been completed. Once again it's a colourful and tasty place to dine, the satay here is the best, just make sure you specify how many sticks (30c a time) you want or they'll assume your appetite is much larger than you will. Near the river and Raffles Quay it's also a pleasant strolling area in the evening.

Right beside the Handicraft Centre on Tanglin Rd is the *Rasa Singapura Centre* where the hawkers were all selected in a special competition to find the best stalls for each individual dish. This centre is promoted heavily for tourists although all the food centres are perfectly safe and healthy – you really can eat anywhere in Singapore. As a result prices are a bit higher than at other centres and some people say the food is not really any better – decide for yourself.

Continue down Orchard Rd and there's another popular centre upstairs in the *Cuppage Street Centre*, The downstairs section is a vegetable and produce market with a wonderful selection of fruit, but the upstairs food stall section includes many of the operators relocated from the famous old Orchard Rd car park (Gluttons' Square) when it was redeveloped. The *Newton Circus Centre*, at the traffic circle at the end of Scotts Rd, is particularly popular at night as it stays open later than usual.

There are other centres on Serangoon Rd, just beyond Rochor Rd, or try the *Albert Centre* on Albert Rd from Waterloo to Queen St. This is an extremely good, very busy and very popular centre with all types of food at low prices. Jalan Besar has two centres, one half way down Jalan Besar near Kitchener St and the *Bugis Square Centre* at the end of Jalan Besar by Lavender St. There's a good centre in the *Peoples' Park Complex* near Chinatown. There's a smaller centre just up from the Raffles Hotel on Beach Rd. There's even a pretty good food centre in the basement of *Changi Airport*!

The *Albert St Complex* at the Bencoolen-Albert intersection, now contains the famous Fatty's Chinese restaurant, *Weing Siong Fatty Restaurant* is at 01-33. Across the street in the basement of the Sim Lim Square complex is *Tenco Food Centre*, a new and very clean establishment, close to the Bencoolen accommodation area. One of the stalls is called *Excellent Duck*. At the other end of Bencoolen, just across Bras Basah Rd on a grassy area, is a small outdoor food centre called *Sweet Home Cafeteria* with a particularly good chicken rice place, *Chuen Chuen*.

In Chinatown, there's a hawkers' centre alongside the *Tanjong Market* not far from the railway station. There's also the *Amory St Food Centre*, where Amory meets Telok Ayer, in Chinatown.

On Kitchener Rd, across from the big President Merlin Hotel near Serangoon Rd is an outdoor food stall area that has steamboats – as does the Satay Club – one of the few that seems to offer it as standard fare. Another centre is at the corner of Serangoon and Bukit Timah Rds.

Quite a different sort of food centre is *Scotts Picnic Food Court* in the Scotts Shopping Centre on Scotts Rd, just off Orchard Rd by the Hyatt Hotel. It's glossier, more restaurant like than the general run of food centres and here the stalls round the dining area are international – as well as a variety of Chinese possibilities there is also Indian, Japanese, Italian, western and vegetarian food available.

The Hawkers' Variety Some typical hawkers' food you may find with average prices includes carrot cake or *chye tow kway* (S$1 to S$2) – also known as radish cake – it's a fried vegetable dish utterly unlike our western health food idea of carrot cake.

Indian *biriyanis* cost S$2 to S$3.50 or you can have a *murtabak* from S$1.20 to S$3. Naturally chicken rice will always be available in food centres (S$1.80 to S$3). Similar to chicken rice is *char siew* or roast pork. All the usual Cantonese dishes are available – like fried rice (S$1.50 to S$3), fried vegetables (S$3), beef & vegetables (S$5), sweet & sour pork (S$3 to S$5), plus other dishes like fish heads with black beans & chilli for S$3 to S$5.

There will often be Malay or Indonesian stalls with *satay* at 25c a stick, *mee rebus* at 80c to S$1, *gado gado* or *mee soto* at similar prices.

Omelettes are available at several stalls at Rasa Singapura from around S$1.50. *Wan ton mee*, that substantial soup dish, costs S$2 for shredded chicken or braised beef. You could try a *chee chong fun*, a type of stuffed noodle dish, costing from S$1.50 depending on whether you want the noodles with prawns, mushrooms or chicken & pork. *Hokkien fried prawn mee* is S$1.50 to S$3, *prawn mee soup* S$1 to S$2, *popiah* (spring rolls) 80c, *laksa* S$1.50 to S$2. There's a whole variety of other dishes and soups.

Or you could even opt for western food like sausage, egg & chips for S$2.40, burgers for S$2.50 or fish & chips for S$2.50. To drink you could have a beer for S$2.50, soft drinks from 30c to 50c, *ais kacang* for 40c or sugar cane juice for 20c to 50c depending on size. Fruit juices range from 50c for melon, papaya or pineapple up to 80c for apple, orange or starfruit may cost up to S$1 or even S$1.50 at some centres. To finish up you might try a fruit salad for S$1.50 to S$2 or just a *pisang goreng* (fried banana) for 20c or 40c.

Chinese Food Singapore has plenty of restaurants serving everything from a south Indian thali to an all-American hamburger, but naturally it's Chinese restaurants that predominate. They range all the way from streetside hawkers' stalls to fancy five-star hotel restaurants with a whole gamut of possibilities in between.

The *Manhill* at 99 Pasir Panjang Rd and its companion the *Hillman* at 159 Cantonment Rd are two more traditional-style Cantonese restaurants with moderate prices in straightforward surroundings. The *Mayflower Peking* at the International Building on Orchard Rd (beside the Thai Embassy) and the *Mayflower* at the DBS Building on Shenton Way are the opposite end of the scale in size and setting. They're huge Hong Kong-style dim sum specialists, but surprisingly reasonably priced for all the carpeting and air-con. Dim sum starts from around S$1 per plate. Also in the DBS Building is the *Swatow Teochew* specialising in Teochew (also called Chiu Chao and Chao Zhou) cuisine – try the roast goose or shark's fin

soup. The Shenton Way area has many other good Chinese eating places.

Other dim sum places include the more expensive *Ming Palace Restaurant* in the Ming Court Hotel or the luxurious *Shang Palace* in the Shangri-La. Remember that dim sum is a lunchtime or Sunday breakfast dish – in the evening these restaurants revert to other menus. Other more expensive Cantonese restaurants include the old-fashioned *Majestic* on Bukit Pasoh Rd near Chinatown.

At 143 and 153 Kitchener Rd, between Jalan Besar and Serangoon Rd, the *Fut Sai Kai* (which translates as 'monk's world') is another spartan old coffee shop where the speciality is vegetarian cooking. Prices are not low, but it offers a good chance to sample a slightly unusual variation of Chinese cuisine. *Kwan Yim* is another traditional and long running vegetarian restaurant, it's at 190 Waterloo St in the South-East Asia Hotel.

Chicken rice is a common, but popular, dish all over town. Originally from Hainan in China chicken rice is a dish of elegant simplicity and in Singapore they do it better than anywhere. *Swee Kee* at 51 Middle Rd, close to the Raffles Hotel, is a long-running specialist with a very high reputation. Chicken and rice is S$3.30 served with chilli, ginger and thick soya sauce. They also do steamboats; a S$20 version has a stock enriched by various Chinese herbs and Mao Tai wine.

A stone's throw from Swee Kee you'll find *Yet Con* at 25 Purvis St which some claim is the best of all Singapore's chicken rice places. This area off Beach Rd is something of a Hainanese stronghold. The *Rasa Singapura* chicken rice stall also does a good job of it – they even offer the chicken as 'regular' or 'boneless'.

Although Cantonese is the most readily available Chinese cuisine in Singapore you can also find most of the regional variations, however, they tend to be more expensive than the common, everyday Cantonese restaurants. If you've got a yen to try Peking duck then the *Eastern*

TIFFIN Room @ Raffles Hotel
Expensive, but FABULOUS

Palace on the 4th floor of Supreme House is one of the best Beijing restaurants.

Sichuan restaurants are relatively common. They include the reasonably priced *Omei* in the Hotel Grand Central at one end of the scale and the decidedly expensive *Golden Phoenix* at the Hotel Equatorial at the other.

Hokkien food is not all that popular despite the large number of Hokkiens in Singapore, but *Beng Hiang* at 20 Murray St is renowned for its Hokkien food. Teochew food is a relatively widely available cuisine – you could try *Guan Hin* at 1 Bendemeer Rd where steamboat is also very popular or the traditional *Chui Wah Lin* at 49 Mosque St. At several of these places there may be no menu, but a request for suggestions and prices will be readily answered. Finally there's Taiwanese food – try the *May Garden* at 101 Orchard Towers or the reasonably priced *Goldleaf* at 185 Orchard Rd.

Singapore has another local variation on Chinese food which it's worth making the effort to try. Seafood in Singapore is simply superb, whether it's prawns or abalone, fish head curry or chilli crabs. Most of the better seafood specialists are some distance out from the city centre, but the travelling is worthwhile. Upper East Coast Rd is one of the best areas where you will find places like *Seaview* at 779A. Or try the *Chin Wah Heng* at 785 Upper East Coast Rd, at about the 14½ km marker. It is moderately priced and has the usual glass tanks containing crabs, eels, prawns and fish all ready to head for the wok.

Others include the *Choon Seng* at 892 Ponggol Rd at Ponggol Point right up at the north of the island or the *Chin Lee* at 18C Jalan Tuas in the small fishing village of Tuas, way out beyond Jurong at the western tip of the island, 30 km from the city. The trip out to Ponggol Point, on bus No 82 or 83 is quite an experience in itself; you pass miles of cemeteries and then chicken and pig farms, surprisingly rural for Singapore.

Indian Food As with everything else some of the best Indian food can be found in the hawkers' centres. This particularly applies to biriyani dishes – in virtually any of the centres, but particularly Telok Ayer – you can have a superb chicken biriyani for just S$2.50 to S$3.50.

If you want to sample eat-with-your-fingers south Indian vegetarian food then the place to go is the Little India district off Serangoon Rd. The famous and very popular *Komala Vilas* at 76 Serangoon Rd was established soon after the war and has an open downstairs area where you can have masala dosa (S$1) and other snacks. The upstairs section is air-conditioned and you can have their all-you-can-eat rice meal for S$3. Remember to wash your hands before you start, to use only your right hand and to ask for eating utensils only if you really have to! On your way out try an Indian sweet from the showcase at the back of the downstairs section.

Two other rice plate specialists are *Sri Krishna Vilas* at 229 and *Ananda Bhavan* at 219-221 Selegie Rd. There are several other Indian eateries on and off Serangoon and a new contender in the local competition for the best south Indian food is *Madras New Woodlands Cafe* at 14 Upper Dickson Rd off Serangoon, around the corner from Komala Vilas. A branch of the well-known Woodlands chain in India, New Woodlands serves freshly-prepared vegetarian food in very clean air-conditioned rooms. The yoghurt is particularly good. Prices are about the same as at Komala Vilas.

There are plenty of modest Indian places in little India along Serangoon Rd. Race Course Rd, a block over, has also become a curry region. Try the *Banana Leaf Apolo* at 56 Race Course Rd for superb non-vegetarian Indian food including Singapore's classic fish head curry.

For north Indian food (chicken biriyani for S$3.50) there are a string of venerable establishements on North Bridge Rd, on the block east from Arab St, near the Sultan Mosque. Each of them has their

Thai food in Restaurant at Intercontinental Hotel - Expensive, but fabulous [handwritten annotation]

year of founding proudly displayed on their sign out front. The *Jubilee* at 771 North Bridge Rd is a great place for biriyani or other north Indian dishes at very low prices. A few doors down at 791-797 the *Islamic* is very similar. Others are the *Victory* (established 1910) at 701, the *Zam Zam* (established 1908) at 699 and the *Singapore* (estabished 1911) at 697. The latter three are all directly opposite the mosque.

Much pricier, but with a great reputation for high-quality food, is *Omar Khayyam* at 55 Hill St, virtually opposite the American Embassy. The food is Kashmiri, a subtle variation on normal north Indian food, but the tandoori dishes are the highlight. There's a small, basic north Indian place called *Sahib Restaurant* at 129 Bencoolen St near Middle Rd, across from the Fortuna Centre. They have very good food and specialise in fish dishes, including fish head curry, but have chicken and vegetable items too. Cost is S$3 to S$4 and they are open 24 hours.

Malay, Thai, Indonesian & Nonya Food You won't find a great deal of Malay or nonya food in the central business or Orchard Rd districts of Singapore although there is the occasional stall or two at some of the food centres. For these cuisines, the place to go is eastwards to the Geylang and Katong districts. Along (and just off) Joo Chiat Rd between East Coast and Geylang Rds in particular are good hunting grounds for all kinds of Asian foods – Indian, Malay, nonya, nasi padang, various kinds of Chinese, Thai, plus Middle Eastern. This area is probably the liveliest local night scene in the city.

There is a place on East Coast Rd just past Siglap Rd called *East Peranakan Inn* that has good nonya and Malay food. Another branch is *Peranakan Inn* at 210 East Coast Rd. Slightly pricier nonya food (S$4 to S$10 per dish) is served in an air-conditioned room at *Guan Hoe Soon*, 214 Joo Chiat, open 11 am to 10 pm.

There are several Thai restaurants along Joo Chiat Rd – *Chiangmai* at 328 Joo Chiat, *Pattaya Eating House* at 402, and *Haadyai Beefball Restaurant* at 455. Closer to town *Her Restaurant* in Serangoon Plaza on Serangoon Rd has excellent Thai food.

Bibi's Restoran on the 2nd floor of Peranakan Place at 180 Orchard Road has a selection of nonya snacks. Satay is available in many centres and you'll find good satay in the *Rasa Singapura* and, of course, at the *Satay Club* on Elizabeth Walk, where many of the stalls specialise in satay.

If you like the fiery food of north Sumatra there are a number of nasi padang specialists, one of the best known being *Rendezvous* at 4-5 Bras Basah Rd, at the junction with Prinsep St. It's open lunchtimes only from 11 am to 3 pm and closed on Wednesdays. They also have a second branch at 02-19 in the Raffles City Shopping Centre which is open until 9.15 pm, but also closed on Wednesdays. *Nasi Padang* at 24 Tanglin Rd, across from the Tanglin Centre, is equally good but also open only for lunch.

Western Food Yes, you can get western food in Singapore too – including a couple of dozen *McDonald's*. You'll find them along Orchard Rd, near Scotts Rd, round the corner on Scotts Rd itself, in front of Plaza Singapura and at the Orchard Rd YMCA. There are lots more all over town including at Peoples' Park and Changi Airport.

There are also *A&W Root Beer*, *Kentucky Fried Chicken* (nearly 40 of them), *Burger King*, *Dunkin' Donuts*, *Dennys*, *Pizza Hut*, *Baskin Robbins* and *Swensen's Ice Cream* outlets so there's no shortage of western fast food.

Slightly more expensive western food can be found at places like *Ponderosa* in the Plaza Singapura centre where you can get a steak and there is a serve yourself salad bar. The very pleasant open air *Wakiki Coffee House & Restaurant* is

— Singapore is multi racial in both dinners & diners —

Top: Old town, Ipoh (JC)
Bottom: Panglima Mosque, Ipoh (JC)

Top: Children on the beach, Pulau Pangkor (TW)
Bottom: Kampung Telok Gedong, Palau Pangkor (JC)

directly across Orchard Rd from Plaza Singapura, in the small park. They have a daily three course lunch with tea or coffee for S$6.50.

For upscale western food, but at bargain prices, there is the *Restaurant Shatec* (tel 235 9533), the Singapore Hotel Association's Training & Educational Centre at 24 Nassim Hill. Now open to the public, the place is really a training centre for hotel dining room food preparation and present-ation. They offer set, five-course meals at lunch and dinner as well as an a la carte menu in a fairly elegant setting. Lunch is S$9.50, dinner S$13.50 with items such as escargot, Scottish salmon and duck a l'orange.

Finally there are the expensive western restaurants at the big hotels. If you really want to think you're in France, even though you're almost on the equator, they'll do a pretty good job of convincing you. Bring your credit cards.

Odds & Ends & Breakfast Naturally Singapore has a lot of personal favourites and obscure odds and ends. If you want a light snack at any time of the day there are quite a few Chinese coffee bars selling interesting cakes which go nicely with a cup of coffee or teh-o. The *Famous Pau Shop* in Peranakan Place at 180 Orchard Rd has an interesting variety of Malay cakes like delicious otak fish cakes, tasty custard tarts and other 'vanishing foods' of Singapore.

For pastries western-style head for *La Boulangerie Restaurant* in the Far East Shopping Centre at 500 Orchard Rd. If you're suffering croissant withdrawal symptoms from 2.30 to 5.30 pm you can eat as many as you like, washed down with unlimited tea and coffee for a flat S$5. The small *L E Cafe* at 264 Middle Rd, under the Sun Sun Hotel almost at Selegie Rd, is an interesting place with European and oriental cakes and pastries, a good place for breakfast or a snack. Or try cakes, cookies, yoghurt and muesli at *Steeple's Deli* at 02-25 Tanglin Shopping Centre on Tanglin Rd. They also do great deli-style sandwiches at S$6 to S$8.

The big international hotels have their big international breakfast buffets of course but there are also lots of little places for breakfast around the Bencoolen St cheap hotel area. Most of them will rustle you up toast and jam without too much difficulty, try the coffee bar right next to Airmaster Travel on Prinsep St.

There are a number of small Indian coffee shops which do cheap Chinese and Indian breakfasts – take your pick, dosa and curry or you-tiao and hot soy milk. Roti chanai with a mild curry dip is a delicious and economical breakfast at *Ming Tong* at 74 Bencoolen St or *Tong Hoe* at 84.

There are many places which do a fixed-price breakfast – continental or American. Try the *Silver Spoon Coffee House* in Supreme House on Penang Rd off Orchard Rd for a S$3.80 or S$4.50 breakfast. *McDonald's* and *A&W* also do fast food breakfasts, you could have a McDonalds' 'big breakfast' for S$3.50 or hotcakes and syrup for S$1.50.

Towards the back of the Empress Place food centre *Neuborne's* is a great place for fish & chips, believe it or not. There are plenty of supermarkets in Singapore with everything from French wine to Australian beer, yoghurt to muesli, cheese to ice cream. A pot of tea on the lawn at the Raffles Hotel is a fine investment and a chance to relive the Singapore of an earlier era. You can get a beer (S$2.50 to S$3) at almost any coffee shop but there are also plenty of bars as well as the big hotels. A beer in the *Long Bar* of the Raffles will cost you S$6.80 with service.

Things to Buy

One of Singapore's major attractions is, of course, shopping. There are plenty of bargains to be had in all sorts of goods, but there are also a number of guidelines to follow if you want to be certain to get your money's worth. First of all don't buy anything unless you really want it and don't buy anything where the hassle of getting it back home will cost you more than the saving you make. Remember that 'duty free' and 'free port' are somewhat throw-away terms. Firstly not everything is loaded down with import duty in your own country, and secondly, Singapore also has some local industries to protect.

Price Before you leap on anything as a great bargain, find out what the price really is. If you're going to Singapore with the intention of buying a camera or a tape recorder, for example, check what they would cost you back home first. Then in Singapore find out what the 'real' price is. It's no triumph to knock a starting price of S$200 down to S$150 if the real price was S$150 to start with. To find out what something should cost, you can check with the main agent or showroom in Singapore, or you can check a big fixed-price department store where the price is unlikely to be rock bottom, but is most likely to be in the ball park. Most importantly, ask around – never buy in the first shop you come to and always check a few places to see what is being asked.

To my surprise on my last visit to Singapore I found the airport duty-free shop was as cheap as anywhere. I wanted a particular model of portable tape recorder which at the airport cost S$195. In town I looked in about a dozen shops and was quoted as high as S$235 for the same model. Even with bargaining only one place beat the airport price and I decided I'd rather buy it at the airport for S$5 more than at that particular grubby little place. Maybe it was due to Chinese New Year but from this limited experience the airport was pretty good.

Bargaining In Singapore you've got to bargain in almost any shop. The secret of successful bargaining is to keep it good humoured and try to make them move rather than you. Your first gambit can be 'is that your best price', for their opening offer certainly won't be. Then when you

have to make an offer go lower than you are willing to spend, but not so low that you seem totally uninterested.

You have to try and give the impression that if the price isn't right you can quite happily do without it; or that if his price isn't right the shop next door probably will be. Also remember that when you've made an offer you've committed yourself. If you really don't want something don't offer anything – you might just end up buying it with a totally ludicrous offer.

Guarantees They're one of the most important considerations if you're buying electronic gear, watches, cameras or the like, and the important point is that the guarantee must be an international one. Usually this is no problem, but always ask before you get down to haggling if the guarantee is international. A national guarantee is next to useless – are you going to bring your calculator back to Singapore to be fixed? Finally, make sure the guarantee is filled out correctly with the shop's name and the serial number of the item written down.

As important as the guarantee is the item's compatibility back home. You don't want a brand or model that has never found its way to your country.

Shops You buy in Singapore on one basis only – price. The goods (high-technology goods that is) are just the same as you'd get back home so quality doesn't enter into it. You're not going to come back for after-sales service, so service doesn't come into the picture either. You're not there to admire the display or get good advice from the assistants. In Singapore it's price, price, price.

As a spin-off from this, Singapore's shops are generally quite unexciting places – 99 times out of 100 it's simply a case of pack the goods in. Nor are the staff always that helpful or friendly – they may be a long way behind Hong Kong shop assistants when it come to out-and-out rudeness, but a few shopping trips in Singapore will soon indicate why the government runs 'be polite' campaigns so often!

Where to Shop Singapore is almost wall-to-wall with shops but there are certain places worth heading to for certain items. People's Park is a large shopping complex, but a little off the regular tourist track. For this reason prices may be a bit lower if you want cameras, film, electrical equipment, watches, etc. This is a good place to try if you are not looking for something highly unusual.

Otherwise the major shopping complexes on and around Orchard Rd – like Plaza Singapura, Specialists Centre, Lucky Plaza, Orchard Towers, Shaw Centre on Scotts Rd, Supreme House on Penang Rd, Tanglin Centre on Tanglin Rd – will all have a very wide variety of shops and goods. Recently opened centres are the huge Daimaru Centre on River Valley Rd opposite the National Theatre and the Parkway Parade complex at Marine Parade Centre. For computer buffs, the top three floors of the Funan Centre on North Bridge Rd between Coleman and High Sts (just south of the Peninsula Hotel) is a must.

Singapore has a number of Chinese emporiums if you're after something from the People's Republic. Try Overseas in the People's Park, Chinese in the International Building on Orchard Rd, or Yu Yi in Orchard Building on Grange Rd. There are also a wide variety of department stores offering both their own brand goods and other items, generally at fixed prices – ideal if you've had enough of bargaining. They include shops like C K Tang, Isetan or Yaohan, all along Orchard Rd.

For oddities you could try Chinatown or the shops along Arab St. High St and North Bridge Rd also provide more traditional shopping possibilities. The famous Change Alley, a narrow tunnel running between Collyer Quay and Raffles Place, is still hanging on in the face of redevelopment, but is now supplemented by a modern, overhead shopping arcade.

The Singapore Handicrafts Centre is the place to look for regional handicrafts and to see many of them actually being made.

What to Buy Anything and everything is the easy answer. Cameras are available throughout the city; when buying film bargain for lower prices if you're buying in bulk – 10 films cost less than 10 times one film. For TVs, stereo equipment, radios, tape recorders, calculators and watches the same story applies – compare prices and check the guarantee. Make sure that you are actually paying less than you would back home – duty free is a somewhat over-used term these days. Camera prices are heavily discounted in the west just as much as in Singapore or Hong Kong.

In the computer realm, software and software manuals were until early '87 very cheap. Now that Singapore is enforcing international copyright laws, all the cheap software is across the causeway in Johore and KL. However, blank diskettes, accessories, and 'cloned' hardware are still bargains. For American-made or Japanese-made name-brand hardware, prices are good, but not necessarily as low as in the countries of origin. The best place to shop for computer gear is Funan Centre on North Bridge Rd.

Clothes, shoes and fashion accessories are widely available in Singapore. You can choose from imported, locally made and made to measure. Some of the best buys include brand-name jeans and clothes (Levis, Wranglers, etc). Orchard Rd is again the place to got to for expensive crafts such as Persian carpets and jewellery.

Getting There & Away

Air Singapore is a major travel crossroads and flights operate in and out of Changi Airport at all hours. See the introductory Getting There section for details on flying to Singapore from all over the world. Singapore Airlines and MAS have flights between Singapore and Kuala Lumpur,

Penang, Kuching and Kota Kinabalu in Malaysia. There are also frequent flights between Singapore and Bangkok in Thailand, Jakarta in Indonesia and Hong Kong.

Singapore is also a good place to look for cheap plane tickets. Two agents Lonely Planet writers have used with entirely satisfactory results are Airmaster Travel at 36B Prinsep St and Student Travel Australia's agency in the Ming Court Hotel. Many others advertise in the *Straits Times* classified columns.

Fares vary with when you want to fly and who you want to fly with. The cheapest fares are likely to be with the least loved airlines (various Eastern European ones, Bangladesh Biman, etc), via inconvenient routes (you're forced to make stop-overs on the way) or with little choice of time (they only fly every other Tuesday and it departs at 3 am).

Some typical cheapest one-way fares being quoted out of Singapore include South-East Asia destinations like Bangkok S$170 to S$210, Denpasar S$375 or S$500 return, Manila S$500 or S$750 return, Jakarta S$175 or S$240 return, Hong Kong S$550 or S$750 return. To the subcontinent you could have Colombo S$380, Madras S$520, Bombay S$520, Kathmandu S$570 to S$600. Fares to Australia or New Zealand include Sydney S$560 or S$800 for more convenient flights, Auckland S$900 or S$1400 return, Perth or Darwin via Bali and Jakarta S$600. London, or other European destinations, costs from S$650 with the Eastern European cheapies or from S$750 with the better airlines, To North America there's Vancouver S$1050, USA west coast S$850 by the northern (Asian) route with stops or S$1600 by the southern (Pacific) route,

There are always some special multi-stop deals on offer such as Singapore, Bangkok, Hong Kong, Taipei, Amsterdam with China Airlines for S$900. Or Singapore, Bangkok, Hong Kong, Taipei, US west coast for about the same price.

You can add in Tokyo and Honolulu on that route for a few dollars more.

Rail Singapore is the southern termination point for the Malaysian railway system although Singapore has no rail system of its own. See the introductory Getting Around section for fare details and timetable. Leaving Singapore you clear immigration and customs at the station so there is no further delay at the causeway when crossing into Malaysia.

Road Although there is a great variety of bus services operating from Singapore there is a much greater choice in Johore Bahru where there is also a wide variety of taxi services. To get to Johore Bahru you can take bus No 170 from Queen St for 80c. Or for S$1 you can take the direct bus which departs every 10 minutes from the nearby Rochor Rd Terminus. It's a red and grey bus and leaves from Albert St across from the food centre. Don't be worried if the bus departs while you're clearing immigration and customs for Malaysia, you can just hop on the next one that comes along. Take it all the way to the Johore Bahru terminus though, don't abandon the bus at Malaysian immigration.

In the same locality in Singapore you will find taxis operating to Johore Bahru at S$4 per person or S$16 for a full car. Foreigners are likely to have to pay slightly more since they take longer to clear the border than Singaporeans or Malaysians.

You can get taxis into Malaysia from Singapore without going to Johore Bahru first. Try the Malaysia Taxi Service (tel 298 3831) at 290 Jalan Besar, for all places in Malaysia. Another is the Kuala Lumpur Taxi Service (tel 223 1889), 191 New Bridge Rd.

To Melaka buses operate from the bus terminal (tel 293 5915) at the junction of Lavender St and Kallang Bahru. Buses leave at 8, 9, 10, 11 am, 1, 2, 3 and 4 pm and the cost is S$11 or S$16 for air-conditioned. Other buses for Malaysia operate from this same terminus. Masmara Travel (tel 294 7034/5) can give you more information about the other buses. Some fares and departure times are:

air-con

Kuala Lumpur	9 am or 9 pm	S$17
Ipoh	6.30 pm	S$25
Butterworth	6.30 pm	S$30
Penang	6.30 pm	S$31
Mersing	9 am, 9 & 10 pm	S$11
Kuantan	9 am, 9 & 10 pm	S$16
Kuala Trengganu	8 pm	S$23
Kota Bahru	7.30 pm	S$31

non air-con

Kuantan	10 am	S$8.50
Kuala Trengganu	8 am	S$19
Kota Bahru	7.30 pm	S$26

There is a money changer at the bus depot – if you don't see him ask at the desk and they will point him out to you.

Many of the air-conditioned Kuala Lumpur buses are new and in immaculate condition having mod-cons such as radio, TV and toilet. The trip takes about eight hours, mainly because the road is very busy in both directions. Parts of it are now divided with toll booths (!), but this widening project will not be completed for a while yet. There's also a lunch and snack break on the way. If you want to hitch into Malaysia get yourself to Johore Bahru before starting.

Boat There used to be lots of shipping services out of Singapore, but very few still operate – it's all airlines today. The only regular passage available today is the Singapore-Kuantan-Kuching service. It departs Singapore on Friday, arrives Kuantan on Saturday, departs on Sunday and arrives Kuching on Monday. The fares from Singapore are Kuantan S$99 in 2nd or S$140 in deluxe, Kuching S$200 in 2nd, S$270 in deluxe. For details, check with Mansfield Travel (tel 737 9688) behind the Ocean Building on Collyer Quay.

You can also take the ferry across to Batam island in the Indonesian Riau island group immediately south of Singapore. This can be a very interesting way to enter or leave Indonesia, see the introductory Getting There chapter for details.

Getting Around

Singapore Airport Singapore's ultra-modern new Changi International Airport is another of those miracles that Singapore specialises in. It's vast, efficient, organised and was built in record time. See airport transport for details on getting to or from the airport. At the airport there are banking and money-changing facilities, post office and telephone facilities (open 24 hours), a free hotel reservation service from 8 am to 11.30 pm, left luggage facilities (S$2 per bag first day, S$1.50 per day thereafter), a variety of shops in the boarding area, and a supermarket in the basement.

On your way through the arrivals concourse pick up the free information booklets, maps and other guides which are available from stands. They give you a lot of useful information and good-quality colour maps of Singapore city and Singapore island. There's even a free booklet listing all flights to and from Singapore, a guide to the airport and the glossy monthly travel rag *Changi*.

If you need a place to rest there are day rooms in the transit lounge which cost S$15 to S$22 per six hours. Or if you just need a shower you can have that for S$5, including towel and soap. You can get your haircut while you wait for your flight too. Bored? Well there's the free Singapore Experience Audio-Visual show at 6, 7, 8 and 9 pm. At 2.30 and 4.30 pm there's even a free two hour tour of Singapore, available for passengers in transit. Kids are catered for with an imaginative play area in the transit lounge too.

There are plenty of places to eat at the airport (this is Singapore after all, food capital of South-East Asia), including a *Swenson's Ice Cream Bar* upstairs, a Chinese restaurant, a Japanese restaurant, a cafe serving Malay, nonya, and Indian food, and the Transit 'Buffeteria' and Wing's Cafeteria both open 24 hours. If you are one of the millions of air travellers fed up with over-priced and terrible food at airports, then Changi Airport has the answer to that too – there is a *McDonald's* at one end of the arrival hall and a *Noodle Restaurant* at the other end. Both at normal prices. To find even cheaper food just take the elevator beside McDonald's on the arrival level and press the button for basement 1 'Food Centre' where you'll find a complete typical Singapore hawkers' food centre! It's essentially the staff cafeteria but the public are quite welcome.

Airport tax ('passenger service charge') from Singapore is S$5 to Malaysia and Brunei, S$12 further afield. You can purchase PSC coupons in advance at airline offices, travel agencies, and major hotels if you don't want to fiddle with counting Singapore currency at the airport. You don't have to pay the charge if you're just in transit so long as you don't leave the transit lounge.

Changi Airport has been rated the world's second most-liked airport (next to Amsterdam's Schipol Airport), according to a survey done by the British travel magazine *Business Traveller*. Singapore is currently undertaking the construction of a second terminal which will be a third larger than the terminal now in use. This terminal will be even more of a self-contained city, with a health club and a fully-equipped medical centre. The two terminals will be connected by a mini-MRT train, part of the larger MRT system now under construction throughout Singapore.

Airport Transport Singapore's Changi International Airport opened in mid-81 and it's at the extreme eastern end of the island, about 20 km from the city. There is no problem in getting into the city because with typical Singaporean efficiency, an expressway was built along reclaimed land.

You've got the choice of a very convenient public bus, taxis or the more expensive limousine services. For the public buses follow the signs in the airport terminal to the basement bus stop. You can take bus No 392 to Somapah for 50c; Somapah is an interchange for other bus services around Singapore. Or you can take bus No 394 to Batu Interchange for 80c.

For budget travellers heading for the Bencoolen St-Beach Rd-Middle Rd cheap accommodation enclave, by far the best bus service is bus No 390, which also costs 80c. You must have the exact change for this bus so when you change money make sure you get some coins. Bus No 390 operates every 12 to 15 minutes, from 6.30 am to 11.45 pm daily, takes about half an hour to the city, and stops at Rochor Canal Rd and Bencoolen St. From Orchard Rd take bus No 7 to Bedok Interchange and from there you can take bus No 390 or 347.

Ignore the other bus services from the airport – amusingly numbered No 727, 737, 747 and 757 – these are intended for airport workers and run to the major housing areas.

Taxis from the airport are subject to a S$3 supplementary charge on top of the meter fare, which will probably be S$7 to S$10 to most places. Note that this only applies from the airport, not from the city. Sintat (tel 235 5855) operate an airport limousine service at S$40 from the airport to your hotel, S$35 hotel to airport. There's a free taxi guide, which lists many fares around town. There are many taxi companies; for radio bookings 24 hours call 293 3111 or 452 5555.

Bus Singapore has an extremely frequent and comprehensive bus network. You rarely have to wait more than a few minutes for a bus and they will get you almost anywhere you want to go. If you intend to do much travelling by bus in Singapore, a copy of the bus guide, which also includes a bus route map, is a vital investment. They cost S$1.50 at bookshops, but shoestring travellers may well find their hotel has a supply left behind by departing visitors. Also helpful is the *Mini Bus Guide* put out by Singapore's two bus companies, Singapore Bus Services and Trans-Island Bus Service. They cost S$1 and list all bus schedules in a convenient pocket-sized guide. Best of all is the street index that gives the numbers of all the bus lines going to each of the listed streets.

The buses follow the same route into and out of the city, and fares start from 40c and go up in 10c increments to a maximum of 80c. There are also OMO (one man operated) buses which charge a flat fare – you must have the exact change as none is given. There are two types of OMO bus – one charges a flat 80c (like the airport bus No 390) while the other operates a step fare system where you pay 80c, 60c or 40c depending on where you board. A sign in the front of the bus indicates the fare to be paid. For information on how to reach a certain place call 284 8866 during business hours.

For those with limited time in Singapore, who still want to see as much of the island as possible for as cheaply as possible there are the Singapore Explorer bus tickets. These provide unlimited travel to anywhere on the island on either Singapore Bus Service or Trans Island Bus Service buses. Six different routes have been named – Historic Singapore, the Temple Route, the Flora and Fauna Route, Island of Contrasts, the Food Trail and the Chinese Touch. You can break your journey wherever you like. You can buy either a one-day Explorer ticket for S$5 or a three-day ticket for S$12. They are available from many hotels including the YMCAs, or phone 2872727 for more details. With the ticket you also get a bus map showing the bus stops and points of interest.

MRT Singapore's ultra modern Mass Rapid Transit system started real operation in early '88 (a two station service started in late '87) and the whole show will be completed by 1990.

Using the subway system is extremely simple. You simply check the map showing fares from your station, put money in the slot and press the button for the fare you want. You can get a single trip ticket or a stored value ticket which is valid until you've used up the value of the ticket. You insert the ticket into the entry gate to enter and on departure the ticket is retained by the exit gate unless it still has 'stored value'. On the first section opened fares varied from 50c to S$1.10. The trains operate 18 hours a day and at peak times there is a train every three to six minutes.

Unusually the platform areas are totally enclosed. When the train pulls in and its doors open a door to the platform opens beside it!

Taxis Singapore has a good supply of taxis – 12,500 of them – and it's usually not too difficult to find one. The exceptions may include rush hours, trips out to the airport (which taxi drivers can be reluctant to make), or at meal times (Singaporeans are not enthusiastic about missing a meal).

It is quite easy to recognise Singapore taxis although they come in several varieties – most common being black with a yellow roof or pale blue. Taxis are all metered and although you should ensure the meter is flagged down it's usually no problem – unlike some Asian countries where the meters always seem to be

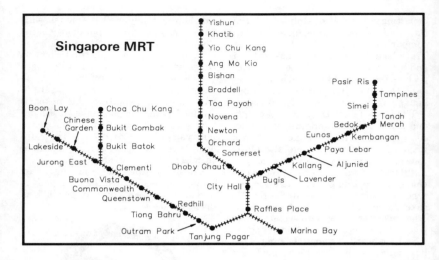

'broken'. Flag fall is S$1.60 (there are still some non-air-con taxis which cost S$1, but most have air-con now) for the first 1.5 km then 10c for each additional 300 metres up to 10 km. After 10 km, every 250 metres is 10c. Add S$1 for any luggage placed in the boot.

From midnight to 6 am there is a 50% surcharge over the meter fare. From the airport there is a surcharge of S$3 for each journey – but not to the airport. You can also book taxis by radio by phoning 293 3111 – this costs an additional 40c. There are other supplementary charges for baggage and additional passengers. Note the information on area licences for the restricted zone. Singapore taxi service is generally refreshingly courteous and efficient, plus the cars themselves are super-clean since drivers can be fined S$30 for driving a dirty cab.

Restricted Area & Car Parking From 7.30 to 10.15 am each morning the Central Business District is a restricted zone where cars may only enter with a licence or if they carry at least four people. A daily licence costs S$5 – not surprisingly this

has dramatically reduced traffic problems in the rush hour! The licence requirement also applies to taxis so if you want to take a taxi into the CBD during these hours you must pay for the taxi licence which costs S$2 – unless somebody else has already done so of course. The area licences are sold at booths just outside the district boundaries.

And if you should carelessly enter the CBD without a licence? Well, there may well be inspectors standing by the roadside noting down the number plates of unlicenced cars as they enter the CBD. A S$50 fine will soon arrive at the car owner's address.

Parking in many places in Singapore is operated by a coupon system. You can buy a booklet of coupons at parking kiosks and must display one in your car window with holes punched out to indicate the time, day and date your car was parked.

Trishaws Singapore's bicycle rickshaws are fast disappearing although you'll find a surprising number still operating in Chinatown and off Serangoon Rd. Today they are mainly used for local shopping trips or to transport articles too heavy to carry. They rarely venture on to Singapore's heavily trafficked main streets.

There are, however, trishaws at many tourist centres in case you really have to try one out. Always agree on the fare beforehand. A recent innovation has been night-time trishaw tours which are operated from a number of the large hotels. Trishaw Tours (tel 223 8809) offer a nightly ride through Chinatown for S$13. On the street a very short ride is S$2 and the price goes up from there. Trishaws had their peak just after WW II when motorised transport was almost non-existent and trishaw riders could make a very healthy income.

Rent-a-Car Singapore has branches of the three major regional rent-a-car operators – Sintat, Hertz and Avis. There are also a large number of small, local operators. If you want a car just for local driving many of these quote rental rates that undercut the major operators. Rates in Singapore are similar to those in Malaysia but it is more expensive to take a Singapore rent-a-car into Malaysia. Addresses of some of the main operators include:

Avis
    204-B Boon Liew Building, Bukit Timah Rd (tel 737 9477)
Best Car Rental
    3-20 Coronation Shopping Plaza, Bukit Timah Rd (tel 468 9777)
Blue Star Car Rental
    2-19 Balestier Complex, Balestier Rd (tel 253 4661)
Budget
    Orchard Plaza, Orchard Rd (tel 734 5511)
Hertz Rent-a-Car
    33 Tanglin Rd (tel 734 4646)
Sime Darby Services
    475 Tanglin Halt Rd (tel 62 3433)
Sintat Rent-a-Car
    1-27 OUB Building, Collyer Quay (tel 224 4155)
Sunrise Car Rental
    107 Bukit Timah Rd (tel 336 0626)

Boats & Ferries There is a wide variety of boating possibilities in Singapore. You can charter a bumboat (motorised sampan) to take a tour up the Singapore River or to go to the islands around Singapore. Speedboats can be hired from Ponggol Boatel to go across to the northern islands or for water skiing. There are regular ferry services from Clifford Pier or the World Trade Centre to Sentosa and the other southern islands. There are also Port of Singapore Authority ferry tours or you can take more luxurious junk tours around the harbour either by daylight or as an evening dinner cruise with operators like Fairwind or Watertours.

Walking Getting around Singapore on foot has one small problem – apart from the heat and humidity that is. The problem, in old Singapore only, is the 'five-foot ways' instead of sidewalks or pavements. A five-foot way, which takes its name from the fact that it is roughly five-feet wide, is a walkway at the front of the traditional Chinese shop-houses, but enclosed, verandah-like, in the front of the building.

The problem with them is that every shop's walkway is individual. It may well be higher or lower than the shop next door or closer to or further from the street. Walking thus becomes a constant up and down and side to side, further complicated by the fact that half the shops seem to overflow right across the walkway forcing you to venture into the street. As well as people parking their bikes or motorcycles across them you are likely to trip over the odd chowkidar asleep on his charpoy at night. (A chowkidar is an Indian nightwatchman and a charpoy is the traditional rope-strung bed which chowkidars seem to spend most of their time horizontal upon.) To further add to the joys of walking in Singapore there are open drains waiting to catch the unwary.

Still, if you can drag your eyes away from where your feet are going, there is plenty to see as you stroll the five-foot ways.

Tours A wide variety of tours are available in Singapore. They include morning or afternoon tours in the city or to Jurong, Changi on the east coast, or the various parks and gardens. These vary in price from around S$20 to S$30. To Jurong Bird Park is S$22 or S$23, a three-hour city tour is S$21, to Sentosa for 3½ hours is S$28. Nightly tours of Chinatown by bicycle trishaw cost from S$25 to S$35 including a preliminary gin sling at the Raffles Hotel although there are also cheaper trishaw tours for S$15.

More unusual tours include a daybreak walking tour of Chinatown for S$15. Port of Singapore Authority tours include a two-hour harbour cruise (10 am or 2.30 pm from Monday to Saturday, departing from the World Trade Centre). The PSA also have evening harbour cruises and there are a number of private operators with junk trips on the harbour or bumboat trips up the river. These start from around S$18 for daytime cruises and cost up to S$40 for dinner cruises including a buffet meal.

Tour East (tel 220 2200) has one for the drinkers, a tour of Malayan Breweries, makers of Anchor and Tiger Beer. After the tour there's a 30-minute tasting session. The same company offers a tour outside of the city with a glimpse at the fast-fading countryside and village life. Gray Line, the international sightseeing tour company, runs trips around town and to local area attractions. They have seven different tours from S$16 to S$147.

Licensed guides are available through the tourist office. They charge S$9 an hour if using any of the four official languages and S$17 an hour for any other. Ask at your hotel about other types of tours.

MALAYSIA

MALAYSIA

Malaysia is a country of beautiful scenery, easy and comfortable travel and friendly people, rather than of deep historical or cultural interest. It's one of the most advanced countries in Asia and offers a wide variety of beaches, mountains and parks for lovers of the outdoors.

For convenience this guide divides Malaysia into four sections. First it's split east and west into East Malaysia and Peninsular Malaysia. Then the peninsula is divided into east and west coasts, and East Malaysia into Sabah and Sarawak.

Population

Malaysia has a population of nearly 14 million. Malays and other indigenous people comprise 54%, Chinese 35%, Indians 10% and others 1%.

It's a reasonable approximation to say that the Malays control the government while the Chinese have their fingers on the economic pulse. Approximately 85% of the population lives in Peninsular Malaysia and the remaining 15% (a bit over two million) in the much more lightly populated states of Sabah and Sarawak.

Geography

Malaysia covers an area of 330,000 square km, 40% in Peninsular Malaysia and 60% in Sabah and Sarawak. Malaysia is densely forested, about 75% of the land area is covered with jungle, and quite mountainous. All of Malaysia is north of the equator although it runs only a short distance south of the southern tip of the peninsula and just south of the southernmost point of Sarawak.

Economy

Malaysia is a prosperous and progressive country and one of the world's major suppliers of tin, natural rubber and palm oil. Indeed, rubber plantations, interspersed with palm oil plantations, seem to cover a large part of the peninsula. In East Malaysia the economy is based on timber in Sabah while in Sarawak oil and pepper

are major exports. Malaysia is self sufficient in oil and also manages to export some. This healthy economic base contributes to Malaysia's position as one of the best-off countries in Asia – only Singapore and Japan have higher per-capita incomes.

THE STATES

Malaysia is a confederation of 13 states and a capital district of Kuala Lumpur. Nine of the peninsular states have sultans and every five years an election is held to determine which one will become the *Yang di-Pertuan Agong* or 'King' of Malaysia.

The states of Sabah and Sarawak in East Malaysia are rather different from the peninsular Malaysian states since they were separate colonies, not parts of Malaya, prior to independence. They still retain a greater degree of local administration than the peninsular states.

Johore

area: 18,984 square km
population: 1,690,000
capital: Johore Bahru
Forms the southern end of the peninsula, connected to Singapore by the causeway.

Kedah

area: 9316 square km
population: 1,210,000
capital: Alor Star
Northern state where much of Malaysia's rice is grown. The island of Langkawi is a popular resort in Kedah.

Kelantan

area: 14,758 square km
population: 860,000
capital: Kota Bahru
Northernmost east coast state, a centre of Malay culture and handicrafts.

Melaka

area: 1650 square km
population: 520,000
A small state centred around the historically important port of Melaka.

States of Peninsular Malaysia

Perak
area: 21,005 square km
population: 1,960,000
capital: Ipoh
The name means silver although the mineral which has created the state's wealth is tin. Important towns are Ipoh, Taiping, Telok Anson and Kuala Kangsar. Pangkor Island is also in Perak.

Perlis
area: 795 square km
population: 150,000
capital: Kangar
Northern border state with Thailand, smallest state in Malaysia.

Sabah
area: 72,858 square km
population: 860,000
capital: Kota Kinabalu
Malaysia's frontier state in north Borneo has the highest mountain in South-East Asia.

Sarawak
area: 121,400 square km
population: 1,294,753
capital: Kuching
North Borneo state of rivers, longhouses and colourful tribes.

Selangor
area: 8203 square km
population: 1,467,441
capital: Shah Alam
State around Kuala Lumpur which includes the satellite town Petaling Jaya.

Kuala Lumpur
area: 244 square km
population: 1,000,000
Federal capital territory.

Trengganu
area: 12,955 square km
population: 541,250
capital: Kuala Trengganu
Popular beach state of the east coast with many beautiful beaches and interesting fishing villages plus the turtle beach strip.

Negri Sembilan
area: 6,645 square km
population: 640,000
capital: Seremban
A federation of nine (negri) states in an area of Minangkabau culture.

Pahang
area: 35,960 square km
population: 750,000
capital: Kuantan
Largest state in the peninsula with varied attractions including a stretch of the east coast, most of Malaysia's hill stations and most of Taman Negara, the national park.

Penang
area: 1021 square km
population: 970,000
capital: Georgetown
The touristically popular island of Penang plus a narrow coastal strip known as Province Wellesley.

CULTURE, CRAFTS & GAMES

It's along the east coast, the predominantly Malay part of Malaysia, that you'll find

Malay crafts, culture and games at their liveliest and most widely practised.

Top Spinning – Main Gasing

Spinning tops hardly seems to be an activity for grown men to engage in but *gasing*, Malaysian tops, are not child's play. A top can weigh up to seven kg and it takes a good deal of strength to whip the five-metre cord back and spin them competitively.

Top spinning contests are held in east coast villages during the slack time of year while the rice is ripening. Contests are usually between teams of fighting tops, where the attackers attempt to dislodge the defenders from a prearranged pattern, or there are contests for length of spin. The record spinning time approaches two hours!

Kite Flying

Flying kites is another child's game that takes on man-size proportions on the east coast. Kite flying contests include events for greatest height reached and also competitions between fighting kites.

The kites, which can be up to 2½ metres wide, are real works of art. There are cat kites, bird kites and, most popular, the *wau balun* or moon kite. An attachment to the front of the kite makes a humming noise and in favourable conditions a kite may be left flying, humming pleasantly, all night. Kites are popular souvenirs of Malaysia and a stylised Kelantan kite is the symbol of Malaysian Airlines System.

Sepak Raga

One of the most popular kampung games, the equipment needed to play *sepak raga* is simplicity itself – a lightweight ball made of strips of rotan. Drawn up in a circle the opposing teams must keep the ball continuously in the air, using legs, head and shoulders. Points are scored for each time a team member hits the ball.

Sepak takraw is a version of the same game where the players hit the ball back and forth over a net just like in volleyball –

but again without using hands. It's a popular sport in a number of South-East Asian countries but the Malays are the champions.

Silat

Also known as *bersilat* this is the Malay martial art which originated in Melaka in the 15th century. Today it is a highly refined and stylised activity, demonstrations of which are often performed at ceremonies and weddings, accompanied by music from drums and gongs.

Wayang Kulit – Shadow Play

Similar to the shadow puppet performances of other South-East Asian countries, in particular Java in Indonesia, the *Wayang Kulit* retells tales from the Hindu epic the *Ramayana*.

The *To'Dalang* or 'Father of the Mysteries' sits behind the semi-transparent screen and manipulates the buffalo-hide puppets whose images are thrown onto the screen. Characters include heroes, demons, kings, animals and, ever favourites, clowns.

Performances can last for many hours and throughout that time the puppeteer has to move the figures, sing all the voice parts and conduct the orchestra – it's a feat of some endurance. There are two forms of Wayang Kulit – the *Wayang Siam* and *Wayang Melayu*. Performances often take place at weddings or after the harvest.

Dances & Other Activities

There are a variety of dances and dance dramas performed in Malaysia. *Menora* is a dance drama of Thai origin performed by an all-male cast dressed in grotesque masks.

Ma'yong is a similar traditional form of theatre but the participants are of both sexes. These performances are often made at Puja Keteks, Buddhist festivals held at temples in Kelantan, near the Thai border.

The *Ronggeng* is one of the oldest and most traditional Malay dance forms.

Rebana Kercing is a dance performed by young men to the accompaniment of tambourines. Other dances, not all of which are from the east coast, include the *Tari Piring, Hadrah* and *Zapin*.

Berdikir Barat is a comparatively recent activity – a sort of poetic debating contest where two teams have to ridicule and argue with each other in instantaneously composed verse!

Musical Instruments
As in other parts of the region Malay music is principally percussion. The large, hollowed-out log drum known as a *rebana* is one of the most important Malay instruments. Drum-beating contests are sometimes held. The *kertok* is a small drum which takes its name from the distinctive sound it makes.

Batik
Although originally an Indonesian craft, batik has made itself equally at home in Malaysia. You'll find it in Penang on the west coast but Kelantan is its true home.

Batik cloths are produced by drawing out a pattern with wax and then dyeing the material. The wax is then melted away by boiling the cloth, and a second wax design is drawn in. By repeating waxing, dyeing and boiling processes an intricate and beautifully coloured design is produced.

Batik can be found as clothes, cushion covers, tablecloths, placemats or simply as works of art. Malay designs are usually less traditional than those found in neighbouring Indonesia. The wax designs can either be drawn out on a one-off basis or printed on with a stencil.

Kain Songket & Other Weaving
A speciality of Kelantan, *kain songket* is a handwoven fabric with gold and silver threads are woven into the material. Clothes made from this beautiful fabric are usually reserved for the most important festivals and occasions. *Mengkuang* is a far more prosaic form of weaving using pandanus leaves and strips of bamboo to make baskets, bags and mats.

Silver & Brasswork
Kelantan is famed for its silverworkers who work in a variety of ways and specialise in filigree and repousse work. In the latter, designs are hammered into the silver from behind. Kampung Sireh at Kota Bahru is a centre for silverwork. Brasswork is an equally traditional skill in Kuala Trengganu.

Peninsular Malaysia – West Coast

The east and west coasts of Peninsular Malaysia are surprisingly different both in population and in geography. The west coast is more heavily populated and connected by more roads and railways. To a large extent this is a factor of geography – the west coast is lower lying and has a larger coastal plain area before the land rises up into the central mountain range. Therefore cities on the west coast were established earlier than on the east coast and roads and communications were also built and developed. It was on the west coast that tin was initially discovered and where the rubber plantations were first developed – the two mainstays of the economy. Since more of the cities are on this side of the peninsula this is also much more the 'Chinese' half of the peninsula.

JOHORE BAHRU

Capital of the state of Johore, which comprises the entire southern tip of the peninsula, Johore Bahru is the southern gateway to Peninsular Malaysia. Connected to Singapore by the 1038-metre-long causeway it inevitably suffers as a poor relation to its more glamorous neighbour. Despite its historical significance and the various points of interest in the city few travellers pause in Johore; it's just the place where you get your passport stamped on arrival or departure in Malaysia.

Johore has had a long and colourful history. When Melaka fell to the Portuguese the sultans fled to the Johore River and re-established their capital there at Johore Lama. In 1536 a Portuguese fleet attacked and sacked the town, but Johore was soon rebuilt another 30 km upriver. Further attempts also failed to destroy the Johore sultanate, but in 1866 Sultan Abu Bakar, who had been educated by the English in Singapore, moved his capital to its present location and renamed it Johore Bahru, New Johore.

Abu Bakar was a modern and progressive ruler and to this day Johore is one of Malaysia's most prosperous states.

Orientation

The road and railway across the causeway run straight into the middle of Johore Bahru through the modern shopping centre of the town. The taxi and bus stations are to the left, the railway station to the right.

A little beyond the station you turn off to the right towards the east coast, a congested trip as far as Kota Tinggi. If you're heading towards Kuala Lumpur or Melaka on the west coast then you turn off to the left almost as soon as you cross the causeway and for the first few km the road runs right along the waterfront with good views across to Singapore Island.

Istana Besar

Overlooking the straits of Johore, the Istana Besar is the main palace of the Johore royal family. It was built in Victorian style by anglophile Sultan Abu Bakar in 1866. The palace houses a collection of royal treasures and is open to the public from 9 am to 12 noon except on Fridays and public holidays.

Advance permission to visit the palace must be arranged, however, with the Controller of the Royal Household or the State Tourist Household, or with the State tourist office. Phone 073-54750, extension 30 for the latter.

Istana Gardens

The Istana Besar stands within the 53-hectare Istana Gardens which includes a fernery, orchid gardens, children's playground, Japanese gardens and a Japanese tea house. The zoo in the gardens is open from 8 am to 6 pm and admission is M$1.

Peninsular Malaysia

Other Attractions

The Abu Bakar Mosque is on Jalan Abu Bakar and was built from 1892 to 1900. The large mosque can accommodate 2000 people and overlooks the Straits of Johore.

With a 32-metre-high tower that serves as a city landmark, Bukit Serene is the actual residence of the Sultan of Johore. The Istana Bukit Serene was built in 1938.

Another city landmark is the 64-metre-high square tower of the imposing Government Offices Building on Bukit Timbalan, overlooking the city centre. The Royal Mausoleum has been the burial site of Johore's sultans since the shift from Johore Lama, but it is not open to the public. On the seafront opposite the court house the Sultan Abu Bakar Monument was erected in 1955.

Kukup

About 40 km south-west of Johore Bahru on the Straits of Melaka, across from Sumatra, is the fishing village of Kukup. The village is famous throughout Malaysia and Singapore for its seafood, especially prawns, and for its open-air restaurants, most of which are built on stilts over the water.

Next to Kukup is Kampung Air Masin (Salt Water Village), renowned for its top-quality *belacan*, shrimp paste.

Both villages are largely inhabited by Hokkien Chinese. Nowadays, Kukup is a favourite stop for package tours from Singapore and abroad. Avoid Kukup on weekends as it is full of day-trippers from Singapore.

Places to Stay – bottom end

Few visitors stay in Johore Bahru; it's too close to the greater attractions of Singapore. On the other hand Johore is an important business centre, in part due to the volume of trade carried on between

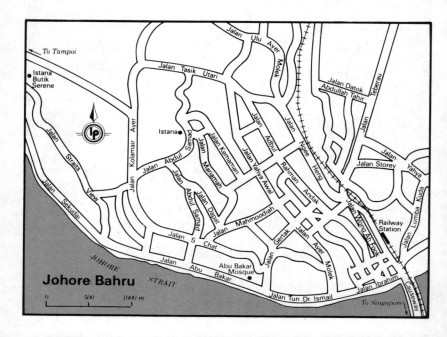

Johore Bahru

Malaysia and Singapore, so there are plenty of hotels.

At the bottom of the price scale there are a number of Chinese cheapies along Jalan Meldrum, which runs parallel to the main Jalan Tun Abdul Razak close to the causeway. The *Nam Yang* and the *Suan Fang* both have rooms for less than M$15. On Jalan Station in the Tan Chang Cheng building slightly more expensive rooms are available in the *First Hotel*.

The *Fortuna Hotel* is handy to the railway and bus terminals and has air-con rooms at M$30. The *New Asia Hotel* has doubles with fan for M$19, or with air-con for M$30. The *Top Hotel* (tel 07-224755) is a middle range place at 12 Jalan Meldrum and also on Jalan Meldrum is the *Malaya Hotel* with rooms from M$18.

Places to Stay - top end

At the other end of the price scale there's the *Johor Baharu Merlin Inn* (tel 07-228581) at 10 Jalan Bukit Meldrum with 104 rooms going for M$65 up. The *Holiday Inn Johor Baru* (tel 07-323800) is on Jalan Dato Century Garden and has 200 rooms, singles M$110 to M$130, doubles M$130 to M$150.

The *Straits View Hotel* (tel 07-224133) at 1D Jalan Scudai has singles from M$65 to M$75, doubles from M$75 to M$85. In the *Regent Elite* (tel 07-223811) at 1 Jalan Siu Nam rooms cost from M$52. The *Tropical Inn* (tel 073-221888) at Johor Tower No 15, Jalan Greja has 160 rooms with singles at M$110 to M$140, doubles M$130 to M$160.

Getting There & Away

With Singapore so close travel connections are important. Due to the hassles of crossing the causeway - customs, immigration and so on - there's a much wider selection of buses and long-distance taxis to other towns in Peninsular Malaysia from JB than there are in Singapore.

The regular bus No 170 operates every 15 minutes between JB and Queen St in Singapore; it costs 90 sen. The Johore

Bahru Express costs M$1 and its Singapore terminus is at Rochor Rd, only a stone's throw from the No 170 bus terminus. Or you can make the trip by taxi for M$4 per person. You may end up paying slightly more for a whole taxi than a party of Malays or Singaporeans would because of the extra hassles at the border.

From JB taxis cost M$7 to Ayer Hitam, M$12 to Muar, M$16 to Melaka, M$22 to Seremban, M$28 to Kuala Lumpur. Buses cost M$10 to Melaka, M$18 to Kuala Lumpur, M$26 to Ipoh, M$30 to Butterworth or M$40 all the way to Hat Yai in Thailand.

Johore Bahru's airport is some distance out of JB on the road to Melaka and KL. Air fares to Kuching and Kota Kinabalu are cheaper than from Singapore, and MAS operate an express bus service from Singapore with high-speed immigration clearance to attract you to fly from JB rather than Singapore.

JOHORE BAHRU TO MELAKA

The main road north from Johore Bahru runs to Kuala Lumpur and Melaka. It's a productive region of oil palms, rubber trees and pineapple plantations.

At Ayer Hitam, an important crossroads, you can turn left to go to Batu Pahat, Muar and Melaka; continue straight on for Segamat, Seremban and KL or alternatively for Segamat and Temerloh; or you can turn right for Keluang and Mersing on the east coast.

Ayer Hitam is a popular rest stop for buses, taxis and motorists so there are lots of small restaurants. Kampung Macap, south of Ayer Hitam, is well known for its Aw Pottery works.

Batu Pahat is a riverine town famed for its Chinese cuisine although it also has a minor reputation as a 'sin city' for jaded Singaporeans. Accommodation can be hard to find on weekends.

Muar, the second largest town in Johore, is another riverside town. Between Muar and Melaka there are a number of kampungs with traditional-style Melaka houses. Muar is a centre of traditional Malay culture, including ghazal music and the Kuda Kepang, 'prancing horse', dances. Keluang is really just a crossroads on the way to the east coast.

Mt Ophir (Gunung Legang in Malay) has a series of waterfalls and pools for swimming on one side. There's also a trail that goes a long way up. 'The falls are a lot nicer than those at Kota Tinggi and they stretch along the mountainside for a longer way', reported a visitor. Local kids camp there and leave a lot of trash. To get there take a Muar-Segamat bus and get out at the 25-mile marker or ask the conductor. It's then a km-plus walk through the plantation to the bottom of the falls.

Places to Stay
Batu Pahat In Batu Pahat the *Government Rest House* has air-conditioned doubles for M$36 or at the *Fairyland Hotel* (great name!) you can get a good large double with fan for less than M$20. The *Asia Hotel* (tel 072-43344) at 1 Jalan Omar is more expensive with rooms priced from M$30 to M$50.

Keluang In Keluang there's another *Rest House* and the *Merdeka Hotel*.

Muar In Muar there is a very good *Rest House* with a restaurant overlooking the river with air-conditioned doubles for M$35.20 or chalets for M$59.40. It is a typical Malaysian town with plenty of Chinese restaurants and hotels but no tourists.

Segamat The *Silver Inn* at 11 Jalan Ros has rooms for M$12. The *Rest House* (tel 07-917199) on Jalan Buloh Kasap has rooms for M$26. For those with a larger budget there is the expensive *Segamat Merlin Inn* (tel 07-914611) at 26 Jalan Ros. Single rooms go for M$65 to M$70 and doubles cost from M$75 to M$80.

Melaka (Malacca)

Malaysia's most historically interesting city, Melaka, has been through some dramatic events over the years. The complete series of European incursions in Malaysia – Portuguese, Dutch and English – were played out there. Yet this was an important trading port long before the first Portuguese adventurers set foot in the city.

Under the Melaka Sultanates the city was a wealthy centre of trade with China, India, Siam and Indonesia due to its strategic position on the Straits of Melaka. The Melaka sultanates were the beginning of what is today Malaysia, and old Malaysia hands say this city is where you find the soul of Malaysia.

In 1405 Admiral Cheng Ho, the 'three-jewelled eunuch prince', arrived in Melaka bearing gifts from the Ming Emperor, the promise of protection from arch-enemies (the Siamese) and, surprisingly, the Muslim religion. Chinese settlers from this earliest contact came to be known as the Babas or Straits Chinese; they are the longest-settled Chinese people in Malaysia. Despite internal squabbles and intrigues Melaka grew to be a powerful trading state and successfully repulsed Siamese attacks.

In 1509 the Portuguese, seeking trading opportunities in the east, arrived at Melaka but after an initially friendly reception, the Melakans attacked the Portuguese fleet and took a number of prisoners.

This action was the pretext for an outright assault by the Portuguese and in 1511 Alfonso d'Albuquerque took the city and the Sultan fled to Johore where he re-established his kingdom. Under the Portuguese, Melaka continued to thrive as a trading post, the fortress of A'Famosa was constructed and missionaries like the famous Francis Xavier strove to implant Christianity.

The period of Portuguese strength in the east was a short one. As Dutch influence

in Indonesia grew and Batavia, modern-day Jakarta, developed as the principal European port of the region, Melaka declined. Finally the Dutch attacked the city and in 1641 it passed into their hands after a siege lasting eight months.

The Dutch built fine public buildings and churches which today are the most solid reminders of the European presence in the city – but like their Portuguese predecessors they stayed in power only about 150 years.

In 1795 the French occupied Holland so the British, allies of the Dutch, temporarily took over administration of the Dutch colonies.

The British administrators, essentially trading men who were opposed to the Dutch policy of trade monopoly, clearly saw that the Dutch and British would be bitter rivals in Malaysia, when and if Melaka was returned. Accordingly in 1807 they commenced to demolish the fortress to ensure that if Melaka was restored to the Dutch it would be no rival to the British Malayan centres.

Fortunately Stamford Raffles, the far-sighted founder of Singapore, stepped in before these destructive policies could go too far and in 1824 Melaka was permanently ceded to the British in exchange for the Sumatran port of Bencoolen (Bengkulu today).

From that time until independence, all of Peninsular Malaysia was under British influence or control except for the period of Japanese occupation during WW II. Under the British, Melaka once more flourished as a trading centre although it was soon superseded by the growing commercial importance of Singapore.

Today it's a sleepy backwater town and no longer of any major commercial influence. It's a place of intriguing Chinese streets and antique shops, old Chinese temples and cemeteries and nostalgic reminders of the now-departed European colonial powers. The traditional Malay kampung house in the Melaka area is distinctive for its colourful arched entrance steps, examples of which can be seen along the river in east Melaka or in the Tanjung Kling district north of the city.

Information & Orientation

Melaka is a small town – easy to find your way around and compact enough to explore on foot, bicycle, or trishaw. Jalan Munshi Abdullah is the main road through Melaka and travelling on this road you could zip through Melaka thinking it was simply another noisy small Malaysian town.

The interesting and older parts of Melaka are mainly closer to the waterfront, particularly around the old Dutch-built Stadthuys (town hall) where you'll also find the GPO, tourist office (tel 06-225895) and the Dutch Christ Church.

The tourist office is open 8.45 am to 5 pm Monday through Thursday, 8.45 am to 12.15 pm and 2.45 to 5 pm on Fridays, 8.45 am to 1.30 pm on Saturdays, and 9 am to 12.30 pm on Sundays.

The long-distance taxi stand is by the bus stand, beside Jalan Munshi Abdullah, on the northern edge of the town centre.

Stadthuys

The most imposing relic of the Dutch period is the massive pink town hall which was built between 1641 and 1660. It is believed to be the oldest Dutch building in the east and is used today for government offices. It displays all the typical features of Dutch colonial architecture, including substantial solid doors and louvred windows. The other buildings around the main square, including the GPO and the old clock tower, also follow the same pink theme.

Christ Church

Between the Stadthuys and the GPO, facing one end of the square, is the bright red Christ Church. The pink bricks were brought out from Zeeland in Holland and faced with local red laterite when the church was constructed in 1753. Under the British the church was converted for Anglican use, but it still has its old Dutch tombstones laid in the floor and its massive 15-metre-long ceiling beams, each cut from a single tree.

St Paul's Church

Bukit St Paul (St Paul's Hill) rises up above the Stadthuys and on top stand the ruins of St Paul's Church. Originally built by the Portuguese in 1571 as the small 'Our Lady of the Hill' chapel, it was regularly visited by Francis Xavier. Following his death in China the saint's body was brought there and buried for nine months before being transferred to Goa in India where it remains today.

In 1556 the church was enlarged to two stories and a tower was added to the front in 1590. The church was renamed following the Dutch takeover, but with the completion of their own Christ Church at the base of the hill it fell into disuse. Under the British it lost its tower, although a lighthouse was built in front of it, and it eventually ended up as a powder magazine. The church has been in ruins now for 150 years, but the setting is beautiful, the walls imposing and fine old Dutch tombstones stand around the interior.

Porta de Santiago

Raffles may have stepped in before the complete destruction of the old Portuguese fortress, but it was a near thing. All that was left was the main gate to A'Famosa, the Porta de Santiago. Curiously this sole surviving relic of the old fort originally constructed by Alfonso d'Albuquerque bears the Dutch East India Company's coat of arms. This was part of the fort which the Dutch reconstructed in 1670 following their takeover. The gate stands at the base of Residency Hill and a path leads up behind it to St Paul's Church.

Melaka National Museum

Housed in a typical Dutch house dating

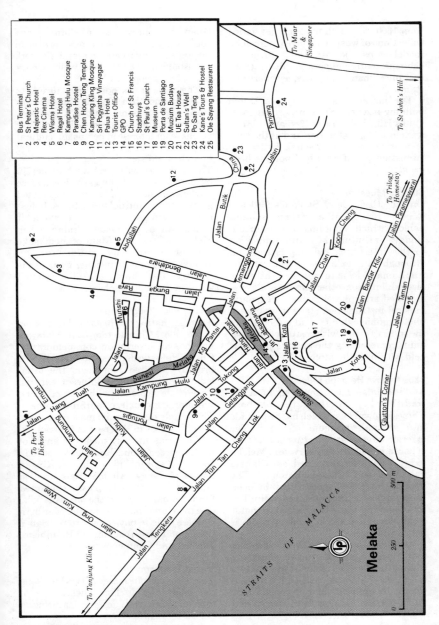

1 Bus Terminal
2 St Peter's Church
3 Majestic Hotel
4 Rex Cinema
5 Wisma Hotel
6 Regal Hotel
7 Kampung Hulu Mosque
8 Paradise Hostel
9 Chen Hoon Teng Temple
10 Kampung Kling Mosque
11 Sri Pogyatha Vinayagar
12 Palua Hotel
13 Tourist Office
14 GPO
15 Church of St Francis
16 Stadthuys
17 St Paul's Church
18 Museum
19 Porta de Santiago
20 Muzium Budaya
21 UE Tea House
22 Sultan's Well
23 Po San Teng
24 Kane's Tours & Hostel
25 Ole Sayang Restaurant

Melaka

STRAITS OF MALACCA

To Muar & Singapore
To St John's Hill
To Trilogy Parameswara
To Port Dickson
To Tanjung Kling

Jalan Panjang
Jalan Chiru
Jalan Bukit
Jalan Temenggong
Jalan Koon Cheng
Jalan Bandar Hilir
Jalan Taman
Jalan Kota
Glutton's Corner
Jalan Chan
Jalan Abdullah
Jalan Bendahara
Jalan Bunga Raya
Jalan Munshi
Jalan Hang Tuah
Jalan Kampung Empat
Jalan Kampung Bunduang
Jalan Ong Kim Wee
Jalan Tengkara
Jalan Portugis
Jalan Kubu
Jalan Tun Tan Cheng Lok
Jalan Tun Tan
Jalan Tokong
Jalan Gelanggang
Jalan Kg Pantai
Jalan Hang Jebat
Jalan Hang Lekir
Jalan Hang Kasturi
Jalan Laksamana
Jalan Kota
Jalan Kg Hulu

Sungai Melaka

500 m
250
0

from 1660, the small museum has varied collections of weapons, knives, porcelain, model ships and fish traps, furniture, cabinets, early maps and illustrations, costumes, shadow puppets, jewellery and stamps.

The museum is housed in a Dutch building near the Stadthuys, next to St Paul's Hill. For most of 1986 and 1987, it was closed for restoration and at the time of writing the new opening hours and admission fee, if any, had not yet been decided.

Cultural Museum

On the other side of St Paul's Hill is a wooden replica of a Melaka sultan's palace which contains the Muzium Budaya or Cultural Museum. Admission to this interesting building is free and although the exhibits concentrate on traditional Melakan culture, there are also exhibits from other parts of Malaysia. Included are apparel, games, weaponry, musical instruments, stone inscriptions, photographic exhibits, and a diorama of the sultan's court, with costumed mannequins representing the various positions held within the hierarchy.

Baba-Nyonya Heritage Museum

At 48-50 Jalan Tun Tan Cheng Lock is a traditional *peranakan* (Straits-born Chinese) townhouse which has been made into a small museum of sorts. The exterior-interior architecture of this type of house, of which many survive in Melaka today, has been described as 'Chinese Palladian' and 'Chinese Baroque'. The interiors of these houses contain open courtyards which admit sun and rain. The interior of the house is arranged so that it looks like a typical 19th century nyonya-baba residence.

It is owned by a baba family who conduct tours of the house. Furniture consists of Chinese hardwoods fashioned in a mixture of Chinese, Victorian, and Dutch designs with mother-of-pearl inlay. 'Nyonya Ware', multi-coloured designs from Jiangxi and Guangzhou provinces in China made specifically for Straits Chinese, is also on display. Nyonya ceramics and tilework are usually a blend of pinks, yellows, dark blues, and greens.

The museum is open from 10 am to 12.30 pm and 2 to 4.30 pm. Admission is a steep M$7, which includes a good 45-minute tour of the house, well worth it if you have an interest in peranakan culture.

Church of St Peter

This unexceptional church was built in 1710 by descendants of the early Portuguese settlers and has some interesting stained glass windows and old tombstones. It does not get much use for most of the year but it comes alive on Good Friday when Melakans flock here. Many of them make the occasion an excuse for an annual trip home from other parts of the country. The church is still associated with the Portuguese church in Macau.

Cheng Hoon Teng Temple

This fascinating temple on Jalan Tokong is the oldest Chinese temple in Malaysia and has an inscription commemorating Cheng Ho's epochal visit to Melaka. The brightly coloured roof bears the usual assortment of mythical Chinese creatures. Entered through massive hardwood doors, the interior is equally colourful and ornate. The temple's ceremonial mast rises above the old houses in this part of Melaka.

The name literally means 'Temple of the Evergreen Clouds' and was founded in 1645 by Kapitan China Lee Wei King, a native of Amoy. All materials used in building the original temple were imported from China, as were the artisans who designed and built it in the southern Chinese style to pay respect to the San Y Chiao, or Three Teachings of Buddhism, Taoism, and Confucianism.

Masjid Tengkera

This 150-year-old mosque, two km along the road towards Port Dickson, is of typical Sumatran design, featuring a square, cake-layered look. In its graveyard is the tomb of the Sultan of Johore who, in 1819, signed over the island of Singapore to Stamford Raffles. The Sultan later retired to Melaka where he died in 1853. Get there on bus No 18 from Jalan Kubu.

Bukit China

In the mid-1400s the Sultan of Melaka's ambassador to China returned with the Ming Emperor's daughter to wed the Sultan and thus seal relations between the two countries. She brought with her a vast retinue, including 500 handmaidens, and Bukit China ('China Hill') was established as their residence. It has been a Chinese area ever since and, together with two adjoining hills, forms a Chinese graveyard covering over 60 hectares which is said to be the largest in the world outside China itself. Some of the ornate graves date back to the Ming dynasty, but unhappily most of them are now in a sorry state.

Chinese graveyards are often built on hillsides because the bulk of the hill shields the graves from evil winds while at the same time the spirits get a good view of what their descendants are up to down below. In our more space-conscious modern world Chinese graves are gradually losing their spacious and expansive traditional design.

Po San Teng & Sultan's Well

Cheng Ho, apart from his real-life role as an admiral and ambassador, is also religiously venerated and this temple is dedicated to him as Po San. Built in 1795, it's at the foot of Bukit China and nearby is the Sultan's Well. The well is said to date back to the founding of Melaka in the 14th century by Raja Iskander Shah. Cheng Ho drank from the well, legends relate, after which its water became incredibly pure and taking a drink would ensure a visitor's return to the city. Today the water is visibly impure and tossing a coin into the well is the recommended way of ensuring a return trip.

Old Melaka

The old part of Melaka is a fascinating area to wander around. Although Melaka has long lost its importance as a port, ancient-looking junks still sail up the river and moor at the banks. Today, however, their cargo is not the varied treasures of the east, but simply mundane charcoal for the cooking fires of the city. There's a good view of the river and boats from the bridge beside the tourist office.

You may still find some of the treasures of the east in the antique shops scattered along Jalan Gelanggang, formerly known as Jonkers St. You'll find a whole assortment of interesting shops and the odd Chinese or Hindu temple or mosque squeezed into this intriguing old street. Melaka is famed for its antique shops and there are several along the street which are worth a leisurely browse.

The Sri Pogyatha Vinoyagar Moorthi Temple, dating from 1781, and the Sumatran-style Kampung Kling Mosque are both in this area. Jalan Tun Tan Cheng Lock, running parallel to Jalan Gelanggang, is also worth a stroll.

River Trips

The tourist centre sponsors two riverboat tours of Melaka which leave from the quay behind the tourist centre. One trip takes 45 minutes, costs M$5, and passes through the downtown area, a few small riverside fish markets and a Malay kampung with traditional Melaka-style houses.

The second trip takes 1½ hours, costs M$10, and adds a trip along the coast to the Portuguese kampung near Medan Portugis. They're not very exciting trips – the high point might be an iguana sighting at the side of the river.

Other Attractions

Although the British demolished most of Fort Santiago they left the small Dutch fort of St John untouched. It stands on a hilltop a little to the east of town, but there's not much to be seen.

A little beyond the fort is the area

known as the Portuguese Eurasian settlement. In this small kampung there are about 500 descendants of marriages which took place between the colonial Portuguese and Malays 400 years ago. There's little of interest for the visitor there except for the cultural shows on Saturday nights at 8 pm at Medan Portugis or Portuguese Square, when Chinese, Portuguese, Indian and Malay cultural ensembles perform for free.

Melaka's beaches offer little attraction either. Tanjung Kling and, a little further out, Tanjung Bidara are the main beaches but the Straits of Melaka have become increasingly polluted over the years and it's worst around Melaka itself. There are also occasional plagues of jellyfish.

The small island of Pulau Besar, a little south of Melaka, is a popular weekend joyride – there are boats operating across from Umbai near Melaka. On a clear day you can see Sumatra from Tanjung Kling – it's only about 50 km away.

Festivals
Major festivals in Melaka include the Good Friday and Easter Sunday processions at St Peter's and the feast in June in honour of the patron saint of fishermen at the same church.

The nationwide bathing festival known as Mandi Safar is exuberantly celebrated at Tanjung Kling during the Muslim month of Safar – usually April.

Places to Stay – bottom end
Melaka At the bottom end of the price scale Melaka has a wide variety of places to choose from although some budget travellers prefer to head 15 km north to the places at Tanjung Kling.

In the town itself you can start at basic and bare doss houses like the *Tong Ah* at 16 Kee Ann Rd where rooms cost from just M$9. Better but at the same rates (M$9 to M$12) is *London Hotel* on Jalan Ong Kim Wee. Both of these have common baths only. Another good one is *Cheng Hoe* (tel 2226102), opposite the Kampung Kling

mosque at 26 Jalan Tokong, where singles are M$9.45, doubles M$12.60; they also have air-con rooms with private baths from M$16.80 to M$21.

Better standards can be found for a few dollars more (M$14 to M$22) at the *Hotel Hong Kong*, 154A Jalan Bunga Raya or a few doors down at the *Hotel Ng Fook* (tel 06-228055) at 154H. However, these latter two also specialise in short-time business.

Close by at 100-105 Jalan Munshi Abdullah the *Cathay Hotel* (tel 223744) is quiet and comfortable with singles from M$14. Or there's the *Federal Hotel* (tel 06-222161) at 60B Jalan Bendahara and the *Valiant Hotel* (tel 06-222323) a few doors down at 41B with rooms from M$14.

The *Malacca Hotel* (tel 06-222325) at 27A Jalan Munshi Abdullah has singles for M$20 – good rooms with fan and attached bathroom. The staff are friendly but the cinema next door and its car park can be noisy at night. Across the road at No 22 the *Hotel Belangi* is fairly quiet and rooms with bath and fan are M$14 to M$18. Air-conditioned rooms are available at both these hotels for around M$25.

The *Central Hotel* on Jalan Bendahara used to be good value but has become more and more of a brothel over the years. The *May Chiang Hotel* on Jalan Munshi Abdullah has similarly low prices (M$10 up), better facilities and friendly proprietors. Several travellers have written to confirm what a pleasant shoestring place this is.

About 20 minutes out of town on the road to Tanjung Kling is the *Westernhay Hotel*, an old colonial-style place with large fan-cooled rooms from M$16. With a private bath, rooms are around $22, and there are also a couple of more expensive air-con rooms. Downstairs there is a dining room that serves simple western breakfasts. Being well off the road toward the beach in the shade of tall trees, this is one of the most economical choices for peace and quiet. Frequent buses to and from the town centre pass the hotel.

Tanjung Kling Melaka's sometime travellers' centre is in the Tanjung Kling area, where you'll find a string of places in every price range. Most are somewhat basic – little more than a mattress on bare boards and not that clean. Once again Malaysian beach accommodation proves to be quite miserable value when compared with Thailand or Bali, although it seems to be improving a bit.

Approximately nine km from Melaka's town centre is the *Melaka Beach Bungalow & Youth Hostel* (tel 06-512935) at 7379C Spring Gardens, just off the road to Pantai Kundor. It can be a little difficult to find but if you call ahead Mr Gan, the proprietor, will look out for you on the main road. He will refund the bus fare (60 sen) out to TK or the taxi fare if you take a room.

The hostel is in a large modern house in a quiet neighbourhood, a few metres from the Straits of Melaka. Dorm beds are M$3.50 a day, singles cost M$8 and doubles are M$12. There are a couple of air-con rooms for M$28 and M$35. Free lockers are provided and there are discounts for longer stays. To get there, take a Patt Hup bus No 41, 42, 43, 44, 46, 47, 49, 51, 52, 53, 54 or 55.

A few km north of the Spring Gardens area, there is a turn-off for Pantai Kundor, the main beach area in Tanjung Kling. You'll pass Shah's Beach Resort (see top end accommodation) and then come to *Motel Tanjung Kling*, which is set right on the beach with a nice sea view and a breezy seaside restaurant. Even though the rooms are not all that special the rates are M$22 for ordinary rooms and M$33 for air-con – just a bit overpriced.

Next there is a row of tumble-down shacks. Whether they are open or not depends on the number of travellers passing through. *SHM* at the southern end of Pantai Kundor has dark single/double huts for M$5/7 or M$10/13 for rooms in a longhouse.

Next is *Yashica Traveller Hostel*, which at the time of writing was the best budget place on Pantai Kundor. Rooms are M$6 per person without bath and M$10 with bath. The restaurant is built right over the beach so that during high tide waves are lapping under your feet. The food at Yashica is cheap and quite tasty and in fact this is a favourite among locals who go there for sunset drinks. They serve the travellers' staples like banana pancakes and salads. They also rent bicycles for M$2 a day.

After Yashica, it's slim pickings – the *Hawaii, Rasa Sayang* and *Sunset* are all on-again off-again, with extremely basic huts at M$5/8 for a single/double. There are, however, several inexpensive seafood restaurants along the north end of Pantai Kundor (see Places to Eat). It is also worth wandering through the local kampungs.

To get to Tanjung Kling take bus No 51 (60 sen) from Melaka. A word of caution – there have been hints of the old Batu Ferringhi-style immigration hassles here although the place has now become quite

Tanjung Kling

well established. It's also somewhat plagued by Malaysia's peeping toms – 'I had to make a couple of surprise night sorties with a solid stick in hand to deter them from prowling around our hut', wrote one visitor.

Hostels Melaka boasts four traveller-oriented hostels with a fifth one to open soon near the bus terminal. The *Paradise Hostel* 4 Jalan Tengkera, is just after the Jalan Kubu intersection on the way north. Dorm accommodation is M$5, singles cost M$8 or M$12 with private bath, and doubles for M$10 or M$15 with bath.

It is a clean and spacious hostel that was once a small hospital. There are 19 rooms and 12 bathrooms. Coffee and tea are free all day. You can have free use of a gas burner, refrigerator and laundry facilities though the staff will do moderate amounts of laundry for you without charge. The proprietors are a young Indian family who are very friendly, helpful and well-organised. The hostel is within walking distance of all the historic sites and many cheap restaurants.

To get there from the Melaka bus terminal, walk west to Jalan Hang Tuah, turn left and walk until you come to a traffic circle, then bear right and walk down Jalan Kubu until it ends at Jalan Tengkera and turn right – the hostel is just a few metres from the corner. It's about a 10-minute walk in all or you can take a trishaw for M$1 to M$2 per person.

The *Trilogy Budget Homestay* is a little out of town on the south side toward Medan Portugis. Their official address is 218-A Jalan Parameswara, though most street signs name this street Jalan Bandar Hilir. To get there from the bus station, take a town bus No 17 for 40 sen and get off at the big convent school on the left. The hostel is across the street on the 2nd floor of a modern shophouse. Rates are basically the same as at Paradise, but there aren't as many rooms.

Kane's Tours & Hostel (tel 06-235124) is at 136A/1 Jalan Panjang. The rates are much the same as the other hostels in Melaka; M$5 for a dorm bed and rooms from M$10.

The *Old City Youth Hostel* at 332 Jalan Kilang, next to the Melaka bus terminal is on the premises of the Livo Hotel, which has closed down. Dorm beds are only M$2.50 and rooms M$12 or M$15 with attached bath. The proprietors of the Old City Youth Hostel also run the Melaka Beach Bungalow & Youth Hostel in Tanjung Kling.

Places to Stay – middle
Best of the places bridging the bottom-to-top gap is the *Majestic Hotel* (tel 06-222455) at 188 Jalan Bunga Raya with rooms at around M$15 to M$20; or with air-con and attached bathroom at M$30 to M$35. This well-kept place is built in true Chinese hotel-style with a central lounge, and it's also well back from the street. Their cheaper rooms are not very good.

The *Wisma Hotel* (tel 06-228311) at the corner of Jalan Munshi Abdullah and Jalan Bendahara has rooms from M$22.

Finally two more middle range places with air-con are the *Lotus Inn* (tel 06-227011) at 2846 Jalan Semabok and the *Sentosa Hotel* (tel 06-228222) further out of town on the north side at 92 Jalan Bachang. The Sentosa, along with the nearby *Dragon* and *Bachang*, cost M$30 to M$40 and are favoured among Malay travellers.

Places to Stay – top end
Melaka The relatively new *Malacca Village Resort* (tel 06-313600) is at Ayer Keroh. It has 160 rooms, all air-con, with singles at M$140 and doubles from M$160 to M$180. There's a swimming pool and all the other usual mod cons.

Other more expensive hotels in town include the *Palace Hotel* (tel 06-25115) at 201 Jalan Munshi Abdullah on the Muar side of town. Singles run M$45 to M$58, doubles M$55 to M$68, all air-con. Even more central at 66 Jalan Munshi

Abdullah, the *Regal Hotel* (tel 06-22282) is cheaper at M$38/48 for singles/doubles. It's quite livable although the rooms are a bit drab and the floors below the noisy bar-restaurant should be avoided.

Then there's the ever-present *Merlin Inn* (tel 06-240777) on Jalan Munshi Abdullah with swimming pool and modern air-con rooms from M$70. More luxurious is the *Ramada Renaissance* (tel 06-248888 on Jalan Bendahara where rooms start at M$95. Ask for a discount – it often works. Melaka's top of the top end is the *City Bayview*, newly built in 1987, opposite the Ramada. Rooms start at about M$100.

The *Malacca Straits Inn* on the waterfront at Jalan Bandar Hilir has closed down as has the *Admiral Hotel* on Jalan Mata Kuching.

Tanjung Kling Just as with the bottom-end hotels there are also a couple of top-end places at Tanjung Kling. One is the delightful beachfront *Shah's Beach Motel* (tel 06-226202) about 10 km north at the 6½ milestone, Tanjung Kling. There are 50 chalets built around a central swimming pool with costs of M$85 for the poolside chalets, M$50 for the rest. There's a pleasant open-air bar and restaurant and it's a very relaxing place to stay although the sea is not clean enough for swimming and you really need a vehicle to get back and forth to the city.

At milestone 10 at the northern end of Pantai Kundor opposite the beach is *Chalet El-Kundor* (tel 06-511015) where for M$35 you get a modern bungalow with a living room, bedroom, kitchen, bathroom with hot water, verandah – and a powerful Japanese stereo! There are only four of them so you should call ahead. At milestone 10½ is the overpriced *Pantai Ria*, where a concrete cell is M$25 – possibly a short-time place.

Places to Eat
All the larger hotels (Wisma, Regal, Palace) have air-con restaurants or coffee lounges with a predilection for fixed-price lunches or dinners in 'English style' for M$6 to M$10. Just the thing if you want soup, chicken & chips and dessert.

Melaka's real eating centre is along the waterfront on Jalan Taman, across from the museum and Porta de Santiago. At night the assortment of stalls along there are all in action and the area is known locally as *Glutton's Corner*. All the usual food centre specialities can be found and some of them are also open at lunch time. Different places to try include the *Bunga Raya Restaurant* which has excellent steamed crabs, the *Sri Pattani* serves Muslim Thai food, and several of the stalls make good oyster omelettes.

Business has been slackening of late since the city started it's land reclamation project – the stalls now face a wooden wall painted with waves rather than the sea. When the walls come down there will be modern development projects.

There are plenty of other food stalls around Melaka. In Lorong Bendahara in particular there are quite a few, including a good steamboat stall, opposite the Rex Cinema on Jalan Bunga Raya. Next to the Capital Theatre the *Capital Restaurant* has great Chinese food for M$5 a dish.

Amongst Melaka's many other restaurants and cafes two worth trying out are the *Tai Chong Hygienic Ice Cafe* at 39/72 Jalan Bunga Raya where a wide variety of ice cream dishes and snacks are available, and the *UE Tea House*, 20 Lorong Bukit China, which is a great place for a dim sum breakfast with prices from 50 sen per plate.

The *Silver Dollar*, at 305 Taman Melaka Raya off Jalan Parameswara (Jalan Bandar Hilir) towards the sea, has western pub food and beer. At night they feature live music, usually country & western. Melaka is famous for its C&W musicians, who are almost always of Portuguese descent. The city actually exports Portuguese-Malay musicians to towns all over Malaysia as well as to Singapore.

The best popiah in Melaka comes from the stall at the end of Jalan Tun Tan Cheng Lock, not far from the Paradise Hostel. The *Ole Sayang* at 193 Jalan Taman Melaka Jaya has good nyonya food for medium to high prices in an air-con dining room. Hours are 11.30 am to 2.30 pm and 6 to 9.30 pm.

Near the intersection of Jalan Temenggong and Jalan Bendahara in the city centre are a few south Indian daun pisang restaurants. The *Sri Krishna Bavan* and *Sri Lakshmi Vilas* are next door to each other on Jalan Bendahara while the *Restoran Veni* is around the corner on Jalan Temenggong. All three offer about the same quality and prices – roti chanai for 50 sen, banana-leaf rice plates for $2 and up.

Finally there's Medan Portugis, Portuguese Square, where you can sample Malay-Portuguese cuisine at tables facing the sea. Prices average around M$6 per entree. One of the best dishes is the baked fish – ask for syakap, one of the tastier local fish, prepared with a tangy red sauce. The best night to eat there is Saturday when they have free cultural performances at 8 pm.

Just outside the square are a couple of Malay-Portuguese restaurants, the *San Pedro* and the *San Juang*. The food is similar to what you find in the square but the atmosphere is more intimate.

On the road between Melaka and Tanjung Kling are a couple of large outdoor Chinese seafood restaurants, the *Seaview* and *Lucky*. There are several smaller seafood places along Pantai Kundor in Tanjung Kling. At night they're often full of Malays from the nearby kampungs – most popular ones are *Gerai Mesraria* and *Roti John* in the middle of the beach.

Further on are more seaside restaurants and a couple of small fish markets where you can select fish to take back to your beach bungalow kitchen.

Getting There & Away

Melaka is 149 km from KL, 216 km from Johore Bahru and just 90 km from Port Dickson. You can fly to Melaka from KL or Johore Bahru.

There is no railway line to Melaka, but there are plenty of buses and long-distance taxis. From KL it's M$5.20 by bus (M$6.50 with air-con), M$13 by taxi. If for any reason you can't get a direct KL-Melaka bus it's usually easy to go to Seremban and change there.

A Melaka to Singapore bus costs M$9 (M$11 air-con). From Melaka the buses run from the Central Omnibus Station on Jalan Kilang.

Johore Bahru to Melaka taxis cost M$15. Buses cost M$1.70 to Muar, M$1.45 to Tampin, M$3.30 to Port Dickson, M$14.50 to Ipoh, M$22 to Butterworth, M$7.50 to Keluang, M$19 to Kuala Trengganu, M$25 all the way to Kota Bahru. A taxi to Muar is M$3.20, to Batu Pahat M$6.50 or to Seremban M$5.80. The bus and taxi stands are off Jalan Hang Tuah, just across the river.

You can also travel to Melaka by ferry from Dumai, Sumatra. Ferries leave once a week – from Dumai each Saturday at 10 am, reaching Melaka at 1 pm and from Melaka back to Dumai at the same hour on Thursdays. Fare is M$80 one-way or M$150 return. You can book tickets at Atlas Travel Service (tel 06-220777) on Jalan Hang Jebat in Melaka.

Getting Around

A bicycle rickshaw is the ideal way of getting around compact and slow-moving Melaka. By the hour they should run about M$7 or M$2 for any one-way trip within the town.

You can easily walk around the central sights or rent a bike from one of the hostels for M$2 a day. To get out to Tanjung Kling take a No 51 Patt Hup bus; the fare is 60 sen.

AROUND MELAKA

There are many fine old Minangkabau-style houses around Melaka. Note the characteristic 'buffalo horn' roof shape, the verandah and lower-level 'pre-verandah' or *anjong*. The steps which lead up to the sometimes intricately carved wooden houses are often decorated with beautiful tiles.

About 40 km south of Port Dickson is the small town of Pengkalan Kempas. Just a short distance on the Lubok China or Melaka side of town a sign indicates the grave of Sheikh Ahmad Majnun, about 100 metres off the road. This local hero died in 1467 and beside his grave, which is sheltered by a structure in the final stages of complete collapse, are three two-metre-high stones standing upright in the ground.

These mysterious stones, known as the sword, the spoon and the rudder, are thought to be older than the grave itself. Immediately in front of the grave is another stone with a hole through it. The circular opening is said to tighten up on the arm of any liar foolish enough to thrust it through.

TANJUNG BIDARA

About 20 km north-west of Melaka on the way to Port Dickson is Tanjung Bidara, one of the west coast's better beach areas. There is a large public beach with toilet and shower facilities, as well as numerous food stalls.

The only accommodation is the rather exclusive *Tanjung Bidara Beach Resort* (tel 06-512201) with its modern chalets and motel, lounge and swimming pool. From Sunday through Thursday rooms in the motel cost M$50 single or double occupancy and chalets are M$70 to M$85. A two-bedroom chalet for four people is M$110. On weekends add M$30.

PORT DICKSON

There's nothing of great interest in Port Dickson itself although it's a pleasant enough small port town. South of the town, however, there is a fine stretch of beach extending for 17 km to Cape Rachado.

There are a number of places to stay along the beach and it's an interesting walk along the coast to the cape.

Originally built by the Portuguese in the 16th century the lighthouse offers fine views along the coast – on a clear day you can see Sumatra, 38 km away across the Straits of Melaka.

The turn-off to the lighthouse is just beyond the 9th milestone, or it's just a short stroll along the beach from the Pantai Motel. Officially you need permission from the Marine Department at the end of the pier in Melaka if you want to ascend the lighthouse.

Places to Stay

There's no reason to stay in Port Dickson unless you stay on the beach, so the hotels in and close to the town itself can be discounted. The beach stretches south of Port Dickson for 16 km to Cape Rachado, but the best beach starts from around the 5th milestone (eight km).

The *Port Dickson Youth Hostel* is on a hill above the road at 3¾ miles. It attracts few visitors although it costs just M$2.50 for the first night, M$2 thereafter. There are a number of food stalls beside the road below it. The *Sunshine Rotary Club* at M$7 as a nice and basic sort of place.

At the 7th milestone *Si Rusa Inn* (tel 06-405244) is a large establishment right by the beach with 220 doubles plus 120 chalets. Rooms cost M$60/66 for singles/ doubles during the week, about twice that on weekends. The *Ming Court Beach Hotel* (tel 06-405244) has 165 rooms with singles from M$110 to M$120, doubles from M$130 to M$140.

At the 8th milestone there are a couple of Chinese hotels. The *Lido Hotel* (tel 06-405273) has rooms at less than M$30, more with air-con. The nearby *Kong Ming Hotel* (tel 06-795239) has some smaller rooms for a few dollars less and some chalets at rather higher prices. This bit of beach is a popular stretch for local holiday-makers and there are food and drink stalls along the beach.

Finally there's another clump of places to stay right at the 9th milestone. You have to follow a dirt road for several hundred metres off the main road to get to the *Pantai Motel* (tel 06-405265) which has a variety of rooms and chalets. They have A, B, C, and D classes of accommodation, starting at M$28.75 for a class D room on a weekday (M$40.25 on weekends and public holidays) and going up to M$64.40 for a class A air-con chalet with bathroom (M$80.50 weekends and holidays). Extra beds in a room or chalet are M$11.50 for adults, M$5.75 for children. It's a quiet, grassy place with steps down to the beach below.

Nearby is the *Holiday Inn* and the *Halcyon Guest House*. From there it's only a short walk along the beach to Cape Rachado; you can see the top of the lighthouse through the trees.

Getting There & Away

Port Dickson is 94 km south of KL, only 34 km south of Seremban and 90 km north of Melaka. You can get there by taxi or bus from any of these places. By bus it's M$3.30 from Melaka, M$3.70 from KL. A taxi would be about M$6.50 from either town. On Sundays only there is a train-bus excursion available from KL – the train leaves at 7.50 am and returns at 5.20 pm and the trip takes two hours via Seremban. From Port Dickson there's a connecting bus which will drop you off anywhere along the beach.

SEREMBAN

South of Kuala Lumpur, Seremban is the capital of Negri Sembilan or 'Nine States' – a group of small Malay lands united by the British. This is the centre of the Minangkabau area of Malaysia. Originating in Sumatra, the Minangkabau people have a matrilineal system whereby inheritance passes through the female rather than the male line. They take their name from the unique architecture of their buildings where the roof sweeps up at each end like buffalo horns or 'minangkabau'.

The small state museum is a good example of Minangkabau architecture. Originally the home of a Malay prince, it was brought to its present location and reassembled in the lake area which overlooks the commercial part of town. Traditionally Minangkabau houses were built entirely without nails.

The museum, is open from 9.30 am to 12 noon and 2 to 5.30 pm daily (9.30 am to 1 pm on Wednesdays, 9.30 am to 6 pm on holidays), and houses a small collection of ceremonial weapons and other regalia.

Lower down towards the town is the new state mosque with its nine pillars symbolising the nine states of Negri Sembilan. Nearby is a huge A&W hamburger drive-in to prove Seremban is really in the 20th century!

Places to Stay

The bustling streets of Seremban have the usual varied assortment of Chinese hotels. The *Ruby Hotel* (tel 06-75201) at 39 Jalan Leman has rooms with and without air-con from less than M$20. The *Carlton Hotel* (tel 06-725336) at 47 Jalan Tuan Sheikh has singles at around M$20, doubles from M$35. The cheaper *Tong Fong* (tel 06-73022) on Birch Rd has rooms as low as M$12. The *Ria Hotel* (tel 06-287744) at Jalan Tetamu is more expensive with singles/doubles at M$85/95.

The *International New Hotel* (tel 06-714957) at 126 Jalan Veloo has rooms in the M$14 to M$25 range.

There are all sorts of restaurants, including the previously mentioned *A&W* drive-in.

Getting There & Away

Seremban is 62 km south of Kuala Lumpur connected by the same modern highway that now extends to Melaka. From KL there are frequent buses (M$2.50) and taxis (M$5). It's a further 34 km south to Port Dickson or 82 km to Melaka.

AROUND SEREMBAN

Kajang, about 20 km south of Kuala Lumpur on the Seremban-Kuala Lumpur

Top: Federal Secretariat, Kuala Lumpur (TW)
Bottom: Railway station, Kuala Lumpur (JC)

Top: Chinese temple, Kuala Lumpur (ST)
Left: Railway station, Kuala Lumpur (MC)
Right: Downtown Kuala Lumpur (MC)

route, is said to have the best satay in all of Malaysia. If your mealtime is approaching it's worth stopping.

If you want to study more Minangkabau architecture take a bus from Seremban east towards Kuala Pilah. Get off eight to 10 km out where there are many traditional houses on both sides of the road. Pantai and Nilai, a short distance north-east of Seremban, also have Minangkabau houses.

Kuala Pilah, 40 km east of Seremban, has an interesting old Chinese temple on Jalan Lister near the bus station. Seri Menanti, 16 km from Kuala Pilah, has a palace or istana in Minangkabau style and also a royal mosque. The central pillars of the istana are impressively carved.

Kuala Lumpur

Malaysia's capital city is a curious blend of the old and new. On one hand it's a modern and fast moving city although the traffic never takes on the nightmare proportions of Bangkok. It has gleaming high-rise office blocks beside multi-lane highways, but the old colonial architecture still manages to stand out proudly. It's also a blend of cultures – the Malay capital with a vibrant Chinatown, an Indian quarter and a playing field in the middle of the city where the crack of cricket bat on ball can still be heard.

KL, as it's almost always called, came into being in the 1860s when a band of prospectors in search of tin landed at the meeting point of the Kelang and Gombek Rivers, and named the place Kuala Lumpur – 'Muddy Estuary'. More that half of those first arrivals were to die of malaria and other tropical diseases, but the tin they discovered in Ampang attracted more miners and KL quickly became a brawling, noisy, violent boom town.

As in other parts of Malaysia the local Sultan appointed a 'Kapitan China' to bring the unruly Chinese fortune seekers

into line – a problem which Yap Ah Loy jumped at with such ruthless relish that he became known as the founder of KL.

In the 1880s successful miners and merchants began to build fine homes along Jalan Ampang, the British resident Frank Swettenham pushed through a far-reaching new town plan and in 1886 a railway line linked KL to Port Kelang.

The town has never looked back and now it's not only the business and commercial capital of Malaysia, but also the political capital. Today with a population of nearly one million it is also the largest city in Malaysia .

Orientation

Just to the south of the confluence of those muddy rivers from which KL takes its name is the modern business centre of KL and the older Chinatown – they simply merge into each other. Across the Kelang River is the railway station and the modern National Mosque.

Starting from the important central junction of Jalan Tuanku Abdul Rahman and Jalan Tun Perak, if you continue along Jalan Tun Perak away from the river you'll end up on Jalan Pudu where you'll find the huge Pudu Raya bus and taxi station.

A left turn will take you into Jalan Bukit Bintang where there's a number of popular mid-range hotels, another left turn leads to Jalan Sultan Ismail and several of KL's top-end hotels and one more left turn brings you into the historic Jalan Ampang. The latter takes you back to your starting point of Jalan Tun Perak.

Turn the other way from that central junction and head up Jalan Tuanku Abdul Rahman (still often referred to as Batu Rd and henceforth known as Jalan Tuanku etc). It runs one-way the wrong way, but there are a number of KL's popular cheaper hotels and more modern buildings along there. The student travel office is in the South-East Asia Hotel at the far end of the road.

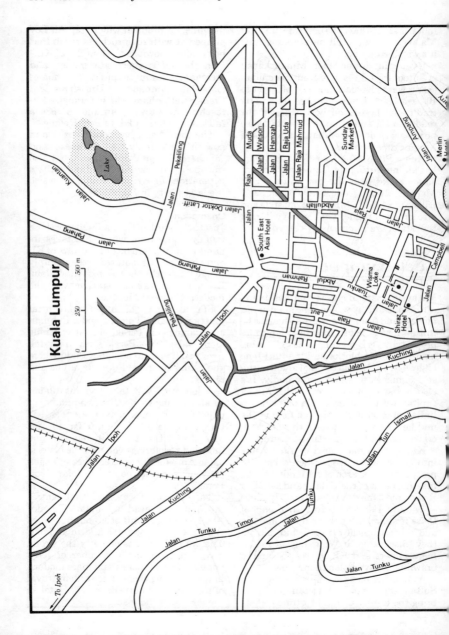

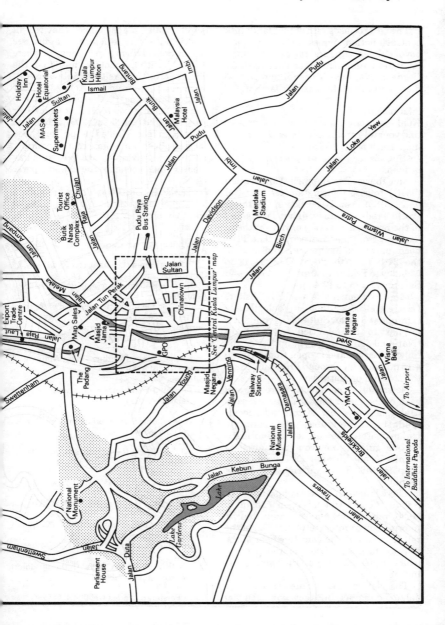

The GPO is just south of that landmark central junction. Across the Kelang River, beyond the mosque and railway station, is KL's green belt where you can find the Lake Gardens, National Museum and Monument and the Malaysian Parliament.

Information

Kuala Lumpur is a relatively easy city to find your way around. It's large but not too large and it never gets overly congested, so getting from place to place is rarely arduous.

The Tourist Development Corporation (TDC) tourist information counter (tel 03-2935188) is on Level two of the Putra World Trade Centre on Jalan Tun Ismail in the north-east section of KL – rather a long way from the town centre. The TDC headquarters is in the same building on the 24th to 27th floors. They're open Monday to Friday, 8.30 am to 4.45 pm and Saturday 8 am to 12.45 pm.

More convenient is the KL Visitors Centre (tel 03-2301369) in Balai Kuala Lumpur at 3 Jalan Sultan Hishamuddin. It's next to the Balai Seni Lukis Negara (National Art Gallery) opposite the railway station and is open from 8 am to 4.15 pm Monday through Friday and 8 am to 12.45 pm on Saturday.

Neither office has much – a brochure on each of the major tourist destinations in Malaysia and a list of top-end accommodation throughout the country. Unfortunately, they do not sell bus maps or bus guides, but you can purchase 'Lani's Kuala Lumpur Discovery Guide Map' for M$3.80; an informative piece of mapping.

There is also an information counter at Subang Airport which is open 9.15 am to 10.30 pm daily; and a small tourist information counter (tel 03-281832) at the railway station. You can store bags at the railway station for 50 sen per item per day, which is safe and very useful if you're just in transit.

The National Map Sales Office is on Jalan Tun Perak, but they won't sell you larger scale maps since they're all 'restricted' – due to fear of communists getting hold of them and finding out where KL is. Visiting scholars may find the library at the University of Malaya useful; buses run there from the Kelang station.

If you're going to the national park, Taman Negara, you must first visit River Park Sdn Bhd (tel 03-2915299), 260-H 2nd Mile Jalan Ipoh, Kuala Lumpur, and book the park boat and your accommodation. You have to leave a M$20 deposit and pay the rest when you leave the national park.

Embassies & Consulates There are quite a few diplomatic offices in Kuala Lumpur and they include:

Australia
6 Jalan Yap Kwan Sweng (tel 03-2423122)
Burma
7 Jalan Taman U Thant (tel 03-2424085)
Canada
Plaza MBS, Jalan Ampang (tel 03-2612000)
Denmark
3rd floor, Denmark House, 86 Jalan Ampang (tel 03-2303895)
Germany (West)
3 Jalan U Thant (tel 03-2429666)
India
Angkasa Raya Building, Jalan Ampang (tel 03-2617000)
Indonesia
233 Jalan Pekeliling, Kuala Lumpur (tel 03-2421011)
Japan
11 Persiaran Stonor, off Jalan Tun Razak (tel 03-2438044)
Netherlands
4 Jalan Megra (tel 03-2431143, 2431341, 2485151)
New Zealand
193 Jalan Tun Razak (tel 03-2486422)
Philippines
1 Changkat Kia Peng (tel 03-2484233)
Singapore
209 Jalan Tun Razak (tel 03-2616277)
Sri Lanka
29 Jalan Yap Kwan Seng (tel 03-2423094)
Sweden
6th floor, Angkasa Raya Building, Jalan Ampang (tel 03-2485981)
Switzerland
16 Persiaran Madge (tel 03-2480622)

Thailand
    206 Jalan Ampang (tel 03-2488222)
UK
    13th floor, Wisma Damansara, Jalan Semantan (tel 03-2541533)
USA
    376 Jalan Tun Razak (tel 03-2489011)

Airlines Silver Travel Service (tel 03-2422181) at 15 Jalan Alor, parallel to Jalan Bukit Bintang, has been recommended as a good agent for cheap airline tickets. They also have a dorm for penniless travellers who are about to leave Malaysia.

MSL (tel 03-2984132) in the South-East Asia Hotel is the Student Travel agent and usually has some interesting fares on offer. They also handle student cards. Some of the airline offices in Kuala Lumpur include:

Aeroflot
    Yayasan Selangor Building, Jalan Bukit Bintang (tel 03-2613231)
British Airways
    Hotel Merlin, Jalan Sultan Ismail (tel 03-2426177)
Cathay Pacific
    Oriental Plaza Building, Jalan Parry (tel 03-2486166)
Garuda
    1st floor, Angkasa Raya Building, Jalan Ampang (tel 03-2483542)
MAS
    UMBC Building, Jalan Sulaiman (tel 03-2308844)
    MAS Building, Jalan Sultan Ismail (tel 03-2610555)
    Dayabumi Complex (tel 03-2748734)
    24 hour reservation (tel 03-7747000)
Qantas
    AIA Building, Jalan Ampang (tel 03-2326544)
Singapore Airlines
    Wisma SIA, Jalan Dang Wangi (tel 03-2987033)
Thai International
    Kuwasa Building, 5 Jalan Raja Laut (tel 03-2937100)

Masjid Jame
The 'Friday Mosque' is built at the confluence of the Kelang and Gombek Rivers. This was the place where KL's founders first set foot in the town and where supplies were landed for the tin mines.

In a grove of palm trees the mosque is a picturesque structure with onion domes and minarets striped in red and white. It was built in 1907 and is at its best when viewed at sunset and early evening from the Benteng street market across the river. There is a new mirror-glass office building which gives excellent reflections of the mosque.

Federal Secretariat & the Selangor Club
Built between 1894 and 1897, the Secretariat building and the adjoining GPO and City Hall are in a Moorish style similar to that of the railway station. Now known as the Sultan Abdul Samad Building, the Secretariat is topped by a 43-metre-high clock tower.

Across the road is the open field known as the Padang. It was there during the colonial days that Malaysia's administrators engaged in that curious British rite known as cricket. Malaysia's independence was proclaimed there in 1957, but despite this, the cricket games still go on.

Beside the padang is the Selangor Club which became a social centre for KL's high society in the tin rush days of the 1890s. It's still a gathering place for KL VIPs.

Chinatown
Just south of the Masjid Jame are the teeming streets of KL's Chinatown. Bounded by Jalan Petaling, Jalan Sultan and Jalan Bandar, this crowded, colourful area is the usual melange of signs, shops, activity and noise. At night the central section of Jalan Petaling is closed to traffic to become a brightly lit and frantically busy pasar malam or night market.

There are many historic Chinese shop-houses still standing in KL's Chinatown and local conservation groups are making efforts to protect them from city development and to restore them to their former glory.

Temples & Pagodas

The typically ornate Chan See Shu Yuen temple stands at the end of Jalan Petaling. Built in 1906, this fine Chinese temple marks the boundary of Chinatown. Dating from 1873, the Sri Mahamariamman temple is a large and ornate south Indian Hindu temple. It's also in Chinatown on Jalan Bandar.

The modern International Buddhist Pagoda is in the south of KL, off Jalan Brickfields. The small temple of See Yeoh, off Jalan Rodger near Central Market, is one of the oldest in KL. Kapitan China Yap Ah Loy himself organised its construction and there's a photograph of him on an altar in the back of the temple. The Shiva temple of Sri Kandaswamy is on Jalan Scott.

Jalan Ampang & the National Museum of Art

Lined with impressive mansions, Jalan Ampang was built up by the early tin millionaires. Today many of the fine buildings have become embassies and consulates so that the street is KL's 'Ambassador's Row'. One of these fine 'stately homes' has been converted into a luxurious restaurant, Le Coq d'Or.

Another is now the National Museum of Art in the Dewan Tuanku Abdul Rahman. The museum houses a collection of works of Malaysian artists and also stages temporary exhibitions. It is open from 10 am to 6 pm daily but closed from 12 noon to 2.30 pm on Fridays. It is sometimes closed for about a week between exhibitions.

Masjid Negara – National Mosque

Sited in 5.2 hectares of landscaped gardens the modernistic national mosque is one of the largest in South-East Asia. A 73-metre-high minaret stands in the centre of a pool and the main dome of the mosque is in the form of an 18– pointed star which represents the 13 states of Malaysia and the five pillars of Islam. Forty-eight smaller domes cover the courtyard; their design is said to be inspired by the Grand Mosque in Mecca. The mosque, which is close to the railway station, can accommodate 8000 people.

Visitors must remove their shoes upon entry and be 'properly' attired – they'll lend you a robe should your own clothing not be suitable. It's open to nonbelievers from 8 am to 6 pm daily except on Fridays when the hours are 2 to 6 pm. Women must use a separate entrance.

Railway Station

If the national mosque is altogether too modern for you then you have only to cross the road to find a building full of eastern promise – Kuala Lumpur's magnificent railway station. Built in 1911, this delightful example of British colonial humour is a Moorish fantasy of spires, minarets, towers, cupolas and arches. It couldn't look any better if it had been built as a set for some whimsical Hollywood extravaganza. It's said that construction of the station was delayed because the original roof design did not meet the British railway specifications that it be able to support three feet of snow!

Across from this superb railway station is the equally wonderful Malayan Railway Administration Building. Almost directly across the station stands the shell of the once-gracious colonial Majestic Hotel. It has been taken over by the government and now contains a national art gallery.

Lake Gardens

The 60-hectare gardens form the green belt of Kuala Lumpur. They were originally founded in 1888 and you can rent boats on Tasik Perdana, the 'Premier Lake', which was once known as Sydney

Lake. They cost M$2 per hour and are available from 10 am to 6 pm Monday through Saturday and 8 am to 6 pm Sundays and holidays.

A Sri Jaya bus No 22 from the 'Toshiba' terminal on Jalan Sultan Mohamed, or a No 10 minibus, will take you to the gardens.

Muzium Negara – National Museum

At the southern end of the Lake Gardens the museum was built on the site of the old Selangor Museum, which was destroyed during WW II. Opened in 1963, its design and construction is a mixture of Malay architecture styles and crafts. It houses a varied collection on Malaysia's history, arts, crafts, cultures and people.

There are interesting sections on the history of Kuala Lumpur, Chinese traditions, the Orang Asli and the country's economy. An unusual exhibit is the elephant's skull which derailed a train. It's doubtful that the elephant actually charged the ironclad monster which was invading its jungle domain.

Another strange sight is an 'amok catcher', an ugly barbed device used to catch and hold a man who has run amok. There are frequent art exhibitions held at the museum and outside there are railway engines, an aircraft and other larger items.

Less than a km along Jalan Damansara from the railway station, admission to the museum is free. It is open daily from 9 am to 6 pm except on Fridays when it closes between 12 noon and 2.45 pm. Minibus No 17, 20, 24, 25, 34 or 37 will take you to the museum as well as most S J Kenderaan buses.

National Art Gallery

The exhibits change regularly and include art from around the world, often quite modern. The art gallery is housed in the former Majestic Hotel, across from the railway station. It's not worth a special trip, but if you're in the vicinity (say waiting for a train), you could while away half an hour or so there.

Admission is free and the hours are 10 am to 6 pm seven days a week except for prayer closing 12.15 to 2.45 pm on Fridays and all day on Hari Raya Haji.

National Monument

This massive monument overlooks the Lake Gardens from a hillside at their northern end. Sculptured in bronze in 1966 by the creator of the Iwo Jima monument in Washington DC, the monument commemorates the successful defeat of the communist terrorists during the Emergency.

Parliament House

Overlooking the Lake Gardens, Malaysia's Parliament House is dominated by an 18-storey office block. There are dress regulations for visitors – no shorts and for women dresses must be below the knee.

Other Attractions

KL has a number of sporting venues, including the indoor Stadium Negara, the Merdeka Stadium, the Royal Selangor Golf Club and the Selangor Turf Club where horse races have been held since 1896.

The Istana Negara is the official palace of Malaysia's 'king' or Yang di-Pertuan Agong, a title which is rotated between the various state sultans.

Kampung Bahru is a Malay section of KL to the north-east and the site, each Saturday night, for KL's Sunday Market – possibly because it continues through into Sunday morning. It's a food and produce market, a handicrafts market and a place to sample a wide variety of Malay foods.

Wisma Loke is an antique shop on Medan Tuanku. One of the oldest buildings in Kuala Lumpur, it was originally owned by Cheow Ah Yeok, a compatriot of the legendary Kapitan China Yap Ah Loy. Later the millionaire philanthropist Loke Yew turned it into one of the finest homes in KL.

Places to Stay – bottom end

Bottom-end accommodation in Kuala Lumpur consists of a variety of Chinese hotels and a choice of hostels. Many of the cheap hotels in town are brothels. Some will rent rooms but others don't want straight business at all. None of them seem to be particularly rough and tough, but women should certainly be aware of the situation. Hotels with signs written only in Malay, Rumah Tumpangan, are, as a general rule, offering more than rooms. Nearly all the ones listed here are straight.

There are a couple of good hunting areas for cheap hotels. The Jalan Tuanku Abdul Rahman area, with a number of hotels along the street, is a good place to look, as is the parallel Jalan Raja Laut. These roads run north from Jalan Tun Perak, by the padang. There are a number of good places around Chinatown, including some excellent traditional old Chinese places, and a few places in the Brickfields area. The hostels are scattered mainly south of the centre.

Around Jalan Tuanku A popular centre for cheap hotels is Jalan Tuanku Abdul Rahman (also called Batu Road) and the parallel Jalan Raja Laut.

Moving up Jalan Tuanku etc from its junction with Jalan Tun Perak there's the *Coliseum* with its famous old-planter's restaurant at No 100. All rooms share common bath facilities and are M$12.60/18.90 for singles/doubles. The cafe and restaurant downstairs are very popular.

At 132 the *Rex* and at 134 the *Tivoli* offer similar rates and accommodation but are not as popular as the Coliseum. The *Paramount*, a long-standing and decrepit cheapie, has mercifully closed its doors. At 142 the *Kowloon* is clean and fairly quiet despite its location – M$37.40 single or double with air-con and rather

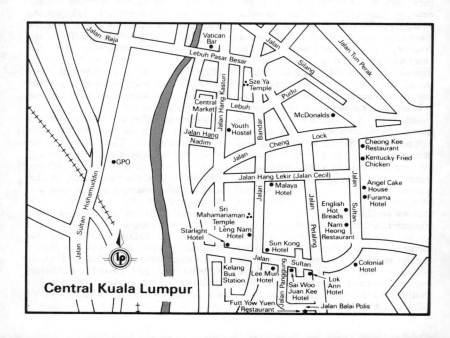

Central Kuala Lumpur

more modern than the others. There are other cheap hotels nearby.

You'll find the *Shiraz Hotel* (tel 03-2920159) on the corner of Jalan Tuanku etc and Jalan Medan Tuanku. There are 60 rooms ranging from M$35 to M$110 and a good Pakistani restaurant downstairs. Next door to Shiraz at 5 Jalan Medan Tuanku is the *Omar Khayam Hotel & Restoran* (tel 03-2988850), with small clean air-con rooms for M$35.70/37.80 single and double.

At 285 Jalan Tuanku is the *Dashrun Hotel*, a modern budget hotel with air-con single/doubles for M$40.25/51.75. Finally, just off Jalan Tuanku etc at the top end is the *South-East Asia Hotel* – it's in the middle price bracket – rooms cost from M$76, but since it houses the student travel office and offers student discounts it attracts some better-off backpackers.

The story is similar over on Jalan Raja Laut where there's a string of places between 316 and 340 including the *Sentosa* (tel 03-2925644) at 316 with rooms from M$27 to M$32 and more for air-con. Across the road there is more accommodation – the *Cylinman* at 110 (the numbers are lower on this side) has rooms for M$20 or M$30 with air-con and hot showers, but its getting rather run-down. The *Sun Ya* is also similar.

In one block nearby are four Chinese hotels, three of which look nice on the outside but accept only short-time visitors – *Tong Kheng, Kong Ming* and *Teong Ah*. The fourth, the *Hotel Rome*, is very good value with large, clean, quiet rooms from M$29. The *City Hotel*, further off Jalan Raja Laut, is in the M$38 to M$63 range. Again this is a short-time area – no real problem but single women travellers should be aware of it.

Chinatown Chinatown also has some cheap Chinese hotels like the very rock-bottom *Sai Woo Juan Kee* on the corner of Jalan Sultan and Jalan Panggang. The *Duni* is for business/pleasure only.

The more expensive *Lok Ann* on the corner of Jalan Sultan and Jalan Petaling has clean air-con rooms with telephone and hot water from M$35 single or double with bath. Opposite the Klang bus terminal on Jalan Sultan, the *Starlight Hotel* has similar rooms and prices as well as air-con rooms with outside bath for M$29. At 83 Jalan Sultan the *Nanyang Hotel* is a good upmarket cheapie at M$30 cold bath, M$35 hot bath and M$40 double.

The popular *Lee Mun Hotel* on Jalan Sultan close to Jalan Petaling and opposite the Mandarin is a good Chinese cheapie. It's a friendly place and costs just M$14.70 single or double. It's a classic old Chinese hotel with wood panelling, soap, towels, free Chinese tea and huge rooms. Although it's noisy it's safe and central.

At 43 Jalan Sultan is the *Colonial* – the bright yellow place. It's also a good one. Walk through the store and upstairs. The place is big, clean and interesting-looking and costs M$16.80 single or double. They also have some air-con rooms for M$25.

Two other convenient and popular places to stay in Chinatown, are the the *Sun Kong* on the corner of Jalan Sultan and Jalan Bandar and the *Leng Nam* at 165-7 Jalan Bandar next to the Sri Mahamariaman temple. The Sun Kong has seven fan-cooled rooms with attached bath and two beds for M$22 single and M$24 double. Rooms at the Leng Nam are very simple, baths are outside, and the beds are a bit hard, but rates are only M$16 single/double. The rooms are off the street and relatively quiet.

Brickfields This district is known as a traditionally Indian neighbourhood, but these days it seems to be about half Chinese. It's less intense than downtown KL and is only minutes away by bus or taxi.

The *Lido Hotel*, just across the street from the Brickfields YMCA, is a big old place with rooms at M$25.30 or M$27.60 with bath, single or double; or M$34.50 with air-con. See the YMCA in the Hostels section for details on getting there. Across the street from the Lido is the *Hotel Mexico* with better-kept rooms for M$25 with private bath or M$39.60/43.70 for single/double air-con rooms.

Down Jalan Thambillai from the Lido and the Mexico are three small Chinese hotels, the *Peng Ann, Selangor* and *Wing Heng*, all with similar accommodation for M$20 – ask for a room off the street as the front rooms can be noisy. All rooms are fan-cooled and have attached toilets and showers. Solo women travellers should be wary of the 'night life' in the area.

Station In 1987 the *Kuala Lumpur Station Hotel* in the central railway station on Jalan Sultan Hishamuddin finally reopened after nearly a year of restoration work. This 70-year-old charmer is the city's oldest hotel and features long skylit corridors, high ceilings, Victorian bathtubs, balconies off every room, and other reminders of a by-gone era, including the original lift!

All 30 rooms have air-con but the lounge and reception lobby are cooled by ceiling fans. There is a restaurant, pub, cafeteria, tea lounge and hawker's corner on the premises, the latter serving inexpensive Malaysian dishes like roti chanai, nasi lemak and mee goreng. Singles go for M$30 and doubles for M$40 – not including service charges and tax of 15%. This hotel could still use some more restoring.

Other Places For medium-price cheapies Jalan Bukit Bintang used to be a good bet but the prices have escalated out of contention. The medium-price places are interspersed with places to eat and also some more expensive hotels. Jalan Bukit Bintang is a short walk from the Pudu Raya bus station.

Starting from the Jalan Pudu end of the street at number 4 you'll find the *Weng Hua* where girls come with the rooms. At 16 the *Mey Wah* has rooms from M$40 to M$49, but seems half-hearted about renting them. The *Sungi Wang* is at 76 with singles/doubles costing M$79/89, all air-con. Continue on to 78 where the *Tai*

Ichi charges M$42/48, or at 80 the *Park Hotel* is M$39 single, M$48 double.

From 172 to 190 Jalan Pudu, from the Pudu Raya bus station, just beyond Jalan Bukit Bintang, there is a string of about 10 brightly painted Chinese hotels. They are all clean and all about M$20 for one bed, M$30 for two – they all have painted ladies. Most of the places will rent rooms and the girls and managers are friendly.

The relatively new 15-storey *Hotel Pudu Raya* (tel 03-2321000), atop the Pudu Raya bus terminal, deserves a special mention. Clean, modern, quiet air-con rooms are M$46 single, M$51.75 double and you couldn't ask for a better location vis a vis outstation travel. It's also within walking distance of Chinatown and the Kota Raya, Sungei Wang, Bukit Bintang, KL Plaza and Plaza Imbi shopping complexes. The hotel can book plane tickets as well as bus travel, and there is a health club with sauna, massage rooms and a small gym.

Hostels Finally there are the hostels. *Wisma Belia* (tel 03-2744833) is at 40 Jalan Lornie (also known as Jalan Syed Putra). It's some way out of the centre but bus No 52 takes you there. There are 115 rooms in this government-operated air-con hostel with rooms for M$20/25 without bath and doubles with bath for M$40. The restaurant is lousy.

Also south of the centre are the YMCA and YWCA. The *YMCA* (tel 03-441439) is at 95 Jalan Kandang Kerbau, just off Jalan Brickfields (now called Jalan Tun Sambanthan). To get there take minibus No 12 or a regular bus No 5, 33, 40, 49, 49A or 243 and ask for the Lido Cinema.

There's a variety of accommodation from M$10 dorm beds to singles/doubles without private bath at M$18/25; and with private bath, air-con and TV they cost M$40/50. You can get an extra bed in any room for M$5. There's a M$1 temporary membership charge to non-members of the YMCA and women and couples are accepted.

The YMCA has a good restaurant with a large menu. The breakfasts are very cheap and the other items are not too unreasonably priced. There are many restaurants and food stalls in the surrounding neighbourhood: south Indian, Chinese, nasi padang, etc, see the Places to Eat section for more details. The Brickfields Y is often full but it's clean and the staff are very helpful with travel advice. You can also take basic language classes (Malay, Chinese, Japanese, Thai and French) for M$100 to M$115 for 10 weeks.

The *YWCA* (tel 03-283225, 201623) is at 12 Jalan Davidson (also known as Jalan Hang Jebat) and has rooms at M$15/25 for singles/doubles but takes women only.

The *Kuala Lumpur International Youth Hostel* (tel 03-6260872) is rather a long way out on Jalan Vethavanam, just off Jalan Ipoh. Ask for a bus that goes down Jalan Ipoh (No 66, 146 or 147 from Pudu Raya, or a No 71 or 143 from Jalan Ampang) and get off at the 3½ milestone or simply tell the conductor you want the YH. For members it costs M$3.50 for the first night, M$3 thereafter; and non-members pay M$5, then M$4. The drawbacks are its distance from the centre and that there's a touch of the 'lights-out' mentality there. A couple of travellers have reported that the staff can be quite unfriendly.

The newest hostel entry is the *Meridian International Youth Hostel* (tel 03-2321428), or, as the sign reads, Asrama Belia Antaranangsa Meridian at 36 Jalan Hang Kasturi. It's between Chinatown and the Pudu Raya area. The staff are generally more helpful than the hostel on Jalan Ipoh but it's more expensive at M$6.50 with a hostel card, M$8.50 if you don't have one.

Places to Stay – middle

In the middle bracket KL has an equally wide selection of places ranging from the second-string 'international' hotels – like the *Furama*, the *Kuala Lumpur Mandarin*, the *Malaya*, or the *South-East Asia* – to the more expensive Chinese hotels. The student travel office is in the *South-East Asia*. The *Ria Hotel* is on top of the Pudu Raya bus terminal on Jalan Pudu. The *Emerald Hotel* is not very good. The venerable old *Majestic*, across the road from the station, has been closed to become a government-run art gallery. *Shah's Village Motel* is a modern motel in Petaling Jaya. If you're stuck out at the airport or have a very early flight the *Subang Airport Hotel* is right by the terminal.

City Hotel (tel 03-2924466), 366 Jalan Raja Laut, 90 rooms, singles M$38 to M$49, doubles M$46 to M$63

Hotel Emerald (tel 03-2429233), 166-168 Jalan Pudu, 45 rooms, singles M$60, doubles M$64 to M$70

Fortuna Hotel (tel 03-2419116), 87 Jalan Berangan off Jalan Bukit Bintang, 100 rooms, doubles M$95 to M$140

Hotel Furama (tel 03-2301777), Kompleks Selangor, Jalan Sultan, 103 rooms, singles M$60 to M$80, doubles M$85 to M$300

Grand Central Hotel (tel 03-2923011), 63 Jalan Chow Kit/Jalan Raja Laut, 150 rooms, doubles M$91 to M$121

Grand Pacific Hotel (tel 03-2982177), 52-56 Jalan Tun Ismail/Jalan Ipoh, 108 rooms, singles M$70 to M$80, doubles M$82 to M$102

Imperial Hotel (tel 03-2422377), 76-80 Jalan Hicks, 90 rooms, singles M$56, doubles M$82 to M$110

Kuala Lumpur Mandarin (tel 03-2304533), 2-8 Jalan Sultan, 150 rooms, doubles M$78 to M$190

The Lodge (tel 03-2420122), Jalan Sultan Ismail, 50 rooms, singles M$88, doubles M$105 to M$195

Hotel Malaya (tel 03-2327722), Jalan Hang Lekir, 250 rooms, singles M$79, doubles M$108 to M$220

Malaysia Hotel (tel 03-2428033), 67-69 Jalan Bukit Bintang, 60 rooms, singles M$75 to M$85, doubles M$85 to M$140

Ria Hotel (tel 03-2387744), Hentian Pudra Raya, 147 rooms, singles M$75 to M$90, doubles M$85 to M$100

Shah's Village Motel (tel 03-7569322), 3-5 Lorong Sultan, Petaling Jaya, 44 rooms, singles and doubles M$80

South-East Asia Hotel (tel 03-2926077), Jalan

Haji Hussein off Jalan Tuanku Abdul Rahman, 208 rooms, singles M$76 to M$80, doubles M$82 to M$190

Subang Airport Hotel (tel 03-7746122), Komplex Airtel Fima, Subang International Airport, 152 rooms, single rooms M$95, doubles M$135

Places to Stay – top end

Kuala Lumpur also has number of very expensive hotels, starting at the very top with the 593-room *Kuala Lumpur Hilton* and the 400-room *Regent of Kuala Lumpur*, both on Jalan Sultan Ismail. The *Kuala Lumpur Merlin* and the *Hotel Equatorial* are also on this road and the *Holiday Inn Kuala Lumpur* is close by. The *Federal Hotel* is round the corner on Jalan Bukit Bintang. On Jalan Ampang there's the relatively new *Ming Court Kuala Lumpur*. The *Petaling Jaya Hilton* is out at Petaling Jaya. In KL like Singapore rooms can be negotiated downward, due to the glut of hotel space as a result of overbuilding and the on-going recession.

Hotel Equatorial (tel 03-2612022), Jalan Sultan Ismail, 300 rooms, singles M$145, doubles M$180

Federal Hotel (tel 03-2489166), 35 Jalan Bukit Bintang, 450 rooms, singles M$125 to M$175, doubles M$140 to M$195

Holiday Inn on the Park (tel 03-2481066), Jalan Pinang, 192 rooms, singles M$120, doubles M$185

Holiday Inn City Centre (tel 2939233), Jalan Raja Laut, 250 rooms, singles M$95, doubles M$150 to M$180

Kuala Lumpur Hilton (tel 03-2422122), Jalan Sultan Ismail, 593 rooms, singles M$160 to M$220, doubles M$200 to M$280

Kuala Lumpur Merlin (tel 03-2480033), 2 Jalan Sultan Ismail, 700 rooms, singles M$135 to M$160, doubles M$135 to M$650

Ming Court Kuala Lumpur (tel 03-2618888), Jalan Ampang, 447 rooms, M$160 to M$229

The Oriental Kuala Lumpur (tel 03-2489500), 126 Jalan Bukit Bintang, from M$180

Pan-Pacific Kuala Lumpur (tel 03-2935555), Jalan Putra, 571 rooms, from M$150

Petaling Jaya Hilton (tel 03-7559122), 2 Jalan Barat, Petaling Jaya, 398 rooms, singles M$160 to M$220, doubles M$200 to M$240

The Plaza Hotel (tel 03-2932255), Jalan Raja Laut, 160 rooms, M$82 to M$110

The Regent of Kuala Lumpur (tel 03-2425588), Jalan Sultan Ismail, 400 rooms, M$160 to M$210

Shangri-La Hotel (tel 03-2322388), 11 Jalan Sultan Ismail, 722 rooms, from M$160

Merlin Subang (tel 03-7335211), Subang Jaya, 162 rooms, M$140 to M$240

Places to Eat

Night Markets KL has some very good night-time eating places. At dusk the tables are set up at the Medan Pasar car park and nearby Benteng, they are across the river from the Masjid Jame, and the food is excellent. Nasi ayam is a speciality and the ais campur is simply the best anywhere. The mosque looks romantically eastern across the river and if it should rain you can shelter in the bank frontages. A drink and a meal is about M$4, satay 30 sen a stick. Unlike Singapore a lot of sugar is added to fruit drinks so if you don't want it, say so.

Other night markets with good food include the Sunday market out at Kampung Bahru, and a street off Jalan Tuanku Abdul Rahman close to the South-East Asia Hotel. Both are good places for Malay food. Across the river from the railway station is another large food stall area. It's wedged between the river and the edge of Chinatown. There is a big indoor market on Jalan Hang Kasturi near the river between the Masjid Jame and the railway station.

Atop Central Market there is a hawkers' centre called *Taman Selera* with all the usual Malaysian standbys.

Indian Food At 15 Jalan Melayu, near the corner of Jalan Tuanku Abdul Rahman and Jalan Tun Perak, there's the *Jai Hind*. Good for Indian snacks and light meals.

Upstairs at 60A Jalan Tuanku etc *Bangles* is an Indian restaurant with a good reputation. Further down the *Shiraz*, on the corner of Jalan Tuanku etc and Jalan Medan Tuanku, is a good Pakistani restaurant. Some prefer the similar *Omar Khayyam* next door. Right across the road from that is the *Akbar* with excellent north Indian food. There are several others there, too. The *Bilal* restaurants – there are branches at 40 Jalan Ipoh, 33 Jalan Ampang and 37 Jalan Tuanku etc – are other good Indian restaurants. They do good roti chanai and murtabaks.

For south Indian food, head to the Brickfields area where there are four or five daun pisang – banana leaf – restaurants serving rice meals with vegetarian, fish, chicken, and mutton curries. One of the best is *Devi's*. In Bangsar on Lorong Maarof is the renowned *Devi Annapoorna*, which is staffed by volunteers from the Indian arts community and is entirely vegetarian. Set breakfasts are M\$1.50, lunches M\$3.50, and dinner M\$5 and M\$10 depending on quantity. Food is served on a *thali*, the traditional stainless steel plate. It is one of the best Indian restaurants in KL.

In Petaling Jaya, *Asha's Home-Cooked Curries* is often recommended by locals for a good daun pisang lunch. It's in 'New Town' PJ next to a claypot rice shop.

Chinese Food Chinese restaurants can be found all over the place, but particularly around Chinatown and along Jalan Bukit Bintang near the Pudu Raya bus station. There is interesting Chinese vegetarian food in the crowded *Futt Woh Yuen* at 2 Jalan Balai Polis, just off the bottom end of Jalan Petaling. There are excellent lunchtime dim sums at the expensive *Merlin Hotel* and also at the *Overseas* in Central Market.

A local speciality in KL is bah kut teh, supposed to have originated in Kelang. It's pork ribs with white rice and Chinese tea and is a very popular breakfast meal.

Malay Food There are Malay warungs and kedai kopis here and there throughout KL, but especially along Jalan Tuanku Abdul Rahman. Several of those in the vicinity of the Coliseum Hotel are excellent and cheap – look for the nasi lemak in the early mornings, coconut-rice topped with dried fish, boiled egg, peanuts, and curry. *Restoran Imaf* is a good bet just down from Minerva Bookshop. The area around Stadium Merdeka is also renowned for its Malay warungs.

Yazmin (tel 241 5655), behind the KL Hilton on Jalan Kia Peng, is a top-end Malay restaurant where a feed costs about M\$22 per person a la carte or M\$35 if you do the buffet and cultural performance.

Restoran Terapung Nelayan Titiwangsa at Lake Titiwangsa Park off Jalan Kuantan in north KL is an amazing place. Huts are built over the lake and the daily-changing menu features six cuisines. It's one of the best 'splurge' restaurants for Malay food.

Western Food KL has a suprising variety of western restaurants. At the bottom of Jalan Tuanku etc, you'll find *Colonel Sanders* and *A&W*. As a matter of fact, KL is said to have the largest KFC franchise in the world. There are several American-style hamburger joints around the bus station including *Wendy's* and, over towards Chinatown, *McDonald's*.

There's also an interesting Malay answer to American fast foods – *Saté Ria* at 9 Jalan Tuanku etc, a take-away satay place with meals from around M\$4.50. Not to be missed on the same street is the restaurant in the *Coliseum Hotel* where they have excellent steaks. For M\$12 you can get a great steak and salad, they also do roast chicken and grilled fillet of sole with chips. The place is quite a colonial experience which has scarcely changed over the years.

Down the street the *KK Cafeteria* by the Paramount Hotel has set lunches for M\$5.50, from soup to tea. The *Ship* near the Regent Hotel is also a splash-out steak place. The *Station Hotel* does good set lunches and dinners for just M\$8 to M\$10 – worth it just to eat in the station's amazing surroundings. There are lots of restaurants along Jalan Bukit Bintang including a *McDonalds* at the junction with Jalan Ismail, a *Dunkin' Donuts* and various bakeries, Indian and Chinese restaurants.

In Chinatown don't miss *English Hotbreads* on Jalan Sultan. They offer all kinds of buns and rolls stuffed with chicken curry or cheeses and fresh from the oven. Also available are pizza, macaroni, fruit tarts and chocolate cakes. Prices are good and there are several branches of Hotbreads throughout KL and PJ. There is another similar place across the street and down a bit called the *Angel Cake House*, downstairs from the Nanyang Hotel.

Just across the bridge from the GPO is a Chinese bar known to the locals as the *Vatican* – it's a popular expat hangout.

The nearby suburb of Petaling Jaya is full of good eating places of all varieties. See the PJ section. The KL airport is well equipped with restaurants including an *A&W Hamburger* stand.

And finally *Le Coq d'Or*, a restaurant in a fine turn-of-the-century mansion on Jalan Ampang, is expensive but not quite as expensive as the elegant surroundings might indicate.

Things to Buy

Karyaneka Handicraft Centre on Jalan Raja Chulan displays a wide variety of local craftwork in quasi-traditional settings. Hours are 9.30 am to 6 pm except Mondays when they close at 5 pm.

Jalan Tuanku Abdul Rahman has a variety of shops including local crafts along the arcade known as Aked Ibu Kota. Jalan Melayu has Indonesian religious goods and also local batik and other art. Pewterware, made from high-quality Malaysian tin, is an important local craft. You can see batik and silver or copperwork being done near the Batu Caves. Purchases can also be made there. Jalan Petaling is, of course, one of the most colourful shopping streets in KL, particularly at night.

The large Weld Supermarket and Fitzpatricks's Supermarket, with a number of other shops in the same complex, are on Jalan Raja Chulan. Two other modern shopping centres are the Bukit Bintang Plaza and the Sungai Wang Plaza, both on Jalan Bukit Bintang. Plaza Imbi, around the corner on Jalan Imbi, is a small complex that contains several computer hardware/software dealers.

The Central Market complex, housed in a cavernous art deco building (formerly a wet market) between the GPO and Chinatown, offers an ever-changing selection of Malaysian art, clothes, souvenirs and more. It's not particularly cheap but is a good place to shop for gifts if you're on your way home and don't have time to make the trek down Jalan Tuanku Abdul Rahman or Jalan Petaling for the fourth time. On the rooftop there are several hawker's stalls and on the river side of the market a couple of outdoor cafes. Occasionally there are free cultural performances as well featuring Malaysian dance, gamelan, or silat.

For a look at some interesting modern Malaysian art, drop by Rupa Gallery at a Lot 158 of the Dayabumi Complex next to the GPO. This small gallery exhibits original painting and lithography, prints, posters and ceramics. Some of the best work is done by Kuala Lumpur's own Victor Chin, who can often be found on the premises and welcomes a chat. Chin lithographs depict old KL scenes, especially of traditional Chinese and Malay architecture. Poster reproductions are quite reasonably priced, with or without framing. This is also a good place to get custom framing done at quite good prices.

Getting There

Kuala Lumpur is Malaysia's principal international arrival gateway and a central travel crossroads for train, bus or taxi travel. The trains arrive at the magnificent Kuala Lumpur railway station. Most long-distance taxis and buses operate from the multi-storey Pudu Raya terminus on Jalan Pudu. The local Kelang bus terminal is beside Jalan Sultan Mohamed in Chinatown and the Jalan Ampang station is opposite the AIA Building.

Air KL is the central hub for MAS's domestic air network – see the introductory Getting Around section for fare details.

Rail It's also the midway point for train services between Singapore and Butterworth, again see the introductory Getting Around section.

Bus There is a wide variety of bus services, the majority of which operate from the Pudu Raya terminal. As usual there are regular buses and very often slightly more expensive air-con services. Fares include Port Kelang M$1.50 (from the Klang terminal), Port Dickson M$3.60, Melaka M$6 to M$8, Johore Bahru M$13 to M$15, Singapore M$15 to M$17, Muar M$9, Ipoh M$7 to M$10, Butterworth M$13 to M$15, Genting Highlands M$5, Cameron Highlands M$7 to M$8, and Padang Besar M$23.

Taxi While the buses depart from downstairs the taxis are upstairs in the Pudu Raya terminal although there are also long-distance taxi offices along Pudu Rd near the bus station. There are lots of taxis, and fares include Seremban M$5, Melaka M$12, Johore Bahru M$30, Ipoh M$15, Kuala Kangsar M$18, Taiping M$20, Butterworth M$30, Alor Setar M$33, Genting Highlands M$7, Kuala Lipis M$12, Kuantan M$20, Kuala Trengganu M$34, and Kota Bahru M$40.

Getting Around

Airport Transport Taxis from Kuala Lumpur's international airport operate on a coupon system. You purchase a coupon from a booth at the airport and use it to pay the driver. The system has been designed to eliminate fare cheating from the airport. Going to the airport is not so simple because the taxi drivers are uncertain about whether they will get a return trip – count on about M$16 to

M$18. Beware of taxi touts at the airport, they'll cost you more.

Or you can go by bus – the No 47 operates every hour from the Klang terminal on Jalan Sultan Mohamed and costs M$1.05. The trip takes 45 minutes though it's a good idea to leave more time since traffic can be bad. The first departure is at 6 am. There's also the non-direct bus No 61.

Bus There are two bus systems operating in KL. Fare stage buses start from 20 sen for the first km and go up 5 sen each two km. City bus companies include Sri Jaya, Len Seng, Len, Ampang, Kee Hup and Toong Foong. There are a number of bus stands around the city including the huge Pudu Raya terminal on Jalan Pudu and the Kelang terminal on Jalan Sultan Mohamed. The faster minibuses operate on a fixed fare of 50 sen anywhere along their route. Whenever possible have correct change ready when boarding the bus, particularly during rush hours.

Taxis Trishaws have virtually disappeared from KL's heavily trafficked streets but there are plenty of taxis and fares are quite reasonable. They start from 70 sen for the first km, then an additional 30 sen for each 0.8 km. Air-conditioned taxis have a 20% surcharge and they tend to use the air-con even when the weather is cool and rainy. From midnight to 6 am there's an additional 50% supplement on top of the meter fare and extra passengers (more than two) are charged 10 sen each.

KL's taxi drivers are not keen on going to the airport or from the station on the meter – in those cases you'll have to bargain your fare. It shouldn't be more than a couple of dollars from the railway station to most places in KL. As KL seems to be suffering from something of a taxi shortage there's a shadow 'pirate taxi' service springing up; you have to bargain with these operators but they're more open to negotiation than the regular ones.

Rent-a-Car There are a number of local car rental organisations in KL with typical rates around M$100 a day. For example, a Datsun 1300 is M$123 a day unlimited mileage or M$49 plus 49 sen per km. The major nationwide rental organisations' addresses in KL are:

Avis Rent-a-Car
  Kuala Lumpur Hilton, Jalan Sultan Ismail
  (tel 03-2743077, 2410561)
Hertz Rent-a-Car
  52 Jalan Ampang (tel 2329125)
Mayflower-Acme Tours
  Angkasa Raya Buildings, 123 Jalan Ampang
  (tel 03-2486739)
National Car Rental
  78 Jalan Ampang (tel 03-2489188)
Sintat Rent-a-Car
  Holiday Inn, Jalan Pinang (tel 03-2743028)
Toyota Rent-a-Car
  Federal Hotel, 35 Jalan Bukit Bintang
  (tel 03-4388387)

Tours MSL Travel in the South-East Asia Hotel have day tours for M$27 or morning tours for M$16.

Hash House Harriers

The internationally known Hash House Harriers was first established in KL in 1938 by a group of British colonials who found themselves drinking too much and needing exercise. Hash house was the nickname for the dining room of the Selangor Club Chambers, a social centre of the times. The harrier idea of a group of runners chasing papers along trails set by an appointed member ('the hare') was not altogether new – previous groups had existed in KL, Ipoh, Johore Bahru and Melaka in colonial Malaya. In Shanghai and Kuching the sport was carried out on horseback. However, it was the original HHH that institutionalised harrying to such a degree that it became an expat tradition all over Asia.

Until 1961 there was only the KL Hash but in the following year a second chapter opened in Singapore, followed by Brunei, Kuching, Kota Kinabalu, Ipoh and Penang. Eventually the first group outside of Singapore/Malaysia was opened in Perth in 1967. There are around 500 HHHs in 70 countries and there are annual interhash meetings at a different place each year.

A hash run: the hare goes to the run site – which changes with each run – a few hours in advance and lays an irregular trail (sometimes including false trails) using paper markers. The point is to allow faster runners to scout for the next bit of trail while slower harriers catch up. The run begins with a call of 'on, on' – the slogan of all HHHs – and when looking for paper markers runners shout out 'are you?' to which runners ahead reply 'checking' to help in trail finding. The typical run lasts one to 1½-hours and is followed by beer drinking at the end of the trail and a meal at a local restaurant. In KL the meals are usually at a Chinese restaurant and each runner contributes about US$3 to cover costs.

There are several branches in the KL area, including one for men only (the original tradition), one for women only (the Hash House Harriettes), the rest mixed. Most of the larger Malaysian towns have their own branches. All of the Malaysian hash clubs have locals amongst their membership. The hash welcomes guest participants and for those so inclined, a hash run would be an interesting way to meet both locals and expats while seeing a bit of the Malaysian countryside since runs tend to be held in secondary jungle areas, or on rubber or oil palm estates. For information write to the Kuala Lumpur Hash House Harriers, PO Box 10182, KL, 01-01, or the contact person in Malaysia is Kon Chee Kong (tel 03-7758455).

AROUND KUALA LUMPUR
Batu Caves

The huge Batu Caves are the best-known attraction in the vicinity of KL. They are just 13 km north of the capital, a short distance off the Ipoh road. The caves are in a towering limestone formation and were little known until about 100 years ago. Later a small Hindu shrine was built in the major cave and it became a pilgrimage centre during the annual Thaipusam festival.

The major cave, a vast open space known as the Cathedral Cave, is reached by a straight flight of 272 steps. For those not feeling up to a steep climb in the tropical heat there's a small railcar which runs beside the steps – at a cost of 50 sen return.

Also reached by the same flight of steps is the long and winding Dark Cave, but this has been closed for the past couple of years because quarrying in the limestone outcrop has made the caves unsafe. There are a number of other caves in the same formation, including a small cave at the base of the outcrop which has been made into a museum with figures of the various Hindu gods; admission is 50 sen.

There's good Indian vegetarian food at the restaurant closest to the caves.

Getting There To reach the caves take the No 11 minibus (60 sen) from Jalan Pudu or Jalan Semarang or Len Seng bus No 70 from Jalan Raja Laut/Jalan Ampang. The bus trip takes about 45 minutes and it's wise to tell the driver you're going all the way to the caves; if there aren't many people it sometimes stops earlier. The No 11 minibus is more frequent and more convenient.

On Saturdays and Sundays you can take a train to the caves – No 140 leaves the KL station at 9 am and No 141 leaves Batu at 11.30 am. Travel takes 35 minutes and the fare is M$2 one-way.

National Zoo & Aquarium
East of KL on the road to Ulu Kelang, about 13 km out, is the 55-hectare site of the National Zoo and Aquarium. Laid out around a central lake, the zoo collection emphasises the wildlife found in Malaysia. There are also elephant and camel rides and other amusements for children.

The zoo is open daily from 9 am to 6 pm and student admission is 30 sen; M$2.50 for others, plus M$1 if you want to use your camera. To get there take a Len Seng bus No 170 or a Lenchee bus No 180 from Jalan Leboh Ampang. Or you can take a No 17 or 23 minibus.

Mimaland
On the road to the Genting Highlands, 18 km from KL, Mimaland is a 120-hectare amusement park – mainly intended for children. It's intended to be a 'Malaysia in Miniature' and amongst the attractions are a fishing and boating lake, a huge natural swimming pool, a small zoo and a collection of full-size dinosaur models.

You can get there on a Len Seng Bus No 168, marked 'Mimaland', from Jalan Ampang. A No 17 minibus will also take you there en route to the zoo. Admission is M$1.40.

Places to Stay You can stay at Mimaland in the lodge (M$12.50 per person), in motel rooms (M$89 for doubles) or in Malaysian cottages known as *bagans* (M$150). Phone 03-632133 for details.

Templer Park
Beside the Ipoh road, 22 km north of KL, Templer Park was established during the colonial period by the British High Commissioner Sir Gerald Templer. The 1200-hectare park is intended to be a tract of jungle, preserved within easy reach of the city. There are a number of marked jungle paths, swimming lagoons and several waterfalls within the park boundaries.

To get there take bus No 66, 72, 78 or 83 from the Pudu Raya terminal. The bus fare is 95 sen and the trip takes 35 minutes. Just north of the park is a 350-metre-high limestone formation known as Bukit Takun and close by the smaller Anak Takun which has many caves.

Petaling Jaya
PJ is a modern suburb of KL. Originally developed as a dormitory town to the capital, it has grown so rapidly and successfully that it has become a major industrial centre in its own right. PJ has a population approaching 250,000. The University of Malaya is en route to PJ.

In recent years, PJ has become a centre of good nightlife and gourmet restaurants, partly because the per capita income is higher than in KL and also because many of the higher-salaried expats working in the KL area live there.

Two clubs featuring good live jazz are *All That Jazz* (tel 7553152) at 14 Jalan 19/36 and *Jazz Boulevard* (tel 7199018), 65 Jalan SS21/1A.

If you're lucky, you might be able to catch a set by Malaysia's own *Asiabeat*, an international fusion-style band that blends regional music forms with jazz idioms. You may come across their cassette, recorded on the Columbia label with shakuhachi virtuoso John Kaizan Neptune, in music stores around KL. Asiabeat can also be seen playing straight jazz in KL hotels.

If your tastes are more country & western, your best bet is *Texas Bar & Dallas Grill* (tel 7193848), on Jalan SS22/25. They serve Texas-style food as well as having live C&W music which is most likely played by Portuguese-Malay musicians from Melaka.

Some of Malaysia's top pop music bands perform at *Piccadilly* in the Kimisawa complex in PJ's Damansara Utama district. This is also the closest KL or PJ comes to a western-style singles scene. Cover charge is M$20 and don't forget that after midnight taxis charge double.

A more low-key music stop is *Treffpunkt*, on the next lane over from Piccadilly. Local legend Alex Peters ('Malaysia's Bob Marley') attracts a mix of Indians, Chinese, expats and a few Malays at this German rathskeller-style pub. Alex, who is an Indian Malaysian, performs material as diverse as Dylan, Dire Straits, Pink Floyd and the Drifters.

PJ's countless restaurants include nyonya-baba cuisine, banana-leaf Indian, Malay, Chinese, and Thai. The food at *Thai Kitchen* in PJ's SS2 district (sections are numbered; SS - 'sub-section') may be the best Thai food in the KL area and the menu is in Thai, Malay and English.

One of the only two Sinhalese restaurants in the KL area is in PJ, too, the *Sri Asoka* at 27 Jalan 20/16 in the Paramount Gardens area. Food is tasty and cheap – specialties are kiri buth, a Sinhalese version of nasi lemak (breakfast only), spicy duck hot fry, seeni sambol, sweet and salty lassis, and appam in the evenings. Hours are 7 am to 9 pm.

Asha's Home-Cooked Curries in 'New Town' is often recommended by locals for a good daun pisang lunch. Also in the same shop is a good Chinese claypot rice vendor. *Devi's* on Jalan Gasing is another good banana-leaf place.

Sheikh Hassan and *Syed*, both across from the PJ Hilton, do good Indian Muslim and Malay food.

Port Kelang

Thirty km south-west of the capital, Port Kelang is the major seaport for KL. Port Kelang is famous for its excellent seafood, particularly chilli crabs. There are good seafood places only a couple of minutes walk from the bus terminus. Public ferries leave for offshore islands and passengers are taken out in curious-looking rowing boats.

Only eight km before Port Kelang you pass through Kelang, the royal capital of Selangor with a royal mosque and istana. Morib, south of Port Kelang and 64 km from KL, is a popular weekend escape and beach resort. The bus from the Kelang terminal in KL to Port Kelang costs M$1.50.

Shah Alam

The newly established capital of Selangor State is undergoing a major construction and development plan with the intention of making it a worthy state centre. It was due for completion in 1986, but the 1985 to 1987 recession slowed things down and it's still not finished.

A new museum, cultural centre, theatre and huge library are being built on a hill overlooking the city's man-made lakes and close to the new state mosque. The sparkling silver and blue mosque, which looks like a lunar station and is as yet unfinished, is worth a look if you have time. So far at least US$14 million has been spent on it. The city of Shah Alam itself is almost deserted except for the bustling campus of the Institut Teknologi MARA.

Other Attractions

On the north-eastern outskirts of the city, on Jalan Pahang, you can visit the

Selangor Pewter Factory between 8.30 am and 4.45 pm daily and see Malaysia's famous pewter products being made.

On the Ipoh road, just north of the turnoff to the Batu Caves, is the Batik Factory Selayang where you can see batik-making demonstrations from 8.30 am to 1 pm and 2 to 5 pm Monday through Sunday.

There are also numerous rubber plantations and tin mines around KL; visits can be arranged.

GENTING HIGHLANDS

Where the style of other Malaysian hill stations is old English, in the Gentings it's modern skyscrapers; where the entertainment at the older stations is jungle walks here it's a casino; instead of waterfalls and mountain views Genting has an artificial lake and a cable car. If that does not sound to your taste then drive straight by, for the Genting Highlands are a thoroughly modern hill station designed to cater for the affluent citizens of Kuala Lumpur, just an hour to the south.

The first stage of the Genting Highlands was opened in the early '70s and there are now three hotels and associated developments. These include Malaysia's only casino in the 18-storey Genting Hotel, with all the usual western games of chance and eastern favourites like keno and tai sai. Patrons must be 21 years old and Malaysian citizens have to pay M$200 to get in. Men must wear a tie or pay M$3 to hire 'Malaysian national dress'. There is a sign denying Muslims entrance by decree of the Sultan of Selangor.

Then there's the four-hectare artificial lake with boating facilities which is encircled by a miniature railway for children. Naturally there's a golf course 700 metres down from the hotels, reached by a cable car (M$2 one-way). Forgetting nothing, the resort also has a bowling alley and a brand new cave temple, the Chin Swee Temple, on the road up to the resort. Of course Genting has cooler weather like

any other hill station; the main part of the resort is at a little over 1700 metres altitude.

Places to Stay

The emphasis is on international standards but there is one place offering if not cheap at least economy accommodation. There are rooms from M$40 in the *Genting Palangi* (tel 03-2113813), and during the week you may be able to get this down as low as M$27. Two other hotels offering economy rates in the past have closed down.

At the top there's the 1100-room *Genting Hotel* (tel 03-2111118) with rooms from M$125 and every mod con imaginable from saunas and swimming pool to tennis courts and a 'revolving disco restaurant'! The *Highlands Hotel* (tel 03-2112812), has 200 rooms from around M$70.

There are often two-day and three-day packages offered at the Genting Highlands, including accommodation and some meals.

Getting There & Away

The jet-set way to the Gentings is by helicopter. A service operates between KL's Subang Airport or the Segambut Helipad in KL to the highlands. Or you can get there by share taxi for M$8 in around an hour; it's about 50 km from KL.

There is also a regular M$4.50 bus service between the Pudu Raya bus station in KL and the Genting Hotel in Genting. There are about nine services daily on weekdays, more on weekends. The Genting Highlands Tours & Promotion Board (tel 03-2613833), on the 9th floor of Wisma Genting on Jalan Sultan Ismail in KL runs day tours to the highlands – M$30 gets you transport there and back, a KL city tour, and M$9 of gambling chips. Buses leave major hotels between 9 and 9.30 am, returning at 3.30 and 8 pm.

FRASER'S HILL

Fraser's Hill takes its name from Louis James Fraser, a reclusive mule-trader who lived there around the turn of the century. It's said he ran a remote and illegal gambling and opium den, but he was long gone when the area's potential as a hill station was recognised in 1910. The station, set at a cool 1524 metres altitude, is quiet and relatively undeveloped – possibly because it's not the easiest hill station to get to.

Information

The information centre (tel 09-382201) is between the golf club and the Merlin Hotel, near the GPO. They can supply maps and information brochures and they will also book accommodation in Fraser's Hill – but not at the rest house which is in Selangor rather than Pahang (the state boundary runs through the town).

There are films on Saturdays and Sundays at the Merlin Hotel which also has a bank which is open at weekends and on holidays. You can hire bicycles for M$1.50 per hour from the Merlin Hotel.

Nightlife on Fraser's consists of hanging out at the outdoor tables in front of the Puncak Inn or sitting before the fire in the Merlin lounge listening to schmaltzy organ music. By 10 pm everyone's in bed.

Things to See & Do

As in the Cameron Highlands there are many beautiful gardens around the town and also many wildflowers carpeting the hills. The jungle walks are much more jungle strolls than real walks. The golf course forms the real 'centre' of Fraser's Hill and there are other sporting facilities which include tennis and squash courts.

About five km from the information centre is the Jerlau Waterfall with a swimming pool fed from the falls. Unfortunately the path leading to the falls is closed. A short walk up from the information centre there's a small zoo – open 9 am to 5 pm, admission is M$1. Its pleasant setting is probably more interesting than the animals, but beware of the monkeys. While the ones in the cages distract you, their wild cousins will make a dash for any edible you're carrying!

Places to Stay

Most of the accommodation in Fraser's Hill is run by the Fraser's Hill Development Corporation, a government-contracted *bumiputra* organisation.

Rates at FHDC lodgings are slightly lower during the designated off seasons, from 15 January to 9 March, 25 June to 14 July and 15 September to 14 November. All rates given are for the off-season – but just add M$5 for peak periods.

The *Seri Berkat Rest House* (tel 09-341026) has rooms from M$30 and the *Puncak Inn* (tel 09-382201) has rooms for M$25 to M$45. The cheaper rooms are very small – just enough space to swing a kitten – while the more expensive rooms are simply larger, no extra facilities. If you do stay at the Puncak, request a room high up and at the back of the inn, as the lower front rooms pick up all the noise from the restaurants below.

Alternatively there are the FHDC bungalows – *Raub* (tel 09-382241), *Temerloh* (tel 09-382242), *Pekan* (tel 09-382213) and *Rompin* (tel 09-382216). The *Semantan Bungalow* is closed.

In some of these you often get excellent, old-fashioned service although the facilities may have seen better days – it rains a lot in Fraser's and rooms tend to be a bit musty. They range in price from as little as M$35 for an off-season double at the Temerloh to around M$55 for a high-season double at some of the others. All FHDC accommodation must be booked at the helpful and informative information centre. On weekends during the peak season you should call ahead to ensure there's space.

At the other end of the scale there's the *Fraser's Hill Merlin Hotel* (tel 09-382279) with 109 rooms from M$80 – during the week you may be be able to ask for a discount. It's overlooking the golf course. There are many other bungalows and a set of condominiums on Fraser's that are privately owned by corporations for employee use or by time-share owners in KL.

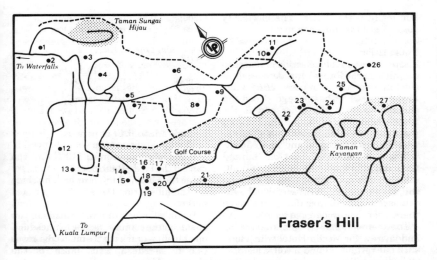

Fraser's Hill

If you're in need of something really reasonably priced try the *Corona Nursery Youth Hostel* (tel 09-382225), the flower nursery about a 25-minute walk from the tourist office. It's run by a friendly Indian family. Rooms with attached bathroom are M\$7 per person and you can use the kitchen and fridge. Beware, however, of the ill-tempered dog belonging to a neighbour – it guards the access road and if you arrive at night pick up a stick with which to warn it off.

On the road which leads to Fraser's highest peak there's the privately-owned *High Pines Bungalow*. The road passes by a nursery and terminates at the bungalows which are owned by a Mr Nashi. Rooms go for M\$5 to M\$10. For the impecunious, the information centre will ring him for you.

If you're stuck at the bottom of the hill there's the relaxed *Gap Rest House* right at the Gap with rooms for M\$22 and up. In fact this wonderfully old-fashioned place is so much better value than anything up the hill that it's worth staying down there and just visiting Fraser's Hill for the day. It's in a pretty setting, has a comfortable lounge, a good restaurant and bathtubs

1	Station Layang-Layang
2	Semantan Bungalow
3	Rompin Bungalow
4	Mini Zoo & Park
5	Temerloh Bungalow (Steak House)
6	Station Murai
7	Station Kenari
8	Lipis Bungalow
9	Station Merpati
10	Station Punai
11	Kuantan Bungalow
12	Nursery
13	Station Muri
14	Tavern
15	Puncak Inn
16	Sports & Golf Complex
17	Pekan Bungalow
18	Tourist Information Office
19	GPO
20	Fraser's Hill Merlin
21	Raub Bungalow
22	Glen Bungalow
23	Pine Resort Condominiums
24	Station Tiong
25	Station Serindek
26	Corona Youth Hostel
27	Station Merbok

with real hot water! There's a Chinese and an Indian restaurant close to the rest house, but really nothing else. The electricity goes off at 11.30 pm each night.

Places to Eat

There's a reasonable selection of places to eat, all near the Puncak Inn. At one end of the inn is the Chinese *Hill View Restaurant* which has quite good food and snacks, while at the other end is the friendly Malay *Arzed Restaurant*. Between the two is the Malay *Restoran Puncak*, which serves roti chanai any time of day.

There's a snack bar in the Golf Club and the straightforward (the name says it all) *Kheng Yuen Lee Eating Shop* right near the gate for 'the gap'. Neither of the Chinese places are open for breakfast. Up a notch there's the *Temerloh Steak House* with steaks at around the M$10 mark. At the top end there's the expensive Merlin Hotel with one restaurant and a coffee shop.

Getting There & Away

Fraser's Hill is 103 km north of Kuala Lumpur and 240 km from Kuantan on the east coast. By public transport Fraser's Hill is a little difficult to get to.

There's a twice-daily bus service from Kuala Kubu Bahru costing M$1.90. The bus is supposed to depart from KKB at 8 am and 12 noon (but usually leaves about 30 minutes late), and from Fraser's Hill at 10 am and 2 pm.

A taxi from KKB is M$30 for the whole taxi. A bus from KL's Pudu Raya station to KKB is M$3; share taxi is M$6. KKB is 62 km north of KL, just off the KL-Butterworth road and the KL-Butterworth railway line.

The last five miles up to Fraser's Hill is on a steep, winding, one-way section. At the Gap you leave the KKB to Raub road to make this final ascent. Traffic is permitted uphill and down at the following times:

Up from the Gap

7.00	to	7.40 am
9.00	to	9.40 am
11.00	to	11.40 am
1.00	to	1.40 pm
3.00	to	3.40 pm
5.00	to	5.40 pm

Down from Fraser's Hill

8.00	to	8.40 am
10.00	to	10.40 am
12 noon	to	12.40 pm
2.00	to	2.40 pm
4.00	to	4.40 pm
6.00	to	6.40 pm

From 7 pm to 6.40 am the road is open both ways and you take your chances!

If you miss the noon KKB-FH bus, you can get the KKB-Raub bus at 2.30 pm, get off at the Gap and try your luck hitching up the hill during the 3 to 3.40 pm 'up' period.

If you get stuck in KKB, there are two cheap hotel/restaurants, one Chinese and one Muslim, at the town's main crossroads (Jalan Merdeka and Jalan Sultan Hamid). There is a small tea shop at the bus stand where you can get cheap refreshments and across the street is a post office.

KUALA LUMPUR TO IPOH

It's 219 km from KL to Ipoh and a further 173 km on from there to Butterworth. Heading north, Kuala Kubu Bahru is the first larger town, but it is just off the main road. This is the place from where buses run to Fraser's Hill. Continuing north you pass through Tanjung Malim and Selim River. During WW II the British forces made a last-ditch attempt to halt the Japanese advance at Selim River, but failed.

Continuing north you reach Bidor, from where you can turn off for Telok Anson, then Tapah, the gateway to the Cameron Highlands. At Kampar you can, if you have your own transport, turn off for Lumut and Pangkor Island, but there are a number of routes to this port. Finally you reach Ipoh, heralded by a number of dramatic limestone outcrops.

Places to Stay

There are rest houses in Tapah, Telok

Anson and Selim River. The Selim River *Rumah Rekat Rest House* is, according to one traveller, 'fantastic value – singles/doubles for M$4/6 includes fan, sheets, towel, soap, mosquito coils, bathroom with bathtub, WC, toilet paper, plus it's clean and quiet. The only catch is there's really no reason for anybody to stop in Selim River!' There is a cinema, however.

In addition to the rest house's popular restaurant, there are many stalls with good cheap food, including Indian food, in the vicinity.

Cameron Highlands

Malaysia's most extensive hill station, about 60 km off the main Kuala Lumpur-Ipoh-Butterworth road at Tapah, is at an altitude of 1500 to 1800 metres. It's a little difficult to pinpoint exactly where the Cameron Highlands are and at what altitude because they consist of a series of villages strung along the main road.

The Highlands take their name from William Cameron, the surveyor who mapped the area in 1885. He was soon followed by tea planters, Chinese vegetable farmers and finally by those seeking a cool escape from the heat of the lowlands.

The temperature rarely drops below 8°C or climbs above 24°C and the area is riotously fertile. Vegetables grow in profusion, flowers are cultivated for sale all over Malaysia, it's the centre of Malaysian tea production and wildflowers bloom everywhere.

The cool weather tempts visitors to exertions normally forgotten at sea level – there's an excellent golf course, a network of jungle tracks, waterfalls and mountains and less taxing points of interest such as a colourful Buddhist temple and a number of tea plantations where visitors are welcome.

Orientation

From the turn-off at Tapah it's 29 miles (46 km) up to Ringlet, the first village of the Highlands. Ringlet is not particularly interesting and although there are a number of places to stay most visitors press on higher up. Soon after Ringlet you skirt the lake created by the Sultan Abu Bakar Dam between milestones 30 and 32.

Soon after milestone 37 (59 km) you reach Tanah Rata, the main town of the highlands. Only a few km further brings you up to the golf course around which you'll find most of the Highlands' more expensive accommodation.

Continue on beyond the golf course and at around the 49th milestone (65 km) you reach the other main Highland town, Brinchang, where there are more restaurants and cheap hotels.

The road continues up beyond Brinchang to smaller villages and the Blue Valley Tea Estate at 56 miles, off to the north-east, or to the top of Gunung Brinchang at 49 miles, to the north-west.

Information

The main town of Tanah Rata has a variety of mainly lower-priced hotels and a wide choice of restaurants. The post office, banks and taxi station are also there and some buses terminate at Tanah Rata.

There used to be a small information centre run by the Cameron Highlands Tourist Promotion Association at the bottom end of Tanah Rata. Of late it has been turned into a small museum and although the sign reads 'museum and information centre' they have no information to offer.

The Boh Tea Factory, beyond Brinchang on the road to the radio station, welcomes visitors. A taxi from Brinchang shouldn't cost more than M$5 if you can't hitch a ride. While you're there visit Mrs Helen Robertson's rose garden and try her delicious rose jam and homemade marmalade.

Walks

There are a variety of walks around the Highlands, leading from place to place or

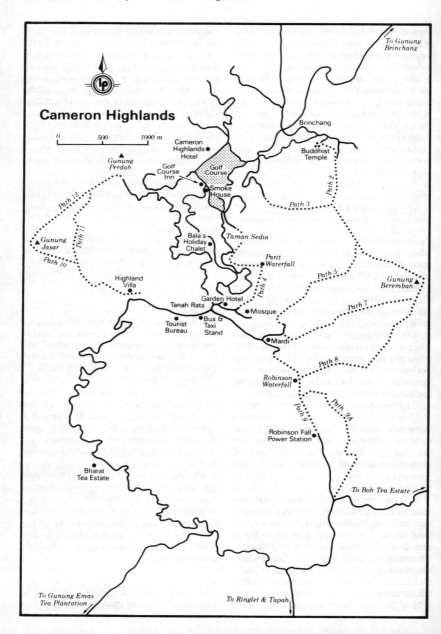

to waterfalls, mountain peaks and other scenic spots. The walks are not all well kept and sometimes can be difficult to follow. In addition there are no high quality maps available. Those supplied by the information centre or from hotels are generally only sketch maps.

You should take care not to get lost and to bring some emergency supplies on the longer or more difficult walks. Walks 4, 9, 11 and 12 (as far as Robinson Falls) are recommended as family strolls taking only about an hour. Walks 3, 5, 7 and 10 are longer walks taking two or more hours; while walks 1, 2 and 8 are 'tough going'.

The walks are generally interesting as they pass through relatively unspoilt jungle and the cool weather makes walking a pleasure. Walk 12 is particularly good for wildflowers – the Highlands are famed for their orchids. The deviation from walk 12 up to the summit of 1576-metre Gunung Perdah is a good short walk.

Although the walks around the Highlands are all relatively short there is obviously great potential for longer walks from there. A glance at the map will indicate what a short, straight-line distance it is from the Highlands down to Ipoh or the main road. Any walk outside the immediate area has to be announced to the local authorities, however, and once again there are no good maps available.

Waterfalls Walk 9 from Tanah Rata leads to some waterfalls, which can also be reached from the road around the golf course Either walk is less than a km. There is a natural swimming pool at the base of the Parit Falls.

You can make an interesting longer walk by taking 9 to the falls, then the steep and 'mildly' challenging 8 to the top of Beremban, then 3 to the golf course or 3 and 2 to the Buddhist temple, finally returning to Tanah Rata on walk 4 past the Smokehouse and the Parit Falls. That makes an interesting round-trip walk taking three or so hours. Another round trip is 10 to Gunung Jasar and back via 12.

Mountains Gunung Brinchang at 2032 metres is the highest point reached by surfaced road on the peninsula. Walk 7 from the Mardi Station will take you the two km to the top of 1841-metre Gunung Beremban. You can also reach the summit by the three km walk 3 from Hopetown near the golf course.

Gunung Jasar is 1696-metres high and is reached on path 10 which runs between the golf course and Tanah Rata. From Tanah Rata there are directional signs from near Highland Villa at the 37th milestone. It's two km from there or coming down from the Hilltop Bungalow at the golf course it's about 2½ km along walk 12 and then walk 10.

The Cameron Highlands' most famous jungle walker was the man who never came back from his walk. American Jim Thompson is credited with founding the Thai silk industry after WW II. He made a personal fortune and his beautiful, antique-packed house beside a khlong (canal) in Bangkok is a major tourist attraction today. On 26 March 1967 he was holidaying in the Highlands and left his villa for a pre-dinner stroll – never to be seen again. Despite extensive searches the mystery of Jim Thompson's disappearance has never been explained. Kidnapped? Taken by a tiger? Or simply a planned disappearance or suicide? Nobody knows.

Tea Plantations

A visit to a tea plantation is a popular highlands activity. The first tea was planted in 1926. The main plantations include the Blue Valley Tea Estate (tel 9847 for an appointment to visit) about 29 km above Tanah Rata. The Boh Tea Estate (tel 996032) is about 10 km below Tanah Rata and they conduct tours between 11 am and 12.30 pm. The plantation owners are happy to show visitors around the estates although you should ring for an appointment. They're closed on Sundays.

Tea bushes are plucked every seven to eight days. A plucker can gather about 40 kg in a day and it takes five kg of leaves to make a kg of tea.

The collected leaves are weighed and 'withered' – a drying process in which air is blown across troughs by fans in order to reduce the moisture content by about 50%. The dried leaves are then rolled to twist, break and rupture the leaf cells and release the juices for fermentation. The finer leaves are then separated out and the larger ones are rolled once again.

Fermentation, which is really oxidisation of the leaf enzymes, has to be critically controlled to develop the characteristic flavour and aroma of the tea. The fermented leaves are then 'fired', a process in which excess moisture is driven off in a drying machine. It is at this time that the leaves become black. Finally the tea is sorted into grades and stalks and fibres are removed before it is stored in bins to mature.

Other Attractions

The new Sam Poh Temple, just below Brinchang and about a km off the road, is a typically Chinese kaleidoscope of colours with Buddha statues, stone lions and incense burners. Mardi is an agricultural research station in Tanah Rata – visits must be arranged in advance.

There are a number of flower nurseries and vegetable farms in the Highlands. There is an Orang Asli settlement near Brinchang and you occasionally see Orang Asli, complete with their hunting blowpipes, while out walking. The Malaysian authorities are not at all happy about western visitors treating the Orang Asli as something to sightsee. Their culture is frail and treating them as snapshot subjects is going to do it no good at all.

The Highlands are famed for their butterflies and there are many colorful species to be seen. They're particularly prevalent around the waterfalls.

Places to Stay

The Highlands can be very busy in April, August and December when many families go there for vacations. At these times it is a good idea to book accommodation. Prices in the cheaper places can be variable with demand – if it's a peak time and few rooms are available you can expect prices to soar.

If it's quiet they will often be negotiable. The four main accommodation areas are:

Ringlet Not many people choose to stay down at Ringlet, which is around 300 metres below Tanah Rata. If you do you could try the base priced *Cathay* or *Hock Sin* or the more expensive *Lake View Bungalows* (tel 05-941630) with chalets and bungalows from M\$50. Right beside the lake, *Foster's Lakehouse* is magnificently 'olde worlde' in style and has singles and doubles from M\$100 to M\$180 plus more expensive suites.

Tanah Rata There are a number of popular cheap Chinese hotels in the main Highlands town. The first hotel upon entering Tanah Rata is the *Federal Hotel* (tel 05-941777) at number 44 with clean, fairly spacious rooms starting at M\$15 for singles/doubles with shared hot water bath.

At 39 Tanah Rata the popular and amazingly clean *Seah Meng* has rooms from M\$16. Next door the *Town House Hotel* (tel 05-941666) at number 41 has singles/doubles at M\$18 or M\$32 with attached hot-water bathroom. The owner of this clean and well-kept place is very helpful. In this same category there's the *Hollywood Hotel*, with rooms from M\$14.

Further up towards the end of town are the *Cameson Hotel*, the *Woh Nam Hotel* and the *Highlands Lodge*. The Woh Nam is rather seedy and overpriced but the Cameson and the Highlands each have quite adequate rooms with shared bath for M\$10.50 single and M\$12.50 double. At all these main street hotels try to avoid the noisy rooms at the front, overlooking the road. There are cheaper and quieter shared-bathroom rooms available if you're persistent.

Up a price notch there's the *Garden Hotel* (tel 05-941911) which is a little further up the road and off to the right. Rooms cost from M\$45 and there are also more expensive chalets. Yes, it does have a beautiful garden, and also its own little cinema. Apart from the weekends, when

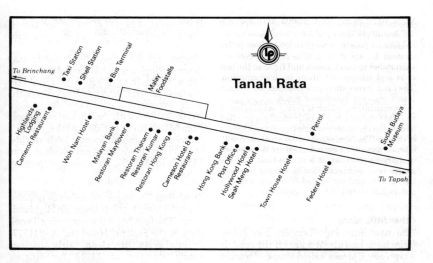

the hotel is often packed out, the prices are negotiable.

The *Rest House* in Tanah Rata is expensive by rest house standards, but pleasant and quiet. Even the ordinary doubles have little sitting rooms as well as attached baths for M$28. For M$40 you can have a suite. The rest house is usually booked out on weekends and holidays.

Brinchang - Golf Course One of the Highlands most popular places for shoestringers is actually between Tanah Rata and the golf course.

At *Bala's Holiday Chalets* (tel 05-941660), there are rooms from around M$5 per person in basic share rooms and the prices go up from there, depending on whether the room has a view of the valley below. Prices also vary to some extent with the season and demand. Doubles cost from M$12 or so, but you may find yourself being steered towards rooms at M$30 and if Bala can convince you to spend M$40 for a 'luxury room', he will!

There's a restaurant and cooking facilities so you can prepare your own food if you want to. There's also a washing machine, a fridge, general travel information available and they'll do bus bookings. Bala is a bit of a businessman, which puts some people off, but for all that it's a popular place, a good meeting point, has a pleasant communal feel to it and most people find it a fine place to stay. It is also quieter than most other accommodation in Tanah Rata and Brinchang. Bala's is about a 20-minute walk from Tanah Rata.

In Brinchang *Ye Olde Smokehouse* (tel 05-941214) looks so much like an old English pub that you'd be excused for thinking it was time-warped there by Dr Who himself. Rooms in Foster's Smokehouse range from around M$60 to M$300 and everything inside is as perfectly in step as the exterior would indicate. This is however, a rather nose-in-the-air establishment. According to one traveller's letter:

We once arrived in jeans and T-shirts (with a reservation) and the arrogant desk personnel started wondering among themselves (but loud enough for us to hear) whether we could afford it. After that, they made our stay as unpleasant as possible; too bad, the place is so beautiful!'

Across the road and about 100 metres further on is the *Golf Course Inn* (tel 05-941411), a modern motel-style place with modern motel-style rooms from M$90 for a single at the back to M$150 for a double at the front. Rooms do look out over the golf course.

Continue around the golf course and you come to the modern *Merlin Inn Resort* (tel 05-941211) with singles from M$80 to M$125 and doubles at M$90 to M$170. Other places around the golf course include the *Golf View Villa* (tel 05-941624) where whole bungalows can be rented.

Brinchang The final accommodation centre is the compact town of Brinchang. There are quite a few straightforward Chinese hotels; often just a little more expensive than those down in Tanah Rata. Prices range from M$10 to M$12 at the *Lido* to M$26 to M$31 for the nicer *Highlands Hotel* (tel 05-941588) at 29-32 Brinchang and *Hotel Brinchang* at 36.

The *Kowloon Hotel* (tel 05-941366) at 34-35 is the nicest place in Brinchang and room rates are M$30 to M$45 off-season, add M$5 during peak periods.

Also at Brinchang the *Wong Villa* is fairly cheap, M$4 to stay in the dorm and M$5 per person in shared rooms. It's a clean and friendly place and they will fix meals for you. You can get rooms for M$10 or less, but they're sometimes packed out with noisy parties of Chinese salesmen. It's also a bit close to the road leading to the tea estates so there is a lot of truck traffic during daylight hours.

Places to Eat

There is excellent Indian food available in the Cameron Highlands, perhaps as a result of the tea plantation influence since the majority of the plantation workers are Indians. In fact this is one of the better places for cheap Indian food in Malaysia.

Some places to try include the *Restoran Kumar* in the centre of Tanah Rata where the murtabaks and roti chanai are simply 'fantastic', and they also do daun pisang,

banana-leaf rice meals. Next door is *Restoran Thanam*, equally good. Up at Brinchang there's the low-priced and excellent *Sri Sentosa* beneath the Sentosa Hotel.

Of course there's also a good selection of Chinese restaurants although they've not as cheap as the Indian places. The *Kowloon* in Brinchang has very good food although you can count on around M$8 a head for food and drinks. Down in Tanah Rata the *Hong Kong* is similarly priced and has really good food.

The Highlands' real taste treat is steamboat, that Chinese equivalent of a Swiss fondue where you get plates of meat, shrimp, vegetables and eggs and brew your soup over a burner on the table. You need at least two people (count on around M$6 a head), but the more the better.

The *Garden Hotel* in Tanah Rata has a very good steamboat in beautiful settings and at prices only marginally higher than the regular restaurants; a worthwhile investment.

For inexpensive Chinese, try the tasty buffet at *Restoran Mayflower* near the Malayan Bank in Tanah Rata, where a

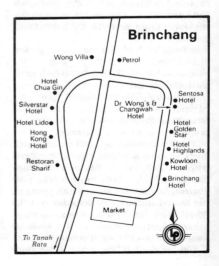

Brinchang

Wong Villa ● ● Petrol

Hotel Chua Gin

Silverstar Hotel

Hotel Lido ●

Hong Kong Hotel

Restoran Sharif ●

Dr. Wong's & Changwah Hotel

Sentosa ● Hotel

Hotel ● Golden Star

Hotel ● Highlands

● Kowloon Hotel

● Brinchang Hotel

Market

To Tanah Rata

Ye Olde Smokehouse, Brinchang

rice plate with three side dishes is about M$2. During the week this is probably the most popular Chinese eating establishment in the highlands.

Near the Highlands Lodge in Tanah Rata there are two smaller restaurants, the *Friendship* and the *Cameron* with similar Chinese buffets – the latter in particular has a wide selection of dishes to choose from.

Also in Tanah Rata are a dozen or so food stalls next to the bus terminal serving inexpensive Malay dishes like nasi campur, mee bandung and so on. In Brinchang the Malay stalls are next to the market near the town entrance.

The *Smokehouse* is 'ideal for homesick Brits' where you can get expensive tea and scones (M$6), sandwiches with the crusts cut off and fairly pricey meals. The *Golf Course Inn* has a restaurant with good and not too expensive Chinese food. Up at the *Merlin* you can get a good hamburger or other lunchtime meals in the open-air area overlooking the golf course.

The Highlands are famous for their luscious strawberries although a strawberry fancier from Georgia wrote to us in outrage to report he was served frozen strawberries once! The Town House Hotel in Tanah Rata has a milk bar where they serve fresh strawberries with whipped cream, ice cream, etc.

If you're preparing your own food, it's reported that vegetables and other food are fresher and cheaper up at Brinchang than in Tanah Rata. They're grown beyond Brinchang at Kampung Raja where there are also a couple of excellent bargain price restaurants. You can get fresh milk from the dairy on the road beside the playground in Tanah Rata. There's also a bakery on Jalan Sultan which does good scones and the food stalls in Tanah Rata have various snacks including delicious dessert pancakes called apam balek.

The *Rest House* in Tanah Rata has a good restaurant and its bar is a local social centre.

Getting There & Away

It's a long and gradual climb from Tapah to the Highlands with plenty of corners on the way. From the Golf Course Inn down to the main road junction one visitor reported counting 653! Bus No 153 runs approximately every hour from Tapah to Tanah Rata; the trip takes about two hours. The fare is M$3 or M$3.30 to Brinchang. A taxi costs M$6.

From the taxi stand in Tanah Rata it's M$6 down to Tapah, M$11 to Ipoh, M$18 to KL, M$22 to Butterworth or just 60 sen per person to Brinchang. There's a daily MARA bus between Tanah Rata and KL for M$8. It departs KL at 8.30 am and arrives in Tanah Rata around 1 pm. A National Express bus departs from the Town House Hotel in TR for KL at 2.30 pm and arrives at 7 pm – fare is M$7.5 – in that direction. Other direct buses also run between KL and the Highlands.

There is no longer a direct bus between Tanah Rata and Butterworth, but the Town House Hotel will book tickets for the Tapah-Butterworth for M$9, not including fare to Tapah. You must leave Tanah Rata by 8 am in order to catch the bus which then gets you to Butterworth around 2.30 pm. There is a later bus that you can book at the Tapah terminal which leaves Tapah at 11 am, arriving in Butterworth around 4 pm. Tapah is on the KL-Butterworth road and there is a railway station at Tapah Road, 20 minutes away by bus.

IPOH

The 'city of millionaires' made its fortune from the rich tin mines of the Kinta Valley. The elegant mansions of Ipoh testify to the many successful Chinese miners. It's an ongoing process since many of the mines around Ipoh are still producing today.

For the visitor Ipoh's mainly a transit town, a place where you change buses if you're heading for Pangkor Island, or where you pause to sample what is reputed to be some of the finest Chinese food in Malaysia. It's worth a longer visit to explore the Buddhist temples cut into the limestone outcrops north and south of the town. 'Old Town' Ipoh is centred along the Kinta River between Jalan Sultan Idris Shah and Jalan Sultan Iskandar Shah and is worth a wander for the old Chinese and British architecture.

To local visitors Ipoh has another side, as this is Malaysia's sin city renowned for its massage parlours and strip clubs and a frequent target of ribald comments and jokes.

Cave Temples

There are a number of cave temples both south and north of the town – several of them close to the main road so it's no problem to pause for a look. Sam Poh Tong is just six km south of Ipoh and is reputed to be one of the largest of the cave temples. There's even a vegetarian restaurant in the upper part of the front facade of this ornate temple. Inside you can wander back through the caves and climb a long series of steps to a lookout over the surrounding countryside.

At Perak Tong there's a 12-metre-high seated Buddha figure and painting of Kuan Yin, the Goddess of Mercy, high on the face of the limestone cliff. Wat Thai or Meh Prasit Sumaki Temple has a 24-metre figure of the reclining Buddha, one of the largest in Malaysia.

Places to Stay – bottom end

There are plenty of hotels in all price categories in Ipoh. At the bottom end of the price scale, the *Beauty Hotel* on Jalan Yang Kalsom near the intersection with Jalan Chamberlain is fairly clean but noisy and has rooms from M$10.50. At number 92 on the same road the *Kowloon* is of a bit higher standard, with fan-cooled rooms for M$18 or air-con for M$23. Or there's the *Embassy* at 37 Jalan Chamberlain with rooms for M$18 and the *Hollywood Hotel* at 72-76 from M$17.

Cheaper still are the *South Eastern Hotel* across from the Lumut bus terminal and the *Cathay Hotel* on Jalan Chamberlain at the Jalan Yang Kalsom junction – both have very basic rooms with common bath from M$13.

Moving into the middle price bracket the *New International Hotel* (tel 05-512699) at 23-25 Jalan Toh Puah Chah in the northern part of the old town has rooms from M$26 to M$80. The *Hotel Diamond* (tel 05-513644) at 3-9 Jalan Ali Pitchay used to be a bargain but has declined of late so that M$27.50 is no longer such good value.

The *Hotel Fairmont* (tel 05-511100) at 10-12 Kampar Rd has large, very clean air-con rooms posted from M$40 but discounts are usually available. The *City Hotel* (tel 05-512911) on Jalan Chamberlain between Jalan Osbourne and Jalan Yang Kalsom is sort of in-between with rooms from M$26.

One of the better value hotels in this category is the *Winner Hotel* (tel 05-515177) at 32-38 Jalan Ali Pitchay which has rooms with air-con from M$26 to M$79. Finally the *Merlin Hotel* (tel 05-541351) at 92-98 Jalan Clare has singles/doubles for M$32/40 and up.

Places to Stay – top end

The *Hotel Excelsior Ipoh* (tel 05-536666) is on Jalan Clarke and has 133 rooms with singles/doubles at M$98/118. Other top-end hotels include the *Eastern Hotel* (tel 05-543936) at 118 Jalan Sultan Idris Shah with singles for M$69 to M$85, and doubles from M$79 to M$95.

The *Hotel Mikado* (tel 05-515855) on Jalan Yang Kalsom has rooms at very similar prices. The larger *Tambun Inn* (tel 05-552211) at 91 Tambun Rd has singles/doubles for M$70/85 plus more expensive deluxe rooms and suites.

The town's intriguing old railway station was built in 1917 and the *Station Hotel* (tel 05-512588) is at the station on Club Rd. Rooms cost from M$40 to M$90.

Places to Eat

Ipoh has plenty of restaurants and the rice noodle dish known as kway teow is reputed to be better in Ipoh than anywhere else in Malaysia. The city's most well-known place for kway teow is *Kedai Kopi Kong Heng* on Jalan Leech between Jalan Market (Pasar) and Jalan Panglima. The kway teow soup there is M$1.50 and has tender strips of chicken and prawns. They also have good roast chicken and popiah. Kong Heng is one of the oldest Chinese restaurants in the city and there are several others like it on and off Jalan Leech.

Another good area for Chinese food is along Jalan Clare. Good Malay food is found on Osbourne St and near the bus stations.

One of the best places in town is *Rahman Restaurant* on Jalan Chamberlain near the Jalan Bendahara junction. This place is actually run by Indian Muslims but they serve traditional Malay dishes like rendang. The Rahman is very clean and cheap – roti chanai for 40 sen, and ayam rendang with rice and vegetables M$1.50. Ipoh-ites take their food seriously and are always ready to give an opinion on which restaurant is particularly worth trying. The *Station Hotel* does a great breakfast for M$6.

Good Punjabi food is available at *Guru's Chapati*, a stall in the Cheong Seng Restaurant complex on Lebuh Raya Ipoh in Ipoh Gardens, north-east of the town centre. The 'Guru' in the stall's name is merely a nickname for the owner, Mr Gurucharan Singh, a Sikh who went into cooking after retiring from Malayan Railways some years ago. For M$2 you get your choice of a variety of curries, plus three to four vegetables, yoghurt, and fresh melt-in-your-mouth chapatis.

In the town centre, there are two south Indian restaurants specialising in vegetarian food, *Krishna Bhawan* and *Makanan Sayor Sayoran Segera* at 8 and 10 Jalan Lahat, not far from the bus terminals. This street is lined with Indian shops selling everything from incense to saris. Further down Jalan Lahat toward the

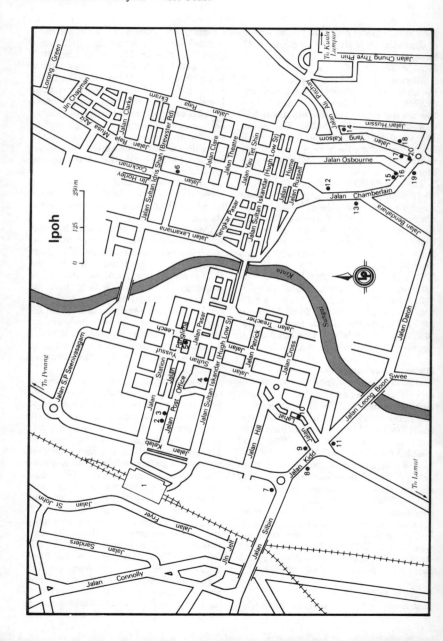

1	Railway Station & Hotel
2	GPO
3	Clock Tower
4	MAS
5	Kong Heng Coffee Shop
6	Taxis
7	City Bus Station
8	Kuala Lumpur, Singapore & Butterworth Bus
9	Lumut Buses
10	Indian Restaurants
11	South Eastern Hotel
12	Rex Theatre
13	Embassy Hotel
14	Winner Hotel
15	Hollywood Hotel
16	Rahman Restaurant
17	Beauty Hotel
18	Kowloon Hotel
19	City Hotel
20	Cathay Hotel

bus area is another Indian place, *Rama Vilas*. At the Jalan Bendahara and Jalan Leong Boon Swee intersection is *Restoran Majeedia*, another Indian Muslim place, convenient to all the hotels on Jalan Chamberlain and Jalan Yang Kalsom.

Getting There & Away

Ipoh is on the main KL-Butterworth road; 219 km north of KL, 173 km south of Butterworth. It's M$8 to M$11 by bus from KL, M$15 by taxi. It's marginally cheaper from Butterworth. There are regular buses from Ipoh to Lumut, 101 km away, for Pangkor Island. The outstation bus terminals and the taxi station are at the intersection of Jalans Kelab, Kidd and Silbin, not far from the railway station in the town centre.

LUMUT

The Malaysian Navy has its principal base in this town – a replacement for the old base in Singapore. In spite of the navy presence, this small river port of 33,000 is little more than a departure point for nearby Pangkor Island.

The rest house, a stone's throw from the

ferry pier, used to have a small museum, but its contents were transferred to the museum in Taiping some years ago. All that's left now is a group of cannons from the Dutch fort on Pangkor and a group of Malay cannons cast in Aceh in north Sumatra about 200 years ago. Lumut is the site for the Pesta Lumut sea carnival in July-August each year.

At Telok Rubiah, not far from Lumut, there's a Marine Farmhouse. Sam Khoo, of Pangkor Island's 'mini camp' fame, also established this place, where he raises tiger prawns, crabs and other seafood creatures. Visitors are welcome to come and have a look at how he's doing. He may also set up a lodging house there.

Places to Stay & Eat

If you get marooned in Lumut because you missed the last ferry to Pangkor, there is a reasonable choice of Chinese hotels and plenty of restaurants.

The *Singa Hotel* with rooms around M$10 is typical. There's good Indian food next door. The *Phi Lum Hooi Hotel*, about ½ km from the bus stand, costs M$8 for a single and is very good, clean and friendly. The restaurant downstairs is decorated with a collection of shark fins! The fine old waterfront *Rest House* (tel 05-935938) is M$15 a double.

Getting There & Away

Lumut is 206 km south of Butterworth or 101 km from Ipoh, the usual place for Lumut buses if you're travelling north on the KL-Butterworth road. There are daily buses Butterworth-Lumut for M$8 or you can get a bus to Taiping about every half hour and another bus on from there.

Probably the best way to go is Ipoh-Lumut. There are buses hourly for M$3. There are also direct buses from KL to Lumut several times per day. The trip takes about six hours and costs M$11 by an air-con bus.

There's also a daily bus from Tapah in the Cameron Highlands to Lumut for M$8, but it only seems to run during the high season, April, August and November to February.

Long-distance taxis would be about M$15 per person for Butterworth-Lumut or M$7 for Ipoh-Lumut.

PANGKOR ISLAND

The island of Pangkor is close to the coast off Lumut – easily accessible via Ipoh. It's a popular resort island for its fine and often quite isolated beaches, many of which can be walked to along an interesting 'around the island' track.

Taking the regular ferry service from Lumut you go out the Dindings River by the Malaysian Navy base. On the mainland coast the huge, almost Singapore-like, apartment complex has been built as naval quarters. Although the base is nearly in full operation it doesn't seem to have made a big difference to Pangkor life. The sailors have their own beach near Lumut, Telok Batik, and about the only time they make it over to Pangkor is for Sunday picnics.

A visit to the island is principally a 'laze on the beach' operation, but there are also a number of interesting things to do.

Information & Orientation

Finding things on Pangkor is very simple. On the east coast of the island, facing the mainland, there's a continuous village strip comprising Sungei Pinang Kecil (SPK), Sungei Pinang Besar (SBK) and Pangkor village.

The ferry from Lumut stops at SPK before Pangkor village which is where you'll find the restaurants and shops. The road which runs along the coast on this side turns west at Pangkor village and runs directly across the island, only a km or two wide at this point, to Pasir Bogak where you find almost all the accommodation. From there a track, suitable for motorcycles for part of the distance, runs right around the northern end of the island, reaching Pangkor's other hotel at Telok Belanga in the north-west.

Pangkor is a fairly conservative place –

it's wise to behave and dress discreetly. It's also a very friendly place and travellers have written of being invited to weddings, festivals and other events even during short visits to the island.

There is no bank on Pangkor; you'll have to cross to Lumut to change money.

Pangkor Problems

Pangkor has two drawbacks. For a start it can get very crowded on weekends and, to a much greater extent, during school holidays. It's a popular local resort, only a short ferry ride from the mainland and close to large population centres so crowds are inevitable.

The other problem is an aesthetic one – most of the island could do with a damn good clean up. Most of the beaches are unpleasantly littered where the tide does not clean them. The paths and roads are strewn with rubbish and Pasir Bogak, the beach with most of the island's accommodation, is a combination of tacky, unplanned buildings and shacks and more of Pangkor's messy garbage problem. It's a shame the island is so uncared for, because basically it's a very pretty place.

Beaches

Pasir Bogak is OK for swimming but during holidays it's crowded, at least by Malaysia's 'empty beach' standards, and, as already mentioned, is somewhat littered. Golden Sands Beach (Telok Belanga) at the other end of the island is pleasant and in between them are a number of virtually deserted beaches which you can reach by boat, on foot or on motorcycles.

Unfortunately Pangkor has its fair share of local young men who come to sit and stare at visitors. Western women may not get too much peace on these beaches. The nicest beach on this side is at Coral Bay, about a 45-minute walk from Pasir Bogak. The water is a clear emerald-green due to the presence of limestone and usually the beach is quite clean and pretty.

Turtles come in to lay their eggs at night on Telok Ketapang beach, only a short walk north of Pasir Bogak. May, June and July are the main months and June is usually best of all if you want to go

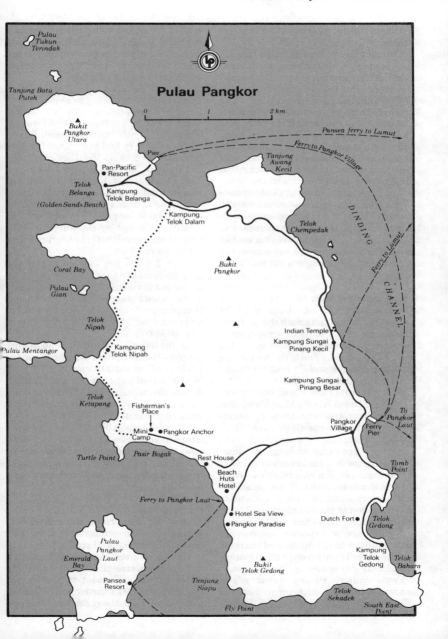

midnight turtle spotting. Sightings are becoming increasingly rare these days.

Emerald Bay on nearby Pulau Pangkor Laut is a beautiful little horseshoe-shaped bay with clear water, fine coral and a gently sloping beach. However, the entire island of Pangkor Laut has been taken over by a French hotel-restaurant conglomerate and as soon as you step off the ferry from Pasir Bogak you'll be hit for a use fee of M$10 per person during the week or M$30 on weekends. The fee includes the use of Pansea facilities, including the swimming pool, beaches, and beach cabanas.

The Pan-Pacific Resort at Golden Sands Beach, run by a Japanese conglomerate, charges M$30 for day admission and it is rumoured that this will be increased to M$50 shortly. The fee does entitle visitors to a M$15 discount in the restaurant, but considering the prices, it's not much of a savings.

Round the Island Walk
Five hours easy walking will take you right around the island, although it's better to make a day of it and pause for a swim at the various beaches you pass along the way. As you walk, admire the jungle, the monkeys and the prolific butterflies and birds - including hornbills.

The path from Pasir Bogak commences right beside Sam Khoo's Mini Camp and it's a two-hour stroll by a string of pleasant beaches to the Pan-Pacific Resort at Telok Belanga. From there you can get a ferry to Lumut or, once a day, to Pangkor village. The path is used by motorcycles the rest of the way around. You may be able to avoid the M$30 entrance fee to Telok Belanga if you're just passing through but it's up to the discretion of the guards there.

Incidentally, according to Malaysian law, public access is allowed to all beaches in the country so the practice of charging admission to Telok Belanga and Pangkor Laut is, strictly speaking, illegal.

From Sungei Pinang Kecil it's a continuous village strip on to Pangkor village - messy but full of interest. There's

boat building, fish being dried or frozen, a colourful south Indian temple - lots to look at. Finally at Pangkor village you can grab a taxi back to Pasir Bogak if your feet won't carry you any further.

Dutch Fort
Pangkor's one bit of history is three km south of Pangkor village at Telok Gedong. There the Dutch built a wooden fort in 1670 - after they had been given the boot from Lower Perak. In 1690 they rebuilt the fort in brick, but lost it soon afterwards. The Dutch retook the fort in 1693 but despite frequent visits did not reoccupy it until 1745 and only three years later they abandoned it for good. The old fort was totally swallowed by the jungle in 1973 when it was rebuilt as far as the remaining bricks would allow.

Near the fort you may encounter the famous 'Snake Man of Pangkor', a Malay snake-handler who keeps various poisonous serpents, including kraits and cobras, and is apparently immune to their venom. He will gladly put on a show for a donation of M$1 to M$2.

On the waterfront a little beyond the fort is a huge stone on which the coat of arms of the Dutch East India Company (VOC) has been inscribed along with some old graffiti. A 'thoughtful' conservationist has painted them all in green and red and added some more recent graffiti for good measure!

The road ends at Telok Gedong and the footpath continues a little further. Note how well kept most of the houses are in this Malay kampung. Drums and tubs of flowers border the houses and more hang from the roof edges.

Places to Stay
Almost all Pangkor's accommodation possibilities are strung out along the beach at Pasir Bogak. On the opposite side of the island from Pangkor village, this quite pleasant stretch of beach would be a whole lot more pleasant if it were not spoilt by the tacky development taking place along it and the grubby way rubbish

is allowed to collect above the high tide mark. The situation does seem to be improving as Pangkor becomes more tourist-oriented.

At the bottom end of the price scale and the far end of the beach is *Sam Khoo's Mini Camp* (tel 05-951164). It's a collection of thatched-roof huts around a central, open restaurant area. In the huts you've just got a bare board to sleep on and the lights all go on at dusk and off at 11 pm – no choice. Single cabins cost M$5; double cabins cost from M$8 to M$10; and there are also 'dorm' huts. Since the huts aren't screened, mosquitoes can be a problem.

This is one of Pangkor's backpackers' centre and you'll meet travellers from all over the world. On weekends and school holidays (April and August) the mini camp can become very crowded and noisy with local students but it's usually quieter on weekdays.

Moving back along the beach from Sam Khoo's there's *Pangkor Beach Camp* (tel 05-951626), with much the same accommodation and rates as Sam's. Same problems, too, noisy holiday revellers and mosquitoes.

The *Pangkor Anchor* (tel 05-951363) is probably Pasir Bogak's best value in accommodation, although it costs a few ringgit more than other beach camps. It has 33 neatly laid-out slightly larger A-frame huts, with simple, mattress-on-the-floor accommodation at a cost of M$8 to M$10 per night per person. The owner of the property, Mrs Wong, is often on the premises and will entertain you with stories, opinions and lots of personality. What makes the Anchor worth a few more ringgit is the fact that the place is spotlessly clean and peaceful – they have a strictly enforced no-noise policy after 11 pm.

Other nice touches include heating the milk for your morning coffee, occasional free snacks of pisang goreng or pandanus cake, and free use of beach equipment. Sim, the manager, is full of information on Pangkor and nearby areas. He has also done quite a bit of travelling, including an

overland trip from Malaysia to Europe back in the days when that was still possible – so he is good about anticipating the needs of backpackers. This is one place that will usually have a bed on weekends since their slightly higher rates and no-noise policy keeps out the student weekenders. Call ahead if you want to make sure.

Continuing up the beach you come to the rather run-down *Pangkor Mini Long House*, which doesn't get much business and probably never will as long as the beach in front of it is the prime location for the drying of ikan bilis or anchovies.

Next is the ramshackle government-run *Pangkor New Rest House* (the sign reads Rumah Rehat Baru Pangkor). There's one room above the restaurant for M$10 or three 'bungalows' at M$20 each. They're quite a bargain since they have a kitchen, lounge, bathroom and two double rooms, so between four or five people they're cheap accommodation. The drawback is that they are dismal and drab in appearance and very poorly kept. There are also dormitory beds available for M$4 per person.

At the south-east end of the beach there's Pasir Bogak's more expensive establishments. Both offer perfectly adequate and fairly reasonably priced accommodation although neither take much advantage of their excellent waterfront positions. A little more imagination is called for.

The newer *Beach Huts Hotel* (tel 05-951359) has rooms from M$40, more with air-con, more again with colour TV. There are also air-conditioned chalets with a TV and fridge. The older *Sea View Hotel* (tel 05-951056), has very friendly staff and offers higher standards at higher prices – air-con rooms or chalets ranging from M$65 to M$75. During the off-season, or at anytime they're not crowded, you can easily get a discount of 30% for the asking. Both places have restaurants and bars and there are boating facilities including windsurfers at the Sea View. The garden area in front of the Sea View is an excellent place to watch the sun set.

Finally, at the extreme end of Pasir Bogak is the newcomer *Pangkor Paradise*, the most basic of the basic, thatched huts with no electricity and little in the way of toilet facilities or security. However, sunset views are even better there than at the Sea View Hotel.

Apart from Pasir Bogak there is also the Japanese-managed *Pan-Pacific Pangkor Resort* (tel 05-951091), formerly the Pangkor Bay Village, at Telok Belanga (Golden Sands Beach) at the other end of the island. The Pan-Pacific has rooms starting at M$150 but off-season discounts are available. There are also package deals from KL which include transport to Pangkor and two or three nights accommodation. There is a variety of sporting and recreational facilities and the hotel is on a very pleasant stretch of beach, nicely isolated from the local development which mars Pasir Bogak.

You can walk from Pasir Bogak to Telok Belanga in about two hours but will have to deal with a possible entrance fee of M$30 because the beach at the hotel is private – it's an attempt to cut down littering and to stop the local cowboys riding their motorcycles along the beach.

Pulau Pangkor Laut, the island across from Pasir Bogak, is totally in the grasp of *Pansea on the Island* (tel 05-951320, in KL 03-2423654), which is managed by a French multinational hotel corporation. Any traveller boarding a ferry for Pangkor Laut from Pasir Bogak or Pangkor village will be interrogated as to the purpose of the trip – are you putting up at the resort or paying for day use (M$10 weekdays, M$30 weekends). Since the French took over from local management, they have been promoting the place through international yacht races and tennis tournaments. There is a small swimming pool, six tennis courts, two restaurants, a disco, and three or four private beaches around the island, including the picturesque Emerald Bay on the side facing away from Pangkor.

Posted rates are M$77 per person double occupancy or M$98 for a single. During the week there are usually discounts available to around M$60 per person.

Places to Eat

All the hotels offer restaurants but the beach camps are more on-again off-again. At the beach camps 'cook's day off' is frequently heard during the week. *Sam Khoo's* usually has consistently cheap and filling meals. Travellers report that the food at the *Rest House* can be excellent – sweet & sour fish, mee hoon, even fish & chips are offered, but be sure to fix the price first. Near the rest house is a string of Malay food stalls, which are generally open only on the weekends.

The *Fisherman's Place* next to the Pangkor Anchor, serves very fresh and tasty seafood. Sim, the young Chinese manager, used to be the general manager for the Pangkor Bay Village (now the Pan-Pacific Resort), and when he left to start his own place and get away from the multinational scene, he brought virtuoso cook Madame Tan with him.

The menu is very flexible and Sim will be glad to make recommendations. Dishes which are especially good are the garlic-fried red snapper, the seafood steamboat, chips (French fries), and barbequed stingray. Groupa and pomfret are also favourite local fish and there are always prawns, crab and squid. Prices vary according to the fish but a medium-sized snapper is M$5 to M$7, stir-fried squid M$3 to M$4 – most dishes will feed two to three people and MSG is not added to the food. Hours at the Fisherman's Place are 5 pm to midnight, or from noon on holidays. This is another good place to have a cold beer and watch the sunset glow over the hills.

The *Pangkor Anchor* next door, also managed by Sim, serves only breakfast (great breakfasts, though) so dinner time finds many Anchor guests at the Fisherman's.

There's a real crowd of restaurants,

predominantly Chinese, at Pangkor village, Sungei Pinang Besar and Kecil. Locals report that each place has a 'best' Chinese restaurant. In Pangkor village it's the *Fook Heng*, in SPK the *Hock Kee* and in SPB the *Wah Moi*. Locals say the Wah Moi has gone downhill since the head cook opened a place in Lumut, but the Hock Kee is still famous for its traditional local-style preparation of seafood – it would be best to go with a Pangkor resident to help you order.

There are two small Indian Muslim restaurants in Pangkor village – locals say the best roti chanai is at the smaller one (no name) on the secondary road out to the Dutch Fort, just before you leave the village. The other Indian place, *Restoran Zainamuddin*, is a bit larger and cleaner.

Getting There & Away

From Lumut boats run every half hour or so from 8 am to 7.30 pm. From Pangkor to Lumut they operate 5.50 am to 6.30 pm. The trip takes 30 to 40 minutes and they also stop at Sungei Pinang Kecil (SPK), the fishing village just north of Pangkor village. Min Lian and Pangkor Feri Ekspres are the ferry operators and the fare for either is M$1 one-way, M$1.50 return.

However, if you buy a return ticket from say, Min Lian, you can't use it on Pangkor Feri Ekspres upon returning to Lumut – you must wait till a Min Lian boat is leaving. Hence if you're on a tight schedule and don't want to wait longer than you have to at the Pangkor jetty, buy one-way tickets.

There are also four boats a day between Lumut and Golden Sands Beach at the north-west end of the island. They cost M$1 and operate from Lumut at 8.30, 10.30 am, 1.30, 4.15 pm; and to Lumut at 9.30 am, 12.30, 3.30, 5 pm. Every morning there is a Pangkor village to Telok Belanga service and each evening a service in the opposite direction; fare is M$1.30.

Ferries from Lumut to Pulau Pangkor Laut are an astounding M$6 return – another way to keep out the riff-raff. From Pasir Bogak there are occasional ferries leaving from the beach between the Beach Huts Hotel and Sea View Hotel directly to the Pansea Resort for M$3.

Getting Around

A taxi – they're almost all old Austin Cambridges – for the 10-minute trip from the ferry pier at Pangkor village to the accommodation at Pasir Bogak on the opposite side of the island costs M$2 to M$3. The drivers may try to charge more, but you shouldn't pay more than M$3, even all the way to the end of Pasir Bogak.

There are also island buses about every half hour or you can walk it in 20 minutes. You can hire bicycles from most of the beach camps or at the bicycle shop in Pangkor village for M$3 a day. The road runs right around the eastern side of the island to Telok Belanga but most of the way it's suitable only for motorcycles. From Telok Belanga a good walking track goes to Pasir Bogak. The Dutch fort and Kampung Telok Gedong are easily reached by bicycle.

You used to be able to hire boats out to Emerald Bay on Pangkor Laut or to Telok Belanga, but now that these are 'private' beaches you will have to pay day use fees in addition to hiring a boat. Between a group the cost of the boat alone is fairly reasonable. From the Sea View Hotel costs range from around M$25 to M$40 for trips to Emerald Bay (return), South Point, Nipah Bay or Telok Belanga. You can bargain for lower prices with other boats.

KUALA KANGSAR

The royal town of Perak state is beside the highway, north of Ipoh. A couple of km out of town is the Ubadiah Mosque with its fine golden onion-dome. It's probably the finest mosque in Malaysia although it looks almost as if it's viewed through a distorting mirror since its four minarets are squeezed up tightly against the dome.

Overlooking the river is the palace or Istana Iskandariah, but it's not open to visitors. There is also an earlier istana and an intricately carved ceremonial hall.

Kuala Kangsar was the birthplace of Malaysia's great rubber industry. A number of rubber trees had been planted at the agricultural station there, from seed stock smuggled from Brazil, but it was not until the invention of the pneumatic tyre in 1888 that rubber suddenly came into demand and rubber plantations sprang up across the country.

All of the trees for the new plantations are descended from the original rubber trees in Kuala Kangsar. You can still see one of those first trees in the district office compound and another near the agriculture department office.

Places to Stay

There is a fine *Rest House* between the town centre and the mosque. It overlooks the Perak River and rooms are M$17.60. The *Double Lion Hotel* at 74 Jalan Kangsar is cheap at just M$8 but also extremely basic.

Getting There & Away

Kuala Kangsar is 50 km north of Ipoh, beside the main KL-Butterworth road. It's 123 km south of Butterworth, 269 km north of KL. A bus from Butterworth takes 2½ hours and costs M$3.80.

TAIPING

The 'town of everlasting peace' hardly started out that way. A century ago, when it was known as Larut, the town was a raucous, rough-and-tumble tin mining centre – the oldest one in Malaysia.

Bitter feuds broke out three times between rival Chinese secret societies with injury, torture and death taking place on both sides. When colonial administrators finally brought the bloody mayhem under control in 1874 they took the prudent step of renaming the town.

Apart from misty, Chinese-looking views Taiping also has quite a number of well-preserved old Anglo-Malay buildings. Along with Penang, this is a favourite spot for wealthy Malaysians to retire to.

Taiping is a low-key town; there's good food in the night market, a great museum and no tourists.

Lake Garden

Taiping is renowned for its beautiful Lake Garden, built on the site of an abandoned tin mine right beside the town in 1890. The well-kept gardens owe some of their lush greenery to the fact that Taiping has the highest annual rainfall in Peninsular Malaysia. There's also a small zoo in the Lake Gardens while in the hills which rise above the gardens is Maxwell Hill, the oldest hill station in Malaysia.

The Prison

At the far end of the gardens is a prison used by the Japanese during the war and later as a rehabilitation centre for captured Communists during the Emergency. Today it houses political detainees under the ISA (Internal Security Act) ruling.

Museum

Just beyond the prison is the Taiping State Museum which is open from 9 am to 5 pm daily, but closed from 12 noon to 2.30 pm on Fridays. It's the oldest museum in Malaysia and its contents include interesting exhibits on the aboriginal people of this area although its fairy-tale architecture is probably its most interesting aspect.

Other Attractions

Taiping was also the starting point for Malaysia's first railway; opened in 1885 it ran 13.5 km to Port Weld, but is now closed.

Taiping has an Allied war cemetery beside the Lake Garden and in the town itself there are some interesting old buildings from the colonial period, including the old town office.

The Ling Nam temple is the oldest Chinese temple in Perak and has a boat figure dedicated to the Chinese emperor who built the first canal in China. On Station St there's an interesting south Indian Hindu temple.

Places to Stay

There are a couple of rest houses in Taiping. The *Rest House* in town is around M$12 for a double including your own bath/toilet, although it is outside the room. Breakfast is served on the verandah and the people who run it are very pleasant.

The other *Rest House* (tel 05-822044) in Taman Tasik is a curious mixture of Sumatran and classical Roman styles. Overlooking the Lake Gardens, it's clean, secure and costs twice as much as the rest house in town.

The *Lake View Hotel* (tel 06-822911) has rooms from M$15. The *Wee Bah Hotel* costs from M$10 and is, according to one traveller, 'a perfect copy of the Tye Ann in Georgetown'. There are other cheap Chinese hotels, like the *Towne Hotel* along the main street or the clean and friendly, but rather noisy, *Kwah Sheong Hotel* opposite the Lido Cinema.

Taiping's large night market has many open-air eating stalls and satay is one of the city's specialties.

Getting There & Away

Taiping is several km off the main KL-Butterworth road. It's 88 km south of Butterworth and 304 km north of KL. If you're heading south from Butterworth to Lumut for Pangkor Island and miss the direct bus it's straightforward to take a Butterworth-Taiping bus and another bus on from Taiping to Lumut.

MAXWELL HILL

The oldest hill station in Malaysia is 12 km from Taiping at an altitude of 1019 metres. It was formerly a tea estate but has now been closed and the quiet little station is simply a cool and peaceful place to be. There are no golf courses, fancy restaurants or other hill station trappings – let alone casinos.

Getting up to Maxwell Hill is half the fun and once there you've got fine views down over Taiping and the Lake Gardens far below. From Cottage, the summit you

can walk to from Maxwell Hill, you can see the coast all the way from Penang to Pangkor on a clear day.

Few people visit Maxwell Hill and in fact the eight bungalows there will only accommodate a total of 53 visitors. During the school holidays of April, August and December all eight are full. The electricity is off from 7.30 am to 6.30 pm and again from midnight to 6 am.

Places to Stay

You can book space in one of the eight bungalows by ringing 05-886241 or by writing to the Superintendent, Tempat Peranginan, Taiping. If you've not booked earlier you can ring from the Land Rover station at the bottom of the hill.

There are two Rest House Bungalows – *Bukit Larut* (also known as the Maxwell) and *Gunung Hijau* (or Speedy), with rooms from M$18. Other bungalows are *Cempaka* (Hugh Low), *Beringin* (Watson) and the more expensive *Cendana* (Hut) and *Tempinis* (Treacher). They're all between the 6th and 7th milestone from the base of the hill. *Watson Rest House* is very cheap although the food is a little expensive. Meals are available at Speedy and Maxwell Rest Houses if you're day-tripping.

Getting There & Away

Prior to WW II you had a choice of walking, pony-back or being carried up in a sedan chair for there was no road to the station. Japanese prisoners of war were put to work building a road at the close of the war and it was opened in 1948.

Private cars are not allowed on the road so if you want to go it has to be in the government Land Rovers that run a regular service from the station at the foot of the hill, just above the Taiping Lake Gardens. They operate every hour on the hour from 8 am to 6 pm and the trip takes about 40 minutes.

The winding road negotiates 72 hairpin bends on the steep ascent and traffic is strictly one-way. You can glimpse superb views through the trees on the way up.

The up and down Land Rovers meet at Tea Gardens, the midway point. Fares from the bottom vary from about 70 sen to the Tea Gardens to just over M$2 all the way to Cottage. Alternatively you can walk to the top in about three hours.

BUTTERWORTH

There's no reason to pause in Butterworth; it's just a port for ferries to Penang Island and the site of an Australian air force base.

Places to Stay

If for some reason you want to stop in Butterworth, there are a number of hotels. The cheap *Ruby Hotel* costs M$12 a double and has a bar downstairs; and the *Ambassadress Hotel* (tel 04-342788) at 4425 Jalan Bagan Luar, has air-con rooms from M$20. At the other end of the scale there's the *Merlin Inn Butterworth* (tel 04-343322), 480 Jalan Bagan Luar, which has singles/doubles at M$60/80.

Penang

The oldest British settlement in Malaysia, predating both Singapore and Melaka, is also one of Malaysia's major tourist attractions. This is hardly surprising, for the 285-square-km island of Penang has popular beach resorts and an intriguing and historically interesting town which is also noted for its superb food.

Penang's major town, Georgetown, is often referred to as 'Penang' although correctly that is the name of the island (the actual Malay spelling is Pinang). It's a real Chinatown with far more Chinese flavour than Singapore or Hong Kong. Those larger cities have had their Chinese flavour submerged under a gleaming concrete, glass and chrome confusion, but in the older parts of Georgetown the clock seems to have stopped 50 years ago. It's an easygoing, colourful city where the bicycle rickshaw is still the most sensible means of transport.

In 1786 Captain Francis Light, on behalf of the East India Company, acquired possession of Penang (Betelnut) Island from the local sultan. It's said that Light loaded his ship's cannons with silver dollars and fired them into the jungle to encourage his labourers to hack back the undergrowth. Whatever the truth of the tale he soon established the small town of Georgetown, named after King George III, with Lebuh Light, Chulia, Pitt and Bishop as its boundaries. Founding towns must have been a Light family tradition because his son is credited with the founding of Adelaide in Australia; which is today a sister city to Georgetown.

Penang has always been a cosmopolitan place and has attracted dreamers, artists, intellectuals, and dissidents. Sun Yat-Sen planned the 1911 Canton uprising from there, probably in a coffee shop run by the local Hainanese. Three of the five social action organisations singled out by Malaysian Prime Minister Mahathir as 'thorns in the flesh of the nation' are based in Penang. In 1816 the first English-language school in South-East Asia was opened in Georgetown.

GEORGETOWN
Orientation

Georgetown has a population of about 400,000 while that of the whole island is 475,000. Georgetown is in the north-east of the island, where the straits between the island and the mainland are at their narrowest.

A vehicle and passenger ferry service operates 24 hours a day across the three-km-wide channel between Georgetown and Butterworth on the mainland. South of the ferry crossing is the Penang Bridge – the longest in Asia – which links the island with Malaysia's north-south highway.

Georgetown is a compact city and most places can easily be reached on foot or by bicycle rickshaw. Two important streets are Lebuh Chulia and Lebuh Campbell. Both run away from the ferry waterfront and terminate on Jalan Penang.

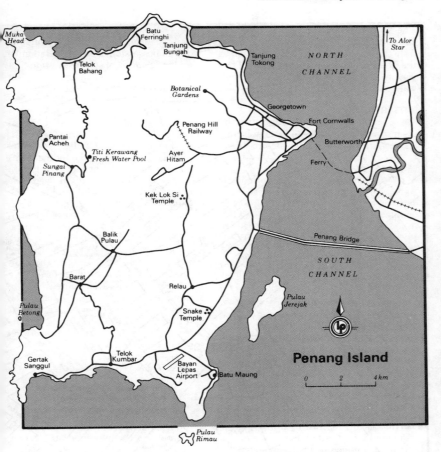

Penang Island

0   2   4 km

You'll find most of Georgetown's popular cheap hotels along Lebuh Chulia or close to it, while Lebuh Campbell is one of the town's main shopping streets. Jalan Penang is another popular shopping street and in this area you'll find a number of the more expensive hotels including, at the waterfront end of Jalan Penang, the venerable Eastern & Oriental Hotel.

If you follow Jalan Penang south you'll pass the modern Kompleks Tun Abdul Razak (KOMTAR), where the MAS office is located, and eventually leave town and continue towards the Bayan Lepas Airport. If you turned west at the waterfront end of Jalan Penang you'd run round the coastline to the popular northern beaches, including Batu Ferringhi. This road runs right round the island and would eventually bring you back into town, via the airport.

Finding your way around Georgetown is slightly complicated by the street names. Jalan Penang may also be referred to as Jalan Pinang or as Penang Rd – but there's also a Penang St, which may also

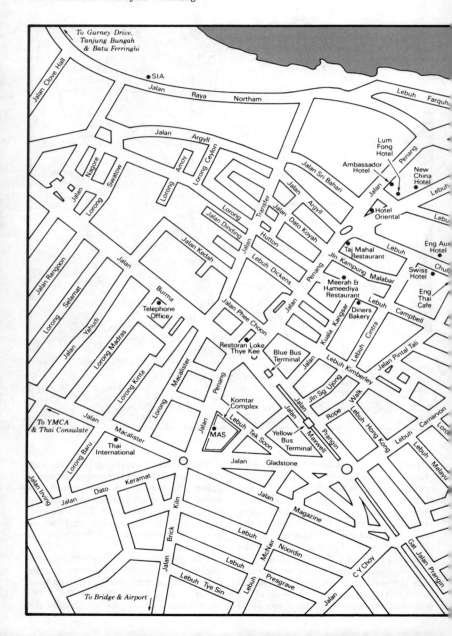

be referred to as Lebuh Pinang! Similarly Pitt St is sometimes called Lebuh Pitt, but Lebuh Chulia is always Lebuh Chulia, never Chulia St. The old spelling for Lebuh is Leboh and some of the street signs still use this spelling.

Information

The Penang Tourist Association (tel 04-366665) is on Jalan Tun Syed Shed Barakbah, close to Fort Cornwallis in the centre of Georgetown. They are a useful information source and also produce a booklet entitled *Penang for the Visitor* which is a worthwhile acquisition. The office is open from 8.30 am to 4.30 pm Monday to Friday and 8.30 am to 1 pm on Saturdays.

The TDC also have an office around the corner of the same building with all the usual TDC literature. Also in this row of offices is the Sanren Delta Marine office (tel 04-619306) for boats to Langkawi and Sumatra.

The immigration office is right across the roundabout from the tourist offices and in this same area you'll also find a number of banks and the GPO on Lebuh Downing. In 1987 the GPO was temporarily moved to the Municipal Office Building on Jalan Padang Kota Lama; when it would be returned to Lebuh Downing was not known.

The Penang Library is on the 1st floor of the Dewan Sri Pinang on Lebuh Duke. It has a large collection of books of local interest and is open from 9 am to 7 pm, Mondays to Fridays and from 9 am to 4.30 pm on Saturdays. There is a good British Council library on Lebuh Pinang, near the Hotel Rio.

For French-language materials, go to the Alliance Francaise library at 32 Kelawai Rd, open 10 am to noon and 3.30 to 7 pm Monday to Friday. The Malaysian German Society Library is at 250B Lorong Madras and is open 9.30 am to 1 pm and 2.30 to 6 pm Tuesday through Saturday, 11 am to 3 pm Monday.

There are several fairly good bookshops along Lebuh Pantai and a good one in the E&O Hotel.

Georgetown's duty-free status was cancelled in 1977. In 1987 Pulau Langkawi was given duty-free status by the Malaysian government in a move to promote tourism on Langkawi. This was usual ethnic politics, under the guise of the National Economic Policy (NEP), of the Malay rulers trying to get the money out of the hands of the Chinese and into their own grasp. On Langkawi the population is primarily Malay, while Penang is Chinese-dominated.

There are still shops offering discounted cameras and electrical goods but prices are not competitive with those in Singapore.

There are traces of Georgetown's seamier past and intrepid travellers can still find opium dens in operation. There are still a lot of drugs in Georgetown, but Malaysia's penalties for drug use are very severe (death for possession of more than 15 grams of any contraband) so beware of those trishaw riders offering a supermarket variety of illegal drugs. Prostitution is also big in Penang and trishaw drivers will try to push girls as much as drugs to unaccompanied male travellers.

Consulates Medan, the entry point from Penang to the Indonesian island of Sumatra, is counted as one of the 'usual' entry points where visitors can be issued a visa on arrival. Which is just as well because the Indonesian Consulate in Penang has long had a reputation for being much less than helpful. The Thailand Consulate, on the other hand, is a good place for obtaining Thai visas.

Indonesia
    467 Jalan Burma (tel 04-25162)
Thailand
    1 Ayer Rajah Rd (tel 04-23352)
UK
    Birch House, 73 Jalan Datuk Keramat (tel 04-27166)

Airlines The addresses of the airline offices in Penang are:

Cathay Pacific
    AIA Building, Lebuh Farquhar (tel 04-620411)
Malaysian Airlines System
    Kompleks Tun Abdul Razak, Penang Rd (tel 04-620011)
Singapore Airlines
    Wisma Penang Gardens, Jalan Sultan Ahmad Shah (tel 04-363201)
Thai Airways
    9 Pengkalan Weld (tel 04-622444)
Thai Airways International
    Wisma Central, 202 Macalister Rd (tel 04-23484)

Penang has many travel agents offering great bargains in airline tickets. Most agents are OK but some aren't totally trustworthy.

Silver Travel has been recommended, and MSL (tel 04-24748), in the lobby of the Ming Court Hotel, is affiliated with Student Travel Australia. While they may not be cheapest they should certainly be reliable – they also have an office on Lebuh Chulia. King's Travel on Lebuh Chulia has also been recommended by several travellers. See the introductory Getting There section for more on airline ticket discounters.

General Information

Phones Outside of Georgetown itself (area code 04) an additional phone code has to be used – Balik Pulau (898), Batu Uban (883), Bayan Lepas (831), Penang Hill (092), Tanjung Bungah (894).

The telephone office for international phone calls is on Jalan Burma at the junction with Lorong Madras.

Hospitals Outpatient medical care is generally inexpensive in Malaysia. The following hospitals are recommended for travellers. Dial 999 for ambulance service.

General Hospital
    Jalan Residensi (tel 373333)
Penang Adventist Hospital
    465 Jalan Burma (tel 373344)

Penang Medical Centre
    1 Jalan Pangkor (tel 20731)
Mt Miriam Hospital
    Jalan Bulan (tel 895322)

Fort Cornwallis

The timeworn walls of Fort Cornwallis in the centre of town are one of Penang's oldest sites. It was there that Light first set foot on the virtually uninhabited island and established the free port where trade would, he hoped, be attracted from England's Dutch rivals. At first a wooden fort was built but between 1808 and 1810 convict labour was used to replace it with the present stone fort.

Today only the outer walls of the fort stand. The area within has been made into a park, but it's liberally studded with old cannons. Many of these were retrieved from local pirates although they were originally cast by the Dutch. Seri Rambai, the most important and largest cannon, faces the north coast and dates back to the early 1600s. It has a chequered history of being passed from the Dutch to the Sultan of Johore to the Portuguese and then to pirates before ending up at the fort. It's famed for its procreative powers and childless women are recommended to place flowers in the barrel of 'the big one' and offer special prayers.

Penang Museum & Art Gallery

From the town's foundation site it's only a short stroll to the museum on Lebuh Farquhar. In front is a statue of Light which was removed by the Japanese during WW II but retrieved and re-erected, minus its sword, after the war. The small museum has lots of old photos and documents, furniture, costumes, the medal collection of Tun Abdul Rahman and numerous other memorabilia.

There's a small, interesting section recounting the bloody wrangles between Chinese secret societies in 1867. Georgetown, it appears, suffered a near civil war before the administrators took a firm hand. The societies were heavily fined and the proceeds used to build police stations which subsequently kept the peace.

The art gallery is upstairs and one of the original Penang Hill funicular railcars is displayed outside the museum.

Opening hours are 9 am to 5 pm daily except Fridays when it is closed from noon to 2.45 pm and Sundays when it is closed. Admission is free.

Kuan Yin Teng

Just round the corner from the museum on Lebuh Pitt is the temple of Kuan Yin, the Goddess of Mercy. The temple was built in the 1800s by the first Chinese settlers in Penang. It's not a terribly impressive or interesting temple, but it's right in the centre of the old part of Georgetown and is the most popular Chinese temple in the city. Perhaps it's Kuan Yin's own reputation as a goddess on the lookout for everyone's well-being or possibly it's the presence of other well-known gods, like the God of Prosperity, that accounts for this popularity.

Whatever the reasons there's often something going on; worshippers burning paper money at the furnaces in front of the temple, a night-time puppet or Chinese theatre performance, or simply offerings of joss sticks inside the temple.

Kapitan Kling Mosque

At the same time Kuan Yin's temple was being constructed, Penang's first Indian Muslim settlers set to and built this mosque at the junction of Lebuh Pitt and

Top: Kek Lok Si Temple, Penang (JC)
Left: Textile house, Penang (JC)
Right: Cathay Hotel, Penang (JC)

Top: Mosque, Penang (ML)
Bottom: Banana-leaf cutter, Penang (JC)

Lebuh Buckingham. In a typically Indian-influenced Islamic style the mosque which has a single minaret is yellow.

Khoo Kongsi

The 'Dragon Mountain Hall' is in Cannon Square close to the end of Lebuh Pitt. A kongsi is a clan house, a building which is part-temple and part-meeting hall for Chinese of the same clan or surname.

Penang has many kongsis but this one, the clan house of the Khoos, is easily the finest. Its construction was first considered around 1853, but it was not built until 1898. The completed building was so magnificent and elaborate that nobody was surprised when the roof caught fire on the very night it was completed! That misfortune was simply interpreted as a message from above that they'd really been overdoing things, so the Khoos rebuilt it in a marginally less grandiose style.

The present kongsi, dating from 1906 and extensively renovated in the 1950s, is a rainbow of dragons, statues, paintings, lamps, coloured tiles and carvings, and is one part of colourful Penang which definitely should not be missed.

Although the Khoo Kongsi is far and away the most well-known kongsi in Georgetown, there are a number of others, including the modern Lee Kongsi on Burma Rd, the combined kongsi of the Chuah, Sin and Quah clans at the corner of Burma Rd and Codrington Avenue, the Khaw Kongsi on Burma Rd and the Yap Kongsi on Armenian St.

Sri Mariamman Temple

Queen St runs parallel to Lebuh Pitt, and about midway between the Kuan Yin Temple and the Kapitan Kling Mosque you'll find another example of Penang's religious diversity.

The Sri Mariamman Temple is a typical south Indian temple with its elaborately sculptured and painted gopuram towering over the entrance. Built in 1883, it's the oldest Hindu temple in Georgetown and testifies to the strong Indian influence you'll also find in this most Chinese of towns.

Wat Chayamangkalaram

At Burma Lane just off the road to Batu Ferringhi is a major Thai temple – 'Temple of the Reclining Buddha'. This brightly painted temple houses a 32-metre-long reclining Buddha, loudly proclaimed in Penang as the third longest in the world – you can take that claim with a pinch of salt since there's at least one other in Malaysia that is larger, plus one in Thailand (at least) and two in Burma. Nevertheless, it's a colourful and picturesque temple and there's a Burmese Buddhist temple directly across the road from it, with two large stone elephants flanking the gates.

Penang Buddhist Association

Completed in 1929 this is a most unusual Chinese Buddhist temple. Instead of the usual gaudy and colourful design of most Chinese temples it is quiet, tasteful and refined. The Buddha statues are carved from Italian marble, and glass chandeliers, made in Penang, hang from above. It's on Anson Rd.

Other Temples, Mosques & Churches

Close to the Kapitan Kling Mosque, the Malay mosque on Acheen St is unusual for its Egyptian-style minaret – most Malay mosques have Moorish minarets.

Also in the centre, St George's Church on Lebuh Farquhar was built in 1818 and is the oldest Anglican church in South-East Asia. The gracefully proportioned building with its marble floor and towering spire was built by convict labour. Also on Lebuh Farquhar is the double-spired Cathedral of the Assumption. The cemetery nearby tells the usual wistful story of the early deaths of English administrators and their families.

The Shiva temple on Jalan Dato Keramat is hidden behind a high wall, but the Nattukotai temple on Waterfall Rd is the largest Hindu temple in Penang and is dedicated to Bala Subramaniam.

On Perak Rd, Wat Buppharam is the oldest Thai temple in Penang and has a pagoda and two 30-metre-long dragons. Out at Tanjung Tokong the Tua Pek Kong Temple is dedicated to the God of Prosperity and dates from 1837. Finally the Penang State Mosque at Ayer Itam is glossy and new and there are good views from the 50-metre-high minaret.

Kek Lok Si Temple

On a hilltop at Ayer Itam, close to the funicular station for Penang Hill, stands the largest Buddhist temple in Malaysia. The construction commenced in 1890 and took more than 20 years to complete.

It's really more of a tourist attraction than a temple and you climb up through arcades of souvenir stalls, past a tightly packed turtle pond and murky fish ponds until you reach the Ban Po Thar or 'Ten Thousand Buddhas' Pagoda.

A 'voluntary' contribution is the price to climb to the top of the seven-tier, 30-metre-high tower which is said to be Burmese at the top, Chinese at the bottom and Thai in between. In the other three-storey shrine there is a large Thai Buddha image that was donated by King Bhumibol of Thailand. Standing high above all the temple structures is a striking white figure of Kuan Yin, the Goddess of Mercy.

Around Georgetown

Georgetown is a delight to simply wander around at any time of day. Set off in any direction and you're certain to find and see plenty of interesting things, whether it's the beautiful old Chinese houses, an early morning vegetable market, a temple ceremony, the crowded shops or a late pasar malam or night market.

Jalan Penang and Jalan Campbell are the main shopping streets with modern air-conditioned shops, but it's along the more old-fashioned streets like Lebuh Chulia or Rope Walk that you'll find the unusual bargains – like a 'Beware of the Dog' sign that adds the warning in Malay

(*Awas – Ada Anjing*) and in Chinese ideograms. At the Lebuh Farquhar end of Jalan Penang there are a string of handicraft and antique shops.

Trishaws are the ideal way of getting around Georgetown, particularly at night when trishaw travel takes on an almost magical property.

All the usual Chinese events are likely to be taking place at any time – a funeral procession with what looks like a run-down Dixieland jazz band leading the mourners, colourful parades at festival times, trishaws wobbling by with whole families aboard, ancient grandmas pushing out their stalls to set up for a day's business. All around you'll hear those distinctively Chinese noises: the clatter of mahjong tiles from inside houses, the trilling of caged songbirds, and everywhere loud arguments and conversations – for Chinese is not a quiet language.

Nor can you miss Georgetown's other inhabitants. Tamils from the south of India cool boiled milk by nonchalantly hurling it through the air from one cup to another. Money changing is almost exclusively an Indian enterprise and a stocky Sikh with an antique-looking gun can be seen guarding many banks or jewellery shops. Altogether Georgetown is a place where there's always something of interest.

Penang Hill

Rising 830 metres above Georgetown, the top of Penang Hill provides a cool retreat from the sticky heat below – it's generally about 5°C cooler than at sea level. From the summit you've got a spectacular view over the island and across to the mainland. There are pleasant gardens, a small cafe and a hotel as well as a choice of a Hindu temple or a Muslim mosque on the top. Penang Hill is particularly pleasant at dusk as Georgetown, far below, starts to light up.

The idea of a hill resort was first mooted towards the end of the last century, but the first attempt at a mountain railway was a dismal failure. In 1923 a Swiss-built funicular railway system was completed and the tiny cable-pulled cars have trundled up and down ever since. The trip takes half an hour with a change of train at the halfway point. A few years ago the original funicular cars were changed for more modern ones, but the queues on weekends and public holidays can still be as long as ever.

Getting There Take bus No 1 from Pengkalan Weld to Ayer Itam (every five minutes, 55 sen), then bus No 8 to the funicular station (30 sen). The ascent of the hill costs M$3 for the round trip. There are departures every 15 minutes from 6.30 to 8.30 am and then every 30 minutes to 9.30 pm from the bottom, 9.15 pm from the top. There are later departures until midnight on Wednesdays and Saturdays.

The energetic can get to the top by an interesting eight-km hike starting from the Moon Gate at the Botanical Gardens. The hike takes nearly three hours so be sure to bring along a water bottle.

Around Ayer Itam

Ayer Itam Dam, three km from Kek Lok Si, has an 18-hectare lake. It's one of several reservoirs on the island. Penang's largest Hindu temple, the Nattukotai Chettiar, is on top of a hill beyond the dam. There's a good view from the top, 233 metres above sea level. This is the most important site in Penang for ceremonies during the Thaipusam festival.

Botanical Gardens

Penang's 30-hectare botanical gardens are off Waterfall Rd and are also known as the Waterfall Gardens after the stream that cascades through them down from Penang Hill. They've also been dubbed the Monkey Gardens due to the many monkeys that appear on the lawn for a feed early each morning and late each afternoon. The gardens also have a small zoo and from them a path leads up Penang Hill.

Festivals

All the usual festivals are celebrated in Penang, but some with special energy. In December the annual Pesta Pulau Penang or Penang Islands Festival is highlighted by colourful dragon boat races. There are also parades, carnivals and all the fun of the fair.

The masochistic Hindu festival of Thaipusam is celebrated in Penang with a fervour to rival Singapore and Kuala Lumpur but without quite the same crowds. The Nattukotai temple on Waterfall Rd is the main centre in Penang for the activities.

At Chinese New Year a wayang or Chinese opera takes place at the snake temple near Bayan Lepas. The number of snakes in residence is also said to be highest at that time of year.

The tourist office can tell you what festivals are approaching, where events occur and can also offer information about their origins and significance.

Places to Stay – bottom end

Hotels There are a great number of cheap hotels around Georgetown, some of them very pleasant. Stroll down Lebuh Chulia, Lebuh Leith or Love Lane and you'll come across them.

One of the most popular is the long-running *New China Hotel* on Lebuh Leith where singles cost M$9 to M$10.50 and doubles from M$11.50 to M$15. There's also a somewhat airless dorm at M$5.50. The whole place is very clean, particularly the toilets, but the bar at the back can be noisy at times. There is also a restaurant serving western food and breakfasts – the food is OK although the prices are a little high. The New China is 'kept almost rat free by an impressive legion of cats'.

Two other popular places, of the same standard as the New China, are the *Swiss Hotel* on Lebuh Chulia and the *Eng Aun*, directly across the road from it. The Swiss Hotel has rooms at M$11.50 single, M$15 double and upstairs there are rooms for M$19.60. The Eng Aun charges M$9.90

for a single or double, and M$11 for a room with bath. They now have a travel agency downstairs. Both of these spacious hotels attract a steady stream of travellers and have large car parks in front (as does the New China) – which also insulates them from street noise.

There are also a couple of places close to the New China with similar standards. The *Lum Fong*, right next door, has a good restaurant/bar downstairs and singles/doubles at M$11/16.50. Facing it across Lebuh Muntri you'll find the *Modern Hotel* with single or double rooms at M$16.50, two beds. The latter is 'excellent, roomy, cheap and clean' reported one traveller, though another added that it was 'friendly but noisy'.

Also nearby, at the corner of Penang Rd and Jalan Argyll, is the *Hock Beng*. It's diagonally opposite the Oriental and has rooms from M$14 to M$15.

Back on Chulia at 509 is the *Eastern Hotel*, a good, clean place where the staff speaks English. Singles or doubles are M$14. Next door is the more basic *Han Chow* run by Indians. Prices are M$14/16 and there is a restaurant downstairs. At 422 is *Lum Thean*, where a modern front off the street encloses a typical Penang Chinese hotel with a courtyard in the middle – rooms are M$12.10.

Further down Lebuh Chulia at 362 is the *Yeng Keng Hotel* with big, cool rooms; singles/doubles are M$10.35/11.50. As the hotel is off the street, the rooms are quiet.

Skip the *Nam Wah* which looks alright at first glance but is a dark brothel feeding off the Hong Kong Bar next door. Likewise the *Sky*, where the manager is unhelpful but the restaurant is OK. Large crowds of Chinese gather there in the evenings to watch Chinese TV serials.

Still further down Lebuh Chulia from the Swiss and Eng Aun there are other places, some even cheaper. The *Yee Hing Hotel* at 302 was 'the best value of my entire trip', according to one traveller; adding that the restaurant downstairs had a menu which featured a 'baked bean on toast'. The staff are friendly and it's certainly cheap at M$8 for a one-bed room, M$9 for two beds, although not the best-kept place around.

At 282 the *Tye Ann* is very popular, particularly for its breakfasts downstairs in the restaurant section. Rooms cost M$11 single or double and there are also M$4.50 dorm beds.

Round the corner on Lorong Pasar, behind the Goddess of Mercy Temple, the very friendly *Noble Hotel* has a novel approach. They charge M$12 for a room – for as many people as you want to cram in. The *Hotel Chung King* is at 398 Chulia directly opposite Lebuh Cintra – you can only see the sign from across the street. It's cheap but noisy.

Love Lane is another popular hotel street, right off Lebuh Chulia. The *Pin Seng* at 82 is OK although the rooms in the new wing tend to be a bit noisy and hot. It's very clean though, and the old section is quiet. Rooms are M$11.50.

At 35 Love Lane the *Wan Hai* (tel 61421), run by Indian Muslims costs M$12 for a room or M$4.40 dorm. It's a quiet place with a travel agency downstairs and a small roof terrace. Nearby are small, interesting light-industrial-type shops, including a place which makes mahjong tiles.

On nearby Rope Walk there are a number of places, usually a bit dingy and/or short-time centres. The *Choong Thean* is OK with rooms for M$11/15. The *Kim Sun* at 86 Lebuh Campbell near Lebuh Cintra is an average sort of place at M$11.50.

Burma Road also has a few hotels like the *Hotel Kim Wah* at 114 where a room with bath and fan costs M$19.80 and it is 'central, clean, has a restaurant and the short-time ladies are well in evidence'. Another is the *Tong Lok* which is owned by the New China Hotel and sometimes used by them as an overflow place.

The *White House*, 72 Penang Rd, charges only M$15 for a large bed, fan, and bath and also has more expensive air-con rooms. There are many, many other hotels around Georgetown – look around and you'll discover them.

The Ys Penang has a well situated, but extremely anonymous, *Youth Hostel* (Asrama Belia) right next door to the gracious old E&O Hotel on Lebuh Farquhar. There are periodic rumours about it completely closing down, but when we were there last they had plenty of space available in the dorm-style rooms for M$4.50 a bed. They even had space when most of the small Chinese cheapies on and off Lebuh Chulia were full (which is common during the high travel seasons – December through to February and August). The reception office is on the 2nd floor at the back of the enormous building. There are discounts for long-term stays.

The *YMCA* (tel 04-372211), at 211 Jalan Macalister, is close to the Thai Consulate which is an important Penang address for many travellers. To get there take a bus No 7. Singles/doubles cost M$17/22 or M$20/26 with air-con. All rooms have attached showers and there are also dorms for M$7 per person. Unfortunately they tend to fill up the noisy dorm rooms in the front before starting on the quieter ones at the back. There's a M$1 temporary membership charge for non-members of the YMCA, but this can be waived if you're a YHA member or have a student card. The YMCA also has a TV lounge and cafeteria.

Finally the *YWCA* is much further out at 8A Green Lane and, unlike the YMCA, it's single sex only.

Places to Stay – middle

For a bit of a splurge you can stay at the wonderful-looking *Cathay Hotel*, halfway between the Oriental and the Merlin near the New China Hotel on Lebuh Leith. The lobby nearly equals the exterior. Prices are M$25/27 singles/doubles, M$29/34 with air-con and attached bath. Also pricey is the *Prince* at 456 Chulia. It's modern, all air-con and the M$40 rooms feature piped-in music. The guy at the

desk told me they could find me 'some company to share my room'.

Other middle-bracket air-con hotels include the *Federal* on Penang Rd at M$26/30 and the *Hotel Fortuna*, also on Penang Rd, at M$36/40. The *Pathe Hotel* (tel 620195) on Light Street near the Esplanade has character and air-con rooms for M$26.40.

In this same price bracket you could try the *Peking Hotel* (tel 04-22455) at 50A Penang Rd or the slightly more expensive *United Hotel* (tel 04-21361) at 101 Macalister Rd. More expensive again, the *Hotel Waterfall* (tel 04-27221) is at 160 Western Rd. At 48F Northam Rd the *Paramount Hotel* (tel 04-63773) has singles from M$26 to M$38, doubles M$48. The *Singapore Hotel* at 495H Penang Rd has large and well-furnished air-con rooms with a shower from around M$20.

Many of Georgetown's original top-end hotels are being squeezed into the mid-priced category by development at Batu Ferringhi, especially those near the Georgetown waterfront.

Places to Stay – top end

Penang's biggest hotels, of the resort variety, are out at Batu Ferringhi. In Georgetown itself you mainly find the older hotels or the second-string places.

Grandest (and oldest?) is the fine old *Eastern & Oriental*, one of those superb old establishments in the Raffles manner – indeed it was built by the Sarkies brothers who also constructed the Raffles, and the Strand in Rangoon. The E&O was built in 1885, is right on the waterfront and has beautiful gardens right down to the water. It has been featured in several Somerset Maugham stories.

While Lebuh Chulia is the main street in Georgetown for cheap hotels, Penang Rd is where you find most of the more expensive places. Virtually across the road from the E&O and at the top of Penang Rd is the much more modern *City Bayview Hotel*, topped by a revolving restaurant with great views over Georgetown. In the basement is the Penny Lane disco which plays all '60s music.

Other central hotels include the *Ming Court Penang*, the *Central* and the pleasant and very reasonably priced *Oriental*. Many of the older hotels along Penang Rd have fallen on hard times recently and so have drastically reduced their rates by as much as 50%. The *Ambassador Hotel* was renting its M$60 to M$70 rooms for M$34.50, tax and service inclusive. Most of the other hotels in this range had similar discounts. The rates listed here are the 'posted' rates and you should be able to get standard rooms for at least 30% off – try 50% first.

On top of Penang Hill there's the small *Bellevue Hotel*, formerly known as the Penang Hill Hotel, which is not only small and quiet with a delightful garden but also very tastefully decorated – its owner is one of Malaysia's foremost architects.

Hotel Ambassador (tel 04-24101), 55 Penang Rd, 78 rooms, singles from M$65, doubles from M$75

Bellevue Hotel (tel 04-892256), Penang Hill, 12 rooms, singles M$60, doubles M$80

Hotel Central (tel 04-21432), 404 Penang Rd, 140 rooms, singles M$45, doubles M$60

City Bayview, 25-A Lebuh Farquhar, 145 rooms, singles M$90 to M$120, doubles M$100 to M$130

Hotel Continental (tel 04-26381), 5 Penang Rd, 120 rooms, singles M$66, doubles M$76, discounts available

Eastern & Oriental Hotel (tel 04-375322), 10 Farquhar St, 100 rooms, singles M$75 up, doubles M$85 up

Hotel Malaysia (tel 04-363311), 7 Penang Rd, 126 rooms, singles M$58 to M$76, doubles M$68 to M$86, discounts available

Ming Court Penang (tel 04-26131), 202A Macalister Rd, 110 rooms, singles M$110 to M$120, doubles M$120 to M$130

Oriental Hotel (tel 04-24211), 105 Penang Rd, 100 rooms, singles M$54 to M$59, doubles M$61 to M$66, discounts available

Merlin Inn (tel 04-376166), 126 Burma Rd, 295 rooms, singles M$95, doubles M$140 to M$150

Towne House Hotel (tel 04-368722), 70 Penang Rd, 50 rooms, M$46 up

Places to Eat

Penang is another of the region's delightful food trips with a wide variety of restaurants and many local specialities to tempt you.

For a start, there are two types of soup or laksa that are particularly associated with Penang. Laksa assam is a fish soup with a sour taste from the tamarind or assam paste. The soup is served with special white laksa noodles. Originally a Thai dish, laksa lemak has been adopted by Penang. It's basically similar to laksa assam except coconut milk is substituted for the tamarind.

Seafood is, of course, very popular in Penang and there are many restaurants that specialise in fresh fish, crabs and prawns – particularly along the northern beach fringe.

Despite its Chinese character Penang also has a strong Indian presence and there are some popular specialities to savour. Curry kapitan is a Penang chicken curry which supposedly takes its name from a Dutch sea captain asking his Indonesian mess boy what was on that night. The answer was 'curry kapitan' and it's been on the menu ever since.

Murtabak, a thin roti chanai pastry stuffed with egg, vegetables and meat, while not actually a Penang specialty, is done with particular flair on the island.

Indian Food Amongst the more popular Indian restaurants is *Dawood's* at 63 Queen St, opposite the Sri Mariamman Temple. Curry kapitan is just one of the many curry dishes at this reasonably priced restaurant, and costs M$2.60. Beer is not available (since it's run by Indian Muslims), but the lime juice is excellent and so is the ice cream. At 166 Campbell St the *Meerah* and at 164A the *Hameediyah* both have good curries and delicious murtabak.

The *Taj Mahal Restaurant* on the corner of Jalan Penang and Lebuh Chulia is another place for murtabak, but this is also an excellent place for a quick snack of roti chanai with dal dip – a cheap and

[handwritten annotations at top of page: "N → POSHNIS THAI FOOD Restaurant / # 3+5, LIGHT STREET / 04-629124 Near Tourist Assn + Fort Cornwallis"]

nourishing meal at any time of the day. Near the corner of Lebuh Chulia and Jalan Penang the *Islamik Restaurant* has delicious food, particularly the murtabaks and biriyanis.

Penang has a 'little India' along Jalan Pasar/Market Street between Lebuh Penang and Lebuh Pitt and along the side streets between. Several small restaurants and stalls in this area offer cheap north (Muslim) and south Indian food. Between Lebuh Queen and Lebuh King on Jalan Market is the easy-to-miss *Krishna Vilas*, good for south Indian breakfasts – idli and dosa – and very cheap. On the corner of King and Bishop Sts you can get a whole selection of curry dishes plus rice and chapatis at *Rio*.

If you're looking for an Indian splurge, the *Kashmir Restaurant* in the basement of the Oriental Hotel on Jalan Penang serves tandoori food and other north Indian specialties in air-con comfort. There is live Indian music in the evenings. A meal for two costs around M$20.

Chinese Food There are so many Chinese restaurants in Penang that making any specific recommendations is really rather redundant.

On Syed Sheh, behind the library and cultural centre, the *Seaview Restaurant* has good breakfast dim sum. On Lebuh Cintra the *Hong Kong Restaurant* is good, cheap and varied and has a menu in English. At the corner of Lebuh Cintra and Campbell St the *Restoran Chup Seng* has excellent chicken rice – as do many of Georgetown's 'excellent Hainanese chicken rice' purveyors. The *Sin Kuan Hiwa Cafe*, on the corner of Chulia and Lebuh Cintra, is one that specialises in this. Georgetown residents claim the best chicken rice purveyor is at the junction by the traffic lights, opposite the RAAF centre at Tanjung Tokong on the way to Tanjung Bungah and Batu Ferringhi.

More good Chinese food can be found at the fancier *Dragon King* on the corner of Lebuh Bishop and Lebuh Pitt which specialises in the not-so-easily-found nonya cuisine. Or try *Sun Hoe Peng* at 25 Lebuh Light. The *Wing Lok*, 300 Penang Rd, is more costly but good. They offer a steamboat for four people at M$20 but give them a day's notice.

Of late one of the most popular outdoor Chinese places is *Hsiang Yang Cafe* across the street from the Tye Ann Hotel on Lebuh Chulia. It's really a hawker's centre, with a cheap and good Chinese buffet (rice with three or four side dishes for M$2.50), plus noodles, satay, and popiah vendors.

Breakfasts & Western Food At breakfast time the popular travellers' hangout is the *Tye Ann Hotel* on Lebuh Chulia. People visit this friendly little establishment for its excellent porridge, toast & marmalade and other breakfast favourites. The manager at the front desk is permanently wreathed with that rarest of Chinese sights – a smile.

Western breakfasts are also available at the *New China, Eng Aun, Swiss* and across from the Wan Hai. Another morning hangout is *Eng Thai Cafe* at 417B Lebuh Chulia, not far from the Eng Aun and Swiss hotels. There are other small Chinese cafes with western breakfast menus.

At *Jaya Supermarket*, Penang Plaza, Burma Rd you can find all the usual supermarket goodies. The *Super Emporium*, on Burma Rd stocks more of the same as does the supermarket in the Komtar complex.

The *Magnolia Snack Bar*, on Jalan Penang, is an excellent place for a hamburger or some other reminder of home. They've also got a wide selection of ice cream flavours. *Diner's Bakery*, across from the Meerah restaurant on Campbell St, has great baked goods ranging from cheesecake to wholemeal bread although there are cheaper bakeries around.

There's more good seafood at *Maple Gardens* on Penang Rd. It's a little pricey if economy is on your mind, but the food is good, the servings large and you select your fish straight from the tank. *Kwikie*

Fast Food at 276 Penang Rd has also been recommended. Burma Rd has a number of places and quite a few western fast food joints including an Italian fried chicken place. There is a *McDonald's* and a *Kentucky Fried Chicken* in the Komtar Complex.

Night Markets Georgetown has a wide selection of street stalls with nightly gatherings at places like Gurney Drive or along the Esplanade. The latter is particularly good for trying local Penang specialities. The big night market, 7 to 11 pm, changes venue every two weeks, so check at the tourist office for its current location. Cold fruit, cakes, pancakes, noodles, and laksa are all on sale.

Medicated tea is a popular item and one Georgetown tea stall has a sign announcing that it will cure everything from 'headache, stomachache and kidney trouble' to 'malaria, cholera and' (wait for it) 'fartulence'.

AROUND THE ISLAND

You can make an interesting circuit of the island either in your own car, on a motorcycle/bicycle, on a tour, or by public transport. On a motorcycle or by car, figure on about four hours with plenty of sightseeing and refreshment stops. If you are on a bicycle allow all day. It's 70 km all the way round, but it's only along the north coast that the road runs right on the coast so you're not beside the beaches all the way. The following takes you from Georgetown in a clockwise direction around the island.

Snake Temple

At milestone 9, a couple of miles before the airport, you reach Penang's famous snake temple, the 'Temple of the Azure Cloud'. The temple was built in 1850 and is dedicated to Chor Soo Kong.

If you fancy it live snakes are draped over you. The snakes are venomous Wagler's Pit Vipers and are said to be slightly 'doped' by the incense smoke which drifts around the temple. There is no admission fee to the temple although 'donations' are requested. The number of snakes tends to vary through the year.

Other Attractions

After the snake temple you soon reach Bayan Lepas, Penang's international airport. A turn-off at the village of Bayan Lepas leads to the small fishing village of Batu Maung, about three km away. Just beyond the village a small shrine dedicated to the legendary Admiral Cheng Ho (see Melaka) marks a huge 'footprint' on the rock which is said to belong to the famous eunuch. Batu Maung is good for seafood and there is a small children's playground with concrete animal figures.

Back on the main road you climb up, then drop down to Telok Kumbar, from where you can diverge to the fishing village of Gertak Sanggul. You'll pass some good beaches, including Pantai Asam, on the way.

A little further on you reach Balik Pulau, the main town you pass through on the island circuit. There are a number of restaurants and cafes but no accommodation – going round the island has to be a one-day operation, unless you bring camping gear. Balik Pulau is a good place to have lunch though, and a must is the local specialty laksa balik pulau. It's a tasty rice noodle concoction with a thick fish broth, mint leaves, pineapple slivers, onions and fresh chillies.

Between Balik Pulau and Sungei Pinang you'll pass through an area of Malay kampungs – if you're on a bicycle or motorbike (the side roads aren't quite wide enough for cars), turn off at Jalan P Pasir and tour the picture-perfect village there, with neatly-kept traditional Malay houses, flower gardens, and coconut groves that look like they've been swept.

Next is a turn-off for Kuala Sungei Pinang, a busy Chinese village built along a stagnant river – the antithesis of the preceding Malay village, but worth a peek. Further on another road turns off to Pantai Acheh, another small fishing village with very little of interest.

From there the road starts to climb and twist, offering glimpses of the coast and the sea far below. The jungle becomes denser and at around the 20th milestone you reach Titi Kerawang, a waterfall just off the road with a natural swimming pool. During durian season, there are stalls set up along the road selling the spiky orbs and you can also see the trees themselves, with durians suspended over waiting nets.

Finally you get back to the coast at Telok Bahang, the village which marks the western end of the northern beach strip. There are a couple of batik factories where you're welcome to drop in and see the processes involved in making batik. They also have showrooms where you can buy a wide variety of batik articles – the prices marked are on the high side but you may be able to bargain.

From there you can also visit the 101-hectare Forest Recreation Park. It's open from 8 am to 6 pm and admission is free. The park is intended to preserve a wide variety of local trees and to conduct forest research, but there are also a number of recreation opportunities, including walking tracks.

From Telok Bahang you can also trek down the beach to Muka Head, the isolated rocky promontory marked by a lighthouse at the extreme north-western corner of the island. South of Muka Head is Keracut Beach, also called Monkey Beach, where there are shelters, pit toilets, and lots of bird and monkey life – camping is possible. Refer to the map for hiking routes.

THE BEACHES

Penang's beautiful beaches are really somewhat over-rated. They're not as clean or as spectacular as the tourist literature makes out. Beaches close to the city also suffer to some extent from pollution. The beaches along the north coast are the most visited and accessible.

They start at the small village of Tanjung Tokong and extend along the north coast to Telok Bahang. Tanjung Bungah (Cape of Flowers) is the first real beach, but it's not attractive for swimming.

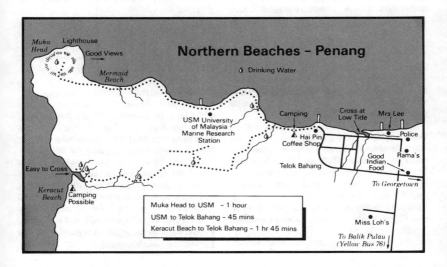

Northern Beaches – Penang

Muka Head | Lighthouse
Good Views
Mermaid Beach
◊ Drinking Water
USM University of Malaysia Marine Research Station
Camping
Cross at Low Tide | Mrs Lee
▲ Hai Pin Coffee Shop
Police
Easy to Cross
Keracut Beach | Camping Possible
Telok Bahang
Good Indian Food
Rama's
To Georgetown
Miss Loh's
To Balik Pulau (Yellow Bus 76)

Muka Head to USM – 1 hour
USM to Telok Bahang – 45 mins
Keracut Beach to Telok Bahang – 1 hr 45 mins

A little further along the coast Batu Ferringhi (Foreigner's Rock) is the resort strip with a number of large hotels. The beach itself is somewhat of a disappointment compared to other beaches in Malaysia and the water is not of the tropically-clear variety you might expect. At the western end the beach slopes off more gradually and the swimming is better.

At the end of this northern beach strip is Telok Bahang (Glowing Bay) where there is little development and it's still principally a small fishing village. There are other beaches around the south of the island, but these are not easily accessible without your own transport.

The two tourist stops in Telok Bahang are the Butterfly Farm and Craft Batik. Both are very touristy but if you're a butterfly freak, the Farm does have 3000 live butterflies representing over 50 species. It's open from 9 am to 5 pm daily, admission is M$2. Craft Batik sells overpriced cotton batik clothing.

Also near Telok Bahang is the Forest Recreation Park, with freshwater pools and trails covering 100 hectares. It's a nice spot and a bit further toward Balik Pulau are durian groves, carefully guarded and with nets strung beneath the trees to catch the valuable fruit.

Places to Stay – Tanjung Bungah

There are a number of small Chinese hotels and restaurants along the coast from Georgetown, but Tanjung Bungah is the first real beach you come to although you can't really swim there.

At the Georgetown end of the beach there is the *Orchid Hotel Penang* (tel 04-803333) which has 323 rooms. Singles cost from M$145 to M$175, and doubles from M$170 to M$200 (peak season rates).

Closer to the village and bus stop is the small *Loke Thean Hotel* with rooms at M$18. Directly opposite the bus stand is the *Eden Hotel* with rooms from around M$10.

Places to Eat – Tanjung Bungah

The beachfront *Eden Hotel* is renowned for its excellent, though a little expensive, seafood. There's also the *Hollywood*, with a variety of dishes including European and Chinese. On the hillside above the road is the *Seri Batik* restaurant which serves Malay food.

Places to Stay – Batu Ferringhi

At the bottom end of the price scale, accommodation at Batu Ferringhi is all unofficial and all found in Batu Ferringhi village, at the end of the international hotel strip. If you wander along to the group of restaurants opposite the Yahong Gallery you'll soon find a room in the village for M$2 to M$5 per night.

The immigration raids of the mid-70s seem to have halted these days, but it's curious that a place like Batu Ferringhi has developed no low-key accommodation facilities to parallel the big hotels. Perhaps it's official policy to discourage grass-roots enterprises like the ones you find at Kuta Beach in Bali, Hikkaduwa in Sri Lanka or Koh Samui in Thailand. Whatever the reason, fewer and fewer budget travellers are staying in BF these days anyway.

Only two places seem to be taking travellers on a regular basis, the *White House* and *Ali's Guest House* (tel 811316). Ali's is the better, with rooms from M$15, clean bathrooms, a restaurant and a nice garden in front.

Batu Ferringhi's 'international standard' hotels, all right on the beach, are strung out along more than a km of coastline. Although Batu Ferringhi is far from the best beach in Malaysia these beach front hotels are relaxed places for a family vacation. There are facilities along the beach for different water sports, including windsurfing and paraflying, offered by the hotels or by independent operators. These hotels have air-con and all except the Lone Pine Hotel have swimming pools. Prices vary depending on whether you're facing the beach or not.

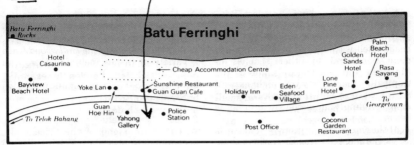

Starting from the eastern, Georgetown end of the beach there's the new *Ferringhi Beach Hotel* which has perhaps the best sea view of all the BF biggies – it's right on a jutting point just before BF proper.

Next comes *Rasa Sayang* – the largest and most expensive of them all. Its design is an exotic interpretation of traditional Malay styles and it's the one place at Batu Ferringhi with real local character.

Right beside it is the smaller, older and quite reasonably priced *Palm Beach*. The large and new *Golden Sands* is next to that and next again is the older and much lower-key *Lone Pine Hotel*. This is the cheapest of these hotels. The Palm Beach, Rasa Sayang, and Golden Sands are all under the same management and if you stay at one you can use the facilities of all three.

There's quite a gap before the *Holiday Inn*, another gap before the *Casuarina Beach Hotel* (both newer places), and finally there's the smaller *Bayview Hotel* at the far end of the beach. The beach slopes into the water a little more gradually there so the swimming is better.

Bayview Beach Hotel (tel 04-811311), 74 rooms, singles M$80 to M$90, doubles M$90 to M$100
Casuarina Beach Hotel (tel 04-811711), 175 rooms, singles M$119 to M$145, doubles M$145 to M$165
Ferringhi Beach Hotel (tel 811289), 136 rooms, singles M$170, doubles M$200
Golden Sands (tel 04-811911), 310 rooms, singles M$140 to M$165, doubles M$165 to M$195

Holiday Inn Penang (tel 04-811601), 159 rooms, singles M$135 to M$150, doubles M$155 to M$175
Lone Pine Hotel (tel 04-811511), 54 rooms, singles M$60 to M$70, doubles M$75 to M$80
Palm Beach Hotel (tel 04-811621), 145 rooms, singles M$80 to M$110, doubles M$100 to M$130
Rasa Sayang Hotel (tel 04-811811), 320 rooms, singles M$130 to M$170, doubles M$155 to M$200

Places to Eat – Batu Ferringhi

All the big hotels have restaurants. The Rasa Sayang has a positive plethora of them, from a Japanese restaurant to a 'British grill room'. There's also the *Coconut Garden Restaurant*, which has typical Chinese food with the accent on seafood, and the more expensive *Eden Seafood Village* with night-time entertainment.

Further along the road is the travellers' centre with a small group of shops and restaurants. You can get a good meal for just a couple of dollars – including all those travellers' favourites like banana-honey pancakes or fruit salad.

Most popular is the *Guan Hoe Hin*, others include the *Yoke Lan*, the *Sunshine Restoran* and the *Guan Guan Cafe*. *Nice*. There's also *Pak Din's Bamboo Restaurant* which is run by an interesting and friendly old gentleman and has excellent, economically priced Malaysian food. The *Malaysian Seafood* is another good place and they also do north Indian food.

Places to Stay – Telok Bahang

Take the beachward road from the round-about, follow it round to just before the Balai Polis and on the right at No 365, Mk 2, is *Rama's* (tel 811179) with beds for M$5. It's run by a Hindu family and is well-kept. Madam Lee is no longer in business but there are still several small Chinese coffee houses there.

Miss Loh has a guest house off the main road towards the butterfly farm. She can be contacted at No 159, Kwong Tuck Hing, the store behind the Shell station. Her house has a fridge, showers, cooking facilities and you can get all your accumulated washing done. A single room costs from M$5 and there are larger rooms up to M$10. It's a bit far from the beach but is quiet and convenient for forest walks.

Places to Eat – Telok Bahang

Food in the shopping area of Telok Bahang is good and you can get 'fantastic' murtabaks for M$1.50 at the *Kassim Restoran* at 48 Main Rd. They also do 55 other dishes, including banana pancakes, steamed crab, south Indian dishes like dosa, and milk shakes.

Getting There & Away

Air MAS fly from Penang to Kota Bahru, Kuala Lumpur and other cities within Malaysia – see the introductory Getting Around section for details of airfares.

Internationally MAS and Garuda fly to Medan in Sumatra – a very popular route for travellers. MAS and SIA have regular flights to Singapore. MAS and Thai Airways or Thai International fly between Penang and Hat Yai, Phuket and Bangkok. Other international connections include direct flights to Hong Kong with Cathay Pacific or to Madras in India with MAS. See the introductory Getting There section for fare details.

Penang is a major centre for cheap airline tickets, but there have also been numerous cut-and-run merchants at work. You'll hear lots of stories of rip-offs. The western agents operating in Georgetown seem to be as much to blame as anybody else so relying on your own is no insurance. Ask around and be careful although Penang is, overall, a good place for buying tickets.

Fares tend to vary with the airline; the cheapest tickets to London, for example, are with Aeroflot or Bangladesh Biman, but some typical one-way tickets on offer in Penang include:

Medan	M$ 95		
Madras	M$550		
Hat Yai	M$ 70		
Phuket	M$112	or	M$ 84
			(student card)
Bangkok	M$210		
Hong Kong	M$476		
London	M$650	to	M$700 from KL
USA West	M$920	to	M$950 from KL
Australia East	M$510	to	M$670 from Singapore

Other quoted fares include Singapore-Jakarta M$224 one-way or M$260 return; Bangkok, Rangoon, Kathmandu M$450; Kuala Lumpur-Perth M$600. Interesting multi-stop or return fares can also be found.

You could take the southern Pacific route Singapore, Jakarta, Noumea, Sydney, Noumea, Auckland, Papeete, Los Angeles for M$1450 to M$1600.

Multi-stop fares to Europe or through Asia are not so easy, but you could do Penang, Bangkok, Delhi for M$625 with extensions on to Europe.

Train The introductory Getting There and Getting Around sections have full details on fares and schedules for the Butterworth, Kuala Lumpur, Singapore services and the international train services to Hat Yai and Bangkok in Thailand.

The station is by the Butterworth ferry terminal and you can make reservations there (tel 04-347962) or at the Railway Booking Station (tel 04-610290) at the Ferry Terminal, Weld Quay, Georgetown. There are good left luggage facilities at Butterworth station.

Bus The bus terminal is also beside the ferry terminal in Butterworth. For long-distance bus information contact MARA (tel 04-345021, 04-349865).

Some travel agents in Georgetown (several are near the Eng Aun and Swiss hotels for example) offer good bargains on bus tickets. Typical fares are Ipoh M\$8, Kuala Lumpur M\$13 to M\$15, Singapore M\$20, Kota Bahru M\$17 to M\$20, Tapah M\$12.50, Kuantan M\$24. The route connecting Kota Bahru on the east coast takes about seven hours by bus.

There are also bus services out of Malaysia to Hat Yai for M\$20 (and about another M\$35 to Bangkok), to Phuket or Koh Samui M\$40.

To Kuala Perlis, for the Langkawi ferry, the bus is M\$5 by Ebban Express from the Butterworth terminal. To Lumut, for Pangkor Island, it is M\$8.50.

Taxi Yes, the long-distance taxis also operate from a depot beside the Butterworth ferry terminal. It's also possible to book them at some of the hot spot backpacker hotels or directly with drivers. Typical fares include Alor Setar M\$7, Ipoh M\$14, Kuala Lumpur M\$30, Cameron Highlands M\$30. Kota Bahru doesn't yet seem to be a main taxi run; fare should be about M\$30.

There are Thai taxis operating to Hat Yai – a convenient way of getting across the border. They're usually big old Chevies and you'll find them at the popular cheap hotels – fare is around M\$25.

Car Penang Bridge, completed in 1985, is the longest bridge in Asia and said to be the third longest in the world. If you drive across you'll have to pay a M\$7 toll at the toll plaza at Prai on the mainland.

Boat The ferry *Gadis Langkasuka* operates twice a week between Penang and Medan in north Sumatra. The crossing takes about 15 hours and costs M\$45. The same boat is used for a weekly service between Penang and Langkawi Island, departing Penang on Friday night

and returning from Langkawi on Sunday night. Sanren Delta Marine (tel 37 9833) are the operators and their office is right next to the tourist office.

Yacht departures are less regular although they're fairly easy to find. There are often yachts passing through Penang looking for paying passengers, most often to Phuket in Thailand but also further afield to places like Sri Lanka. Some run almost regular services between Penang and Phuket, only a few days north. You'll find ads and notices pinned to the wall in the cheap hotels and restaurants along Lebuh Chulia.

Getting Around

Airport Transport Penang's Bayan Lepas Airport with its Minangkabau-style terminal is 18 km south of Georgetown. A coupon system operates for taxis from the airport. The fare to Georgetown should be M\$13.50 for an ordinary taxi and M\$15.40 for one with air-con. To reach Batu Ferringhi it should cost M\$20 and M\$22.50.

You can get a yellow bus No 83 to the airport from Pengkalan Weld Quay for M\$1.25 – they operate on this route from 6 am to 10 pm. Taxis take about 30 minutes from the centre of town, the bus an hour.

Ferry There's a 24-hour ferry service between Georgetown and Butterworth on the mainland. Passenger ferries and ferries for cars and trucks operate from adjacent terminals. Ferries operate every 20 minutes from 6 am to midnight, every hour after midnight. The vehicular ferries operate only slightly less frequently, but do not operate at all between 10 pm (10.20 pm from Penang) and 6.30 am, except on Saturdays, Sundays and public holidays when they continue to 1.30 am.

Fares are only charged from Butterworth to Penang; the other direction is free. The adult fare is 40 sen, and cars with driver cost from M\$4 to M\$6 depending on the engine capacity.

Around the Island Getting around the island is easiest with your own transport, particularly since the road does not actually run along the coast except on the northern side and you have to leave the main road to get out to the small fishing villages and isolated beaches.

For around M$3 to M$4, depending on where and when you stop, you can make the circuit by public transport. Start with a yellow No 83 bus for the Bayan Lepas Airport and hop on and off at the snake temple. This bus will take you all the way to Balik Pulau from where you have to change to another bus, a No 76 for Telok Bahang.

There are only six of these daily and the last one leaves in the mid-afternoon so it's wise to leave Georgetown early and check departure times when you reach Balik Pulau. At Telok Bahang you're on the northern beach strip and you need a blue bus to Tanjung Bungah and another blue bus for the short trip into Georgetown.

Bus There are three main bus departure points in Georgetown and five types of buses. The city buses (MPPP Buses) all depart from the terminal at Lebuh Victoria which is directly in front of the ferry terminal. Fares range from 25 sen to 55 sen and the main routes are:

1 Ayer Itam – every 5 minutes, 55 sen
2 Bagan Jermal – every 10 minutes, 45 sen
3 Jelutong – every 5 minutes, 45 sen
4 Jalan Yeap Chor Ee via Jalan Perak – every 10 minutes, 55 sen
5 Green Lane via Dhoby Ghaut – every 1 hour 5 minutes, 55 sen
6 Green Lane via Jalan Patani – every 16 minutes, 55 sen
7 Botanical Gardens – every 30 minutes, 45 sen
8 Penang Hill Railway from Ayer Itam – every 20 minutes 30 sen
9 Green Lane via Caunter Hall Rd – every 16 minutes, 55 sen
10 Kampung Melayu – every 16 minutes, 55 sen
11 Bukit Glogor – every 1 hour 10 minutes, 55 sen
12 Ayer Itam from Jelutong – every 20 minutes, 45 sen
13 Bagan Jermal from Jelutong – every 30 minutes, 55 sen

From Pengkalan Weld, the waterfront road by the ferry terminal, you can take Sri Negara Buses around Georgetown. The other main stand is at Jalan Maxwell where you can take green, blue or yellow buses. These are the buses to take if you want to do a circuit of the island or get out to Batu Ferringhi and the other northern beaches.

From the Jalan Maxwell bus stand take a blue No 93 bus to Tanjung Bungah and change there for another blue bus on to Batu Ferringhi or Telok Bahang. You buy a 75 sen ticket on the first bus for the whole trip.

The green buses run to Ayer Itam like the No 1 MPPP bus. Blue buses run to the northern beaches although a change of bus is required at Tanjung Bungah. Yellow buses go to the south and west of the island including the aquarium, snake temple, airport and right round to Telok Bahang.

Taxi Penang's taxis officially cost 70 sen for the first mile and 30 sen for each additional half mile. In practice, however, the drivers are none too keen on operating by the meter and you may have to bargain fares, particularly for longer trips. Meter fares can be loaded by 50% from 1 to 6 am. Some sample fares from Georgetown are Batu Ferringhi M$12, Botanical Gardens M$6, Penang Hill/Kek Lok Si M$8, Snake Temple M$12, and the airport M$15.

Trishaw Bicycle rickshaws are ideal in Georgetown's relatively uncrowded streets and cost around 40 or 50 sen per half mile. The fare table displayed doesn't have too much in common with reality – agree to the fare before departure.

If you come across from Butterworth on the ferry, grab a trishaw to the Lebuh Chulia cheap hotels area for M$2 although you can walk there in five or 10 minutes. The riders will know plenty of other hotels if your selected one is full. For touring, the rate is M$6 to M$8 an hour.

Bicycles & Motorcycles If you want to pedal yourself you can hire bicycles from various places. The Eng Aun Hotel in Georgetown has them for M$5 per day or there are various places at Batu Ferringhi where you can hire them at more expensive rates. The New China has a couple of bikes, or try Hire a Bicycle at 206 Prangin Rd, just off Penang Rd. You can also try renting from any repair shop you see around town. They sometimes have the big, heavy-duty grocery bikes at a good rate.

Motorcycles can also be hired for around M$20 per day. Most of the places renting motorbikes are in BF, but on Lebuh Chulia Yasin, a bookstore/money changer next to the Eng Thai Cafe has a few well-maintained 70 to 125cc bikes for rent, as well as bicycles.

Rent-a-Cars
Avis Rent-a-Car
    E&O Hotel, 10 Lebuh Farquhar (tel 04-373964)
Hertz Rent-a-Car
    38 Lebuh Farquhar (tel 04-375914)
National Car Rental
    17 Lebuh Leith (tel 04-629404)
Sintat Rent-a-Car
    Lone Pine Hotel, Batu Ferringhi (tel 04-830958)

Tours Many companies offer local tours – you'll see sandwich boards along the sidewalks. MSL Travel in the Ming Court Hotel is reliable and has a 3½-hour tour for M$18. A Penang Hill trip, including the train up, takes four hours and costs M$27. They also have an office on Lebuh Chulia. The tourist office also has official guides for personal tours.

Watertours (tel 362315), do a daytime and a sunset cruise. The day cruise is from 11 am to 1 pm, tours the waterfront and Penang Bridge while the night cruise from 7 to 9 pm includes a buffet dinner.

ALOR STAR
The capital of Kedah state is on the mainland north of Penang on the main road to the Thai border and it's also the turn-off point for Kuala Perlis, from where ferries run to Langkawi Island. Few people stay very long in Alor Star although it does have a few places of interest.

The Padang
The large open town square has a number of interesting buildings around its perimeter. The Balai Besar or 'Big Hall' was built in 1898 and is still used by the Sultan of Kedah for ceremonial functions. On the other side of the square is the Zahir Mosque; it's the state mosque and one of the largest in Malaysia, and was completed in 1912.

The Balai Nobat, an octagonal building topped by an onion-shaped dome, houses the nobat, or royal orchestra. A nobat is principally composed of percussion instruments and the drums in this orchestra are said to have been a gift from the Sultan of Melaka in the 15th century.

On the main road north is the State Museum, built in a style similar to that of the Balai Besar. The museum has a good collection of early Chinese porcelain and artefacts from the archaeological excavations made at the Bujang Valley. Next to the museum is the royal boathouse where royal barges and boats are housed.

Places to Stay
There are a number of cheap hotels around the bus and taxi stations in the centre of town.

The *Kuan Siang Hotel* on Jalan Langgar, across the street from the local bus terminal, is becoming a favourite rest place due to the highly informative and fluent English-speaking Mr Kim who can fill you in on what to see and where to eat in Alor Star. It's a basic place actually, with share baths and rooms for M$8/12 single/double. There's a good Malay restaurant downstairs and they have a counter selling express bus tickets.

On the corner with Lorong Selamat is the equally cheap *Yuan Fang Hotel*. Head north up Jalan Sultan Badlishah and the

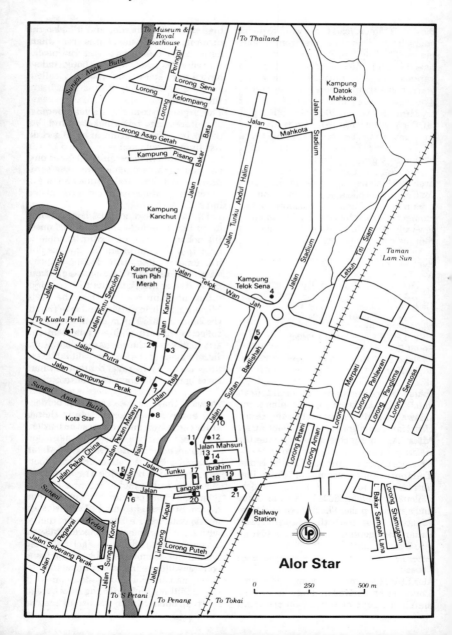

Alor Star

1	Hotel Miramar
2	Federal Hotel
3	Hotel Samilla
4	Thai Temple
5	Express Bus Station
6	Zahir Mosque
7	Balai Nobat
8	Balai Besar
9	National Bank
10	MAS Office
11	Merlin Inn
12	Regent Hotel
13	Rose Restoran
14	Hajjah Restoran
15	GPO
16	Hotel Mahawangsa
17	Restoran Empire
18	Yuan Fang Hotel
19	Kuan Siang Hotel
20	Taxis
21	Local Buses

Regent Hotel (tel 04-721291) at 1536 has air-con rooms from M$26. The *Hotel Mahawangsa* (tel 04-721433) at 449 Jalan Raja, diagonally opposite the GPO, has similar rooms at similar rates, though the Regent is slightly better value. A little north of the padang at 429 Jalan Kancut, the *Federal Hotel* has air-con rooms from M$25.

Alor Star has a *Government Rest House* at 75 Pumpong with rooms from M$12. Moving upmarket the *Hotel Miramar* (tel 04-738144) at 246 Jalan Putra has air-con rooms which start at M$30.

Across the road from the Federal is one of Alor Star's more expensive hotels. The *Hotel Samila* (tel 04-722344) at 27 Jalan Kancut has singles/doubles for M$58/66. Right at the top there's the *Kedah Merlin Inn* (tel 04-735917) at 134-141 Jalan Sultan Badlishah with singles/doubles at M$85/95.

Places to Eat

Alor Star has some surprisingly good and economical restaurants. Two blocks from the Yuan Fang Hotel up on Jalan Tunku

Ibrahim is *Restoran Empire*, a hawkers' centre in a restored wet market, where there's a good selection of fruit juices, chicken rice, rojak, appam balik, curry sambal rice, and a local specialty called mee jawa, spicy noodles in a sauce of bean curd, potatoes, squid, peanuts, bean sprouts, and appam chips – very tasty.

On Jalan Sultan Badlishah south of the Merlin is a popular Thai Muslim place, *Hajjah Restoran*.

Along Jalan Langgar near the local bus terminal are several coffee shops serving inexpensive Malay and Chinese food.

Getting There & Away

Alor Star is 91 km north of Butterworth and is served by MAS. The road between Butterworth and Alor Star carries a surprising amount of traffic. By bus it's M$3.30 to Butterworth, M$10 to Ipoh, M$16 to KL and M$31 to Singapore. A taxi costs M$3 per person to Kuala Perlis, M$6 to Butterworth.

There are also buses to Hat Yai in Thailand for M$10 – go to the Tunjang Ekspress office at the bus station. Although you can easily get to Changlun, the Malay border post for Thailand, by bus or taxi, it is then very difficult to cross the long strip of no man's land to Sadao, the Thai border post, as there is no regular transport that just goes across the border.

If, however, you go to Padang Besar, where the railway line crosses the border, you can simply walk across and take a bus from there into Hat Yai. Padang Besar can be reached by road, although the main road to Thailand crosses the border at Changlun-Sadao.

Padang Besar can also be reached from Alor Star by train for only M$2.30. Most of the passengers on this route are petty smugglers, who may make several return trips per day. An estimated 3000 to 4000 kg of Thai rice is smuggled aboard the train every day hidden in secret compartments throughout the KTM coaches.

The Malays don't go to the Thai border empty-handed either; cooking oil, biscuits, flour, garlic and kerosene are favourite items that end up in Pekan Siam, the Thai border counterpart to Padang Besar.

Malaysia's green-uniformed Anti-Smuggling Unit occasionally makes an arrest, but the overall trade is hardly affected. If the smuggling were somehow halted, Pekan Siam and Padang Besar would become ghost towns virtually overnight.

There is no longer a through train from Alor Star to Hat Yai, except for the International Express from Singapore, which doesn't take passengers at Alor Setar.

KEDAH & PERLIS

In the north-west corner of the peninsula the states of Kedah and Perlis are the rice bowls of Malaysia. A green sea of rice paddies stretches away from the road for much of the distance through the state. Perlis is also the smallest state in Malaysia and both states are important gateways into Thailand.

For travellers the most important towns in the state are likely to be the large town of Alor Star and the small fishing port of Kuala Perlis, from where ferries operate to Langkawi. Other places of interest include:

Gunung Jerai & the Bujang Valley

Kedah Peak or Gunung Jerai is the highest peak in the north-west at 1206 metres. It's between the main road and the coast north of Sungai Petani and is topped by a 6th-century Hindu shrine.

The area around the Bujang River which flows off the mountain is the location of important archaeological sites where statues, inscriptions and ancient tombs left by a Pallava cultural outpost of south India have been discovered.

There is a museum at Bukit Batu Pahat where the Candi Bukit Batu Pahat temple has been reconstructed. Other finds are displayed in the Alor Star State Museum.

Kangar & Around

Kangar, 56 km north-west of Alor Star, is the main settlement in the state of Perlis. It's a low-lying town surrounded by rice paddies.

North of there is Padang Besar, a border town to Thailand. It's a popular place to visit because of the duty-free market that operates there, in the no-man's land between the two countries. It's most active on weekends.

Arau, near Kangar, is the royal capital of Perlis and has an istana and a royal mosque. Kaki Bukit in the extreme north-west corner of the state has some interesting limestone caverns from which tin is mined.

Places to Stay Kangar has number of hotels including the *Hotel Malaysia* (tel 04-761366) at 65-67 Jalan Jubli Perak where rooms begin at M$20. The more expensive *Federal Hotel* (tel 04-751288) at 104 Jalan Besar has air-con rooms from M$35.

The cheapest is *Hotel Ban Cheong* (tel 04-751074) at 79A on the same street where rooms start as low as M$10. There is also a *Rest House* on Jalan Kangar (tel 04-751183).

KUALA PERLIS

This small port town in the extreme north-west of the peninsula is visited mainly as the departure point for Langkawi. You can also use Kuala Perlis as an unusual gateway into Thailand.

The main part of Kuala Perlis is just a couple of streets with plenty of restaurants and shops, one hotel and no banks. Kangar is only 10 km away if you need more facilities.

If you've got some time to kill waiting for a boat there's plenty to see. Beside the dock there's an ice works and fish are packed into ice-filled crates on the quay. You can cross the river by a foot bridge to the other part of town where the houses and mosques are built on stilts over the water around the mangrove swamps.

Places to Stay

Kuala Perlis' one and only hotel is the

Soon Hin opposite the taxi stand where a room will cost you M$10.

Getting There & Away

There are direct buses from Butterworth at 8.30 and 11 am for M$5. They connect, more or less, with ferry departures. A taxi between Butterworth and Kuala Perlis costs M$9. From Alor Star there are buses at regular intervals for M$2.60 or taxis at M$3 per person (M$12 for an entire taxi). Buses also depart from Kuala Perlis to Padang Besar (for Thailand) for M$1.90 (taxi M$3.30) and to Kuala Lumpur for M$18. The short taxi ride into Kangar costs 60 sen.

LANGKAWI

The 99 islands of the Langkawi group are 30 km off the coast from Kuala Perlis, at the northern end of peninsular Malaysia. They're accessible by boat from Kuala Perlis, Georgetown (Penang), and Satun in Thailand; or by air from Penang, 112 km south, and Kuala Lumpur.

The islands, strategically situated where the Indian Ocean narrows down into the Straits of Melaka, were once a haven for pirates and could easily have become the site for the first British foothold in Malaya instead of Penang. Earlier they were charted by Admiral Cheng Ho on his visit to Melaka in 1405.

Today they're a quiet and relatively unspoilt place with a population of around 30,000. Attempts to promote Langkawi as a tourist destination have not been very successful, perhaps due to the island's relative remoteness. Whatever the reason, this does mean that visitors have the beaches pretty much to themselves.

The islands of the group often rise sheer from the water and only narrow channels separate one island from another.

In January 1987, the Malaysian government conferred duty-free status on Langkawi as part of a renewed effort to promote Langkawi tourism. An airport large enough for MAS flights was built, and the ferry service from Penang was made more or less regular. These efforts are slowly beginning to take effect and during Malaysia's high travel months, November to January and April, Langkawi does get quite a few visitors.

As in Penang, the monsoon season is July to September. During these months the island is relatively empty because of the occasional heavy rains. Weekends and school holidays are when Langkawi gets the most local visitors.

Information & Orientation

Kuah, with a population of about 2000, is the main town and the arrival point for the ferries from Kuala Perlis. There are a few places to stay but the best beaches are elsewhere on the island, which can make transport logistics a little difficult.

Apart from building their money-losing hotel, the TDC has confined other work on tourist development on the island to erecting a fairly comprehensive, but often rather misleading, collection of signposts. The locals have begun taking matters into their own hands, though, and inexpensive and comfortable accommodation is appearing in the beach areas.

Remember that Langkawi is part of Kedah state and as such banks and government offices are closed on Fridays. Saturdays are half-days and Sundays regular business days.

Kuah (Pekan Kuah)

The island's main town is a one street affair along the waterfront. The bay is dotted with sunken fishing boats – the remains of confiscated Thai poachers or unlicensed local boats, which have sunk while the government slowly got around to prosecuting the fishermen.

Kuah's only 'sight' is the picturesque waterside mosque with its golden dome and Moorish arches and minarets rising prettily above the palm trees.

There are also many small duty-free shops in Kuah. Cigarettes and liquor, including Malaysian beer, are quite cheap as evidenced by the fact that fishermen

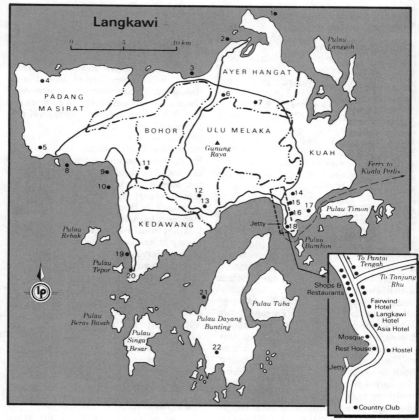

sitting in local coffee shops can be seen smoking Dunhills, Benson & Hedges and Peter Stuyvesant – only M$1.50 a pack. Even Japanese motorcycles are duty-free in Kuah, but they can't be taken off the island!

Durian Perangin

From Kuah you pass through a long series of rubber plantations before the turn-off to this waterfall at the 9th milestone. There's a small sign by the shop there and a larger sign by a second turn-off a bit further on.

The falls are three km off the road – the first part of the path is passable by motorcycle. The falls are best seen at the end of the monsoon season, late September, early October.

Telaga Air Panas

These hot springs are towards the north of the island, 13 km from Kuah, and like so many places in Malaysia there's an intriguing legend to go with them.

The island's two most powerful families, so the story goes, became involved in a bitter argument over a marriage proposal.

1	Gua Cherita
2	Pantai Rhu
3	Pasir Hitam
4	Datai
5	Telaga Tujuh
6	Telaga Air Panas
7	Durian Perangin
8	Pantai Kok
9	Kuala Teriang Village
10	Airstrip
11	Burnt Rice Area
12	Mahsuri's Grave
13	Golf Course
14	Kuah Town
15	Hotel Langkawi
16	Rest House
17	Pantai Dafo'Syed Omar
18	Langkawi Country Club
19	Pantai Cenang
20	Pantai Tengah
21	Gua Langsir
22	Tasik Dayang Bunting

A fight broke out and all the kitchen utensils were used as missiles. The gravy (kuah) was spilt at (yes!) Kuah and seeped into the ground at Kisap (seep). A pot landed at Belanga Perak (broken pot) and finally the saucepan of hot water (air panas) came to land here.

The fathers of these two families got their come-uppance for causing all this mayhem – they are now the island's two major mountain peaks. The hot springs themselves are no tourist attraction – just an ugly little clump of green buildings by the roadside.

Telaga Tujuh

Water cascades nearly 100 metres down a hillside through a series of seven (tujuh) wells (telaga). You can slide down from one of these shallow pools to another near the top of the falls.

To get there you can hire a fishing boat at the fishing village of Kuala Teriang or at Pantai Cenang, or get there by bus and a three-km walk. The boats go to the beach, Pantai Kok, from where there is short walk to the foot of the falls.

If you're staying at or near the Semarak Beach Resort on Pantai Cenang they will drive you to the falls in their van for around M$8 per person.

By motorcycle it's an interesting trip along roads with varying surfaces from Kuah or Pantai Cenang through Pantai Kok. You no longer have to ride from Ayer Hangat in the north of the island since the road now connects all the way from Kuala Teriang village to the falls. For part of the way you ride on a red dirt track through marvellous jungle where monkeys may scamper across the road. The effort's worthwhile – 'I had a fun that I haven't had since I was a child' wrote a Danish visitor.

Mahsuri's Tomb & Padang Masirat

Mahsuri was a legendary 10th-century Malay princess unjustly accused of adultery and sentenced to death. All attempts to execute the indignant Mahsuri *agreed* to die, but not before issuing the curse that 'there shall be no peace or prosperity on this island for a period of seven generations'.

A result of that curse can still sometimes be seen at nearby Padang Masirat, the 'field of burnt rice'. There, villagers once burnt their rice fields rather than allow them to fall into the hands of Siamese invaders and heavy rain, it is said, still sometimes brings traces of burnt rice to the surface.

Pantai Cenang

This beautiful two-km-long strip of beach lies at the south-west corner of Langkawi connected by partly unsurfaced road to Kuah (25 km).

A sandbar appears at low tide where you can see fascinating local sea-life – conches inching their way along, hermit crabs, urchins, sand dollars, live starfish and more. Between November and January, you can walk across this sandbar to the nearby island of Rebak, but be sure to walk back before the sandbar disappears – you only have about two hours.

Another nearby island is Pulau Tepor which can be reached by a hired boat from Cenang beach. Pantai Cenang is where most of the local beach chalet development is happening and it can get a little crowded during weekends. Still, it's a long beach and you can usually find a piece for yourself. If you walk along the beach towards the north, you'll round a bend and come to a small fishing village where a freshwater stream empties into the ocean – very pretty at sunset.

In the distance you can just make out the hump of Koh Adang, an island on the Thai side of the border inhabited by sea gypsies – *orang laut*.

Pantai Tengah

Only about one-km long, Pantai Tengah is just south of Pantai Cenang over a small rocky point and very similar. So far there is only one bungalow development so fewer people are there than on Pantai Cenang.

Pantai Kok

On the western part of the island, 12 km from Pantai Cenang, Kok Beach fronts a beautiful bay surrounded by limestone mountains and jungle. Telaga Tujuh is only a 2.2-km walk away. The water is a bit clearer there than at any of the other beaches during the monsoon season.

Pantai Rhu

On the north coast of the island, 23 km from Kuah, this was once one of Langkawi's better known beaches. The water is shallow and at low tide you can walk across the sand bank to the neighbouring island, except during monsoon season. The water swirls across the bank as the tide comes in.

Around the promontory, accessible by boat, is the Gua Cherita cave. Along the coast for a couple of km before the beach the tiny fish known as ikan bilis are spread out on mats to dry in the sun.

There's a failing beach resort at Pantai Rhu and the company developing the area is virtually on its last legs, so abandoned vehicles and unfinished construction mar the scenery, to say the least, and it's all a pitiful waste. Another problem is that Pantai Rhu is so isolated from the rest of the island that there is not even a village near the beach.

Pasir Hitam

A couple of km west of Pantai Rhu, this beach is noted for its black sand although it's not a real black sand beach – simply streaks of black through the sand. The waters off Pasir Hitam are dotted with huge boulders.

Tasik Dayang Bunting & Gua Langsir

The 'Lake of the Pregnant Maiden' is a freshwater lake with good swimming on Pulau Dayang Bunting, the large island south of Langkawi itself.

A legend states that a childless couple, after 19 years of unsuccessful efforts, had a baby girl after drinking from this lake. Since then it has been a popular pilgrimage centre for those in search of children! Legend also says that the lake is inhabited by a large white crocodile.

Nearby is Gua Langsir, the 'Cave of the Banshee', which is inhabited by thousands of bats. Marble is quarried on the island and shipped to the mainland for processing. To get to this island you must hire a boat from the Kuah jetty or Pantai Cenang.

Boat trips to Pulau Dayang Bunting usually add in a stop at Pulau Singa Besar, where there is reasonable snorkelling. During the monsoon season, July to mid-September, the seas are usually too rough and unpredictable for boat trips to Dayang Bunting. From Cenang boats can be hired for about M$10 per person, eight to a boat.

Pulau Bumbon

Only 10 minutes from the Kuah jetty, this island has five bungalows and some longhouse rooms which you can rent for M$10. There's a pleasant beach nearby and another about 15-minutes walk over the hill. Ask for Pa Wan or Omar at the Kuah jetty to get out there – if they're not around you should be able to find someone else to shuttle you across for around M$5 to M$8.

Places to Stay – Kuah

A short ride by share-taxi will take you from the pier to any of Kuah's cheaper accommodation, all of which is strung out along the waterfront around the bay. Kuah is practically a one-street town and that street follows the bay all the way.

On past the mosque, about a km from the pier, you'll come to Kuah's first two hotels. The *Asia Hotel* (tel 04-788218) has fan-cooled rooms for M$20, and air-con rooms for M$30 and M$48. A few doors down at the *Langkawi Hotel* (tel 04-788248), rooms start at M$15.

The Fairwind Hotel was not in operation at the time of writing, though they still have a sign up, but the Rose Restaurant downstairs is still open.

Further away from the jetty, just over the Kuah town limit in Pokok Assam is *Malaysia Hotel & Restaurant* (tel 788298), a travellers' favourite run by Mr Vellu and his family. Rooms are M$12, there's an Indian restaurant downstairs, and they also hire taxis, motorbikes and bicycles at lower rates than just about anyone else on the island. At the jetty, look for a taxi with plates reading KH3960 for free transport to the hotel and discounted transport elsewhere.

In the top end bracket is the *Langkawi Island Resort* (tel 04-788209), which you pass just before docking as you arrive at Langkawi. The TDC-operated hotel has been a sad white elephant ever since its opening in 1973 – people simply don't come to Langkawi in large enough numbers yet. Its got a fine waterfront position, swimming pool, bars, restaurants, 100 rooms with all the usual mod-cons, but not enough customers to even come close to making money. Singles start at M$95, doubles M$115.

Places to Stay – the beaches

Pantai Cenang There are five 'budget' places to stay and one 'deluxe' place on Cenang, though prices at either end lean toward the middle.

Coming from Kuah, the first you'll come to is *Rebak Cabins*, rather unattractive brick bungalows set too far back from the beach. Next is the well-designed *Semarak Langkawi Resort* where large bungalows (or 'chalets' as they are generally called in Malaysia) with attached bath are M$44.

Just south of Semarak is the *Sandy Beach Hotel* where clean and roomy chalets are M$15 with common bath or M$20 to M$25 bath attached. The atmosphere at Sandy's is relaxed and friendly and they do boat trips to all the nearby islands, including Pulau Adang, just over Thailand's marine border. (It's an interesting island with a population of *orang laut* or sea gypsies.) The open-air restaurant at Sandy is very popular locally because of their five Thai cooks.

After Sandy Beach Hotel are three nondescript places that thus far get little business outside of the high season when accommodation can be a little tight all along Cenang. The *AB Motel*, the *Samila Motel* and the *Delta Motel* all charge the same rates as Sandy's.

Pantai Tengah Only one place to stay there so far. *Charlie's* has standard but well-kept chalets for M$15. They have a small restaurant also.

Pantai Kok There are two places to choose from: the *Pantai Kok Motel & Restaurant* and the *Country Beach Hotel*. Chalets at the former are only M$10 with attached bath which, is the best deal on Langkawi. At the other end of the beach, the Country Beach charges M$20 for fancier chalets.

Pantai Rhu Only one place there, the ill-fated *Mutiara Beach Hotel*, attractive on the inside but a disgrace on the outside. Modern air-con rooms cost from M$70 to M$120.

Places to Eat

Chinese food is available in the restaurants at the *Asia* and *Langkawi Hotels* and also at the *Rose Restaurant* (open 6.45 pm to midnight) under the closed Fairwind Hotel.

There are a number of other Chinese and Indian restaurants and stalls along the road through Kuah. You can buy excellent roti chanai in the various Indian places, also dosa and other south Indian foods in the restaurant below the Malaysia Hotel at 66 Pokok Assam. As in so many other Malaysian towns Kuah has a far greater number and variety of eating places than its size would indicate.

Getting There & Away

Air MAS have daily flights between KL and Langkawi via Penang. The one-way fare is M$112.

Boat The *MS Gadis Langkasuka* operates a weekly (fortnightly during monsoon season) service between Penang and Langkawi. The boat departs the Swettenham Pier in Georgetown at 11 pm Friday nights and arrives in Langkawi at around 7 am the next morning. It departs Langkawi at 9 am Sundays and arrives in Penang about 4 pm the same evening.

The one-way fare is M$45 for a berth or M$35 for a seat. During the monsoon season (July to September) sailings may be cancelled due to rough weather – August is usually the worst month. This ferry docks at Telok Ewa on the north shore rather than at Kuah.

Ferries between Kuala Perlis and Langkawi leave hourly in either direction between 8 am and 6 pm. Fares depend on the speed of the boat. Some boats are gender-segregated, with males in the front half of the boat, females in the rear. The slower boats are M$8 and take about 1 hour 15 minutes; the fast boats are M$10 and take about 45 minutes.

A recent innovation is supposed to be a 10-times-daily hovercraft operating 9 am to 5 pm from Kuala Perlis to the Langkawi resort for M$12 one-way. This was announced a couple of years ago and a ticket booth has been set up in Kuala Perlis, but the service has yet to materialise on a regular basis.

There is now a once-a-day ferry service between Langkawi and Satun, Thailand. The fare is M$10 and the trip takes about 45 minutes.

Between the jetty and Kuah town itself a share taxi costs 60 sen.

Getting Around

You've got to get out and about on Langkawi since there's little of interest in Kuah itself. This can be a problem because although the buses are cheap enough (M$1 will take you almost anywhere on the island), departure times and, more important, return times, are very uncertain. You can also get out to the beaches by taxi (say M$12 to Pantai Cenang/Tengah), but once again you have to get back.

The easiest way to get around is to hire a motorcycle (usually Honda 70 step-thrus) for the day. At Chuan Hin motorcycle dealer in Kuah they cost M$20 but you must show a motorcycle license (from any country) – an international license is preferred. For hires of more than a day you can get a discount. They also hire bicycles and, it is said, you can ride around the island in a day.

The Malaysia Hotel also does motorbike and bicycle hire – at lower rates than Chuan Hin. You can hire a boat to get across to Pulau Dayang Bunting for around M$70 to M$90 per day – get a group together. The Malaysia and Asia Hotels in town organise boat trips, as do most of the beach places.

Peninsular Malaysia – East Coast

Whereas the western side of the peninsula is the more crowded, enterprising, strongly Chinese-influenced part of the country, the east coast is open, relaxed and very Malay in character. It's a long series of gleaming beaches, backed by dense jungle and interspersed with colourful and easygoing fishing villages or kampungs.

Along this coast you also have the opportunity to see some traditional Malay handicrafts and culture or even stay in a small kampung and watch the scarcely changing rituals of village life.

To some extent, the east coast's slower development is a result of its relative isolation. There were few roads along the coast until WW II and it was well into the '70s before the last of the ferries across the many east coast rivers was replaced by a bridge. Today you can follow an excellent 730-km road all the way from Johore Bahru, across the causeway from Singapore in the south, to Kota Bahru, close to the Thai border in the north.

The east-west road, running across the top of the peninsula, has also brought about an increase of visitors to the east coast. With the completion of the new central highway, which runs parallel to the old railway line through the dense jungle, it's possible to get to Kota Bahru from Kuala Lipis in five or six hours – the jungle train takes a lot longer but, with all the locals and their produce on board, it's a more interesting and colourful trip. There is some spectacular scenery along this route.

The east coast is affected by the monsoon – November through January (particularly December) – and the heavy rainfall sometimes floods rivers and makes road travel a difficult proposition. From May through to September it's a busy time on the east coast as this is the season when the giant leatherback turtles,

and their smaller relatives, come ashore to lay their eggs.

Remember that the east coast is predominantly Malay and Muslim, therefore, Friday will be the day of rest. Solo women travellers should exercise a little caution in some of the cheaper hotels and rest houses – several travellers have reported a number of peeping toms and other unwanted attention along the east coast.

KOTA TINGGI

The small town of Kota Tinggi is 42 km from Johore Bahru on the road to Mersing. The town itself is of little interest but the Kota Tinggi waterfalls, 15 km north-west of the town, are a very popular weekend retreat.

The falls, at the base of 624-metre-high Gunung Muntahak, leap down 36 metres and then flow through a series of pools which are ideal for a cooling dip. The smaller pools are shallow enough for safe use by children.

A couple of km from Kota Tinggi town is Kampung Makam, where the Sultans of Johore have their mausoleums.

Places to Stay

At the falls you can stay at the *Waterfall Chalet* where rooms cost from M$27 to M$42 per night, complete with cooking facilities and fridges. To book ring 07-421957. Day chalets are also available at a cost of M$18 per day – weekend bookings are heavy. There is a restaurant on the hillside facing the falls.

If you're desperate for somewhere cheaper to stay, you could try the noisy *Hotel Koko* which has grubby, smelly rooms for about M$10. There's at least one other Chinese hotel in town which has rooms around the same price as Hotel Koko.

Getting There & Away

There are regular buses (No 41) and taxis

from Johore Bahru to the town. From there you can take bus No 43 or a taxi to the waterfalls. From Johore Bahru the taxi fare to Kota Tinggi is about M$8, the bus fare is M$2.

JOHORE LAMA

Following the fall of Melaka to the Portuguese the Malay kingdom was transferred to Johore Lama, about 30 km down the Johore River from Kota Tinggi. The town was built as a fortified capital between 1547 and 1587 but later abandoned as Johore Bahru rose in prominence. There were a number of skirmishes between Malay and Portuguese fleets along the Sungai Johore and on two occasions the town was sacked and burnt.

Today the old fort of Kota Batu, overlooking the river, has been restored but getting to Johore Lama entails arranging a boat for the downriver trip.

JASON'S BAY (Telok Mahkota)

A turn-off 13 km north of Kota Tinggi leads down 24 km of rather rough road to the sheltered waters of Jason's Bay. There are 10 km of sandy beach but few facilities at this relatively isolated spot.

DESARU

On a 20-km stretch of beach at Tanjung Penawar, 88 km north-east of Johore Bahru and also reached via Kota Tinggi, this is a new beach resort area which is being heavily promoted and developed. It's popular as a weekend escape for Singaporeans but it's not particularly interesting for international visitors to Malaysia.

Places to Stay

There are three large resorts right on the beach. The *Desaru Merlin Inn* (tel 07-838101), has 100 rooms priced between M$115 and M$280; the *Desaru View Hotel* (tel 07-838221), has 134 rooms from M$150 to M$650; and the *Desaru Holiday Resort* has chalets from M$70 to M$200.

You can camp with your own or rented equipment for M$5 per person, or there's a dormitory (for groups of at least 15) for M$10 per person. There's a day visit charge of 50 sen.

Getting There & Away

Buses and taxis operate from Kota Tinggi.

MERSING

Mersing is a small fishing village on the east coast of Peninsular Malaysia. It's the departure point for many of the small boats which travel between the mainland and the beautiful islands lying just off the coast, in the South China Sea. The river bustles with fishing boats and there's plenty to see. Mersing has an impressive-looking mosque on a hill above the town and some good beaches such as Sri Pantai and Sekakap – six and 13 km south; and Ayer Papan and Panyabong – 10 and 50 km to the north.

Mersing is a very small town and it's quite easy to find your way about. Travellers' cheques can be changed at the Bank Bumiputra Malaysia Berhad, near the E & W Bakery on Jalan Ismail, or, if it's closed, you can go to the licensed moneychanger on Jalan Abu Bakar.

Places to Stay

Most people only stay overnight in Mersing on their way to Pulau Tioman, or one of the other nearby islands. There is plenty of accommodation in town and, as usual, the basic family-run Chinese hotels are the cheapest.

The *East Coast Hotel* (tel 07-791337), at 43A-1 Jalan Abu Bakar, is run by an English-speaking Chinese lady. The rooms are clean and cheap at M$8.40 for a two-bed room and M$13.65 for a triple room. Just across the road, a nice old man runs the *Syuan Koong Hotel* (tel 07-791498) and charges M$11 for a three-bed room – there is also a cheaper room which is very small.

The *Mersing Hotel* on Jalan Dato Mohammed Ali has fan-cooled double rooms without bathroom for M$13, fan-cooled double rooms with bathroom for M$17 and rooms with air-con and bathroom for M$28.

On Jalan Ismail, the *Hotel Tiong Hwa* has basic doubles with bathroom from M$13 and triples from about M$17; the *Kwang Hong Hotel* has clean rooms from M$15; and the *Hoy Seng Hotel* has rooms from about M$13. At 2 Jalan Ismail, you'll find the popular *Embassy Hotel* (tel 07-791301) with non-air-con rooms at M$21 and air-con rooms at M$32.

The *Mandarin Hotel*, opposite the bus station is another travellers' favourite. It's fairly clean and has fan-cooled rooms from M$12 as well as some more expensive rooms with air-con. Downstairs in the cafe, you'll be accosted by touts trying to round up passengers for the boats to Tioman.

The Tourist Boat Association, down by the jetty, can arrange for you to spend a night or two at a Malay kampung close to Mersing town, at a cost of M$5 per person.

The most expensive hotel in town is the *Mersing Merlin Inn* (tel 07-791311), 1st Mile, Endau Rd. This hotel has 34 fully air-conditioned rooms priced from M$70.

The *Mersing Rest House* (tel 07-791103) is overlooking the six-hole (yes, six) golf course and rooms cost about M$35 per night. As the Rest House is often booked out, you may have to fall back on the cheap hotels in the centre of town.

Places to Eat

Restoran Malaysia, opposite the bus stop where Singapore-bound buses stop for a break, stays open throughout the night – very useful if you arrive on one of the late-night long-distance buses. The people working there are nice and don't seem to mind if you fall asleep next to your coffee. A couple of other nearby cafes also stay open to serve passengers from the late-night buses.

For breakfast, the *E & W Bakery* on Jalan Ismail is OK, but for a better selection of fresh cakes and bread, try the *Sri Mersing Cafe* on Jalan Sulaiman.

If you're looking for Chinese food, there are lots of cafes on Jalan Sulaiman or Jalan Abu Bakar. None of them serve outstanding food but they are cheap. One of the better ones for Chinese-style seafood is the cafe downstairs in the Hotel Embassy.

For cheap, tasty Indian food, try the *Taj Mahal Restoran* on Jalan Abu Bakar and the *Sri Laxmi Restoran* at 30 Jalan Dato Mohammed Ali – the latter has great vegetarian meals for around M$2.

Getting There & Away

Mersing is 133 km north of Johore Bahru and 189 km south of Kuantan. The taxi station and the local bus station are in the centre of town on the corner of Jalan Sulaiman and Jalan Abu Bakar.

Taxi fares from Mersing are M$11 to Johore Bahru, M$3 to Endau, M$5 to Kuala Rompin, M$8.50 to Keluang (for the west coast), M$33 to Kuala Lumpur, M$15 to Kuantan, M$18 to Kota Tinggi, M$11.50 to Pekan, M$33 to Kuala Trengganu, and M$46 all the way north to Kota Bahru.

The express bus to Johore Bahru is about M$6 and the regular bus is around M$5. There are also buses to and from Singapore for S$11. Buses from Mersing to Kuantan cost M$10.50 and from there, you can catch a bus to KL for M$11.

Long-distance buses to Kuantan or Singapore depart from outside Restoran Malaysia and tickets can be purchased from inside. As the buses only pass through Mersing on their way to/from Kuantan or Singapore, sometimes there are no spare seats – the staff at Restoran Malaysia won't sell any tickets until about 30 minutes before the bus is due to pass by.

Tioman

The largest of the east coast islands, Tioman is 19 km long and 12 km wide. It is mountainous, Gunung Kajang is 1049 metres high, densely wooded, ringed with beautiful beaches and fine coral, and best of all is relatively unspoilt.

Tioman is lightly populated – there is just a handful of small kampungs dotted around the coast and the hilly inland area is virgin forest with no settlements at all.

The island's only road runs from the telecommunications tower one km south of the Tioman Island Resort to the airstrip at Tekek, about two km north. A few cars use the road and the number of motorbikes is growing but no vehicles can travel beyond the headland, a couple of km north of the airstrip.

Tioman has beautiful beaches, clear water and coral for snorkelling or diving enthusiasts, but its major attraction has to be the contrasts and diversity it offers – high mountains and dense jungle are only a short walk away from the coast. As evidence of the island's abundant natural beauty it's generally quoted that this was the setting for the mythical Bali Hai in the film *South Pacific*.

Two thousand years ago, Arab traders noted Tioman on their charts as a place with good anchorages and fresh water. It's an island that would be hard to miss with spectacular peaks like Batu Sirau and Nenek Si-muka at the southern end of the island. To this day the streams run rapid and clear from the high peaks of the island.

Tioman has also been blessed with some delightful names. The highest peak, Gunung Kajang is 'Palm-Frond Hill'. Gunung Chula Naga is 'Dragon-Horn Hill' and the villages are equally imaginatively named. There's Kampung Tekek (Lizard Village), Kampung Lalang (Elephant Village), Kampung Juara (Catfish Village) and even Kampung Merkut (Village of Doubt).

Pulau Tioman has become a very popular travellers' centre and at certain times of the year it can get quite crowded, especially at Kampung Ayer Batang, where the majority of backpackers tend to stay. If you want to get away from it all,

head for the isolated Kampung Juara on the other side of the island.

Information & Orientation

The island is wilder and more mountainous at the southern end. The single strip of road, the one big hotel and most of the smaller, cheaper places are along the west coast. There's a good trail across the 'waist' of the island to a settlement on the east coast, where there is also cheap accommodation.

If you want to read more about the wildlife and plant life of the island get a copy of *The Natural History of Pulau Tioman* a University of Malaya research project published by the Merlin Hotel (now the Tioman Island Resort).

The Tioman Island Resort has the only phone on the island, which can be used by anyone in an emergency but otherwise is not for general use.

Walks

Using Tekek as a base you can walk south to the Tioman Island Resort at Lalang in about 30 minutes either by the road (it's steep) or by rock-hopping around the headland. From there you can continue another 30 minutes south to the deserted beach beyond the Telecom tower. It's further south to Kampung Paya where the climb up Gunung Kajang commences. There is no actual trail to follow when climbing the mountain.

Heading north from Tekek, you follow the coast round a series of beaches and headlands to Monkey Bay. Alternatively, you can head inland on the easiest of the cross-island tracks which starts near the mosque in the main part of Kampung Tekek. At Tekek, pass the mosque on your left and take the path which is marked by faded white crosses on rocks.

It's a relatively steep climb through dense jungle following the course of the Sungai Besar river to the highest point. Then it slopes down more gradually and soon leaves the damp, dark jungle for the cooler and brighter area of a rubber

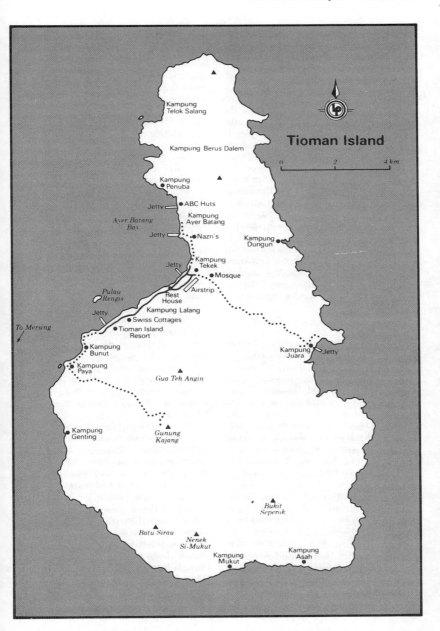

Tioman Island

plantation and then coconut palms as you reach the coast. The walk across the island to Kampung Juara takes two to three hours.

Wildlife

Tioman is of great interest to biologists because of its relative isolation from the similarly forested terrain of the peninsula. Some common animals are completely missing from the island while others are present in unexpectedly large numbers.

Tioman has a very large mouse deer population, for example, and also has a wide variety of lizards in larger than usual numbers. You've got a good chance of seeing some wildlife while you are on Tioman, particularly bats which come out in force each evening.

The waters around Tioman shelter the usual technicolour assembly of fish and a surprising number of turtles. At Kampung Nipah, Juara and Pulau Tulai you have a good chance of seeing turtles come ashore to lay their eggs.

Places to Stay

There is a lot of cheap accommodation on Tioman and the island is so delightful that it's likely more 'big' hotels will also be built in the future. At present you've got a choice of the top-end Tioman Island Resort, a few mid-range chalets or a host of little local places with rock-bottom prices and facilities to match. The latter are generally found at Kampung Tekek and further north at Kampung Ayer Batang. If you'd like a beach to yourself, try Kampung Juara on the east coast.

Lalang The *Tioman Island Resort* (tel 09-2305266), is the only 'international class' hotel on the island. It has 68 rooms from around M$85 to M$175. The rooms have air-con but are relatively simple which is OK since the hotel's number one attraction has nothing to do with the hotel itself – it's the delightful location that counts.

The beach is just a few steps from the hotel, the water is clear and ideal for snorkelling, there are plenty of opportunities for water sports and there's a small island within swimming distance of the shore. This hotel can be heavily booked, particularly during school holidays. The restaurant there is very good, though by no means cheap.

Tekek Strung along the beach at Tekek and to the north are a whole series of places to stay and there are a lot more under construction. Most of them are in the M$7 to M$12 per person bracket although there are a few at higher prices.

For what is offered, Tioman's prices are definitely higher than on the mainland and a little bargaining is often in order. The basic places are just that. There are no fans or mosquito nets, often no electricity, and toilets and washing facilities are communal.

Finding accommodation is fairly simple – the Mersing boatmen will undoubtedly have some contacts to tell you about. Often, when you arrive at the island, people with rooms to spare will be down at the wharf looking for customers. If not, you can simply wander around and ask at likely-looking places. There are virtually no signs out saying 'This is a hotel'.

Most places have their own small canteen, serving good, cheap food. In season, you'll find plenty of fruit all over the island.

One of the nicest places to stay at is *Swiss Cottages*, on a beautiful stretch of beach, a little further north of the Tioman Island Resort. Accommodation is chalet-style and prices start from about M$15 per person.

Tekek Chalets and *Manap Chalets* are similarly priced while cheaper places, charging between M$5 and M$8, include the *Azman Chalets*, *Yahya Chalets*, *Rallay's Chalet* and *Aris Chalets*. The more expensive places usually have private bathrooms, otherwise, there is little difference between any of them.

On the beach at Tekek is the *Rest House*, rooms with fan and attached bathroom cost between M$10 and M$18.

It's still really run down and decrepit, the furniture is all falling apart, it's surrounded by ugly and rusting barbed wire and is desperately in need of a coat of paint. Check with the last of the small shops to the left of the jetty to see if there's space (it's often booked out).

The *Razali Guest House* and the *Wan Endut Guest House* have six-bed rooms costing around M$7 for a bed. The *Jumaat Guest House* has rooms from M$7 to M$16 and the *Tekek Inn* has four-bed rooms costing M$7 or M$8 per person.

There are a number of other places along the beach and more under construction. In Tekek there's electricity from 6 am to 6 pm; further along there's no power unless places have their own generator. Several of the kedais (shops) in Tekek have coldish drinks and you can get meals at the kedai nearest the jetty.

Ayer Batang If you keep walking north from Tekek, you'll come to Kampung Ayer Batang. This is where most travellers end up and some people stay for

weeks on end. The beach is great and gets better the further north you walk.

Accommodation in this kampung is at its most basic. A typical A-frame hut is equipped with two mattresses on the floor and nothing else – definitely no fan or electricity (though you can borrow kerosene lamps). There are communal toilets and washing facilities.

Most boats drop passengers at *Nazri's* jetty which is probably why his chalets are often full. Nazri has about a dozen chalets near the jetty and charges M$8 per two-bed hut and slightly less if only one person stays in a hut. There are also some more expensive bungalows.

There are plenty of cute little A-frame huts dotted along the whole length of the beach between Nazri's jetty and a second jetty further north, close to ABC huts. It's worth walking beyond Nazri's to some of these places – it's quieter and the beach is much nicer.

Some of the smaller places include *Zahara's Place*, *Aziz House*, *Osman Chalets*, *Hamidon Chalets* and *Mokhtar*

Chalets. They're all clean and well-kept with friendly people running them. Prices are M$4 to M$5 per person, sometimes even cheaper when business is slow. Most of these places have their own little cafes serving delicious food at very low prices.

The most popular place to stay in Kampung Ayer Batang seems to be the *ABC* huts at the northern end of the beach. Many a weary traveller has got off the boat at Nazri's jetty and trudged 20 minutes further up the beach to ABC. Accommodation costs M$4 per person and is in basic A-frame huts equipped with mattresses but no fan or light. The beach is great, far less crowded than the area near Nazri's. Some boats drop passengers at Nazri's jetty and then continue to the jetty near the ABC huts – check before you board the boat.

Salang Kampung Salang is the settlement at the north-west end of the island and it's the place to head for if you're into diving. There's a lot of beautiful live coral and some spectacular fish to see.

Salang is where you'll find *Ben's Diving Centre*, run by a Malay guy who lived in Germany for several years. He has a few chalets costing M$5 to M$6 per person. You can also stay at *Bidin's Guest House* for about M$6 a night.

The Tourist Boats Association (tel 07-792501) has boats which drop passengers at Nazri's jetty and ABC's jetty for M$15. If you make the arrangements beforehand, they can also drop you at Salang for an extra M$5.

Juara If you really want to get away from it all you can stay at this small kampung on the other side of the island. There are some beautiful, long, isolated beaches around Juara. A walking track links this village with Tekek, across the other side of Tioman – it takes about two to three hours to walk from one kampung to the other.

The *Happy Cafe*, with its delightfully cheerful proprietor, is right by the jetty. It's a spotlessly clean and tidy little

establishment where one small room with a double bed and mosquito net costs M$5 per person. If the room should be in use he'll arrange for you to stay in his own house nearby.

Ali Awang's Chalets are well-kept and a bargain at M$3 to M$4 per person. *Sanny Hussein's Chalets*, which are also nice, cost slightly more with rooms from M$6 to M$16. There are quite a few other places to stay in Juara, all similar in terms of facilities offered (or rather, facilities not offered) and the price of a bed seems to hover around M$4 per person.

Boat trips to other beaches on this coast can be arranged. You can charter a boat from Tekek to Juara for M$70. If you do this, you will pass the Mukut Waterfall at the southernmost point of Tioman. You can only see this waterfall from a boat as it cannot be reached on foot due to the rocky headland.

Paya Kampung Paya is a few km south of the Tioman Island Resort. You can stay in any of the cheap chalets and A-frame huts which cost around M$7 per night. It's a nice place but there are no regular scheduled boats going there so unless you can afford to charter a boat from Tekek, which costs at least M$60, you're in for a very long, hot walk.

Getting There & Away

Air Tioman Island is now part of MAS's domestic flight network. There are daily flights between the peninsula and Tioman, costing M$100 one-way. You can also fly direct from Singapore to Tioman. The flight from Singapore takes about 30 minutes and the flight from KL slightly longer.

Boat It's about 50 km from Mersing to Tioman and several boats make daily trips back and forth. The fastest boat is the Tioman Island Resort's hydrofoil which takes around one hour (plus time-consuming boat transfers at each end of the trip) and costs M$30 one-way. There is a hovercraft which takes 1½ hours and is

Top & Bottom: Pantai Cenang, Pulau Langkawi (JC)

Top: Fishing boat, Marang (VB)
Bottom: Village, Marang (VB)

cheaper at M$25 one-way; and there are also small fishing boats which make frequent daily trips from Mersing to Tioman for M$15.

The jetty is about five-minutes walk from the town centre and you'll find the offices for boats to all the islands in this area.

The Tourist Boats Association (tel 07-792501), 1 Jalan Abu Bakar, is pretty reliable – ask for Shuco. They can arrange boats out to several of the islands as well as to Tioman. They operate a fast launch to Tioman costing M$25 which takes about 1½ hours and regular slow boats throughout the day costing M$15 and taking three to four hours. Shuco insists that he has boats going to Tioman at all times of the day.

Rawa Bird Sdn Bhd (07-792589) at 5 Jalan Abu Bakar and Tioman Chalets and Boats Services (07-793048) at 3 Jalan Abu Bakar also have regular boats going to Tioman and the standard one-way fare is M$15. You can also arrange your boat trip downstairs in the cafe at the Hotel Mandarin.

Boats can be chartered for M$150 one-way. If you want to return the same day, the round trip costs M$280. The trip tends to get a bit choppy once you get about a third of the way to Tioman.

During the monsoon, seas can be very rough and departures may be delayed or cancelled. Despite this, the monsoon period is not a bad time to visit Tioman – it's a lot less crowded and the weather can be very pleasant for most of the time. The worst part is the boat trip out – one traveller lived to tell the tale after battling against one to two-metre-high waves in a small fishing boat bound for Tioman. As their boat approached the bar, they spotted a 10-metre boat surfing back in!

At the island it's possible to charter boats for excursions around Tioman or to nearby islands but, expect to pay at least M$80 per day.

OTHER ISLANDS

Although Tioman is the largest and best-known of the islands off Mersing, there are many others, most of them uninhabited and often too rocky and precipitous to land on. Most islands off the coast of Mersing have beautiful white sandy beaches and are surrounded by crystal-clear water.

Pulau Rawa

This tiny island owned by the Malaysian royal family is the second most developed island of the 64 islands. There are simple chalets and bungalows which cost M$40 to M$60 per day. Only 12 km from the peninsula, it takes just over an hour to get there and costs M$16 return.

Day-visitors to the island are charged M$3 and the island operators stipulate that there is to be no camping or picnicking without prior arrangement with the management (and it's likely that you'd be refused should you try to make such arrangements). You can hire the necessary equipment for windsurfing, canoeing, scuba diving, snorkelling and fishing – Rawa is not an ideal place for diving as most of the coral is dead. You can make reservations at Rawa Safaris Sdn Bhd (tel 07-791204) at the Tourist Centre in Mersing.

Pulau Babi Besar

This island is larger than Pulau Rawa and lies closer to the peninsula. Boats take about an hour to reach the island from Mersing and cost M$80 to charter one-way. If you charter the boat to take you there and back, the cost is slightly cheaper at M$150. For day trips, you must pay an extra M$100 for the boat to wait for you to return.

There are some expensive chalets on Pulau Babi Besar, costing M$44 per night and a few cheaper huts at M$7 to M$8 per person. As there are cooking facilities on the island, you can bring your own food. Meals can also be arranged in advance with the owners of huts.

Pulau Tengah

This is a small, privately-owned island with a few huts available at M$5 per person. No one lives there so there are few facilities. You can bring your own food as there are cooking facilities or you can make arrangements for supplies to be brought if you decide to stay for a week or so. You can eat the fruit which grow there.

If you'd like to stay on Tengah, ask at the Tourist Boats Association by the jetty in Mersing. They will drop you at the island and pick you up a day or so later on their way to Pulau Tioman. The fare from Mersing to Pulau Tengah to Tioman is M$15 one-way and M$30 return.

Pulau Sibu

This island is becoming quite popular and there are several bungalows for rent. Two-bed A-frame huts cost M$18 each and more upmarket ones cost from M$25 to M$35 a night. There's a canteen at the Sea Gypsy Chalets.

To get to Sibu, you have to charter a boat from Mersing which costs about M$120. There are some beautiful beaches on the island.

Pulau Hujung

Another small island which you can visit from Mersing. It's remote and has no facilities to offer. No one lives here but there are a couple of beach huts. If you want to stay you can either camp or find someone to open a hut for you – the Mersing boatmen may be able to help.

MERSING TO KUANTAN

The 133 km from Johore Bahru to Mersing are surprisingly uninhabited, but you pass through more settlements on the 189 km from Mersing to Kuantan. This was the last stretch of the east coast road to replace river ferries with bridges and there were still a number of ferry crossings in the early '70s. Even the wide Pahang River has now been bridged, with a 50 sen toll to cross the river. At a number of places the road touches the coast and there are good beaches. You can catch a bus or taxi from town to town along the coast.

Endau

There's little of interest in Endau itself, but you can hire boats to make trips up the remote Endau River to the Orang Asli settlements in the interior.

You can get about 110 km upriver in fair size boats, almost to Kampung Patah which is the last village up the river. From there smaller boats are required to negotiate the rapids into Orang Asli country. Smaller boats can be hired at Kampung Punan, about 100 km from Endau.

Kuala Rompin & Nenasi

Again there is nothing to see or do in the town, but with a four wheel-drive vehicle you can go inland to Iban, 10 km, and a further 25 km to Kampung Aur where there are Orang Asli settlements.

At Nenasi boats can be hired and you can go upriver to the Orang Asli village of Kampung Ulu Serai.

Places to Stay Near Kuala Rompin at the 122½ milestone the small *Government Rest House* (tel 09-565245), has rooms at M$14, more for air-con. The *Mee Chew Hotel* in Kuala Rompin costs M$10.

Pekan

The royal town of Pahang state has a couple of well-built white-marble mosques and the Sultan's palace, the modern Istana Abu Bakar. The istana is on the Kuantan edge of town.

The Pahang River, crossed at this town by a lengthy bridge, is the longest river in Malaysia and was the last east coast river to be bridged. At the river mouth on the other side there's the small fishing village of Kuala Pahang.

A road follows the Pahang River to Kampung Melayu or Mempelas, 60 km upriver. From there, you can take boats out onto the Tasik Chini (see the Around Kuantan section). Buses run along this road.

Silk weaving can be seen at Kampung Pulau Keladi, only about five km out of Pekan.

Places to Stay The *Pekan Hotel* (tel 09-571378) at 60 Jalan Clifford and the *Ching Hiang Hotel* (tel 09-571378) have rooms for around M$10. There's also the equally cheap *Pekan Rest House* (tel 09-571240).

Kuantan

About midway up the east coast from Singapore to Kota Bahru, Kuantan is the capital of the state of Pahang and the start of the east coast beach strip which extends all the way to Kota Bahru.

Kuantan itself, has little to offer the visitor but is a useful stop-over point when you are travelling north, south or across the peninsula. It also has plenty of hotels and restaurants and, nearby, a number of interesting places to visit.

Although the town of Kuantan is not particularly interesting, the Kuantan area is noted for its handicrafts, including batik, and there are a number of shops selling local craftwork along Jalan Besar near the bus stand.

Further up and across the road from the bus stand, you'll find a string of colourful shops selling dried fish and other seafoods – the smell of dried fish and open drains is a memorable combination!

Take a stroll along the riverbank and watch the activity on the wide Kuantan River. From a jetty a little downstream from the bus stand, near the fish market, you can get a ferry across the river for about 45 sen to the small fishing village of Kampung Tanjung Lumpur.

Information & Orientation

Kuantan is essentially a three-street town. Jalan Besar runs close to the river and changes name to Telok Sisek partway along. You'll find the long-distance bus station on Jalan Besar, along with most of the cheaper hotels. Jalan Mahkota runs parallel to Jalan Besar/Telok Sisek – these two streets are both one-way, in opposite directions.

The tourist office, the GPO and most of the banks are up the far end of this street. Also on Jalan Mahkota is a bookshop with English-language books and the local bus station. The taxi station is between Jalan Mahkota and Jalan Besar.

The third main street, Jalan Butik Ubi, runs perpendicular to Jalan Besar and Jalan Mahkota. There are some cheap hotels and restaurants along this street. The MAS office is on Jalan Gambut which runs off Jalan Butik Ubi.

Telok Chempedak

Kuantan's major attraction is Telok Chempedak beach, about four km from the town. The beach, bounded by rocky headlands at each end, is quite pleasant but not that good for swimming – there are much better beaches on the peninsula. A short track leads from the southern end of the beach over the hill to the Telok Chempedak Rest House on the river side of the promontory. There are a number of walking tracks in the park area on this promontory.

Telok Chempedak, which was a quiet little place until the early '70s, now has a two international hotels and a sleazy row of bars, clubs and restaurants. On the Hyatt's beachfront is a small wooden junk which carried 162 Vietnamese boat-people on their hazardous voyage to the west – it's now the 'Sampan Bar' where you can pay over the odds for a beer or coke!

Places to Stay

Kuantan has the usual quota of cheap Chinese hotels and a few upmarket places, but the big international hotels are a few km out of town at Telok Chempedak.

One of the most convenient hotels in town is the *Hotel Raya Baru* (tel 09-522344), opposite the long-distance bus station on Jalan Besar. It has basic fan-cooled rooms, some with peepholes, from

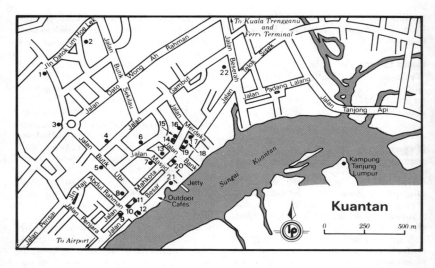

Kuantan

1	Hindu Temple
2	Stadium
3	Hotel Pacific Kuantan
4	MAS
5	New Capitol Hotel
6	Immigration
7	Local bus station
8	Min Heng Hotel
9	Taxi station
10	Hotel Raya Baru & Indian Restaurant
11	Hotel Tong Nam Ah
12	Bus station
13	Food Centre
14	Malayan Banking
15	Tourist Office
16	GPO
17	Suraya Hotel
18	New Embassy Hotel
19	Chartered Bank
20	Tiki's Restoran
21	Samudra Hotel
22	Mitra Hotel

M$23 single or double. It's hardly good value, but you can check in at all hours of the night – good news when you reach Kuantan at 1 am on one of the night flights or night buses.

Further down the street, there's the *Hotel New Embassy* (tel 09-524277), formerly the Moonlight, which has very basic but clean rooms from M$13. More expensive air-con rooms cost about M$21.

The *Sin Nam Fong* (tel 09-521561) at 44 Jalan Telok Sisek has clean rooms and friendly owners. The price of a room varies from M$12 to M$21 and they are reasonably comfortable.

Back down the street towards the bus station, you'll find the *Tong Nam Ah Hotel* (tel 521204) which has reasonable rooms from M$11 to M$15.

On Jalan Mahkota, there's the *Ming Heng Hotel & Bakery* (tel 09-524885), where basic rooms start at M$11. At the far end of Jalan Mahkota, near the banks, there's the the *Hotel Malaysia* (tel 09-521587) which has small double rooms for M$15 and larger triples for M$17. The *New Capitol Hotel* (tel 09-552422), next to the Capitol Cinema on Jalan Bukit Ubi has single rooms for M$15 and double rooms for M$19. There are also a few air-con rooms for M$27.

Opposite the GPO on Jalan Mahkota, there's the more upmarket *Suraya Hotel*

(tel 09-524266) with air-con single rooms for M$45 and doubles from M$52. Another hotel in this price bracket is the *Samudra Hotel* (tel 09-522688) with 75 rooms priced from M$53 to well over M$100.

There is also a Government Rest House on Jalan Telok Sisek called the *Annex Rest House* which has fan-cooled rooms from M$19. Some rooms have their own sitting room and cost M$25 – good value.

Places to Stay – Telok Chempedak The alternative to staying in Kuantan itself is out at Telok Chempedak beach where there's a wide variety of accommodation possibilities.

Until the beachfront 'international' hotels were built, the popular little *Asrama Bendahara* used to look on to the beach. It's the lowest-priced place therewith rooms at M$12, dorm facilities and a cheap restaurant downstairs – a friendly place popular with many travellers.

Nearby is the *Kuantan Hotel* (tel 09-524755) with 22 rooms priced from M$30 to M$70. Round on the main road there's the *Hill View Hotel* (tel 09-521555) with rooms for M$35.

Finally there's a group of 'motels' in the street behind the Hill View. Some are very seedy and ill-cared-for but the *Wally Motel* (tel 09-522646) is reasonably well kept and friendly – a good little travellers' centre. There are six small rooms from M$15 to M$18. You can also rent good, clean rooms from the family next door; or you can try the *Sri Pantai Motel* (tel 09-524749) which has fan-cooled rooms from M$15.

More expensive places include the *Samudra Beach Hotel* (tel 09-522688) which has air-con rooms for M$54; the *Merlin Hotel* (tel 09-522388) which has 106 rooms priced between M$85 and M$190; and the *Hyatt Kuantan* (tel 09-525211) where rooms sky-rocket from M$130.

The *Telok Chempedak Rest House* (tel 09-521711) is a modern, motel-like place with rooms at M$25. It's round the promontory from the main beach and at low tide the beach is messy and covered in garbage, and the water is rather shallow. Officially, it's only for government workers and their families but you could always ring to see if they have any extra space. There is a public pool nearby which costs around M$1 to use.

Places to Eat
There are several small cafes around Kuantan serving good Chinese or Malay/Muslim food. At the Indian cafe downstairs in the Hotel Raya Baru, you'll get tasty vegetarian food served on a huge banana leaf. Further down Jalan Besar, inside a huge shopping complex across the road from the taxi station, is the *Teruntum Bakery & Cafe*. There's also a good supermarket in the complex.

For breakfast, try *Tiki's Restoran* up the far end of Jalan Mahkota. It's a friendly little place run by two brothers who always seem to be busy. Western-style breakfasts and other meals are available for around M$2. They also serve excellent local dishes for similar prices.

Not far from Tiki's Restoran is the popular *Restoran Cheun Kee* which serves good Chinese food for M$2 to M$3. On the

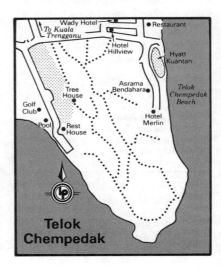

Telok Chempedak

opposite side of the road, further down the street (heading away from all the banks) there are lots of interesting food stalls, even one catering for vegetarians.

Jalan Bukit Ubi is a busy street lined with several restaurants, hotels and quite a few bakeries, emporiums and super-markets. Try the *Swan Bakery Cafe* for a variety of fresh cakes and pastries or the *Istimewa Moon Cake Bakery*, almost opposite.

If you have time to spare, it's really nice to sit down and relax at the small Malay cafes dotted along the riverbank, behind the long-distance bus station. All the cafes look out on to the river and you have the choice of sitting undercover or in the sun. It's easy to spend an hour or so just watching the boats pass by on the river – one observant traveller saw the same pile of rubbish float by twice, in opposite directions, within about two hours. The only unpleasant thing about this area is the smell of open drains when the wind changes direction.

Places to Eat – Telok Chempedak The big hotels have the usual selection of restaurants and there is also a collection of Chinese open-air restaurants further up the beach – good seafood at the *Sea View Restaurant*.

The flashy-looking Chinese restaurants along the road to the beach are actually much cheaper than they look. The *Asrama Bendahara* has a restaurant with low prices for food and drinks.

Getting There & Away
Kuantan is on MAS's flight network. Examples of bus fares from Kuantan (non-air-con/air-con) include: M$4.30/5.10 to Temerloh, M$9/11 to KL, M$16.50/19.50 to Ipoh, M$12.50/15 to Johore Bahru, M$10.40/12.50 to Kuala Lipis and M$16 (air-con only) to Singapore. Along the east coast it's M$5.50 (non-air-con only) south to Kuala Rompin, M$7/8 north to Kuala Trengganu and M$13.20/15.80 to Kota Bahru.

Taxis cost M$4 to Pekan, M$9.50 to Kuala Rompin, M$15 to Mersing. Heading north it's around M$5 to Kemaman, M$9 to Kuala Dungun, M$15.50 to Kuala Trengganu or M$29 to Kota Bahru. Across the peninsula it's about M$8.50 to Temerloh, M$13 to Jerantut, M$17.50 to Raub and M$19 to KL.

Getting Around
Bus No 39 will take you to Telok Chempedak for less than 50 sen. For Kampung Cherating, take the grey and red bus marked 'Kemaman' from the main bus station for M$2.20. The trip takes about 45 minutes.

AROUND KUANTAN
Beserah
The small, interesting fishing village of Beserah is only 10 km north of Kuantan and is a centre for local handicrafts including batik, carvings and shell items from the village of Sungai Karang Darat, a little further north. Kite-flying, top-spinning and other east coast activities can also be seen there. Batu Hitam is a good beach just north of Beserah.

Places to Stay The popular shoestring travellers' place in Beserah is known as *Jaafar's Place*. It's a kampung house about a half km off the road on the inland side. A small sign points it out and bus drivers know it. Accommodation costs M$9 a night including bananas, bread and tea for breakfast (lunch is an extra M$3). Youth Hostel members pay only M$4 a night. Facilities are rudimentary – you sleep on the floor, wash in the river and there are squat toilets.

Reactions to this place are varied – some travellers feel it's restful, easy-going and friendly while others claim it's a 'pack-them-in rip-off' with 'bad food and zero facilities'. If you want to stay kampung-style you obviously have to make some adjustments, but there's no denying that the places at Cherating, 40 km north, offer a lot more for little more.

Plus points for staying in Beserah include the interesting kampung life and the local activities you can join in. There is a number of local batik and other handicraft activities. You may well see top-spinning contests and coconut-collecting monkeys, and it's very easy to arrange to go out on fishing trips in the morning – bring back some fish to cook.

Getting There Although any bus travelling north from Kuantan towards Kuala Trengganu will pass through Beserah, it's easiest to catch a bus marked 'Beserah' from the main bus stand for 50 sen.

Berkelah Falls

The Berkelah Falls are about 50 km from Kuantan – the final six km involve a jungle trek from the main road. The falls come down a hillside in a series of eight cascades. The Marathandhavar Temple is the site for a major Hindu festival in March or April each year. It's on the Maran-Jerantut road taken by visitors to the Taman Negara.

Getting There Catch a bus to Maran from the main bus station for M$3.35. At Kampung Maran, you'll see a bridge by the river. This is where the walk to the falls begins (there is a sign indicating the direction). The jungle track is very overgrown due to the lack of walkers and lack of maintenance! The walk takes about three hours.

Charah Caves

The caves are similar to the Batu Caves near Kuala Lumpur, except they are Buddhist, not Hindu. It's a steep climb up an external stairway to the caves' entrance. In the more enclosed cave there's a nine-metre-long reclining Buddha and other Buddhist statuary. There's a M$1 admission charge to the caves, which should include a small boy with a torch to show you around. It's best to take your own torch.

Further on at Sungai Lembing there's Malaysia's deepest tin mine, but a visit requires advance arrangements.

Getting There & Away If you're driving or hitching, head out on the Panching road towards Sungai Lembing and when the road finally forks in two, veer to the right – it leads directly to the caves through palm oil and rubber plantations.

Alternatively, catch the Sungai Lembing bus from the main bus station in Kuantan. Get off at Panching town, walk to your right until you reach the end of the road where you'll find the caves.

A bus from Kuantan to Panching, halfway to Sungai Lembing, costs about M$1.50. From the bus stop in town it's a 3½-km walk each way, but someone *always* stops and offers you a lift. The caves are just OK but the trip to and from Kuantan is very interesting.

Tasik Chini

Turn south from the Temerloh road 56 km west of Kuantan, and a rough road will take you to Kampung Tasik Chini. From there you can hire a boat to cross the Pahang River and get out onto the often lotus-covered expanse of Tasik Chini.

The lake, which is renowned for its superb fishing, is said to contain a Malaysian monster of the Loch Ness variety. It's a beautiful area where you can go swimming and walk for miles in jungle territory. There are also several Orang Asli settlements in the Tasik Chini area.

If you're interested in trekking around Tasik Chini, ring Johnny Tan (tel 09-311173) in Kuala Lipis.

Places to Stay There are a couple of free rest houses near Tasik Chini, but they're not near the main tourist area. Club Med have their own expensive area where they bring bus loads of their Kuantan Club Med guests for the day. There are chalets available for about M$40.

Getting There From Kuantan, you either have to hitch, or take a taxi for a hefty

M$100 to Kampung Tasik Chini. Then you have to hire a boat to take you down the Pahang River to the lake itself.

You can also reach the lake via Kampung Melayu which is connected by road with Pekan. An alternative route is to take a taxi from Maran to Kampung Tasik Chini for about M$30 one-way. Hitching is difficult as not many cars use the road to the lake.

KUANTAN TO KUALA TRENGGANU

The 218 km between Kuantan and Kuala Trengganu is probably the most interesting stretch of road along the east coast although it now embraces miles of new petro-chemical developments. The road runs close to the coast most of the way, and there are many good beaches and a number of interesting offshore islands.

There are many places to stay along the coast, as well as several interesting small towns and fishing villages.

North of Beserah, the small island of Ular, 'Snake Island', is only a short distance offshore and easily reached by a local fishing boat. It's then only a couple of km north of there to the kampung of Cherating, a very popular backpackers' accommodation centre. Just round the promontory from Cherating is accommodation at the other end of the scale – Malaysia's Club Mediterranée at Chendor.

Chendor is the start of the turtle beach area of Malaysia, although the species that come in to lay their eggs are not the giant leatherback variety you find further north at Rantau Abang.

Places to Stay – Beserah to Chendor There is

a wide variety of places to stay along the coast from Kuantan. At the 9¼ mile marker the *Hotel Simjifa* (tel 09-523254) is a run-down motel on the beach with 51 over-priced rooms from M$35 to M$60.

Only four km further north is the *Titik Inn* (tel 09-531329), a pleasant beachfront place with chalets at M$45 or two bedroom

chalets for M$90. All the chalets have bathrooms, small verandahs and fans, but they're rather expensive for what you get.

At the 45-km marker you come to the small kampung of Cherating where there are a number of places to stay. (Refer to the following section on Cherating.) Just beyond Cherating there's a headland, then the turn-off to the Chendor Motel and the Club Mediterranée at the 29th mile (46 km).

The *Chendor Motel* (tel 09-531369) has 58 rooms from M$54 to M$120, but it's not particularly good value and the restaurant is very expensive. There are some dormitory beds available for around M$6.

Nearby is the large (325 room) and securely guarded *Club Mediterranée* complex. This was the first Club Mediterranée holiday resort in Asia and the majority of people who stay there come to Malaysia from Europe or Australia on all-inclusive package deals. However, if you've always wanted to try a Club Mediterranée there are often short-stay packages offered in Malaysia. Regular cost? Over M$1000 a week!

Cherating

This beautiful little haven has become a popular traveller's centre for kampung-style accommodation. Cherating is the name given to the type of sand crab found on the beach. There are several places to stay in this kampung and there's always a steady stream of young travellers passing through.

Many people visiting Cherating settle down and stay for weeks. At this kampung it's no trouble to let days just drift by. You can watch the kampung life, stroll along the beach or swim either off the long stretch of beach in front of the kampung or from the secluded bays just to the north towards Club Mediterranée.

You can arrange minitreks, river trips and barbecues on the beach with the locals who run the guest houses. The locals are always willing to teach travellers how to play Malaysian board games and sports and, sometimes, they will arrange shadow-puppet shows so you can sample some of the local culture.

The Coconut Inn and the Kampung Inn arrange a river trip/trek on the Cherating River for about M$9. It involves a one-hour boat ride upstream, followed by a pleasant 40-minute walk through jungle to a tiny kampung consisting of only five houses. Common wildlife to look out for includes monkeys, yellow and black snakes (hanging in trees and swimming in the water), large lizards, wild boar, colourful kingfishers, otters, fish and giant crabs.

At night, turtles come ashore to lay their eggs at Chendor beach, right by Club Méditerranée. These turtles are smaller cousins of the giant leatherbacks found further north at Rantau Abang. Ask the people you stay with about the turtles and they may be able to arrange for someone to check the beaches at night for you. You cannot walk along the beach to Chendor due to the rocky headland. If any turtles come ashore, locals will spread the word pretty quickly and you may be able to arrange a lift.

A few km along the beach towards Kuantan, beyond the Cherating river, there's a Kampuchean refugee camp. To walk to the camp, you have to cross the Cherating River – you can wade across at low tide, but be prepared to swim back.

Places to Stay & Eat Accommodation ranges from basic A-frame huts, each with a double mattress and light, but without a fan, mosquito net or bathroom to air-conditioned 'chalets' with a bathroom but often not worth the extra ringgits. Most of the A-frame huts cost around M$10 and sleep two people; the more expensive chalets cost around M$14 or M$15; and the air-con chalets are in the M$25 to M$30 range.

As with all kampung-style accommodation, the toilets and bathrooms are outhouses shared by everyone. The overnight fee may include meals but usually meals are extra and must be ordered in advance. A couple of places have their own restaurants which anyone can eat at – the food is simple but good.

The guest houses are either close to the main road (convenient but noisier) or by

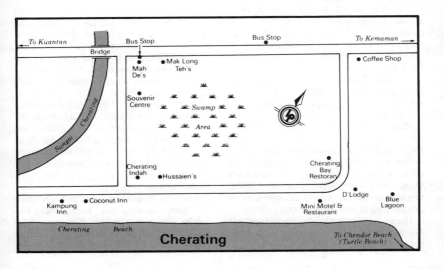

the sea. The former include *Mak Long Teh's* and *Mak De's House*. Both places charge M$10 to M$15 for chalet-style accommodation, breakfast and dinner. Apparently, meals at both places are excellent. Mak Long Teh's is affiliated with the Malaysian Youth Hostel Association.

Closer to the beach there's *Cherating Indah* and *Hussaien's Bungalows* where clean double rooms are M$8 to M$10. Hussaien, reported to be more than 100-years old, is presently extending and a few more upmarket chalets are underway.

A little further down the road, in the direction of Kuantan, you'll find the *Coconut Inn*, perhaps the nicest place to stay in the area. The Coconut Inn has A-frame huts (double bed) for M$10, chalets with verandah for M$12 and larger bungalows for M$14. Meals must be ordered in advance and can be expensive. The owners, Ilal, Marina and Bob, are really nice people and will make you feel at home.

Next door, there's the relatively new *Kampung Inn* run by a very friendly and helpful person named Nain. The Kampung Inn is clean and comfortable. Chalet-style huts vary in price from M$12 a double for the most basic to M$28 for one with bathroom, mosquito net and fan. Cabins are available at M$14 (communal bathroom) and a four-bed room costs M$24. There is also a building where one large room has been partitioned off into several rooms – beds cost M$4 per person. The Kampung Inn and the Coconut Inn have a restaurant and bar under construction by the beach.

Right on the beachfront is the *Cherating Mini Motel* where rooms range from M$8 for a two-bed bungalow without electricity or bathroom to M$35 for a four-bed room with electricity and bathroom. There are a few chalets for M$25. The Mini Motel has a good restaurant which is reasonably priced and serves tasty food.

Other places on the beachfront are *D'Lodge* and *Blue Lagoon* which have rooms from M$8 to M$10.

Besides the restaurant at the Mini Motel, you can eat at the *Cherating Bay Restoran* which is on the road behind the Mini Motel. The food is very good, but it's not cheap. There's also a small coffee shop on the corner of the Kuantan-Kemaman road and the entrance road to the kampung.

A van brings fresh fruit, vegetables and sometimes fish to the kampung several days a week. You can buy whatever you like and cook it yourself on an open-air barbecue.

Getting There & Away To get to Cherating, catch a grey and red bus marked 'Kemaman' from the main bus station in Kuantan. Buses leave every hour, the fare is M$2.20 and the journey takes around 45 minutes. From Cherating to Kuantan, wave down a bus to Kuantan from the bus stop outside Mak Long Teh's.

If you're on the bus, the driver will automatically drop you at one of the entrances to the village. If you hitch from Kuantan, look for a large sign on the right advertising the Coconut Inn; if you're hitching from the north, look for a sign on the left advertising the Mini Motel.

Kemaman

Kemaman is the first town of any size north of Kuantan and also the first town you reach in Trengganu. It's about 25 km north of Chendor and has a very glossy new mosque on the north side of town.

There are a few cheap Chinese hotels with basic rooms for M$10 to M$12. The *Duin Hotel* (tel 09-591801) on Jalan Kampung Tengah has reasonable rooms from M$16 and the *Muni Hotel* (tel 09-592366) on Jalan Che Teh has rooms from M$70 to M$120 with air-con. The bus fare from Cherating to Kemaman is less than M$1.

Kuala Dungun

From Kemaman there are more stretches of beach, more small kampungs and fishing villages at river mouths, before you reach Kuala Dungun which is actually a couple of km off the main road.

The beaches where the giant leatherbacks come in to lay their eggs stretch north of there. From Kuala Dungun you can make a 2½-hour boat trip out to Pulau Tenggol, 29 km offshore.

Places to Stay There are some cheap Chinese hotels in Kuala Dungun itself, otherwise there's the *Surra Resort* (tel 09-841280) on the main road with rooms from around M$25 per night. *Hotel Kasanya* (tel 09-841211) at 225-227 Jalan Tambun has large, clean and cheaper rooms from M$15.

RANTAU ABANG

This is the principal turtle beach and the prime area for spotting the great leatherback turtles during the laying season. The beach is beautiful and you can laze about on the white sand, go for long walks or go swimming. It's pleasant sitting on the beach at night, waiting for the turtles to make their nightly appearance.

A little north of the village itself is the Rantau Abang Visitors' Centre – part hotel-restaurant-bar and part handicraft centre and turtle museum. It's not all that interesting and the museum has had much more effort put into flashy appearance than worthwhile content; apart from which all descriptions are only in Malay, considerably reducing its worth to non-Malay speakers. Note that the nearest bank is at Kuala Dungun, 22 km south.

Turtles

Turtle watching is one of the big attractions of the east coast; in fact it's one of Malaysia's biggest attractions. There are seven species of turtles and all seven pay annual visits to the coast from 35 to 150 km north of Kuantan.

The area around Rantau Abang, just north of Kuala Dungun, is prime turtle watching territory for it's there that the giant leatherback turtles make their annual excursion onto dry land. At other times of the year the leatherbacks can wander as far away as the Atlantic Ocean, but each year from May to September they return to this one Malaysian beach to lay their eggs.

Late August is the peak laying season, but in June and July you can count on seeing turtles on the beach almost every night. Full moon and high tide nights are said to be best.

The egg-laying process is an awesome one, for the female leatherbacks can weigh up to 750 kg (three quarters of a ton!) and reach over three metres in length. They crawl laboriously up the beach and, well above the high-tide line, dig a deep hole in the sand for their eggs. Usually they dig a false decoy hole first and fill it in again before digging the real hole.

Into this cavity the turtle lays, with much huffing and puffing, about 100 eggs which look rather like large ping pong balls. Having covered the eggs she then heads back towards the water, leaving tracks as if a tank had just driven down the beach. It all takes an enormous effort and several times the turtle will pause to catch her breath as 'tears', to keep sand out of her eyes, trickle down.

Finally the giant turtle reaches the water and an amazing transformation takes place. The heavy, ungainly, cumbersome creature is suddenly back in its element and glides off silently into the night.

The whole process can take two or more hours from start to finish and in each laying season an individual turtle may make several trips to the beach before disappearing until the next year.

The eggs take about 55 days to hatch. It's a fraught process, for many eggs are taken by crabs and other predators. Newly-hatched young turtles are seized by birds on their perilous crawl to the sea and those that reach the water are easy prey for fish and other creatures. It's a long time before they rival their parents in size.

Turtle-watching isn't as simple as it could be. You either wander along the beach with your own torch, searching for an emerging turtle or their tracks in the sand, or, you go to sleep and let the locals do the searching and ask them to wake you when, or if, they find one.

The organisation is hopeless and the story often goes like this: you are woken as soon as a turtle has been spotted, but find there is only one car (or no car!) available to take *everyone* to the exact spot which is a few km away. Several car trips and nearly one hour later, the last load of people are dropped near the stretch of beach where some poor unsuspecting turtle is busy laying her eggs. Someone tries to lead the way and before long the entire group gets hopelessly lost, the turtle returns to the water and disappointed tourists have to find the van or spend a couple of hours walking back to Rantau Abang along the beach. The best time to find turtles seems to be between about 11 pm and 3 am.

Western visitors usually come away with mixed impressions. The turtles are an amazing sight, but the behaviour of some local turtle watchers can be quite gross – pulling the turtles' flippers, shining lights in their eyes, even riding on the turtles' backs is all part of the fun and games. Thursday night, start of the weekend in Muslim Kuala Trengganu, is the worst time.

Also, while the poor turtle is straining to lay the eggs, somebody else will be busy collecting them straight from the hole. Unable to focus its eyes out of water, the turtle cannot see any of the spectators, nor does it realise the immediate theft of its eggs.

Fortunately this is not the conservationist's nightmare one might expect. Around 40,000 young turtles must be hatched out and returned to the sea before the eggs can be collected for consumption or sale in the local markets. Eggs to be hatched are collected and incubated in enclosed hatching areas along the beach. Although you have less chance of seeing turtles early or late in the season, you do get far fewer crowds at that time.

Places to Stay & Eat

There are both expensive and cheap places to stay in the area. Thirteen km north of Kuala Dungun the elegant *Tanjung Jara Beach Hotel* (tel 09-841801) is a 100-room beach resort built entirely of wood to a design claimed to be copied from an ancient palace. There's a pool, bar and restaurant and rooms cost M\$140 to M\$350. There are also some more expensive bungalows.

Rantau Abang's other upper-notch establishment is the *Rantau Abang Visitors' Centre* (tel 09-841533), built on stilts over the lagoon behind the beach. It's just a km north of Rantau Abang itself and the 10 chalets cost M\$80 to M\$90 per night.

At the cheaper end of the scale, there's the *Sri Dungun Hotel* (tel 09-841881) on Jalan Tambun. It has rooms priced between M\$16 and M\$38. Right on the beach, there are several travellers' places which have chalets from M\$8 to M\$15.

Awang's (tel 09-842236) has cute little double huts for M\$5 (M\$2.50 per person) and a few larger chalets each with their own bathroom and verandah for M\$10. There's reasonable food and cold drinks available from the restaurants. *Ismail's* has basic wooden huts on the beach for M\$15 and a few cheaper huts at M\$8. The people running these places are friendly and easy-going.

Washing facilities consist of showers with water pumped from the well and the toilets are Asian-style. Despite these places being so basic, for on-the-beach convenience they just can't be beat. During the turtle season a string of food stores operate along the beach in the evenings.

There's a new place which falls between the top and bottom stratas. The *Merantau Inn* (tel 09-841131) is midway between the Tanjung Jara and the Visitors' Centre and has clean two-bed bungalows with bathrooms and fan for M\$35. There's also a restaurant.

Getting There & Away

Rantau Abang is only about 22 km north of Kuala Dungun, which in turn is 80 km south of Kuala Trengganu and 138 km north of Kuantan.

Any Kuantan-Kuala Trengganu or Kuala Dungun-Kuala Trengganu bus will go right through the village and there's a bus stop right where the cheap accommodation places are. From Kuantan to Rantau Abang, the non-air-con bus costs M\$7 and the air-con bus M\$8. From Kuantan to Kuala Dungun a taxi costs around M\$10; they're cheaper from Kuala Trengganu.

MARANG

From Rantau Abang the road continues to skirt the coast. Many of the small fishing kampungs along the east coast are found at river mouths, and at Marang the road runs across a long bridge over a wide river.

The kampung of Marang, on this river mouth, is very picturesque. The river is dotted with brightly painted boats, the water is crystal clear and thick with fish, and over on the beach the kampung huts are interspersed with swaying coconut palms. It's a beautiful place to relax for a few days.

You can charter boats from Marang to take you to nearby islands.

Places to Stay

Kamal's, once known as Ibi's, is a great little place by a small river and about 100 metres from a beautiful beach. Kamal is the young Malay guy who runs the place with another friend. He's very friendly and helpful and tries to make everyone feel at home. Dorm beds costs M$4, a room to yourself costs M$10 and a chalet is M$13. The place is very clean and comfortable and you'll find all sorts of useful information stuck on the walls.

For most of the time you'll probably have the place to yourself – Kamal works part time at the petrol station down the road. Besides relaxing in the garden or on the beach, you can arrange a trip to the river, to the waterfall, or you can go fishing. To get to Kamal's, turn right out of the bus station and follow the road by the river for about five minutes – the guest house is on the left.

Another popular place to stay at is the *Zakaria Guest House* (tel 09-682328), two km south of Marang on the Kuala Trengganu-Kuala Dungun road. Zakaria is a fisherman who runs the guest house with his family. Dorm beds cost M$5 and double rooms cost M$10. Breakfast and dinner cost M$5 – tea and coffee are free of charge. They'll even cut your hair for free, or drive you to the night market in town.

At Zakaria's, you can also arrange trips to the nearby islands of Kapas, Redang and Tinggo. Expect to pay M$15 to M$20. You may be able to go deep sea fishing too – ask Zakaria about it. Zakaria's Guest House is past the mosque, about two km south of the Marang bridge.

You can also go to the District Office in Marang and get the key for the *Marang Rest House* which is a little way out of town. There are two rooms which both

cost M$5 and sleep six people. There are cooking facilities and you can buy food to cook and drinks (tea and coffee) at the nearby shops.

In the middle to top-end bracket, there's the *Mare Nostrum Holiday Resort House* (tel 09-682417), at Kampung Rhu Muda, two km south of Marang village. Accommodation ranges from M$10 to M$50 per night.

The *Beach House* (tel 09-682516) is a nice place to stay, right on a great beach with crystal-clear water. The cheapest hut costs M$7 for one person or M$10 for two, and there are more expensive rooms – the top of the range sleeps three people, is fully air-conditioned and costs M$70 per night.

Getting There & Away

Marang is 45 minutes south of Kuala Trengganu and buses depart Kuala Trengganu every hour from 7 am to 6 pm. The fare is M$1. If you're intending to stay at any of the places in Kampung Rhu Muda, you need to take the Kuala Dungun bus and get off just past the mosque, about two km beyond the Marang bridge. From Kuala Dungun, there are regular buses to Marang which cost M$2.40 and take about 1½ hours.

Pulau Kapas

Offshore from Marang is the island of Kapas with good swimming and snorkelling, fine coral and good seashell collecting. There's not much on the island apart from fresh water, so bring food with you if you plan to stay. You can sleep on the beach for free or in one of the two-bed chalets for about M$28.

Boats out to Kapas can be arranged in Marang. The Beach House has a speed boat which can take you to Kapas for M$15 return. The trip takes about 15 minutes compared with 45 minutes by slow fishing boat from the village.

Pulau Raja

This island has been designated a marine park and you can enjoy excellent snorkelling in crystal-clear water with live coral and beautiful fish.

You can hire a boat from Marang to take you to Pulau Raja or, you can go on the Beach House's speed boat for M$15 (you can visit both Pulau Kapas and Pulau Raja). They can arrange lunch for you if you're just going on a day trip. If you want to stay for one or more nights, arrange for the same boat that drops you off to pick you up at a later date.

KUALA TRENGGANU

Halfway between Kuantan and Kota Bahru on the east coast, the town of Kuala Trengganu is delightfully easygoing. You can almost feel how slow-moving the pace of life is. It's hardly surprising that there are no local taxis and that trishaws are the usual means of transport around town.

Like the other east coast towns, Kuala Trengganu has little of great tourist interest or historical importance, but there's plenty to keep you amused during a short stay.

Information & Orientation

The town stands on a promontory formed by the sea on one side and the wide Trengganu River on the other. There are two main streets in the town centre which together form a complete loop. Coming in from the south you find yourself on the wide, modern Jalan Sultan Ismail. Along this street there are a number of hotels, the MAS office, the bus station and banks. Jalan Sultan Ismail ends at the river where you will also find the long-distance taxi station.

If you turn left there, you'll be heading north towards Kota Bahru – if you turn right, you'll find yourself on a street as narrow and old-fashioned as Jalan Sultan Ismail is modern. Now known as Jalan Bandar, but still often referred to as Jalan Kumpung China, this street changes name at the market to Jalan Pantai and continues around the waterfront by the GPO to the roundabout where it meets Jalan Sultan Ismail.

Around Town

Most of Kuala Trengganu's colourful atmosphere can be appreciated along Jalan Bandar. Wander along the street from the taxi station end and you'll find interesting little Chinese shops, a bustling Chinese temple and narrow alleys leading to jetties on the waterfront. The clock tower marks the change point from Jalan Bandar to Jalan Pantai.

The municipal market is one of the most colourful and active in Malaysia with fruit and foods of all types on sale and hordes of trishaws outside waiting to take marketers and their purchases home. When they say the fish is fresh, they really mean it – the fishing boats dock right outside! The best time to visit the market is early in the morning. There are lots of shops upstairs in the market building.

Continuing along Jalan Pantai, you pass the Istana Mazia on your right. Parts of this old palace are still utilised by the Trengganu royal family. There are some beautiful examples of traditional wood-carving in the old palace buildings. Behind the Istana is the gleaming new Zainal Abidin Mosque. The steep road up Bukit Besar on the southern outskirts of town takes you to a viewpoint offering excellent views of the town and the South China Sea.

River Trips

There is a series of jetties behind the taxi station and beside the market from which small ferries shuttle across the river or to the many islands in the estuary. The jetty behind the taxi station is the place for a 30 sen ferry ride to Pulau Duyong Besar, the largest island in the estuary. Fishing boats are built there using age-old techniques and tools; it's always worth a wander around.

A boat from beside the market will take you across to Kampung Seberang Takir on the other side of the river mouth. In this fishing village you can see fish being dried and processed. Five km upriver is Kampung Pulau Rusa which has a

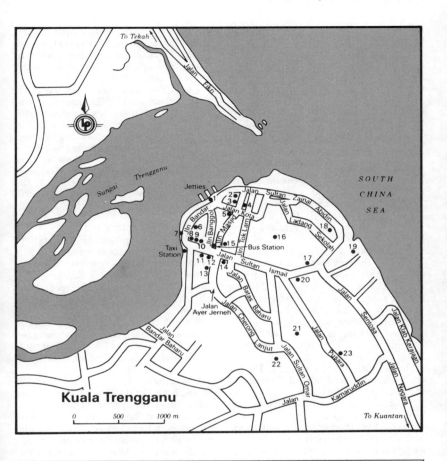

Kuala Trengganu

0   500   1000 m

1	Central Market	13	Government Offices
2	GPO	14	Hotel Warisan
3	Istana Mazia	15	Rex Hotel
4	Seaview Hotel	16	Government Offices
5	Mosque	17	Sri Trengganu Hotel
6	Chinese Temple	18	Tourist Information Centre
7	Kopi Cheng Cheng	19	Pantai Motel
8	Trengganu Hotel	20	Muslim Cemetery
9	MAS	21	Chinese Cemetery
10	Hotel Lido	22	Motel Desa
11	Hotel Tong Nam	23	Government Offices
12	Hoover Hotel		

number of interesting old traditional houses. Ferries and buses go there.

You can hire a boat on an hourly or daily basis to explore further upriver. Kuala Berang is a good starting point for trips much further up into the interior. If you just want to get away from city life you can cross the river for about 50 sen from the ferry jetty behind the taxi stand to Kampung Dijong on the other side of the river.

Islands & Beaches

There are a number of pleasant islands and beaches accessible from Kuala Trengganu. Boats can be arranged to Pulau Kapas although that beautiful island is more easily reached from Marang, a few km south.

Pulau Redang, also with good swimming, snorkelling and jungle walks, is about 50 km offshore from Kuala Trengganu, or only about 30 km from Kampung Merang further north. There's a good chance of finding a boat going across to this inhabited island on Thursdays or Fridays.

Pulau Bidong is 34 km off Kuala Trengganu but only about 16 km from Kampung Merang although it can be difficult to get boats out there. Do not confuse Merang, north of Kuala Trengganu, with Marang, to the south.

Swimming at Pantai Batu Burok, the beach immediately south of the town, is not so good and there are strong undertows. A three-day beach festival is held there each year in May. The swimming is better at Chenering Head, 10 km south.

There are also some good beaches north of Kuala Trengganu at Batu Rakit (rather dirty beach) and Kampung Merang. Both places are off the main road, Batu Rakit is 25 km north and Kampung Merang, with a good beach and swimming in the bay, is a further 15 km north. There's a pleasant guest house at Batu Rakit.

Other Attractions

The Sekayu Waterfalls are 56 km west of Kuala Trengganu. You have to walk three km from Kampung Ipoh, a little beyond Kuala Berang, to the falls where there are pleasant natural swimming pools. In Kuala Berang you can stay at the *Selasi Hotel* for around M$14.

Kuala Trengganu has a wide variety of handicrafts made in and around the town. At Rusila, 13 km south, you can see palm leaves woven into mats, baskets or bags in the process known as mengkuang weaving.

Traditional brocade songket weaving is done at Kampung Pulau Rusa, upriver from Kuala Trengganu, and at Kampung Tanjung on the north bank of the Trengganu River. Brasswork and batik are other popular local crafts.

Places to Stay – bottom end

The *Rex Hotel*, opposite the bus station, has reasonable rooms sleeping up to four people from M$17. A few doors down the street, there is the *Hotel Evergreen* (tel 09-622505). Single fan-cooled rooms start at M$14.70. The owners are helpful people.

Two blocks north of the bus station, past the mosque, is the recently renovated *Nam Tan Hotel* (tel 09-621540) at 29-B Jalan Sultan Ismail which has clean rooms from M$14.

One of the most popular places to stay is on the island in the river at *Awi's House* (also called the 'yellow house'). It is a relaxed guest house and it is a good opportunity to experience kampung life, although mosquitoes can be a nuisance on windless nights. At Awi's House, accommodation is dormitory-style and costs M$5 per night. You can help yourself to tea and coffee at all hours of the day and you even get a small breakfast – all for M$5.

There are several cheap hotels in the area of Jalan Sultan Ismail. Nearby, there's the *Trengganu Hotel* (tel 09-622900) where single fan-cooled rooms cost M$17 and doubles are M$21. Air-con rooms are also available and cost M$26. The *Lido Hotel* (tel 09-621752) at 62 Jalan Sultan Ismail has two-bed rooms for M$12 and three-bed rooms for M$16.

A little further along the street is the *Mali Hotel* (tel 09-623278) where single rooms with fan and bathroom cost M$11, doubles with fan and bathroom cost M$17 and a large triple room costs M$19. The hotel is managed by a friendly and helpful Malay guy. There's a restaurant downstairs.

Other cheapies with rooms from M$12 to M$16 include the *Seaview Hotel* (tel 09-621911 on Jalan Masjid, the *Hotel Tong Nam*, the *Hotel Bunga Raya* (tel 09-621166) and the *City Hotel* (tel 09-621481) both on Jalan Banggol.

Places to Stay – middle

The *Sri Hoover Hotel* (tel 09-624655) and the *Meriah Hotel* (tel 09-624655), both on Jalan Sultan Ismail, have reasonable rooms from about M$20 to M$32.

The *Motel Sri Marang* (tel 09-632566) at Kampung Pulau Kerengga has air-con rooms from M$40 and the *Sri Trengganu Hotel* (tel 09-634622) has similarly priced air-con rooms and a few cheaper fan-cooled rooms for M$20. There's also the *Hoover Hotel*, 49 Jalan Sultan Ismail, rooms with bath cost from M$40 to M$70.

Places to Stay – top end

The *Pantai Motel* (tel 09-622100) on Jalan Persinggahan is Kuala Trengganu's number one hotel. It's on the beachfront about a km from the centre on the Kuantan side of town. The Pantai Motel has 173 rooms with air-con from M$115 to M$300. There's a swimming pool and an old Vietnamese refugee boat that is now a bar. On the ceiling of every room in the motel there's an arrow indicating the direction of Mecca! Before you contemplate swimming and lying on the beach in front of the motel, walk 100 metres or so towards the town and see what the villagers use the beach for every morning!

Alternatively there's the *Motel Desa* (tel 09-622100) on top of Bukit Pak Apil, a steep hill close to the town. Singles/doubles cost M$90/100. The motel is fully air-conditioned and there is a swimming pool.

Places to Eat

A great place to head for is *Kedai Kopi Cheng Cheng* at 224 Jalan Bandar, down near the jetties. It's an extremely popular restaurant, always crowded at meal times and very reasonably priced. All sorts of interesting vegetable and meat dishes are displayed and there's a huge pot of soup boiling furiously at one side of the restaurant. The friendly staff/owners give you a plate of rice or noodles and you help yourself to the rest of the food. The staff will price your meal using their colour-coded peg system – when you've finished eating take the plate with peg to the counter and pay. Delicious food and different from the stuff served up at most Chinese cafes.

There are plenty of other Chinese restaurants along Jalan Bandar and Jalan Bunga Raya. If you feel like a minor extravagance the *Pantai Motel's* restaurant sometimes puts on an excellent smorgasbord of Malay food. It's a good opportunity to try all sorts of unusual local specialities and the cost is less than M$20 for a complete meal including desserts and coffee.

You could also try the *Sinafaz Restoran*, 38 Jalan Masjid Abidin, which has been recommended by a couple of travellers.

Getting There & Away

The taxi stand is at the bottom of Jalan Sultan Ismail, right at the waterfront. Fares include M$1.50 to Marang, M$8 to Jerteh (for Kuala Besut), M$6 to Kuala Dungun, M$12 to Kota Bahru, M$15 to Kuantan, M$30 to Mersing, M$60 to Penang, M$25 to Temerloh and M$35 to Kuala Lumpur.

By bus it's about M$6 to Rantau Abang, M$7 to Kuantan, M$7 to Kota Bahru, M$20 to Kuala Lumpur, M$24 to Johore Bahru and M$25 to Singapore.

Small ferries cross the river mouth from wharfs behind the taxi stand (40 sen to cross) or from along the waterfront behind Jalan Bandar. The best way to get to Kuala Trengganu's airport is probably to take the ferry across the river and then take a taxi for about M$3.

KUALA TRENGGANU TO KOTA BAHRU

At Kuala Trengganu the road leaves the coast and runs inland to Kota Bahru, 165 km north. There are, however, a number of minor roads branching off to the coast with several good places for swimming. Batu Rakit and Kampung Merang have already been mentioned. Further north there is Kuala Besut, the departure point for trips to Pulau Perhentian. Kuala Keluang, about 10 km south of Kuala Besut, also has good beaches.

The final stretch into Kota Bahru runs through fertile rice-growing areas, mirroring the similar area in Kedah and Perlis at the northern end of the peninsula on the other, western, side.

KUALA BESUT

Kuala Besut, on the coast south of Kota Bahru, has a reasonably pleasant beach and is an interesting, though grubby, little fishing village. A visit to this kampung is usually just a preliminary to a trip to Perhentian Island. Since fishing boats out to Perhentian leave only in the mornings, most travellers spend the night at the Kuala Besut rest house.

Kuala Besut is actually in two parts, separated by a river. The northern part (the turn-off is at Pasir Puteh) is the fishing village and has small shops and a market. The southern part, reached by the main road turn-off at Jerteh, has the rest house and various government offices.

The small ferries which used to shuttle back and forth across the river have now been replaced by a large bridge. There's a new fisheries centre on the south side of the river and you can catch fishing boats out to Pulau Perhentian from the large dock there.

Places to Stay

The *Rest House* is quite close to the beach on the south side of the river. It's fairly spacious and has double rooms with bathroom and fan at M$16. There are also some small, basic rooms around M$8. It's a friendly place but the restaurant food is expensive for what you get, though they do make excellent tea.

About a km north of the rest house, right by the bridge, the *Banana Leaf Restaurant* has good food.

Getting There & Away

From Kota Bahru take bus No 3 to Jerteh (M$2.80), from where you can get another bus through Kampung Raja to Kuala Besut.

There are also out-station taxis which cost M$1 from Jerteh to Kuala Besut. They'll stop in Kampung Raja for you to check on the rest house bookings for Pulau Perhentian. Heading north a share-taxi Jerteh-Kota Bahru costs M$4.50.

PULAU PERHENTIAN

A two-hour boat trip from Kuala Besut, south of Kota Bahru, will take you to the beautiful islands of Perhentian Besar and Perhentian Kecil, just 21 km off the coast of Peninsular Malaysia. There, you can escape from the hustle and bustle of the mainland and although you can take a day-trip to the islands, it's better to stay a few days.

A narrow strait separates the besar, or big island from the kecil, or small island. Both have accommodation but as far as things to 'do and see' go, staying on Pulau Perhentian is simply a case of lazing around and watching the coconuts fall.

There are beautiful beaches, though rather littered around the rest house, and excellent snorkelling. There are also some walking trails although they don't go too far since most of the island is covered with impenetrable jungle. Bring plenty of books and suntan lotion.

Places to Stay

On Pulau Perhentian Besar there is a *Rest House* with four double rooms which can be booked through the District Office in Kampung Raja, just a couple of km from

Kuala Besut. The booking system is a little haphazard.

Nightly cost is M$12 per room and they have flush toilets and a generator which operates from 6.30 to 11 pm each night. There are other chalets and bungalows priced between M$20 and M$40 per night.

There is a fishing village on the small island and some very basic chalets on the beach which cost between M$5 and M$10 – you can wash with water from a well but will have to find a convenient bush for a toilet. The caretaker managing the cheaper chalets will take good care of you and is a real character.

You can also camp, although campers report that a tent is preferable to sleeping out on the beach – unless you don't mind being trampled on at night by metre-plus iguanas! The island also has flying foxes and a variety of monkeys.

There's no need to take your own food to either of the islands as there are a few shops and restaurants. It's recommended that you boil all drinking water.

Getting There & Away

Getting out to the island is fairly simple. In Kuala Besut there are plenty of fishing boats going out and they will take passengers. The usual price is M$5 to M$10 per person although bargaining will probably start from a higher level. If you have to charter a boat, you'll be up for at least M$60 to M$80 for the day.

Getting back can be a little difficult as you just have to wait for a boat to come by – but there are worse places to be stranded. Ask the fishermen about accommodation on the island – they'll tell you who to contact.

Kota Bahru

In the north-east corner of the peninsula, Kota Bahru is the capital of the state of Kelantan, the end of the east coast road and an alternative gateway to Thailand.

It's also Malaysia at its most Malayan – Kota Bahru is a centre for Malay culture, crafts and religion. It's the place to see kite-flying contests, watch batik being made, admire traditional woodcarving, photograph the colourful marketplace and marvel at the skills of songket weavers and silversmiths.

Information & Orientation

The Kota Bahru tourist office (tel 09-725533) is open Saturday to Wednesday from 8 to 11.45 am and 2 to 4 pm, Thursday from 8 am to 12.45 pm, closed Friday. It's on Jalan Ibrahim, just a stone's throw south of the clock tower and a little north of the GPO. The tourist office has some useful information sheets which you may find in boxes outside the office if it is closed.

In Kelantan, state public offices and banks are all closed Thursday afternoons and Fridays, but open on Saturdays and Sundays.

The Royal Thai Consulate (tel 09-722545) is on Jalan Pengkalan Chepa and is open from 9 am to 4 pm from Sundays to Thursdays, but may be closed for lunch between 12.30 and 2.30 pm. Banks are open between 10 am and 3 pm Saturdays to Wednesdays, 9.30 to 11.30 am Thursdays and closed on Fridays.

Like Kuantan and Kuala Trengganu, the town is beside a wide river, in this case the Kelantan River, but Kota Bahru is not on the coast – it's about 10 km inland. The riverfront is, sadly, neglected and messy.

The centre of town is a busy area, north of the clock tower, bounded by Jalan Pintu Pong, Jalan Kebun Sultan/Jalan Mahmud, Jalan Hospital and Jalan Temenggong.

The long-distance bus station is in the south of the town while the Kota Bahru railway station is several km away at Wakaf Bahru, across the river. The railway line continues on to terminate at Tumpat. A little north of the city centre is Merdeka Square, around which are a number of the town's points of interest.

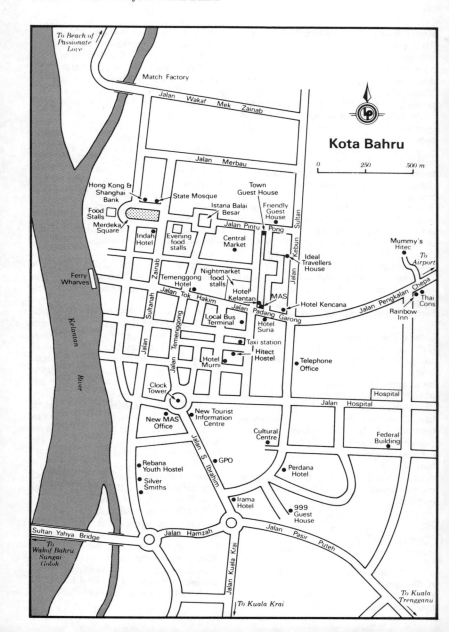

Around Merdeka Square

The central Merdeka Square was built as a memorial following WW I. There are several points of interest nearby and at night the car park at the end of the square becomes a popular open-air eating place.

On one side of the square is the State Mosque, completed in 1926. Next to that is the Hong Kong & Shanghai Bank building which is the oldest brick building in the town. Constructed in 1913, it was used by the Japanese army as their headquarters during WW II.

Beyond the car park at the end of the square is the entrance to the Istana Balai Besar or 'Palace of the Large Audience Hall', which dates from 1844. Constructed largely of timber, the palace contains an opulent royal barge that was used only once for a cruise on the Kelantan River in 1900. The adjacent Istana Jahar was constructed in 1889.

Handicrafts

Kota Bahru is a centre for Malay crafts and there are many to be seen around the town. Batik factories and warehouses are dotted around town; much of the batik comes from Kuala Trengannu, Thailand and even Indonesia. Some of the batik products available are sarongs from M$6, wall-hangings from M$4, shirts from M$12 and skirts from M$16. There's an interesting batik factory at Samasa, down the road beside Lee's Garage which you reach on local bus No 5.

Silverwork is another local speciality and you can see silversmiths at work just out of town at Kampung Sireh. Songket weaving can be seen in a number of places along the road to Pantai Cinta Berahi; take bus No 10 or 28.

Along the same road, there are a number of places making and selling those fantastic Malaysian kites. Look for the signs saying *wau bulan* (moon kites). They cost M$10 and up but can be difficult to pack and mail. Traditional woodcarving can be seen out on the airport road; take either bus No 4, 9 or 13.

Activities

Every Wednesday and Saturday, except during the fasting months of Ramadan, there are performances of top spinning, traditional dance dramas, wayang kulits, and other east coast activities from 3 to 5.30 pm and from 8 to 11.30 pm. They're held at Gelanggang Seni, across the road from the Hotel Perdana on Jalan Mahmud. Check with the tourist office for more details. The performances are free but the hours seem to vary with the season.

Each year in June, Kota Bahru has a bird-singing contest when you can see the prized Merbok or Burong Ketitir birds perform. There are also contests every week in a village about seven km downriver from Kota Bahru. It starts around 8 am with numerous categories of competition. Ask in pet shops.

Places to Stay – bottom end

There is a good selection of cheap hostels and guest houses in Kota Bahru, but there are very few upper-notch places. Finding places in the city however, is somewhat complicated by the curious street-naming and numbering procedures.

Jalan Tok Hakim changes name to Jalan Padang Garong and then becomes Jalan Pengkalan Chepa all within the space of a couple of hundred metres. The numbering process is even worse; you only have to walk a few doors down to find street numbers in the thousands while the other side of the street is numbered completely differently.

There are several friendly traveller's guest houses well worth recommending. All offer simple dorm accommodation, share bathroom facilities, free tea and coffee (and often free breakfast), lots of interesting travellers' information and a relaxed atmosphere. Most of these places will lend bicycles to guests free of charge.

The *Ideal Traveller's House* on Jalan Padang Garong has been highly recommended by many travellers and is a great little place where dorm beds cost M$4 and rooms go for M$10 a double or M$8 for a single. The people running the place are very helpful and make you feel at home.

The nearby *Town Guest House* remains one of the most popular places to stay and at times it gets quite crowded. The owners are really nice people who will go out of their way to make your stay enjoyable. Dorm beds are M$4, single rooms M$8 and double rooms M$10. You can entertain yourself by reading travellers' comments and stories featured in various notebooks belonging to the guest house.

In the same area, you'll find the *Friendly Guest House & Restoran*, run by the owners of the Ideal Traveller's House. Prices are similar, though there are some rooms for M$15 which come with double bed, mosquito net and own bathroom.

Slightly out of town on the airport road, there's the *Rainbow Inn* where dorm beds cost the usual M$4 and double rooms cost M$10. Breakfast is available for a couple of ringgits and there is a nice garden to sit in. The manager of the place is a friendly, relaxed person and he'll show you some great artwork on the walls, courtesy of inspired travellers.

The Thai Consulate is just next door and across the road is the inimitable *Mummy's Hitec Hostel*. Despite rampant rumours to the contrary, Mummy's Hitec is still going strong and is one of the most popular hostels in town. Mummy is a real character and enjoys a night out with her guests. Mummy's rooms cost M$10, M$4 in the dorm, breakfast is included in the price and there is free tea and coffee all day. Bicycles can be hired for M$2 per day. A trishaw to the Rainbow Inn or Mummy's Hitec should cost about M$1.

Right in town, near the taxi station is another *Hitec Hostel* (formerly Hitect and nothing to do with Mummy's) which is run by a very pleasant, helpful and friendly man. This hostel has basic fan-cooled rooms for M$8 to M$10 but lacks the homely atmosphere of the other hostels/guest houses in town. The people there will probably tell you that Mummy's Hitec is no longer in business.

Another highly recommended place to stay is the *Rebana Hostel* on the other side of town. It's behind the Caltex Station on Jalan Sultan Zainab – a bit of a walk from the town centre (M$1 by trishaw) but definitely worth the effort. The Rebana has dorm beds for around M$4 and double rooms for M$8 or M$10. It's a lovely house, decorated Malay-style with lots of batik around the place. You can help yourself to tea and coffee, read books from the library, contribute to the travellers' information board or just relax in the garden by the bar.

Not far from the Cultural Centre and the post office, behind the Irama Hotel, there's the *999 Guest House* on Tahan Sri Bayam. This guest house has recently been recommended by several travellers. Dorm beds cost M$4 and rooms are around M$10. Tea and coffee are free and you can use the cooking facilities.

Apart from all these places, there are the usual bottom-end Chinese hotels in Kota Bahru. On Jalan Tok Hakim, there is a string of hotels with rooms in the M$10 to M$12 price bracket; the *Kelantan Hotel*, the *Ah Chew Hotel*, the *Thye Ann Hotel*, the *Hotel Maryland* and the *Mee Ching* – all fairly basic but OK.

Places to Stay - middle

The *Hotel Aman* (tel 09-743049) on Jalan Tengku Besar is a friendly place with air-conditioned double rooms from M$28.

Next door is the *Indah Hotel* (tel 09-785081) where rooms cost M$48 to M$80. *Hotel Suria Baru* (tel 09-746567) on Jalan Padang Garong has good single rooms for M$28, doubles for M$39 and triples for M$48. Nearby is the *Hotel Irama* (tel 09-722722) with rooms from M$35.

On Jalan Tok Hakim, there's the *Hotel Tokyo Baru* (tel 09-749488) run by a very pleasant and helpful man. It's a recently renovated hotel with a rather strange system for pricing rooms; four-bed rooms with air-con cost M$35 for the first person, M$5 for each additional person and, if up to four people share, the fourth person stays free of charge. For the non-air-con four-bed rooms, the first person pays M$26 and each extra person pays M$4, while the fourth person still gets to stay for free.

The *Hotel Intan* (tel 09-721277) on Jalan Datuk Pati has air-conditioned rooms from M$24 and rooms without air-con for M$19.

Other hotels in the mid-range price bracket are the *Kencana Inn* (tel 09-747944) on Jalan Padang Garong, the *Kobaru Hotel* (tel 09-749397) on Jalan Doktor and the *Temenggong Hotel* (tel 09-783130) on Jalan Tok Hakim. All have air-conditioned rooms from about M$60.

Places to Stay – top end

At the top end, the 136-room *Hotel Perdana* (tel 09-785000) on Jalan Mahmud, has rooms from M$65 to M$400. It's the biggest and most expensive hotel in Kota Bahru and is fully air-conditioned with swimming pool, tennis courts and so on.

Right in the centre of town on Jalan Datuk Pati, the architecturally eccentric *Hotel Murni* (tel 09-782399) has rooms ranging from M$52 to M$150.

Finally, out at the Beach of Passionate Love, the *Pantai Cinta Berahi Resort* (tel 09-781307) has beachfront chalets with air-con, as well as other rooms with and without air-con. Prices start from around M$60. It's rather run down and is expensive for what you get – the beach is nothing special either. You can try bargaining.

Places to Eat

Despite the town's overwhelmingly Malay character there are plenty of Chinese restaurants around, particularly near the bus stop and along Jalan Kebun Sultan and Jalan Padang Garong. The *Kuan Ah Cafe* on Jalan Datuk Pati has been recommended by travellers and there are also a couple of good Chinese bakeries near the bus station.

For good Indian food, try the *Banana Leaf Restaurant* across from the Ideal Traveller's House or the *Murugan Cafe* behind the supermarket. Both restaurants

cater for vegetarians. The *Razak Restaurant* is also very good.

Without doubt, the best and cheapest Malay food in Kota Bahru, and probably the entire peninsula, is found at the night market in the centre of town, opposite the local bus station. Nearly all the locals eat there and there's a wide variety of delicious, cheap Malay food being cooked before your very eyes.

There are tables set up around all the food stalls and you can sit anywhere. As the traditional way of eating is with the fingers of the right hand, each table is equipped with a jug of water and a roll of tissue paper to clean your fingers with. If you can't do without a fork and spoon, most of the stalls do keep a supply. You can eat well at the night market for around M$2; drinks cost about 50 sen and meals cost M$1 to M$2 – try the delicious chicken pancakes which are very filling and cost M$1.20.

The food centres in the car park by Merdeka Square and at Taman Sekebun Bunga (the 'floating house') are good places for satay and other Malay dishes.

Getting There & Away

Bus & Taxi The opening of the long-awaited east-west highway has brought Kota Bahru and Penang much closer together. Previously you had to make a 1000 km detour south through KL, a slightly less circuitous trip north through Thailand, or fly. Now it's a straightforward day trip.

Air-con buses depart from the Butterworth bus terminal by the ferry between 9 and 9.30 am and cost around M$20, depending on the company. Departures from Kota Bahru are at about the same time. With a couple of meal stops the trip takes seven or more hours.

A taxi between Butterworth and Kota Bahru costs M$30 and there are four departures between 7.30 and 10 am every morning. See the Coast to Coast section at the end of this chapter for details on places along the road.

Air-con buses from Kota Bahru cost M\$7 to Kuala Trengganu, M\$10 to Kuala Dungun, M\$16 to Kuantan, M\$25 to Kuala Lumpur, M\$30 to Singapore and M\$30 to Johore Bahru.

Taxis from Kota Bahru cost M\$12 to Kuala Trengganu, M\$25 to Kuantan, M\$35 to Kuala Lumpur, M\$52 to Johore Bahru, M\$3.50 to the Thai border and 120B from there to Hat Yai.

If you are heading for Singapore, it is best to take a taxi as far as Johore Bahru and from there catch a bus to Singapore.

Train The Kota Bahru station is at Wakaf Bahru, a 50 sen trip on bus No 19 or 27. If you're travelling to Kota Bahru by train, get off at Pasir Mas and take a taxi or bus into town – this saves an hour of train travel. Buses go from Wakaf Bahru to Kota Bahru frequently throughout the day and cost 50 sen.

If you're heading through to Thailand you can travel straight from Pasir Mas to the border at Rantau Panjang; the taxi fare is around M\$2. Malaysian currency can be spent at Sungai Golok and Hat Yai in Thailand.

Refer to the introductory Getting Around section for train timetable and fare details.

Getting Around

There's a wide variety of local bus services from Kota Bahru. Take bus No 2 to the coastal village of Bachok for M\$2. The trip takes about one hour. For Kuala Besut take bus No 3 to Jerteh for M\$3. Kuala Krai is reached by bus No 5 for M\$3.50. To Pantai Cinta Berahi, the Beach of Passionate Love, take bus No 10 for 60 sen. Tumpat to the north is reached by bus No 19 or No 27 for M\$1.

Local taxis run to the airport (whole taxi) for M\$9 or M\$10, to Kuala Krai for M\$5, Tanjung Merah for M\$4 and on a share-taxi basis they go to Machang for M\$3.

AROUND KOTA BAHRU
Beaches

Kota Bahru's best-known beach has a name that's hard to forget. Pantai Cinta Berahi, the 'Beach of Passionate Love', is 10 km north of the town. It's actually just a normal beach with a few casuarinas and palm trees which hardly lives up to its exotic name. Furthermore any overt passion is likely to be looked on with extreme displeasure in this strict Muslim area. Foreigners are generally ignored but local Malaysians have to follow Muslim code.

Pantai Dasar Sabak, 13 km from Kota Bahru and three km beyond the Pengkalan Chepa Airport, is a beach with a history. On 7 December 1941 the Pacific Theatre of WW II commenced there when Japanese troops stormed ashore, a full hour and a half before the rising sun rose over Pearl Harbor.

Other beaches close to Kota Bahru include Pantai Dalam Rhu near the fishing village of Semerak, 19 km from Pasir Puteh, near Kuala Besut. It's sometimes known as Pantai Bisikan Bayu, the 'Beach of Whispering Breeze'. Pantai Irama, the 'Beach of Melody', is 25 km south of Kota Bahru. North of Kota Bahru there's Pantai Kuda, 'Horse Beach', 25 km away in the Tumpat area.

Waterfalls

There are a number of waterfalls in the Pasir Puteh area. Jeram Pasu is the most popular; to reach it you have to follow an eight-km path from Kampung Padang Pak Amat, about 35 km south of Kota Bahru en route to Pasir Puteh. Other falls in this same area include Jeram Tapeh, Cherang Tuli and Jeram Lenang.

Kuala Krai

Kuala Krai, 65 km south of Kota Bahru, used to be the end of the road but now it continues on to Gua Musang. On the way to Kuala Krai you can stop at Labok, a natural hot springs two km off the road.

Kuala Krai has a zoo specialising in local wildlife. It's open from 8 am to 6 pm and admission is 50 sen.

Places to Stay The *Kiew Shi Hotel*, next to the prominently advertised Bata shoe shop, is two-minutes walk from the railway station. It's quiet for a Chinese hotel and very clean. Rooms cost M$9.

River Trips

You can make a number of river trips from Kota Bahru. A short trip takes you downriver to Kuala Besar and you can then return on bus No 28. Longer trips can be made from Kuala Krai.

From Kota Bahru, take bus No 5 to Kuala Krai at 8 am (about M$3) and then a boat from Kuala Krai to Kuala Balah (M$4) at around 11 am – no boat on Fridays. It's a two-hour trip through dense jungle.

From Kuala Balah you can hitch or pay for a ride (around M$4) to Jeli, near the Thai border, then bus to Tanah Merah (M$2) and from there back to Kota Bahru (approximately M$2). Buses on the new east-west highway also pass through Tanah Merah.

It's worth staying in Kuala Balah overnight so you have time to look around. You can catch a boat back to Kuala Krai very early the next morning.

Another alternative is to get off the boat at Dabong, before you reach Kuala Balah. Dabong is on the railway line and you can get a train back to Kota Bahru around 2.30 pm. The train takes three long hours to reach Kuala Krai and a further two hours from there to Wakaf Bahru. From Wakaf Bahru, you need to take a bus into Kota Bahru. It's much easier to leave the train at Kuala Krai and to catch a taxi from there to Kota Bahru for M$5 – the taxi trip takes about one hour.

From Dabong, it's a one-hour walk to some caves. Ask locals for directions to the caves and to the waterfall which is in the same area (maybe 30 minutes further on). You can sleep in the caves for free.

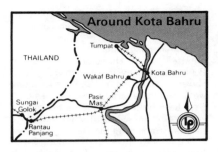

Places to Stay Kuala Balah has recently been rebuilt a km or so away from its previous flood-prone site. You can stay at the *Rest House* for about M$5 per night.

Wildlife

There are a number of salt licks in Kelantan where you may see deer, goats and even elephants in search of these naturally occurring salt deposits. There's one at the Jenut Sira area, about 1½-hours walk from Lubok Bongor which is between Kampung Balah and Jeli. The salt lick near Jenut Ibu is close to the banks of the Sungai Ibu river and can only be reached by boat.

Tumpat

Around Tumpat, in the region bordering with Thailand, there are a number of interesting Buddhist temples. Kampung Berok, about 12 km north of Kota Bahru, has Wat Phothivihan, a Buddhist temple with a 41-metre-long reclining Buddha statue, claimed to be one of the largest in South-East Asia. It was built in 1973. There is a rest house available for use by sincere devotees for a donation. The abbot is a soccer fan, 'which he watches on his splendid colour TV'!

To get to Wat Phothivihan, take bus No 19 or No 27 to Chabang Empat for M$1. Get off at the crossroads and turn left. Walk along this road, through interesting villages and paddy fields, until you reach the reclining Buddha (takes about one hour).

Other Thai-influenced temples or 'wats' include Wat Mai Suwan Kiri.

Masjid Kampung Laut

Reputed to be the oldest mosque in Peninsular Malaysia, this mosque is not, however, at Kampung Laut as its name would indicate. The mosque is said to have been built about 300 years ago by a group of Javanese Muslims as thanks for a narrow escape from pirates.

It originally stood at Kampung Laut, just across the river from Kota Bahru, but each year the November to January monsoon floods caused considerable damage to the wooden mosque and in 1968 the decision was made to shift it to a safer location. It now stands about 10 km inland at Kampung Nilam Puri, a local centre for religious study.

Adjacent to the mosque is the State Religious Council building, a fine example of Kelantan craftsmanship. It was originally established in 1914.

Taman Negara

Peninsular Malaysia's great national park covers 4343 square km and sprawls across the states of Pahang, Kelantan and Trengganu. The part of the park mostly visited, however, is all in Pahang and virtually all visitors enter the park in Pahang.

Reactions to the park depend totally on the individual's experience. Some people see lots of wildlife and come away happy, others see little more than leeches and find the park hardly worth the effort.

The park headquarters are at Kuala Tahan. There are a number of jungle walks to hides and salt licks from the headquarters where you may see animals.

Getting well away from it all requires a few day-long treks and/or expensive trips upriver by boat. The 60-km boat trip from Kuala Tembeling to Kuala Tahan (park headquarters) takes three to four hours, depending on the level of the river. You reach the park boundary near Kuala Atok, 35 km from Kuala Tembeling.

Along the river, you'll see several Orang Asli kampungs, domestic water buffalo and local fishermen. Other animals you might see from the boat include monkeys, otters, kingfishers and hornbills. It's a beautiful journey.

Taman Negara has recently been taken over by a private organisation, River Park Sdn Bhd, who plan to upgrade the park to cater for more affluent tourists.

Information & Orientation

Make arrangements for your visit to Taman Negara at the River Park Sdn Bhd office (tel 03-2915299), 260-H 2nd Mile Jalan Ipoh, Kuala Lumpur. You have to pay a M$20 deposit to confirm bookings for the park boat and accommodation at Kuala Tahan. You pay the balance at reception the day before you leave Taman Negara. On arrival at Kuala Tahan you must pay a M$1 entry fee and a M$5 camera fee. If you intend to go fishing, a fishing licence will cost M$10.

The park headquarters has a reception centre, a couple of restaurants, a hostel, some chalets and two shops selling a small range of tinned foods, toiletries, batteries, local cakes and snacks. You can rent camping and hiking gear from the shop near reception. Every Monday, Tuesday and Wednesday night, a free slide show is shown during which a free map of Taman Negara and its trails is handed out.

The best time to visit the park is between March and September. It's closed in the rainy season from mid-November to mid-January and also at Muslim New Year for about one week.

Although everyday clothes are quite suitable around Kuala Tahan, you'll need heavy-duty gear if you're heading further afield. Jungle attire is a good idea both as protection and to make you less conspicuous to the wildlife you want to see. River travel in the early morning hours can be surprisingly cold. Mosquitoes can be

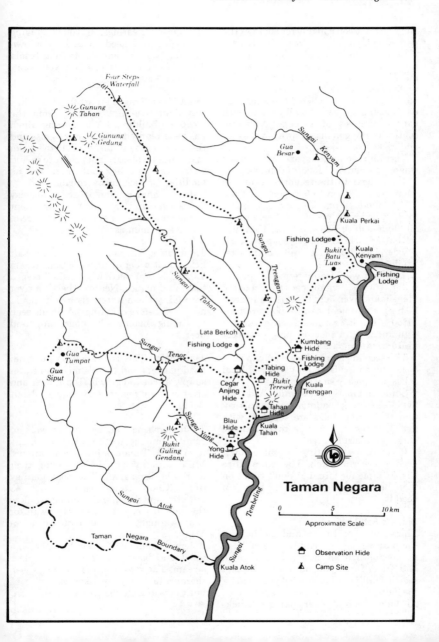

Taman Negara

0   5   10 km

Approximate Scale

⌂ Observation Hide

▲ Camp Site

annoying but you can buy repellent at the park shop if you're not already prepared.

Leeches are generally not a major problem, although they can be a real nuisance after heavy rain. There are many ways to keep these little blood-suckers at bay – mosquito repellent, tobacco, salt, toothpaste and soap can all be used with varying degrees of success. A liberal coating of Baygon insect spray over shoes and socks works best.

There are two shops at park headquarters where you can buy food and provisions. The one next to the reception centre is open from 8.30 am to 6.30 pm and from 8.30 to about 10 pm. You can buy tinned food, tinned milk, noodles, coffee, sauces, oil, flour, soft drinks and fruit. They also sell batteries, insect sprays, soap, washing powder, toothbrushes and toothpaste, bandages, etc.

This shop will hire out tents, day packs, water bottles, small cookers, cooking utensils and even light boots (small sizes). Fishing equipment can be borrowed for M$50 deposit, refunded on return if equipment is in tact. Fishing rods cost M$10 to hire.

The second shop at Kuala Tahan sells basic tinned foods and a variety of local cakes and pastry snacks.

Some members of the Orang Asli tribe live close to park headquarters. Locals say that the Orang Asli's are supplied with free food to encourage them to settle in the park headquarters area.

If you're overnighting in a hide you'll need a powerful torch. The camp office has a couple for hire, but don't count on there being one available at the time you need it.

Hides & Salt Licks

There are several hides and salt licks in the park which are readily accessible. A number of them are close to Kuala Tahan and Kuala Terenggan, but your chances of seeing wildlife will increase if you head for the hides furthest from park headquarters. All hides are built overlooking salt licks

and grassy clearings. If you're staying overnight, you need to take your own sleeping bag, or some sheets from Kuala Tahan (lent free of charge); you won't need blankets.

Jenut Tahan This is an artificial salt lick less than five-minutes walk from the reception building. It's a clearing which has been planted with pasture grass and there's a nearby waterhole. There's room in the hide for about eight people to sit and watch the salt lick but there are no facilities for sleeping overnight.

Jenut Tahan is often packed with noisy locals who find this hide a convenient venue for all-night parties – no chance of seeing any animals there!

Jenut Tabing The hide at this natural salt lick, about a one-hour walk from Kuala Tahan, is equipped with eight beds, a toilet and mandi. Nearby, there's a river with fairly clean water (though it should be boiled before drinking). Animals seen at Tabing include wild boar, tapir and deer.

Jenut Belau This is 1½-hours walk from headquarters and there's no clean water supply at the hide itself. Tapir, deer and civet cats are reported to frequent Jenut Belau.

Jenut Kumbang You can either walk to Jenut Kumbang, it takes about five-hours from Kuala Tahan, or hire a boat (around M$60) to take you up the Tembeling River to Kuala Terenggan. The boat journey from Kuala Tahan takes about 45 minutes, and then it's a 45-minute walk to the hide. If you want the boat to wait for you overnight, it will cost an extra M$40.

Jenut Kumbang has six bunk beds, a toilet and basin and nearby is a clear stream. The most common animals seen there are tapir, rats, monkeys and gibbons but tigers and elephants have been seen.

Jenut Cegar Anging Once an airstrip, this is now an artificial salt lick established to attract wild cattle and deer. There are four bunk beds, a toilet and mandi (no water of course!). A nice, clear river runs a few metres from the hide. Jenut Cegar Anging is 1½-hours walk from Kuala Tahan.

Each hide costs around M$3 per person per night. Even if you're not lucky enough to see any wildlife, the fantastic sounds of the jungle are well worth the time and effort taken to reach the hides. The 'symphony' is at its best at dusk and dawn.

A powerful torch is necessary to see any animals that wander into the salt-lick area. It's probably best to arrange shifts where one person stays awake, searching the clearing with a torch every 10 to 15 minutes, while everyone else sleeps until it's their turn to take over.

Rats can be a problem at some of the hides. They search for food during the night and have been known to move whole bottles of cooking oil (one of their favourite treats) from hides to their nests. Either hang food high out of reach, or, as one traveller suggested, leave some in the centre of the floor so you can see them – some of the rats are gigantic.

Rivers & Fishing

Lubok Simpon, only 10 minutes on foot from the park headquarters, has a good natural bathing pool. Anglers will find the park a real paradise. Fish found in the park rivers include the superb fighting fish (known in India as the Mahseer but here as the Kelasa).

Popular fishing rivers include the Sungai Tahan, the Sungai Kenyam (above Kuala Terenggan) and the remote Sungai Sepia. February through March and July through August are the best fishing months. A fishing permit costs M$10 and hiring a rod costs M$5 per day.

Several boat trips can be arranged at park headquarters but they're all expensive. Expect to pay at least M$60 return for the shortest trip.

From Kuala Tahan you can hire a boat to Lata Berkoh, a powerful set of rapids on the Sungai Tahan. There's a natural swimming hole below the rapids and there's a Visitors' Lodge 185 metres downstream. The boat trip takes around one hour.

Another trip takes you from Kuala Tahan to Kuala Terenggan. It's a really spectacular journey through virgin jungle, gorges and rapids. There are seven sets of major rapids to be negotiated by highly skilled boatmen – this is why it costs so much to hire the boat in the first place. The trip takes about 45 minutes and everyone gets wet. There's a Visitors' Lodge at Kuala Terenggan.

A 1½-hour boat trip will take you from Kuala Terenggan to Kuala Kenyam. There are plenty of fruit trees at Kuala Kenyam. From there, you can walk inland to Bukit Batu Luas (130 metres of limestone) where there is a marked trail to the top of the rock. It takes around two hours to walk to the rock. There are some caves you can explore at the rock.

Mountains & Walks

Trails around park headquarters are well-marked, though some of the paths are hard going. Trails are sign-posted and have approximate walking times marked clearly along the way. If you're interested in birdlife, it's best to start walking before 8 am.

There are two daily walking tours conducted by park officials. The first walk commences at Kuala Tahan and continues to Bukit Teserik and then on to Tabing Hide. From there, you take a boat to Lata Berkoh (minor rapids) and then walk back to Kuala Tahan from Lata Berkoh. The cost is around M$40 per person – the guide won't go unless there are at least four people lined up – and lunch is included.

The second organised walk starts from

Kuala Tahan, stops at Bukit Indah where you take a boat through major rapids to Kuala Terenggan and then walk back to Kuala Tahan. This walk costs M$40 per person (minimum of four people) and includes lunch. Both trips begin at 9 am and finish between 3 and 4 pm.

Gunung Tahan at 2187 metres is the highest mountain in Peninsular Malaysia, but to climb to the summit requires a 2½-day trek from Kuala Tahan to Kuala Teku at the foot of the mountain and another 2½ days to the summit. A guide is not compulsory but is a good idea if you're not familiar with Gunung Tahan. You can climb 590-metre Gunung Gendang in a day-trip from Kuala Tahan.

Places to Stay

If you have your own tent, you can camp at park headquarters for M$3, otherwise, you can hire a tent for M$2.50. Beyond park headquarters, you can camp anywhere in Taman Negara.

The park hostel, *Asrama*, has nine rooms, each clean and comfortable with four bunk beds, overhead fans and personal lockers. Men and women share the dormitory rooms but there are separate toilets and showers. No toilet paper is provided. The hostel costs M$7 per person.

There are 12 older chalets and a long block of a dozen or more new chalets. Each chalet costs M$40 and sleeps two people. Mosquito nets are provided and you get your own bathroom. Further into the park, you'll find *Visitors' Lodges* at Kuala Atok, Kuala Terenggan and Kuala Kenyam. At Kuala Perkai and Lata Berkoh, there are two *Fishing Lodges* which cost around M$4 per person.

Places to Eat

There are two restaurants at Kuala Tahan with similar menus and prices. The food is ordinary and expensive, though they do have western-style breakfasts for those who can't face pork and fish porridge in the morning.

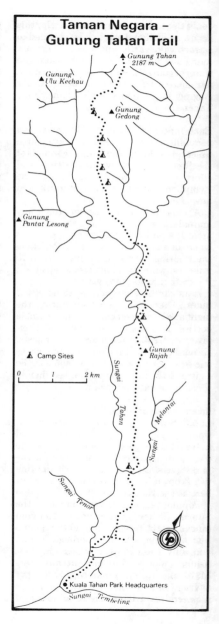

Taman Negara – Gunung Tahan Trail

For tasty local dishes, try the noodle stalls which set up outside the main restaurant at night – you can get delicious mee soup and prices are much less than those at the restaurants. The ais kacang is excellent at these stalls. There are two shops in Kuala Tahan where you can buy basic supplies.

Getting There & Away

The entry point into the park is Kuala Tembeling, near Tembeling Halt on the central railway line. To get there you can take the train north or south and get off at Tembeling Halt. The train departs Singapore at 9 pm and arrives in Jerantut around 6.30 am. Tembeling Halt is the station between Jerantut and Kuala Lipis and you must make arrangements in advance if you want the train to stop there for you.

Travelling south, the day train from Kota Bahru doesn't get to Tembeling Halt until after 6.30 pm so you may as well spend the night in Kuala Lipis (the station before Tembeling Halt) or in Jerantut (the station after Tembeling Halt). It's then either a short bus trip or a 30-minute walk from Tembeling Halt to Kuala Tembeling.

Alternatively you can go by bus to Kuala Lipis, then catch the train to Tembeling Halt or go by road direct to Kuala Tembeling. Buses run frequently between Jerantut and Tembeling but there's no timetable – buses go when full. A taxi will be M$3 to M$4 per person. Temerloh to Tembeling takes about two hours by bus.

You can also arrange for the River Park Sdn Bhd bus to take you from Kuala Lumpur to Kuala Tembeling for M$14. The bus departs KL at 9 am daily and returns to KL at 2 pm daily.

It's a three-hour boat trip from Tembeling to the park headquarters at Kuala Tahan. The trip upriver costs M$16, the trip downriver M$14.

There are as many boats going as required (according to the booking lists of River Park Sdn Bhd) so if you turn up without a booking you might find all the boats are full. No matter how many boats there are, they all leave together, 2 pm from Kuala Tembeling to Kuala Tahan and 11 am from Kuala Tahan to Kuala Tembeling. Occasionally, there is an extra boat from Kuala Tembeling to the park which leaves at 11 am but don't count on it!

On leaving the park, if heading north, the train from Singapore to Kota Bahru passes through Jerantut between 5.45 and 6 am, through Tembeling Halt from 6.15 to 6.30 am and through Kuala Lipis around 7.30 am. Going south, the train passes through Kuala Lipis at 6.30 pm, Tembeling Halt from 7 to 7.30 pm and Jerantut at 8 pm. Check these train schedules though, as apparently the timetable changes every year.

Getting Around

Around Kuala Tahan there are plenty of jungle tracks and once you've paid your M$30 for the return boat trip to Taman Negara, you can spend all your time walking and camping in the park, cooking your own food, etc. If you've money to spare, hire a boat (around M$60 return) for the interesting upstream trip from Kuala Tahan to Kuala Terenggan.

COAST TO COAST

With the completion of the northern east-west highway there are now three routes from coast to coast, apart from the crossing in the south between Ayer Hitam and Jemaluang, a little south of Mersing.

East-West Highway

The new east-west road starts near Kota Bahru and runs roughly parallel to the Thai border, eventually meeting the little-used road north from Kuala Kangsar to Keroh on the Thai border at Grik. The views from the highway are often superb.

The road runs through jungle which

was the last area of the peninsula to be controlled by Communist guerrilla forces so they're rather touchy about it. There are, supposedly, 62 army posts on one 117-km stretch! Furthermore the road is only open from 6 am to 6 pm daily and you must start out by 4 pm. If you're travelling with your own transport you have to fill out two forms that you surrender at the end.

Hitching is fairly easy along this stretch if you're on the road early. The road may be subject to closure during the monsoon.

Grik

Grik was once just a logging 'cowboy town' but the east-west highway and the huge Temenggor Dam hydropower scheme has really put it on the map. For WW II buffs there are many associations with the exploits of Force 136.

The *Rest House* has ancient but spacious doubles with attached bath for M$12 and is probably the best place to stay. The much more central *Sin Wah Hotel* has basic but large rooms for M$8.

Getting There & Away There are buses from Ipoh or Kuala Kangsar to Grik every two hours or so. Taxis to or from Kota Bahru cost about M$18. See the Kota Bahru section for Butterworth-Kota Bahru transport.

The Jungle Railway

The central railway line goes largely through aboriginal territory. It's an area of dense jungle offering magnificent views.

Commencing near Kota Bahru, the line runs to Kuala Krai, Gua Musang, Kuala Lipis, Jerantut (access point for the Taman Negara), and eventually meets the Singapore-Kuala Lumpur railway line at Gemas. Unless you have managed to book a sleeping berth right through, you'll probably find yourself sharing a seat with vast quantities of agricultural produce, babies and people moving their entire homes. Allow for at least a couple of hours delay, even on the expresses.

The line's days are probably numbered as roads are rapidly being pushed through. The road now goes all the way from Singapore, through Kuala Lipis to Kota Bahru. The train is a lot slower but definitely more interesting. The trains are poorly maintained and most of the rolling stock looks as old as the line – about 50 years.

See the introductory Getting Around section for timetable and fares on the jungle railway. Taxis from Kota Bahru to Gua Musang cost M$14, from Kuala Krai M$12.

Kuala Lumpur to Kuantan

This busy road runs 275 km from KL past Bentong and through Temerloh. A bustling Chinese town, Temerloh has several cheap hotels and a good rest house. There's also an active and colourful market there each Saturday afternoon.

The town is on the Pahang River and you can sometimes find boats going downriver to Pekan on the coast. You can also use Temerloh as a starting point for trips south to Tasik Bera. It's normally approached through Bahau and Ladang Geddes, which can also be reached from Seremban through Kuala Pilah.

As an alternative to the direct KL-Kuantan route, you can start north from KL on the Ipoh road and turn off to Fraser's Hill. Continuing from The Gap you reach Raub, a busy gold mining area where the hunt for gold continued right up to 1955, and eventually Kuala Lipis.

You can turn off the road just before Raub and rejoin the main KL-Kuantan road at Bentong or, turn off at Benta Seberang for Jerantut, en route to the national park. At Jerantut you can turn south to Temerloh or continue on to rejoin the KL-Kuantan road midway between Temerloh and Kuantan.

Tasik Bera

Tasik Bera is the largest lake in Malaysia and around its shores are five Orang Asli

Top: Kuala Lipis (RN)
Bottom: Juice stand near Beserah (CK)

Top: View from Tioman Island (VB)
Left: Market, Kota Bahru (VB)
Right: Taman Negara (ST)

kampungs. Around 800 people live at Tasik Bera and it's worth visiting.

You have to get police permission to visit the area in Temerloh. Permits are obtained from the police station between the hours of 8 am and 4.30 pm. They are issued free of charge but a recent passport-size photo is required. You can get cheap black and white photos from Lee Nam Photo in Temerloh.

Once you have the permit, the problem is getting to Tasik Bera. There are no buses and very few cars visit the area. Most of the Orang Asli people get about on motorbikes. Taxis are a little reluctant to go to the lake and will ask a hefty price (about M$50) to cover their return journey. They're not interested in bargaining. Hitching is possible but traffic is scarce.

The easiest way to get to Tasik Bera is by bus or share-taxi from Temerloh to Triang and then chartered taxi from Triang to Tasik Bera. The most accessible kampung is Pos Iskandar, where there's a Government Rest House. The school teacher, *guru sekolah*, is a friendly, English-speaking Malay called Haris.

Unfortunately, unless you can arrange a lift to Temerloh or Triang on the back of a motorbike, the only way out of the kampung is to hitch or walk the 30 km.

Gua Musang

This former logging camp is now rapidly on its way up. Planners see it as eventually becoming the second largest town in Kelantan, centre of a huge new agricultural area. Early British jungle explorers came out here when they made their way across the main range by river-rafting and jungle tracks.

The *Rest House* was once the police station and looks like it. It's now very decrepit and overpriced at M$16 for a double with shared bathroom, but it's friendly and from the verandah you can watch the whole life of swinging Gua Musang – you are, in fact, right opposite the volleyball court. Singles are around M$10.

Other Chinese hotels in the main street are a little cheaper but equally basic and less colourful. A pointer for the future is the newly built *Kesada Inn* just outside town with rooms in the M$30 range and all mod cons. Their van will fetch you from the station.

Jerantut

If you're stopping there en route to Taman Negara there are several places to stay. The *Jerantut Hotel* at 36 Jalan Besar has rooms for about M$14. The *Sri Damak Hotel* is a little more expensive. There's also a cheap, but run down and unfriendly, *Rest House* with mosquito nets and an erratic water supply. Single rooms are M$14 and it's reasonably quiet once the traffic on the road stops at night.

There are lots of reasonable Chinese and Malay restaurants around town. You can eat well for around M$2.

From Jerantut, there are buses to Temerloh every 15 minutes before 10 am and then at least one every hour until the late afternoon. Taxis cost M$5.

To Kuala Tembeling, there are regular buses from Jerantut costing M$1.20 and taxis for M$3. If a bus is waiting, don't let anyone try to tell you it won't depart for another hour, just get on and wait patiently as the locals do. There is no fixed timetable, buses just depart when full.

Kuala Lipis

The road from Fraser's Hill through Raub meets the railway line at this town. There's not much to do in Kuala Lipis itself, though it's a pleasant enough place. It's a meeting place for travellers waiting to take one of Johnny Tan Bon Tok's jungle treks.

Female travellers should be extremely careful as we have received a number of letters from women saying they were drugged and raped while on jungle treks from Kuala Lipis. If you intend to go trekking in this area, go with other travellers and make sure you are not separated from them at any time.

Places to Stay There are several cheap hotels in Kuala Lipis. There are bungalows where travellers can stay while waiting to go on a trek. Alternatively if they're full trekkers usually get taken to the *Sing Sing Hotel* or the *London Hotel*. Both hotels are cheap and fairly clean with basic rooms for around M$8.

The *Hotel Jelai* is slightly upmarket with single rooms for M$14 and double rooms for M$16. There are also some air-con rooms available.

The *Rest House* has the best rooms around, but they tend to up the prices when they spot an *orang putih*, especially if it's late at night. Don't pay more than M$16 and watch out for extra charges.

Other cheap hotels are the *Central Hotel*, the *Hotel Paris* and the *Southern Park*.

Places to Eat There are plenty of small cafes where you can get reasonable Chinese food and delicious pancakes are available at the market for about 20 sen.

Getting There & Away Buses from KL to Kuala Lipis depart Puda Raya bus station daily from 8 to 8.30 am and at 1 pm and cost M$7.40.

If you're heading for Taman Negara, you can take the train, a bus or a taxi to Jerantut and then a bus from Jerantut to Kuala Tembeling. Alternatively, you can take a bus from Kuala Lipis to Kuala Merah (a tiny town between Tembeling and Jerantut) where another bus will take you straight to the jetty at Kuala Tembeling.

For Kota Bahru, take the 7.30 am train from Kuala Lipis for M$9.40. The trip takes seven to eight hours. Heading south, the Singapore train passes through Kuala Lipis around 6.30 pm.

There is a bus from Kota Bahru to Kuala Lipis departing at 10 am daily and costing M$14. The same bus continues to Jerantut for an extra M$4. Buses depart at the same times when going from Kuala Lipis to Kota Bahru.

Mentakab

The railway station town where the jungle railway crosses the KL-Kuantan road just before Temerloh has a horde of cheap Chinese hotels. The *Hotel Walto* on the right-hand side of the main road from KL has double fan-cooled rooms for M$10.50 and communal bathrooms with western-style toilets.

The best value in town is probably the *Hotel London* where clean twin rooms with own bathroom are M$14.70. The *Orient Hotel* has three-bed rooms with attached bathroom for M$23. Double rooms are M$21, single rooms M$19.

The *Hotel Supreme* has reasonable fan-cooled rooms from M$15 and air-con doubles from M$27. You can also stay at the *Cosy Inn* and the *Yien Wah Hotel*, both in a street running parallel to the main road. Interesting food stalls set up along this street at night.

There are several Chinese and Malay restaurants in town – try the one below the London Hotel.

If you're on your way to Taman Negara, there are a couple of supermarkets in town where you can stock up on basic supplies.

Buses to Temerloh leave every 20 minutes, cost 70 sen and stop at the stand almost opposite the London Hotel. Buses to KL cost M$5.80 and the journey takes about 2½ hours.

Raub

This town, between Fraser's Hill and Kuala Lipis, has a few cheapies including the very basic *Raub Hotel* and the *Dragon Hotel* where singles cost about M$10. There may also be a rest house.

Temerloh

There are a number of cheap Chinese hotels in Temerloh on the KL-Kuantan road with a variety of rooms under M$20.

They include the very cheap *Swiss Hotel*, out past the police station on the way to Mentakab, which has rooms with attached bathroom for M$10. There are a couple of cheap Chinese hotels nearby.

The nicest place to stay is the *Rest House* on a hill overlooking the river. It's very clean and comfortable with spacious fan-cooled double rooms for M$27 – worth the splurge.

Other hotels are the *Ban Hin Hotel* which has very basic rooms for about M$14. The *Hotel Ibis* has better rooms with fan for M$17 and with air-con for M$27.

The *Sin Lan Chin Hotel* on Jalan Tengku Bakar is the best value in town with large rooms and clean communal

bathrooms for M$6.50. The manager is a friendly person. You can also stay at the *Temerloh Hotel* on Jalan Kuantan and the *Hotel Tropicana* on Jalan Tengku Bakar.

The usual cafes serving cheap Chinese-style food are all over town; the one below the Sin Lan Chin Hotel serves reasonable food and there are some cheap food stalls selling good satay near the fire station.

The bus from KL to Temerloh costs M$5.90 and takes two hours. To Kuantan, buses take two hours and cost M$5.10. They leave from the bus station near the mosque. Taxis cost M$11 from KL to Temerloh and M$9 from Temerloh to Kuantan.

Sarawak

Sarawak's period as the personal kingdom of the Brooke family of 'White Rajahs' ended with the arrival of the Japanese in WW II. Following the war the Brooke family handed Sarawak over to the British government, thus putting Britain in the curious position of acquiring a new colony at the same time they were shedding others. Sarawak remained under British control when Malaya gained its independence in 1957, but then joined Malaysia when it was formed in 1963.

Today, with its oil production plus timber, pepper and some rubber, Sarawak is of great economic importance to the nation. Although Sarawak suffered even more than Peninsular Malaysia from the Emergency and then the Confrontation, today things are quite peaceful.

For the visitor, Sarawak's interest is in its diversity of tribes and the many areas of still untouched jungle. Many of the tribes up the great rivers of Sarawak live in longhouses – 'villages' where the entire population live under one roof with separate rooms leading on to one long communal verandah. Hospitality to visitors is a way of life in these longhouses and many travellers in Sarawak stay overnight at one during their travels.

Visas & Permits

Even though Sarawak is a part of Malaysia it has its own immigration controls which are designed, in theory, to protect the indigenous tribal people from being swamped by migrants from the peninsula and elsewhere. This means that

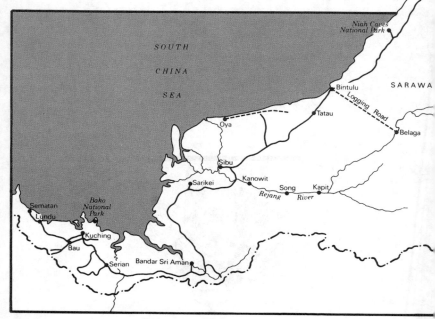

244

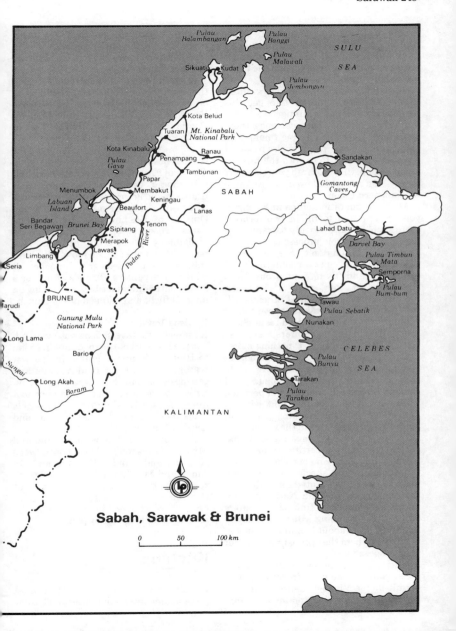

Sabah, Sarawak & Brunei

0   50   100 km

if you're flying into Kuching, Miri, Bintulu or Sibu from the peninsula or from Sabah you will have to go through immigration again even though the flight is officially an internal one.

On arrival you will probably be granted a two-week stay. It's easy to get this permit extended at the immigration office in Kuching, provided you can show them an onward ticket and ample finances (a credit card is fine). You may also be asked whether you want to go into the interior and if you do, they'll stamp your passport to say you're not allowed to go there without permission.

At the immigration office in Kuching, you are required to fill in two forms – there's no fee and no photographs are required. The whole process takes about 30 minutes. If you don't have an onward ticket, tell them you're travelling overland to Sabah and flying out from Kota Kinabalu. At this stage, if you can produce a credit card, most officials will be satisfied. The Sarawak state government is touchy about unannounced researchers, journalists, photographers, etc, so remember you're a tourist, nothing more.

If you plan to visit any of the longhouses above Kapit on the Rejang River, or to trek overland between Belaga and Bintulu then you'll need special permits. These are obtainable in Kapit without fuss or fee, but the trekking permit to Bintulu is not available in the wet season. Officially, you need an international cholera vaccination certificate for these permits but usually no one checks this.

You also need a special permit if you intend to visit the 'Painted Cave' (but not the main cave) in Niah National Park. Permits are obtained from the curator's office at the Kuching Museum. They're free and it takes about 10 minutes, but you have to tell them the approximate date of your proposed visit.

Alternatively, you can wait until you reach Niah, where you can get the same permit at the Visitors' Centre, from the warden at the hostel. If coming west from Sabah or Brunei, you can get these permits from the national park office in Miri, where permits for Gunung Mulu are also available.

A special permit is also required from the immigration office in Kuching in order to cross the land border between Sarawak and Kalimantan (if heading for Pontianak) and it's unlikely you'll get it. An Indonesian visa is also required.

General Costs

Travel in East Malaysia is not cheap and you should beware of assuming that transport and accommodation costs are on a par with those of Peninsular Malaysia. Outside of Kuching and the national parks, where hostel accommodation is available, you'll be up for at least M$20 per night and often much more. Likewise, transport on buses and launches is relatively expensive. There's often not a great deal of difference between taking an internal flight and taking a bus or launch.

Overland Travel

It's possible to traverse Sarawak overland, but the last part of the road, linking Sibu to Bintulu, is pretty rough. In the wet season, it is often a muddy mess and getting out and pushing is part of the trip. Expect to get a lot more than your feet muddy. Usually when one vehicle gets stuck those behind will have to stop and help push it out.

Parts of the road between Bintulu and Miri are just as rough. The roads between Kuching and Lundu, Kuching and Sri Aman and Miri to the Brunei border are sealed and in good condition, but elsewhere they're atrocious or non-existent. Most travel in the interior is by river launch, longboat or plane.

Kuching

Kuching is without doubt one of the most pleasant and interesting cities you'll come across in East Malaysia. Built principally on the south bank of the Sungai Sarawak (River Sarawak), it was the centre of the White Rajah dynasty which ruled Sarawak until 1945, when the state became a British Crown Colony.

Kuching contains many beautifully landscaped parks and gardens, historic buildings, an interesting waterfront, colourful markets, one of Asia's best museums, and a collection of Chinese temples, Christian churches and the striking state mosque.

Orientation

By comparison with the state capitals of Peninsular Malaysia, Kuching is small and compact and almost all places of interest or importance to travellers are within easy walking distance of each other.

You would only need to use public buses or taxis when travelling to and from the airport (about 12 km); the Police Marine Base at Pending for boats to Sibu (about six km); and to the state government complex to buy maps for trekking purposes or, to visit the immigration office for a permit extension.

Information

There are several tourist offices. The Sarawak Tourist Association (STA) tends to be more helpful than the Tourist Development Corporation (TDC).

The main office for the STA (tel 240620) is on the 2nd floor of the Sarawak Plaza, Jalan Tunku Abdul Rahman. There is also a kiosk at the airport, where you can pick up maps and information pamphlets. The STA staff are very friendly and knowledgeable and are pleased to answer all of your questions.

At the airport, travellers sometimes miss the STA desk outside the immigration/customs hall and end up at a second information desk which is only for flight information. The people there may not tell you about the STA tourist information kiosk.

The TDC (tel 246775) have their office on Song Thian Cheok Rd, near Ban Hock Rd. The friendly staff will give you maps and printed information on Kuching and the national parks.

For information on the national parks, including advance booking of accommodation and transport, go to the national parks office (tel 2466477), on Jalan Mosque, opposite the Sikh temple. The office is open Monday through Thursday from 8 am to 12.30 pm and 2 to 4.45 pm, Saturdays from 8 am to 12.45 pm and is closed on Sundays. Accommodation in Bako National Park must be booked and paid for at least three days in advance.

Visas & Permits The visa/permit extensions office (tel 240301), has moved out of town to immigration headquarters. Catch bus No 6 or 17 to the state government offices on Jalan Simpang Tiga. Visas can be extended Monday through Friday from 9 am to 4.30 pm and on Saturday from 9 am to 12 noon. No photos are required but you do need to complete two forms and you may be asked to show your money and an onward ticket.

Permits to visit the 'Painted Cave' at Niah National Park can be obtained while you wait and free of charge at the curator's office on the museum grounds. You need to tell them the approximate date you intend to be there (I was never asked for my permit when I got there but you'd be wise not to take this for granted). You can now obtain a permit for the 'Painted Cave' at the national park's Visitors' Centre.

If you want to travel from Kapit to Belaga along the Rejang River, you must first get a permit from the state government complex in Kapit.

If you want to continue to Bintulu via the logging road, you should go to the police station in Belaga to obtain permission. Locals will tell you that it's necessary to hire a guide, but we've had letters from travellers who managed without.

For Indonesian visas, take bus No 5A or 6 Chin Lian Long (CCL) to the Indonesian Consulate on Pisang Rd.

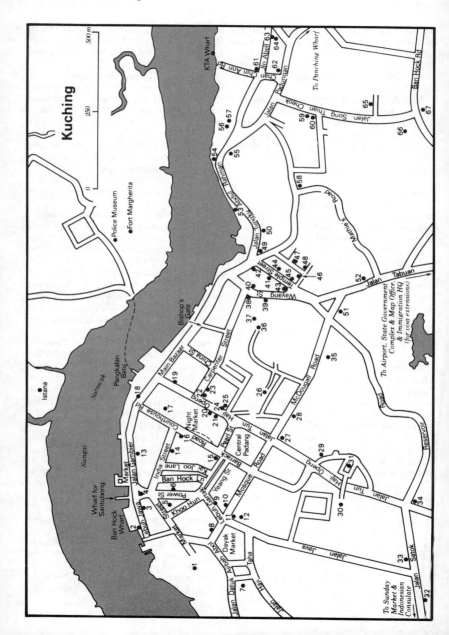

Kuching

1	Masjid Negara	36	Diocise Office
2	Long Distance Bus Station	37	Anglican Hostel
3	Miri Sin Ching Shipping Company	38	Hong San Temple
4	Taxis	39	Sarawak House
5	Open Air Market	40	Ho Cafe
6	Electra House	41	Rex Cinema
7	Arif Hotel	42	Sarawak Batik Art Shop
8	Bus to Bau	43	Hua Jang Cafe
9	Bus Stop	44	Kuching Hotel
10	Section Forest Office	45	Sin Hwa Travel (Tickets to Indonesia)
11	Sikh Temple	46	Southern Navigation Sdn Bhd
12	Information Office	47	Selamat Lodging House
13	Indian Mosque	48	Green Mountain Lodging House
14	Kiaw Hin Lodging	49	Tua Pek Kong Temple
15	Central Police Station	50	Kuching Hilton Hotel
16	Bus Stop	51	Fata Hotel
17	Law Courts	52	Borneo Hotel
18	Bus Stop	53	Tan Boon Tien Shell Station
19	HK & Shanghai Bank	54	Singapore Airlines & British Council
20	Fook Hoi Restaurant	55	Chartered Bank
21	Hock Hwa Bank	56	Holiday Inn
22	Chinese Temple	57	Sarawak Plaza
23	National Islamic Cafe		(Sarawak Tourist Association)
24	Bus Stop	58	Odeon Cinema
25	GPO	59	TDC Tourist Office
26	Anglican Cathedral	60	MAS
27	Aurora Hotel	61	SE Asia Shipping
28	Kuching Plaza	62	Kapit Hotel
29	Curators Office	63	Longhouse Hotel
30	New Museum Building	64	Hwa Kwang Hotel
31	Museum	65	Immigration (No visa extensions
32	Bank Bumiputra		– passport problems only)
33	Radio Television Malaysia	66	Lee Huo Theatre
34	Food Stalls	67	Indian Temple
35	St Thomas' School		

Banks For changing money (travellers' cheques) the best places to go are the Hong Kong & Shanghai Bank or the Overseas Union Bank, both on Jalan Tun Haji Openg near the junction with Main Bazaar. Banking hours are 9.30 am to 3 pm on weekdays and 9.30 to 11 am on Saturdays. Have your passport handy when changing travellers' cheques as, for security reasons, banks are not allowed to cash travellers' cheques without sighting your passport first.

On Sundays and public holidays, you can change money at the bookstore in the Holiday Inn and also in the Sarawak Plaza.

Airlines MAS (tel 244144) is near the TDC on Jalan Song Thian. Singapore Airlines (tel 20266) is at Jalan Tunku Abdul Rahman (in the high-rise building next to the Holiday Inn). The Indonesian airline Merpati (tel 243276) and Jalan Air Lines are handled by the travel agent on Temple St opposite the Rex Cinema, two doors from the Kuching Hotel. This office also handles MAS bookings. British Airways is at 92 Jalan Green Hill.

There are charter companies which fly to the more remote areas of Sarawak; Hornbill Skyways (tel 411737) is on Jalan Rubber and Borneo Skyways (tel (085) 334242) has an office in Miri.

Maps & Books If you're thinking of trekking in Sarawak and need good maps take a taxi (M$2.50 to M$3) or a local bus to the State Government offices near the end of Jalan Simpang Tiga. Take a blue CCL bus (Nos 6, 14 or 18) and the fare is about 25 sen. The map sales office (Bahagian Katografi) is on the 2nd floor on the left.

Excellent large-scale maps – 1:1,000,000 and 1:500,000 of the whole of Sarawak, plus 1:50,000 (Series T735) of various parts of the state are available, but you need security clearance from the police headquarters in the centre of town for the sectional maps.

If you intend buying any of these ask for the relevant forms and a form of recommendation at the map sales office. The people there are very friendly and will help you fill in the forms. Security clearance takes a day. Take your passport with you to the maps sales office.

One of the best bookshops is H N Mohd Yahia & Son inside the Holiday Inn on Jalan Tunku Abdul Rahman. It has an interesting range of books on Malaysia and neighbouring regions. Another good bookshop is the Berita Book Centre on Jalan Haji Taha, not far from the state mosque. There are other bookshops in town, but most only stock books in the Malay language. One which has a small selection of English-language novels is the Kwang Hwa Bookstore on Carpenter St.

The Istana
Sometimes spelt 'Astana', this shingle-roofed palace, set amid rolling lawns on the north bank of the Sungai Sarawak, was built by the second White Rajah, Charles Brooke, in 1870. It's no longer open to the public as it's now the Governor of Sarawak's residence. It's looking rather run-down and is plainly visible from the small park (Pangkalan Batu) on the opposite side of the river.

Fort Margherita
Built by Charles Brooke in the mid-19th century and named after his wife, the fort was designed to guard the entrance to Kuching in the days when piracy was commonplace. It is now a police museum (Muzium Polis) which houses a collection of weapons, uniformed dummies, memorabilia of the Japanese occupation and the Communist insurgency as well as currency-forging equipment seized at various times.

It's well worth a visit and is open every day except Fridays and public holidays from 10 am to 6 pm. There's no entry charge. To get there take one of the small ferry boats (tambangs) which ply back and forth all day until late in the evening from Pangkalan Batu. The fare is 15 sen each way. Instead of getting off at the landing near the Istana grounds you can get off at the Malay kampung (village) landing site.

From around 2 pm to sunset stalls set up along the path to the fort and sell many different kinds of home-made Malay cakes at 10 to 20 sen. There's also an ais kacang shop there.

Sarawak Museum
This is one of the best museums in Asia and should not be missed. It consists of two segments, the old and new, connected by a foot bridge over Jalan Tun Haji Openg. The old part was built in 1880 in the style of a Normandy town house and was strongly influenced by the anthropologist Wallace, a contemporary of Darwin, who spent two years there at the invitation of Charles Brooke.

The new section was opened towards the end of 1983 and is large, modern and air-conditioned. Together they house an incredible collection of tribal artefacts, stuffed animals and birds from the Borneo jungles, a shell collection, whale skeletons, a recreation of a longhouse complete with head-hunting skulls, wild photographs of even wilder tribal people from the beginning of the century and a whole section on the exploration and processing of oil.

Also included are ceramics, brassware,

Chinese jars and furniture and a great section on some of the tribal peoples – their arts, tools, clothes and so on. There's a cave replica and a description of gathering birds' nests for soup. Through the day, various video and slide shows are offered in the new section. There's also a souvenir and gift shop with some interesting items.

In the old section, look for the python that was killed in Kuching – it's strung up on the wall. The gable ends of the upper floor in this section are painted with beautiful motifs inspired by those found in a longhouse at Long Nawang.

You can easily spend a few hours there and to top it all, it's free. The museum is open Saturday through Thursday from 9.15 am to 6 pm, closing for lunch between 12 noon and 1 pm. It's closed all day Friday.

Temples, Mosques & Churches

The most interesting of these are the Chinese temples and the best of these is perhaps the Hong San at the junction of Jalan Carpenter and Jalan Wayang at the back of the Rex Cinema. It was built in 1897 in honour of Kuek Seng On, a native of Hokkien province in mainland China who was deified about 100 years ago.

Others include the Tua Pek Kong at the junction of Jalan Temple and Jalan Tunku Abdul Rahman, which was built in 1876 and is the oldest in Kuching. The Kwan Yin on Jalan Tabuan was built in 1908 in honour of the goddess of mercy. Visitors are welcome at any of these temples.

The Masjid Negara (state mosque), completed in 1968, is visually impressive, particularly from across the river, but otherwise uninteresting. There is no admission for non-Muslims Thursday 3 pm through Friday 3 pm, Saturday 4 to 6 pm and Sunday 2 to 5 pm.

Of the Christian churches perhaps the most interesting is the futuristic, single-roofed Roman Catholic Cathedral past the Sarawak Museum on Jalan Tun Haji Openg.

Court House & Brooke Memorial

The Court House was built in 1871 and was the seat of the White Rajahs' government. It was used until 1973 when the new government complex on Jalan Openg opened. The clock tower was added in 1883. Also at the Court House is a memorial to Charles Brooke, the second White Rajah.

Other Attractions

The site of the former bus station has now become Kuching's open-air market. It's small and not particularly interesting unless you hit a good day and some villagers are in town. At the waterfront, there is an outdoor area and a clothes and hawkers' centre in a large white building. Nearby is an information bureau, but only for family planning. Along Gambier are open-air food stalls and fresh vegetables and food stuffs can also be bought there.

The very busy Sunday morning market is a bit of a walk from town, but worth it. It's along Jalan Satok, turn away from the museum at the corner of Satok and Jalan Tun Haji Openg.

The Dayaks bring all their produce and live stock to this area late on Saturday afternoon – so the Sunday market actually begins on Saturday night. The Dayaks sleep at their stalls overnight and resume trading around 5 am on Sunday morning.

You'll see all manner of food including some vegetables and herbs you probably haven't seen before. Wild boars are butchered, and chopped-up turtles are on display. You'll see fantastic orchids, live fish hanging in suspended plastic bags of water, cassowaries, monkeys, bats, lizards – you name it, it's for sale. There are all kinds of live birds, also plastic toys, clothes and other odds and ends usually reserved for Woolworths.

Jalan Carpenter is interesting to wander through, with its many little shops, businesses and laneways. There are also a couple of restaurants and a bake shop. Sundays are pleasant for strolling as the streets are remarkably quiet – good for taking pictures. It seems a day for those eternal Chinese pastimes – mahjong and card playing.

The Hero's Grave commemorates Allied soldiers from World War II who died in and around Kuching at the hands of the Japanese who controlled the area in 1944. The Supreme Court, near the market area, was built in 1874 during the second White Rajah's time.

If you're looking for somewhere pleasant to relax then try either the grounds of the Anglican cathedral or the Sarawak Museum gardens, at the back of the museum itself.

Places to Stay – bottom end

One of the most popular places is the *Anglican Cathedral Hostel* (tel 414027), on the hill at the back of St Thomas's church. A 'donation' of M$20/25 for a singles/doubles with fan, or M$15/20 for singles/doubles without fan, gets you a large, spotlessly clean room with polished wooden floors, comfortable beds, cane chairs, clean toilets and showers and good views. There are a couple of cheaper, smaller rooms on the upper level. The number of rooms is not great and if a conference or something is on it could well be booked out. Otherwise, a room for a traveller is no problem.

There are also a couple of self-contained flats for hire which cost about M$45 per night and four or five people can stay in each flat. The man to see is a friendly chap named Pulin Kantul who lives next to the hostel. The hostel is not registered as a hotel, so be a little discreet about using it.

The *Methodist Guest House* on Jalan Pisang is excellent value at M$10 for a clean room with air-con and private bathroom. Bus No 6 will take you there for about 30 sen. If you can hire a bicycle, it's a short ride from the town centre.

Another good place to stay is the *Kuching Hotel* (tel 413985), across from the Rex Cinema on Jalan Temple. Rooms are M$17 for singles and M$21 for doubles. All rooms are equipped with fan

and sink and there are reasonably clean, communal bathrooms. The manager and staff are very friendly and helpful.

Kiaw Hin Lodging (tel 246981) on Jalan India, has basic air-con singles for M$21 and rooms with fan only from M$15. Another basic cheapie is the *Ah Chew Hotel* at 3 Jalan Jawa, down near the river. It's typical of cheap Chinese hotels and rooms cost around M$20.

Places to Stay – middle

The *Kapit Lodging House* (tel 420091) on Jalan Padungan, has air-con singles for M$38 and doubles for M$50. The *Palm Hotel* is cheaper with reasonably clean rooms priced at M$25/40 for singles/doubles.

A couple of nice places on Jalan Green Hill are the *Selamat Lodging House* (tel 411249) and the *Green Mountain Lodging House* (tel 415244). Both are well-kept and have double rooms with air-con for M$33.

Still on Jalan Green Hill, there's the more upmarket *Metropole Inn* (tel 412561) which has fully air-conditioned rooms from M$40 to M$80. The *Borneo Hotel* (tel 244121), Jalan Tabuan has good rooms from about M$40.

You can also stay at the *Government Rest House* (tel 242042), Jalan Crookshank, for M$32/42 for singles/doubles. As always, government officials are given preference.

A couple of more expensive hotels in the middle price bracket are the *Longhouse Hotel* (tel 249333) on Jalan Abell, where singles start from M$65, doubles from M$75, and the popular *Fata Hotel* (tel 248111) on McDougall Rd where rooms cost M$55/70 for singles/doubles. They also have a new wing where rooms start from M$70.

Places to Stay – top end

During quieter periods, many of Kuching's top-end hotels reduce rates drastically, sometimes by as much as 40%, to attract customers. If you usually stay in middle-range hotels, it's worth checking out some of the top-end prices.

The main hotels are the *Aurora Hotel*, the *Liwah Hotel* and the *Country View Hotel*. The most luxurious hotels are the *Holiday Inn* and the big, new, international *Sheraton Damai Beach Resort* out at Santubong.

Aurora Hotel (tel 20281), Jalan McDougall, 84 rooms, singles M$95, doubles M$115
Country View Hotel (tel 247111), Jalan Tan Sri Datuk Ong Kee Hiu, singles M$90, doubles M$100
Holiday Inn (tel 423111), Jalan Tunku Abdul Rahman, 312 rooms, singles M$135, doubles M$155
Liwah Hotel (tel 249222), Jalan Siong Thien Cheok, 62 rooms, singles M$98, doubles M$118
Sheraton Damai Beach Resort (tel 411777), Santubong, 202 rooms, singles M$180, doubles M$210

Places to Eat

The best food you'll come across in Sarawak is in Kuching, so make the most of it. There are many excellent restaurants, hawker centres and small food stalls around town serving all manner of food.

For tasty Indian food, head for Jalan India and eat at any of the little coffee shops. The *Malaya Restaurant* has good, cheap food and the *Madinah Cafe* is great for vegetarians.

Not far away on Jalan Carpenter, you'll find the *National Islamic Cafe* which serves tasty, cheap Malay food. The Sunday market is another good place for Malay food. There are all sorts of interesting food stalls and an amazing variety of local cakes and sweets – the peanut pancakes are delicious.

You can get excellent satay at the open-air food market on Jalan Market and at the SEDC food stalls on the corner of Jalan Mosque and Jalan Datuk Ajibah Abol. The SEDC food stalls sell great laksa as does the museum kiosk.

There are quite a few eating places inside Wisma Saberkas where you can buy reasonable mee dishes, ice cream desserts, cakes, buns and western-style hamburgers, chicken and chips. At the *Permata Food Centre*, Jalan Padungan, you can gorge yourself with excellent local, Indonesian and Filipino food.

For Chinese food, one of the best places is the *Mei-San Restaurant* in the Holiday Inn. It specialises in dishes from the Sichuan province and is expensive but worth the splurge.

At the cheaper end of the scale, the *Jin Ming Cafe* on Jalan Sekama serves reasonably good Chinese food and so does the *Hua Jang Cafe*, on the corner of Jalan Temple and Jalan Wayang. The *Fook Hoi Restaurant*, opposite the GPO, isn't as good as it used to be, but it is still very popular with travellers and locals.

The *Supersonic Coffee House*, also opposite the GPO, serves fairly plain Chinese food and assorted western dishes but it's not cheap. It is, however, a nice place to relax for an hour or so to escape the heat and hustle and bustle of Kuching.

The *Ruby Cafe* on Jalan Green Hill is reasonably priced and they usually have a better supply of fresh vegetables than many of the small Chinese cafes.

Most of the larger hotels have their own expensive restaurants which serve a mixture of Malaysian and western food. There's a nice Japanese restaurant in the Aurora Hotel as well as the usual western coffee shop. If you like Thai food, try the *Bangkok Thai Seafood Restaurant* on Jalan Pending, close to the end of Jalan Padungan.

For cakes, buns and pastries, there are numerous bakeries in town, most of which can be found in any of the large shopping complexes. *Sugar Bun* is a popular fast food chain which basically sells fried chicken, but they do have tasty coconut buns.

And a Cold Beer The cheapest beer in Kuching is Anchor draught but there are few places which sell it chilled. The price of bottled beer depends on whether it's refrigerated or not, although it's very unlikely you'll want to settle for anything but a cold beer in this climate.

Cold bottles of Anchor cost M$3.60

(small) and M$5.20 (large); cold Carlsberg is a bit more. Heineken and Tsingtao (an excellent lager beer brewed in mainland China) are usually a little more expensive.

Things to Buy
Kuching is one of the best centres in Sarawak for buying tribal artefacts. Shops selling arts and crafts are scattered around the city but be warned that prices are very high.

Hog charm sticks go for M$80 to M$100; larger, crudely carved totems for M$400 to M$1000 and intricately patterned baskets for up to M$800 depending on quality, source and age. Another very fine item is the woven textiles. Older ones go for about M$200 and up. Jewellery is likewise expensive. Spend several days browsing before you commit yourself to a purchase.

A couple of shops to try are Sarawak House, 35 Wayang St; Sarawak Batik Art Shop, which is across the road from the Kuching Hotel and seems to be more often closed than open; and the shop in the new section of the museum which is very expensive.

Alternatively, you can try Eeze Trading (tel 419024) on Jalan Ban Hock; Borneo Art Gallery (418290) in the Sarawak Plaza; and the Melody Store (tel 51932) on the ground floor of Electra House, Kuching. There is a handicraft shop close to the Sunday market which has some reasonable prices.

For pottery there are a few places along Jalan Penrissen. Also try Loo Pan Arts at 83 Jalan Ban Hock and the Sarawak Pottery Centre (tel 451709) at 313 Kuching By Pass. Look for the beautiful Borneo pottery with traditional Sarawak designs. There are a few pottery factories and warehouses out towards the airport.

Getting There & Away
Air – To/From Singapore & Peninsular Malaysia The regular MAS fare from KL to Kuching is M$231. There are early morning flights, economy fare, at M$162. From Singapore the fare is S$170.

Skipping over to Johore Bahru from Singapore drops the fare to M$147. To encourage people to fly from Johore Bahru MAS has a direct bus service from their Singapore office to the airport for S$8. Passports are collected at the MAS office and returned to you at the airport where you also go through a security check. There are no customs to clear until you get to Kuching.

Fares from Kuching to Singapore and Peninsular Malaysia are similar. MAS also have a 14-day (sometimes more) advance purchase fare which can lower prices even further.

From Kuching flights to Bandar Seri Begawan are M$192 regular fare.

Air – To/From Indonesia Merpati operate one flight per week on Fridays from Kuching to Pontianak (Kalimantan) and Jakarta. They also fly the same route in the opposite direction on the same day. The fare is about M$123 to Pontianak and M$323 to Jakarta.

The ticket agent in Kuching is Sin Hwa Travel (tel 246688), 8 Jalan Temple, opposite the Rex Cinema. Pontianak is not a 'no visa' entry point to Indonesia, you must have a visa before you arrive.

Air – Around Sarawak MAS have a fairly extensive provincial network with about 20 regular destinations. Flights are sometimes a little more expensive than land transport.

Boat *Feri Malaysia* commutes between the peninsula and East Malaysia twice weekly. From Kuching, you can take the ferry to Singapore for M$200 (standard cabin), M$235 (deluxe cabin) or M$355 (suite). Return fares are double these one-way fares.

Alternatively, you can go from Kuching to Kota Kinabalu for M$140 (standard cabin), M$195 (deluxe cabin) or M$300 (suite).

For reservations or more information, contact Malaysia Shipping Agencies (tel

429480), Block E, Lot 33 Taman Sri Sarawak Mail, Jalan Tunku Abdul Rahman.

Boat – Kuching-Bintulu-Miri Cargo boats depart Kuching fairly regularly, but there is no fixed schedule. Miri Sin Ching Shipping Company (tel 240599), 2A Jalan Jawa, operates a boat which takes about 48 hours to reach Miri and costs M$50. Food is included but it's pretty bad.

The Siam Company (tel 242832) at 28 Main Bazaar has a boat which travels beyond Miri to Marudi, Limbang and Lawas. If you start from Kuching, the whole trip takes 36 hours and costs M$50, including awful food.

Boat – Kuching-Sarikei-Sibu You have a choice on this run of fast launch or cargo/ passenger boat. The launch is considerably faster as the cargo boats have to load and unload at the various ports of call (Sarikei and Binatang). If you have the time, the cargo/passenger boats are the more interesting way to cover this part of the journey. The trip takes at least 16 hours.

The *Pomas Hovermarine* departs Kuching daily at 12 noon from Bintawa wharf at Pending, which is about six km east of the city centre. The fare is M$25 and the trip takes about 3½ hours. You can book a day in advance at the Tan Boon Tien Shell Station (tel 24601) on Jalan Tunku Abdul Rahman, just below the Tua Pek Kong temple.

On the ticket you'll be allocated a seat number but this doesn't mean you'll get a seat, as you'll discover when you get to the launch. The service is usually cancelled if seas are very rough. To get to Bintawa wharf, take bus No 16 for 60 sen.

To return to Kuching, the boat departs Sibu daily at 7 am. The agents are K T Leong Sdn Bhd (tel 22616) and Chop Lim Hup Choon (tel 22044). On Sundays or public holidays, contact the Hoover Ice Factory (tel 311573) at 50A Jalan Lanang, Sibu. All Kuching to Sibu passengers must change boats at Sarikei.

An alternative launch is the *Sibu Kuching Union Express* (tel 484824) which departs from the Police Marine Base (Kuching) daily at 8.30 am, costs M$20 and takes about five hours to reach Sibu.

The agents are the Hwa Kwang Cafe (tel 56890) behind the Longhouse Hotel and the Sarawak Coastal Express Association (tel 484824) at Bintawa Wharf. There's no need to buy a ticket in advance as you can buy it on the boat itself. Take bus No 17 or 19 to the Police Marine Base. The fare is about 60 sen. In Sibu, the agent to contact is at 3 Jalan Channel.

For all launches, there's an incredibly rapid change of boat at Sarikei, where all passengers, luggage, livestock, food supplies, etc are unloaded from one boat and reloaded on to another in about four minutes flat. Grab your pack and make a run for the connecting cabin.

From Kuching to Sibu, Sarikei is the last stop along the Rejang River before it flows into the sea; it's the point where you must leave an ocean-going boat for a river boat. All launches dock at Delta Wharf in Sibu.

There are a few companies which operate cargo/passenger boats to Sibu and even further along the coast. Finding out about them and when the ships leave can be a real hassle though. The Sarawak Tourist Association are quite helpful with information about these cargo boats.

Southern Navigation Sdn Bhd (tel 242613), Jalan 21 Green Hill, are agents for the *M V Soon Bee* which departs Kuching for Sarikei and Sibu every Tuesday and Saturday at 6 pm. The trip takes about 18 hours and costs M$10 on deck or M$20 for a cabin.

South East Asia Shipping (tel 242966), Lot 175 Jalan Chan Chin Ann, operates the *M V Rajah Mas*. This boat departs Kuching every Monday and Thursday at 6 pm and takes about 18 hours to reach Sibu. There are no cabins available and the fare is M$10 on deck.

Other cargo boats making regular trips between Kuching and Sibu via Sarikei, are the *Sing Soon*, *Sri Lanjut*, *Sri Sabtu*,

Sri Gadong, Sri Muhhibah and *Swee Joo.* Inquire at the KTS wharf where all the cargo boats depart from.

Bus Long-distance buses depart from the terminus on Jalan Jawa which is a continuation of Jalan Gambier. Fares include Kuching-Bau M$2.25 (departures every 20 minutes), Kuching-Betong M$13 (one bus only), Kuching-Kampung Segu M$1.85 (three buses), Kuching-Lundu M$4.20 (four buses), Kuching-Pandawan M$4.30 (twice daily), Kuching-Serian M$3.60 (departures every 30 minutes), Kuching-Sri Aman M$11.20 (three buses daily).

Connecting buses include Betong-Debak M$3.70 (five buses daily), Betong-Spaoh M$3 (seven buses daily), Lundu-Bau M$3.60 (six buses daily), Lundu-Biawak M$2.20 (eight buses daily), Lundu-Sematan M$2.80 (10 buses daily), Serian-Tebakang M$1 (departures every 30 minutes), Sri Aman-Batu Lintang M$2.50 (four buses daily), Sri Aman-Betong M$5.20 (four buses daily), Sri Aman-Engkili M$2.70 (10 buses daily), Sri Aman-Lubok Antu M$5.60 (five buses daily), Sri Aman-Saratok M$8.50 (two buses daily), Sri Aman-Sarikei M$11.60 (two buses daily).

If you're heading east from Kuching by bus you cannot reach Sibu in one day since you will not arrive in Sarikei until the early evening and will have to spend the night there. As there's precious little of interest in Sarikei itself, and as the road from Sri Aman to Sarikei and Sarikei to Sibu is one hell of a bone shaker, most travellers prefer to take a launch or boat from Kuching to Sibu.

The alternative is to stop-over in Sri Aman and to explore the surrounding area since it's possible to reach Sibu from Sri Aman in one day. Where there are only a few buses each day to a certain destination it's advisable to book in advance at the ticket office on Jalan Jawa.

Getting Around

Airport Transport A taxi between Kuching airport and the city centre costs about M$12 and 50% more after midnight. Buses are available between the airport and the centre of town for about 80 sen. The only bus going to the airport is Bus No 12A – No 12 goes to the *old* airport. These buses are run by the Sarawak Transport Company and depart regularly between 7 am and 8 pm.

Bus At first, bus transport around Kuching may seem chaotic as there's no longer a bus terminal. There are two types – the privately-owned, blue Chin Lian Long buses (tel 32766) and the green Sarawak Transport Company buses (tel 242967).

You'll probably only need to take buses to the airport, immigration, or to the wharfs where launches to Sibu depart from. Most local bus fares are under 60 sen. The tourist offices can supply you with exact routings.

Some useful routes covered by CLL buses are: Jalan Mosque to the state government complex (Bus No 6, 11, 14 or 14A – fare 40 sen); Jalan Satok to the Holiday Inn and Sarawak Tourist Association (Bus No 1, 19 or 23A – fare 35 sen); Jalan Satok to the Police Marine Base wharf (Bus No 17 or 19 – fare 60 sen); Jalan Tunku Abdul Rahman to Bintawa Wharf (No 16 – fare 60 sen). A useful route covered by STC buses is city to Kuching Airport (No 12A – fare 80 sen). The STC deals with long-distance travel.

Taxi Taxis wait around the market and the area where long-distance buses drop passengers. A taxi to Police Marine Base costs at least M$6.

Boat Small boats and express boats serve the Sarawak River, connecting the small villages around Kuching. You can also charter boats. Ask other passengers what the fare should be and be prepared to bargain. Make sure you agree on the fare before you take the ride.

Tours There is an incredible array of travel agents and tour operators in town. Besides the usual day trips in and around Kuching town, many travel agents offer longer trips out to national parks or to longhouses along the Skrang and Rejang Rivers.

Sarawak Travel Agencies (tel 243708), 70 Pandungan Rd, is a well-established agency with a variety of tours available. Interworld Travel (tel 55494) and Borneo Transverse (tel 57784) have been recommended by travellers. The latter is at 10B 1st floor, Jalan Wayang and arranges jungle/river safaris. Overseas Express (tel 429323), on the 1st floor of the Sarawak Plaza, is a helpful place. None of the travel agencies in Kuching are cheap.

AROUND KUCHING
Santubong
North of Kuching on the coast, this is the nearest beach 'resort' to Kuching, other than the beaches in the nearby Bako National Park, and is very popular with local people on the weekends. It is 32 km from Kuching and there is a small village. Nearby at Sungai Jaong, about 1½ km upriver from the coast, rock carvings can be seen.

You can stay at the very expensive, new *Sheraton Damai Beach Resort* or at the government rest houses but the rest houses must be booked in advance at the Kuching District Office (tel 242533). Launches leave early in the morning (around 8.30 am) from the docks behind the market in Kuching for the trip to Santubong. Ask for the pangkalan panjang (long jetty). The fare to Santubong is about M$2.

Dayak Longhouses
As you might expect, the most interesting and unspoilt longhouses are to be found furthest from the main urban centres, in particular, along the upper reaches of the Skrang, Rejang, Balai and Baram Rivers.

If you're not planning on going that far, or would like a preview, then the nearest longhouse to Kuching is at Kampung Segu Benuk which is a 35-km bus ride south of the city followed by a short walk. Don't expect too much of this place as all the package tours include it on their itinerary so it's very commercialised. A better choice would be the one on the banks of the Sungai Kayan reached by boat from Lundu.

Lundu & Sematan
Sematan is a tiny coastal village near the extreme western end of Sarawak. It has a very laid-back and relaxing atmosphere with a good deserted beach, warm sea and safe swimming. Many years ago it was a bauxite mining area, but that's all long since gone. A tourist hotel complex is planned, based around the lake left by the bauxite mine, but it will be years before that gets anywhere near completion.

Off-shore are two forest-covered islands, one of which is a turtle sanctuary. Permission is needed to go there and you would have to hire a boat from the village. There's also a crocodile sanctuary near the village which was established by a local group and, further up the coast, a wildlife sanctuary is being set up with the help of VSO volunteers. The latter is difficult to get to however, as boats seldom go there. If you're interested in visiting any of these sanctuaries, write to the Director of the Sarawak Museum (tel 244236) for permission.

In addition to the sanctuaries there is a longhouse about 15 minutes by car from Sematan. Try hitching a ride, or asking people around town if they know anyone going to the longhouse – a taxi would be expensive as you'd have to hire the whole vehicle and pay the return fare. If you don't mind walking, the round trip will take you about three hours.

Places to Stay The people are friendly and you may well be offered a free room at Sematan, but you can rent a room at the *Thomas Lai Bungalows*. There are seven of these altogether, set in a coconut palm grove next to the sea. The cheapest unit

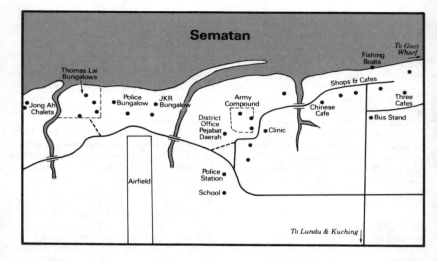

has two rooms, kitchen and bathroom and costs M$40 a night (maximum of 10 people). The most expensive units have three rooms, kitchen and bathroom and cost M$100 a night (maximum of 15 people). Naturally, at these prices you'd need to get a small group together before setting out from Kuching.

You can either rent them from the caretaker on arrival in Sematan or book in advance through Mrs Doris Lai (tel 45174) or through the tourist office. Mrs Lai is very helpful and can offer tips on how to get there and what to do.

The best food in Sematan is served at the Muslim restaurant – try their seafood and omelettes. This cafe also has Sematan T-shirts for sale at M$6.

Getting There & Away The return bus fare from Kuching is about M$14. First take an STC bus No 2B from Kuching to Lundu for about M$5. The journey takes 1½ to two hours. The road is sealed from Kuching to Bau, but quite rough from Bau to Lundu.

There are also six ordinary 'milk-run' buses daily, the first at 6.50 am and the

last at 3.10 pm. From Lundu there are several daily buses to Sematan; it's a one-hour journey over a rough road at a cost of M$2.

If you have to wait around in Lundu and would like to eat, excellent Chinese meals are available at the *Siong Kee Restaurant*, close to the bus stand – look for the large Guinness sign.

Semmongok

This is where you'll find Sarawak's answer to the orang-utan sanctuary at Sepilok in Sabah. Semmongok sanctuary, 22 km from Kuching, is a rehabilitation centre for orang-utans, monkeys, honey bears and hornbills who have either been orphaned or kept illegally by locals.

A permit is required in order to visit the sanctuary and can be arranged, free of charge, at the Forestry Department (tel 248739), Jalan Mosque, Kuching. Hours are 8 am to 4.15 pm Monday through Friday, 8 am to 12.45 pm on Saturdays and closed on Sundays.

It takes about 30 minutes to reach the entrance to the sanctuary by car and then another 30 minutes to walk right into the park. From Kuching, an STC bus No 6 will take you there.

Serian
Serian is a very small town south-east of Kuching. There is a series of nice rock pools and a waterfall at the river, a short distance from the village itself. On weekends, it's a very popular destination for locals who come to Serian to swim and to escape from the heat for a while. To get there from Kuching, take STC bus No 15. The journey takes about an hour and the fare is less than M$4. If you go on a weekend, try hitching as there's lots of traffic. There is a rest house in Serian which costs M$25 for a room.

Bako National Park
This is the national park closest to Kuching and it is highly recommended. For details see the National Parks section.

Sibu

Sibu is the main port city on the Rejang River – Sarawak's longest and largest river. Sixty km upriver from the ocean, its bustling waterfront sports all manner of craft from motorised dugouts to ocean-going liners. It's there that the raw materials of the interior – lumber, gravel, minerals and agricultural products – are brought for export. Manufactured goods from the outside world also arrive there for distribution along the Rejang and its tributaries.

Sibu is the starting point for a trip up the Rejang to visit the longhouses which are scattered along its entire length, the most interesting, naturally, being those furthest from the urban centres.

There's not a lot to do in Sibu itself unless you like hanging around waterfronts or vegetable markets, and although both of these are quite entertaining, most travellers only stay overnight and head off up the Rejang the next day. A new 36-hectare township near Sibu, to be called Seduan Park, is still under construction.

Information
There is no tourist office in Sibu. The Information Centre at the junction of Jalan Cross and Jalan Channel can tell you all about family planning, though presumably that's not why you're there.

At the Sarawak Hotel, a man named Johnny Wong acts as a representative for the Sarawak Tourist Association. For changing money, the best place to go is the Chartered Bank on Jalan Cross. Some of the other banks won't change American Express travellers' cheques.

All the launch and shipping agents are either along Jalan Khoo Peng Loong which faces Delta Wharf or along Jalan Channel which runs parallel to it. MAS is close by, opposite the huge Premier Hotel on Kampung Nyabor Rd.

Places to Stay – bottom end
The majority of budget hotels in Sibu are pretty seedy places and it's hard to choose between them. The Methodist guest house, *Hoover House*, is next to the church on Jalan Pulau and reception is in the building behind. It's excellent value at M$10 per person for clean, well-kept rooms with polished wooden floors, fan and attached western-style bathroom. Fresh drinking water, guest towels and soap are brought to your room.

The *Sibu Hotel* (tel 21784), 2 Jalan Kampung Pulu, has basic rooms without bathroom from M$14. The *Raman Hotel* on Raman Way is dingy and seedy-looking but doubles are cheap at M$18.

The *Miramar Hotel* at 47 Jalan Channel is still quite popular with travellers. Fan-cooled rooms with private bathrooms start at M$18 and towels and soap are provided. The *Diman Hotel* (tel 337887) at 27 Jalan Kampung Nyabor has non-air-con rooms for M$16, while the nearby *Federal Hotel* is more expensive with rooms starting from about M$18.

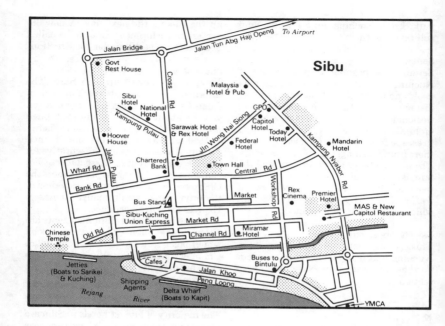

The *Bilik Untuk Sewa Lodging House*, near the bus station, has been recommended as having good, clean rooms for M\$12 and dorm beds for only M\$4 – a bargain in Sarawak. Apparently, you can cook your own food in the kitchen.

Places to Stay – middle

Many of the hotels in the middle price bracket are of the same standard as bottom-end hotels except more expensive.

The *Capitol Hotel* (tel 336444), 19 Jalan Wong Nai Siong, has reasonable rooms from M\$37. The popular *Rex Hotel* (tel 330933) at 32 Jalan Cross has double rooms from M\$33.

The *Today Hotel* (tel 334468) at 40 Jalan Kampung Nyabor has reasonably clean rooms for M\$28 and a few cheaper ones under M\$20. The *Maling Hotel* on Jalan Brooke Drive is good value with clean, spacious rooms with own bathroom for about M\$40.

The *New World Hotel* (tel 330678) at 1 Jalan Wong Nai Siong has good single rooms for M\$30 and doubles for M\$35. A little further along the street is the *Merrido Hotel* (tel 331411) where rooms cost between M\$23 and M\$70.

The *Malaysia Hotel* (tel 332299) at 8 Jalan Kampung Nyabor is quite good with single rooms starting from M\$45.

The *Ban Hin Hotel*, 12 Jalan Pulau, has recently been recommended by a couple of travellers. Single rooms costs M\$27 and doubles costs M\$30.

The *Government Rest House* has good rooms which are very expensive at M\$40/50 for singles/doubles. It's on Jalan Pulau, near the junction with Jalan Bridge.

Places to Stay – top end

Hotel Zuhra (tel 310711) on Jalan Kampung Nyabor is one of the cheaper top-end hotels with air-con rooms for M\$55/65 singles/doubles. The staff are very friendly and helpful. There's a coffee shop downstairs and a clean, airy Chinese cafe next door. The *Sarawak Hotel* (tel 333455) is a popular place to stay on Jalan Cross. Single rooms start from M$52 and doubles start from M$60.

The *Li Hua Hotel* (tel 24000) at the Longbridge Commercial Centre has 77 fully air-conditioned single rooms from M$60 and doubles from M$95.

The top of the range is the enormous *Premier Hotel* (tel 23222) on Jalan Kampung Nyabor. All rooms have air-con and private facilities, and prices are between M$100 and M$200 per night. This hotel has its own nightclub, bars, coffee lounges and even a travel agency.

The *Sarawak Hotel* (tel 23455), 34 Cross Rd is a much smaller hotel with 24 rooms with and without air-con at M$62 to M$80 for singles, M$70 to M$90 for doubles.

The *Li Hua* (tel 2400), at the Longbridge Commercial Centre, has singles at M$70 to M$90, doubles at M$105. The *Hotel Malaysia* (tel 22298), 8 Kampung Nyabor Rd, has 21 rooms at M$45/60.

Places to Eat

Virtually all the restaurants in Sibu are small Chinese cafes and very few of them have anything to recommend. The vast majority serve uninteresting, tasteless rubbish that will either provoke you into fasting or into spending hard-earned cash on a decent meal.

An exception is the *Sing Hai Seafood Restaurant* at 13 Jalan Maju. The seafood served is tasty, fresh and reasonably priced. A good place for cheap, Chinese food is the *Hung Guan Cafe* at 17 Jalan Channel, next to the River Swan Hotel. The cafe on the corner of Jalan Kampung Nyabor, opposite the Premier Hotel, makes good satay in the evening.

Around the corner from the Phoenix Hotel on Jalan Tunku Osman are several very clean cafes. The *Seafood Garden* and the *Tasty Cafe* are quite good. The *Sugar Bun*, diagonally opposite the church on the large roundabout, not far from the bus

station, is OK for breakfast or western-style snacks.

If you're trying to find food around 7 pm, it's worth eating at the food stalls near the market which set up late in the afternoons. Most restaurants/cafes are closed for the evening by this time. The *New Capitol Restaurant* opposite the Premier Hotel serves reasonably priced food.

Getting There & Away

Air If you're flying from Sibu to Bintulu note that this sector is usually heavily booked – plan ahead if you're on your way up the Rejang River. If you have no booking it's well worth trying standby at the airport since there are seven flights a day to Bintulu and MAS are notorious for 'fully-booked' flights which leave half empty.

If you're travelling by boat from Sibu to Belaga and want to fly back, book your flight as far in advance as possible because the Belaga-Sibu sector is only covered twice a week by one 12-seater plane.

Road The road from Sibu to Bintulu has been completed and this, being the last stretch, means the entire coast of Sarawak is now connected right through to Brunei. This last section to Bintulu is a long, tough slog and could hardly be called a road in some places.

Two bus companies run buses from Sibu to Bintulu twice daily around 6.30 am and 12.30 pm. The journey takes about 4½ hours and costs M$15 (no air-con) or M$18 (with air-con).

There is also a local bus which goes to Bintulu via Stapang, Selangau, Nanga and Tepus Bridge. There are two daily buses costing M$15 which depart Sibu around 6 am and 12 noon.

Whichever bus you take, you're in for a really rough, uncomfortable trip where the bus bounces along the pot-holed road (which is lined with all sorts of rubbish) for 90% of the journey. At one stage of the bus trip, the seat I was on came right off it's hinges!

There is one air-con and one non-air-con express bus departing Sibu for Miri daily at 6.45 am and this incredibly bumpy journey takes about 7½ to eight hours. The fares are M$29 (non-air-con) and M$35 (air-con).

See the Kuching section for details about road transport between Kuching and Sibu.

Boat – To Sibu-Sarikei-Kuching The fast launch to Kuching via Sarikei (where you change launches) departs from the Delta Wharf daily at 8.30 am, costs M$20 and takes about five hours. You can book tickets at Kuching-Sibu Union Express (tel 331593), 3 Jalan Channel or, at Tieng Gine Baru Office (tel 323751) but it's easier to buy your ticket on the boat itself. The hovermarine departs Sibu for Kuching daily around 7 am and costs M$25.

Several cargo boats make trips from Kuching to Sibu to Bintulu and beyond. See the Kuching section for further details.

Boat – To Kapit Getting to Kapit is the first leg of the journey up the Rejang River and the trip offers a fascinating insight into life along Sarawak's mightiest river and the rain forests which border its banks.

The super-fast launches which do this trip, known as the *Kapit Express* are narrow, steel-bottomed boats powered by enormous twin diesels which generate one hell of a thrust. They cover the 130 km or so from Sibu to Kapit in a mere 3½ hours! Unfortunately the video craze has hit these boats – unless you sit outside you'll find no way of escaping from third-rate Kung Fu films.

The launches depart Sibu daily between 7 am to 1 pm – times are not exact since they like to leave full – and the fare is M$12. There's no need to book in advance, simply go down to Delta Wharf about half an hour before one is due to leave and pay on board. You can sit anywhere you like – on the seats inside, on the bench at the back, on the deck at the front or on the roof.

The launches call at Kanowit and Song as well as a number of smaller settlements and logging camps en route, but only long enough to let passengers on or off. Often, the boats will slow down to a crawl as they pass the jetty and then start speeding off before the alighting passenger has both feet safely on the wharf!

The launches used to stop at two jetties in Kapit, but now stop only at the main concrete jetty in town.

Boat – To Bintulu & Miri Cargo/passenger boats are the only ones which do this run and they do not operate on any regular schedule – departure times depend on demand – so you may have to wait around for several days.

The fare to Bintulu is between M$40 and M$50 and the journey takes about 18 hours. To Miri the fare is about M$50 (including food) and the journey takes at least 36 hours.

If you're interested in a boat along this route enquire at Miri Sin Ching Shipping Company (tel 240599), 2A Jalan Jawa, Kuching or the Siam Company (tell 242832), 28 Main Bazaar, Kuching.

Going the other way, contact Tan & Sim (tel 33545) in Miri. If no large cargo ships are leaving for several days, ask around at Delta Wharf in case there's a smaller vessel going that way.

Boat & Walking – To Bintulu See the Belaga section for details on the Sibu, Kapit, Belaga, Tubau, Bintulu trip.

Getting Around
If you arrive in Sibu by launch (from Kuching or Sarikei) or by cargo/passenger boat (from Kuching, Sarikei, Bintulu or Miri) then you will dock at Delta Wharf, which is only a few minutes walk from all the main hotels and restaurants. Delta Wharf is also where the launches to or from Kapit dock.

If you arrive by air take either a taxi or bus No 1 to the terminus in the centre of town. Buses to Bintulu depart from the area at the far end of Jalan Khoo Peng Loong, not far from Jalan Workshop.

UP THE REJANG RIVER

Other than a visit to Kuching and one or more of the national parks, the Rejang is the principal travel destination in Sarawak. Scattered along this river and its tributaries, particularly the upper reaches, are the longhouses of the Iban tribe.

Some people have reported that some of the longhouse inhabitants between Kapit and Belaga are decidedly unfriendly towards visitors. No doubt they're sick to death of strangers turning up out of the blue and expecting to be welcomed with open arms, fed and entertained. One traveller was stuck for words when an old Iban lady asked: 'Where in Europe can I go and be welcomed into a stranger's house?'

Don't let this put you off, as generally, the Iban are very friendly, hospitable people who welcome foreigners and are pleased to invite you into their homes. Just smile a lot, be friendly and take along a few small gifts and some food towards your keep.

Ask the boatmen if there's a longhouse they can recommend and then, when you're dropped off, ask someone to take you there and introduce you to the *kepala* (chief). You'll probably be offered a place to stay for the night and you'll be invited to join them for a meal.

If you want to get a real feel for life in the longhouses then you should plan on staying at least one night. Staying at a

Tanjong Ben Osad - HEADMAN

longhouse is one of the highlights of any trip to Sarawak.

You will most likely have to sleep with the chief's family, or the family of the person who brings you to the longhouse. If there is no bathroom or toilet at the longhouse, do as the locals do and bathe in the river. Don't jump in wearing your bathing-suit or worse without your bathing-suit, wear a sarong. The locals are very conservative when it comes to communal bath time.

It's polite to 'pay' for your stay in terms of gifts (food and cigarettes), but there's no need to offer any money. You should take some cash with you as you may want to buy handicrafts, soft drinks or beer. Make sure you find out the cost before you consume the goods, or, as one traveller wrote, 'you may find the longhouse bottle of Anchor beer costs more than the same in the main lounge of Singapore's Mandarin Hotel!'.

Naturally the more 'authentic' long-houses are to be found on the upper reaches of the river, furthest away from 'civilisation'. Most travellers head for the stretch of river between Kapit and Belaga.

Going beyond Belaga tends to present difficulties in the form of red tape. Special permits for travel between Kapit and Belaga are a mere formality and will take only an hour or two of your time at Kapit, but if you want to travel beyond Belaga then you will need another permit which isn't quite as easy to obtain.

KAPIT

This bustling little town dating from the days of the White Rajahs and still sporting an old wooden fort built by Charles Brooke, will be your first stop on the journey up the Rejang. To anyone from outside it's just a sleepy riverside village tucked into the rain forest, but to upriver people it's the 'big city' to which they come to buy, sell and exchange goods as well as for entertainment – there are two cinemas.

There isn't a great deal to do or see in Kapit though the waterfront and the market are interesting and the Chinese temple works up a sweat on the big drums some evenings. Kapit is the terminus for the *Kapit Express* launches from Sibu and the place to which you must come to obtain the permit for travelling to Belaga.

There are two longhouses about six to seven km from town along Jalan Selerik, but they're thoroughly urbanised and nothing like the more traditional ones you'll find further upriver.

Information

If you need to change money (ie travellers' cheques) there are two banks in town – one in the same block as the Kapit Longhouse Hotel overlooking New Bazaar and the other not far from the new Hotel Meligai. Their charges for changing travellers' cheques are heavy.

You can get good maps of the area on the top floor of the government complex. MAS has an office at the back of the block opposite the jetty and is open Monday through Saturday from 8.30 am to 12 noon and 1.30 to 5 pm, Sundays and public holidays from 8.30 to 11 am.

Permits for Travel Beyond Kapit The first step in this process is to go to the 'Pejabat Am' office on the 1st floor of the State Government Complex and collect the necessary forms. Fill them in and take them to the top floor of the police headquarters where they will be stamped and you'll be asked to fill in a visitors' book. One of the questions on the forms asks if you have a valid international cholera vaccination certificate, but nobody seems to check this.

Take the stamped forms back to the State Government Complex and present them at the office of the 'Residen' which is next door to 'Pejabat Am'. There the forms will be filed and a typed permit issued to you.

There's no charge for the permits but if you're planning on going beyond Belaga

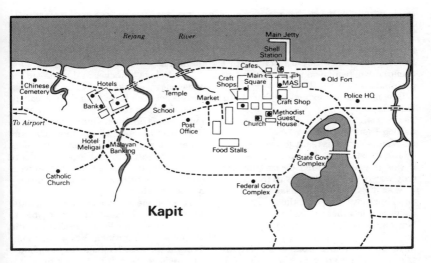

Kapit

you'll need an additional permit – ask about it there. Unless you're going as far as Belaga, however, nobody will want to inspect your permit.

Places to Stay

The place to head for is the *Methodist Guest House*, the double-storey building to the left of the blue church near the centre of town. It's a pleasant place and the people who run it are friendly, though rooms are a little dingy and the bathroom is grotty. Still, it's a bargain at M$7 for a single room and M$10 for a double.

The *Rejang Hotel* (tel 796709), 28 New Bazaar, has clean rooms with fan and western-style bathroom from M$26 per night. The *Kapit Longhouse Hotel* (tel 796415) on Jalan Berjaya, has single or double rooms (all with air-con) for M$25.

The *Hiap Chiong Hotel* (tel 796213), 33 New Bazaar is a lot cheaper at M$17 for fan-cooled rooms, and clean common bathrooms from M$17. They also have a few air-con rooms from M$25 and the management are friendly.

The new top-end hotel in town is the *Hotel Meligai* (tel 796611) on Jalan Airport, near the town centre. Rooms start from M$43 a double.

Places to Eat

Kapit is a dreadful place to be when you're desperate for a reasonable meal. Most of the small cafes serve basic, tasteless rice or noodles with some fatty meat. No matter what you ask for, you're likely to end up with an outrageously expensive plate of greasy rice and chicken. Vegetarians will no doubt leave Kapit having eaten enough vegetable stalks to last them a lifetime!

The *Kah Ping Cafe* is better than most others – at least they have a variety of food available. Their sweet and sour pork is still popular and an added bonus, according to one traveller, is the nightly cabaret put on by the enormously overweight family who run Kah Ping – a performance of howling and squabbling rivalled by none!

You can get excellent mee dishes (especially soup) at the *S'ng Ee Ho Restaurant*.

For breakfast, try the *Kiew Ming Cafe* on Jalan Court, the *King Hung Cafe* across the road from MAS or the *Ding*

Chou on the left-hand side of the street as you approach the Methodist Guest House.

The *Weng Dong Bakery*, in the centre of town, has a range of delicious plain and sweet buns. It's run by a family with a friendly, English-speaking daughter who has studied in Australia.

Beer is a lot more expensive than it is in Kuching.

Getting There & Away

Air When the river is really low you will not be able to get a launch or boat to Belaga, so if this is your intended destination the only way of getting there is to fly.

MAS fly Sibu-Kapit-Belaga and back on Thursdays and Sundays. The free baggage allowance on the small Britten-Norman Islanders is officially just 10 kg.

Road The only local road transport are taxis and there are very few of these. It isn't surprising since there's hardly anywhere you can go by road. If you arrive by air you'll have to take a taxi for the two km into town.

Launches & Boats - To Sibu There are frequent departures of the *Kapit Express* from 5.45 am to 1 pm. Times vary as the boats like to leave when full. If you want to catch the first launch back to Sibu, go down to the wharf really early as the boat often leaves before the first scheduled departure time. There is a cheap cafe right opposite the wharf where you can enjoy coffee and cakes before the trip.

The Kapit-Sibu fare is M$12 and the journey takes four hours. You can buy your ticket on the boat. The launch calls en route at Song, Kanowit and a number of smaller settlements and logging camps.

Launches & Boats - To Belaga Launches and boats leave daily from the main jetty whenever the river is high enough to allow them to negotiate the several sets of rapids which are encountered between there and Belaga. The rapids are the main reason why there are no boats when the river is low.

The launches to Belaga cost M$12 or more and take six to 10 hours to get there depending on the tides. Make inquiries the day before at the Shell Station at the main jetty.

The Belaga launches and boats are the same ones you take to visit the Iban long-houses between Kapit and Belaga, except that when the river is low you'll have to make use of tribesmen's motorised dugouts. The latter are usually considerably more expensive than the launches so it makes sense to be part of a small group in order to share costs. It's also a good idea to wear protective clothing and a hat as there may not be any shade.

To recommend any particular longhouse as opposed to another would be to encourage a travellers' bottleneck and overload the traditional hospitality to be found at these settlements. Iban longhouse culture is very sensitive to such pressures from outside and although changes are inevitably being forced on these people from other quarters – development, commerce, government activity – there seems little justification for augmenting the process. Presumably you haven't come this far up the river just to see the plastic smiles of a tourist trap.

BELAGA

Belaga is just a small village and government administration centre on the upper reaches of the Rejang where the river divides into the Belaga and Baleh rivers.

Along these rivers are many interesting Kayan and Kenyah longhouses. If you start talking to a friendly local on the boat, you're bound to be invited to stay at their longhouse. Don't forget to offer food, cigarettes, or some small gift as a contribution towards your keep. There is a Kayan longhouse within walking distance from Belaga town.

You cannot travel beyond Belaga without official permission and unless you have a written invitation from someone living further up the river, it's highly unlikely that you'll be granted permission.

Travellers have been known to go ahead without a permit, however, if you do this it might be an idea to let someone else know where you are heading.

Places to Stay
The *Huan Kilah Lodging House* is the cheapest hotel in Belaga, with basic rooms for M$15. The *Sing Soon Hing Hotel* isn't much better with fan-cooled rooms at M$20 and rooms with air-con at M$30. The *Belaga Hotel* has a few cheap rooms for M$15 and more expensive air-con rooms costing M$25. There's a communal bathroom.

You can also stay at the logging camp near Belaga and use their transportation to get to Bintulu. Accommodation is usually free, but they may charge you around M$15 for the ride to Bintulu.

It's probably not worth going to either of the government rest houses in Belaga, as one is strictly reserved for government officials and the other seems to be for longhouse *bumiputras* only.

Getting There & Away
It's possible to trek in the dry season from Belaga to Bintulu – or in the opposite direction. This has been made a lot easier in recent years due to the rapid growth of logging in the area. You still need a permit from the Resident at Belaga (or Bintulu if you're coming the other way).

The journey takes a few days and is fairly strenuous. If you want to hire guides at various longhouses, or boats on the rivers, it's advisable to get a small group together before you start.

The route you take will depend largely on how much water there is in the river, but the usual route is to head up the Belaga River until you get close to the Tibang Rapids where you get off the boat.

From there walk a rough six hours over the mountains to cut out the rapids and then hire another boat up to one of the longhouses where you hire a guide to take you over the mountains to the Tubau River on the other side of the watershed.

The usual destination is the longhouse at Long Unan. From there it's generally possible to charter a motorised boat down to Tubau for about M$50 – a journey which takes several hours.

From Tubau, there are launches down to Bintulu which cost M$12 per person and take about three hours. If you like, you can stay overnight at the Belaga Sawmill which is about 15 minutes downriver from Tubau but you should bring your own food.

Alternatively, there's a logging camp about an hours boat-ride up the Belaga River. You can stay there overnight and then take one of their logging trucks to Tubau for M$10 to M$15, depending on your bargaining skills.

One traveller says that it's quite easy to hitch along this stretch. From Tubau, you can catch one of the launches downriver to Bintulu.

Another traveller sent us the following report on making this trip, from the Bintulu end:

After taking the boat up to Tubau you can continue on to Belaga via one of the logging camps set up along the Belaga River. They usually maintain daily Landcruiser connections with their dumping camps in Tubau. The loggers are friendly and cooperative and you can try to get a ride back to one of the camps with them. Their logging concessions are limited in time and place so the camps tend to move fairly frequently.

Once you get to the Belaga River it is possible to travel down to the town of Belaga, where the Rejang River starts, in one day of river paddling and jungle walking. There are several jungle paths you can choose from but you'll have to use the services of a local boatman at some point or other, either to travel along the river or to cross it. No matter how experienced a jungle walker you may be, you will find it helpful to take along a trustworthy local guide. He can help you bargain with the boatmen along the way.

Even for local people there is no fixed price for hiring a boat on a given stretch of the river; the prices vary with the weather, the strength of the currents, the time of the day and willingness of the boatman to leave his farmwork to take you up or down the river.

Nevertheless, when foreigners appear on the scene the locals are likely to ask for outrageous fares. And their bargaining position is certainly strong! Just for reference I paid M$100 for two of us to travel from a logging camp all the way down to Belaga. This included three boat rides and the fees for two young Kenyah guides. The whole trip took seven hours. It turned out to be one of the most exciting jungle trips I have ever had, partly due to the Belaga River being rather swollen at the time.

Police permits are still necessary and are partly meant for your own safety. The police may tell you the story of the German guy who ventured on his journey without a permit and disappeared never to be seen again. Local touts will tell you the same story but stress that the unfortunate German didn't have the good sense to hire a guide!

Bureaucratically the river seems to be a sort of one-way road because the permit is apparently easy to obtain in Bintulu for the Tubau-Belaga trek, but not so easy to to get in Kapit for Belaga-Tubau. We did not have a permit and nowhere were we asked to produce one.

I should think it is possible to do it alone, without guides and at the 'local price', even if you don't speak the local language. Make sure, however, that you have a good map, food, water, clothing, possibly a sleeping bag and maybe simple cooking utensils. Mosquito coils would be a good idea and mosquito net still better – Belaga is a bad malaria area.

There are three rest houses (read stilted platforms topped by an attap roof) along the Belaga River, conveniently placed before and after the 'impassable' rapids. This is where you are most likely to get stuck if there is no boat or if it's too expensive.

If you stay at the rest houses you are likely to meet small parties of travelling Kayans, perhaps families engaged in shifting agriculture or groups of young men who leave their longhouses in the Belaga basin and go to look for work in the logging camps. If they like you they may share their food with you and perhaps the boat they are going to charter next morning too. Be patient and be prepared to wait a few days for a passage which money could buy immediately.

This trip is likely to become easier as the logging roads are slowly pushed further down the river. There's even talk of a government plan for a Bintulu-Kapit road.

BINTULU

Bintulu is an air-conditioned boom town which is best to pass through as quickly as possible, unless you want holes burned in every pocket.

Construction is going on everywhere – a new international airport, deepwater port, residential suburbs, more shops, new hotels – thanks to all that oil and lumber money which is pouring into the place. The town is jam-packed with migrants from all over Sarawak and abroad who have come here hoping for a piece of the action. Due to these developments, prices have hit the sky and cheap accommodation is really difficult to find.

There isn't anything to see or do in Bintulu, except perhaps shed a lot of money in expensive nightclubs, but the street markets which mushroom in the evenings are pretty lively.

Places to Stay

Everything is outrageously expensive and since all the hoteliers are trying to make a killing while the boom lasts there's nothing you can really call a 'budget' hotel. Unfortunately, money is only half the story. The other half is finding a room at all, especially if you arrive in the evening, since many hotels are more or less permanently full with oil, lumber and construction workers and businessmen.

The *Hock Chuhn Lodging House* does, however, have pigeonhole-like rooms for M$15 and it's a stone's throw from the Tubau Express pier if you're going upriver.

Perhaps the best place to head for is the small, separate annexe of the *Kemena Lodging House* (tel 333777) where there are three or four comfortable, clean double and triple rooms costing M$15 – no matter whether one, two or three people occupy a room. This annexe backs on to the airport which isn't as noisy as you might imagine, since there are no planes arriving or departing from about 8.30 pm to 7.30 am. If you want to stay at the annexe, you have

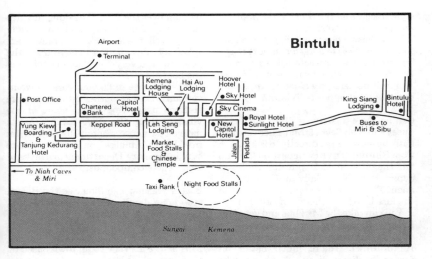

to see reception at the main Kemena Lodging House on Jalan Keppel first.

Also on Jalan Keppel, there's the *Hai Au Lodging House* (tel 31728) which is a bit seedy and dirty and has rooms with air-con but without bathroom for M$40. You're better off saving this one for when you're on skid row.

Much better places are the *Capitol Hotel* (tel 31167) and the *Leh Seng Lodging House* (tel 31431), both on Jalan Keppel with reasonably clean, fan-cooled rooms from M$20. There are more expensive rooms with air-con, TV and telephone for around M$40. Other hotels with rooms around the M$40 mark are the *New Capitol Hotel* and *Kiang Siang Lodging*.

The *Sunlight Hotel* (tel 32577) on Jalan Pedada has fully air-conditioned rooms, each complete with bathroom, TV and video. Singles start from M$80, doubles from M$90 and there is a coffee shop downstairs.

A few doors down is the *Royal Hotel* (tel 32166) which has single rooms for M$100 and doubles for M$115. The *Kemena Lodging House* (tel 333777) at 78 Jalan

Keppel is one of the cheaper top-end hotels with air-con rooms starting from M$71 single and M$75 double. The *Hoover Hotel* (tel 31355) is slightly more expensive with prices starting at M$80 for a double room.

At the top of the heap, there's the *Li Hua Hotel* (tel 35000) where rooms cost from M$100 to M$300 per night, and the *Aurora Beach Hotel* (tel 31622) on Jalan Tanjung Batu which has 108 rooms from M$125 to M$260.

Places to Eat

There are plenty of restaurants attached to the various hotels and others around the centre of town, but the best selection, very popular with local people and travellers, are the night food stalls next to the taxi rank, between the riverfront and the first road which runs parallel to it. You can eat well and cheaply depending on what you choose. Just wander round the stalls and sit down when you see something you'd like to eat.

Two popular bakeries are the *Bakewell Bakery*, near the bus station, which has a good selection of cakes, local and western-style snacks and the *Glory Cake Shop* for anyone craving western food.

If you have a bus to catch, you can pass time at the *Seaview Restoran* next to the bus station and opposite the waterfront. For delicious but expensive fruit juices and fruit desserts, try *Honey Bun*, on the corner almost opposite Telecom.

Getting There & Away
Buses – To Niah Caves & Miri There are two daily buses which go directly to Batu Niah from Bintulu. The first departs at 7.30 am and the other at 12.15 pm. Return buses depart Batu Niah daily at 7 am and 12 noon. The trip takes about 2½ hours and the fare is M$10 – there is no air-con.

You can take the Miri bus and get off at Batu Niah, but you cannot pay a sector fare, you have to pay the for the entire trip Bintulu-Miri. You're much better off taking the direct Bintulu-Niah bus. The Park hostel is a long walk from Batu Niah junction.

To Miri, there are five buses daily, the journey is rough and takes around four hours. Departures are at 7, 7.30, 8 am and 12 noon. The 7.30 am bus and one of the 12 noon buses have air-con and cost M$18. The non-air-con buses cost M$15. It's also possible to get taxis to Miri for about M$30.

Buses – To Sibu There are three non-air-con buses departing daily from Bintulu to Sibu at 6, 9 am and 12 noon and two additional air-con buses also departing at 6 am and 12 noon. The bus fares are M$15 without air-con and M$18 with.

Boats – To Sibu It's sometimes possible to find cargo/passenger boats from Bintulu to either Sibu or Miri. The fare to either place is M$35 and the journey takes about 18 hours. Check with the agents along the waterfront.

There are also launches up the Kemena River as far as Tubau when there's sufficient water in the river. The journey takes about 3½ hours and you should

bargain over the fare. 'The kung fu video tapes played in the express boats', wrote one traveller who took this route, 'are specially designed to out-noise the powerful and very noisy diesel engines of the boat.'

If you decide to do your ears a favour, you can break the journey into two or more sections by getting off at some of the villages along the way. Sebauh has a native rest house where you can stay for free. In other places you may be able to stay in Forestry Department barracks or local school compounds.

Boat & Walking – To Sibu See the Belaga section for details of the Bintulu, Tubau, Belaga, Kapit, Sibu trip.

MIRI
Miri is just another boom town based on oil money which has managed to attract a large number of expatriates, prostitutes and transvestites. Much of the town is being redeveloped and only the old centre remains. It's a pleasant enough town though there's precious little of interest to keep you there and, as in Bintulu, everything is air-conditioned and expensive.

Most travellers stay only overnight when heading to Brunei, to the Niah Caves, or to Gunung Mulu. The only real point of interest in the town is the Chinese temple down by the waterfront at the end of Jalan China.

Information & Orientation
If you're heading to the caves, call at the national parks office for a permit to visit Niah's 'Painted Cave'. You also need a permit for Gunung Mulu National Park.

The national parks office is in Kingsway behind the blue and white Majlis Islam building. Keeping this building on your left, walk down the Bintulu-Brunei road towards Brunei, past the various government offices and the Land & Survey Department (which has detailed maps of Sarawak) and you'll come to the national parks office.

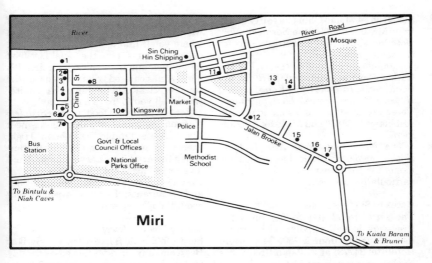

Miri

1	Chinese Temple
2	Seaview Cafe
3	Tai Tong Hotel
4	Thai Foh Lodging
5	Malaysia Lodging House
6	Park Hotel
7	Wisma Pelita
8	Borneo Hotel
9	SE Asia Lodging
10	Chartered Bank
11	King Hua Restaurant
12	Gloria Hotel & Pub Disco
13	Halaman Kabor
14	MAS
15	Miri Hotel
16	Hotel Plaza Regency
17	Fatimah Hotel & Malang Sisters Travel Agency

Everything in Miri is within easy walking distance of everywhere else so there's no need to take taxis or local buses.

Places to Stay - bottom end

Miri is a fairly sleazy town and many of the cheaper hotels are full-time brothels housing male and female prostitutes of various nationalities.

An exception is the *Thai Foh Lodging House* at 18 Jalan China. The English-speaking manager is quite helpful and will let you sleep on one of the beds permanently set up in the hall for M$5. So long as you ask, he'll also clear out a locker for you to keep your valuables in. If you prefer, there are single rooms for M$16 and doubles for M$20. It's very basic, but quite OK for a night or two.

A couple of doors down, the *Kheng Nam Lee Lodging House* has a similar set up, but beds are M$4 and the whole place is rather dingy, smelly and dirty – OK for desperados.

The *Tai Tong Lodging House*, opposite the Chinese temple on Jalan China, is better value with clean, well-kept bunk beds in the hall costing M$5.50 and good double rooms for about M$28.

Near the ferry terminal, a short walk from the centre of Miri, is the friendly *Red Cross & Crescent Society* which has one guest room with fan and bathroom for M$10. If the room is occupied, they will put mattresses on the floor for M$3 per person. Bus No 1 will take you there.

The *Malaysia Lodging House* (tel

34300) at 1-C Jalan China has dirty rooms from M$20 a double; the *Sarawak No 7 Hotel* on Kingsway has better rooms for the same price.

Around one side and to the back of the Cathay Cinema, you'll find the *Ruby Air-Conditioned Inn*, the *Hong Kong Lodging House* and the *Sarawak Lodging House*. These are all of a similar standard and cost between M$30 and M$40 for a double room.

The *New South-East Asia Lodging House* on Jalan China has reasonable rooms for M$42 per night, but it's not particularly good value.

Places to Stay - top end
The *Park Hotel* (tel 32355) on Jalan Kingsway is still popular with air-con rooms starting from M$80. The *Gloria Hotel* (tel 34773) at 27 Jalan Brooke has single rooms starting at M$92 and doubles starting at M$120.

The *Ria Fatimah Hotel* (tel 32255), 15 Jalan Brooke has 64 rooms from M$64 to M$250. The Malang Sisters' Travel Agency (tel 38141) is downstairs.

The *Hotel Plaza Regency*, next door to the Ria Fatimah Hotel, is the newest international hotel and has rooms starting from around M$100.

You can also try the *Million Inn* (tel 34344) at 6 Jalan South Yu Seng, where single rooms start at M$92 and doubles start at M$120.

Places to Eat
Other than hotel restaurants there are plenty of good food places in Miri, especially in the new blocks between Brooke Rd and the waterfront. For the best selection – Chinese, Muslim, seafood – try any of the ones around Halaman Kabor.

Max's Coffee House, on the 1st floor of Wisma Pelita, the big new shopping complex by the bus station, has a range of western and Malaysian food at reasonable prices. It's not the place to head for though if you're starving as the portions are quite small.

On the ground floor, there's a branch of Malaysia's fast food chain *Sugar Bun*, where you'll find a selection of pastries, cakes and buns, plus the usual fast food hamburger and fried chicken section. It's very Americanised right down to the squeaky clean kids behind the counter who'll tell you to 'have a nice day'.

For tasty Muslim food, try the *Seaview Cafe* on the corner of Jalan China, near the Chinese temple. On Jalan High, there's a popular Chinese restaurant called the *Jun Lian Cafe* where you'll find a variety of meat and fish dishes. Most of the large hotels have their own good cafes and restaurants; their food is usually very good, though expensive.

Getting There & Away
Road - To Bintulu & Batu Niah The Syrikat Bas Company operates five buses per day to Bintulu. Air-con buses depart at 7.30 am and 12 noon and the fare is M$18; non-air-con buses cost M$15 and depart at 7, 8 am and 12.30 pm. The trip takes about 4½ hours.

The same company also operates four buses daily direct to Batu Niah (for the Niah Caves) which cost M$9 and take about 2½ hours. Buses depart from Miri at 7 am, 10.30 am, 12 noon and 2 pm. From Batu Niah to Miri, the last bus leaves around 1 pm. It's advisable to book a day in advance – the company's office is across the street from the main bus stand offices. It's a rough road.

You can go by air-con taxi to Batu Niah early in the morning for about M$15 per person. Hitching is quite easy.

Road - To Sibu There are two buses daily, going all the way to Sibu, which takes eight to nine hours along an incredibly bad road. The non-air-con bus departs at 7 am and costs M$30 and the air-con bus departs at 7.30 am and costs M$35.

Road - To Brunei The Miri Belait Transport Company (office at the main bus stand) operates six buses daily to

Top: Mosque in Kuching, Sarawak (ST)
Left: Shopfront in Kuching, Sarawak (GC)
Right: Pepper tree, Sarawak (ST)

Top: Chinese temple in Kuching, Sarawak (ML)
Bottom: Kapit on the Rejang River, Sarawak (ST)

Kuala Belait – the first town in Brunei – from 7 am to 3 pm. The fare is about M$12 and the trip takes about 2½ hours.

Alternatively, you can take the bus as far as the Sarawak-Brunei border for M$5.15 and then hitch (but it's probably easier and more convenient to take the bus right to Kuala Belait).

The road is sealed from Miri to Kuala Baram where a river crossing is made. Vehicles often have to queue for some time before reaching the ferry, so most passengers get out and wait for their bus/car by the edge of the water. You can leave your bags on the bus.

Just across the river, you go through the Malaysian immigration checkpoint and continue on the same bus to the Brunei immigration checkpoint. You must take all your belongings off the bus and go through passport control and customs.

Once through customs, you board a new Brunei bus which will take you to the Belait River for another ferry crossing. If there is a long queue, as there usually is, you can be stuck there for three or four hours in the heat of the day. In this case, the best thing to do is to take everything off the bus and take one of the local motor boats across the river (about B$1), then walk or hitch to Kuala Belait town. It's only a 20-minute walk.

Alternatively, you could try asking drivers near the front of the ferry queue if they would mind taking you across with them – the car ferry is free. Government officials are allowed to drive straight to the front of the queue and will sometimes take travellers across the river into town (especially at times when the queue appears to be endless).

At Kuala Belait, you will be dropped at the Belait United Traction Company bus stand, where you can take another bus to Seria. This is preferable to staying in Kuala Belait overnight as the cheapest hotel in Kuala Belait charges B$100 for a single room!

Buses depart Kuala Belait for Seria frequently throughout the day and cost

B$1. The last bus goes at 7.30 pm and taxis cost between B$3 and B$4. The journey takes about 45 minutes.

If you need to change money – no one is interested in the Malaysian ringgit – the Hong Kong & Shanghai Banking Corporation is opposite the bus stand in Kuala Belait.

From Seria, you must take another bus to Bandar Seri Begawan, the capital of Brunei Darussalam. Several bus companies do the run and there are many buses daily. The fare is B$4 and the journey takes one to 1½ hours. It's a good sealed road all the way. From Kuala Belait or Seria to BSB it's easy to hitch.

Early in the morning, you can also get taxis from Miri to Kuala Belait for about M$30 per person. One traveller wrote to us saying that 'illegal' taxis also make the trip between Miri and Kuala Belait for around M$10 per person – ask around.

Boats Cargo/passenger boats operate between Miri and Bintulu, Sibu and Kuching. If you're interested in taking one of these start your enquiries at Sin Ching Hin Shipping, River Rd, Miri. There is a notice board on the wall outside the office with details of current sailings.

INLAND FROM MIRI

If you're heading out for a long trek into the mountains along the Indonesian border to such places as Bareo, Lio Matoh and Long Akah the first stage of the journey will be by road to Kuala Baram. The fare to Kuala Baram is M$2.10 and buses depart Miri hourly (at least) from 6 am to 5.30 pm.

If you're heading for Gunung Mulu National Park, take the 6 am bus if you want to get there in one day. From Kuala Baram, you can take a fast launch up the Baram River to Marudi for M$12 and the journey takes about 45 minutes. Launches leave Kuala Baram at 8, 10 am, 12 noon and 2 pm. There are regular launches to Long Lama, further up the Baram River.

For Gunung Mulu National Park, take

the express boat from Marudi to Long Panai or Kuala Apoh (depending on the level of the river) for M$12. There's only one departure per day at 12 noon.

From Kuala Apoh or Long Panai, take a private longboat to Long Terrawan (prices vary a great deal, but should be no more than M$12) and another private longboat to the national park.

If you're travelling with other people, the latter boat trip should cost about M$35 per person, but if you have to hire the whole thing yourself, you'll be up for about M$150. The price you pay for private boats is negotiable and journey times vary considerably.

From Long Lama to Long Akah reckon on about M$25 and one to 1½ days and from there to Lio Matoh about the same.

There are airstrips at Marudi, Lawas, Limbang, Long Seridan, Long Lellang, Bareo, Long Sukang, Long Semado and Bakelalan. MAS operate a good network of local flights between these places. Permits are required to visit most of the places up in the mountains. Apply for these at the office of the Resident, 4th Division, Miri.

Marudi

There are good views of the river from the hilltop Fort Hose, built in 1901. Permits for Bareo, Long Lellang and Long Seridan are issued by the district officer there. You can also get visas extended in Marudi and there are two banks for changing foreign currency.

There is a road network around Marudi and you can visit longhouses at Long Selaban, Long Moh and Leo Mato – you can either hitch or take a taxi.

Places to Stay The popular *Grand Hotel* (tel 55712), Marudi Bazaar, is very nice and even meets the launches with a car to drive you the four or five blocks to the hotel. The cheapest room (single or double) is M$13.50 and for that, you get your own bathroom and toilet as well as clean sheets. It's about the tallest building

in town so the sunset views from the roof are good.

The *Hawaii Hotel* and the *Marudi Hotel* have both been recommended and have basic rooms from M$10. The *Alisan Hotel* (tel 55911) on Queens Square, has a few cheap rooms for M$13 and many more expensive ones between M$30 and M$100.

There is also the *Mayland Hotel* (tel 55106), Kampung Dagang, which has single rooms from M$30 and doubles from M$45. The *Government Rest House* is another place you can try – contact the district officer in town.

Getting There & Away The express boats from Kuala Baram to Marudi cost M$12, with no extra charge for Kung Fu or American wrestling videos.

Bareo

Bareo sits on a beautiful high valley floor in the Kelabit Highlands, close to the Indonesian border. A four-hour walk on a wide trail takes you to Pa'Lungan, a friendly longhouse with a pleasant river to swim in. The headman has a room for visitors with mats, blankets, pillows and mosquito net.

From there you can hire guides and bearers to climb Gunung Marudi, at 2423 metres (7946 feet) the highest peak in Sarawak. Or you can walk to Bakelalan and cross the uncontrolled Indonesian border to Long Bawan in east Kalimantan. The Kelabit people live on both sides of the border and ignore it. They are getting away from the traditional tattoos and stretched earlobes, although you will still see these on the elders.

A six-day walk from Bareo takes you to Long Lellang via Pa'Dalih and Ramudu with a night or two in the jungle with the nomadic Punan people. You can fly out from Long Lellang.

The longhouse guest books are full of good information. Many Kelabits are hard-core Christians and don't smoke so bring sugar, seeds, tea, kerosene or anything imaginative for the headman.

From Bareo, you can also hire a guide and porters to climb Gunung Marudi, one of the highest mountains in Malaysia. It takes about five days to complete the ascent and descent.

Places to Stay The *Bareo Lodging House* is M$8 per person but it's nothing special and you may want to head straight out to the longhouses.

Getting There & Away MAS flies Twin Otters from Miri to Bareo and from Marudi to Bareo, Long Seridan (for Gunung Mulu National Park) and Long Lellang. Marudi to Bareo flights operate almost every day of the week. There are no roads and walking takes at least a week.

The National Parks

The Malaysian jungles are some of the oldest undisturbed areas of rainforest in the world. It's estimated that they've existed for about 100 million years since they remained largely unaffected by the far-reaching climatic changes brought on elsewhere by the Ice Ages. In recent years, however, vast areas of this virgin forest – particularly in Peninsular Malaysia and Sabah – have been devastated by the uncontrolled and thoughtless activities of lumber and mineral concerns.

While the government is slowly moving in the direction of reafforestation and forcing companies which negotiate concessions to invest in this, it's obvious that much goes by the board and that a more intelligent approach to these magnificent forests is a long way off.

Fortunately, quite large areas of some of the best and most spectacular of these rainforests have been made into national parks in which all commercial activities are banned. These parks are, in effect, the essence of a trip to Borneo, other than visits to longhouses. A lot of effort goes into maintaining them and making them

accessible to visitors, and you cannot help but be captivated by the astonishing variety of plant and animal life to be found.

In Sarawak itself at the moment there are six such parks – Samunsan at the extreme western tip near Sematan; Bako north of Kuching (27 square km); Similajau on the coast, north-east of Bintulu (75 square km); Niah of Niah caves fame, about halfway between Bintulu and Miri (31 square km); Lambir Hills just south of Miri (69 square km); and Gunung Mulu south-east of Marudi near the Brunei border (529 square km).

The Lambir Hills park is for day use only; no overnight lodging or camping. Due to the limited and often primitive road system in Sarawak, Samunsan and Similajau are difficult to reach for those without their own four-wheel drive transport. Similajau is temporarily closed to the public.

GUNUNG MULU NATIONAL PARK

Since Gunung Mulu National Park reopened in late 1985, it has become one of the most popular travel destinations in Sarawak. Unfortunately it's also one of the most expensive places to visit.

Gunung Mulu National Park is Sarawak's largest national park covering 529 square km of peat-swamp, sandstone, limestone and montane forests. The two major mountains are Gunung Mulu (2377 metres of sandstone) and Gunung Api (1750 metres of limestone).

The park contains hundreds of species of flowering plants, fungi, mosses and ferns. It has around 10 different species of pitcher plants, which attract botanists and scientists from around the world.

Gunung Mulu has a variety of mammals, birds (eight different types of hornbill), frogs, fish and insects, but it's not the place to head for if you want to see loads of exotic wild animals.

The park is noted for many underground caves. Cave explorers recently discovered the largest cave chamber in the world, the Sarawak Chamber and the 51-km long Clearwater Cave, one of the longest in the world. At present, only the Deer Cave and the Clearwater Cave are open to the public, but, if you're lucky, you may be able to find a guide who will take you to see others.

Many of the caves closed to the public are inaccessible, or considered dangerous while some contain fragile formations that park authorities want to preserve and protect from further deterioration.

Permits & Information

Permits for Gunung Mulu National Park can be obtained at the national parks office (tel 33361) in Miri. The staff at this office don't seem to know much about Gunung Mulu.

For better information, visit the Malang Sisters' Travel Agency (tel 38141) on the ground floor of the Ria Fatimah Hotel on Jalan Brooke, Miri. See the Getting There section for more about this travel agency.

Other helpful agencies are Gua Mulu Tours (tel 37278), 31-G Park Arcade, Miri; and Philip Enterprise (tel 411611) on the 2nd floor of Lot 1342, Lorong 3, Jalan Jee Foh, Krokop, Miri.

Besides getting a permit for the park, visitors must book and pay a deposit (M$20 per group) for accommodation. On arrival at the park, you must report to the head ranger. It's unlikely that you would be sent away if you turned up without confirmed reservations but as facilities at park headquarters are very limited, it's better to book in advance.

There are two hostels at the park, each providing beds for 10 people at M$5 per night each. You can cook your own food as there are gas cookers, and you can use the cutlery, crockery, pots and pans. There is a small canteen at park headquarters selling basic tinned foods, bread, milk, eggs and margarine. The prices are not too expensive when you consider all the hassle of transporting goods to the park.

There are no walking trails around park headquarters and, unfortunately, you cannot go anywhere without taking a guide which is annoying as you often don't need one. Guides' fees vary between M$20 and M$30 per day. If you are hiring a guide for a few days, make sure you agree on the total price before you start off.

The Caves

Deer Cave, 2160-metres long and 220-metres deep, has the world's largest cave passage. The passage is illuminated, though a strong torch is useful for the darker areas. Water cascades from openings in the roof after very heavy rain.

You enter the cave on one side of the mountain, exit from the other and it takes about 30 minutes to walk the entire length. Guides are compulsory and charge M$20 to take you through the cave, but they don't care how many people there are in a group, so round up as many as you can.

The Deer Cave's biggest attraction is the spectacular black cloud of free-tailed bats which emerges from the entrance between 5 and 6 pm each night and returns early in the morning. If you want to see this incredible sight, camp overnight at the entrance to the cave.

The Deer Cave is a pleasant, easy walk from the park headquarters through some beautiful forest. It's worth spending a couple of hours in the forest areas around the cave.

The Clearwater Cave is 51-km long (the longest cave passage in South-East Asia) and 355-metres deep. It's very dark inside and you need a really strong torch to see the finer details of its various features and limestone formations. There are several river crossings and you should be prepared to wade through waist-deep water at times.

To get to the Clearwater system, you must hire a boat to take you about two hours up the Melinau River – if the river is running low, you might have to help the boat along for most of the way.

It costs about M$60 to hire the boat with a boatman and a guide, but then you have

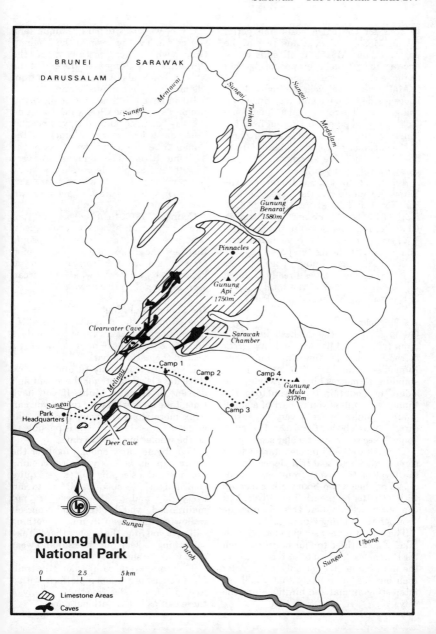

BRUNEI
DARUSSALAM

SARAWAK

Sungai Mentawai

Sungai Terikan

Sungai Medalam

Gunung
Benarat
1580m

Pinnacles

Gunung
Api
1750m

Clearwater Cave

Sarawak
Chamber

Camp 1

Camp 2

Camp 4

Gunung
Mulu
2376m

Melinau

Camp 3

Sungai
Park
Headquarters

Deer Cave

**Gunung Mulu
National Park**

0   2.5   5 km

Limestone Areas

Caves

Sungai

Sungai Tutoh

Sungai Ubong

to consider the extra costs like petrol (about M$25) and wear and tear of the engine (about M$15). It all adds up so once again try to get a few people together to make things easier money-wise.

Make sure you wear strong walking shoes inside the cave and keep an eye on the ground. There are some dangerous-looking jagged points jutting out from the limestone floor. There is a swimming hole at the entrance to the cave where you can spend an enjoyable afternoon. You can camp overnight if you like.

According to tourist literature, the Sarawak Chamber is the largest cave in the world and 'is about the size of 16 football fields'. At present, the Sarawak Chamber remains closed to the public.

There are several other caves in the park, many are still being 'prepared' by the national parks organisation. They estimate that the number of caves already explored represents only 30% of the total number in the Gunung Mulu National Park.

The Pinnacles

Gunung Api is the highest limestone mountain in Malaysia and its great attraction is its towering limestone Pinnacles – an incredible stone forest standing 45-metres high, halfway up the side of the mountain. If you want to see the Pinnacles – unless you're part of a small group – you're in for a very expensive three-day trek by boat and foot. However, you will see some spectacular scenery.

The trek to the Pinnacles starts with a three to four-hour boat trip (depending on the level of the river) from park headquarters, then a two-hour walk to a camp with a shelter by the Melinau River. You can sleep overnight at this picturesque spot before climbing Gunung Api.

The ascent is very steep in parts and it takes a good three to four hours to reach the Pinnacles. It's best to start out early in the morning as it's not only a lot cooler then but it's more likely that you'll see interesting animal and birdlife along the way.

On the way back to park headquarters, you can follow the river to the Melinau Gorge which lies north-east of the Pinnacles. The Gorge is at the end of the walking track, about 1½-hours walk from the previously mentioned camp.

If you have the time (and money) you can also stop at the Clearwater Caves on the way back. If you do this, you need at least a day to look around. Members of the Punan tribe live along the banks of the Melinau River. The Punans are very friendly and hospitable people who enjoy the company of visitors – they are also very poor, so make sure you have your own food supplies.

Count on M$100 to M$120 per group per day for the guide's fees, boatmen's fees, boat hire, petrol, etc. The more people there are, the cheaper it gets. Ask the men for a break down of the total price, so you know exactly what costs what and you can start beating the price down.

The Gunung Mulu Trail

The climb to the summit of this 2376-metre mountain takes three to five days and is the highlight of many a traveller's visit to the national park.

If you are reasonably fit and healthy, three days is adequate for the ascent and descent of Gunung Mulu. If you have time, take an extra day or two so you can relax more along the way. For any star athletes pressed for time, it is possible to do the whole thing in two days.

You should carry enough food for the entire trip, as well as your own cooking utensils and a sleeping bag (it gets quite cold at night). It's not unusual for it to rain every day and as the tracks are not maintained, you'll often find yourself wallowing knee-deep in mud – nothing will save you from the leeches there! Take something to keep out the rain and wear good walking shoes.

There are several camps along the trail. Most consist of a wooden platform with a roof – it's free to sleep overnight at any of these camps in the national park.

If you leave headquarters very early in the morning, you can reach Camp No 1 in about three hours. This camp is beside a beautiful river. A further four to five-hours walk will take you as far as Camp No 3 which is where most people sleep overnight. A simple canvas roof over a rough floor provides shelter but the water is very brown and should be boiled before use.

On the second day, you're faced with an extremely steep climb from this camp to Camp No 4. The walk to Camp 4 takes four or five hours and there's a shed you can sleep in. If it hasn't rained, there won't be any water at Camp 4, so try to remember to carry some muddy water up from Camp 3.

On the third day, leave your pack at Camp 4 and climb to the summit. You can either sleep at the camp another night, or descend the mountain in the one day. The latter is quite tough on the legs, but at least you can cool down in the river along the way.

Here is one traveller's recent account of the Gunung Mulu ascent:

On the first day, we walked from park headquarters to Camp No 3. We started out on a flat trail, walking through a great forest with huge trees. It took about two hours to reach Camp No 1, then 40 minutes to reach Camp No 2 (not really a camp, just a clearing).

From there, the trail becomes almost vertical and, after rain, it's just a mud chute in places. It gets so steep that you have to pull yourself up by grabbing tree roots, but if you make an early start you can have frequent rests – it was a two-hour slog for us, but I've heard of people taking at least twice that time.

The other handicap is the leeches; I counted 54 of them from headquarters to Camp 3 and my socks were stained red. Try to pull them off as soon as you feel them – the trek is hard enough without having to give blood. Check your shoes often, they get in through the holes for your laces and have a feast.

The second day, Camp 3 to Camp 4, is easier and takes about 2½ hours. The forest changes from tall trees to moss-covered, stunted growth. Look out for the many varieties of pitcher plants and stop and listen for any wildlife – you might see monkeys and birds. When we were climbing the mountain, it was cloudy, damp and humid – it must be like that for most of the year as everything is covered in moss.

Have a rest at Camp 4 and then start the 1½-hour walk to the top. There are a few steep areas with ropes and then you'll find yourself amongst colourful bushes, scrambling over roots. At the top, you can wander around and look for orchids.

Sleep at Camp 4 again overnight and climb up to the helipad to see the sunrise in the morning. You can walk all the way to headquarters in one day, but you'll wonder how you made it up some of the steeper parts. You can swim in the river down by Camp 1.

Getting There & Away

Air MAS fly Miri-Marudi daily and the flight costs M$29 one-way. From Marudi, you'll have to take boats to Gunung Mulu Park.

Road/Boat Miri is the starting point for the journey to Gunung Mulu, as this is where you obtain a permit and book your accommodation. From Miri, take a bus to Kuala Baram for M$2.10. Buses depart Miri regularly but if you want to get to the national park in one day, take the 6 am bus. Alternatively, you can stay in Marudi for the night.

From Kuala Baram, there are express boats to Marudi for M$12. Departures are at 8, 10 am, 12 noon and 2 pm. The trip takes about three hours and you'll be subjected to some horrible Kung Fu videos. From Marudi, you can take the 12 noon express boat to Long Panai for M$12. There is only one departure per day.

From there on, the journey to Gunung Mulu is completed by use of tribesmen's longboats. The prices vary a great deal and depend heavily on your bargaining skills.

If you can get a few people together, you can get Philip Ube of Mulu Tutoh Travel Services (tel 55676) to arrange a longboat (about M$30 per person) to take you all the way from Long Panai to park headquarters.

If the river is running low, you can get a private boat to take you from Long Panai to Long Terrawan for M$7 to M$10 and then another boat to the park for about M$35. You may have to help move the boat in the shallow areas.

In Long Terrawan, ask for the park boat man who takes supplies to the park canteen. He goes to the park regularly and will take passengers for M$35.

You can also arrange transport and a tailor-made tour at the Malang Sisters' Travel Agency (tel 38141), ground floor of the Ria Fatimah Hotel, Miri. It's a family business and they're very friendly, helpful people who can chat for ages about Gunung Mulu. They can give you plenty of information about the park and surrounding areas – ask them about places of interest along the Upper Baram River. If you like, they'll help you plan an individual tour to suit your needs. They'll even pick you up at Miri airport and can transfer you straight to Niah Caves or Gunung Mulu. Their prices are quite reasonable.

BAKO NATIONAL PARK

This park is at the mouth of the Bako River, north of Kuching, and contains some 27 square km of unspoilt tropical rainforest. The coastline has many fine sandy beaches, cliffs and mangrove swamps while the interior sports seven types of vegetation, each very different from the others.

Due to the different vegetation types many animals – notably the rare and protected species of hornbill and the proboscis monkey – have made their homes in this park.

Well-marked trails have been laid through the park to make it accessible and all of them are colour coded with a paint mark on trees adjacent to the path. On some of the longer walks you should plan your route before leaving and aim to be back at the hostels at Telok Assam before dark at 6.45 pm.

If you're thinking of walking to the end of the longest trail (Jalan Telok Limau)

you will need to arrange transport to collect you since it's impossible to do the return trip on foot in one day. Transport can be arranged with the park warden. The main trails in the park are:

Name of Path	Destination	Time Required
Jalan Lintang	circular path	3-4 hours
Jalan Tanjung Sapi	cliffs/viewpoint	½ hour
Jalan Telok Delima	mangroves	¾ hour
Jalan Telok Pandan	cove beaches	1½ hours
Jalan Telok Paku	cove beach	¾ hour
Jalan Serait	park boundary	1½ hours
Jalan Tanjor	waterfalls	2 hours
Jalan Tanjung Rhu	cliffs/viewpoint	2½ hours
Jalan Bukit Keruing/Jalan Bukit Gondol	mountain path	7 hours
Jalan Ulu Serait/Jalan Telok Limau	Pulau Lakei (island)	8 hours

You can book accommodation for Bako at the national parks office (tel 248988), Forest Department, Jalan Gertak, Kuching. Telephone bookings are accepted but must be confirmed and paid for at least three days before your intended departure. It's actually a lot easier to go to the national parks office in person. People have been known to turn up to the park itself without any bookings and as far as we know they haven't been turned away.

The park canteen has a variety of goods for sale (mainly tinned food) but there is also fresh bread and vegetables. There's no need to bring a lot of food with you, although prices are higher at the park than they are elsewhere.

Places to Stay

There are three types of accommodation available at the park. Rest houses include a fridge, gas burners, all utensils and bed linen. It costs M$22 per rest house; one has two bedrooms with a total of six beds and

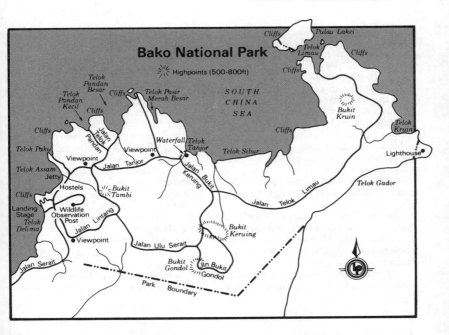

the other has three bedrooms with a total of seven beds.

Hostel cabins sleep five to a room and a bed costs M$1.10 per person. Linen, cooking utensils, a few cups and plates are provided.

Lastly, there are permanent tents (basically fly sheets) on raised platforms with open fireplaces which cost M$1.10 each. Bring your own supplies/utensils and sheets or sleeping bags. Two or three people can sleep under these.

From November to February, the sea is often rough and at times it may not be possible for boats to approach or leave the hostel area at Telok Assam.

Getting There & Away

The park is 37 km from Kuching and can be reached by bus and boat. First, take Bus No 6 from outside the national parks office (near the Sikh mosque) in Kuching town. The fare is M$2.10 one-way (M$2.50 return). The trip to Kampung Bako takes about 45 minutes and buses depart hourly from about 7 am to 5 pm.

From Kampung Bako, you must charter a private boat to the national park for about M$25. The boats can take eight to ten passengers and the costs can be shared. The journey takes about 30 minutes.

NIAH NATIONAL PARK & NIAH CAVES

A visit to the Niah Caves is one of the most memorable experiences available in East Malaysia. The Great Cave, also one of the world's largest, is in the centre of the Niah National Park which is dominated by the 394-metre-high limestone massif of Gunung Subis, visible from far away.

Since 1958, when archaeologists discovered evidence that humans have been living in and around the caves for some 40,000 years, they have been under the protection of the Sarawak Museum.

The rock paintings found in the 'Painted Cave' were the only ones known to exist in Borneo at the time and were associated with several small canoe-like boats which were used as coffins, indicating that this part of the caves was used as a burial ground. A reconstruction of this cave together with some of the remains found there can be seen in the Sarawak Museum in Kuching.

More recent human activity in the caves has centred around the fact that they are the home of three species of swiftlet, numbering some four million, and 12 species of bat, of which there are also several million.

The swiftlets construct their nests in crevices in the roof of the Great Cave and it's these nests which are used in the preparation of that famous Chinese dish, bird's nest soup.

The collection of these nests, which are sold for over a $250 a kg, is supposed to be limited to certain times of the year, but is apparently carried out quite regularly. Scattered throughout the Great Cave are many flimsy poles, up which men have to scramble to get to the nests. The poles stretch from the floor to the roof and some are well over 30-metres.

Another activity which has been going on since 1928 is the collection of guano – the bird and bat excrement which is used as a fertiliser. The guano is collected each week on Mondays, Tuesdays and Wednesdays and carted laboriously along the plankwalk to the depot at Pangkalan Lubang where it is weighed, rebagged and boated down to Batu Niah for sale.

If you're heading up to the caves on these days you may well have to give way to the collectors sweating it out down the plankwalk, each with a huge bag of guano on his back.

The millions of winged inhabitants of the caves provide an unforgettable spectacle

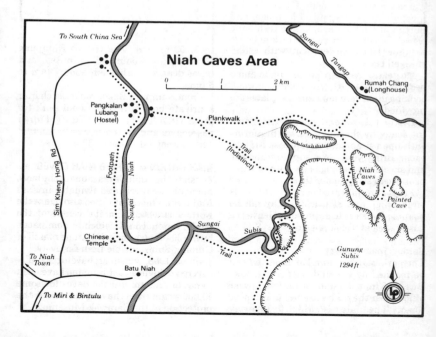

as evening comes along. Swiftlets are day flyers and bats are nocturnal animals, so if you arrange to be at the mouth of the cave around 6 pm you can watch the shift change as the swiftlets return home and the bats go out for the night. You might even be lucky enough to see one of the large predatory birds, such as the bat hawks, swoop into the cave for a meal.

If you go up to the caves at this time be sure to bring a strong torch for the return trip. It's an exciting night-time jungle experience, but made easy by the plankwalk. Though you are certain to hear and see plenty on the way you'll probably remember most the many luminous mushrooms that grow beside the plankwalk.

If you go up to the caves at this time of day, you'll probably find that the gate to the caves, at the point where the plankwalk forks for the caves and the nearby longhouse, is locked when you return. There's a simple remedy for this which involves lifting the gate off its hinges and putting it back on again. The technique was shown to me by two of the longhouse children! The alternative is to climb through the gap at the top of the gate.

The three-km-long plankwalk is made of Belian wood, which is very durable and so heavy that it cannot be transported by water since it doesn't float. This plankwalk starts at Pangkalan Lubang, about four km from the village of Batu Niah opposite the Niah Park hostel, and passes through primary rainforest all the way to the Niah Caves. If you do the trip in the rainy season take care because the plankwalk gets very slippery.

The first part of the walk is also subject to flooding – if you stay at the park hostel ask if anyone has photographs or slides of what it's like when it really floods around there. Quite a sight!

Unfortunately, most visitors are so intent on reaching the caves that they miss out on the life in the forest around them. If you break your trek and spend some time just watching and listening you

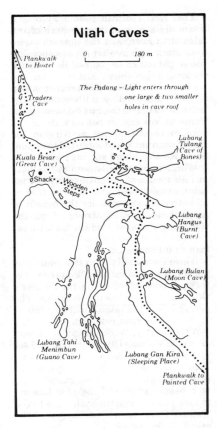

Niah Caves

0 ———— 180 m

Plankwalk to Hostel

Traders Cave

The Padang – Light enters through one large & two smaller holes in cave roof

Kuala Besar (Great Cave)

Shack

Wooden Steps

Lubang Tulang (Cave of Bones)

Lubang Hangus (Burnt Cave)

Lubang Bulan (Moon Cave)

Lubang Tahi Menimbun (Guano Cave)

Lubang Gan Kira (Sleeping Place)

Plankwalk to Painted Cave

may be lucky enough to see such animals as the long-tailed macaque monkeys, hornbills, squirrels and flying lizards, as well as the many hundreds of species of butterflies which inhabit this forest. Even if you don't, you'll certainly hear much more than you see.

The area around the park hostel itself is not without interest. While you're relaxing in the cane chairs on the verandah four km from Batu Niah and about 17 km from the sea, keep an eye on the river.

The river level can change by over a metre depending on the strength of the tides out to sea, and the current varies from static to quite strong – something you might notice as you paddle across to the shop in someone's boat.

Logging is widespread in this area and several times a day you'll see large, log-laden barges chug their way downstream. These barges are almost as wide as the river. Once at the river mouth they are loaded onto ships and exported to Japan, South Korea, Taiwan and the Philippines.

Wildlife occasionally seen in the river include monitor lizards (up to two-metres long), crocodiles and snakes, but they're all extremely shy and, for the benefit of those who are thinking of swimming in the river, rarely seen around the hostel area.

Permits & Information

No permit is needed to visit the Great Cave but if you wish to visit the 'Painted Cave' then you need a permit from the Curator's Office, Sarawak Museum, Kuching. The permit is free and takes about 10 minutes to issue if you're in Kuching.

Alternatively, you can wait until you get to the Visitor's Centre at Niah and get your permit from the ranger at the hostel. That's the official story, anyway. In practice, if you hire a local guide at the park headquarters at Pangkalan Lubang to take you through the main cave to the 'Painted Cave', then it's unlikely you'll be asked for the permit.

Guides cost M$30 (shared between however many comprise the group) and however much you fancy yourself as a speleologist they're well worth it.

Sketch maps of the cave give the impression that it's relatively easy to find your way around inside, but this isn't the case. There are innumerable blind alleys which look like main thoroughfares – some of them quite dangerous. There are also a number of overhanging walls literally crawling with scorpions.

Whether you go with a guide or not (we didn't – but it took us several hours to find the right path – and many hours to find our way out again!) you need a *strong* light and spare batteries. A pair of stout shoes wouldn't go amiss either – don't go in thongs. Ask the park warden or his assistant if you want a guide.

You can book accommodation for Niah at the national parks office (tel 248988), Forest Department, Jalan Gertak, Kuching. Telephone bookings are accepted but must be confirmed and paid for at least three days before your intended departure.

It's a lot easier to go to the national parks office in person, though people have been known to turn up to the park itself without any bookings. If you decide to do this, don't do it on weekends when all of Sarawak seems to head for the Niah Caves.

Around Niah

There is an 80-door Iban longhouse called Rumah Chang, about 40-minutes walk down the plankwalk, where many of the guano and birds' nest collectors live. To get there take the left-hand fork where the plankwalk divides in two. Be warned though that they may charge you M$5 to look around.

In addition to the plankwalk there are a number of vague trails through the jungle which will take you to the summit of Gunung Subis. They're supposed to be marked with blue and white paint strips on the trunks of trees, but these are not at all obvious. Other walks in the area are also worth investigating.

Places to Stay

It would be a strange traveller who would want to stay anywhere other than the *Visitors' Hostel* at Pangkalan Lubang, across the river from the start of the plankwalk.

The hostel can accommodate 25 people in three dormitory rooms and costs M$2.50 per person per night. Bedding, cooking utensils and crockery (latter in very short supply!) are provided and the hostel is equipped with toilets, showers, cooking stoves and electricity in the evenings until 10 pm. If you're lucky there may be an overseas volunteer working there who will put on a slide show for you in the evening – you have to ask.

The hostel is rarely full so you can turn up without prior booking, but if you want to make sure then you can book in advance at the Forest Office (Pejabat Hutan) (tel 085-36637) in Miri. Weekends and holidays can get quite busy.

Meals cannot be bought at the hostel or across the river so you will have to prepare your own at the hostel. It's a good idea to bring canned foods, vegetables and cooking oil with you from Batu Niah although there's a store across the river from the hostel which sells a very limited range of canned meats, rice, noodles, onions, eggs, potatoes, soft drinks, beer and a few other things. They also have torches and batteries for sale in case you didn't pick one up earlier.

If for some reason you don't want to stay at the Visitors' Hostel or your time of arrival stops you getting there that night, there are three hotels in Batu Niah. The *Niah Caves Hotel* is clean, reasonably cheap at M$18 for a double and has good basic food in the restaurant downstairs. The *Yung Hur Lodging House* is similarly priced and the *Hock Sen Hotel* has a dormitory.

If you need to go into Batu Niah for supplies from Pangkalan Lubang you can either hail a boat going upriver (the one-way fare should be about M$2 though they'll naturally start higher) or walk along the track which follows the river. If you walk, it will take about an hour, but be careful of the bridges along the way. Some of them are decidedly unsafe – though children walk along them every day on their way to school.

Getting There & Away

From Bintulu There are two direct buses daily from Bintulu to Batu Niah – the first departs at 7.30 am and the other at 12.15 pm. The fare is M$10 and the journey takes about 2½ hours. It is possible to take the Bintulu-Miri bus but you cannot pay sector fares – you have to pay the entire fare for Bintulu-Miri.

The Bintulu-Batu Niah buses drop you right at the Visitors' Centre. If you take the Bintulu-Miri express bus in either direction, you will be dropped at the Batu Niah junction. From there, it's a 13-km walk to the Visitor's Centre. You can also try hitching, or waving down a taxi (about M$8 right to the hostel).

There are other buses which charge M$1 from the junction to Batu Niah. From Batu Niah to Bintulu, there are two buses daily leaving at 7 am and 12 noon.

From Miri There are four daily buses from Miri direct to Batu Niah. They depart at 7, 10.30 am, 12 noon and 2 pm, cost M$9 and the trip takes about 2½ hours.

Coming in the other direction, there are also four buses daily and the last one leaves Miri at 1 pm. Taxis cost around M$15 per person and leave regularly in the mornings. Don't bother looking for them; they'll find you.

On the way to Batu Niah you can stop at Lambir National Park, about 50 km from Miri. There's a pleasant waterfall about 20-minutes walk in from the park buildings on the road. At the waterfall there's an empty house where you can stay for free – no beds or cooking facilities. Check with the forest officer in Miri or at the park.

Batu Niah to Pangkalan Lubang (Visitors' Hostel) Whether you come from Bintulu or Miri you will end up at Batu Niah. From there the best way to get to the Visitors' Hostel (or the start of the plankwalk if you're not staying at the hostel) is to take a motorised boat down the river to Pangkalan Lubang. The fare should be about M$2 per person (M$10 for the boat) though they'll start higher, so haggle.

If you booked national park transport in Miri someone will collect you from Batu Niah in the hostel's own longboat for M$5 per boat load per return trip.

The alternatives are to walk along the track which follows the river to the hostel (about 45 minutes to one hour) or, if you have your own transport, to drive to the end of Sim Kheng Hong Rd, leave your car there, and walk 10 minutes along the track to the hostel.

It's possible to get a ride from Batu Niah to the end of the road for M$2 per person. It's about three km from Batu Niah to the hostel.

Sabah

Prior to independence, Sabah was known as North Borneo and operated by the British North Borneo Company. After WW II, both Sabah and Sarawak (which had been ruled by the Brooke family) were handed over to the British government and they both finally gained their independence when they merged with Malaysia in 1963.

There was some trouble after independence as Sabah's existence was disputed not only by Indonesia but also by the Philippines. There are close cultural ties between the people of the Sulu Archipelago of the Philippines' Mindanao province and the neighbouring people of Sabah. To this day there is a busy smuggling trade operated from Sabah into Mindanao and Mindanao's Muslim rebels often retreat down towards Sabah when pursued by government forces.

Post-independent Sabah was governed for a time by Tun Mustapha who ran the state almost as a private fiefdom and was often at odds with the central government in Kuala Lumpur. In 1976 he slipped from power and since then Sabah has moved closer to the central government. Sabah's economic strength is based on timber and agriculture.

For the visitor Sabah offers scenic grandeur, Mt Kinabalu and an interesting tribal culture. Unfortunately it's an expensive place to travel around compared to the Peninsula. The population of Sabah is just over one million.

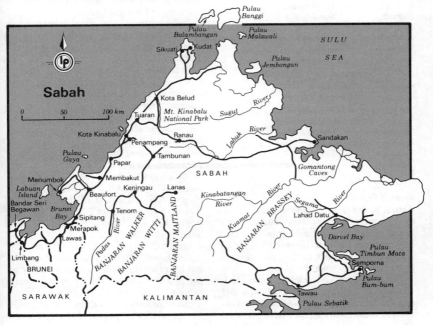

Tamus

The local weekly markets (known as *tamus*) held at various small towns all over Sabah are a colourful local attraction. Tamu days are:

Babaggon	Saturday
Beaufort	Saturday
Keningau	Thursday
Kinarut	Saturday
Kionsom	Sunday
Kiulu	Tuesday
Kota Belud	Sunday
Kota Merudu	Sunday
Kuala Penyu	1st Wednesday of month
Kundasang	20th of month
Mangis	Thursday
Mattunggon	Saturday
Membakut	Sunday
Mersapol	Friday
Papar	Sunday
Penampang	Saturday
Putatan	Sunday
Ranau	1st of month
Sequati	Sunday
Simpangan	Thursday
Sindumin	Saturday
Sinsuran	Friday
Sipitang	Thursday
Tambunan	Thursday
Tamparuli	Wednesday
Tandek	Monday
Telipok	Thursday
Tenghilan	Thursday
Tenom	Sunday
Tinnopok	15th & 30th of month
Toboh	Sunday
Topokom	Tuesday
Tuaran	Sunday
Weston	Friday

Visas & Permits

Sabah is semi-autonomous and has its own immigration controls, but they are much more relaxed than Sarawak. These days you are likely to be given a month's stay permit and it's rare to be asked to show money or onward tickets.

Permits can be quickly and easily renewed at an immigration office, which can be found at most points of arrival, even at small riverine places like Merapok near Beaufort. If you miss them it's no problem, you simply report to another immigration office, even several days later, and explain the situation.

No further permits are required to visit the interior. If you're going to Sandakan you're supposed to have a permission slip to visit the Orang-Utan sanctuary outside the city at Sepilok, but when you get there no one asks for it.

General Costs

Sabah is an expensive place to travel around. Only at Kinabalu National Park and Poring Hot Springs will you find accommodation that could be classed as 'budget'. Elsewhere it's the familiar story of $M20 per night and often much more.

Lodging is also complicated by the fact that many of the cheaper places are often full with semi-permanent boarders, which means you may have to stay in places which would normally be outside the range of budget travel.

If you're prepared to rough it there is the alternative in many places of staying overnight in churches, religious missions and schools – ask for permission first. The only trouble with this is that you have to cart your baggage around all day. Churches and missions generally don't charge overnight fees but donations are always appreciated.

The other alternative to budget accommodation in Sabah is the series of government rest houses which cost M$12 per person per night. There are rest houses in Keningau, Kota Belud, Kota Merudu (tel 61321), Kudat (tel 61133), Kuala Penyu (tel 231), Lahad Datu, Papar, Ranau, Semporna (tel 7781709), Sipitang (tel 426), Tambunan (tel 74339) and Tuaran (tel 788511).

Generally, the rest houses are for government officials and their families, but if a place is not full, travellers are often permitted to stay. Bookings are made through the district officer of the appropriate town and there are listings in the government pages of the telephone directory.

Top: Flora, Kinabalu National Park, Sabah (ST)
Bottom Left: Pitcher plants by the Mt Kinabalu trail (GC)
Bottom Right: Orang-utan sanctuary, Sepilok, Sabah (GC)

Top: Sunset in Kota Kinabalu, Sabah (ST)
Bottom: Mt Kinabalu, Sabah (ST)

Kota Kinabalu

Known as Jesselton until 1963, Kota Kinabalu was razed during WW II to prevent the Japanese using it as a base. Nowadays it's just a modern city with wide avenues and tall buildings without any of the historical charm of Kuching. All the same, KK, as the locals call it, is a pleasant city, well landscaped in parts, and its coastal location gives it an equitable climate.

One of Asia's fastest growing cities, with a population approaching 250,000, KK is an interesting blend of European, Malay and Chinese cultures. It's worth spending a few days in KK if only to sample the excellent variety of cuisines – something which is sadly lacking elsewhere in the state. You must also go to KK to book accommodation and guides for the trip to Mt Kinabalu – Sabah's number one attraction.

Orientation

Although the city sprawls for many miles along the coast from the international airport at Tanjung Aru to the new developments at Tanjung Lita, the centre itself is quite small and most places are within easy walking distance of each other. This includes the bulk of the hotels and restaurants, banks, travel agents, the tourist office, the national parks office and the new GPO.

There is no bus station in town, instead there are two or three areas in central KK where you can find the bus you want, or at least be directed to the right area by the runners who accost you as you walk along. Taxis are all over town, but seem to conglomerate in the area between the GPO and the council offices.

The city can be roughly divided into two halves split in the middle by a large pedestrian walkway or bridge. East of this bridge is the older, cheaper part of town. The other side has the bulk of the better hotels and restaurants as well as offices,

airline companies and the more western-type shops.

Information

Tourist Office The Tourist Office (tel 211484) is in Block L of the Sinsuran Kompleks and has a good range of information, with plenty of glossy leaflets and sketch maps available. Probably the most useful thing they have is a loose-leaf folder packed with up-to-date info on most of the hotels in Sabah, available transport in the form of taxis, buses, Land Rovers, launch services, etc, and many other titbits you'd find hard to come across elsewhere.

The staff are friendly and helpful and will photocopy information for you if you need it. Hours are 8.30 am to 12.45 pm; 2 to 4.45 pm Monday to Friday; 8 am to 12.45 pm Saturday; closed Sundays.

National Parks The Sabah Parks office (tel 211585, 211652), PO Box 10626, Kota Kinabalu is on Jalan Tun Fuad Stephens. Before going to Mt Kinabalu or Poring Hot Springs you must go to this office to make reservations for accommodation (and guides, if required).

The further ahead you do this the more chance you have of being able to go there when you want. Mt Kinabalu is a very popular place both with overseas visitors and local people, and accommodation at the park HQ is often booked up a week in advance.

The office is open Monday to Thursday from 8 am to 12.45 pm and from 2 to 4.15 pm; on Fridays from 8 to 11.30 am and 2 to 4.15 pm; and again on Saturdays from 8 am to 12.45 pm. The staff are helpful and in addition to handling reservations they stock a range of guidebooks and information pamphlets on Mt Kinabalu National Park and Tunku Abdul Rahman National Park. They also sell postcards and T-shirts.

Airlines Offices MAS (tel 51455, 53560) is on the ground floor of the Karamunsing Complex, one km out of town en route to

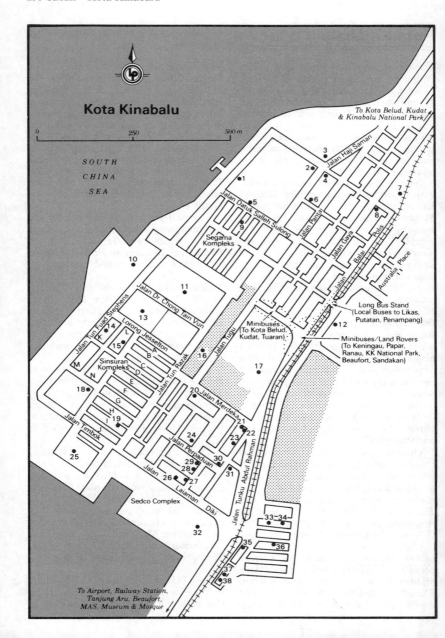

Kota Kinabalu

SOUTH
CHINA
SEA

To Kota Belud, Kudat
& Kinabalu National Park

Long Bus Stand
(Local Buses to Likas,
Putatan, Penampang)

Minibuses
(To Kota Belud,
Kudat, Tuaran)

Minibuses/Land Rovers
(To Keningau, Papar,
Ranau, KK National Park,
Beaufort, Sandakan)

Segama
Kompleks

Sinsuran
Kompleks

Sedco Complex

To Airport, Railway Station,
Tanjung Aru, Beaufort,
MAS, Museum & Mosque

1	Lucky Food Paradise
2	Wisma Merdeka
3	Wisma Sabah
4	Hotel Capital & Capital Restoran
5	Hyatt Kinabalu International
6	Ang's Hotel
7	Post Office
8	Hotel Jesselton & Wishbone Café
9	Bilal Hotel
10	Central Market
11	GPO
12	Police Station
13	Night Market
14	Sabah Parks Office
15	Tourist Office
16	Night Food Stalls
17	High Court, Council Offices & Library
18	Night Food Market
19	Hotel Rakyat
20	Central Hotel
21	Putera Hotel
22	Great Wall Restaurant
23	Hotel Federal
24	Pine Bay Hotel
25	Centre Point
26	Sri Melaka Restoran
27	Ruby Inn
28	Full On Resthouse
29	Islamic Hotel
30	Sri Intan Restoran & Diamond Inn
31	Immigration
32	Cinemas
33	Asia Hotel
34	Hotel Pertama
35	Noodle Inn
36	Hotel Fortune
37	Shangri-La Hotel
38	Grand Palace Restaurant

the museum. Take any bus along Jalan Tunku Abdul Rahman. Cathay Pacific (tel 54733, 54758/9) is at 59 Jalan Gaya; Singapore Airlines (tel 55444), 20 Jalan Pantai Tempahan; Philippine Airlines (tel 57870) and Garuda Airways have offices in Wisma Sabah; British Airways (tel 2426177) has its office in Wisma Merlin; Royal Brunei Airlines (tel 54042, 54830).

Unlike Singapore, Penang or Hong Kong there are no real bargains to be found in the form of discounted airline tickets. There's an abundance of travel agencies in KK, none of which offer incredible bargains to the budget traveller, so if you're planning to fly on from Sabah to Hong Kong or Manila enquire about tickets in Singapore first.

Other Offices The Immigration Office is on the 4th floor of the tall government building, near Jalan Tunku Abdul Rahman and around the corner from the Sri Intan Restoran. As long as your entry permit is still valid, they don't seem to mind if your passport lacks the official entry stamp for Sabah. Permits can be easily extended in less than an hour, though you may be asked for your onward ticket.

The poste restante service at the GPO is efficient and reliable. The clerk will give you the whole pile of letters to sort through.

The Indonesian Consulate (tel 54100) is at Jalan Sagunting in the Wing On Life Building.

Banking hours are Monday through Friday from 9.30 am to 2.30 pm and Saturdays from 9.30 to 11 am. The banks are closed on Sundays and public holidays.

You can make international phone calls at Telecom, Block C of Kompleks Kuwusa, corner of Jalan Tungku Abdul Rahman and Jalan Kemajuan, in the Karamunsing area. The office is open seven days a week and closes quite late at night. Collect calls can only be made from hotels and private houses.

Books Good bookshops are hard to find in Kota Kinabalu. The best one is the Rahmat Bookstore in the Hyatt Hotel. It is very small but it has a good selection of books of Sabah and other parts of Malaysia. The next best choice is probably the Arena Book Centre in Block L of the Sinsuran Kompleks, just down from the tourist office. There are other bookshops in town which stock new and secondhand English-language books but they sell little more than second-rate novels.

The State Mosque

As an example of contemporary Islamic architecture at its best, this mosque is well worth a visit. It's on the outskirts of town and you'll see it if you're on your way to or from the airport. It's much more interesting than the mosque at Kuching.

Visitors are allowed inside though, naturally, shoes must be removed before entering and you should be appropriately dressed. If you are refused entry, chances are a recent western visitor breached the code of etiquette resulting in a temporary ban for all foreigners.

Sabah Museum

The museum, completed in 1984, is next to the State Legislative Assembly Hall. The main building is a four-storey structure built in the longhouse style of the Rungus and Murut tribes. Inside are good collections of tribal and historical artefacts, including ceramics. Another section has flora and fauna exhibits from around the country. There's also a souvenir shop in the main building.

The Science Centre, next to the main building, sometimes holds temporary exhibitions and demonstrations of the latest in computer technology. Next to the Science Centre is the Art Gallery & Multivision Theatre. The Multivision Theatre is the place to see the slide show *Sabah. The Land Below the Wind*. Viewing times vary, so enquire at the entrance desk.

There is also a restaurant and coffee shop with views over the gardens and man-made lakes in the grounds. Definitely worth a visit. Hours are 10 am to 6 pm Monday to Thursday; closed Friday; and from 9 am to 6 pm on Saturday, Sunday and public holidays. Catch a red bus along Jalan Tunku Abdul Rahman for 35 sen and get off just before the mosque. The museum is on a hill on the left side of the road.

Tunku Abdul Rahman National Park

The park is made up of the offshore islands of Gaya, Mamutik, Manukan, Sapi and Sulug. Only a short boat ride from the centre of the city, they offer good beaches, crystal-clear water and a wealth of tropical corals and marine life.

You'll find the Park Headquarters on Pulau Gaya, the largest island which has 20 km of marked hiking trails and the well-known Police Beach at Bulijong Bay. If you're lucky, you may see monkeys pangolins or even what's known as the bearded pig.

Pulau Gaya is inhabited by about 500 Malaysians and 4700 Filipino refugees who live in stilt villages on the water. The water village is quite interesting, but as there are few walkways, you may have to take one of the local boats which ferry people about.

Close by is the most visited and most developed island, Pulau Sapi, which also has good beaches and trails and day-use facilities. There's a three-km nature trail on the island and apparently there are some monkeys living in the forest who sometimes go down to the beach to swim and look for crabs. You may also see the white-bellied sea eagle around this island.

Pulau Mamutik is a small, uninhabited island which is being pushed as a 'Robinson Crusoe experience'. There is a rest house on the island and little else. The nearby Pulau Manukan has a couple of interesting reefs for snorkellers, but most of the coral around this island was damaged in the days of fish bombing before the area became a national park.

Pulau Sulug is the least visited island of this group, probably because it's the furthest away from KK. It has some beautiful coral reefs and tropical fish.

Places to Stay There is a *Rest House* for up to 12 people on Pulau Mamutik which costs M$60 per night. You can camp on all of the islands, though some have better facilities than others. At present, it's best to bring all your own camping equipment and food. If you want to camp on Pulau Sulug, you must first get permission from the Sabah Parks Office in KK.

Getting There & Away The Tanjung Aru Beach Hotel (tel 58711) controls the boats to and from these islands. Boats depart KK daily, on the hour, from 8 am to 4 pm and return every hour until 5 pm. The return fare to Pulau Sapi is M$20, while the return fare to each of the other islands is M$16. You cannot go to more than one island for M$16. You may be able to find local boats willing to take you out to the islands, but they won't be cheap.

Tanjung Aru Beach
Several km south-west of KK centre is Tanjung Aru Beach, adjacent to Prince Philip Park and close to the international airport. It's not bad as beaches go and the area is dotted with open-air food and drink stalls and the occasional pile of rubbish. You can find much better beaches as well as Rungus longhouses at Kudat way up near the northern tip of Sabah.

To get to Tanjung Aru Beach, take a red bus displaying 'beach' from Jalan Tunku Abdul Rahman. It costs 55 sen and will drop you near the yacht club, a pleasant ½-km walk from the international hotel at the other end of the beach.

Other Attractions
If you'd like a view over the city go for a stroll up Signal Hill at the eastern end of the city centre above the former GPO. It's best at sunset. Prince Philip Park, by the beach, has some food stalls and is close to downtown.

You'll often see tourist literature in Sabah adorned with photographs of the Sabah Foundation's cylindrical, mirror-fronted, 31-storey building at Likas Bay, with its revolving restaurant and ministerial suites. The literature gushes breathlessly about this landmark and insists that you include it in your programme but it isn't

worth the effort. Anyway it can be seen from a distance, en route to Kinabalu National Park, standing in the middle of a vast, devastated landscape.

There is also the market which is in two sections – the waterfront area for fish and an area in front of the harbour for fruit and vegetables. Around dusk, it's quite nice to walk along the beach front to this area where the local people are packing up their market stalls for the day and the fishermen are unloading their catch. There are some food stalls around the waterfront area.

Places to Stay
After Kuching and Brunei, Kota Kinabalu seems positively overflowing with hotels but most of them are fairly expensive. Sometimes, you'll find mid-range hotels with cheaper fan-cooled rooms on the higher floors – it's worth asking.

Places to Stay – bottom end
Finding a decent budget hotel in KK is not easy. Essentially to get a good room you have to pay for it. The *Putera Hotel* on Jalan Merdeka, near the corner with Jalan Tunku Abdul Rahman, is a fairly clean Chinese hotel with air-con singles from M$30 and fan-cooled singles from M$20. They often try to get rid of the worst rooms first, so ask for something better if you're shown a grotty hole.

The *Islamic Hotel* on Jalan Perpaduan is still a popular choice among travellers, though it's rather run down. It has rooms for around M$30. A much better choice is the *Hotel Rakyat*, Block I, Sinsuran Kompleks, run by friendly Muslims. It's spotlessly clean and well kept. Rooms vary in price from M$20 for a fan-cooled single and M$30 for a fan-cooled double. The couple who operate White Waters Adventures (Borneo) Sdn Bhd also run a hostel which can accommodate up to 34 people. Their hostel and office (tel 231892), where you can arrange tours, is on the 3rd floor, Block L, Sinsuran Kompleks. You can stay in their 14-person dorm with bunk beds for M$15 per night. The dorm is a bit noisy until 11.30 pm when the nearby night market closes but the other rooms are OK. Double rooms cost $34/42 for fan-cooled/air-con but when occupied by one person they cost M$28/36. Prices also include breakfast.

The *Pine Bay*, across from the Islamic Hotel, has some rooms for M$21 but most are in the M$30 range and none are particularly good value.

Hotel Bilal isn't bad and has rooms from M$25 for a fan-cooled double. It's on the 2nd floor of a block in the Segama Kompleks, across from the Hyatt Hotel. The Segama Kompleks houses several bottom-end hotels, many of which double as brothels.

If you're willing to stay a little way out of town at Kampung Likas, there are two places highly recommended by several travellers.

One is Cecilia and Danny Chew's *Home Away From Home* (tel 35733), 328 Jalan Saga, Kampung Likas. They offer bed & breakfast to travellers from M$18 per night. Breakfast is huge and the owners are very helpful. It's six km out of KK town and accessible by minibus for around 60 sen.

The other favourite is the *Likas Guest House* (tel 31706) at 371 Jalan Likas, Kampung Likas, which has a friendly owner who charges M$15 for a single room and M$20 for a double. Breakfast can be ordered the night before and costs M$2.50.

Places to Stay – middle

Hotel Eden (tel 53577) on the corner of Jalan Sentosa and Jalan Merdeka has clean air-con rooms from M$50. They also have cheaper fan-cooled rooms. The *Diamond Inn* (tel 225222) on Jalan Haji Yakub has reasonable rooms from M$42 but one traveller says that it seems to be in the process of becoming a 'short-stay' place as rooms can now be rented by the hour.

The nearby *Ruby Inn*, behind the Islamic Hotel, is recommended. It's very clean with nice staff and rooms cost M$75 a double. Sometimes, they let an extra person sleep on the floor at no extra charge.

Ang's Hotel (tel 55433) on Jalan Bakau has good rooms with air-con for around M$50. Don't bother with the restaurant downstairs though, unless you eat nothing but pork. The *City Inn*, 41 Jalan Pantai, is new and clean – they even change the sheets each day. Double rooms start from M$51.

The *Full On Rest House*, 10 Jalan Perpaduan, Kampung Air, has good clean rooms for M$56 a double. It's not far from the Islamic Hotel. The *Jesselton Hotel* has a run-down annexe on Jalan Gaya, but the rooms are definitely not worth M$55.

Back on Jalan Merdeka, near Jalan Tugu, you'll find the *Hotel Nam Tai*. It's fairly clean and has double rooms for around M$40. The *Asia Hotel* (tel 53533) on Jalan Bandaran Berjaya, is better value with rooms from M$36.

Other hotels you could try are the *Central Hotel* (tel 51544) on Jalan Tugu, the *Federal Hotel* at 16 Jalan Haji Yaacub, and the *Nan Xing Hotel* on Jalan Haji Saman, all with rooms from about M$40.

Places to Stay – top end

Kota Kinabalu has a number of hotels with prices right up there with the leading hotels in Singapore, Kuala Lumpur and Penang. The five top hotels are the *Hotel Capital*, the *Hotel Jesselton*, the *Hyatt Kinabalu International*, the *Hotel Shangri-La*, and the big and very expensive beachfront *Tanjung Aru Beach Hotel*.

Other top range hotels, but below this stratospheric level, include the *Sabah Inn*, the *Winner Hotel*, and, once again out at Tanjung Aru Beach, the *Borneo Hotel*.

Borneo Hotel (tel 55255), 13 Jalan Selangor, Tanjung Aru, 31 rooms, singles M$90, doubles M$110 to M$140

Hotel Capital (tel 53433), 23 Jalan Haji Saman, 102 rooms, singles M$150, doubles M$160

Hyatt Kinabalu International (tel 51777), Jalan Datuk Salleh Sulong, 344 rooms, singles M$185, doubles M$250

Jesselton Hotel (tel 55633), Jalan Gaya, 49 rooms, singles M$140 to M$155, doubles M$180; for annexe rooms see middle bracket

Sabah Inn (tel 53322), 25 Jalan Pantai, 40 rooms, singles M$58, doubles M$78

Hotel Shangri-La (tel 56100), Bandaran Berjaya, 120 rooms, singles M$140, doubles M$155

Tanjung Aru Beach Hotel (tel 80752), Tanjung Aru, 300 rooms, singles M$210, doubles M$230 to M$1400

Winner Hotel (tel 55211), 9-10 Jalan Haji Saman, 45 rooms, singles M$100, doubles M$140

Places to Eat

For the variety of restaurants and the quality of food available, KK is probably the best city in Borneo. There are Chinese, Indian, Malay, Indonesian, Spanish, Filipino, Japanese, Korean and western restaurants right in the centre of town.

If you've forced down one too many of the bland, monotonous Chinese meals served up in the backwoods of Sarawak, you may be prepared to splurge on a 1st class meal. If this is the case, you can have a real feast at the *Grand Palace Chinese Restaurant* in the Shangri-La Hotel, the *Great Wall Restaurant* on the corner of Jalan Tunku Abdul Rahman and Jalan Merdeka, the *Shiraz Restaurant* in Block B of the Sedco Kompleks, or any of the restaurants in the big international hotels.

Moving down the price scale, one of the best places is the *Sri Melaka Restoran*, 9 Jalan Laiaman Diki, Kampung Air, around the corner from the Ruby Inn. Friendly English-speaking staff will help you choose something from the menu. They have an excellent range of tasty dishes for low prices – try their laksa.

The *Noodle Inn*, between Kentucky Fried Chicken and the Shangri-La Hotel on Jalan Berjaya offers a variety of spicy dishes for around M$5. The *Sri Intan Restoran*, downstairs in the Diamond Inn serves delicious, tasty food with pint-size glasses of hot Chinese tea, for about M$5.

The *Sinsuran Food Centre*, opposite the waterfront, further up the road from the Sabah parks office, is very clean and has reasonable vegetarian dishes for M$2 to M$3. Most restaurants in the Sinsuran Kompleks offer good seafood at reasonable prices.

Over in the Segama Kompleks, there's a great Indian restaurant called the *Banana Leaf* which serves some very tasty meals for M$3. It's on the 2nd floor. Also in the Segama Kompleks, down at street level, is *Sat's Ice Cream Parlour* where you can get freshly-squeezed fruit juices and local-style ice-cream desserts.

If you walk along the road that follows the waterfront, past the Hyatt Hotel, in the direction of Kota Belud, you will come to the Marine Police building. Opposite, is the *Lucky Food Paradise* which houses about 30 individual hawker stalls. There's a variety of cheap food available at reasonable prices.

On the 2nd floor of Wisma Merdeka, you'll find the very popular *Merdeka Food Stall Centre* where food is varied and cheap.

If you go to MAS or telecom at Karamunsing, you can eat at the *Avasi Cafeteria*, opposite the telecom office in Kompleks Kuwusa. It's very popular with workers and is often crowded. Just help yourself to any of the dishes you fancy and pay at the end of the counter. You can eat well for less than M$5.

There are several western-style fast food places around town and some of the middle to top-end hotels have western restaurants. The *Wishbone Café & Restaurant* on Jalan Gaya, is not bad – it's downstairs in the Hotel Jesselton and serves both western and Asian food.

Things to Buy

Though a major centre, KK isn't a great

place for handicrafts. There is a small shop in the Tanjung Aru Beach Hotel which has some fairly expensive handicrafts and souvenirs for sale. The Hyatt's bookshop has a range of books on various parts of Malaysia and some of them are excellent.

Unfortunately, the weekly tamus don't seem to have much to offer in the way of tribal handicrafts, though occasionally you may find something. You can sometimes buy handicrafts from tribal people when you visit longhouses. Some of the Filipino refugees on Pulau Gaya, sell their handicrafts for reasonable prices.

Getting There & Away

Peninsular Malaysia & Singapore The cheapest way of getting from Peninsular Malaysia to Kota Kinabalu is by purchasing an advance purchase ticket (M$256) from Johore Bahru; regular fare is M$301. There are also economy night flights from Kuala Lumpur. Advance purchase tickets must be paid for 14 days in advance while the night fares only apply to certain flights.

Similar fares are also available from Kota Kinabalu to the peninsula. MAS operate a special direct bus from their office in Singapore to Johore Bahru which makes the flight from there not only cheaper but also quite convenient. The MAS office is one km out of town at Karamunsing.

There used to be regular shipping services with Straits Shipping between Singapore and Sabah but now there is only one service operated by Feri Malaysia Sdn Bhd which you can book through Harrisons & Crossfields (tel 215011) in KK.

The ferry departs Kuching on Mondays and arrives in KK on Tuesday morning at 8 am. It departs KK around 2 pm on Tuesdays, arriving in Kuantan at 12 noon on Thursdays and Singapore at 10 am on Fridays. The cheapest one-way fares from KK are: M$140 to Kuching, M$265 to Kuantan and M$310 to Singapore. For these prices you get a bed in a standard share-cabin. Deluxe cabins are more expensive and family suites cost almost double the standard fares.

Hong Kong MAS and Cathay Pacific each have two flights weekly between Kota Kinabalu and Hong Kong. The fare is approximately M$660, but you will probably find cheaper tickets on Philippine Airlines. The flight time is a little under four hours.

The Philippines MAS and Philippine Airlines fly KK-Manila daily; the fare is US$189 and flight time is just under two hours. From time to time there have been flights between KK or other towns in Sabah and Zamboanga in the southern Philippines' island of Mindanao. At present they are, once again, out of operation.

Buses There is no longer a main bus station in KK. Instead, there are two or three areas from where buses, minibuses and Land Rovers depart. These areas are marked on the map.

The area north of the council offices and east of the GPO is the departure point for minibuses to Kota Belud, Kudat and Tuaran. Just east of this, in the area where Jalan Tunku Abdul Rahman changes name to Jalan Balai Polis, is a long bus stop for local buses to Likas, Penampang, etc. Behind and beside this bus stop you'll find minibuses and Land Rovers for Ranau, Mt Kinabalu National Park, Papar, Keningau, Beaufort and Sandakan.

All minibuses leave when full and there are frequent early morning departures. There are fewer departures later in the day and for some destinations, such as Ranau, the last bus departs around lunchtime. For long-haul trips, like KK to Sandakan, the last bus may leave as early as 8 am, so unless you're up at the crack of dawn, you could find yourself stuck for another night. Following are some examples of minibus fares from KK:

To Beaufort (90 km), regular departures up to about 3 pm, two hours on a very good road for M$7.

To Kota Belud (77 km), departures up to 2 pm daily, two hours on a road that is sealed nearly all the way for M$5.

To Kudat (122 km), departures to about 1 pm, four hours on a road which is partially sealed for M$12.

To Sandakan (386 km), departures early morning only, about eight hours for M$25. Land Cruisers and some buses make the same trip for M$35. The road is sealed as far as Ranau but it's a pretty rough ride the rest of the way to Sandakan. It's paved in and around Sandakan.

To Keningau (128 km), regular departures to about 1 pm, about 2½ hours on a road which is surfaced to Tambunan, then a rough gravel road the rest of the way.

To Ranau (156 km), early morning departures, the last bus leaves at 12.30 pm and takes about two hours. All buses pass Kinabalu National Park. The road is not too bad.

If you're heading for Kinabalu National Park from KK you can get there by taking either the minibuses for Ranau or Sandakan and getting off at the park HQ, which is right by the side of the road. Ask the driver to drop you off there. Occasionally, the driver goes right into the park and drops passengers at the reception.

The fare to the park HQ costs between M$5 and M$8 depending on whose minibus you take. You can buy tickets for the M$5 minibuses from the offices beside the long local bus stand on Jalan Balai Polis.

Many of the minibuses are in fairly poor condition and no wonder considering the state of some of the roads. From KK, one of the worst roads you'll come across is the stretch between Papar and Keningau, where cars have to dodge potholes, stray rocks and the occasional mud slide.

Besides the minibuses, there are share-taxis and Land Rovers to most places.

They also go when full and their fares are at least 25% higher than the minibuses. It's usually not worth the extra money to travel by Land Rover. If you're willing to pay a bit more for comfort, you're probably better off flying.

Getting Around

Airport Transport The only occasion in which you'll need to use local public transport is to get to the airport at Tanjung Aru, south-west of the centre. To get there take a 15-minute taxi ride for M$10, or a red 'Putatan' bus for 65 sen from Jalan Tunku Abdul Rahman and ask to be dropped at the airport. This bus stops opposite the road which leads to the airport and from there it's a 10-minute walk to the terminal. Alternatively, take a 'Putatan' minibus right into the airport for about M$1.50.

Heading into town from the airport, there's a bus stop to the right as you leave the airport. Taxis operate on a coupon system and prices are listed at the airport desk. It's quite easy to hitch into town from the airport.

The airport is new and modern, with an efficient MAS office, post office, a small bookshop and an overpriced restaurant upstairs.

Taxis Local taxis are plentiful in the extreme. Fares are generally 10% to 15% more for air-con and 50% more from 1 to 6 am. Taxi stands are all over town, but most can be found in the large area between the council offices and the GPO.

Car Rentals Most of the more expensive hotels have connections with car hire companies around town and will be able to arrange something for you.

AROUND KOTA KINABALU

Penampang

Home of the popular Kadazan people, Penampang is a pretty village about 13 km from KK. Some handicrafts can be found and if you're lucky, you might catch the local dancers performing the *Sumazau* (harvest dance). Occasionally, these young dancers perform in KK.

Take a look at St Michael's Church, the largest and oldest church in Sabah, or visit the Kadazan graveyards where you'll see some burial jars.

There is an authentic Kadazan restaurant called the *Yun Chuan Restaurant* in Block L, Penampang Newtownship. Prices are reasonable and the food is good.

To get to Penampang, take a 'Penampang' bus from the long bus stop on Jalan Balai Polis for 70 sen. Minibuses also ply back and forth at a slightly higher cost.

Papar

South of KK, this is a coastal Kadazan village where they make coconut wine. There's a beach in Papar and the Papar River where you can take a boat ride. It's worth going on a Sunday so you can experience the weekly tamu. To get there, take a minibus for M$2 from the area around Jalan Balai Polis, near the long local bus stand.

BEAUFORT

Beaufort is a quiet little provincial town on the River Padas with a fair amount of charm, although there's absolutely nothing to see or do so it's unlikely you'll stay more than one night.

If you're heading to or coming from eastern Sarawak by either the Brunei-Labuan-Mempakol or Lawas-Merapok-Sipitang routes then you will pass through Beaufort. The railway line from Tanjung Aru (Kota Kinabalu) to Tenom also passes through Beaufort so you can take the train in either direction.

Information

There's a branch of the Hong Kong & Shanghai Banking Corporation in Beaufort which will change travellers' cheques. There is no bank at Sipitang. If you

entered Sabah via the Lawas-Merapok-Sipitang route and missed immigration at Merapok (it's actually about a km beyond Merapok at Sindumin), the nearest immigration office is at Kota Kinabalu.

Places to Stay

There are only a couple of hotels in Beaufort and they're often full. The *Hotel Beaufort* (tel 211911) is clean and safe with good air-con rooms, each with an attached bathroom and many with a TV (often not working). Rooms start from M$42.

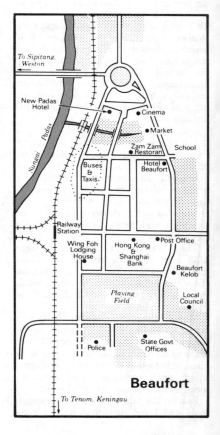

Beaufort

The *New Padas Hotel* (tel 211441) has reasonable rooms from M$18 for a single and M$24 for a double. The people running the place are helpful and provide towels and soap.

Places to Eat

For good food, try *Restoran Zam Zam*, near the market. It's spacious, has friendly staff and prices are reasonable. Another popular restaurant is under the Beaufort Hotel. The food is not bad but it's definitely overpriced. Otherwise, there are numerous Chinese coffee shops around town offering the standard rice or mee dishes.

Getting There & Away

Train Sabah is the only place in East Malaysia where you will find railways and even here there's only one line. The 154-km track connects Tenom to KK (Tanjung Aru) via Beaufort. For a while, the service between Beaufort and KK was discontinued, but now it's possible, though not recommended, to take the train right through.

It's a spectacular trip between Beaufort and Tenom, where the train follows the Padas River through steamy jungle. At times the dense jungle forms a bridge over the narrow track. The ride from Beaufort to KK is not so exciting and takes too long for the trip to be convenient or worthwhile.

There are two types of passenger trains available. The railcars are the best for comfort, speed and views, and the ordinary diesel trains are the ones to take if you want a slower, more colourful journey packed in with the local people and their produce.

The railcar is a single car with a single class which has been designated '1st class' and therefore gets a 1st-class price. The number of people travelling on it often exceeds the number of seats available and if there are children on board, it can be quite crowded because generally children are not given seats. You'll probably be squashed beside one or two extra bodies for at least part of the way. The schedule is:

Beaufort-Tenom
diesel train	Mon-Sat 10.50 am, 1.55 pm
	Sun 6.45 am, 2.30 pm
rail car	Mon-Sat 8.25 am
	Sun 9.10 am, 3.40 pm

Tenom-Beaufort
diesel train	Mon-Sat 7.30 am, 1.40 pm
	Sun 7.55 am, 3.05 pm
rail car	Mon-Sat 3.10 pm
	Sun 7.20 am, 1.55 pm

Between Beaufort and Tenom the 1st-class fare is $8.35, plus 50 sen booking fee, and the economy fare is M$2.75. The trip takes 1½ to two hours. From Tenom through to KK, trains depart daily at 7 am and the fare is M$7.50. In the reverse direction, trains depart KK at 8 am daily.

Road There is a good road all the way from KK to Beaufort and there are regular bus services between the two towns; the fare is M$7. Elsewhere there are minibuses and share-taxis. These leave every morning for Papar/Kota Kinabalu. If you're heading for Labuan take a minibus or taxi (M$8) to Mempakol. If you're heading for Merapok and Lawas (M$7) take a taxi or minibus to Sipitang.

There's no problem in finding transport as the drivers will approach you. Drivers who are heading for Mempakol will be shouting 'Labuan'. They connect with the launch to Labuan (M$7). If you're heading for Lawas you'll be able to get a taxi (M$3) or a van (M$2) to Merapok from Sipitang in time to connect with a boat to Lawas.

AROUND BEAUFORT

Tiga Island

Off coastal Kuala Penyu, which sits on a peninsula, is Tiga Island. There is a good beach and a government rest house. Expensive boat charters are available.

Labuan Island

Off the coast from Menumbok, Labuan is the departure point for one of the ways of getting to Brunei. Labuan is a Federal Territory and is governed directly from Kuala Lumpur. The island acts as a duty-free centre and as such attracts many of Brunei's population, as well as Malaysians, for quick shopping sprees.

Victoria is the main town and it is the place where the ferries tie in. There really isn't anything to see unless you're into the bloody Sunday cockfights, though there are some nice beaches. Labuan is the place where the Japanese forces in north Borneo surrendered at the end of WW II. There's an appropriate memorial on the island.

Places to Stay Accommodation is expensive. The cheapest hotel on the island is the *Kim Soon Lee Hotel* (tel 42544) on Jalan Okk Awang Besar. Rooms start at M$50. Slightly more expensive is the *Victoria Hotel* (tel 42411) on Jalan Tun Mustapha, where prices start from M$70.

The *Hotel Emas-Labuan* (tel 413966), on Jalan Muhibbah, has about 40 rooms ranging in price from M$90 to M$125. Also on Jalan Muhibbah, is the *Hotel Apollo* (tel 412822). The top of the range is the *Hotel Labuan* (tel 421311) on Jalan Merdeka, where rooms prices start from M$160.

Getting There & Away The government car ferry from Menumbok to Labuan costs M$5.30 and there are daily departures at 10.30 am and 4 pm. In the other direction, ferries depart Labuan at 8 am and 1 pm daily. Students pay about M$2.50. Power boats leave more frequently, take less time and charge M$8 to M$10.

From Brunei to Labuan, there are daily express-boat departures at 8 am and 2 pm. The trip takes an hour and 45 minutes and costs B$15 (or M$15 going the other way). See the Brunei section for more details. There is also a daily hovermarine service at 8 am which costs B$18. From Menumbok, you can get minibuses to Beaufort for M$7, or right through to KK for M$14.

From Sarawak, boats depart Lawas for Labuan Tuesdays and Saturdays at 7 am, and return the same day at 12 noon.

TENOM

Tenom is the home of the friendly Murut people, most of whom are farmers. Soyabeans, maize and a variety of vegetables are grown in this fertile area and there are several cocoa plantations.

It's a very pleasant rural town, with much more old world charm than Beaufort, and is also the railhead on the line from Tanjung Aru (KK).

But, although it has that perennial attraction of a 'backdrop of forested mountains' (as the tourist literature is fond of reminding you), there's absolutely nothing to do unless you enjoy a game of pool. If you do then you're in luck because there's an excellent pool hall, but the game is very popular with locals so get there early and chalk your initials up if you want a game before it closes.

Information

Tenom is a compact little place and it's very easy to find your way around. There is a taxi stand in town but many taxis just wait around the train station. There's no bus station, the minibuses just cruise around the block until they've filled all the seats.

There's an immigration office at Tenom but it no longer deals with visa extensions and the officer I saw was not interested in the fact that I had missed the Sabah entry checkpoint at Merapok. If you need to extend your visa, wait until you reach KK.

Murut Longhouses

There are some interesting longhouses around Tenom but they can be a bit difficult to reach. The best longhouses are along the Padas River towards Sarawak, as far as Tomani and beyond.

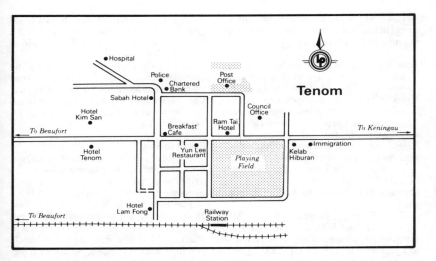

To Beaufort

To Keningau

To Beaufort

Tenom

Hospital

Police

Chartered Bank

Sabah Hotel

Hotel Kim San

Hotel Tenom

Post Office

Council Office

Breakfast Cafe

Ram Tai Hotel

Yun Lee Restaurant

Playing Field

Immigration

Kelab Hiburan

Hotel Lam Fong

Railway Station

There are buses going to Tomani for around M$4 or you may be able to get a boat there.

Cocoa Research Centre

This centre is run by an Australian guy and is about 10 km out of Tenom. Strangely enough, the main reason for visiting the plantation is to see their beautiful orchids which attract tourists from all around the valley. You can get a minibus to drop you there but it's easier to hitch.

Places to Stay

If you can get in, the *Government Rest House* is good value at M$12. Otherwise, one of the cheapest hotels in Tenom is the *Hotel Sym Nam Tai* on Jalan Keningau. It's very central and has reasonable single rooms for M$15 and doubles for M$20. *Hotel Nam Fong* and *Hotel Sabah* have fan-cooled rooms starting from M$20.

Hotel Kim San has moved to the area opposite the Hotel Tenom. Rooms are clean, cost M$25 and the owner is a friendly Chinese man. *Hotel Tenom* on Jalan Tun Datu Mustapha, has rooms

with air-con and attached bathroom for M$42.

Places to Eat

Probably the best place to eat is the *Yun Lee Restaurant*, Jalan Tun Datu Mustapha. It isn't the cheapest place to eat in Tenom, but it does have the best menu, the food is excellent and the staff are very friendly. You'll find everything from sweet & sour pork to nasi goreng.

Downstairs in the *Sabah Hotel* there's a good and very reasonably priced Muslim restaurant serving excellent Indian-style food.

Nearly all the Chinese restaurants have bread and cakes if you can't face mee with fish balls for breakfast.

Getting There & Away

Train Although the railway line goes as far as Melalap, which is further up the valley, Tenom is the railhead as far as passenger trains are concerned. The journey down to Beaufort is the most spectacular part of the journey and recommended if you've come from Tambunan or Keningau and are on your way to Sarawak or Brunei.

The train schedule and fares can be found in the Beaufort section. This service is unlikely to survive much longer.

Road The only place to go by road from Tenom is up the valley to Keningau and Tambunan. The ride through the scenic Crocker Range is quite spectacular.

Minibus owners often employ young boys to run around town shouting destinations at the top of their voices. They'll soon find you and point to their bus. As buses move continuously through town, you may find yourself and a couple of other would-be passengers, running through the streets to catch up with one.

From Tenom to Keningau it costs M$5 by minibus and M$6 by taxi. There are frequent departures to mid-afternoon and the journey takes about an hour. If you're heading for Kota Kinabalu you can get there easily from Tenom in a morning.

KENINGAU

The provincial capital of the Interior Residency, Keningau is a lumber and agricultural town deep in the heart of Murut country, though it's most unlikely you'll see anyone dressed in traditional tribal wear. Attracted by the prospects of well-paid employment, migrants have flocked there from neighbouring districts and the town's population has doubled since the 1960s.

Sabah tourist brochures rave on about Keningau, and the nearby towns of Tenom and Tambunan, as being popular excursion centres with a fascinating cultural heritage. They're really nothing of the sort. Indeed they're quite dull and uninteresting – and expensive – and it won't be long before you wonder why you went there at all. They're a perfect example of tourist organisations' over-enthusiasm for something which survives only as a fond memory.

Keningau is simply a mini-boom town which is being torn apart to provide new business premises, shops, hotels, adminis-

trative offices and the like. If you enjoy sport there's a large sports complex with a good swimming pool opposite the Hotel Perkasa Keningau.

Other than that, the only worthwhile experience Keningau offers is the journey there over the forested Crocker mountains. Get there soon though, if you want to see any trees because they're logging at an alarming rate.

Places to Stay

Like other boom towns in East Malaysia, accommodation is expensive and the price you pay for a room doesn't necessarily reflect the facilities it offers.

The best value is the *Government Rest House* (tel 31525) which costs M$12 per night if it's not full with Government officials. The *Hotel Hiap Soon* (tel 31541) has nice staff and clean, rooms with air-con from M$30.

The *Tai Wah Hotel* has basic rooms from M$21.50 and for slightly higher prices, so do the *Wing Lee Hotel* and *Hotel Ling Ling*.

Mass Lodging has overpriced rooms from M$40. *Hotel Alisan* and *Hotel Rai* have better, cheaper rooms. The *Hotel Perkasa Keningau* (tel 31044) is the most expensive hotel in town, with 44 air-con rooms from M$75.

Places to Eat

Finding decent food is difficult in Keningau and after 6.30 pm you're lucky if you can find a restaurant open at all. The *Keningau Restoran*, near the post office, is very popular with locals but is often packed with avid TV fans.

The night market, which sets up in front of the post office around 4.30 pm, has reasonably cheap food and soups. The *Mandarin Restaurant* serves good Chinese food, which makes a nice change from the standard greasy fare dished up at the smaller places around town.

Getting There & Away

Share-taxis, minibuses and Land Rovers

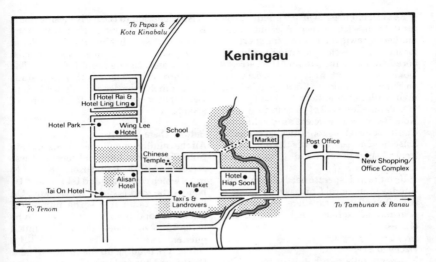

Keningau

are the only transport available and can be found around the central square where the market is. The cheapest way to travel between Keningau and KK is to go by minibus for M$10. The journey takes about 2½ hours. Land Rovers and taxis make the same trip but charge about double the minibus fare.

There are some great views as the road cuts through the spectacular Crocker Range, but it's really rough in parts. Occasionally, you pass small areas devastated by logging, fire or both. The best scenery is between Tambunan and KK.

Keningau-Tenom costs M$4 by minibus and takes about one hour along a good gravel road through forest and rubber plantations. A taxi will cost about M$5. There are also taxis and minibuses to Tambunan and Ranau. From Ranau you can go either to Sandakan or Kinabalu National Park.

KOTA BELUD

The town is the venue of Sabah's largest and most colourful tamu and as such is a magnet for travellers. The tamu takes place every Sunday – get there early.

Tamus are not simply open-air markets where tribal people gather to sell their farm products of fruit and vegetables and to buy manufactured goods from the Chinese and Indian traders. They are also social occasions when news and stories are exchanged.

The tamu at Kota Belud attracts all manner of traders from quasi-medical commercial travellers selling herbal remedies and magic pills to water buffalo owners who haggle all morning over the price of a cow or a calf.

For keen photographers the tamus provides a never-ending procession of colourful characters and situations and, if you're lucky, the Bajau 'cowboys' may turn up on their caparisoned horses looking like mediaeval knights at a tournament.

Unfortunately, those looking for tribal handicrafts will be disappointed. You may have more luck in that department at the Sunday tamu at Sikuati, 23 km from Kudat, which is attended by the Rungus people who live in longhouses in the surrounding area.

Kota Belud itself is just a small, sleepy rural town with a vegetable and meat market; a town where everything except for the pool halls close down very early and bored adolescents roam the streets looking for something to do. Once a week on Sunday it comes to life as people from many miles around flock to the tamu.

Looking a little out of place in downtown Kota Belud, is an efficient air-conditioned camera store selling sophisticated cameras, lenses and accessories. It's the only glass-fronted shop in town and it stocks print and slide film.

If you're in desperate need of cash at the Sunday tamu, local Chinese businessmen will often change travellers' cheques at a poor rate of exchange. Ask in shops and offices.

Places to Stay

There are only two hotels in town. The *Hotel Tai Seng* which has 20 rooms from M$20 upwards and the *Hotel Kota Belud* (tel 976576) which has clean air-con rooms from M$28.

If you can't afford to stay at the hotels you can sleep free at the school near the police station – ask for the school teacher. Your 'bed' will be a table tennis table.

There is also a faint possibility of staying at the *Government Rest House* (tel 67532) which costs M$12 per person per night, but it's officially for government officers only. The police station can be most helpful if you're stuck for accommodation.

Places to Eat

Most of the restaurants, and there are very few, close at the latest by 5.30 pm and unless you've eaten by then you're up for a 'meal' of peanuts, confectionery and beer bought from the stalls on the sports ground side of the central square/market.

Even the restaurant on the ground floor of the *Hotel Kota Belud* closes by 5.30 pm, regardless of how many people are staying in the hotel! They do serve good mee soup but asking for anything else is useless.

An exception to the early closing hours is the popular *Indonesia Restoran*, in the gravel car park behind the Kota Belud Hotel, which does simple dishes like nasi goreng and is open until 8 pm. The standard of hygiene in other food stalls leaves much to be desired. All in all, Kota Belud has very little to offer in terms of good food.

Getting There & Away

All the minibuses and share-taxis operate from the main square and most of these serve the Kota Belud-Kota Kinabalu route which costs M$5 and takes about 1½ hours. The road is sealed all the way. On Sundays – tamu day – the number of minibuses and taxis has to be seen to be believed. On other days it's much quieter.

If you're heading up the coast to Kudat there is one bus daily which departs about 10 am from outside the petrol station, costs M$10 and takes about two to 2½ hours.

If you want to get to Kinabalu National Park then take any of the minibuses or share-taxis which are going to Kota Kinabalu and get off at Tamparuli about halfway there. The trip takes about 1½ hours and costs M$4.

From Tamparuli there are several minibuses and taxis to Ranau every day up to about 2 pm. The taxis cost M$10 to M$12 and the minibuses cost M$4 to M$6 (you have to haggle and play a waiting game for the lower prices).

The journey to the National Park HQ takes about two to 2½ hours along a good sealed road. Tell the driver to drop you off there.

AROUND KOTA BELUD
Mengkabong Water Village

About halfway along the coast from Kota Kinabalu to Kota Belud is the beautiful little Bajau water village of Mengkabong where the houses are built on stilts in the sea. Transport around the village is by canoe or sampan. It's well worth making a

Top: Mosque, Kota Belud, Sabah (ST)
Bottom: Fish market, Kota Belud, Sabah (ST)

Market, Kuala Trengganu (TW)

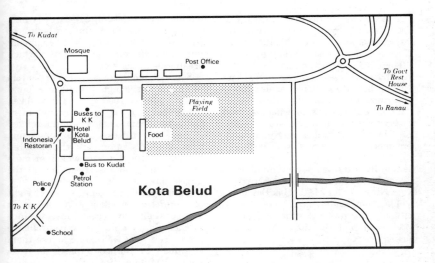

Kota Belud

detour to see this place if you're passing by.

First head for Tuaran and then take local transport from there. There is a tamu held in Tuaran on Sundays which is also worth visiting – you might be able to pick up some local handicrafts. Transport to Tuaran from either Kota Kinabalu or Kota Belud is no problem. From Tuaran it's a short taxi ride to Pantadalit Beach, where there's a *Government Rest House* which costs M$15.

Kudat

Kudat, near the north-eastern tip of Sabah, has some of the best beaches in Sabah. The beaches are definitely for those who want tranquillity and who expect little in terms of facilities; very few people find their way up to this part of Sabah. Unfortunately, the beach at Bak Bak is being transformed into a resort. For unspoilt beauty, the beaches to head for are north of Bak Bak.

The Kudat area is the home of the Rungus people, tribal cousins of the Kadazans. The Rungus people continue to live in their traditional manner. The older women wear black sarongs and colourful, beaded necklaces. On festive occasions, heavy brass bracelets are worn as well. The Rungus tribes produce some excellent, elaborate beadwork and you can sometimes buy their handicrafts at the Sunday tamu held at Sikuati, a town 23 km from Kudat.

More and more Rungus people are building their own houses in preference to living in a traditional longhouse. There are still some interesting longhouses around Kudat and, if you visit one, it's polite to take a few small gifts of food or cigarettes. It's also better to be invited to a longhouse by a local, than to invite yourself – but this is easier said than done.

Places to Stay If you're planning on staying in Kudat there are three main hotels. *Hotel Sunrise* (tel 61517) is the largest and best with 20 rooms and its own good restaurant. Rooms cost from M$29 up to M$57 with air-con and attached bathroom. The *Kudat Hotel* (tel 61600), Little St has air-conditioned rooms from M$30 to M$55 but the more expensive rooms have their own bathroom.

At the bottom of the heap is the *Hasba Hotel* (tel 61959) with rooms, without own bathroom or air-con, from M$16 to M$25. The rooms are airless, hot and dirty.

There is also a *Government Rest House* (tel 61304) with seven rooms at M$12 per person, but the usual warning about 'government workers' only applies.

If you're stuck for somewhere to sleep, it's worth asking if you can stay at one of the Christian churches in Kudat – but remember to leave a reasonable donation.

Getting There & Away Several minibuses a day make the three to four-hour trip from Kota Kinabalu for M$10. Bak Bak beach is 11 km from Kudat and difficult to get to without your own transport – count on M$6 for a taxi out there, M$12 to be picked up!

Kinabalu National Park

Towering 4101 metres (13,455 feet) above the lush tropical jungles of North Borneo and the centrepiece of the vast 767-square-km Kinabalu National Park, Mt Kinabalu is the major attraction in Sabah. It is the highest mountain between the snow-capped peaks of the Himalaya and those of New Guinea and, although 50 km inland, its jagged granite peaks are visible most mornings from many places along the coast.

Yet, despite its height, it is one of the easiest mountains in the world to climb. No special skills or equipment are required. All you need is a little stamina. Given this, you will be rewarded with one of the most memorable experiences of your life. The views – even before you get to the top – are magnificent and the sunsets equally incredible. Where else could you see the rays of the setting sun shining *up* through the clouds below you?

Exhilarating though it undoubtedly is, merely being able to climb to the top of this mountain isn't the only experience which awaits you. Mt Kinabalu is a botanical paradise stocked with a phenomenal number of different plants, many of which are unique to the area.

Some of the more spectacular flowers belonging to the orchid family are found there – almost 1000 species have been discovered so far with many more blooming unnamed among still-unexplored gullies and ridges. There are many unusual rhododendron and the giant red blossoms of the *Rafflesia* which, at more than 70 cm in diameter, are one of the largest flowers in the world.

Even if you don't manage to catch sight of a *Rafflesia* you will certainly see one or more of the many types of insectivorous pitcher plants which grow in profusion there. You may well come across them elsewhere in Borneo – particularly in Gunung Mulu National Park, Sarawak – but there's nowhere else they grow in such numbers.

They come in all manner of elaborate shapes, sizes and colours, although you probably won't be as lucky as the late-19th century botanist, Spencer St John who found one that was 30 cm in diameter. He reported finding a *Nepenthes Rajah* pitcher of this size which contained 2½ litres of watery fluid and a drowned rat!

Most, however, are only large enough to catch unwary insects which are attracted to nectar which the plants secrete, but then find themselves unable to escape up the slippery inner surface of the pitcher. While on your way to the summit, try exploring a few metres in the undergrowth on either side of the trail – you're bound to come across a pitcher plant sooner or later.

From its immense size you might imagine that Mt Kinabalu is the ancient core of the island of Borneo but in fact the mountain is a relatively recent arrival. Its origins go back a mere nine million years to when a solidified core of volcanic rock began swelling up from the depths below, pushing its way through the overlying

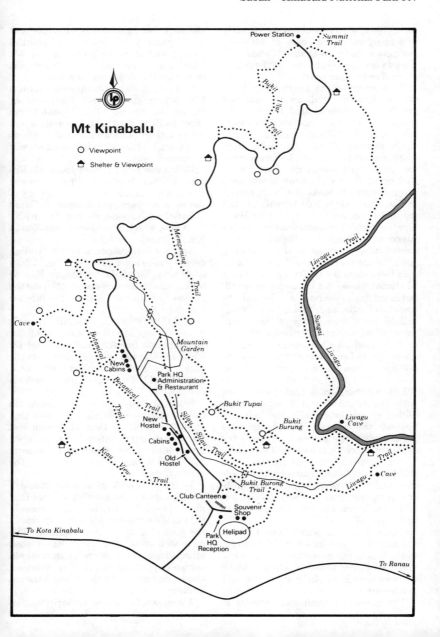

rock. This upward movement is apparently still going on and a team of Japanese geologists have estimated that the mountain continues to grow at the rate of about five mm per year.

On account of its youth, very little erosion has occurred on the exposed granite rock faces around the summit, though the effects of glaciers which used to cover much of Kinabalu can be picked out by the trained eye. The glaciers have disappeared but, at times, ice forms in the rock pools near the summit – it gets pretty cold up there at night-time so you need warm clothing to make the final ascent.

The first recorded ascent of the mountain was made in 1851 by Sir Hugh Low, the British colonial secretary on the island of Labuan. The highest peak is named after him as is the mile-deep 'gully' on the other side of the mountain.

In those days the difficulty of climbing Mt Kinabalu lay not in the ascent itself, but in getting to the base of it through the trackless jungles and finding local porters willing to go there. None of the Dusun (now called Kadazan) tribespeople who accompanied Low had ever climbed the mountain before, believing it to be the dwelling place of the spirits of their dead.

Low was therefore obliged to take along with him a guide armed with a large basket of quartz crystals and teeth to protect the party. The ceremonies performed by the guides to appease the spirits on reaching the summit gradually became more elaborate as time went on so that by the 1920s they had come to include the sacrifice of seven eggs, seven white chickens, loud prayers and gunshots, but in recent times the custom appears to have died out.

These days you won't have to hack through the jungle for several days to get to the foot of the mountain like the early explorers did as there's a sealed road all the way from Kota Kinabalu to the park headquarters.

The accommodation and catering at the park headquarters is excellent and well-organised. It's built in a beautiful setting with a magnificent view of Mt Kinabalu when the clouds are not obscuring the slopes and summits.

You should make advance reservations for accommodation both there and at Poring Hot Springs at the Sabah Parks office in Kota Kinabalu, however, if you arrive without a booking and all the beds are taken, it's highly unlikely that you will be turned away.

Before you go to the park you might like to read a little about what's in store for you on the mountain by purchasing a copy of the national parks publication, *A Guide to Kinabalu National Park* by Susan Kay Jacobson, which is on sale at the office in Kota Kinabalu for M$5.

Another book which is worth reading even if you're not a botanist is *Nepenthes of Mount Kinabalu* by Shigeo Kurata which sells for the same price. (Nepenthes is the botanical name for pitcher plants.)

A M$10 climbing permit is now required for Mt Kinabalu, M$2 for students and free for children under 13. There are also vehicle entry charges to the park, M$5 for a large bus, M$2 for a minibus, M$1 for a car or jeep, 50c for a motorcycle.

Scientists and botanists wanting to collect specimens for research must first apply for a permit on form A1, available at the Sabah parks office. You are then issued with a form A2 permit which costs M$50 and is valid for a single visit to the national park.

When you check in at reception, ask them to screen the slide show later that night. The slides introduce you to some of the plant and animal life you might see in the park and up on the mountain. The man who shows the slides has a good knowledge of the park and often brings in samples of pitcher plants. The slides are shown downstairs in the administration building.

Also downstairs, is an ecologist's office

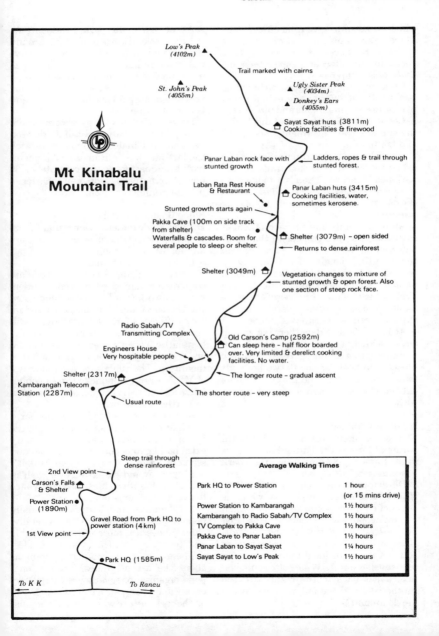

Mt Kinabalu
Mountain Trail

Low's Peak
(4102m)

Trail marked with cairns

St. John's Peak
(4055m)

Ugly Sister Peak
(4034m)

Donkey's Ears
(4055m)

Sayat Sayat huts (3811m)
Cooking facilities & firewood

Panar Laban rock face with
stunted growth

Ladders, ropes & trail through
stunted forest.

Laban Rata Rest House
& Restaurant

Panar Laban huts (3415m)
Cooking facilities, water,
sometimes kerosene.

Stunted growth starts again

Pakka Cave (100m on side track
from shelter)
Waterfalls & cascades. Room for
several people to sleep or shelter.

Shelter (3079m) – open sided

Returns to dense rainforest

Shelter (3049m)

Vegetation changes to mixture of
stunted growth & open forest. Also
one section of steep rock face.

Radio Sabah/TV
Transmitting Complex

Old Carson's Camp (2592m)
Can sleep here – half floor boarded
over. Very limited & derelict cooking
facilities. No water.

Engineers House
Very hospitable people

Shelter (2317m)

The longer route – gradual ascent

Kambarangah Telecom
Station (2287m)

The shorter route – very steep

Usual route

Steep trail through
dense rainforest

2nd View point

Carson's Falls
& Shelter

Power Station
(1890m)

1st View point

Gravel Road from Park HQ to
power station (4 km)

Park HQ (1585m)

To K K

To Ranau

Average Walking Times	
Park HQ to Power Station	1 hour
	(or 15 mins drive)
Power Station to Kambarangah	1½ hours
Kambarangah to Radio Sabah/TV Complex	1½ hours
TV Complex to Pakka Cave	1½ hours
Pakka Cave to Panar Laban	1½ hours
Panar Laban to Sayat Sayat	1¼ hours
Sayat Sayat to Low's Peak	1½ hours

which is open during normal office hours. There are also some noticeboards displaying up to date prices of accommodation, porter and guide fees and some interesting newspaper clippings.

Upstairs in the administration building, is a small but informative exhibition of plants, insects, mammals and birds in the national park. There's a map displaying the summit trail, overnight huts, caves and landmarks.

It's well worth spending a day or two exploring the well-marked trails around park headquarters. There's a rough map available at the reception desk which shows all the trails and points of interest.

All of the trails link up with others at some stage, so you can spend the whole day walking at a leisurely pace through the beautiful jungle. Some interesting plants and, if you're lucky, the occasional animal can be seen along the Liwagu Trail, which follows the river of the same name. When it rains, watch out for slippery paths and armies of leeches.

At 11.15 am each day, there is a guided walk which starts from the main administration building (near the new hostel) and lasts for one to two hours. It follows an easy path and the guide points out flowers, plants and insects along the way.

Poring Hot Springs

The other main feature of Kinabalu National Park is the Poring Hot Springs near Ranau, 43 km from the park headquarters.

Developed by the Japanese during WW II, the steaming, sulphurous water is channelled into pools and tubs which attract people who go there to relax tired muscles after the trek to the summit. Each pool has hot and cold water taps so you can mix your ideal temperature. As one traveller put it, 'Where else could you take a hot bath in the night with the southern stars above and the sounds of the jungle around?'

As at Kinabalu park headquarters, there are several km of forest trails around the springs which lead to some attractive waterfalls and dark caves. You can swim in the pool at the base of one waterfall, a 35-minute walk. There's also a swimming pool set among gardens, flowers, trees and hordes of butterflies.

However, if you want to relax in the hot springs in the late afternoon of the day you descend Mt Kinabalu, you need to catch the last minibus to Ranau which passes park headquarters at approximately 2.30 pm. Alternatively, you can charter a private minibus or hitch.

Hiring Guides & Porters

Hiring a guide (at least from Panar Laban to the summit) is supposedly compulsory although a lot of people get away without one. Porters are optional.

Neither the guides nor the porters are employees of the national park organisation, but they work closely together and when you book accommodation at the national parks office the form you are handed will specify that you have 'requested' a guide to stand by at the park headquarters at 7 am on the day you intend to climb the mountain. The guide's fee is a minimum of M$25 per day (for one to three people), M$28 for four to six people, M$30 for seven to 12 (the maximum).

A porter's fee is M$25 per day for a maximum load of 11 kg (24 lbs) up to the Panar Laban Huts and M$1 for every extra half kg (one pound). For the second segment up to the Sayat-Sayat huts it's M$28 per day and M$1.20 for every half kg over 11 kg. It's advisable to pay in advance to avoid arguments later.

Local guides and porters are usually members of the Kadazan tribe. Generally, older guides are more efficient, reliable and knowledgeable than younger guides.

There are many conflicting opinions about the use of guides. The national parks organisation says they're compulsory because climbers can 'easily lose their way on the rock surface when the fog and mist start covering the upper part of the mountain', which is probably true if you've never climbed mountains before.

Another theory is that in making it compulsory to hire a guide, the chances of people stealing pitcher plants and smuggling them out of the country are drastically reduced.

They've installed a gate at the power station, manned to keep people from going without guides, but if you start early you pass the gate before the guard gets on duty. It's an expensive nuisance if you can't share the cost of a guide with others.

The best compromise you can make is to tell the Sabah parks office that you intend to share a guide with other people when you get there – this is no problem. Alternatively, try tagging on to the end of a group as they pass the gate with their guide, then break away and climb on your own.

Booking Accommodation

Overnight accommodation is provided at the park headquarters itself on the Ranau road, at Poring Hot Springs, in the new rest house on the mountain and in mountain huts at 3360 metres (11,200 feet) and at 3750 metres (12,500 feet) on the summit trail.

Try to book as far in advance as possible (at least several days to a week) and note that on weekends, school and public holidays all the accommodation may be taken up.

You can, if you like, make your reservations by post or phone, but they will not be confirmed until fully paid for. The postal address is Sabah Parks (Reservations), PO Box 626, Kota Kinabalu, Sabah. In Kota Kinabalu you can reach the reservation clerk at (tel 211585) and the administrative clerk on (tel 211652).

Most travellers, however, make their reservations by calling at the Sabah parks office, Jalan Tun Fuad Stephens, which is round the corner from the tourist office on the seafront in Kota Kinabalu.

The office is open Monday through Thursday from 8 am to 12.45 pm and 2 to 4.15 pm; on Fridays from 8 to 11.30 am and 2 to 4.15 pm, and on Saturdays from 8 am to 12.45 pm.

In making up your mind on how long you want to stay at Mt Kinabalu you should bear in mind that the weather on the mountain is very unpredictable. You can be in bright sunshine one minute and soaked to the skin the next. The first two hours after dawn is the most likely time to catch the summit free of clouds. You might be lucky and get a clear dawn the first morning you go to the summit, but if you don't or it's raining you'll see absolutely nothing and will feel bitterly disappointed at having to go back down. If at all possible, book for four nights with two of them in the mountain huts.

You can shorten your walk by taking a truck up to the power station, saving about 500 metres of vertical climb. It costs M$20 to hire the entire vehicle.

One fit traveller wrote that he walked from the park headquarters to the summit and back down again in one day – but I wouldn't recommend it as you get to the top in the afternoon when it's likely to be cloudy. In any case Mt Kinabalu is quite high enough for altitude sickness problems to occur; some acclimatisation is worthwhile.

Places to Stay & Eat

Park Headquarters There's a variety of excellent accommodation at the park headquarters. The cheapest place to stay is the *Old Hostel* which costs M$6 per person, or M$3 for students with official ID.

The *New Hostel* costs an extra ringgit, M$8 for non-students and M$4 for students. Both hostels are clean and comfortable, have cooking facilities and a dining area with an open fireplace. Blankets and pillows are provided free of charge. In the early hours of the morning, you get a brilliant view of Mt Kinabalu from the balcony of the New Hostel.

The rest of the accommodation at park headquarters is very expensive. The twin-bed cabins are M$100 and annexes for up to four people are M$200. There are two-bedroom chalets which can sleep up to six people and they cost M$200 per night. Then there are the deluxe cabins, single storey for five people and double storey for seven people, costing M$200 and M$300 respectively.

Top of the range, is the *Kinabalu Lodge* where one unit costs M$360 per night and sleeps eight people. The *Hotel Perkasa Kundasang* (tel 79511) has 74 rooms starting from M$70.

There are two places where you can buy meals at park headquarters. The cheaper and more popular of the two is the *Club Canteen*, down below reception, which offers Malay, Chinese and western food at reasonable prices. There's also a small shop which sells a limited range of tinned foods, chocolate, beer, spirits, cigarettes, T-shirts, bread, eggs and margarine.

The other restaurant is in the main administration building just past the hostels. It's more expensive than the Club Canteen, though the food is quite good.

Valuables can be deposited in the safe at reception and any excess baggage can be stored there until you return from the mountain. A small selection of crafts and books is also available. Prices compare well with those elsewhere.

On the Mountain Although the information sheet put out by the Sabah National Parks says otherwise, there are no raincoats available for hire. Being soaked to the skin in a cold mountain hut at 3300 metres (11,000 feet) is no joke so *bring rain gear with you*.

On your way up to the summit you will have to stay overnight at one of the mountain huts or the new *Laban Rata Rest House* at Panar Laban which costs M$25 per person in four-bed rooms. It's possible to sleep for free in the cave at 3150 metres (10,500 feet), but you'd have to carry your own bedding.

The mountain huts are equipped with wooden bunks and mattresses, kerosene stoves, cooking facilities and some cooking utensils. You can hire sleeping bags for M$2, so there's no point in lugging your own all the way to the top of the mountain. Take a torch and your own toilet paper. Don't expect a warm Swiss-type chalet with a blazing fire at these huts. They're just aluminium sheds with the absolute minimum of facilities.

The first hut is at 3240 metres (10,800 feet) and has 20 bunks. There are two huts at 3300 metres (11,000 feet), one with 10 bunks at Panar Laban and the other with 40 bunks at Gunting Lagadan. The hut at Sayat-Sayat 3750 metres (12,500 feet) has 10 bunks.

A bed in any of the mountain huts costs M$4 per person, M$1 for students and, if the huts are full, M$1 for anyone sleeping on the floor.

Sayat-Sayat is the more popular of the mountain huts since it's only 1½ hours from the summit, whereas Panar Laban is about 2¾ hours from the top. If you stay overnight in the Sayat-Sayat hut, you don't have to get up in the middle of the night in order to reach the summit by dawn.

On the other hand, many people not used to climbing may find they've had enough for one day by the time they reach Panar Laban. Possibly the extra effort on the first day is worth the reward of a slightly easier day on the next.

As far as sleep is concerned, it doesn't make much difference where you stay; unless you've spent a lot of time in the mountains recently, you'll probably sleep quite fitfully – the air is quite thin up there. It's *very* cold in the early mornings, so take warm clothing with you!

Poring Hot Springs The *Poring Hostel* costs M$8 per person (less for students) and blankets and pillows are provided free of charge. Each open-sided hut contains eight beds and there is a clean, spacious kitchen with gas cookers (plates, cups, etc can be borrowed). There's a campground which costs M\$2 per night. Pillows and blankets can be hired for 50 sen each.

There are more expensive cabins; the *Poring New Cabin* costs M\$80 per night and has two bedrooms for four people, while the *Poring Old Cabin* costs M\$100 per night with three bedrooms for up to six people.

There are cooking facilities at Poring with firewood provided, but you should take your own food as there's only one small, expensive shop outside the Park. Get your food in Ranau.

Getting There & Away

From Kota Kinabalu There are several minibuses daily from KK to Ranau which depart up to about 1 pm. The trip as far as Park HQ takes about two hours and the fare varies from M\$5 to M\$8 depending on whose minibus you take. You can get tickets for M\$5 at the ticket office next to the long local bus stop, on Jalan Balai Polis.

You can also get a Land Rover from KK to the Park HQ for about M\$8. The Land Rovers leave around 7 am from behind the local bus stop on Jalan Balai Polis.

From Kota Belud/Tamparuli Tamparuli is where the road up the coast to Kudat branches for Kota Belud and Ranau. If you've been visiting Mengkabong Water Village or Kota Belud and are heading for Kinabalu National Park, then first go to Tamparuli.

From Tamparuli there are several minibuses and share-taxis daily to Ranau which, like the ones from KK, pass right by the Park HQ. The minibuses cost about M\$4 and a taxi will cost you at least double. The journey to the park headquarters takes about two hours.

If you want to get from the park headquarters to Ranau, wait at the side of the main road for a minibus going to Ranau or Sandakan (about M\$3), or hitch. There is a minibus to Ranau which passes HQ around 8 am and one heading for Sandakan which passes HQ between 8.30 and 9 am. There are other minibuses which pass Kinabalu National Park on their way to Ranau, but the last one goes by before 2 pm.

Ranau-Poring Hot Springs On weekends it's easy and cheap to get to the hot springs from Ranau. Drivers in pick-ups cruise round the blocks shouting, 'Poring, Poring!'. The price is more or less fixed at M\$3 per person and the transport leaves when it's full (which doesn't take long, as many Ranau people go there for the afternoon and return in the evening).

On weekdays it isn't quite so easy, especially if you arrive in Ranau during the afternoon. If this happens you'll have to ask around the cafes and shops to see if anyone is going there and you can share the cost.

Taxis *are* available – and the drivers will approach you muttering, 'charter, charter', but they will ask a high price for taking you. If you're not willing to pay this price (about M\$15) then you'll have to stay in Ranau overnight and try again the next morning when your chances of reasonably priced transport are much better. The road to Poring is a dead-end so hitching a ride is difficult.

Chartered Transport If you're part of a large group and are able to fill a Land Rover (up to 12 people) or a 28-seater minibus then you can charter vehicles from Kota Kinabalu to the national park or the hot springs at competitive prices.

Land Rovers and minibuses depart KK for the national park between 7 and 8 am and the national park for KK around 1 pm. You can charter a Land Rover for about M\$20.

National Park-Kota Kinabalu If you're heading back towards KK, minibuses pass the park headquarters around 8 am and 12 noon to 1 pm daily. Stand by the side of the main road and wave them down. The fare to KK is around M\$5. If you can't be bothered to wait, hitching is quite easy.

National Park-Sandakan Minibuses leave KK for Sandakan every 1½ to two hours from about 7 am to 12 noon, and pass by the national park HQ approximately two hours later. Ask the people at the HQ reception desk what time they think the next minibus will pass, then just stand by the side of the main road and wave them down. They'll fit you in even if there are no seats (people always get off at Ranau so you'll have a seat from there if it's 'full').

The fare to Sandakan is M$27 in a minibus and the journey takes about seven hours. You can also get Land Rovers from KK for M$35. In bad weather the road disintegrates until you get within sight of Sandakan. Along the way you'll be treated to the spectacle of devastated jungle landscapes raped to oblivion by the logging concerns.

RANAU

Ranau is just a small provincial town half way between Kota Kinabalu and Sandakan. Nothing much ever happens yet it has some remarkably friendly people. We were offered unrequested discounts on food we bought at a Chinese store, followed by an offer of free accommodation for the night and, at a cafe nearby, the owner fell over backwards to make sure we were perfectly satisfied with what we ate there. In the morning he refused to accept payment for the breakfast we had.

Few travellers stay overnight since the big attraction is Poring Hot Springs about 18 km north of the town. If you arrive late in the afternoon during the week, however, you may be forced to stay overnight, as the only transport available to Poring would be chartered taxis which are far from cheap. Although it's usually quiet, Ranau does have a very colourful and busy tamu on the first of each month.

Places to Stay

The *Ranau Hotel* is the first place you will see when you enter the town opposite the petrol stations. Rooms start at M$23 for a single without air-con.

There is also a *Government Rest House* (tel 75534) which costs M$12 per person for rooms with attached bathroom and air-con. Very friendly people, but it's a little way from the centre.

People have been known to stay at the Catholic church which has one guest room, but it's not really for travellers. If you do stay there, make sure you offer a donation to the priest.

The most expensive hotel in Ranau is the *Mt Kinabalu Perkasa Hotel*, Kundasang, which has 74 rooms ranging in price from M$71 to M$200.

Places to Eat

Probably the best place to eat is the Chinese restaurant around the corner from the Ranau Hotel on the top side of the first block. The food is good, the menu varied and prices very reasonable.

The *Leang Leang Restaurant* is also very good and there are at least half a

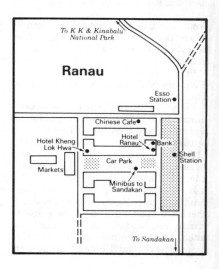

dozen others, but most close early – there simply isn't the clientele.

Getting There & Away

To Poring Hot Springs On weekends there's no problem getting to Poring, as pick-ups cruise round the blocks with their drivers shouting the word you want to hear. They cost M$3 per person and go when full. You may also be able to get to Poring for this price in the early mornings on weekdays, but usually you will have to ask around the cafes and small stores for a lift or hire a taxi (available anytime) for around M$15.

To Kota Kinabalu Taxis and minibuses depart daily up to about 2 pm, cost M$7 to M$10 and take about three hours.

To Sandakan Minibuses leave Ranau for Sandakan around 7.30 am, cost M$20 to M$25 and take about seven hours. If you get there later in the day, you can take one of the minibuses which travel between KK and Sandakan every morning. The last minibus to Sandakan leaves Ranau around 2.30 pm and, even if there are no spare seats, it's unlikely that they'll refuse to take you.

Sandakan

The former capital city of Sabah, Sandakan, is today a major commercial centre where the products of the interior – rattan, timber, rubber, copra, palm oil and even birds' nests from the Gomantong Caves – are brought to be loaded onto boats for export.

The city lies at the entrance to a huge bay and its docks sprawl along the waterfront for many miles. The bay itself is dotted with islands some of them with excellent beaches. There is always the hustle and bustle of boats, large and small.

Outside the city, at Sepilok, is one of the world's three orang-utan sanctuaries. There's another one in Sumatra, west of Medan, and one in Semonggok, Sarawak. The Sepilok sanctuary is well worth visiting.

There's also the Gomantong Caves across the other side of the bay, where edible birds' nests are collected for that famous Chinese delicacy, and offshore there's one of the world's few turtle sanctuaries where giant turtles come to lay their eggs. Unfortunately, both these attractions are more or less inaccessible unless you have plenty of money to spend or are part of a large group which can charter its own transport.

Orientation

The centre of Sandakan is very compact and consists of three main blocks built between the seafront and the wooded hills on which the Governor's residence sits. In these blocks, you'll find many of the hotels and restaurants, banks, post office, MAS office, the local bus stand and the long-distance minibus stands.

The minibus stands are on the waterfront, round the back of the Mayfair Hotel and near the market and the local bus stand.

West of the main area of the city off to one side or the other of Jalan Leila, the main road, lie other hotels and restaurants. The immigration office is where the footbridge crosses the road. Considerably further along this road is the national parks organisation.

All the main truck routes into and out of Sandakan start from the large roundabout at the junction of Jalan Tiga/ Jalan Leila and Jalan Utara. Jalan Utara is a dual carriageway which heads north-west out of the city and passes the airport turn-off.

Information

If you want to cash travellers' cheques, change them at the Hong Kong & Shanghai Banking Corporation rather than at the Chartered Bank where they

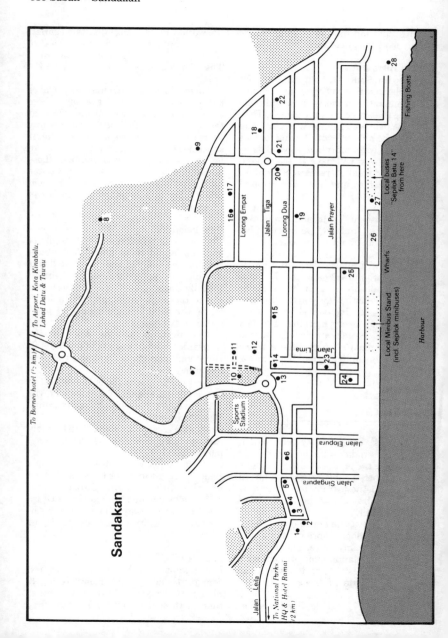

Sandakan

1	Sandakan Community Centre
2	Buses to KK, Tawau, Lahad, Datu, Semporna
3	Immigration
4	Federal Hotel
5	Hotel New Sabah
6	Hotel Gaya
7	Police
8	Istana
9	Mosque
10	Post Office
11	Town Hall
12	MAS
13	Hong Kong & Shanghai Bank
14	Chartered Bank
15	Hotel Paris
16	Hotel London
17	Cosmo Hotel
18	Emas Seafood Restoran
19	Malaysia Hotel
20	Superman Ice Cream Parlour
21	Merlin Hotel
22	Hotel Hung Wing
23	Hotel Nak & Apple Fast Food
24	Port Authority
25	Mayfair Hotel
26	Market
27	Shell Station
28	Shopping Complex

charge commission. Most of the banks are around the intersection of Jalan Tiga and Jalan Pelabohan. Banking hours are from 10 am to 3 pm Monday to Friday and from 9.30 to 11 am on Saturdays.

If you intend to visit the orang-utan sanctuary at Sepilok, you're supposed to get a permission slip first, but when you get there no one asks for it. You'll save much time and energy by going to Sepilok without bothering about the permission slip.

The national parks office (Pejabat Taman Negara) (tel 42188) is a 30 sen ride out of town along Jalan Leila – ask to be dropped at the Kapitol Cinema (Punggung Kapitol) or the Hotel Ramai. In the new block next to the Hotel Ramai, look for the 'SKE Carpet House'. Above this on the 1st floor is the national parks office; there are no signposts.

This office is also the place to get permission to visit the turtle sanctuary if you're intending to go there, but refer to the info on getting to the island before you trail up to this office.

The immigration office is next door to the Sandakan community centre, Jalan Leila, where the footbridge crosses the road. This is also the area where long-distance buses for Tawau, Ranau, KK and Lahad Datu leave from. The MAS office (tel 42211), on the ground floor, Rural District Council Building, Jalan Tiga, is often very busy.

Waterfront

The waterfront at Sandakan, with its motley collection of fishing boats, barges, ferries and ocean-going container ships as well as the vegetable and fish markets, is worth wandering around for a morning or afternoon, but apart from this there isn't a great deal to see in Sandakan itself.

War Memorial

There's an Australian War Memorial between Sandakan and Sepilok which was built lest we forget the 'death march' of WW II, when thousands of soldiers were forced to march from the prison camp in Sandakan to their deaths in Ranau.

Orang-Utan Sanctuary

Located at Sepilok, about 25 km from Sandakan, this is one of only three orang-utan sanctuaries in the world. It was established in 1964 and now covers 4000 hectares.

Apes are taken there to be rehabilitated to forest life and so far the centre has handled about 80 of them. Only about 20 still return regularly to be fed. It's unlikely you'll see anywhere near this number at feeding time – three or four is a more likely number.

The apes are fed from a platform in the middle of the forest about 30-minutes walk from the centre. Feeding time is 10.30 am and 2.30 pm daily.

The orang-utans who turn up for the

two daily feedings are usually six to eight-year olds. They're fed milk and bananas day after day, year after year, until finally, they decide it's time to venture into the forest to look for their own food.

Of the ones which have returned to the wild, females often come back to the feeding platforms when they're pregnant and stay near the sanctuary centre until they've given birth, after which time they go back to the forest.

Entrance to the sanctuary is free, although officially you need a permission slip to visit the sanctuary from the national forests office in Sandakan.

Visiting hours are Monday through Thursday from 10 am to 12 noon and 3 to 4.15 pm; on Friday from 10 to 11.10 am and 2.30 to 4.15 pm; and on Saturday and Sunday from 10 am to 12 noon and 2 to 4.15 pm.

No one seems to adhere strictly to the official visiting hours; the sanctuary remains open all day, though most of the staff may disappear during lunch hours.

You are allowed to wander through the forest at your own pace and risk. Although the orang-utans are not aggressive animals, the proboscis monkeys, who live in the mangrove swamps, have been known to attack humans. It's not uncommon to see snakes and lizards in the forest.

Don't be in so much of a hurry to see the orang-utans that you miss the forest and if it's been raining watch out for leeches! If you're taking photographs you'll need to have ASA 400 film available (it's quite dark in the forest).

The reserve also has a Nature Education Centre which is open to the public. Some information is displayed about the animals of the reserve and, if you ask, they may show you the free slide show which is quite interesting. There are some information pamphlets available at the reception desk at the entrance to the reserve.

Peace Corps and CUSO volunteers have helped to establish a small museum as well as a library and film theatre. They

have also set up a self-guided nature trail and longer trails, one leading to a good spot for swimming.

To get to the centre, take the service bus marked 'Sepilok Batu 14' from the local bus stand next to the central market on the waterfront. The fare is M$1.20 and the journey takes about 45 minutes. The 9.20 am bus gets you to the sanctuary in time for the first feeding. This is one of the only buses which takes you right up to the gate. Buses go every hour.

Don't miss this place; it's well worth a visit.

Orangutan

Turtle Sanctuary

The turtle sanctuary comprises three small islands which lie 32 km north of Sandakan. Pulau Selingan, Pulau Bakungan Kecil and Pulau Gulisan are visited by marine turtles who come ashore to lay their eggs, mostly between the months of September and November each year.

The green turtle is a strong, slow-moving creature, commonly found on Pulau Selingan and Pulau Bakungan Kecil. It weighs between 50 and 90 kg and lays around 180 eggs. The hawksbill turtle lays it's eggs on Pulau Gulisan. It's much smaller than the green turtle, weighing between 25 and 55 kg.

Places to Stay There is a *Government Rest House* on Pulau Selingan which costs M$120 for four-bed accommodation with own bathroom and cooking facilities.

Alternatively, you can stay in a cabin without cooking facilities for about M$20 per person per night.

Enquire at the district office in Sandakan. You may be allowed to camp on the islands, but you would have to get permission from the national parks people first.

Getting There & Away Unfortunately, getting out to the islands is not an easy task. There are no regular services, so you'll probably have to charter an expensive boat to take you there. If you can manage to round up a few people who also want to visit the sanctuary, it's well worth chartering a boat.

Gomantong Caves

These caves are across the other side of the bay from Sandakan and about 20 km inland. They are famous as a source of swiftlets' nests, which are raw material for that famous Chinese delicacy, birds' nest soup.

You can watch the nests being collected from the roof of the cave, as they are at Niah in Sarawak, by men climbing long, precariously placed bamboo poles.

The problem is getting there. Travel agencies will arrange a trip, but their costs are high and outside the range of most travellers' budgets.

One way of doing it more cheaply would be to enquire at a place where you see the nests on sale or being unloaded and ask if you can go along on the next trip over there. If you haven't the time to do this or draw a blank on enquiries wait until you get to Niah Caves.

This is another of the 'attractions' of Sabah where the tourist literature neglects to mention the high costs and difficulty in getting there.

Places to Stay – bottom end

It's difficult to find a reasonable, cheap hotel in Sandakan. Many are overpriced and very poor value. One of the better places is the *Hung Wing Hotel* (tel 218855) on Jalan Tiga, towards the mosque. It's a middle-range hotel with some cheaper rooms which are great value. Generally, the higher the floor, the cheaper the room. If you're willing to climb to the 5th or 6th floor, you'll find clean, spacious rooms with attached bathroom and fan for M$15 to M$20. Air-con rooms range from M$30 to M$60 but most people are given what seems to be an automatic discount of about 25%.

Also on Jalan Tiga, is the *Hotel Paris* (tel 218488) which has clean rooms from M$21. Further up the street at 51 Jalan Tiga, you'll find good rooms from M$40 at the *Kin Nam Sing Hotel*.

The *Mayfair Hotel* is on 24 Jalan Prayer and has 12 rooms from M$32 to M$42, but is often full as it's very close to the minibus stand.

There's also the *London Hotel* (tel 216366), on Lorong Empat, which has rooms ranging from M$30 to M$40.

You can still stay at the Catholic school, 10 minutes out of town, but you have to sleep on the floor. A taxi to the school shouldn't cost more than M$2.

Places to Stay – middle

The middle-range hotels are all similar in standard and their cheaper rooms go quickly. The *Federal Hotel* (tel 219611) on Jalan Tiga has rooms with air-con and own bathroom from M$43 (4th floor) to M$58 (2nd floor). No rooms are available on the 1st floor.

The *Gaya Hotel* (tel 212292), 9-11 Jalan Tiga has good rooms from M$44. The *New Sabah Inn* (tel 218711) at 18 Jalan Singapura is popular and clean with rooms from M$48. All rooms are air-conditioned and have an attached bathroom.

There's also the *Malaysia Hotel* (tel 42277) at 32 Lorong Dua which has rooms from M$38.

Places to Stay – top end

The *Sabah Hotel* (tel 213299) at Mile 1, Jalan Utara is on the hill out of town and has a considerable amount of old world charm. All 28 rooms have air-con and cost from M$160. There is an Indonesian and a Chinese restaurant.

In the centre of town, there's the *Nak Hotel* (tel 216988) on Jalan Pelabohan with rooms from M$100. The *Hotel Hsiang Garden* (tel 43191) has 45 rooms with air-con and prices starting from M$100.

Places to Eat

Eating in Sandakan depends on what you want to pay. The town is full of cheap Chinese restaurants and coffee houses serving the standard rice or noodles with fried vegetables, but none of them are worth recommending.

If you'd like a break from this sort of high-carbohydrate fodder then go to the *Silver Star Ice Cream & Cafe* where, in the evenings, you can buy satay at 30 sen per stick with hot peanut sauce. It's a friendly place and popular with local people. They also have ice-cold beer!

The *Emas Seafood Restaurant* on Jalan Tiga, near the town hall, has good Chinese food at reasonable prices. The *Happy Restaurant*, also on Jalan Tiga, does good satay in the evenings. Another restaurant for good satay is *Satay House*, next to the Hung Wing Hotel.

The *Apple Fast Food Centre*, under the Nak Hotel, is a reasonably cheap place for a quick lunch or snack. The Filipino waitresses are friendly and helpful.

Drink House, opposite the Shell Station on Jalan Tiga, is good for cheap noodle dishes, freshly squeezed fruit juices and expensive beer. Nearby, is the *Superman Ice Cream Parlour* where you can get delicious local-style ice-cream desserts.

Down on Jalan Sim Sim, there's the *Fat Cat* for cheap hawker food, and western-style breakfasts. A couple of doors away is the *Parking Food Centre* – part of a local fast food chain. On the same street, *Tat Teck Vegetarian Restoran*, serves vegetarian food, though there's not much variety.

There are several places to eat in Wisma Sandakan, the huge mushroom-pink building at the end of a court running off Jalan Tiga. On the 1st and 2nd floors of this complex, there are a number of small restaurants and coffee shops selling cheap and tasty local dishes. There are also a couple of ice cream parlours in the complex.

Getting There & Away

Air Sandakan is on MAS's domestic network. If there are flights in operation, for they are notoriously unreliable, then the cheapest flights to Zamboanga in the Philippines operate out of Sandakan.

Road All long-distance minibuses leave from the area next to the footbridge over Lebuh Tiga; local minibuses leave from round the back of the Mayfair Hotel, parallel to the waterfront. Most minibuses depart for their destinations between 5 and 6 am.

There are buses and Land Rovers to Kota Kinabalu which cost about M$35 and take eight hours. You can take the same transport to Kinabalu national park headquarters for M$27. Minibuses to Ranau cost M$25 and the journey takes five to six hours.

There is one large bus which departs Sandakan for Lahad Datu daily at 4.30 and costs M$12. Several minibuses also make the trip, departing Sandakan from 5 to 6.30 am. They charge M$15 and the trip takes about five hours, depending on the length of the queue waiting for the ferry.

The road between Sandakan and Lahad Datu is abominable; potholes, huge rocks, stray dogs, stubborn cows – you name it, it's on the road. At times, it's so dusty that you can't see beyond 50 metres.

From Lahad Datu, you can catch one of the regular minibuses to Tawau for M$8 and the journey takes 3½ hours. If you really want to torture yourself, take the direct bus from Sandakan to Tawau for M$20. It departs at 4.30 am daily and

Top: Pangkor sunset (JC)
Bottom: Emerald Bay, Pangkor Laut (JC)

Top: Rooftops, Penang (JC)
Bottom: Penang at dusk (JC)

takes at least eight uncomfortable hours.

Getting Around

If you're arriving or leaving by air, the airport is about 11 km from the city. There are minibuses throughout the day connecting the two which tout for customers outside the Mayfair Hotel. The fare is 70 sen and the journey takes about 15 minutes. Look for a bus displaying 'Batu 7'. At the airport, any bus coming from the right as you leave the terminal building, will be going into Sandakan town. A taxi to or from the airport costs M$8 to M$10 depending on the age of the car. Taxis can be found in the side streets which run off Jalan Tiga and Lorong Dua.

LAHAD DATU

Lahad Datu is a busy little town of 20,000 people. There are very few tourists but at least 10 hotels – all of them as expensive as the ones in Sandakan. Probably the only reason you would have for going there would be to take a boat across Darvel Bay and explore some of the many islands between there and Semporna which have been declared a national park.

Places to Stay

For budget accommodation, the best place to stay is the *Government Rest House* (tel 81177, 81536) which is at the airport, less than a km from the town centre. If you're coming from Sandakan or Tawau by bus ask the driver to stop there. Overnight cost per person is M$12.

If you can't get in at the Government Rest House, then the *Liang Ming Lodging House* (tel 81419), Kampung Sawmill has reasonable rooms from M$22.

The *Deluxe Hotel* (tel 81500) and the *Winning Hotel* (tel 81200) have basic rooms from M$30. The *Perdana Hotel* (tel 81400) on Jalan Seroja, has fan-cooled rooms from M$35 and the *Venus Hotel* (tel 81900) is similarly priced.

The *Lahad Datu Hotel*, on Jalan Kemboja, is slightly cheaper with clean, single rooms at M$32.

In the middle range, there's the *Ocean Hotel* (tel 81700) on Jalan Timur, which has 19 rooms with prices starting at M$40. Otherwise, you can stay at the expensive *Hotel Mido* (tel 81800), 94 Jalan Main. All rooms have air-con and have attached bathrooms.

Places to Eat

As at Sandakan there are plenty of Chinese rice or noodle places, all more or less of the same standard. If you're determined not to eat another plate of tasteless rice and vegetable stalks, there are a couple of fried chicken restaurants in town.

There's also a reasonable Chinese place, the *Restaurant Hong Kong*. It's behind the Esso petrol station and serves good food, though it's not cheap.

Getting There & Away

Air MAS fly to Lahad Datu. They have an efficient office beneath the Mido Hotel.

Road The long-distance minibus stand is next to the Esso filling station by the market. Most depart for their destinations early – around 6 am.

Buses are available to Sandakan (M$12), Kunak (M$4), Semporna (M$6) and Tawau (M$8). There are also large buses which cost M$8 from Lahad Datu and Tawau.

The bus to Tungku, east of Lahad Datu, goes past a really fine beach about 20 km out of Lahad Datu. The beach is worth visiting although getting back is a problem.

Boats There are no longer any scheduled boats going to Semporna and Kunak, although if you're lucky, you may find a local boat owner who's willing to take you for a high price.

SEMPORNA

Semporna, between Lahad Datu and Tawau, has a stilt village and there's a cultured pearl farm off the coast there. The only hotel in town is the *Island View Hotel* (tel 781638). There are 40 air-conditioned rooms ranging from M$40 to M$50.

TAWAU

A mini-boomtown in the very south-east corner of Sabah close to the Indonesian border, Tawau is a provincial capital and centre for export of the products of the interior – timber, rubber, manila hemp, cocoa, copra and tobacco.

There's precious little to do or see, but the town has retained some of its old world charm. You'll pass through Tawau if you're on your way south to Tarakan in Kalimantan.

Tawau is still a small, compact town with virtually everything in or near to the centre. The only time you may need to use public transport is to get to the airport which is a km out of town.

Places to Stay – bottom end

So called budget hotels in Tawau are, like those elsewhere in Sabah, outrageously priced and poor value for money. The *Soon Yee Hotel*, next to the market, has single rooms with fan but no bathroom for M$21 and doubles from M$27. Air-conditioned rooms start from M$30 and all the rooms are small and basic.

The *Hotel Kuhara* on Jalan Kuhara has reasonable rooms for M$29. The *Hotel Foo Guan* (tel 771700) at 152 Jalan Chester, is not much cheaper at M$25 a fan-cooled double.

The *Lido Hotel* (tel 74547), Jalan Stephen Tam, has rooms from M$30. The *Hotel Ambassador* (tel 72700) at 1872 Jalan Paya Tawau, has similarly priced rooms, each with air-con and own bathroom. The *Hotel Malaysia* (tel 72800) at 37 Jalan Dunlop is slightly more expensive at M$32 for a single room.

Moving up the scale, there's the *Hotel Far East* (tel 73200) on Jalan Masjid, which has fully air-conditioned rooms from about M$45 and the *Hotel Tawau* (tel 771100), at 72 Jalan Chester, where rooms start from M$50.

Places to Stay – top end

The cheapest top-end hotel is the *Hotel Oriental* (tel 71500), 10 Jalan Dunlop, where prices start at M$70. There's also the *Royal Hotel* (tel 73100), Jalan Billion, where single rooms start from M$110 and doubles start from M$130. *Hotel Emas* (tel 73300) on Jalan Utara, has 100 rooms costing from M$105 to M$200.

The most luxurious hotel in town is the *Marco Polo Hotel* (tel 777615) on Jalan Clinic. There are 150 rooms, most of which have their own TV and in-house video collection. Prices range from M$125 to M$1000!

Places to Eat

The choice as in many other places, is between a cheap meal in one of the many Chinese rice and noodle places or spending considerably more money on a decent meal.

If you can afford it, the best restaurant in town is the *Kublai Restaurant* in the Marco Polo Hotel. The food is excellent and staff are friendly. There is also a coffee shop serving western-style food inside the hotel.

For tasty, cheap Indian dishes, try the *Charis Banana Leaf Restaurant* opposite the foodstalls on the road parallel to the waterfront. The foodstalls are set up late in the afternoon and serve reasonable Malay food.

Another cheap Indian restaurant is the popular *Restoran Sabah*. It's on Jalan Dunlop, not far from the Oriental Hotel. There are also a couple of the usual fried chicken restaurants in town.

Getting There & Away

Road From Tawau to Semporna (110 km) you have a choice of minibuses, taxis or Land Rovers. Taxis and minibuses depart

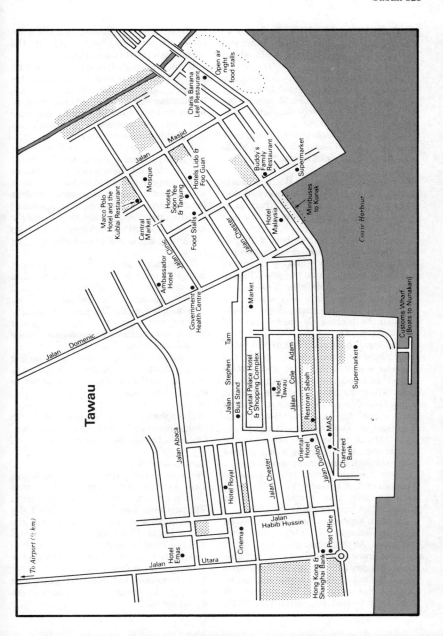

Tawau

To Airport (½ km)

Jalan Emas

Jalan Utara

Cinema

Jalan Habib Hussin

Hong Kong & Shanghai Bank

Post Office

Jalan Dunlop

Chartered Bank

MAS

Oriental Hotel

Restoran Sabah

Hotel Tawau

Jalan Cole Adam

Crystal Palace Hotel & Shopping Complex

Jalan Stephen Tam

Hotel Royal

Jalan Chester

Jalan Abaca

Bus Stand

Jalan Domenic

Market

Government Health Centre

Jalan Clinic

Ambassador Hotel

Central Market

Food Stalls

Marco Polo Hotel and the Kublai Restaurant

Mosque

Jalan

Masjid

Hotels Soon Yee & Tanjung

Hotels Lido & Foo Guan

Charis Banana Leaf Restaurant

Buddy's Family Restaurant

Supermarket

Hotel Malaysia

Minibuses to Kunak

Supermarket

Customs Wharf (Boats to Nunakan)

Cowie Harbour

regularly and take about 2½ hours to reach Semporna. The taxi fare is around M$12, while the minibus costs about M$4.

For Tawau-Lahad Datu (176 km), shared taxis leave daily up to 7.30 am, cost M$15 and take three hours. Minibuses ply back and forth regularly throughout the day and cost only M$6.

There is a direct bus to Sandakan departing daily at 5 am, which costs M$20 and takes about eight hours.

To Kalimantan (Indonesian Borneo). Boats depart Tawau for Nunakan every second day or so – services are fairly irregular as boats only go when there are enough 'legal' passengers.

There are countless numbers of 'illegal' passengers, usually Indonesians working unofficially in remote logging camps of Sabah. Each day, at least one small 'illegal' boat travels to and from Tawau and Nunakan. These boats take alternative routes, skirting the immigration checkpoints on both sides. Of course, they will not take tourists.

The 'legal' boat costs M$25 and takes three hours. Boats depart from the customs wharf at the back of the MAS office. The immigration staff will probably know when the next 'legal' boat will be going. From Nunakan you can get another boat south to Tarakan. Boats from Nunakan to Tarakan depart daily and cost 8000 rp. The boat ride is quite spectacular, as you move along narrow rivers through dense mangrove forests.

There are also flights from Tawau to Tarakan and, at present, it's OK to travel between the two towns (in either direction) by boat or plane.

Tarakan seems to come and go as an officially recognised entry point into Indonesia. At the moment, it's quite OK to enter Indonesia at Tarakan, but this could change without warning. Tarakan is not on the list of places where you can be issued a visa on arrival. You can get one from the Indonesian consulate (tel 72052)

on Jalan Kuhara, Tawau, but it's a lot easier if you get your visa at the Indonesian consulate in KK.

If you find yourself stuck in Tawau for a day or two and are on your way south, try hanging around the customs wharf. Indonesian sailors often introduce themselves and you may be able to talk your way into a passage – if that's an acceptable means of entry.

The Indonesian visa/entry point question has always been a hazy one. It's a bit complicated as there are certain places where you can enter and depart Indonesia without obtaining a visa in advance. Just because a place is not on this 'approved list' does not mean it is not a valid entry or exit point. What it does mean, is that you must have organised a visa before you get there.

There are two additional important points to consider. You must enter and exit through approved points – even if you're coming in to Indonesia at an approved place (like Denpasar, Jakarta or Medan) you must still have a visa if you intend to exit through a non-listed place (like Jayapura or Tarakan).

Secondly, although visa-on-entry people get a free extension, people with visas still have to pay the expensive landing tax to extend their visas.

To Philippines There are on-again, off-again flights between Tawau and Zamboanga. Check Sabre Air Services in Tawau.

Getting Around
Probably the only time you'll need to use local transport is if you're going to or from the airport, which is a km from the centre. The best thing to do is take one of the hotel buses into town. They are provided by the Royal Hotel, Hotel Emas, Tawau Hotel and the Marco Polo Hotel. They're all free and there's no obligation to stay at the hotel which runs the bus.

To go from town to the airport may not be so simple. Hitching is easy or you can take a taxi for M$2.

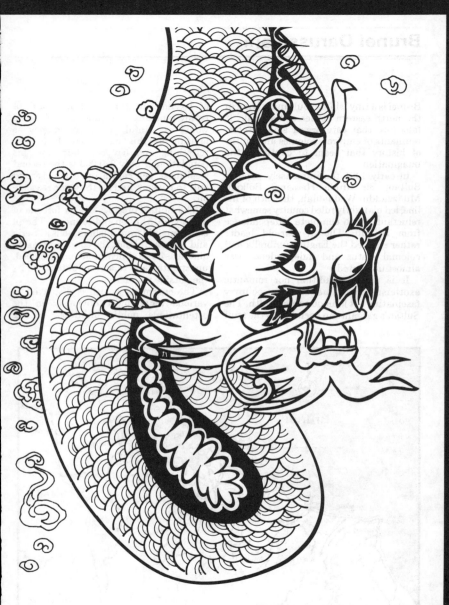

 BRUNEI

Brunei Darussalam

Brunei is a tiny Islamic Sultanate lying in the north-eastern corner of Sarawak. It falls into that category of small states, remnants of empires, colonies and quirks of history that seem to captivate the imagination.

In early 1984 the immensely popular Sultan, Sir Muda Hassanal Bolkiah Mu'izzaddin Waddaulah, the 29th of his line, led his tightly ruled country somewhat reluctantly into complete independence from Britain. The 37-year-old leader rather enjoyed the English umbrella and colonial status and independence was almost unwanted.

It is neither tradition nor romantic exoticism that makes this country fascinating – it is astounding wealth. The Sultan's gargantuan spending is the stuff of legends. In this skinflint world of penny-pinching it is unheard of, some would say sinful, to expend money as lavishly as this man does. It is also refreshing and few complain, for this population of only 220,000 is the second wealthiest per capita on earth, second only to Kuwait, and for the same reason – oil.

The Sultan presides over a fortune of about US$15 billion and counting. The oil comes mainly from offshore wells at Seria and Muara. Inland, the country remains almost as it has always been – undeveloped, unexploited and relatively untouched by the outside world.

The enormous wealth is displayed in various ways, most obviously in the ostentatious public buildings of the

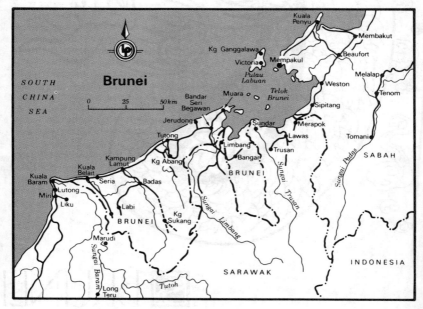

capital, Bandar Seri Begawan. The airport is suitable for a country 10 times the size of Brunei. Everything is done big here.

Perhaps more outlandish are the Sultan's personal buys: a US$350 million palace; a fleet of Italian exoticars said to be serviced by a mechanic flown in from Italy; and his grand passion – a fabulous polo farm with 200 Argentine ponies, some enjoying air-conditioned stalls.

On the other hand everyone in Brunei benefits from oil money. There are no taxes, there are pensions for all, free medicare, free schooling, free sports and leisure centres, cheap loans, subsidies for many purchases including cars and the highest minimum wages in the region.

The government with Brunei Shell Oil (the only oil company there in any substantial way) is by far the country's largest employer. All government workers get subsidised holidays and trips to Mecca. All in all, not too shabby an arrangement. When there is any criticism, the government-owned newspaper stifles it.

The traditional pattern of agriculture in Brunei is that of shifting cultivation, which continues in the more remote areas. Farming is largely a part-time occupation and there are no large estates. About 80% of the country's food requirements have to be imported.

Some diversification plans for the economy are now being instituted for that fearsome day when the pump runs dry. These plans include more rice farming, some forestry and eventual self-sufficiency in beef production.

To this latter goal the government purchased a cattle station in Australia's Northern Territory which is larger than Brunei itself! Fresh beef is flown into Bandar Seri Begawan daily.

Brunei is also one of the world's largest exporters of liquefied natural gas. A small amount of rubber is also exported.

History

In the 15th and 16th centuries Brunei Darussalam, as it's formally known, was a considerable power in the area and its rule extended throughout Borneo and into the Philippines.

The Spanish and the Portuguese were the first European visitors, arriving in the 16th century. The Spanish actually made a bid to take over but were soon ousted.

The arrival of the British in the guise of James Brooke, the first White Rajah of Sarawak, in the early 19th century, spelt the end of Brunei's power.

A series of 'treaties' were forced onto the Sultan as James Brooke consolidated his hold over Kuching with the aim of developing commercial relationships and suppressing piracy – a favourite Bruneian and Dayak occupation.

The country was gradually whittled away until, with a final dash of absurdity, Limbang was ceded to Sarawak, thus dividing the country in half.

In 1929, just as Brunei was about to be swallowed up entirely, oil was discovered. The Sultan's father, who abdicated in 1967, kept Brunei out of the Malaysian confederacy, preferring that the country remain a British protectorate, which it had been since 1888.

Since the 1960s, when there was a failed coup attempt, the country has been under emergency laws, but you'll see little evidence of this.

Population

The total population of Brunei is about 220,000 composed of Malays, Chinese, Indians and around 25,000 Iban, Murut and other tribespeople of the interior.

Brunei is quite a strict Muslim country; there is little alcohol and apparently government men prowl the streets after dark looking for unmarried couples standing or sitting too close to each other. Getting nailed for this crime, known as *khalwat*, can mean six months in jail.

The official language is Malay but English is widely spoken.

Geography

Brunei consists of two separate areas, bordered by the South China Sea to the north and bounded on all other sides by Sarawak.

It covers an area of 5765 square km and other than the capital, Bandar Seri Begawan, the oil town of Seria and the commercial town of Kuala Belait, Brunei is mainly jungle.

Climate

From November to January, during the north-east monsoon, temperatures are somewhat lower than the 28°C average. With an average humidity of 82% it's a pretty warm place.

Money

The official currency is the Brunei dollar but Singapore dollars are more or less equally exchanged and can be used. There's about 9% difference between the Brunei dollar and the Malaysian ringgit. Banks give 10 to 20% less for cash than they do for travellers' cheques.

Bandar Seri Begawan

The capital, Bandar Seri Begawan, is the only town of any size and really one of the few places to go in the country. It's a neat, very clean and modern city with some fine, overstated buildings.

You won't see any bicycles, trishaws or even motorcycles there. Everybody has an air-conditioned car and they're nearly all new; you'll notice the quietness, because they all have working mufflers.

The historical water villages surrounding the city are quite fascinating and offer some contrasting tradition. A big plus is the friendly people; even young women will smile and say hello. There are a few things to see and do around town but, unless you stay at the youth centre, the city can be expensive to linger in.

Information

Tourist Information There is a tourist information booth (tel 31794) at the airport which isn't bad and has maps. Although they are helpful, they can't answer questions about the rest of the country.

You can also chat to the friendly Public Relations Officer at the customs wharf. She's in Room 13, up the stairs around the back of the white building on the corner of Jalan McArthur and Jalan Sungai Kianggeh. There is a sign in front of this building which says *Jabatan Penyiaran Dan Penerangan, Negara Brunei Darussalam*.

The Public Relations Officer is in charge of providing 'information' on Brunei to foreign or local visitors. Everyone stresses that her office is *not* a tourist office and that, unfortunately, there is no tourist office in BSB. Despite this you will find a lot of useful information here.

Embassies The Chop Teck Guan Complex houses the US Embassy on the 3rd floor and the Australian Embassy on the 4th. American Express has an office on the 1st floor. The British High Commission (tel 26001) is in the Hong Kong Bank Chambers building and the West German Embassy (tel 25547) is in the UNF building. The Malaysian Embassy (28515) is at Lot 12-15 Tingkat 6 Bang. The Thai Embassy (tel 29438) is in Kampung Kiarong, the Philippines Embassy (tel 51622) is at 277 Kampung Telanai and the Indonesian Embassy (tel 30180) is at Lot 4498, Kampung Sungau Hanching.

Airlines Singapore Airlines is on Jalan Sultan and there is an agent for Qantas, Royal Brunei and Cathay Pacific on the ground floor of Britannia House, corner of Jalan Cator and Jalan Sungai Kianggeh. Royal Brunei Airlines (tel 29438) is in the RBA Plaza, Jalan Sultan and Thai International (tel 23862) is at 93 Jaian Pemancha. MAS is also on Jalan

Pemancha. British Airways (tel 43911) have an office on Jalan Kianggeh.

Omar Ali Saifuddin Mosque

Named after the 28th Sultan of Brunei, the mosque was built in 1958 at a cost of about US$5 million. Designed by an Italian architect, the golden-domed structure stands close to the Brunei River in its own artificial lagoon and is the tallest building in Bandar Seri Begawan. For my money it's one of the most impressive structures in the east.

As is customary, the interior is simple but tasteful although certainly no match for the stunning exterior; but what other mosque anywhere has an elevator and an escalator?

The floor and walls of the mosque are made from the finest Italian marble, the stained-glass windows were handcrafted in England and the luxurious carpets were flown in from Saudi Arabia. The small pools and quadrants surrounding the main building are beautiful. The ceremonial boat sitting in the lagoon/moat is used for special occasions, including Koran-reading competitions.

The elevator to the top of the 44-metre (146 feet) minaret was broken last visit, but ask in the mosque and someone will open the door and let you walk up the long, winding staircase without charge. The view over the city and nearby Kampung Ayer or water village is excellent.

The mosque is closed to non-Muslims on Thursdays and on Friday mornings. From Saturday to Wednesday, you may enter the mosque between the hours of 8 am and 12 noon, 1 and 3 pm or 4.30 and 5.30 pm. Remember to dress appropriately and to remove your shoes before entering. Muslim travellers can enter the mosque to pray at any time.

Winston Churchill Memorial Museum

The museum was built by Sultan Omar Ali Saifuddin and houses a collection of articles which once belonged to Churchill. It's all very boring, but if you're desperate

it's open from 9 am to 12 noon and 2 to 5 pm daily, except Tuesdays when it's closed all day. Admission is free.

Aquarium Hassanal Bolkiah Brunei

Adjacent to the Churchill museum is the far more interesting aquarium which has a total of 47 exhibition tanks, both fresh and seawater, one of them nearly eight metres long. There's an interesting and colourful collection of tropical fish from the local reefs. The aquarium is open from 9 am to 12 noon and 1.15 to 7 pm daily except Mondays. Admission is 30 sen.

Constitutional History Gallery

On the other side of the aquarium is the history museum, created to mark the independence of Brunei in 1984. The history of Brunei is traced from the 1800's to the present day. There are even action scenes set up where buttons may be pressed to light up part of the scene and start off a recorded commentary describing the 'action' – typically, none of these buttons work. This museum is rather dull.

Opening hours are 9 am to 12 noon and 2 to 5 pm daily, except for Tuesdays when the museum is closed. Entry is free.

The Library

There is a general reference library in the Churchill complex which houses a fairly good collection of books on South-East Asia and, of course, several books written by Sir Winston Churchill.

Brunei Museum

Located at Kota Batu, three km from the centre of Bandar Seri Begawan, the museum is housed in a beautifully constructed building on the banks of the Brunei River. It has a collection of historical treasures from the 15th century together with artefacts of the cultural heritage of Brunei, including an Iban longhouse. It also has a natural history section. The wildlife section exhibits animals, birds and insects.

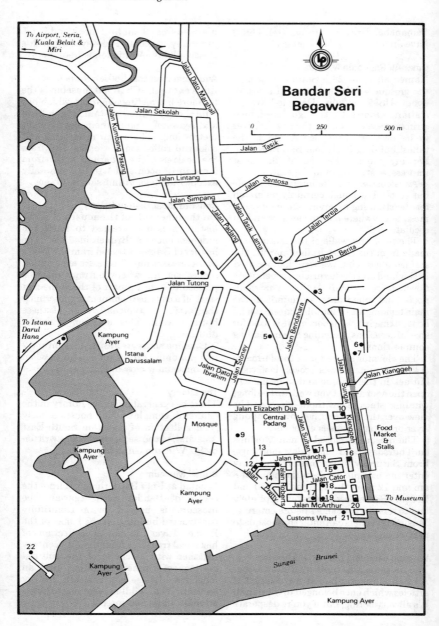

Bandar Seri Begawan

0   250   500 m

To Airport, Seria, Kuala Belait & Miri

Jalan Dato Marshall

Jalan Sekolah

Jalan Kumbang Pasang

Jalan Tasik

Jalan Lintang

Jalan Sentosa

Jalan Simpang

Jalan Tereja

Jalan Padang

Jalan Tasik Lama

Jalan Berita

● 2

● 1

Jalan Tutong

● 3

Jalan Bendahara

To Istana Darul Hana

● 4

Kampung Ayer

Istana Darussalam

● 5

● 6
● 7

Jalan Kianggeh

Jalan Dato Ibrahim

Jalan Stoney

Jalan Sungai

● 8

Jalan Elizabeth Dua

10 ●

Mosque

Central Padang

Jalan Sultan

Jalan Kianggeh

Food Market & Stalls

● 9

13

11

Jalan Pemancha

16

12

Jalan Petti

14

Jalan Roberts

15

Jalan Cator

17 18
19

To Museum

Jalan McArthur

20

Customs Wharf

21

● 22

Kampung Ayer

Kampung Ayer

Kampung Ayer

Sungai Brunei

Kampung Ayer

1	Immigration
2	Ang's Hotel
3	Sheraton Hotel
4	High Court
5	Churchill Museum
6	Capital Hotel
7	Pusat Belia (Youth Centre)
8	Post Office
9	Car Park
10	Chinese Temple
11	Hong Kong & Shanghai Bank
12	MAS
13	Chartered Bank
14	Malayan Bank
15	Bus Station
16	Brunei Hotel
17	Teck Guan Complex
18	Creamery
19	Darussalam Complex
20	Harrisons & Crossfield
21	Information Office
22	Makam Di-Raja (Mausoleum)

There is an extensive section on oil with an amusing vignette showing local life with and without the 'benefits' that oil brings. Best is the ethnography section with good examples of musical instruments, baskets and brassware. Also check the coffins of the Kenyah people's chiefs. There is a large collection of Chinese ceramics from 1000 AD to more recent times. Brunei's first gunboat is on display under a traditional roof by the riverbank in front of the museum.

The museum is open Tuesday, Wednesday, Thursday, Saturday and Sunday from 10 am to 5.30 pm; Friday from 9.30 to 11.30 am and 2.30 to 6.30 pm; and is closed Mondays.

City buses depart from the downtown depot; the fare is 50 sen, but buses are not that frequent as they only go when they are full. Taxis cost B$6 but you can hitch quite easily or even walk one way. After visiting the museum, you can keep going in the same direction to the beach at Muara.

Ancient Tomb of Sultan Bolkiah

Near the museum, about a km closer to town, is the tomb and mausoleum of the fifth Sultan of Brunei, known as the 'Singing Admiral' who died returning from a voyage to Java. He lived from 1473 to 1521, during a period when Brunei was the dominant power in the region.

Kampung Ayer

This collection of 28 water villages, built on stilts out in the Brunei River, has been there for centuries and at present houses a population of around 30,000 people. It's a strange mixture of ancient and modern; old traditions and ways of life are side by side with modern plumbing, electricity and colour TVs. A visit to one of the villages is probably the most rewarding experience you'll have in Brunei, though the garbage which floats around them has to be seen to be believed.

To get there, go down to the main wharf and take any one of the many launches which ply back and forth all day. Bargain over the fare, it shouldn't be more than 50 sen. You don't need a boat to visit the section of Kampung Ayer nearest the mosque; all the houses in this area are connected by a maze of wooden planks and it's fascinating to wander around for an hour or so – even if you do keep finding yourself in the middle of someone's kitchen.

When Bandar Seri Begawan was being modernised, it was suggested that the people from the water villages be relocated to the mainland. These people refused to move and in enlightened fashion were permitted to stay. Schools and hospitals, of cement rather than wood, were then built on the water for the villagers.

There are all sorts of shops and businesses amongst the houses in Kampung Ayer. If you're lucky, you might come across handicraft shops selling silverware, brass, woven cloth and baskets. If not, you can always ask the boatmen to take you to these places.

A boat trip right around Kampung Ayer takes at least 30 minutes and the boatmen will probably want B$30 for their efforts – bargain hard.

Handicraft Centre

The preposterously large and grandiose handicraft centre was built to help develop local craftwork. It's along the waterfront toward the museum, visible from town and an easy walk. However, if you are interested in traditional crafts, it is disappointing. Only new silverwork and weaving are available and everything is very expensive, even hundreds of dollars. There's not much variety either. You can visit workshops upstairs.

A Short Town Walk

From town it's a short walk to a small waterfall and a view. Past the Ang's Hotel, going away from the town centre, turn right at the next traffic light. Go up the road to the parking lot, through the gate by the parking lot and continue for about 15 minutes. Continuing past the flowers and picnic tables follow the stream to the falls. They are best in the wet season when the water is deeper; you can swim there. Another road by the gate leads to a 15-minute walk uphill to a view over the water reservoir.

Other Attractions

There is a Chinese temple on the corner of Jalan Elizabeth Dua and Jalan Sungai Kianggeh with some colourful, pictorial tilework and plenty of carved, gilded wood.

The Istana Nurul Iman, the magnificent Sultan's palace, larger than the Vatican Palace, is said to be due for inclusion in the *Guinness Book of Records* for its nearly 1800 rooms. It's an impressive sight, especially when illuminated at night, and you can be sure no expense has been spared in its construction. Unfortunately, the Istana is only open to the public on the Sultan's birthday, and even then, there are restricted areas.

The Istana is four km out of Bandar Seri Begawan on the Tutong road. You can either spend a leisurely hour walking to it or you can try hitching. The Tutong and Seria buses pass the Istana but they run infrequently. On the hill opposite the Istana are homes belonging to other members of the Royal Family.

All over town you'll notice uniquely designed, oversized federal buildings – the GPO, the Government complex opposite the youth centre, the Royal Ceremonial Hall, the Arts and Handicrafts Centre and the Supreme Court. Try to see the Royal Ceremonial Hall (*Lapua*) where traditional events are held and the Sultan's golden throne sits. The Legislative Assembly (Dewan Majlis) has been moved to the Istana.

Visitors are welcome to attend traditional Malay weddings; ask the Public Relations Officer for more information.

For books and magazines try the third floor of the Teck Guan Plaza Building, on the corner of Jalan Sultan and Jalan McArthur. There are also STP distributors at the corner of Jalan Pemancha and Jalan Sultan and the Rex Bookstore around the corner on Jalan Sungai Kianggeh.

There is a popular food market on one side of the river, parallel to Jalan Sungai Kianggeh, near the intersection with Jalan Pemancha.

Lastly, watch out for the meter maids all over town wearing blue suits, white gloves and usually sporting umbrellas. They ticket cars incessantly with parking charges and collect the money when the driver returns.

Places to Stay - bottom end

Pusat Belia (tel 23936), the youth centre on Jalan Sungai Kianggeh, is a short walk from the town centre. It's one of the cheapest places to stay in town and definitely the place to head for when you arrive.

In the past, a problem with the youth centre has been getting in. In fact, it's quite simple for anyone with a membership card for any youth or student organisation. The difficulties start when someone turns up without a 'membership card' and expects to be able to stay. There are two large dorms, one for each sex, both nearly always empty, and vacant beds are available for travellers who happen to be 'members'.

The place was set up for local and visiting youth groups and registered clubs, and this is its main function. If there is a local group staying, it's likely you won't be given permission to stay, even if all the beds are not taken.

First, look as respectable as possible. Second, be very polite, courteous and calm. Remember that in letting you stay, the management is doing you a favour, not helping you exercise your God-given right. It is not a hotel. I was told some horror stories of tantrum-throwing, screaming western travellers behaving like spoiled brats. Remain calm, bring out a student/youth card and quietly state why and how long you would like to stay. Most importantly, be friendly and do not start a confrontation which will only make things difficult for travellers in the future.

There are two men in charge – the boss, with a desk in a private office out the back, and another man at the desk in the front office. (The latter is often surrounded by several other men who apparently have little else to do). The men in charge respond to a light handshake, a smile and a little formal decorum. Unfortunately, locating these gentlemen is not always easy and may require some waiting. There is always somebody on duty, so ask to see the officer in charge.

There is room for 60 men and at least 20 women in dorms that have seen better days. Maintenance is non-existent. Some fans don't work, showers are broken, the water system is erratic and is often cut off at night – take your shower early or you might not get one.

However, the price is only B$10 for one to three nights (same price for one, two or three nights) and then B$5 for each night after that. Don't stay one night and then demand B$6.66 back! It's B$10 flat rate. Downstairs there is a small cafeteria-type restaurant for cheap, fairly well-balanced, passable meals served up by friendly people. The swimming pool has been repaired and is now open.

There is also a *Government Rest House* (tel 23571) on the same side of Jalan Sungai Kianggeh as the youth centre, not far from the Chinese temple. It costs around B$8 per night and the rooms are in much better condition than the youth centre's dorms. They don't always accept foreigners.

Despite stories you may hear, there is really no accommodation at St Andrew's Church, although the minister is friendly. If you're really desperate, he has a very small, old shed you can use but there are no beds and no screens. The mosquitoes will love having you.

Places to Stay – middle

The jump in price from bottom to middle range places to stay is enormous.

The next cheapest place to stay in Bandar Seri Begawan is at the *Capital Hostel* (tel 23561), off Jalan Tasik Lama just behind Pusat Belia. It's the one you'll most likely have to use if you're on a budget and cannot get into the youth centre or the Rest House. Rooms cost B$70 single, B$85 double and all have air-con, TV and fridge. The restaurant and bar downstairs serve reasonably priced meals from B$5 to B$8. The continental breakfast is B$3.50 or B$6 with eggs and is handy if you're at the youth centre.

A more recent middle to top addition is the *National Inn* (tel 21128) on Jalan Tutong, out of the town centre, across the Brunei River behind the mosque. It features fine, modern rooms, all with air-con and prices from B$70. The hotel offers free transport to the airport and a regular shuttle service into town. The restaurant serves expensive meals.

Places to Stay – top end

There are more hotels in this category than in any other. The relatively new *Sheraton-Utama* (tel 27272) is the country's top hotel and has all the modern amenities, including a pool. It is centrally located on Jalan Bendahara. There are 170 rooms with singles from B$186 and doubles from B$205. Deluxe suites cost B$775 per night.

Ang's Hotel (tel 23553) on Jalan Tasik has its own restaurant and bar and is fully air-conditioned, of course. The 84 rooms start at B$118 single and B$128 double.

Right downtown is the *Brunei Hotel* (tel 22372) at 95 Jalan Pemancha. Each room has air-con, a private bath and TV and the hotel has a restaurant and bar. Rates are B$130 single and B$145 double.

Places to Eat

All the hotels and the youth centre have their own restaurants. The meals at the Capital Hotel are pretty good and quite cheap. You can get tasty Hokkien Mee and other noodle dishes for B$4.50. There's not much of a menu at the canteen in the youth centre; what you see is what you get and the choice is very limited.

A nice place to eat, especially in the evenings, is at the food stalls by the riverfront, near the bridge. Looking out to the stilt villages while you eat is a very pleasant experience. Soups are a speciality and cost B$2. Various rice and noodle dishes also cost B$2. Soft drinks are B$1, as they are all over town.

Another place to head for is the food stalls by the river, near the intersection with Jalan Sungai Kianggeh and Jalan Pemancha. You can get some really delicious Muslim dishes from B$2 to B$4 – the fried rice and the pancakes are wonderful.

Along the main street, Jalan Sultan, you'll find a few places to eat. *The Creamery* has ice-cream, milkshakes, pastries and the *Wisma Bahru* has cheap Muslim-style food.

Chop Jing Chew Bakery, opposite the customs building on Jalan McArthur sells cakes, bread and ice-cream. There are also some cheap Chinese and Indian places. The *Darussalam*, toward the McArthur end, is the only place in town I saw fresh Indian breads being made.

There's an English-style pub in Ang's Hotel as well as a Chinese restaurant which serves the most fantastic laksa – not cheap but definitely worth the splurge.

Right in the centre of town, there's the *Carnation Country Bake Corner* on the corner of Jalan McArthur and Jalan Sultan. Across the road in Darussalam Complex, you'll find the more upmarket *Grill Room* and the busy *Chin Lian Restaurant* where you can get cheap, tasty Malaysian food.

Restoran Rosanika on Jalan Roberts has great Malay food for around B$3. On Jalan McArthur the *Seri Indah* has the usual items; nasi goreng is B$3.50. It's quick and the local office crowd frequents the place. The *Chop Chuan Huat*, on Jalan Roberts, is an Indian place where you can get a good, tasty meal for under B$4. Drink a refreshing lemon ping for B$1.40.

For a better meal try the *Lucky Restaurant*, where Chinese food may be had at about B$40 for two without alcohol. There are very few bars in town and only Chinese restaurants carry a liquor licence. Muslims are not allowed to drink. Nevertheless beer, wine and spirits are *much* cheaper in Brunei than in Sarawak or Sabah.

Getting There & Away

Air Airlines which fly into Brunei include Royal Brunei, MAS, SIA, Cathay Pacific, Qantas and British Airways.

Qantas have direct flights between Brunei and Darwin while British Airways have a weekly flight between London and Australia which goes via Brunei.

Royal Brunei flies to Bandar Seri Begawan from Singapore, Hong Kong,

Manila, Darwin and other destinations. It's actually cheaper to fly Manila-BSB than Manila-Kota Kinabalu, even though it's further. Being a good Muslim airline Royal Brunei serve no alcohol on their flights.

None of the airline offices offer student or other discounts but some of the travel agents (such as the one next door to the Brunei Hotel) will offer small discounts.

The standard economy fare to Singapore is B$320 one way. To Kuching the airfare is M$192, KK M$65, Manila US$196, Kuala Lumpur M$372, and to Bangkok about M$500.

For Qantas, Pan Am and Cathay Pacific, tickets can be bought at the Borneo Company Travel at the corner of Jalan Cator and Jalan Sungai Kianggeh.

Road The only roads which exist in Brunei are the ones linking Bandar Seri Begawan to Seria, Kuala Belait and the Sarawak border near Kuala Baram. There is now a road to Lawas but not to Limbang. The only way to reach Limbang is by launch. It has been said that the government purposely keeps the roads out of Brunei in such miserable condition to make any invasion by land difficult!

The bus station in Bandar Seri Begawan is on Jalan Cator, near Britannia House, at the back of the Brunei Hotel. There are many buses every day to Seria. The fare is B$4 and the journey takes 1½ to two hours.

From Seria to Kuala Belait there are frequent buses daily and the fare is B$1. The journey takes about 30 minutes. On both of these legs beware of bus conductors trying to charge you extra for your bags.

It's very easy, to hitch from Bandar Seri Begawan to Seria or Kuala Belait because there are plenty of air-conditioned cars and very few hitch-hikers.

If you want to reach Miri in one day from Bandar Seri Begawan, start out early in the day. There are taxis leaving very early in the mornings which charge around B$30 per person. Apparently, there are also a few 'illegal' taxis willing to take passengers for B$10 each.

There are now four or five buses daily from Kuala Belait to Miri. These are operated by the Sharikat Berlima Belait bus company. The fare is B$11 and the journey takes about 2½ hours and involves river crossings.

From Kuala Belait, it's a five-minute bus ride (20 minutes walk) to the Belait River where the car ferry plies back and forth. Sometimes the queue is incredibly long and it's easier to collect your things from the bus and take one of the small motorised boats across the river for B$1. Otherwise, you could ask one of the drivers near the front of the queue if they would mind taking you across with them.

Once you cross the river, there's another bus ride to the Brunei immigration checkpoint. After going through Brunei customs, you board a Malaysian bus which will take you to the Malaysian immigration checkpoint. From there, it's a very short ride to the queue at the next river which usually takes 15 to 30 minutes to cross.

From Kuala Baram to Miri, the road is sealed all the way and is in fairly good condition.

Launches & Boats Unless you are going to fly to Labuan or Kota Kinabalu, the only way to get to Sabah or the isolated eastern Sarawak outposts of Limbang or Lawas is to use riverboats or riverboat/taxi combinations.

If you really want to know what makes this part of Borneo tick then take the riverboats. It's a fascinating journey whichever route you take. Some of the possibilities include:

Brunei-Limbang There are several private speed boats which do this run at various times of the day – departure times depend on demand. The fare is B$7. The trip takes about 30 minutes, ask at the dock.

There isn't much to see or do in Limbang and the town has a bit of a reputation as a sin spot. One of the cheapest places in town is the *Bunga Raya Hotel* opposite the wharf. Basic dormitory accommodation costs M$10 per night and you are provided with soap and a towel.

Other hotels include the *Muhibbah Inn* and the *Borneo Hotel*, the latter with reasonable rooms for M$15 per night. You can either stay at Limbang overnight or take another boat to Punang, further up the coast.

Boats for Punang depart every day around 11 am except Sunday. From Punang you can get a connecting share taxi to Lawas. Total fare from Limbang to Lawas will be about B$15.

Brunei-Labuan Labuan is a duty-free island off Brunei from which you can get ferries to Sabah and then a bus into Kota Kinabalu. For more details, see the section under Sabah.

From Bandar Seri Begawan there are several boats to Labuan, all costing B$15. The *Serai Sungai Express* leaves Bandar Seri Begawan at 8 am every Sunday, Tuesday and Thursday, arriving at Labuan around 9.45 am.

You can buy tickets on the boat or at Oriental Travel, down a little alley off Jalan McArthur, opposite the dock area. The alley is beside G L Amour, a store selling sporting goods. The agent is beside the Borneo Hardware.

You can also pre-book tickets there for the *Sri Labuan Express* which leaves Mondays, Wednesdays, Fridays and Saturdays at 8 am and returns around 2 pm. The *Raji Wali Express* does the same trip, also leaving in the morning. All boats take 1½ to two hours and it's usually a good idea to book a day ahead.

You can get private boats to take you. They'll probably settle for B$15 or so. With triple outboard engines they are fast. Stand around the dock area and touts and boat owners will approach you or call out.

Top: Council workers, BSB, Brunei (ST)
Bottom: Cinema posters, Brunei (ML)

Top: Chinese temple, BSB, Brunei (ST)
Left: Omar Ali Saifuddinn Mosque, BSB, Brunei (ML)
Right: Entrance to mosque, BSB, Brunei (ST)

The *Serai Sungai* docks at the end of the wharf near the tourist office; the others leave from beside the tin-roofed building with the yellow sides, just before the market stalls. Normally you can get tickets the morning of departure, but on holidays and weekends it can get busy. You can book ahead at Oriental Travel.

Labuan Island is an expensive place to linger in and there is virtually nothing of interest there, so if you don't want to shed a lot of money on partially duty-free consumer items then catch a launch to Menumbok on the Sabah mainland. There are several launches every day and the fare is M$9. They depart from the dock opposite the Hock Hua Bank, several blocks to the left after you clear Labuan immigration. It is intended that government car ferries will soon start operating this service.

From Menumbok, share taxis and minibuses are available to either Beaufort (about M$7 per person) or Kota Kinabalu.

Brunei-Lawas There are usually one or two launches daily to Lawas which cost B$25 and take about two hours. The one which most travellers take departs at 11 am on Tuesdays, Thursdays and Saturdays and returns on Sundays, Mondays, Wednesdays and Fridays. Runners will accost you as you enter the wharf – no problem finding a boat, just ask around the area near the bridge over the canal.

You can stay the night at Lawas, in which case the *Government Rest House* on the airport road is good, but recently all Sarawak rest houses have had their prices for non-government workers increased dramatically and the cost is now M$30. Failing that there's the *Federal Hotel* which is similarly priced.

Alternatively, you can take a bus to Merapok, which will cost M$3.50 and take about 40 minutes. The road to Beaufort and KK now connects down to Lawas, but there is not a lot of traffic. You can apparently get lifts with trucks. If you're lucky and have no particular interest in going to Lawas, you may find that the launch from Brunei will hail a motorised longboat in mid-river on the way to Lawas and transfer you to it so you get to Merapok without having to wait in Lawas.

Merapok is a strange one-street hamlet in the middle of nowhere and you get the distinct impression that you could be there forever trying to get out. At least that's the case if you arrive by somewhat unorthodox methods – as we did. But there are two billiard halls, with beautiful tables made in Australia, and a cafe while you wait!

From there it's a question of hassling for a lift to Sipitang (the usual price is M$2 per person for the half-hour journey) which isn't difficult – *someone* will be going there so long as you don't arrive too late in the day.

Note that Sabah immigration is a few hundred metres out of the hamlet and that you're supposed to report there for immigration formalities. If you happen to drive past it, like most people do, it doesn't really matter. Sabah immigration is pretty easygoing, unlike Sarawak immigration, and you can report to another office in Sabah, such as Sipitang or KK (but not Tenom or Beaufort) even several days later.

If you take the 11 am launch from Brunei to Lawas then you'll arrive in Sipitang too late for any scheduled transport (taxis or buses) out of there and, if you want to get to Beaufort or KK that night, you'll have to hitch – which is not easy as there's very little traffic.

If you have to stay in Sipitang for the night there's a *Government Rest House*, about a km from the centre on the Merapok road, which costs M$12 per person. A more basic flea-pit in the centre of the village costs less than this.

Share-taxis depart for Beaufort every day around 7 to 8 am and cost M$7 per person. From Beaufort there are buses, taxis and trains to KK or Tenom.

Getting Around

Airport Transport There are no buses to the airport so if you're flying into or out of Brunei you will have to hire a taxi or hitch (which is quite easy). Taxis do not have meters so fix the fare in advance. Taxis to or from the airport and town are B$15; very expensive for just four km. The airport is big, new and modern and you can change money there.

Buses Local buses around Bandar Seri Begawan are few and far between and only leave when full. The bus station is next to the central market, behind the Brunei Hotel.

Rent-a-Cars At the airport are two car rental agencies, Sharikat Yuran (tel 24054) and Avis. Other offices are located in town. Rates for a car are B$75 a day (Toyota or Datsun 1600cc) or B$150 for a jeep. Gas, need I say, is ridiculously cheap. Sharikat can be found at 144 Jalan Pemancha.

Around Brunei

MUARA

This is a small town north from Bandar Seri Begawan at the top of the peninsula. It's a new oil centre with not much to see but there is a pretty decent beach.

The World Wide club is basically for expats and is a good place to have a beer and to meet someone who lives in the country. The *Tropicana Seafood Restaurant*, Block 1, Ground Floor of Pang's building is a nice place to eat. There are also a lot of yachts in Muara, for you opportunists.

The bus from Bandar Seri Begawan takes about 40 minutes and costs B$2 or you can try hitching. There are other beaches on the north coast, but these are not as pleasant and the buses are less frequent.

BANGAR

Bangar is another small town, but it is reached only by boat. You can get launches there from Bandar Seri Begawan. Bangar is the district centre and is on the Temburong River, east of the capital, toward Sarawak. The town has a couple of shops and a market.

There is a *Government Rest House* which travellers can use at a cost of B$8 per night. Apparently you can organise some sleeping arrangements in town, perhaps through the information office in Bandar Seri Begawan.

There's one road going inland from Bangar to Limbang and another follows the river upstream for a distance to the village of Batang Duri.

There are several Iban longhouses along the upper reaches of the river. While there are basic cafes in Bangar, take food with you if you're going upstream. You can get one of the three taxis in town or a private car to take you to longhouses. The fare should be no more than B$1 per km.

The nearest longhouse to Bangar is about 13 km away, and, as you'd expect, the further up the river you go, the more 'authentic' the longhouses become. You might even find a nice new Volvo parked outside the more urban longhouses! Most of the longhouses in this area are homes of the friendly Murut people.

Between 7 am and 3 pm daily, you can get launches to Bangar from Bandar Seri Begawan. Go to the customs wharf and bargain – the fare should be B$6 to B$7 and the journey less than one hour. It is also possible to catch an early boat to Bangar (7.30 am) and a late boat back to Bandar Seri Begawan (4 pm) but, unless you have access to private transport or can afford expensive taxis to take you about, you'll be rushed.

SERIA

Seria is the main town on the north coast, situated between Tutong and Kuala Belait, quite close to the Malaysian border. There are at least three banks i town and a few interesting cafes and cake shops.

Before Seria a road branches off inland to Labi. About halfway to Labi is Luagan Lalak with good views and a lake. From Labi there are several Iban longhouses which you can go to. The main one is called Rumah Panjang Mendaram Besar and it's worth visiting. There is a road but, as very few cars use it, you may have to walk. Take a few small gifts. On the way, you'll pass Rampayoh where there is a waterfall.

Places to Stay
The *Hotel Seria* has fan-cooled singles for B$35 and doubles for B$40. If you're just passing through Brunei from Sabah to Sarawak, and can't stay in the Pusat Belia, then it's quite a saving to spend your last Brunei night here rather than at the extremely expensive Bandar Seri Begawan hotels.

At the other end of Seria's price scale the *Sea View Hotel* is completely modern at B$85 for singles and B$90 for doubles.

Getting There & Away
The road from Bandar Seri Begawan is good; there are about 10 buses daily taking two hours. The last one leaves Seria at 4 pm. From Seria there are buses to Kuala Belait for B$1.

KUALA BELAIT
The last town before Malaysia, Kuala Belait is where you get buses for Miri in Sarawak. There are two banks in town and an efficient GPO.

You can hire a motor launch by the market for trips up the river to Kuala Balai, a small river village. The 45-minute trip (one way) goes by good, jungle vegetation at the river's edge. Near Kuala

Balai you'll see sago palms growing. Along the way ask the driver to stop at the wooden case of skulls mounted on stilts, left over from the head-hunting days.

Places to Stay
At the cheap end of the scale there's a *Government Rest House* where, if you're permitted to stay, rooms are about B$12. Rooms are generally reserved for government officials, but occasionally travellers may be allowed to stay.

Otherwise, there's the *Sentosa Hotel* at 92 Jalan McKerron which is all air-conditioned and has single rooms from B$100 and a Chinese restaurant downstairs which serves excellent seafood. The *Seaview Hotel* by the beach has rooms for well over B$100.

Getting There & Away
For Malaysia there are quite a few buses daily, mostly in the morning, and the fare is just under B$11 for the 30-minute trip. Just out of town the road ends and you take a ferry over the Belait River. The road then continues along the coast to the border. At the border you change to a Malaysian bus and head to the Baram River, from where there's another ferry crossing. From there to Miri it's a good road.

Other Attractions
There are walking trails to various villages and their longhouses in the interior jungle, particularly along the Belait River. Villages such as Buau, Punan and Melilas see few foreigners. These three towns are all south of Batu Sawat, which is on a branch of the main road leading from the coast to Labi.

Getting enough time on your visa for such touring could be a hassle.

Index

MAPS

Temperature

To convert °C to °F multiply by 1.8 and add 32

To convert °F to °C subtract 32 and multiply by ·55

Length, Distance & Area

	multiply by
inches to centimetres	2.54
centimetres to inches	0.39
feet to metres	0.30
metres to feet	3.28
yards to metres	0.91
metres to yards	1.09
miles to kilometres	1.61
kilometres to miles	0.62
acres to hectares	0.40
hectares to acres	2.47

Weight

	multiply by
ounces to grams	28.35
grams to ounces	0.035
pounds to kilograms	0.45
kilograms to pounds	2.21
British tons to kilograms	1016
US tons to kilograms	907

A British ton is 2240 lbs, a US ton is 2000 lbs

Volume

	multiply by
Imperial gallons to litres	4.55
litres to imperial gallons	0.22
US gallons to litres	3.79
litres to US gallons	0.26

5 imperial gallons equals 6 US gallons
a litre is slightly more than a US quart, slightly less
than a British one

°C		°F
50		122
45		113
40		104
35		95
30		86
25		75
20		68
15		59
10		50
5		41
0		32

Thanks to:

Jane Adams (Aus); Per Ahlin (Sw); Terry Anderson (USA); Kjell Backvall (B); Balfroid (B); John Benedict (USA); Rick & Carol Blighton; Kevin Bonnie; Jimmy Lim (M); Ingrid Bremer (D); Steve Brooks (B); Kaarin Buhrmann (Can); Glen Burns (Aus); Frances Cincotta & Grame Brown (Aus); J Collins (Aus); Larry & Sandra Davidson (USA); Alan Davis (Can); Jeni Dick & Lars Christense (Dk); Diane Edwards (UK); Jeffrey Ehrlich (Aus); Lesley Fidler (UK); Favaro Terezita Garcia; Libby Gawith (NZ); Richard Gregory-Smith (PNG); Dave Griswold (USA); Debbie Haigh (USA); Thomas Hanrahan (USA); Bill Harvey (NZ); Bill Hazell (Aus); Roger Heading (Aus); Susanna Hedenborg (Sw); Sandra Higgs (UK); John Holland (Aus); Armin Husse (D); Ismail Ibrahim; Soren Jeppesen (Dk); Ian Johnston (Aus); Julia Moss (M); Eric Kabel (M); Sam Chuan Kang (M); Michael Keith (USA); Coral & Mike Kernick (Aus); Gunnar Kihlberg (Sw); Mike Kruppa-Charherr; Rosli Latif (M); Gretle & Kay Lauritsen (Dk); Martin Law (M); Chris & Irene Laws (Aus); Nair Ibrahim (M); Karl-Ulrich Lechner; Lene & Jens (M); S Leong (M); Ms L Lim (Aus); Siang Piow Liu (S); A Lor (Can); Carl Magnus Lundberg (Sw); Michael MC Gowan (Aus); Justine Mickle & Cath Lovelock (Aus); Adele Millard & Bob Persons (Aus); Sandy Moritz & Phil Sinclair (Aus); Paul Moulder (UK); Berthy Muller (Ch); A & C Mulls-Werk (D); Steven Nimmo (UK); Mathew Ong (M); Mirjam Otte (Nl); Hauri Philippe (Ch); Otto Prause (A); Jon Rees (M); Pru Robbie (Aus); Carla Rufelds (Can); Darren Russell (Aus); Caryll Sefton (Aus); Debra Shadovitz (USA); Jessica Snell (UK); Andrea Spignesi (USA); Alex Stewart (Aus); Robert Stuart; Tahanga (Aus); Rose Tan (M); Johnny Tan (M); Edward Teja (USA); Chantal Thompson (UK); Roxi Timm (USA); Bala Velusamy (M); Roy Vinnicombe (Aus); R Walter (HK); Damian White (Sw); Robert Whittle (Aus); Razra Yasok (M); Tony Yates (UK);

A – Austria; Aus – Australia; B – Brunei; Can – Canada; CH – Switzerland; D – West Germany; Dk – Denmark; HK – Hong Kong, M – Malaysia; Nl – Netherlands; NZ – New Zealand; PNG – Papua New Guinea; S – Singapore, Sw – Sweden; UK – UK; USA – USA

Dear traveller

Prices go up, good places go bad, bad places go bankrupt ... and every guide book is inevitably outdated in places. Fortunately, many travellers write to us about their experiences, telling us when things have changed. If we reprint a book between editions, we try to include as much of this information as possible in a Stop Press section. Most of this information has not been verified by our own writers.

We really enjoy hearing from people out on the road, and apart from guaranteeing that others will benefit from your good and bad experiences, we're prepared to bribe you with the offer of a free book for sending us substantial useful information.

Thank you to everyone who has written, and to those who haven't, I hope you do find this book useful – and that you let us know when it isn't.

Tony Wheeler

1990 has been declared 'Visit Malaysia Year' and the Malaysians are are getting ready for a big year of celebrations, festivals and cultural events. Our researchers will be in Malaysia later in the year to work on a new edition.

Since this edition was published, there have been no major changes. Although general costs have risen, Malaysia, Singapore and Brunei remain cheap countries to travel in. The most important update for Brunei is that *Pusat Belia*, the youth hostel in Bandar Seri Begawan, has reopened having been redecorated and modernised over several months. It's still the cheapest place to stay in town.

This is the second stop press we have done for this edition of *Malaysia, Singapore & Brunei – a travel survival kit*. It was compiled using information sent to us by these travellers: Joe Doherty (Ire), F Gali (Can), Derek Langley (Aus), Geoff Mann, Per Rahbek (Dk), Carol Rubenstein (Sin) and Kerry & Melanie Underwood (UK).

In Malaysia you will come across several towns with many hostels and guests houses catering specifically to foreign travellers. In Kota Bahru there is fierce rivalry among these establishments. Most of the hostels are excellent, offering a similar standard of cheap, safe and comfortable dormitory accommodation, free breakfast, travellers' information, and friendly surroundings. Despite this, we often receive letters from hostel owners running down rival hostels with all sorts of slanderous trivia. Keep an open mind and check places for yourself. The most up to date reliable sources of information are first hand experiences of other travellers.

Money & Costs

A few years ago when the economy was booming, shopping complexes and high-rise buildings were going up all over the place, especially in West Malaysia. Over the past couple of years, work on many of these buildings has been halted due to lack of funds, and now these half finished buildings stand empty and abandoned.

In Malaysia, the current exchange rate is around US$1 to M$2.71. In Singapore and Brunei (their currencies are interchangeable) US$1 is equivalent to S$1.88. Costs have not increased dramatically.

Dangers & Annoyances

Warning Some months ago, we received number of letters from women travell saying they had been drugged and raped while on jungle treks from Kuala Lipis. If you intend to go trekking in this area, go with other travellers and stay with them at all times.

Generally, Malaysia, Singapore and Brunei are safe countries to travel in. Be careful in crowded areas (bus and train stations, markets, shopping centres, etc) where pickpockets thrive.

A couple of people have complained about trishaw drivers in Melaka offering tours around town for M$15, and then at the end of the tour insisting the cost was M$15 per hour. In Georgetown, Penang, travellers say that newspapers have published reports of travellers being drugged and robbed.

Getting There
It seems to be much cheaper to fly out of Kuala Lumpur than Singapore. The STA office on Chulia Rd in Georgetown has been recommended as a good place to buy cheap tickets. Another popular travel agent is the Silver-Econ Travel Agency.

If you are going to Indonesia, you can take the boat from Penang to Medan, Sumatra, on Mondays or Wednesdays at 6.30 pm. The fare is M$55, plus M$10 departure tax.

Buses from Singapore to Malaysia leave from Lavender St, not New Bridge Rd. Most buses are booked well in advance, however, some passengers book their seats from Johore Bahru, just over the border, to Kuala Lumpur. It's worth asking the driver to take you from Singapore to Johore Bahru as some of the Johore to KL passengers may not turn up. In this case, you can stay on the bus until you reach your destination.

Border Crossings
Kalimantan-Sarawak It is possible to cross the Indonesian border with East Malaysia at Pontianak with a social visit visa. If you have an Indonesian tourist visa, you must first obtain written permission from immigration in Pontianak.

In Pontianak, cross the river by speed boat for 150 rp to Pasar Lintang, where the main long distance bus station is. Buy a ticket to Entikong for 5500 rp. The dusty trip takes eight to nine hours. The border closes at 5 pm, so you might not make it in one day. We've heard that a direct bus service from Pontianak to Kuching (fare 40,000 rp) has just started. You can also fly between the two cities for M$160 on either Merpati Airlines or Malaysian Airlines.

Sabah-Kalimantan The Indonesian Consulate in Kota Kinabalu, Sabah, readily hands out 30-day visas for travel to Kalimantan. The visas cost M$10 and you need three photos and an onward ticket.

You take the weekly boat from Tawau to Tarakan for M$50, and then take the Pelni boat from Tarakan to Balikpapan or Samarinda. The Pelni boat goes once every two weeks only. You can also fly from Sabah to Kalimantan for 70,000 rp.

Taman Negara National Park
As the privately owned company River Park Sdn Bhd has gone bankrupt, the Malaysian government has once again taken over the running of Taman Negara National Park. To book the park boat and park accommodation, ring the Wildlife National Park Department (tel (03) 905 2872 or (03) 905 2873). Prices for beds are now M$10 in a hostel dormitory, M$5 in a hide and M$8 in a fishing lodge.

Park boats now leave from Kuala Tembeling to Kuala Tahan at 9 am and 2 pm and return at the same times from Kuala Tahan. The park officials no longer conduct walking tours, the noodle stalls have disappeared and, according to one disgruntled traveller, restaurant meals should be ordered at least two hours in advance!

Apparently, foreign cash and travellers' cheques are not accepted at Taman Negara, so take ringgits.

Gunung Mulu National Park
You must obtain a permit to visit Gunung Mulu National Park from the administrative complex in the centre of Miri. You do not

have to be definite about what you want to do and you are usually given a week to see the park.

When applying for permits in Sarawak, it is important to remember never to say that you are a journalist, biologist or scientist. Such people might be interested in the environment or the indigenous people and therefore (because of the Bruno Manser case) are regarded as troublemakers. Bruno Manser is the Swiss shepherd who disappeared into the jungle in 1984, later appearing with the Penans, a nomadic tribe roaming the jungle.

Bruno is supporting the Penans in a protest against the disastrous logging of the rainforest. The logging not only threatens the life and welfare of these peaceful people but also the welfare of our planet.

The Penans have been blocking logging routes and sabotaging roads, creating worldwide attention to the destruction of the rainforests in Borneo and to the shortsightedness of the Malaysian politicians.

At Gunung Mulu you are not allowed to enter the caves unless you are with a licensed guide. If you do, you risk never coming out again. You are not allowed into the jungle without a guide either, probably partly due to the Bruno Manser case and partly because they want to make money. It costs M$20 per day to hire a guide. This can be shared among the number of people travelling in your group.

To get to Gunung Mulu National Park from Miri take a bus to Kuala Baram and from there take a half-hour boat trip for M$12 to Marudi. At Marudi take another boat to Long Panai. This leg costs M$10 and takes two and a half hours. At Long Panai (a longhouse) a longboat will be waiting to take you to Gunung Mulu headquarters. The trip takes two to three hours, depending on the tides, and costs M$35.

Mt Kinabalu National Park

It is no longer compulsory to hire a guide if you sign a piece of paper at headquarters claiming that you are climbing the mountain at your own risk. One traveller claims that you can walk all the way to Laban Rata blindfolded! Apparently, from Laban Rata to Sayat Sayat the trail is easy to follow but from Sayat Sayat to the summit the trail can be missed in bad weather.

Travellers' Tips & Comments

White Water Adventures (tel 231 892) is on the 3rd Floor of Block L, Sinsuran, Kota Kinabalu. Their postal address is PO Box 13076, Kota Kinabalu 88834, Sabah. The company is run by a young couple with just the right combination of knowledge and skills. John is English and Elmer is a local Bajan. They operate tours and a hostel for budget travellers. The hostel is in the heart of Kota Kinabalu and the tours, although expensive, are tailored to suit your needs.

J & N Sheppard – England

I recommend *Uncle Tan's Guest House*, Mile 6, Sandakan, Sabah. It costs M$15 for accommodation in a big house in a middle class suburb of Sandakan. Uncle Tan is a veteran of the British Army and has extensive knowledge of history, jungle trekking, wildlife and places of interest in Sabah. Uncle Tan prepares all the food you can eat and can organise trips to places such as Turtle Island for you.

Derek Langley – Australia

The orang-utan sanctuary in Sandakan has had a population increase. I saw 13 orang-utans in one day walking around. I met one of them going the other way on the trail and he stopped, shook my hand, kissed my foot and continued on his way. These sociable creatures were raised in captivity but should be watched rather than played with as they are trying to adjust to forest life. New arrivals are given wheelbarrow trips through the jungle and the rangers have to teach them how to climb trees.

Eric Telfer – USA

Guides to South-East Asia

South-East Asia on a shoestring
The well-known 'yellow bible' for travellers in South-East Asia contains detailed travel information on Brunei, Burma, Hong Kong, Indonesia, Macau, Malaysia, Papua New Guinea, the Philippines, Singapore, and Thailand.

Bali & Lombok – a travel survival kit
This guide will help travellers to experience the real magic of Bali's tropical paradise. Neighbouring Lombok is largely untouched by outside influences and has a special atmosphere of its own.

Burma – a travel survival kit
Burma is one of Asia's friendliest and most interesting countries. This book shoes how to make the most of a trip around the main triangle route of Rangoon-Mandalay-Pagan, and explores many lesser-known places such as Pegu and Inle Lake.

Thailand – a travel survival kit
Beyond the Buddhist temples and Bangkok bars there is much to see in fascinating Thailand. This extensively researched guide presents an inside look at Thailand's culture, people and language.

The Philippines – a travel survival kit
The friendly Filipinos, colourful festivals, and superb natural scenery make the Philippines one of the most interesting countries in South-East Asia for adventurous travellers and sun– seekers alike.

Indonesia – a travel survival kit
Some of the most remarkable sights and sounds in South-East Asia can be found amongst the 7000 islands of Indonesia – this book covers the entire archipelago in detail.

Papua New Guinea – a travel survival kit
Papua New Guinea is the last inhabited place on earth to be explored by Europeans. From coastal cities to villages perched beside mighty rivers, palm-fringed beaches and rushing mountain streams, Papua New Guinea promises memorable travel.

Also available:
Thai phrasebook, *Burmese* phrasebook, *Pilipino* phrasebook, and *Indonesia* phrasebook.

Lonely Planet Guidebooks

Lonely Planet guidebooks cover virtually every accessible part of Asia as well as Australia, the Pacific, Central and South America, Africa, the Middle East and parts of North America. There are four main series: 'travel survival kits', covering a single country for a range of budgets; 'shoestring' guides with compact information for low-budget travel in a major region; trekking guides; and 'phrasebooks'.

Australia & the Pacific
Australia
Bushwalking in Australia
Papua New Guinea
Papua New Guinea phrasebook
New Zealand
Tramping in New Zealand
Rarotonga & the Cook Islands
Solomon Islands
Tahiti & French Polynesia
Fiji
Micronesia
Tonga
Samoa

South-East Asia
South-East Asia on a shoestring
Malaysia, Singapore & Brunei
Indonesia
Bali & Lombok
Indonesia phrasebook
Burma
Burmese phrasebook
Thailand
Thai phrasebook
Philippines
Pilipino phrasebook

North-East Asia
North-East Asia on a shoestring
China
China phrasebook
Tibet
Tibet phrasebook
Japan
Japanese phrasebook
Korea
Korean phrasebook
Hong Kong, Macau & Canton
Taiwan

West Asia
West Asia on a shoestring
Trekking in Turkey
Turkey
Turkish phrasebook

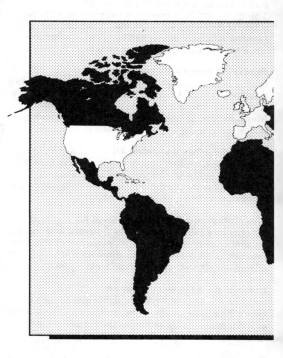

Indian Ocean
Madagascar & Comoros
Maldives & Islands of the East Indian Ocean
Mauritius, Réunion & Seychelles

Mail Order

Lonely Planet guidebooks are distributed worldwide and are sold by good bookshops everywhere. They are also available by mail order from Lonely Planet, so if you have difficulty finding a title please write to us. US and Canadian residents should write to Embarcadero West, 112 Linden St, Oakland CA 94607, USA and residents of other countries to PO Box 617, Hawthorn, Victoria 3122, Australia.

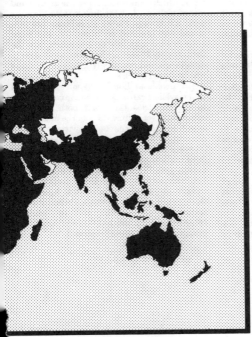

Eastern Europe
Eastern Europe

Indian Subcontinent
India
Hindi/Urdu phrasebook
Kashmir, Ladakh & Zanskar
Trekking in the Indian Himalaya
Pakistan
Kathmandu & the Kingdom of Nepal
Trekking in the Nepal Himalaya
Nepal phrasebook
Sri Lanka
Sri Lanka phrasebook
Bangladesh
Karakoram Highway

Africa
Africa on a shoestring
East Africa
Swahili phrasebook
West Africa
Central Africa
Morocco, Algeria & Tunisia

North America
Canada
Alaska

Mexico
Mexico
Baja California

South America
South America on a shoestring
Ecuador & the Galapagos Islands
Colombia
Chile & Easter Island
Bolivia
Brazil
Brazilian phrasebook
Peru
Argentina
Quechua phrasebook

Middle East
Israel
Egypt & the Sudan
Jordan & Syria
Yemen

Lonely Planet

Lonely Planet published its first book in 1973. Tony and Maureen Wheeler had made a lengthy overland trip from England to Australia and, in response to numerous 'how do you do it?' questions, Tony wrote and they published *Across Asia on the Cheap*. It became an instant local best-seller and inspired thoughts of a second travel guide. A year and a half in South-East Asia resulted in their second book, *South-East Asia on a Shoestring*, which they put together in a backstreet Chinese hotel in Singapore in 1975. The 'yellow book', as it quickly became known, soon became *the* guide to the region and has gone through five editions, always with its familiar yellow cover.

Soon other writers came to them with ideas for similar books – books that went off the beaten track with an adventurous approach to travel, books that 'assumed you knew how to get your luggage off the carousel,' as one reviewer put it. Lonely Planet grew from a kitchen table operation to a spare room and then to its own office. Its international reputation began to grow as the Lonely Planet logo began to appear in more and more countries. In 1982 *India – a travel survival kit* won the Thomas Cook award for the best guidebook of the year.

These days there are over 70 Lonely Planet titles. Over 40 people work at our office in Melbourne, Australia and another half dozen at our US office in Oakland, California.

At first Lonely Planet specialised in the Asia region but these days we are also developing major ranges of guidebooks to the Pacific region, to South America and to Africa. The list of walking guides is growing and Lonely Planet now has a unique series of phrasebooks to 'unusual' languages. The emphasis continues to be on travel for travellers and Tony and Maureen still manage to fit in a number of trips each year and play a very active part in the writing and updating of Lonely Planet's guides.

Keeping guidebooks up to date is a constant battle which requires an ear to the ground and lots of walking, but technology also plays its part. All Lonely Planet guidebooks are now stored and updated on computer, and some authors even take lap-top computers into the field. Lonely Planet is also using computers to draw maps and eventually many of the maps will be stored on disk.

The people at Lonely Planet strongly feel that travellers can make a positive contribution to the countries they visit both by better appreciation of cultures and by the money they spend. In addition the company tries to make a direct contribution to the countries and regions it covers. Since 1986 a percentage of the income from each book has gone to aid groups and associations. This has included donations to famine relief in Africa, to aid projects in India, to agricultural projects in Central America, to Greenpeace's efforts to halt French nuclear testing in the Pacific and to Amnesty International. In 1989 $41,000 was donated by Lonely Planet to these projects.